D0975238

HQ
734          Blumstein, Philip.
.B659        AMERICAN COUPLES
1983         05418

| DATE | |
|------|---------|
| | ISSUED TO |
| | |
| | |
| | |
| | |
| | |
| | |
| | |

LIBRARY
ROSEBRIDGE GRADUATE SCHOOL
OF INTEGRATIVE PSYCHOLOGY
1040 Oak Grove Road • Concord, CA 94518

HQ          Blumstein, Philip.
734          AMERICAN COUPLES
.B659        05418
1983

# AMERICAN COUPLES

PHILIP BLUMSTEIN, Ph.D.
& PEPPER SCHWARTZ, Ph.D.

## MONEY

## WORK

## SEX

LIBRARY
ROSEBRIDGE GRADUATE SCHOOL
OF INTEGRATIVE PSYCHOLOGY
1040 Oak Grove Road • Concord, CA 94518

WILLIAM MORROW AND COMPANY, Inc.     1983
New York

05418

The case histories reported in this book are true. They are all based on actual, voluntary interviews given for the purposes of this publication. However, names, locations, and other identifying material have been changed to protect the identity of the subjects. Similarities in names or other physically descriptive characteristics between any of the subjects of this book and other persons is purely coincidental.

Any opinions, findings, and conclusions or recommendations expressed in this publication are those of the authors and do not necessarily reflect the views of the National Science Foundation.

Copyright © 1983 by Philip Blumstein and Pepper W. Schwartz

All rights reserved. No part of this book may be reproduced or utilized in any form or by any means, electronic or mechanical, including photocopying, recording or by any information storage and retrieval system, without permission in writing from the Publisher. Inquiries should be addressed to William Morrow and Company, Inc., 105 Madison Avenue, New York, N.Y. 10016.

Library of Congress Catalog Card Number: 83–62066

ISBN: 0–688–03772–0

Printed in the United States of America

First Edition

1 2 3 4 5 6 7 8 9 10

BOOK DESIGN BY BETTY BINNS GRAPHICS

# Acknowledgments

A large study takes the cooperation, goodwill and hard work of more than just the primary investigators. This study could not have been done without an enormous amount of collaboration and we want to thank everyone who helped us. We have had as many as thirty people working on this project at any one time. Getting these data collected and analyzed has required dedication, ridiculous hours, and endless patience. We are indebted to the people who supported us by giving graciously of themselves.

We would like to thank the federal agencies and the private foundation who gave us support. We are grateful to the Russell Sage Foundation and to Tony Cline, who was then its president, who gave us our earliest grant for instrument development. The National Science Foundation funded the actual research (grant SES-7617497). Roland Liebert who administered our grant at NSF was a great help in innumerable ways. We did not accept funds from the National Institutes of Mental Health, but we wish to thank their review team, Murray Straus and Patricia Gurin, who gave us helpful suggestions, almost all of which we followed.

People at the University of Washington have given us support economically, intellectually, and emotionally. We would like to thank our colleagues who gave us helpful criticism over the years, especially Herbert Costner whose advice along the way and critique of the grant proposal were invaluable. Charles Hill, Judith Howard, and George Bridges read drafts of parts of the manuscript and James McCann gave us advice on statistical issues. We are also grateful to Frederick Campbell, chairman of the Sociology Department, for being a good friend, helping us field countless problems the study created, and supporting us every inch of the way.

We were also blessed with Virginia Alldred, administrative assistant of the Sociology Department, who helped us negotiate the university system. We are grateful to Tim Trusty, Gail Morris, Martha Perla, Karola Henry, Joanne Radmore, Sylvia Moul, Francine Carroll, Julie Page, and Nancy Hulbert for various office responsibilities well done. In addition, there were times when help from the administrators of the university was necessary, and we are especially in debt to Frank Miyamoto and Joe Creager for their help with the problems a large grant produces for the investigators and for the university.

We had a large and able staff. We are particularly indebted to Charles Williams who spent three months in New York and three months in San Francisco interviewing couples. The questionnaire and the preparation of data for retrieval bear the mark of his fastidious organizational skills. Blair Kangley gave many hours of his time managing the data and overseeing the entire project. Thanks to Deanna Strom who also interviewed in the Bay Area and whose help on the questionnaire made it a better document. Diane Knuckles helped interview in the Bay Area, recruit volunteers and organize our Bay Area research operation. We were also fortunate in having Ann Northrop and Meredith Gould as our New York staff. They interviewed couples and Ann also did a fantastic job of getting the New York media to help us find participants.

We have had a large group of talented and dedicated interviewers in Seattle. Special thanks go to Mary Gillmore, Karen Hegtvedt, Blair Kangley, Lauren Aaronson, Christina Mumma, Dennis Lacy, Amnon Schoenfeld, Anne Martin, Mary Leber, Elaine Thompson, Roger Brooks, Kathleen Hellum, Tami Gillman, and Suzanne Domnick. We are also grateful to people who worked on the early design of the study and questionnaires: Steven Mount, Marie Jones, Charles Williams, Deanna Strom, Judith Little, and Barrett Lee. We are greatly indebted to Wagner Thielens who reviewed the original draft of the questionnaire and helped refine it and condense it. Additional help in preparing the data for the computer came from Louis Blumstein, Kenneth Pike, Katherine Diaz, Brian Galvin, and Michael Peterson. David Sampson helped us design our charts and Allen Auvil helped lay out the questionnaires. We are particularly lucky to have talented help with the university computer system. Fred Nick gave us creative solutions to difficult data problems. Peter Kollock, Lisa Lake, and Jerald Herting put in hundreds of hours of work. They worked late at night, on weekends, during crises, and often with frustrating equipment. This book could not have been done without their willingness to give unstintingly of their time and talent.

One of the great advantages of being on a university campus is the ability to get critical feedback. We are part of an ongoing group that studies gender, and their critical review of our research and this manuscript has been extremely helpful. This book has benefited from their ideas about gender and we have personally benefited from our discussions over the years. We would like to thank Barbara Risman, Mary Gillmore, Mary Seidel, Judith Howard, Laura Bailey, Charles Hill, Anne Martin, Laurie Hatch, Linda Williams, Nancy Durbin, and Mary Leber for their contributions. We also want to thank other special readers, particularly Graham Spanier for his review of our chapter on *American Couples* in *Historical Perspective*.

There are a number of people who helped us get our call for volunteers out to the country. We cannot remember everyone who did a story or who got us on a news show, but we would like to thank them all. We are grateful to Jane Brody whose story in *The New York Times* was circulated on their wire service and drew thousands of volunteers from around the country. We also want to thank Betsy Osha, then talent coordinator for the *Today* show who put us on the program and, again, helped us attract people from all over the country. Charles Brydon and the National Gay Task Force were a great help in generating our gay sample. We are also indebted to the many people—gay and heterosexual—who believed in our study and allowed us to seek participants in their businesses, churches, unions, and civic groups.

There are also a great many people who helped the study become a book. We are grateful to our agent, Lynn Nesbit, who believed in this project and who helped us get an enthusiastic reaction from the publishing world. Edmund White, Christopher Cox, and Jane Adams gave us encouragement and advice. We are fortunate to have a publishing house that shares our vision of the project and gave us talented people to work with. We want to thank Lawrence Hughes and Sherry Arden for giving us all the support authors could ask for. We want to thank all the people at Morrow—Betsy Cenedella, Joan Amico, Al Marchioni, Carolyn Reidy, and Lela Rolontz—whose careful attention to the book has profited it greatly. We are also thankful to Cheryl Asherman for the jacket and to Betty Binns for her design of the book. Our greatest debt by far, however, is to Maria Guarnaschelli, our editor, who is a rare and gifted teacher as well as a special human being. She shepherded this project from the moment she heard about it. She has lived and breathed this book with us. We have become better thinkers as well as better writers by responding to her critical eye. What flaws remain are not her responsibility but merely reflect our own limitations.

Finally there are all the people at home whose belief in the importance of this project helped us so much over the years. We would like to thank our parents, Louis and Myrtle Blumstein and Gertrude and Julius Schwartz, for being wonderful people, wonderful parents, and a source of inspiration. We would like to thank our friends who were understanding when we went "underground" to write and forsook all our obligations as companions. We would like to thank Cynthia and Don Roberts for a hundred different services that supported this book. We would also like to thank Arthur Skolnik and Cooper Schwartz-

Skolnik for being troupers and giving up their wife and mother graciously.

Finally, we would like to thank each other. We enjoy a special partnership. This book is the product of mutual dedication to a large and sometimes overwhelming project. It has required many years of learning from one another, dividing tasks, arguing creatively, and building on each other's strengths. We have listed our authorship alphabetically and not by any other schema because there is no hierarchy in our relationship. Although this book does not cover our kind of partnership, we feel a kindred spirit with the couples we write about. We have worked hard over the years to create a durable and equal friendship and colleagueship, and we feel we have succeeded.

To our parents who gave us models of successful relationships, and to all the people who shared their experiences with us and trusted us, we dedicate this book.

—PHILIP BLUMSTEIN
PEPPER SCHWARTZ

# CONTENTS

# Introduction: How the Study Was Done

T HE couple is a basic unit of society. It is the unit of reproduction, the wellspring of the family, and most often the precinct of love, romance, and sexuality. The majority of adults in contemporary Western society will court, form emotional and economic alliances, and live with, one adult at a time. When Americans marry, they hope they are making a lifetime commitment. Those who choose to live together may have more ambiguous motives, but all the same, they expect the kind of love and support traditional marriage promises. If these attempts at a long-term intimacy fail, the desire to be part of a couple is so strong that most usually try again. People carry around with them a complicated set of aspirations, the central focus of which is developing an intimate and enduring relationship with another human being. As people get older, some become disenchanted with a particular partner or find it impossible to create a relationship that will last. But these are only disappointments. People would like their relationships to be permanent.

The frustrating fact is that there is no guarantee of permanence. All kinds of couples—married and unmarried, heterosexual and homosexual—are seeking guidance because their relationships are in jeopardy. For husbands and wives, many of the existing traditions have lost their meaning, and few reliable criteria have been offered in exchange. Cohabitors and same-sex couples have no models to help them live out their lives.

This study is the culmination of our career-long interest in the nature of relationships. In 1975 when we began work, scholarly journals were full of articles about the rising divorce rate, the impact of changing male and female roles, and the search for novel answers to the question of how couples should live. These articles grew out of a long tradition. Since the 1920's family researchers have sought to explain what made marriages happy and likely to last. In the past thirty years, other topics have appeared in the literature: Which partner possesses greater power? What happens to a marriage when the wife is employed outside the home? What is the context of the partners' sex lives? As a consequence of seeing many of these questions remaining unanswered, we took on the task of looking at couples ourselves. While we agreed that it was necessary to discover what makes relationships happy, we also wanted to investigate, more closely than any existing study did, just how couples put their lives together. In the 1970's, the theme of gender emerged and we wished to include that in our examination.

In addition, the social change of the past twenty years has given rise to new options in living as couples, options not generally sanctioned in previous generations. We considered it important, even urgent, to apply the customary marriage-research questions to other types of couples as well, to see what we could learn about the nature of all kinds of relationships.

We chose a broad range of issues. We wanted to look at the everyday lives of couples, to find out who buys the groceries, how much free time they spend together, when they decide to have sex. People may think these matters inconsequential, but we consider them the building blocks of all relationships. We also knew that out-of-the-ordinary circumstances can be highly significant. A decision that a wife will return to work, or a partner's choosing to explore outside sex, can change the meaning of a relationship and the degree to which it satisfies one or both partners.

We wanted to do more than merely describe the lives of couples. We wanted to discover why they make the choices they do, and if those choices prove gratifying. Couples may agree to pool their money or they may refuse. Partners may allow each other the right to propose sex, or they may feel that only one of them should assume that role. They may elect to share all their leisure activities or to maintain certain areas of privacy. We wanted to know why a couple would choose one pattern or another, and if the choice has significance for their future.

Taking our cue from hundreds of articles in our field, we knew that the diverse opinions and values people have about love and living together help to shape their goals for their relationships. For example, some husbands and wives want their marriages to resemble their parents' as closely as possible. They want few or no changes in the customary division of male and female roles. Others yearn to depart from tradition. They want men and women to be, if not similar, at least guided by personal preference rather than by the dictates of the past. We expected that the different contracts and values of nontraditional couples would manifest themselves in every aspect of their lives together, and so we focused on a number of beliefs and attitudes, to assess their effect on the course of a relationship.

We also sought descriptions of the emotions aroused within relationships. What circumstances give rise to possessiveness, suspicion, and competitiveness, for example? Why do some couples have problems in these areas while others do not? What happens when these emotions are present?

Finally, we wanted to learn how couples actually behave: how often they have sex, spend money, quarrel, how their jobs affect their relationship. And how is the life of the couple affected by the individual behavior of each partner in such areas as ambition, monogamy, devotion to career?

Choosing what we wanted to concentrate on in our study was a devilish task; potentially we could look at every single thing that might occur in a couple's life together. We elected to inquire into those concerns we considered inescapable. Some of them, such as housework, earning a living, raising children, communicating affection, having sex, and resolving conflict, had been researched by others, so that the groundwork in formulating questions had been laid for us. Other areas, such as money management, sexual jealousy and suspicion, and competition between partners had been examined negligibly, if at all. Here we had to come up with totally new questions.

One area of interest earlier researchers had explored became an important focus of our study: the dynamics of influence, and the negotiation of control between partners. The study of gender roles has, in part, been the study of the subordination of women to men. Family researchers have examined this topic in marriage, and we have looked at it in the broader context of intimate associations in general. In every area of a couple's life we asked who had the right or authority to exert control, how it had come to be that way, and how that control affected the relationship. We learned, from criticisms leveled at family researchers who went before us, that it is difficult to measure accurately the balance of power within a couple's life. Therefore, in addition to relying on each partner's individual assessment of his or her own power, we looked at how influence is exerted in many areas of their lives. Control may be exercised by a man in one area, by a woman in another. One partner may govern financial and career matters, but cede authority in the bedroom.

Which brings up the question of why we have concentrated on money, work, and sex. Why not other areas? We should say that to some extent this choice of themes is arbitrary. Many aspects of couple life are important, and our selection of these three does not imply that they have more consequence than others. Indeed, our study covers all the topics we have mentioned: kin, friends, children, communication, and the resolution of conflict, as well as money, work and sex. It is only that we have decided to write about these three subjects first.

It is true, however, that we settled on these three matters in particular because they are critical issues in couple life. Money and work are aligned, even though they present different problems. In a capitalist society, it is impossible to study power without understanding people's relationship to the worlds of finance and work. It is impossible to study changing gender roles without looking at how control of money and entry into the labor force change the relationship of partners to each other. In addition, we wished to leaven this perspective with at least one glimpse into the need for affection and trust in a private area of couples' lives. Sex is a personal, but also regulated, component of any intimate union. It has rules and patterns, even if they are not explicitly stated. A couple's sexual interaction tells us a great deal about their values, attitudes, emotions, and distribution of power.

Our interest in power, in gender, and in diversity led us to feel dissatisfied with our discipline's established preoccupation with married couples. Sociologists, examining gender in couples comprised of one male and one female, have tried to comprehend the differences between men and women and the ways in which these differences shape intimacy. While we have always found these inquiries fascinating, we have also found them limiting. The concentration on married couples made it hard to disentangle the conflicts and resolutions built into the institution of marriage from those that are common to any two people trying to create a life together. Is a particular instance of male domination the result of husbands' time-honored authority over wives, of Woman's subjugation by Man, or only of one man's ability to exert personal power? Does the pattern of one homemaker, one wage earner recur because it is pragmatically efficient or because the partners both adhere to historic male/female traditions?

If people are to be happy and their relationship is to last, should household tasks and everyday decisions be shared equally or should each partner stick to a specialty? Should men do some jobs and women others, or should tasks be assigned irrespective of gender? We decided that in order to answer questions like these, we had to look not only at marriage but also at *its alternatives:* cohabitation and same-sex relationships, which could provide a "naturally occurring experiment." By comparing cohabitors with married couples, we gain perspective on the impact of the institution of marriage on heterosexual relationships. By contrasting homosexual couples with both types of heterosexual couples, we can see how relationships function when there are no male/female differences to contend with. By comparing gay men to lesbians, we explore differences in male and female contributions to relationships.

We felt that recent social change necessitated our looking at alternatives to marriage. While most people still believe in marriage, some no longer automatically trust it as a perfect vehicle for fulfilling aspirations for intimacy. We need to know if other kinds of couples, unrestricted by marital traditions, find solutions that make them happier, or more committed, or more stable, or more egalitarian. If all four kinds of couples are pursuing similar goals—love, sexual satisfaction, emotional intimacy, and trust—then successful relationships should all look alike . . . *if* there is only one way to attain these goals. If, however, unmarried and same-sex couples look quite different, and yet achieve success—perhaps in realms where marriage has failed—there may be alternative strategies all couples could use and everyone should know about. On the other hand, if nonmarried couples are doing things differently, and are more dissatisfied than husbands and wives, this may tell us something about the nature of intimacy and how few options are really available to those who wish to create enduring relationships.

# How the study was done

The study was designed with several objectives: first, to include a large and diverse sample of respondents, people of every income level, age, educational background, length of relationship, and from large cities and small towns all across the country. We wanted people with a wide array of values: conservative and liberal political views, religious and nonreligious people, feminists and traditionalists, gay activists and gay people who desired no involvement with the gay world. And we wanted people who had chosen very different styles of life: childless couples and those with big families, one- and two-paycheck couples, couples who are sexually monogamous and those who are not, the gregarious and the solitary. In order to assure ourselves enough of each kind for statistical analysis, we needed to start with an enormous number of couples. Some sorts are rarer than others, and it was necessary to cast a wide net to get them. For example, it was important to find wives who earn more than their husbands, not because they are in the majority but because they allow us to answer a very important question: What is the impact on a marriage when the woman has economic clout?

Our second objective was to secure detailed data that would allow us to see couples from several vantage points. We wanted data that would permit statistical analysis. So we designed a long and detailed questionnaire for each partner to fill out. And for in-depth discussions of their relationship in their own words, we also conducted face-to-face interviews with couples in their own homes. These sessions lasted from two and a half to four hours, and each person was interviewed privately as well as together with his or her partner. We also wanted to know how a couple solved problems without an observer present, so when we were in their home, they were left alone with a tape recorder and several dilemmas which they were asked to resolve. Finally, the two interviewers would both note their personal impressions of each partner, how the individuals interacted with each other, and the style in which they lived.

Our last aim was to see if the information we garnered from the questionnaires and interviews enabled us to predict which couples would stay together and which would not. Therefore, we chose a large number of the original couples and mailed to each partner a brief follow-up questionnaire approximately eighteen months later.

Our study was designed to avoid some of the problems earlier researchers had encountered. Most prior research sampled either wives or husbands. On those occasions when both husbands and wives were included, the researchers rarely matched a husband's answers to those of his wife. In our study, each partner filled out a questionnaire privately and neither saw the other's answers. The two questionnaires were given the same identification number to eliminate the possibility that one partner might be mistakenly compared to someone from another couple. The questionnaires were usually returned to us together, although the partners could, if they preferred to do so for the sake of privacy, send theirs in individually. The identification numbers ensured that the questionnaires would eventually be rematched.

---

## Participants

Among the first questions we are asked by other social scientists—questions rightly asked of any researcher—are: How representative is your sample? Are all of your respondents members of the same religious sect? Are they all part of the same club or organization? Do they all live in the same part of the country? Is there something that makes them special or unique or in any way grossly unlike the population in general?

If the answer to any of these questions is yes, then the study's findings might have very narrow applicability. Recognizing this, we tried to get a large and diverse sample that avoided any systematic bias.[1] Our task was complicated because we wanted to include people who were indeed very private about their lives. For same-sex couples, this meant people who are "closeted" about their homosexuality, because we felt that this feature of their existence might have repercussions on their relationships. Therefore we needed to develop a rapport and mutual trust that is seldom necessary in a researcher-respondent relationship. In fact, good rapport was necessary with *all* our couples because the questionnaires and interviews were to be long and demanding, and would cover a number of topics that people would be unlikely to discuss with anyone but their closest intimates. Indeed, many respondents mentioned that they talked to us about matters they had never discussed before even with their partners.

In seeking the best sample possible, we wanted first to achieve a broad geographical spread. We chose as bases of operation three locales that would provide access to a number of lesbians, gay men, and cohabitors, as well as married couples. We picked Seattle because we were established there and had, through earlier research, established goodwill with the gay communities, people in the media, local clergy, and community leaders. The Seattle area also has within easy driving distance small towns and rural communities where we might interview people. We chose San Francisco because of its large gay and lesbian population who live uncloseted lives and are therefore more readily comparable to married couples. Where gay people are a stigmatized minority, their relationships might be influenced in ways we could not detect. In San Francisco a gay couple might have a gay landlord, a gay butcher, and a lesbian pharmacist. New York gave us East Coast representation and a diverse array of couples within an hour's travel.

Moreover, as the media capital of the United States, New York also gave us a chance to appeal for participants nationwide in interviews on talk shows and news programs on local and national television and radio, and in newspapers and magazines. We received extensive media coverage in Seattle, San Francisco (the entire Bay Area), New York, Chicago, Washington, D.C., Los Angeles, Wichita, Atlanta, and Dayton.

Stories sent out by the *New York Times* wire service appeared in hundreds of newspapers in metropolitan areas like Houston and Philadelphia as well as in small towns and rural areas all over the United States. Soon after our appearance on the *Today* show, the mailroom at the University of Washington was inundated. As requests to take part in the study flowed in, we were impressed by the geographical diversity and the variety of life-styles. There were letters from presidents of *Fortune* 500 companies and their wives, from ranchers, members of the clergy, and people in the military (a story had appeared in *Stars and Stripes*), just to name a few.

In addition to the media we used more familiar social-science methods, similar to those used by Alfred Kinsey in his study of human sexuality. We appeared before such groups as Democratic and Republican clubs, PTAs, service clubs like the Rotary and the Junior League. We spoke at churches and synagogues, attended union meetings, went anywhere we could find a receptive ear. We canvassed neighborhoods and put up notices in public places like supermarkets and movie theaters. A breakdown of how couples came to participate in the study is found in the Appendix (Table 1).

We sent a pair of questionnaires to every couple who made a request, and a total of 22,000 questionnaires were mailed or left at places where they could be picked up anonymously. Eventually we had to set a cutoff date for their return in order to begin analyzing the data. At that time we had over 12,000 usable questionnaires.[2] To be included in the study, questionnaires had to be filled out and returned by *both* partners of a couple who lived together and had a sexual relationship at least some time in their life together.[3] They also had to consider themselves a couple, not just roommates. Tabulations of characteristics of people in the study appear in the Appendix.[4]

Every study needs to address the question of whether the participants are special because they *volunteered* to take part. This is a serious methodological issue for *anyone* but the Bureau of the Census—which can compel people to fill out a questionnaire. It poses an especially sticky problem if the researcher wants to ask about anything more serious than a person's favorite soft drink, and ours was particularly difficult because we asked both partners to finish a lengthy questionnaire which dealt with intimate issues. We tried to get maximum participation by making the questionnaires as interesting and inoffensive as possible. We made it easy for partners to hide their answers from one another and we worded the questions in a nonjudgmental fashion. We could not overcome the volunteer issue entirely, but one of the difficulties of the study turned out to be a strength. It was not uncommon for people to take part in the study only to please their partners. People often told us that they would not have participated without their partners' urging, but that once they had agreed, they found it a positive experience. Frequently when we interviewed couples and asked how they had originally heard about the study, one partner would remark that the questionnaires "just showed up in the mailbox one day." We knew this could not be true since we had never sent out a questionnaire that was not requested. At the time, we did not comment on the questionnaires' "just showing up," because one of the partners had obviously chosen an indirect way of getting the couple to participate.[5]

From this large group of returned questionnaires, we selected three hundred couples for intensive interviewing.[6] Some topics, we felt, could be better covered in face-to-face conversation; we feared they might be off-putting to some people if they appeared on the questionnaire. Then too, we wanted to give people a chance to elaborate on their answers. We had questionnaire data from all over the country, and ideally we would have liked to conduct interviews everywhere. That was financially impossible, however, so we chose a diverse sample of people who lived within an hour's travel of our three bases of operation; Seattle, New York, and San Francisco. We grouped the couples in each area according to whether they were married, cohabiting, gay male couples, or lesbian couples. We then subdivided each of the four types into three groups: couples who had been together a short time (less than two years), those of medium duration (between two and ten years) and those of long duration (ten years and more).[7] The importance of this distinction is obvious: Couples just starting out cannot be expected to have the same problems or the same solutions as longtime couples who have accumulated property, reared children, experienced changes in who and what they are to each other. Sociologists have long noted the different stages in the life cycle and we wanted to be able to record the cycles of relationships.

We also broke down the couples available for interviews according to level of education—because we thought that level would reflect their social class[8]—into three divisions: one where neither partner had gone beyond high school, one where at least one partner had attended college, and one where at least one partner had a degree higher than a B.A. Much sociological research has shown the importance of social class as a distinction in predicting the ways people act and feel. Education not only affects the way people look at the world and react to daily events, but also directly affects the type of employment available and the direction life-courses take.

Once we had all the couples in the Seattle, San Francisco, and New York vicinities divided according to education, number of years together, and type of couple, we chose randomly from within each category. Eventually we interviewed 120 heterosexual couples (72 married and 48 cohabiting), 90 lesbian couples, and 90 gay male couples.[9]

Approximately eighteen months after their interviews, we sent each of these people a follow-up questionnaire. In addition, we randomly selected a large number of couples who had completed questionnaires, but whom we had not interviewed, to receive follow-up questionnaires also.[10]

## The questionnaire and interview

All couples began their participation with questionnaires of approximately thirty-eight pages, including questions on a variety of subjects. The four different versions of the basic questionnaire differed little. Married and cohabiting couples received one Male Questionnaire and one Female Questionnaire. The only basic differences between these two were the gender of the pronouns used throughout and a few questions about giving and receiving alimony or child-support payments. Several special sections within each questionnaire specifically queried married people only or cohabitors only. The lesbian version used only female pronouns and asked some extra questions about lesbian life-styles, and the gay-male version had male pronouns and special gay-male questions. An important consideration in creating the questionnaires had been to ensure that all types of couples were asked exactly the same questions in exactly the same way. A composite of the four kinds of questionnaires appears in the Appendix.

Each partner was required to give two assurances in order to participate: first, that they would complete their questionnaires without consulting their partners, and would not show them to their partners after completion, so that the sincerity of their responses might not be compromised. Second, they attested that they lived together more than four days a week.

All couples were assured that our study had passed a rigorous set of standards, set by our university and by the federal government, which assured proper protection of their rights and their privacy. Before filling out the questionnaires, the couples read a pledge from us telling them exactly what they were getting involved in and what kinds of questions we would ask; reminding them that the questionnaires were totally anonymous (we destroyed names and addresses of respondents as soon as their questionnaires were mailed out, so that our only identifiable respondents were those who indicated on completed questionnaires their interest in further participation); and noting that they were free to skip questions or to end their participation at any point in the project.

Few significant aspects of a couple's life went untouched in the questionnaire, which covered the history of the couple's relationship, their attitudes and feelings about a number of issues pertinent to relationships in general, and questions about how their relationship operated on a daily basis in such realms as housework, emotional support, finances, sexual relations, conflict, leisure activities, satisfaction, dominance, children, relations with kin and friends, and so on. Space was also provided to write, if they chose to, additional comments that might help us understand their relationship.

From our main office at the University of Washington we selected the couples to be interviewed in the three parts of the country. Once appointments were arranged, two interviewers went to the couple's home. In most cases the interview team consisted of one male and one female, and a coin was tossed to decide which interviewer talked with which partner.[11] In approximately one quarter of the interviews, one or both of us took part.

Interviews took from two and a half to four hours and were tape-recorded and transcribed. The tapes were kept under lock and key until they were destroyed. After introducing themselves, the interviewers informed the couple that they would need two relatively soundproof rooms in which to interview the partners separately. Later they would interview them together. Since privacy was an uncompromisable part of our design, the request for separate rooms sometimes caused a problem: Some couples had only one suitable room, and so several interviews were conducted without heat, or with a flashlight, in backyards and even bathrooms. We came to call these our bathtub interviews.

The individual interviews allowed each person to recount the exact history of his or her relationship, from first meeting to the present, as well as the histories of other important previous relationships, especially if an earlier relationship was felt to have affected the current one. A number of topics too delicate to be approached in the relatively impersonal questionnaire, and questions too cumbersome to fit the questionnaire format, were raised in the interview. These included, particularly, questions about areas of conflict and how conflict was managed and resolved, and about sexual behavior and satisfaction. Individuals were encouraged to elaborate on any topics they wished.

Following the individual interviews, both partners met with both interviewers. Then, as part of the joint interview, couples were given a set of problems to resolve. For example, one of the problems asked them how they would spend a gift of $600. After each problem was described, the couple was left alone with the tape recorder running in order to capture their ways of making decisions and resolving disagreements. After these exercises, additional questions were asked of the couple together: How did they feel about their relationship, and about relationships in general.

After they had left, the interviewers compared notes on what they had seen and learned. A few recurring impressions cropped up time and again. Sometimes the interviewers had difficulty believing they had been talking to members of the same couple, so divergent were the partners' accounts. Though we might have expected this, we were sometimes surprised at just how much divergence was possible. In most cases, however, we got much the same view of things from both partners, except that the missing pieces in one person's story—perhaps too sensitive to discuss—were often filled in by the partner, an advantage of asking the same questions independently of both. Another common reaction interviewers had was a sense of enormous responsibility. We found out things about people that no one else knew—even the other partner—and we were very moved by the trust people placed in us. In the course of an evening we had changed from strangers to confidants. When we left their homes, we would again be strangers, but we carried with us our sense of the importance of doing justice to these people and their stories.

We feel indebted to the couples who took part in the study, particularly to those whom we interviewed. We were unable to repay all the people who filled out our questionnaires, but our research grant did allot $20 for the interview couples, hardly enough to compensate them for the time they spent with us, and many refused to take even that.

Follow-up questionnaires, sent out eighteen months after the interview, asked whether or not the couple was still together, and in what ways any aspects of their relationship had changed. Additional data were also collected to fill in any gaps sensed by the interviewers.[12]

*The data*

The questionnaires and interviews generated an enormous amount of information. Twenty-eight computer cards per couple were required for the data from questionnaires alone. Each interview took approximately twenty-five hours to transcribe. At times the study has employed more than thirty people to code questionnaires, punch cards, code interviews, type transcripts, and prepare the data for computer analysis. The data have been analyzed wih multivariate statistical techniques.[13]

# How to read this book

This book begins with an overview of the history of American couples, followed by three sections on money, work, and sex. Then we discuss which couples broke up, and why. The last chapters comprise relationship histories of each kind of couple, and a brief conclusion.

With the discussion of money, work, and sex, we present in figures the data that led us to our main conclusions. Numerous smaller conclusions drawn from data are presented in notes at the end of the book, along with further statistical elaborations for the academic reader. The end notes also include finer points about the argument that seemed inappropriate within the text. Many of our points are illustrated by direct quotations from the interviews. In every case, the name of the speaker has been changed as well as his or her occupation and any identifying details. A similar occupation has been substituted, so that the change will not distort the reader's perception of the actual person. We have been particularly careful to disguise identities in the four chapters of relationship histories. In these chapters, which have nothing to do with our analysis of the data but are included only for their illustrative value, we have occasionally added an incident from another couple's life if it typifies an issue relevant to this kind of couple. We have thus disguised our couples, in order to make them less recognizable to any reader who might be acquainted with them, and sometimes even to each other. Although details in some histories have been added, deleted, or rearranged, we have not distorted the essentials of the couple's relationship. Social class, general type of occupation, style of life, basic values, and issues critical to them have not been changed.

A word is in order about some of the language we have chosen. We often use the word *partner* to refer to one member of a couple. We do this because it was hard to find one term appropriate to all four kinds of couples, and we hope the usage does not lend an aura of big business to our discussion. Other possibilities included *mate, lover, spouse, significant other,* and *posslq* (census terminology for "People of Opposite Sex Sharing Living Quarters"), but none of these seemed satisfactory. We also do not like using the word *cohabitors,* but could find no more felicitous term. We use the words *gay men* for male homosexuals and *lesbians* for female homosexuals, and *same-sex couple* to describe them both. Other terms exist but we opted for these because we found them most acceptable to the people we were describing.

In the sections on money, work, and sex, we use the phrase *we find* . . . in presenting a conclusion based on statistical analyses of data from the questionnaires. When we feel the data are inconclusive, or subject to more than one interpretation, we begin our discussion with the words *we think.* . . . In these cases we are operating on what we believe is a good hunch, usually informed by related pieces of questionnaire data or by statements heard frequently in interviews. The interview data help us interpret our questionnaire findings, but unless we are using one of the parts of the interview that is readily quantifiable, we do not afford them the same trust we grant to information derived from the questionnaires.

The interviews serve another purpose. We use the interview material to illustrate both majority patterns and important exceptions. When we present tabulations of data from the questionnaires, we generally present statistical averages, which obscure the amount of variation that really exists. The central pattern is given and tells what is most commonly occurring, but the reader may forget that many people may be contained in the minority pattern. For example, if we were to say that most husbands are older than their wives, we would not be denying that there are quite a few marriages where the reverse is true. We would spend more time discussing the majority pattern, but if there was an interesting lesson to be learned, we might, with the help of some quotations, discuss the exceptions to the rule. If we say, for example, that married couples fight more over an issue than do cohabitors, again we are using a statistical average. We do not mean that every married couple fights more than any cohabiting couple. Readers who find themselves in the minority, rather than the majority, on a particular issue should realize they are an exception and not an oddity. No single person fits the average on every issue and everyone is an exception in one way or another.

There are many factors in couples' lives that we felt might affect their relationship. We tried to include, both in our analysis and in the writing, as many of these factors as we could think of, or could derive from scholarly writings or popular articles. For all four kinds of couples, we included: how long they have been together, partners' ages, income, whether each partner is employed, each partner's education level, church or synagogue attendance, whether or not they have children living with them (except gay men), and their own assessment of their masculinity or femininity. Some factors were considered only for the married couples, such as how many times they have been married, what opinions they have about marriage and its permanence, and their values concerning men's and women's roles in heterosexual relationships. For cohabitors, we sought to know whether either had ever been married, if this relationship was a "trial marriage" or not, and again their values concerning men's and women's roles in heterosexual relationships. For the gay men and lesbians, we included the question of how "closeted" they are, and how much they are involved in the gay or lesbian culture.

Some of these factors proved truly important, while others disappointed us by explaining less than we had expected. Only a few of our findings indicate that relationships can be affected by attendance at church or synagogue, the presence or absence of children and previous marriages of heterosexual couples. Among the same-sex couples, covertness about their homosexuality or involvement in the gay culture seldom mattered to relationships. Thus, when we discuss an issue, we present only the factors that did have an impact on the couple. If any factor is not mentioned, it means that we considered its impact a possibility but could find no concrete evidence of it.

# The American Couple in Historical Perspective

T HE American family has changed more in the last thirty years than in the previous two hundred and fifty. That is not an exaggeration. We do not have very precise information about personal life in the earliest days of the nation, but beginning with the census of 1790 one fact emerges quite clearly: The American couple—and its family—has been remarkably stable.[1]

Two things can be said about our knowledge of American marriages in the past: As we move farther back in time, the evidence gets sparser and the picture less clear, and in general we know more about the "facts" of marriage—the age at which people married, the size of their households—and less about the internal dynamics of their marriages, the emotional tone of the relationship, how happy people were, who made the decisions, etc.

But whatever the limitations in the quality of information on married couples over the last three hundred years, we are in much worse shape when it comes to evidence or even descriptions about people who lived together without marriage or about male couples and female couples. We know that such couples did exist: We have learned this from an occasional diary or courtroom account, and from physicians' notes which have surfaced from time to time. These scraps of evidence tell us something about alternative ways of living among a probably small and certainly clandestine group of people, but they give us a much less clear and detailed picture than we would like. Because of the lack of such information, much of this chapter will focus on the evolution of the heterosexual married couple of today. Wherever possible we will introduce what little is known about gay couples and other couples who were unmarried.

Except in times of war and other terrible disruptions of human life, the American couple has been a stable and predictable unit. It is, and has always been, fairly small; even in the 1700's it consisted of a husband, a wife, and approximately three children. The American couple guarded its privacy. This sense of a private, inviolate enclave was respected even by the children in the family as they reached the age of maturity. As soon as they were of age they left the household in which they were raised, either because of their own passionate desire for privacy or because their parents wished to reclaim their household, lands, or adult relationship. Most adult offspring struck out to form new households as soon as they could afford to or as soon as their parents could help them establish themselves.

As families (and the country as a whole) became more wealthy and as land opened up and became available in the West, young people married earlier: Poverty no longer held back the formation of new families. This situation is in sharp contrast to that in nineteenth-century Ireland, where farms were small in comparison to the large number of people they were expected to support. The soil was of poor quality, so it took as much land as the family could jointly afford and the labor of adult children as well as parents to produce enough food to survive. It took a long time for young Irish men to acquire enough money or land to support families of their own. Hence the average age of marriage in Ireland was extremely high, even in comparison to today's standards: middle to late twenties for women and middle to late thirties for men. But such constraints did not operate in rural America to keep young people in the homes where they were born. Land was more plentiful and parents encouraged their young people to form independent households and start their own families.

American families stayed small. There is no strong tradition in this country of the "extended family," where several generations *were expected* to live in the same dwelling. Afro-Americans had a cultural preference for the extended family but this was undermined by slavery and the social disruption after the Civil War. Other ethnic minorities, the Chinese and Japanese for example, occasionally adopted multigenerational living arrangements. But the only major exception among Caucasians is found during the great waves of immigration from eastern and southern Europe toward the end of the nineteenth century. Different cultural traditions combined with economic necessity to encourage larger families with relationships that went beyond the nuclear group (parents and offspring). But for these new arrivals, one of the first goals—and one of the clearest signs that they had become Americans—was surrendering their extended families to create their own households. And as the country developed and the Midwest and the West Coast were settled, children left their families and headed out to farm or to seek other opportunities. If moving from Boston to Philadelphia did not result in liberation, moving to California might. Americans revised the commandment "Honor thy father and mother" to read "Honor thy father and mother—but get away from them."

A small two-generation family is not our only cultural consistency; the American view of the family, and the couple at its core, has remained remarkably constant. In America, the home was a family's castle. What happened there among family members was considered the sole and exclusive province of those involved (usually the husband with advice and consent from the wife) and not of the state. How children or spouses or parents were treated, abusively or lovingly, has traditionally been left to the discretion of adult family members, and was not a legitimate area for interference by the government or the courts.

Moreover, within the family, the duties, expectations, and position of each member were always clearly understood and unquestioned. This held true even if everyday reality differed in some respects (as it did in most farming families where men and women were likely to share the same chores). In American families the husband was expected to be responsible for the economic support of the household, and the wife for all the "interior" considerations, e.g., child rearing, emotional support of the husband, household chores, relations with friends and kin. When the balance between the husband's responsibilities and wife's responsibilities tipped because of illness or economic exigency, it was generally viewed as a temporary departure from the ideal brought on by unavoidable and extraordinary circumstances. The notion of the "good life" was comprised of the hardworking and prosperous husband, the nurturing wife and mother, and the small and happy troop of children for whom she cared while preparing them for an independent future of happiness and achievement.

It was also assumed that the husband-wife relationship, and the entire family structure, was based on, and stabilized by, the affection all the members held for one another. The couple came together and the family stayed together because they all *loved* and respected one another. Because romantic love was the basis for a marriage (rather than money or property), young adults were more or less left alone to choose a partner. But because marriage also entailed the beginning of a lifetime commitment with accompanying responsibilities, parents tried to make sure that their children met only the right kind of potential mate. Falling in love with the wrong person would have a devastating impact on one's offspring's chances in life. It was considered appropriate, therefore, for parents to intervene in courtships they disapproved of. Other institutions (for example, schools and universities) were expected to act *in loco parentis,* which meant that they enforced parental values, as much as possible, especially regarding courtship and sexuality.

A tension developed between unsupervised dating (having a good time while acquiring self-knowledge and social skills) and courtship (dating that could result in marriage). Since what had started out as unsupervised dating might easily turn into courtship, parents feared democratic environments that exposed their child to someone who could be endured as a date but would never be accepted as a son- or daughter-in-law. Thus, sometimes openly, but more often unconsciously, parents supported a double standard that allowed their children to experiment with "exotic" partners, but subtly directed their children's serious romantic commitments toward people who met parental standards. A son who wanted to explore sexuality before marriage (a troublesome, yet expected male pursuit), was encouraged, at least tacitly, as long as his adventures did not jeopardize a "proper" marital alliance in the future. Prostitutes and women from very different social classes were accessible and permitted sexual partners for young men in the middle  or upper-middle class. The relationships between these men and women were clearly arranged and understood to be outside the context of romance or extended emotional commitment. Such experimentation was not considered necessary or appropriate for respectable young women. They were to encourage men of "good" family (the definition of "good" depending on one's race, class, religion) and to discourage any sexual relations. Premarital sex, in the woman's case, would not be tolerated. She would be considered "soiled" and her marriageability would be jeopardized.

Thus, romantic love—in the *right* context and with the *right* type of person—is and has been glorified in our country. Marry someone handsome and wealthy and you will be congratulated, but say you are not in love with that person and your cynicism will earn you the censure of all around you. At the same time it is clear that people accrue great benefits (often in terms of an improved standard of living) by the marriages they contract. "Marrying up" is applauded as long as one does not consciously admit to having made this the foundation for choosing a mate. We, as a people, still firmly believe that arranged marriages and marriages of convenience, are un-American.

And Americans have always married "forever." If the marriage contract was abrogated because of desertion, death, or divorce, this was seen as a personal and community tragedy. No one ever thought of marrying for one year or for ten years, and "Till death us do part" is still part of most contemporary marriage ceremonies. This may be no more than a pious hope today in the face of the current divorce statistics, but at the same time that the witnesses to the wedding are feeling a certain cynicism about the couple's future, the couple themselves cling tenaciously to the belief and hope that theirs will be a marriage of permanence. The American tradition is to hope for the best, which means a lifetime of loyalty to and from one's marriage partner.

This partnership was expected to find its ultimate expression in the establishment of a family. But having children required giving up past freedoms and the prospect of making one's way in the world as an independent agent. The decision to have children (and before the widespread use of contraceptives, deciding to have children was synonymous with having sex) was predicated in part on the absolute assurance that the paternity would be acknowledged, that economic support would be guaranteed, and that a paternal presence would be maintained. The family was, consequently, bonded both emotionally and legally; informal expectations were upheld by law and public opinion.

This exceptionally stable ideal of the American family was challenged and changed at two historical periods. Events democratized marriage by giving each member of the couple an opportunity to leave the household and establish a life elsewhere. Traditionally, partners were not allowed the choice of maintaining or terminating their marriage contract. But when the husband "got the vote," the institution of marriage became less stable. When the wife got the vote as well, the institution began to crumble. The institution was no longer larger than the sum of its parts.

What events began the progressive "getting of the vote" for husband and wife? The first was the Industrial Revolution. The latter part of the nineteenth century ushered in new forms of technology that drew men away from the farms and into the cities and factories. The interdependent farm couple (where each partner needed the other for cooperation in the daily survival chores) began to disappear. Husbands left the farm community, and its familiar faces and relationships, and began to see the big, wide world and what it had to offer. The first step in what ultimately was to become the suburbanization and isolation of the American woman had begun.

The second historical event was the Second World War, which accelerated a process that had already been under way during the Depression years. The war made it necessary for hundreds of thousands of women to enter the labor force in order to support their families. They also had to take over jobs, vital to the American economy, that had been vacated when their husbands went into the armed forces. After the war industry worked hard and with some success to "defeminize" the work force; nevertheless, many women remained on the job—or at least recalled what it was like to work for compensation outside the home. Things were never the same again in the American family. Both husbands and wives were out of the home and developed new opportunities, new skills, and new acquaintances. Family life began to change.

The changes were not apparent at the time. On the contrary. While the divorce rate had actually been rising since the turn of the century, it had done so at such a slow and steady pace that few observers were alarmed. Marriage and divorce rates shot up briefly right after World War II, but they fell again sharply and then gradually returned to their previous levels. By the 1950's the United States had entered the most family-oriented period of the century—the generation of the Feminine Mystique and the Baby Boom—and couples married at the youngest ages in recorded American history. During the 1950's, 96 percent of people in the childbearing years married.[2] Women's magazines, newspapers, movies, and television were all extolling the perfect family life: zany, if one watched *I Love Lucy;* warm and wise, if it was *I Remember Mama;* or somewhere in between, for *Father Knows Best* or *My Three Sons.* No one recognized that the family was in transition and that couples would never again be the same.

But by the end of the fifties and early sixties, radical changes were becoming evident. The marriage rate began to fall and the divorce rate, which had been fairly level, accelerated its historical trend upward.[3] Now, imagine if you will a movie that takes three hours to unreel the credits, four hours to introduce the characters, and only five minutes to reveal the entire plot. This is an analogy to the history of the modern American couple. Changes that had taken a hundred years to germinate suddenly began to appear at a startling rate, and new family problems were full-blown before we had any idea that they existed.

In the late sixties and early seventies, fertility began to decline. It has stayed low—16.0 live births per 1,000 in 1982.[4] This was not entirely due, as some social scientists have suggested, to the emergence of the Pill on American college campuses, in family clinics, and in private physicians' offices. The Pill did enable women to make childbearing a choice, and after 1974, access to legal abortions became a way for some estimated 13 to 20 percent of the population to terminate unwanted pregnancies. But, in point of fact, the national trend of having fewer children had been developing over the past two hundred years; the baby-boom years were the exception, not the rule. The most profound impact made by the Pill was that it allowed women to have sex without linking it to reproduction, introducing them to the idea that making love could be spontaneous, enjoyable—and above all, an act whose consequences they could control. Accepted views about fertility—how large a family to have and when—had been changing before the Industrial Revolution and the new values were simply enhanced, not created, by the new scientific method of contraception.[5]

In the early seventies, the marriage rate for people under forty-five was as low as it had been at the end of the Depression. By 1974, the average age of marriage was a full year higher than it had been in the 1950's, and the proportion of women who remained unmarried until they reached the ages of twenty to twenty-four had increased by one third since 1960. The divorce rate had soared to the level it had attained only for a moment right after the Second World War, and one out of every three marriages of women at least thirty years old (the rate varies depending on the age group) was ending in divorce.[6] This information is particularly dramatic if one recalls that divorce statistics do not include desertion statistics.

Americans suddenly looked around and saw that social change seemed to have gotten out of hand. The statistics from the early seventies indicate enormous changes in social trends bearing on the meaning of marriage. The statistics of the eighties suggest that while some of the rates of change are slowing down a bit, the direction of change is persistent.

# The present situation

In 1960, 28 percent of American women between the ages of twenty and twenty-four had not yet married. By 1979, the figure had jumped to 49 percent. (This was a return to pre-1940 levels.[7]) In 1981, 52 percent of women that age were single.[8] This fact alone can have enormous repercussions. First, a woman's fertility (the number of children she will bear over the course of her life) is strongly related to the age at which she marries. The later the marriage, for the most part, the later childbearing begins, and the smaller the family. We are already seeing later childbearing and smaller families. In 1970, 16 percent of the women twenty-five to twenty-nine years old who had ever been married were childless.[9] In 1981, that number rose to 25 percent. The greatest rise in the fertility rate was among women thirty to thirty-four years old. But that is not changing the larger picture. The actual fertility replacement rate in 1981 was about 1.8, well below the level of 2.1 that is needed to replace the present population.[10] There was an increase in 1982 of about 2 percent, but this merely indicates more women of childbearing age, not a change in the size of families.[11] Second, the smaller the family, the less difficult it is for a woman to divorce. Delaying marriage gives a woman more opportunity for advanced education and training, reduces the number of children she will have, and ultimately gives her more independence and flexibility in making life choices. Its secondary effect is to give exactly the same advantages to her husband.

Two explanations are generally offered for the decline in marriage rates and the rise in age of marriage: First, a much higher percentage of the population is going to college and beyond, and extended education tends to delay marriage. Second, men and women are being affected by what Paul Glick, formerly senior demographer at the U.S. Bureau of the Census, has referred to as the "marriage squeeze." By this he means that more people want to marry than can be accommodated. For example, women tend to marry men who are two or three years older than themselves. This works out well when the size of the population at each of these ages is approximately the same—for example, if there is an approximately equal number of twenty-year-old women and twenty-three-year-old men.

But that is not how the population took shape in the years following the maturing of the baby-boom children. From 1945 to about 1960, couples were having rather large families. Girls from these families are now women in their twenties and thirties looking for either their first or second husband. They lament—and their comments are echoed in the popular magazines—that a "good man is hard to find." Why? Because there were fewer men born to the generation directly preceding them, and so the ratio of women to men who are a few years older than themselves is unfavorable. In addition, men in their second marriages tend to marry women five or more years their junior, and the statistics show that if a man remarries in his forties, he may choose a partner *ten* years younger than himself. In 1980, 94 percent of all men aged fifty were married! Marriage, even remarriage, is not possible for every woman born in the baby-boom years unless she marries someone younger than herself, or unless there is a great deal of rotation among the available men.[12] The high divorce rate, in an ironic sort of way, is helping these women by "recycling" men into the marriage market. These ratios are even more lopsided for black women. Interracial marriage increases the difference, with black men marrying white women approximately twice as often as black women marry white men.[13]

By the time women are in the forty- to forty-four-year age group, there are 300,000 fewer men than women or 141 single women to every 100 men, and if we include separated and divorced women, it is 213 women to 100 men. If we consider only those who are widowed, it is about 644 widows to 100 widowers. So as people enter their forties there are 233 unattached women for every 100 men.[14]

Age is a particularly strong impediment to remarriage for women. If a woman is divorced in her twenties, she has a 76 percent chance of remarriage. In her thirties her chances drop to 56 percent, and in her forties they plunge to 32 percent. If she is in her fifties or older she has less than a 12 percent chance of remarriage. Men fare better, particularly if they are well-off, educated, and in a prestigious profession. Such men are often described as "catches," and the evidence shows that they do indeed get caught. Data from 1970 indicate that more than 90 percent of these men (both white and black) were currently married. Only 2 percent of high-achieving white men and 5 percent of similar black men had never married. And the highest earners among divorced men remarry most quickly; they are not on the market very long.[15]

Age, however, is not the only impediment. Another factor that diminishes a woman's chance of remarrying is success at work: The more she achieves in her job, the greater her chance of divorce and the smaller her chance of remarriage. For example, in 1977 women between the ages of thirty-five and forty-four with postgraduate degrees and personal incomes above $20,000 had four times the divorce rate of women with lower achievement. They also had a 20 percent greater chance of never remarrying. This was especially true if the woman had a relatively late first marriage. Let us consider men in the same category. They do just fine: A man with a postgraduate degree is half as likely as his female counterpart to get divorced.[16]

Children complicate the situation. While awards of custody are changing a bit, a single-parent household is still most likely to be headed by a woman. In 1981, 24 percent of all children were living with only one parent, and 90 percent of these children were living with their mothers.[17] At present, relatively few fathers go to court to get custody, and courts still show a pronounced tendency to award custody to the mother. The major exception to this is the concept of joint custody which is becoming more common and gives *each* parent an equal voice in major decisions affecting their children. Even here, however, the child tends to live with the mother.[18]

While we are supposed to be a nation that loves its children, remarriage statistics indicate that the financial and emotional tasks that accompany child rearing may deter many suitors. A woman with no children has a 73 percent chance of remarriage. With two children her chances dip to 63 percent, and with three they drop to 56 percent. It is interesting, however, that her age has a stronger impact on her remarriageability than the number of children she has. If she has three children but is still in her twenties, she has a 72 percent likelihood of marrying again. If she is childless but in her thirties, her chance of remarrying is only 60 percent.[19]

This may mean that youth and beauty outweigh the man's fear of taking on additional dependents. Or it may have something to do with the age of the children. Younger women are more likely to have younger children, and a man may be more interested if the children are young enough to accept him in a parental role. Or it may be that thirty-year-old women are more established in careers and therefore less willing to marry after having tasted independence. The woman in her twenties with children may not have developed a career or found a job with a great deal of security. With several children, she probably cannot afford the luxury of being choosy about her next husband. Being the head of a large household is very demanding and without the support of a sizeable income, a woman may consider men she would not have looked at before her first marriage. Thus, she and a thirty-year-old divorcée without children may have completely different needs and therefore completely different romantic interests.

Marriages *are* increasing but perhaps not everyone still has the same chance to make that commitment. In 1982, there were 2 percent more marriages than in 1981 and 16 percent more than in 1975. We have reached a new national record.[20] But this is not necessarily a comforting statistic because the divorce rate is almost three times what it was in the 1960's. Demographers project that half of first marriages now taking place will end in divorce and that, nationwide, 41 percent of all people now of marriageable age will at some time experience a divorce.[21] There seems to be some connection to geography. In 1971, the divorce rate was lowest in the Northeast (3.6 per 1,000 people), increasing through the North Central States (6.0 per 1,000) and the South (6.1 per 1,000) and becoming highest (at 6.6 per 1,000) on the West Coast.[22] It prompts one to wonder if a couple could save their marriage by moving from California to Maine.

This kind of divorce rate terrifies people who are trying to plan a lifetime relationship and distresses those who have a durable marriage and want the same kind of permanence for their children. No one is immune from the fear that a divorce may befall someone in his or her extended family or circle of friends. Even the elderly do not seem to be totally free from risk. While it is true that the highest probability of divorce falls between the second and sixth years of marriage (and between the first and fourth years in second marriages), the rate is still quite high throughout the entire life cycle.[23] Comparing 1978 statistics with those for 1968, the greatest *increase* in the rate of divorce is in people between the ages of twenty-five and thirty-nine, where it has risen 65 percent. People under twenty-five have experienced an increase of 50 percent, as have people between forty and sixty-five. Divorce has even risen by 35 percent among men and women over sixty-five.[24] It is commonly believed that second marriages are safer, on the assumption that people must necessarily learn something from their first ventures. But actually the divorce rate for second marriages is even higher than for first marriages.[25] Even though the latest available national statistics finally showed a slowdown in divorce in 1982 (for the first time since 1962), it is hard for people to feel safe. Three percent fewer people divorced in 1982 than in 1981, but the rate is still very high.[26] Is it any wonder that we saw a need for this study?

This change in the permanence of marriage must also be considered in connection with its impact on the entire family. The number of children involved in divorces is now more than 1 million a year. The number of children below the age of eighteen in households headed by women increased from 8.7 million in 1970 to 9.4 million in 1976 and 10.3 million in 1980. This represents one quarter of all American children. While the average number of children in each divorce is declining, this is still a distressing figure. Many children these days stand a good chance of becoming part of a "broken" family. Andrew Cherlin believes that if current rates of divorce continue, one third of all white children and three fifths of all black children born between 1970 and 1973 will be in a household affected by divorce by the time the child is sixteen years of age.[27]

Today many children require some form of care from someone other than their parents. This is because their mothers will want or need to work, and their fathers, if present, will also be out in the labor force. In 1982, approximately 52 percent of all women were working.

Forty-eight percent of all married mothers with children under the age of six work outside the home.[28] In a recent study, a national sample of high-school seniors favored full-time or half-time work for childless wives. The majority, however, still preferred that mothers with pre-school children stay at home, working part time at most.[29] But statistics indicate that, like it or not, many of these mothers *will* work outside the home.

This causes a great deal of reorganization of the family. Young children are placed with relatives or in formal or informal child-care environments. Both men and women worry about the quality of care their children are receiving, and husbands often criticize their wives for leaving the children to go to work, or lose respect for themselves for needing their wives' income. The home is empty during the day and many housekeeping chores are not done until after work—if at all. Men and women come home from a workday tired and often under a great deal of stress, and so their interactions with their children are frequently brief and spoiled by less than ideal amounts of energy and patience.

All this is occurring at a time of intense dialogue about men's and women's roles. The women's movement has established itself so well—in national political organizations as well as in local interest groups—that there is both large-scale and locally organized opposition. The right to work, control over fertility and birth, the presence of egal-itarian role-models in books and in movies, the ordination of women—are all hotly contested issues.

Sexual behavior is a major focus for all this political activism. The "sexual revolution" is being attacked by groups who blame the changes in the family on new sexual mores. There is, however, no evidence of a trend to sexual conservatism. Alfred Kinsey alerted the general public to patterns of male and female sexuality in the late forties and early fifties. In the years since his studies, national women's magazines, such as *Redbook* and *Cosmopolitan*, and men's magazines like *Playboy* have done surveys showing that substantial changes have occurred in women's sexual behavior, and smaller but significant changes were observed among men. How-to books like Alex Comfort's *The Joy of Sex* (followed by Charles Silverstein and Edmund White's *The Joy of Gay Sex*, and Emily Sisley and Bertha Harris's *The Joy of Lesbian Sex*) became best sellers.[30] Serious and scientific study of sexuality (such as Masters and Johnson on heterosexual and homosexual sexuality, and Helen Singer Kaplan on sex therapies) were important contributions to public un-derstanding and to the new and growing field of sexual counseling.[31]

From our overview of the current state of couples in the United States one overwhelming conclusion must be drawn. Families are in a significant state of flux, and the uncertainty reverberates throughout society. One consequence is that people are apprehensive about the future—the future of personal relationships in general, and the future of the specific relationships that nourish them. They do not know how to design what they want or protect what they have. They are unsure about the future of marriage.

That unsureness is reflected in experiments with new ways of structuring intimate relationships. One way that has been increasing in popularity and visibility is *cohabitation*. While we have a great deal of useful information about marriages, we know a good deal less about unmarried cohabitation in the United States during the last fifteen years, and we have almost no information about it before that time.

What information we do have is particularly recent. Graham Spanier, using data from the March 1981 population survey, estimated that there were about 1.8 million unmarried couples of the opposite sex living together in the United States, about 4 percent of all couples.[32] That was an increase of 14 percent over 1980 and a threefold increase since 1970. Between 1977 and 1979 the increase was 40 percent![33] It is possible that part of this marked acceleration is because earlier researchers did not try as hard to locate the couples, and also because the couples themselves were reluctant to reveal their living arrangements. Nevertheless, the rapidity of change in the number of couples living together is striking.

This is not to say that this increase will continue indefinitely. If that happened, America would quickly become a nation populated solely by cohabitors. However, one thing is clear: Now that cohabitation no longer attracts as much disapproval as it once did (and therefore no longer entails as many social costs for the individual, such as parental outrage or punitive job discrimination), it will probably become more visible and more common than ever.

Critics have warned that cohabitation is a dangerous new form that will replace marriage. They hold out the prospect of large numbers of children born without "legitimacy." Right now, however, cohabitation continues to be primarily a *childless* life-style. While many cohabitors may have full or partial custody of children from a previous marriage, or visitation rights, all evidence points to the fact that when cohabitors consider adding children to their relationship, they are very reluctant to do so without first becoming legally married. Seventy-two percent of the cohabiting couples in 1981 did not have any children living with them.[34] There has been, however, a slight increase in cohabiting couples where one person has full-time custody of children. Thus, cohabitation may become less of a childless life-style than it has been in the past.

Richard Clayton and Harwin Voss conducted a study in 1977 that found that 18 percent of a random sample of American men had at some time lived with a woman for six months or more without being married to her. Only 5 percent of their respondents were living with a woman at the time they were interviewed. It was a more common occurrence among black men than white, and more prevalent among urban than rural men. The majority of men who were cohabiting had been married at least once in their lives, but the majority of the men did *not* plan to marry their present partners, and indeed did not marry them. If the man had been previously married, there was a slightly higher probability that he would marry the woman he was living with.[35]

The cohabiting couples in our study make an interesting comparison to the men Clayton and Voss reported on. Ours is not a random sample and therefore we must rely on works such as theirs for orientation. Among our cohabitors only 38 percent of the men considered it a strong likelihood that they would marry their partners, while 58 percent professed the desire to marry them eventually. These responses are not vastly different from the one derived from the earlier study, but it becomes much more interesting when we take into account our women. They are slightly less likely than the men to *expect* to marry their partners (35 percent), but they are somewhat more *eager* to marry them (65 percent).

The pattern strikes us as especially provocative when we look separately at the cohabitors who have never been married and compare them with those who have been divorced or widowed. The previously married women are less eager to marry (61 percent) than the women who had never been married (68 percent). Previous marriage had no negative impact on the men.

These findings bring to mind sociologist Jessie Bernard's insightful observations on marriage in her book *The Future of Marriage*.[36] She argues very forcefully that for most American couples, being married is a much better "deal" for the husband than for the wife. She concludes this from her reading of a large number of studies which show that married men are healthier, happier, and saner than the unmarried—while just the opposite is true for wives.

Other research on cohabitation has in general confirmed our own findings: At present, cohabitation for most couples is not a lifetime commitment. Clayton and Voss's study found that most cohabiting couples either got married or ended their relationship in a relatively short time.[37] While our study has many couples who have lived together between five and eight years, we had a very difficult time finding couples who had lived together for as many as ten years. (Fewer than 2 percent had lived together ten years or more.)[38] This is consistent with other researchers' findings. But it is difficult to interpret what is happening. On the one hand, it is possible that most cohabiting couples do marry or break up before they reach the tenth year. On the other hand, it may be that our eight-year cohabitors were among the first to deliberately adopt living together as a very new and daring life-style. We shall have to wait several years to see if that first generation survives to celebrate their tenth or fifteenth anniversary.

In spite of the five-to-eight-year cohabitors in our sample, most of our couples have lived together a much shorter time (54 percent had been together for two years or less). This is consistent with the study by Glick and Spanier who found that the majority of cohabiting couples shared the same housing for less than two years. Unfortunately, their data did not show whether the couples broke up or married.

There are other interesting statistics from Spanier's 1983 article on cohabitation. Cohabitors who have never been previously married are relatively young: About 81 percent of the males and 88 percent of the females are under thirty-five. However, if the couple has been previously married, the age profile changes. Only 36 percent of the males and 46 percent of the females are under age thirty-five; 40 percent and 31 percent, respectively, are thirty-five to fifty-four years old; and 24 percent and 22 percent, respectively, are sixty-five or older.[39] When we consider the effect age has on life-styles and on personal needs, we can see how misleading it would be to think of all cohabitors as wanting the same things or behaving in the same ways for the same reasons. Unfortunately, in-depth studies of cohabitation have been almost exclusively concentrated on college students or other young people. Our information on older cohabitors should help this situation (14 percent of our male cohabitors and 9 percent of our female cohabitors are over forty).

Thus, while cohabitation is not well chronicled and is not historically a major pattern among American couples, it interests us now because of its dramatic increase and also because it may tell us something new about intimacy between adults. The number of people involved may be small (between 2 percent and 3.8 percent of couples, depending on which demographer is making the estimates), but their significance is out of proportion to their numbers. If we look at households where the man is under twenty-five, the picture becomes more impressive. The percentage of cohabitors more than doubles—to 7.4 percent. While this is still far fewer couples than in some countries (such as Sweden where the cohabitation rate is estimated at 12 percent of the couple population), it may mean that the future will contain more cohabiting couples than the present statistical pattern would indicate.[40] We cannot know whether this means more "trial marriages" leading either to breakups or "real marriages," or more people adopting cohabitation as a permanent life-style.

Demographer Judith Blake has reasoned that because marriage is now less predictably secure—both in its emotional and its financial benefits—the line between cohabitation and marriage is becoming blurred.[41] This is especially true in states where an unmarried partner has been given the right to sue for division of property. If the couple were married this might be called a part of the alimony. In the case of cohabitors, the media have had a lot of fun with the concept and have coined the term "palimony." The reality of going into court after living together, however, is not very funny. People who choose to live together to *avoid* economic interdependence and obligation are learning that it may be out of their control. A very important and widely publicized legal decision stated the case for the financial accountability of ex-cohabitors to one another. This was the suit of Michele Triola against Lee Marvin, and it was the Supreme Court of the State of California that rendered the following opinion:

> The mere fact that a couple have not participated in a valid marriage ceremony cannot serve as a basis for a court's inference that the couple intended to keep their earnings and property separate and independent.

Under this interpretation of the legal obligations of cohabitation, Lee Marvin was assessed $104,000 for Ms. Triola's "rehabilitation." Rehabilitation, in this case, was the opportunity to establish herself as an economically independent person. This is the same logic behind spousal support, given for a limited period following a divorce, to allow the ex-wife time for training or education that will allow her to earn an independent living.

This means that the courts are recognizing cohabitation as an unspoken business partnership, at the very least. In earlier decades, the moral stance of the country might have allowed the woman to be left penniless because she was blamed for entering into a sordid arrangement. At present, the judicial system, by allowing cohabitors to appear in court and make claims against each other, is in a sense legitimizing this kind of living arrangement. Indeed, some have argued that while the courts are not making it *the same* as marriage, they are certainly making it a type of marriage.[42] Ironically, at the same time, the courts generally seem unwilling to sanction living arrangements between pairs of men or pairs of women, in spite of the fact that many gay men and lesbians feel they deserve legal recognition.

Lesbian couples and gay male couples make up a significant and integral part of our study. When we first began this project, writings by social scientists on homosexual couples were essentially nonexistent, and it was necessary for us to base our questions entirely on our own observations and our discussions over the years with many gay people. Although same-sex *couples* had not been studied, there was already a voluminous literature about gay men and lesbians as individuals. Almost all the competent, nonmoralistic research on homosexuality has been conducted during the last ten years, and gay men have tended to receive more attention than lesbians.[43]

Until the 1970's, gay men and lesbians were a fairly invisible part of the American population. Before that time, almost all gay people wished to avoid the risks that would come with a disclosure of their sexual preference. Hostility and discrimination at the hands of an unaccepting society created a climate of secrecy that did not permit challenges to the prevailing stereotypes.

Historical evidence on this matter is particularly difficult to gather. Western society has a long tradition of fear and hatred of homosexuality. It is such an ardent aversion that the reaction has been termed *homophobic*. While some non-Western societies tolerate homosexual behavior or see it as appropriate for certain people (such as the young or for men when women are not around),[44] Judeo-Christian cultures have labeled sex between two people of the same sex *an abomination*. Therefore, since any form of living arrangement except marriage was totally condemned in Europe and then in the New World, homosexuals had no other choice but to make their existence as invisible as possible.

Most of what we know about homosexuals in the past is from those unfortunate individuals who were unable to keep their lives private and suffered the consequences. Most of our information comes from court trials and other public documents announcing punishments for sexual offenses. If discovered, homosexuals could lose their lives, since homosexuality was often a capital offense. Specific punishments varied by location in Colonial times and throughout the sixteenth, seventeenth, and eighteenth centuries, but court records and memoirs record punishments that range from public execution, drowning, castration, and court-martial to imprisonment and lobotomy. The very best a homosexual might hope for was to be discharged from work and to be publicly ostracized. Even with this great need for discretion, there is evidence that communities of gay men existed in the late 1800's, and social commentators will often refer to certain occupations (such as "counter jumpers" in the dry-goods trade) as being filled by gay men. Books mention homosexual houses of prostitution and the use by gay men of special clothes so that other homosexual men could recognize them.[45] What we do not know are what kind of intimate relationships existed within the "gay life." We do not know how the need for subterfuge affected the ability to create long-term bonds.

Historians have more insight into the history of homosexual women. In Colonial times women were allowed and encouraged to have female friendships, and those who were unlucky enough to stay single would not have been censured for moving in with another spinster lady. Even close romantic relationships between women were allowed because they were never imagined to be sexual. Recent research into literature, diaries, and letters of women of the last three centuries affords a glimpse of women's most personal and intense feelings for one another. Written in the sentimental style of their time, these documents lead modern readers to conclude that these women were lovers who had sexual contact with one another. They describe their longing for one another in the same sensuous terms female lovers today would use. For example:

> Molly ended her letter to Helena, "I shall return in a few days. Imagine yourself kissed many times by one who loved you dearly."[46]

Such passionate language, however, is felt by some scholars to be merely the heartfelt evocation of love as it is known in friendship rather than in sexual rapture.[47] Women were allowed such latitude of emotional expression that they could use words reserved for lovers and not be aware that their affection and commitment could also be sexual. There is a great debate as to whether these women actually had sex with one another, but it is agreed that the friendships they made were serious, loyal, long-lasting, and like marriages, except—perhaps—for sexual contact. Women would write adoring letters to each other over a lifetime. They might live together as young women, separate when they married, have children, and then rejoin when they were widowed. Most of these women could carry on regular existences as wives and also maintain these special friendships. It was only in bohemian or literary circles of the late 1800's and early 1900's that a few women actually wore men's clothes or adopted male prerogatives such as having a career, traveling alone, or creating an identity as an independent person. These women evoked a more severe reaction from those who observed them.[48] Still, from the accounts we have read (such as the life of Natalie Barney) women were allowed more license than their male counterparts would ever have been granted. They might be seen as odd or even insane, and their families might reject them, but they, unlike the men, were rarely subjected to violence and punishment.

Women were protected for most of history because they were assumed to be pure and chaste—uninterested in sexual expression. Close relationships, even if suspected to be sexual, were not regarded as a threat to the established order since no illegitimate heir could result from a woman's relationship with another woman. Author Lillian Faderman argues that romantic friendships between young women in previous centuries were often encouraged as "training" for heterosexual marriage.[49] Sensitivities could be developed so that women's gentler nature would blossom even more and be of great benefit to their future husbands. Among the upper classes, men and women occupied separate worlds during marriage, which made a wife's desire to keep the company of other women very understandable and socially convenient. It was never feared that these relationships would compete with the marital household. After all, a woman's place was in the home, so there was little worry that they would leave for some other way of life.

In the late nineteenth century, the secrecy that shrouded gay male relationships began to lift. Dialogues on sexuality that had heretofore existed only within the religious, academic, and medical professions began to be more open. Homosexuality became an interest for physicians in particular because they saw it as an unhealthy biological condition they could reverse. At the time, this was considered to be an enlightened approach because it offered an alternative to incarceration and physical punishment. They categorized homosexuality as an illness, not a crime.

The medical profession began to take on responsibility for a number of other judgments regarding sexuality and health. It was the medical establishment that launched the Victorian campaign against masturbation, based on the erroneous notion that "self-abuse" would produce all manner of physical and mental deterioration. They also considered marital sexual relations potentially dangerous to a healthy body and warned that they should occur only in moderation and preferably for procreation. Masturbation, excessive intercourse, and most especially, homosexual behavior headed the list of injurious sexual practices warned against by "modern medicine."

In this climate, competing theories about sexuality and homosexuality sprang up. One posited that homosexuality was determined before birth, and so homosexuals might be "degenerates," but they were not personally to blame for their condition. Nevertheless, it was still considered necessary to isolate them from the rest of society. Anti-homosexual laws were strengthened and prosecutions increased in Germany, England, and the United States. "Moral entrepreneurs," people who took it upon themselves to guard the public's moral health (as defined by themselves), set out to discover and punish gross indecency. The "medical" approach to homosexuality became increasingly entrenched. A number of physicians argued that homosexuality was a disease, but they were not in agreement about whether it was communicable. In 1886, an influential work on the subject appeared. In *Psychopathia Sexualis,* the German physician Richard von Krafft-Ebing argued that homosexuality was the result of a congenital problem in the central nervous system and was unchangeable. Homosexuals were, therefore, "sick," but not through any fault of their own. They should be treated therapeutically by the medical profession rather than criminally by the courts.[50]

Krafft-Ebing was, in a sense, an intellectual forefather to Sigmund Freud. In true Oedipal fashion, Freud took him on, criticized his work, and attempted to redefine the nature of human sexuality.[51] Freud saw sexuality as normal, and indeed necessary for good "mental health." Homosexuals, according to Freud, were stuck at one point in sexual development, a stage that "normal" people passed through on their way to "mature" (hetero)sexuality. He saw homosexuals, accordingly, as "regressed" but not "sick." He rejected genetic explanations and indeed said that "inversion" was not disabling; rather, he felt that it was often found in people of high intellectual ability and impeccable moral character. In a letter to the mother of a homosexual son, he said that "homosexuality is assuredly no advantage, but it is nothing to be ashamed of, no vice, no degradation, it cannot be classified as an illness." These conclusions were largely ignored by the medical/psychiatric profession that otherwise shaped itself according to Freud's views. Therapists considered homosexuality a problem in need of cure—in part because they were usually exposed to troubled people, who came to them confused, unhappy, and guilt-ridden. Psychiatrists, starting from the proposition that there could be no such thing as a healthy homosexual, prescribed long-term therapies, shock treatments, and even brain surgery. Rates of change were extremely low.

The definition of what homosexuality is, and what attitude society ought to have toward homosexuals, continues to be an important social debate. On one side are a group of psychoanalysts and psychiatrists who vehemently support the view that homosexuality is a diagnosable sickness which can be cured through psychiatry. On the other side of the debate are other psychoanalysts, and a large number of psychiatrists, psychologists, and social scientists who follow a more "live-and-let-live" approach to homosexuality. These professionals have been guided by recent scientific research that indicates that homosexuality is not the result of any personal problem or family deficiency and does not indicate any psychological maladjustment.[52]

This tradition began in the 1940's and 1950's. Alfred Kinsey and his associates—Wardell Pomeroy, Clyde Martin, and Paul Gebhard—published the findings from their large surveys of male and female sexuality in 1948 and 1953.[53] For the first time the public was exposed to more statistical information than had ever before been gathered about the actual sexual practices and attitudes of Americans. They had before them summaries of the detailed sexual histories of more than sixteen thousand men and women. Homosexuality and bisexuality were placed on a continuum of sexual behavior and found to be a great deal more common than anyone had suspected. It was particularly shocking to learn that large numbers of heterosexual people had had more than incidental homosexual experience. Kinsey insisted that homosexual behavior was well within the norm of ordinary sexuality. The book was a landmark because it was descriptive and nonjudgmental. The public reaction was not: Readers and commentators were upset about the extent and variety of sexual practices in the United States. American moral pride was hurt, and once again moral entrepreneurs attempted to censor Kinsey's findings and to destroy his research operation. But Kinsey was widely read, and despite methodological flaws, his findings were replicated in other studies.

Since the publication of Kinsey's work, a number of important psychological and sociological studies have attempted to lay to rest the question of the normalcy of homosexuals and homosexual conduct. The Wolfenden report, a study commissioned for the British Parliament in 1957 and based on expert testimony from hundreds of people, recommended that homosexuality be decriminalized in Britain. Homosexuality, the report concluded, was not harmful, was not a disease, and was not a therapeutic problem.[54] Psychologist Evelyn Hooker compared a group of homosexual men who were not in psychotherapy (in contrast to the homosexuals who had been studied by earlier researchers) with a group of heterosexual men with the same background (age, education, etc.), and she found no difference in psychological profiles.[55] Psychologist Mark Freedman had similar results with women.[56]

Ultimately, the American Psychiatric Association and the American Psychological Association convened panels to review all the available data on homosexuality so that a general statement might be made about the health of homosexual people and the nature of homosexual conduct. Both these organizations agreed that while homosexuality is a minority pattern, it is not a manifestation of psychological problems. The majority of the psychological community had finally and clearly stated that homosexuality is not an illness nor is it a cause, in and of itself, for medical intervention.

These conclusions have at last allowed researchers as well as clinicians to concentrate on other aspects of same-sex preference. A good deal of research has now been done on why people become homosexual and how homosexual people live, on gay communities, gay history, and gay politics. There are many books by individuals who have come to terms with being gay in a society that, at best, practices toleration of diversity, and at worst, makes life miserable for people who are not heterosexual. But there has been very little research on the relationships between homosexual people. This has been particularly true of books that reach the heterosexual reader. Traditionally, researchers and the media have concentrated on the ways that gay people are different. The fact that gay men and lesbians form long-term relationships and face the same problems as do heterosexual couples has not been well explored. As a result, except for a few good articles on gay couples, there is a paucity of academic information, with almost no appeal to a general readership.[57] Gay couples have been even more invisible in American life than have gay individuals.

It is very difficult to document recent historical changes in the lives of same-sex couples. But it does seem that gay men and lesbians have been following the same course as heterosexual couples. It is our impression that homosexual couples went through the familial fifties right along with the rest of the country. At a time when traditional assumptions about sex roles in marriage remained unchallenged (husband as protector and provider, wife as homemaker and nurturer), many gay and lesbian couples fell into a pattern of role playing. The terms "butch" and "femme," which were used in the lesbian community, reflected a very stringent division of roles between the masculine and the feminine. A "butch" woman was expected to perform male tasks and be the greater financial support of the couple. She was also expected to project a masculine demeanor and style of behavior. The "femme" was her feminine counterpart. Although gay men did not use such terms, there was a sense that one partner in a couple should be more masculine and the other more feminine. How prominent or how widespread these patterns were among lesbians and gay men in the 1950's and earlier is impossible for us to know because of the lack of research, but it is probably true that they were more common when gender roles were more rigidly adhered to by everyone.

Role playing, however, is no longer in vogue. While many gay and lesbian couples had already rejected role playing on ideological grounds, the women's movement and the reevaluation of sex roles in our society affected lesbians and gay men just as they affected heterosexuals. So all the issues that are bringing challenge and change to heterosexual couples are, and have been, present among homosexual couples.

Homosexuals and heterosexuals alike are now trying to understand their relationships in a society that offers them more options than ever before. People enter on long-term commitments wanting them to work and to last. But they hear many stories of failed relationships and wonder if theirs will survive. And this is just as true for gay men and lesbians as for heterosexuals. In a study done at The Kinsey Institute in the late 1960's, it was found, for example, that 71 percent of their sample of gay men between the ages of thirty-six and forty-five were living with a partner.[58] In the seventies Bell and Weinberg found that one quarter of the lesbians they interviewed said that being in a permanent relationship was the "most important thing in life"; 35 percent more felt it was "very important." Eighty-two percent of the women they talked to were currently living with someone.[59] Other studies have shown that gay men and lesbians who are not in relationships report that they have been in one previously and that they envision being in one in the future. "Couplehood," either as a reality or an aspiration, is as strong among gay people as it is among heterosexuals.[60]

# The issues today

A common set of questions and challenges confronts *all* "types" of couples today. The changing nature of male and female roles creates problems as couples go about even the most mundane tasks. For example: Who should do what within the household? The question is not simply who cooks, who takes out the trash, and who repairs the leaky faucet. Such task arrangements are really only a small part of the division of chores in a partnership. The larger question is much more profound and less amenable to easy answers. The household provides symbolic occasions for the establishment of territory and authority. Couples are trying to grapple with how men and women, how men and men, how women and women, should relate to one another. Where is fairness and justice? Where is compromise? What is the "rightful" province of male or female expertise? Whose needs—or perceptions of needs—will guide the relationship? To what extent is it right or fair that one person take responsibility for earning a living for the household while the other takes care of the housework, the children, and the emotional well-being of the couple? And forgetting what is right or fair—what works? What would make couples happy regardless of ideology or cultural expectations? There are many couples in America today who would accept any division of household chores, of emotional skills, of dominance, if they could just protect, preserve, or restore their relationship.

A relationship today can be compared to a smorgasbord, while yesterday's unit was more like Sunday's chicken dinner. Perhaps the older arrangement, in retrospect, was not so glorious, but it was structured and orderly. There were few choices and it was not considered appropriate to complain. Now there are so many decisions that one is liable to make serious errors in judgment. Everything is in flux and the priorities are not clear. Modern couples face a new and difficult set of questions—on the division of power and authority, on the responsibility for making decisions, and on emotional obligations, to name only a few. They also have questions about trust, loyalty, possible choices of life-style. If they have passed their mid-twenties, they may also have accumulated experience from earlier relationships, or they may be accustomed to being alone. Suddenly they are supposed to integrate all this past education and experience with the demands brought by the person with whom they are currently in love and with whom they are trying to maintain an intimate relationship.

Couples who have been together a long time may look around and realize that they are the only "survivors" among their acquaintances. All the promising, optimistic couples they have known seem to have disbanded. Some of these survivors have told us they feel somewhat besieged. People around them want to know not only *how* they managed to stay together but, indeed, *why*. They suspect that outsiders are holding their relationship up to some standard to see if it *deserves* to remain intact. In a society where marriage was once the central and most taken-for-granted institution, there seems to be a new need to justify the very existence of any kind of relationship.

Then there is the problem of work when both partners are equally committed to earning a living and both derive satisfaction from being in the economic marketplace. Complications for two-career couples emerge because many American cities do not offer the same opportunities for advancement for each member of the couple. When traditional assignments were made, with one partner taking care of the home and the other "out in the world of work," this dilemma never arose. If the primary wage earner's career required a geographical move, the homemaker could be uprooted with less trauma than if she had a career of her own to maintain. At this point in history, when so many couples have two careers, the place they choose to settle in and whose work opportunities they pursue become serious new issues that must be negotiated. Two careers challenge the traditional structure of family life. Other issues have arisen as well, including the question of how each person's work should affect the time available for the relationship, and the question of whether the money that is earned will be the "couple's money" or the private property of each individual to spend in any way he or she decides.

Some of the most obvious and unfortunate victims of recent social change are men and women in their late thirties or older who entered relationships with a clear and untroubled sense of their rules, operations, and understandings. They often find that in mid-relationship— and in mid-life—they have to make serious adjustments. It has been difficult for both men and women, but perhaps most disquieting for "displaced homemakers," who cultivated only the skills society told them were best and most appropriate, the skills associated with being a wife and mother. When the prospect of divorce arises, they are the most surprised, the most vulnerable. When divorce actually occurs, they are unprepared to face a world they had been told they would never need to enter. They have few if any abilities with which to generate significant income, and what skills they did possess have been dulled by many years in a relatively sheltered home situation. They actually have fewer resources and less confidence than they did twenty years before. Not only must they enter a new and inhospitable world of work, with few of the necessary qualifications, they must also face a romantic or sexual marketplace for which they are unprepared. Dating at forty-two is different from dating at eighteen, and twenty years of marriage is not always the best training ground for a reentry. The idea of being single in mid-life makes the threat of divorce an especially terrifying prospect.

This brief and selective chronicle of the recent history of American couples has led to the inescapable conclusion that couples today are in a state of transition. But transition to what? There is a political struggle under way, focusing on the question of what rules and expectations should prevail for all couples. The women's movement, including such diverse organizations as the National Organization for Women and the Young Women's Christian Association, and gay rights groups like the National Gay Task Force are struggling to extend and broaden the definitions of couple and of family. Groups such as these endorse pluralism and advocate a couple's right to depart from traditional expectations. They want to give new forms of relationship a chance to survive.

In reaction there are organizations and individuals who staunchly support traditional values and a return to the family unit of earlier days, as they remember it. Such groups as the right-to-life (antiabortion) organizations, the anti-E.R.A. movement, the antigay activists, and Fascinating Womanhood all feel that the recent changes in the definitions of intimacy and family relationships herald undesirable directions in American society.

These two different forces clashed head-on in the early seventies in the organization of the White House Conference on Families. Representatives of the two opposing approaches to family life came face to face and displayed enormous ideological conflict. It was not uncommon to see members of both sides shouting, screaming, and cursing one another. It was clear that how they mate, pair, and love are central to people's lives, and the emotions that coursed through the conference meeting halls in each state reflected how strongly people feel about their vision of couple and family life.

This brings us to our task in the following chapters. We are not taking a position on how couples ought to live. We are simply looking at those areas of life that concern couples nowadays. We are chronicling how individual couples and families solve the problems they confront, to their *own* satisfaction. When they fail, they fail on their own terms, not ours. The dreams that couples have are too diverse to be accomplished or satisfied by one simple formula or prescription. We will try to emphasize the rich diversity of solutions people have found. If many of our couples are very different from ourselves, different in what they want and how they seek to achieve it, then we will treat these differences with respect and with gratitude for what they have shared with us.

Our task here is to take relationships as we find them: diverse, inconsistent, and changing. We take as our mandate, description of what is actually going on among different kinds of couples and analysis of how these different patterns work for the individuals who have created them. Men and women, in this moment of challenge and change, are aware that their own relationships, and those of the people they love, are in a critical period. To borrow medical terminology, many of them are "at risk." The rest of this book is about couples today—what we have learned about them and what information we can offer to help them survive the risks.

# MONEY

**E**CONOMIC factors tend to be involved in every aspect of a couple's life. Although it is widely accepted that the *amount* of money available to a couple has a bearing on their happiness and the amount of conflict they experience, this is not the only important financial issue. Even couples who are relatively well off must deal with the day-to-day management of their finances. They must decide what money, if any, is to be personal, what money is to be shared, who will manage the books, how much consultation is appropriate when purchases are made—they must ask themselves whether they even have similar values about money. If a couple discovers, as many do, that they have very different ideas about how money is to be earned, managed, and spent, then these may become areas of contention. While the romantic in us might argue that money should not create significant problems in committed relationships, the scientist in us must argue to the contrary: Money is significant indeed.

How do people ever come together if they have different values about money? After all, isn't money the mover and shaker of society? In fact, most couples pay little or no attention at first to each other's financial values. Money is often a more taboo topic of conversation than sex, and courting couples may discuss their prior sex lives while never raising the question of their economic histories. After all, it is not very romantic or interesting to talk about net worth or projections of income or one's indebtedness, so money becomes the last frontier of self-disclosure even though each partner may hold strong feelings about how money should be dealt with. Discussion of premarital sexuality has far outdistanced fiscal awareness.

This was not always the case. Traditionally, in the negotiations between a male suitor and the parents of his prospective bride in middle- and upper-middle-class families, money was a major area of discussion. The husband was usually expected to be the economic provider, and his value in society was determined by his worth in that role. In working-class families, the prospective groom was required to have steady employment or to earn an income equal to or better than the bride's father's.

This notion of the husband as major provider has not changed very much. Sociologist Ivan Nye conducted a recent study that showed that both married men and married women still feel it is the husband's responsibility to provide for his wife.[1] In our study, fewer than a quarter of the wives felt it was not important for their husbands to furnish them with financial security.[2] What has changed is that parents have lost control over the selection of their children's suitors. Gentlemanly haggling over the dowry, or the father's right to know the groom's future job prospects, is a thing of the past. Nowadays, there is practically no guarantee that people will enter a relationship knowing their partners' economic history or outlook. Indeed, there is no guarantee that they will even start out with similar economic backgrounds. The matchmaking that currently takes place—on college campuses, at parties given by mutual friends, in singles bars—operates less openly on the gold standard.

The chances of being in the same economic bracket and of having the same economic values may be even further reduced for lesbians and gay men. Both these groups, particularly gay men, often meet potential partners in settings that are organized around their gayness, rather than around their tastes or social backgrounds. In small cities, where there are only one or two places where gay people can meet, the social mix will be very diverse in terms of occupation, income, or class. In larger metropolitan areas, gay and lesbian places are more specialized: One can choose a gay bowling group or a gay yachting club. But apart from these, there are not as many socially homogeneous meeting places for gay men and lesbians as there are for heterosexuals.


Money matters are the most commonly discussed issues among married couples. In study after study, going back several decades, between one quarter and one third of all married couples ranked money as their primary problem.[3] Consequently, we expected to find dozens of research studies that explored in depth the ways married life is affected by finances. But researchers exhibit the same reluctance to discuss money as do courting couples, and a standard textbook on marriage and the family is unlikely to devote more than five pages to the subject. We suspect that ours is the first large study to analyze the financial aspects of intimate relationships and their impact on the lives of couples.

# Income and power

## *A struggle for control*

Does the distribution of money in a relationship affect each partner's ability to make decisions and enforce his or her will? This seemed to us the first and most critical question. Is it merely tradition that grants a husband power over his wife, or has his ability to earn more been the key to the usual hierarchy in marriage? If a wife earns as much money as her husband, does she gain an equal share of power and control? Do these same questions yield different answers from couples without marital traditions to shape their lives? If partners are of the same sex, does money become more or less influential in their lives?

Discovering how money bestows power tells us crucial things about the institution of marriage and why some people object so strongly to it.

*Money establishes the balance of power in relationships, except among lesbians.*[1]

In three out of four of the types of couples we studied, we find that the amount of money a person earns—in comparison with a partner's income—establishes relative power. This seems a rather cynical finding, one that does not accord well with cherished American beliefs about fairness and how people acquire influence in romantic relationships. Most people like to think that the right to affect decisions is based on the demands of daily events, on which partner is wiser on a certain issue, or on special gifts of persuasion. They do not like to think that income, something that comes into the relationship from the outside, imposes a hierarchy on the couple. But it does.

For example, among married couples, wives with high incomes gain greater financial autonomy, and the higher a wife's income, the freer she becomes to spend money as she sees fit, and the less accountable she feels for how she allocates her own spending money.[2] Furthermore, wives with large incomes are more likely to have personal savings accounts to which their husbands have no access.[3]

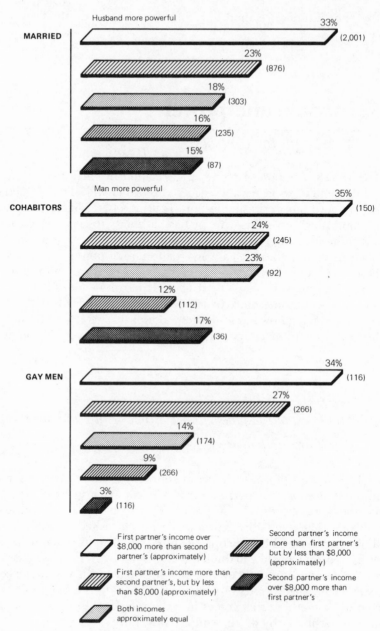

MARRIED

Husband more powerful

33% (2,001)

23% (876)

18% (303)

16% (235)

15% (87)

COHABITORS

Man more powerful

35% (150)

24% (245)

23% (92)

12% (112)

17% (36)

GAY MEN

34% (116)

27% (266)

14% (174)

9% (266)

3% (116)

First partner's income over $8,000 more than second partner's (approximately)

Second partner's income more than first partner's but by less than $8,000 (approximately)

First partner's income more than second partner's, but by less than $8,000 (approximately)

Second partner's income over $8,000 more than first partner's

Both incomes approximately equal

Note: For married and cohabiting couples the bars represent the number of couples in which the man (first partner) is more powerful, as opposed to power being equal or the woman (second partner) more powerful. For gay male couples the bars represent the number of couples in which a particular man (first partner) is more powerful, as opposed to power being equal or the other man (second partner) more powerful.

Numbers in parentheses are the number of couples on which the percentages are based.

FIGURE   1

Lesbian couples are a notable exception to this finding: Their power balance is not determined by either woman's income. Since women in this society are not accustomed to judging their *own* worth by how much money they make, we feel that lesbians do not fall into judging their partners by such a standard. Moreover, because women historically have not earned much money, they may be unaccustomed to using wealth to "throw their weight around." Men on the other hand have a long tradition of feeling they have the right to exercise control if they have proved their worth by being financially successful. They are accustomed to having their wishes honored by people in the outside world as well as at home. We believe that many lesbians, particularly younger women, fully understand the power that money bestows on men, but they do not agree that it should do so. They make a conscious effort to keep their relationships free of any form of domination, especially if it derives from something as impersonal as money. Rebecca, twenty-seven, is a law student, who had worked for several years as a kindergarten teacher. She has been living for four years with Lynn, thirty, who is an office manager. Rebecca said:

> In her other relationship she had always been the boss, always the one who ended up controlling the money. When she came into this relationship, she said that "I don't want to do this anymore." . . . We both want the right to speak our mind, but we aren't going to base it on who has the bigger paycheck. I could see that temptation in her every now and again. Because I'm a student right now and I am bringing in a lot less than I used to, and she could be a drag about it if she wanted to be and say that I should give in to her because she's carrying things right now. But we have that worked out real well. I think the reason we never argue is that we respect each other for who we really are and have left all that power-tripping behind.

We should not be surprised that money brings power. When we look at other areas of life, we recognize how true this is. Moreover, feminists have long pointed out that wage disparities between men and women are related to the disparity of power within marriage. They have observed that it is more than mere coincidence that husbands generally have superior incomes and financial resources as well as greater power and control within the family. What we have found vigorously supports this position: In marriages, and among heterosexual couples who live together, when women earn more, they win more clout.

But it is not simply money combined with the tradition of male dominance that establishes the balance of power. By noting that even gay male couples gain advantage over one another when one partner has a high income, we see that money may create inequality even when there is no gender difference. But we also see, by looking at lesbian couples, that money need not have that effect. These patterns have led us to conclude that it is men—who for generations have learned in the work place the equation that money equals power—who have re-created this experience in the home. Wives and cohabiting women fall prey to the logic that money talks. But women seem capable of escaping the ruthless impact of money when no man is present.

---

*In marriage, adherence to the male-provider philosophy*
*grants greater power to husbands.*

The balance of power in marriage is affected not only by income but also by a very central aspect of marriage: the traditional male-provider role. Because of it, husbands are generally accorded more power than wives. In some cases, even if a wife earns a great deal of money— perhaps even more than her husband—she will not necessarily acquire a proportionate amount of power.

The degree to which married couples accept the validity of the male-provider role varies greatly. For some, it is a thing of the past, but for many couples it is still very important.[4] We measured our couples' acceptance of it by asking whether they agreed or disagreed with the following statements:

> The two partners should share the responsibility for earning a living for the household.

> It is better if the man works to support the household and the woman takes care of the home.

By using their agreement or disagreement with these statements, we determined how each person felt about the male-provider role as a guiding marital principle.[5] In couples where either husband or wife endorses the male-provider role philosophy, we find the husband is more powerful, regardless of the income of each partner.[6] When the husband believes in his provider role, he has the greater say in the important decisions. If his wife shares the same view, then she yields to his wishes. Even if she is employed full time, and earns more money than he, she places their financial destiny in his hands, granting him ultimate control over their money.

Marlene and Art have been married thirty years. Marlene, fifty, has worked in an executive position for the telephone company for almost twenty years, and Art, fifty-one, is a farm-equipment dealer. While Marlene earns a good salary, sometimes as much as Art, she still orients her life to his work. Both agree that Art has the last word in how they spend their money.

> MARLENE: Art makes the major economic decisions in our household. We are as consulting of one another as possible, but I realize that in the final push comes to shove that he is the one who

shoulders the responsibility for this family. It's not as important now because the children are in their own families, but he has always felt a great sense of responsibility to do the best we could for them, and I respect what it has cost him in time and worry. My job is important and he has always respected my work, but we made a decision right from the beginning that what I contributed would be additional and what he did we would depend on.

ART: I would say that I make the decisions when it comes to money and I guess I would also say that if there is an argument and we cannot totally work it out so that we both agree, then I have more to say in the relationship. Someone has to finally make a decision and we have always done it this way.

**BELIEF IN THE MALE PROVIDER ROLE AND THE BALANCE OF POWER IN MARRIED COUPLES**

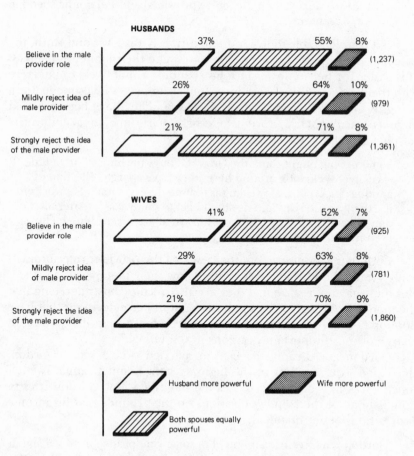

Numbers in parentheses are the number of people on which the percentages are based.

FIGURE 2

Some husbands feel that because they make the money, they can spend it in any way they like. Ruth and Vic are a young couple who have very different ideas about how money should be spent. Vic, eighteen, is currently employed as a night watchman on a pier and Ruth, nineteen, is a homemaker. They live in a very modest apartment because Vic's wages are low. After a year of married life, their biggest fights are about how money is spent and who has the right to make decisions about it. Vic expressed what he feels are his rights as the breadwinner:

> All my paycheck goes into the bank and I don't see none of it. . . . I had a hundred-and-forty-dollar check coming. So I went out and bought me a vest and shirt and a pair of pants. She got mad because I went out and did it because I didn't go out and do it with her. I says, "I work for the money. I get the shit beat out of me for it [he was recently attacked on the job by prowlers] and I'm gonna spend it the way I want to."

If a couple is able to live more luxuriously than Vic and Ruth, the wife may back up her husband's right to spend their money as he likes. It is easier for her to do so since his spending is not likely to interfere with their style of life. Aaron, forty-four, who makes investments for a living, is given free rein by his wife, Marla. They have been married eighteen years. Marla, forty-two, works part time in a children's-hospital gift shop. Marla said:

> Some people might think the "toys" he buys for himself are a little excessive. Well, look around here [they have a large collection of antique clocks]. . . . My feeling is that he deserves it all. He works for it. He takes the risks and he should get to enjoy it. . . . After all, we don't live forever. . . . I support him on almost everything he buys, even if I think it is outrageous.

Both these couples accept the view that the provider role automatically grants the husband power over how their money will be spent. But they may not realize that they are also unconsciously agreeing that the money he brings in gives him the right to make decisions that have little or nothing to do with finances. He is more than likely to be in charge of most important decisions in the family.[7]

Gordon and Leanna have been married twelve years. Gordon, thirty-one, is a sergeant in the highway patrol, and Leanna, twenty-nine, works in a delicatessen. Leanna described how Gordon tries to dominate all of the couple's decisions on the grounds that his income proves he is better qualified:

> Gordon is aggressive, and me, I'm somewhat passive. And while that has equalized some over the years, Gordon still has to have the last word on everything. We get annoyed with each other over that, but when I start to push back, he reminds me just who supports me and the children. He doesn't always bring that up, but if I start to win an

argument or make more sense about something we should do, I think he gets frustrated and so he gives me his big final line which is something like, "If you're so smart, why don't you earn more money?" or how dumb I am 'cause if I had to go out and support myself I'd be a big fizzle. . . . He's only lousy like that when he thinks I'm winning and he gets threatened.

*In gay male couples, income is an extremely important force in determining which partner will be dominant.*

Gay men do not rely on the idea of a "provider role" to define their relationships. Such a view requires a nonworking partner, or at least someone whose work and income are considered subordinate to the provider's. It comes out of the structure of traditional marriage which assigns men and women specific responsibilities in family life: In return for the man's economic support, the woman raises the children and does the household chores. Few gay men want to participate in such a rigid exchange where one man would be assigned all the female jobs.[8]

In gay couples, each man is used not only to earning his own income but also to making his own decisions. And in couples with two decision-makers, wills are likely to collide. Hence gay men find some way to establish the balance of power, and find it in the belief they share with heterosexual men—that the right to dominate in the decision-making process is based on one's financial contribution to the relationship.

In our interviews with gay men, they talked a great deal about money, fairness, and decision-making. For example, Garrett, thirty-eight, is eleven years older than Boyd and considerably more successful. He is an established architect and comes from an upper-middle-class background. Boyd earns a modest living as a salesman, and his education and social class suffer in comparison with Garrett's. After three years, Garrett's financial superiority and hold over Boyd continue to be a major issue between them. While Garrett is always generous, he expects in exchange complete and absolute control over financial decisions. Since what the two of them spend is largely his money, he feels he should have complete authority over how much is expended and what is bought. He commented:

> It bothered Boyd if I gave him money to get coffee, clothing and stuff. Because he didn't have anything. . . . I always felt I was dressing him the way I wanted him to look rather than giving him money to buy his own clothing. . . . If I gave him a thousand dollars he'd go out and buy something wild and foolish. I thought he'd come back with all the wrong things.

Garrett feels Boyd should be given a say only if his income warrants it:

I'd like him to come up with some ideas for free time together. But then he can't come up with ideas for free time that require spending money, which he doesn't have. Like theater, plays, travel. If he made those decisions, he wouldn't have the money to do it. . . . So we do those things when I suggest it and feel like doing it.

---

*Lesbians do not use income to establish dominance in their relationships. They use it to avoid having one woman dependent on the other.*

Most lesbians have grown up with an awareness of the provider-role logic, part of which emphasizes women's financial dependence on men. Many of these women eventually come to reject this attitude, partly because they have chosen not to marry and partly because some think married women are subordinated to their husbands because of their acceptance of it. Younger lesbians, in particular, told us they feel it is important to avoid dependency, especially in the financial realm.[9] Lesbians whom we interviewed frequently expressed concern, sometimes even preoccupation, with the idea of keeping money matters equitable and in balance. Julia and Lois have lived together three years. Julia, twenty-five, works as a dental technician, and Lois, twenty-three, is a payroll clerk. Julia said:

[Lois is] a real dependent independent. She wants me to take charge of the big decisions but also have a voice in things. I have to fight her tendencies, because I don't want this to look like a husband and wife with her saying, "Yes, dear." I make her take full responsibility for every decision we make, just as I take full responsibility. We are women together and we don't have to get into a situation where one person overpowers the other. . . . We got into a lot of trouble when we had to decide to buy this apartment. It was a real deal to people in the building and it required her and me going to our parents and asking for some help. She wanted to leave every decision to me and was going to go with whatever I wanted. I said no way, we are going up or down with this thing together.

Another woman, in her early thirties, reflected on her concern that both partners contribute equally to the relationship:

We have problems when she doesn't think I'm doing my share and when I don't think she's doing her share. I was real reluctant to move in with her because she makes a lot more money than I do and I was afraid that I wouldn't be able to participate equally and I didn't want to be in a relationship where I was beholden to anyone. We had a lot of discussions about how to contribute so that I didn't feel that she was carrying me. We give her a little more of the vote if it's something that uses more of her surplus income than mine but mostly it's fifty percent. I think it's real equal most of the time.

Sharing financial responsibilities equally, neither partner becoming dependent on the other, were common goals we heard from lesbians. When a relationship was seen as out of balance—with one woman contributing less to household bills than the other—it was disturbing to both partners. Each expressed a strong dislike of such a potential for power imbalance.[10] Phyllis gave a bitter description of how the problem of unequal incomes had affected her ten-year relationship with Joan. Phyllis has been continually out of work for the last few years. It has been a constant source of anxiety for her:

Right now I'm not bringing in much money and I don't like it. We don't fight about it. Most of the uproar around is my feeling really awful because I don't have any money. This morning Joan had to put all the money into the household account instead of me putting my half in and that upset me.

The expectation of equal contribution was so great that when Phyllis had trouble living up to it, the relationship was jeopardized. We were impressed that the problem stemmed from Phyllis's self-recrimination rather than from any critical reactions on Joan's part.

*Cohabiting women use money to achieve equality in their relationships.*

The most provocative evidence we can offer on the link between power and money comes from the cohabitors. The impact of income differences on the balance of power among these couples is substantial. Although both male and female partners are very keen on giving privileges based on who has more money, their approach to money and power does not parallel that of the married couples. They are more like the gay men and lesbians. As it does to the gay men, money represents power to them and both partners seem to want to be on the right side of that equation, and like the lesbians, cohabitors believe strongly in each partner's contributing his or her *equal* share.

For the cohabitors, the male-provider image loses its importance and other values take precedence. Most of these women are anxious to sustain their independence, avoiding the financial (and symbolic) domination they believe marriage allows men to impose on women.[11] The males, too, are wary about living with a dependent partner. They prefer to be financially responsible only for themselves.[12]

Jane, thirty-two, is a pediatrician who lives with Morton, thirty-seven, a lawyer with an appointed position in city government. When they met three years ago, Jane was still a medical resident and not earning much money. Now, since Morton has accepted a government position, Jane earns the bigger income. She feels it entitles her to a certain freedom in decision-making, even if Morton does not always like it.

> JANE: I work very hard. I love my work, but it has long hours and often when I see people they are very worried, which can be emotionally exhausting for me as well as for them. . . . I feel I earn my salary, and especially with this last raise, I felt I could do whatever I wanted with it. Morton was not particularly thrilled when I took the bonus and traded in the Volvo for the Alpha. Well, too bad. I let him alone and I expect him to let me alone. No, I expect him to respect me for being able to afford what I want. . . . I would never tolerate a single moment of "You can't do that because I don't think it's appropriate." I have a hard time accepting the logic of women turning their paycheck over to men.

> MORTON: We argue about money occasionally. I would not always make the same decisions she does. I would save and invest more. But it's her money and I don't dare interfere. We have a pot we put together for joint plans and that is the only money we can make equal decisions on.

As with the wives, the larger the female cohabitor's income, the more likely she is to keep a private savings account and the less likely she is to discuss her discretionary spending with her partner.[13] Cohabiting women are watchful and independent in financial matters, the possible loss of power being the driving force behind their caution.

---

*When financial decisions concern expensive items, the partner with the larger income exercises greater control, except among married couples.*

Power is the ability to get one's way, to influence important decisions. The power that income bestows in a relationship is strikingly evident when we look at who has the upper hand when it comes to how the couple spends its money. This is most obvious if the proposed expenditure will affect the general economic welfare of the couple. The purchase of a living-room set, for instance, demands so much deliberation between the partners that it reveals a great deal about the internal dynamics of the couple.

Since spending decisions are one of the best windows we have on the way power operates between two partners, we asked couples to tell us which partner usually has more influence over the amount of money spent on furniture. In most instances, we found that the partner with the larger income tends to dominate this kind of purchase.[14] In marriages, however, the dynamics involved are less clear-cut. A large income does not translate into simple control. Although most husbands earn more than their wives, if only one partner decides how much will be spent on home furnishings, it is the wife.[15] This is because the husband understands his authority to include the right to delegate responsibility to his wife. He may decide to do this for large one-time expenditures as well as for lesser decisions that routinely fall to wives, such as how much to spend on food or on the day-to-day needs of the children.[16] The provider role gives husbands the right to tell their wives, "You do it," and expect it to be done. A good example of how everyday spending decisions are made is the way a couple discusses what will be spent on groceries. Tina, twenty-nine, is an editor in a publishing house, and her husband, Matt, thirty-nine, is a vice-president in a large public-relations firm. They have been married for eight years. Even though they are both extremely career-oriented and busy, both agree that grocery shopping is Tina's job.

> MATT: I let her do everything pertaining to keeping food in our tummies and clothes on our back. I promise to eat everything and agree with everything she buys. It works fine.
>
> TINA: I hate shopping for food and I always do it at the end of the day when I'm grouchy. Usually, I just go to the stores in the building even though they are too expensive, just because they are convenient. . . . I don't cook the big fancy meals I used to because it can kill half a day just going around to get the right ingredients. . . . Sometimes I con him into doing it on the weekends but basically it's my job. We usually manage my aggravation by spending a little more and using the convenience of this store rather than thinking about price.

Sometimes we see a wife making decisions about very costly items, but she can do so because of the trust she and her husband have built up between them over the years. She is really acting as an agent for the couple because her husband has learned that she will act in their best interest and in accordance with the values they share. Although his trust may give her control over big purchases, it is control that is assigned and not a sign of a more fundamental power. A wife may choose to interpret her control over the checkbook as a measure of her clout, whereas her husband sees it a different way. This is illustrated by a highly volatile married couple. The husband thinks he has solved the delegation problem:

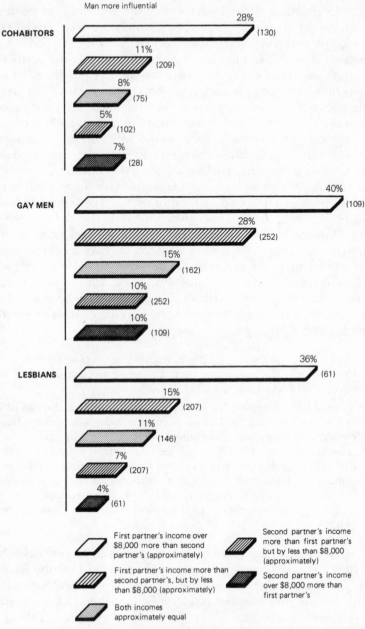

FIGURE    3

We don't argue about money because that's usually the biggest cause of arguments. We don't argue about money because she pays all the bills. I give her the money and she pays the bills. . . . I don't have to worry about it, do I? I don't see the bills so I don't worry about them, so it's a cop-out on my part. I let her worry about them. She's got the bookkeeping background, so that's the official reason, but the more I think about it and look at it, I'm copping out. I'm giving her all the responsibility and she enjoys it; apparently, it gives her a sense of power. It's beautiful.

He regards the delegation of control to his wife as giving her a false sense of power.

---

*The partner with the higher income controls the couple's recreational activities, except among married couples.*

When one partner has a great deal of money, we might expect that both would benefit, especially when there are ample funds for leisure-time activities. This is precisely the case in most marriages. The institution of marriage confers on each partner the right to the other's money, even though some couples may keep some property and funds separate. Married couples make the presumption that if the provider makes an income that pays for more than the essentials in life, both partners are entitled to think of ways to use it.

Other kinds of couples do not assume such a claim on each other's finances. As a result, the person who can afford to do more things than the other may unilaterally dictate the recreational activities for the couple.[17] For example, Dan, forty-one, and Patrick, forty-seven, have lived together for seventeen years. Dan is manager in a packing business and Patrick is a contractor whose business has been in a slump lately. Dan feels that since he pays for the couple's entertainment, he has more right to decide what they do:

I buy all the subscriptions—we go to plays and dance and opera and I buy all of that, usually at the beginning of each season. He occasionally suggests a movie and I can hardly refuse. . . . I arrange our social schedule really, just by getting everything lined up and by paying for it all. He goes along with it, even the opera, which he doesn't really like very much.

The person with fewer resources may resent having the other dictate how they will spend their leisure time. Even if the activities themselves are congenial, a sense of indebtedness may result and create a division between the partners. The division can deepen if the partner who pays makes it clear that he or she finds the other's dependency a source of irritation. Celeste and Rosa, a couple who have lived together

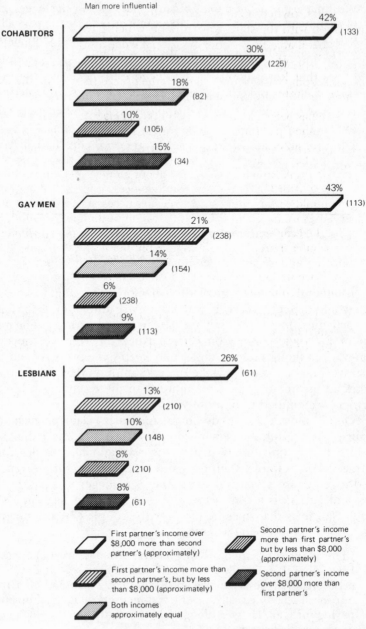

Man more influential

COHABITORS

42% (133)

30% (225)

18% (82)

10% (105)

15% (34)

GAY MEN

43% (113)

21% (238)

14% (154)

6% (238)

9% (113)

LESBIANS

26% (61)

13% (210)

10% (148)

8% (210)

8% (61)

First partner's income over $8,000 more than second partner's (approximately)

First partner's income more than second partner's, but by less than $8,000 (approximately)

Both incomes approximately equal

Second partner's income more than first partner's but by less than $8,000 (approximately)

Second partner's income over $8,000 more than first partner's

Note: For cohabiting couples the bars represent the number of couples in which the man (first partner) is more influential, as opposed to influence being equal or the woman (second partner) more influential. For gay male and lesbian couples the bars represent the number of couples in which a particular person (first partner) is more influential, as opposed to influence being equal or the other person (second partner) more influential.

Numbers in parentheses are the number of couples on which the percentages are based.

FIGURE    4

for six years, owned a small variety store until it failed. Celeste then found a job with the state government, which pays a good salary. But Rosa has been able to get only occasional work as a typist. They have a mortgage and other living expenses they have difficulty meeting. Celeste feels that Rosa should be doing more to meet her share of the expenses. Celeste spoke in the interview about Rosa's indebtedness:

> There has been a lot of door slamming lately. . . . I keep a ledger every time I pay for something for the house and we have a special sheet for entertainment expenses . . . for example, I have been loaning her money for our card games that we go to each week. . . . I don't think Rosa has been good about money, spending on things we can't afford and then sometimes expecting me to bail her out. So I withhold certain things that I feel are necessary for important expenses we have and she feels that I am pushing her around. Well, I am the economically responsible person right now and when she contributes more, I can relax some, but not now. . . . I don't want to hurt her and we argue about money more than anything else, but only since we lost the store. . . . I can't wait until she gets a job she wants and things get back to normal.

Resentment may grow to the point where one partner will not underwrite joint vacations or other shared outings—and may simply go off and do these things alone. On the other hand, this person may offer to pay the other's way only to have this generosity refused. In either case, the two have lost an opportunity to share a pleasant experience. More important, they have deprived themselves of each other's company and their life together may be the poorer.

In the next sections we explore how important financial success is for the happiness and commitment of any couple. Money—how much there is and how much people want—can be a significant problem in a couple's life. Partners not only gain power by bringing money into the relationship; they may also find themselves at odds when the money they bring in is not sufficient or is less than one or both expect.

---

*When partners are disappointed with the amount of money the couple has, they find their entire relationship less satisfying, except among lesbians.*

It is difficult to be poor but happy. Financial deprivation does indeed take its toll on a relationship[18]—and not just because money is a way to survive and to acquire goods. It is also a symbol of a couple's success. A thirty-five-year-old wife told us how money problems had damaged an earlier marriage:

**DISAPPOINTMENT WITH COUPLE INCOME AND
SATISFACTION WITH THE RELATIONSHIP**

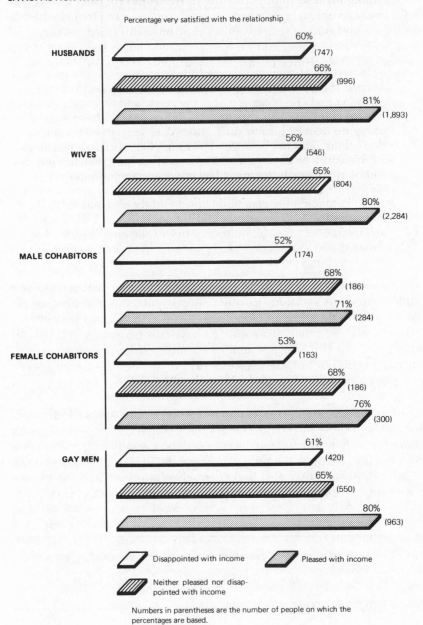

Percentage very satisfied with the relationship

HUSBANDS
60% (747)
66% (996)
81% (1,893)

WIVES
56% (546)
65% (804)
80% (2,284)

MALE COHABITORS
52% (174)
68% (186)
71% (284)

FEMALE COHABITORS
53% (163)
68% (186)
76% (300)

GAY MEN
61% (420)
65% (550)
80% (963)

Disappointed with income          Pleased with income

Neither pleased nor disappointed with income

Numbers in parentheses are the number of people on which the
percentages are based.

FIGURE     5

I can't tell you how bad it was in my last marriage. There was nothing my husband could do right. He set us up so many times. He would go out and get a fancy job and then he would buy a hundred things because he thought he could afford it. So we'd have instant debt as soon as we had instant money, and then he'd get fired and all we had were debts. The highs weren't worth the lows. When you really have no money and you're afraid to answer the phone because it's some collection agency or some bad check and you dread the mailman or whenever the doorbell rings it might be somebody who wants to take something away, it was hell. . . . And don't tell me you can have a marriage through all that. When you're furious at each other all the time and you can't afford to go to a goddamned movie, don't tell me love conquers all. It got to where we couldn't stand the sight of one another. Leaving each other was an incredible relief.

In a capitalist society money is often equated with goodness, ability, talent, drive, even moral uprightness. One homemaker who has been married twenty years told us how proud she and her husband are that he has made a good living:

He takes a lot of pride in what he's been able to accomplish and he needs to get thanked for it. He will bring up, from time to time, what he's given to the kids or what he's given to me, just so that we can tell him we know and are grateful. . . . And even though I sometimes tell him how great he is just so he can hear it, it is true that we can enjoy a good life because he has worked hard for us. The fact that all four of our kids can go to the colleges they want to go to is no small feat. You have to remember, we started out with nothing. . . . It feels very sweet to look at each other and know how much we have done.

People who are poor are sometimes considered in our society to be the architects of their own failure, and many are unable to resist this definition of themselves. Even though it may not be their fault (for example, workers who are laid off in failing industries, or a person who is fired because his or her boss does not like women, or blacks, or homosexuals), they may blame themselves just the same. They judge themselves only according to their success or failure, not according to the obstacles that have been placed in their paths. We came to this view from talking to couples like Nick and Larry. Nick is a thirty-one-year-old gay man who is currently unemployed. He and Larry have lived together six years. Nick told us how devastated he feels about not earning a living:

I left my job with the Fed to go out and consult and, I thought, to make a little more money. Well, wouldn't you know, I picked the beginning of the recession. Being a consultant out there is like being in Buffalo during the winter without a parka. It's bad enough to be in Buffalo but picking the winter to be out there uncovered is real dumb, right? So here I am not reading one economic sign and figuring that everything is going to turn around. Wrong. Wrong. For

six months I try to make this thing go and then I go back to the Fed
to see if I can have my old job back, but naturally jobs are scarcer
than hen's teeth. So I look at a *lower* paying job figuring I will do
them a favor—they'll be getting something great cheap, right? Yeah,
well nothing doing there either. . . . So it's been a downer and it's
going on almost a year since I've been able to work in my old field. I
feel pretty awful about myself most of the time even though I know
it's not my fault and Larry tells me it's not my fault. . . . There is a
job in Florida that might be open to me and if I have to I will think
of going there and maybe commuting back here once a month. I
can't go on like this, making no money, using up Larry's and feeling
shitty.

Married couples who feel they are doing well financially often see
this as a joint accomplishment, proving that they chose each other
wisely. The wife has selected a man who has proved he can survive,
even prosper, in his job. For example, Holly and Leonard have been
married seventeen years. They are both forty-seven and it is the second
marriage for both. Leonard is an engineer with a large manufacturing
company and Holly is a homemaker. They live on a small farm, which
they tend on weekends. Holly described her marriage with pride:

Oh, we never have any fights about money. I wish every part of our
life were that easy. . . . He has always made a good living. He's had
to change jobs a few times to do better, and it's always worked
out. . . . He's very careful and he has never gotten fired or had any
problems that I know of. . . . We put away money for retirement and
he's always made sure that we had a good health policy and good
insurance. I think we're quite well organized. I know other couples
where the man brings home the bacon but they squander it and
don't provide for their retirement or old age. . . . He has been a
wonder. There's always been enough to live on and to save for the
future.

And *he* feels he has married someone who budgets, spends, and
perhaps earns, in ways that cause his efforts to culminate in the good
life. Leonard said:

She's a great budgeter—one of the great shoppers. She collects
coupons. I think she belongs to a club that tells you how to get a lot
of free things from coupons and she makes a lot of the things we
use. She made this suit. Yes, she did. She made our daughter's
wedding dress, she makes shirts . . . she keeps a garden. . . . She's
responsible for our having a fine life. I give her money and she
makes it go farther than I could ever make it go. She makes a lot
more money for us at home than she could if she gave up what she
does here and went out to work.

A twenty-three-year-old husband spoke of his wife's ability to budget their money:

She's great with money. She handles all our money. I do the books for other people but she does the books for us. I would spend it and never see anything from it, but she makes sure it accumulates and we can do things with it. If it had been up to me we never would have been able to vacation in Hawaii last spring. But miracle Sally over there figured a way we could do it.

The traditional vision of married life is that partners sink or swim together. Few wives would be likely to say, "I'm doing okay financially, and it doesn't reflect on me how my husband does." Traditionally, society has judged them and they have judged themselves as a unit. When married couples are disappointed with the amount of money they have, what they usually mean is that they are displeased with the husband's income. We infer this because we find that no matter how much or how little a wife earns, her income has much less impact on how each of them feels about the family income.[19] It is up to the man to make the *couple's* mark in the world.

Male and female cohabitors, on the other hand, are much more likely to deal with one another as independent economic entities and are less likely to measure economic success as a joint enterprise. We find that the more each individual cohabitor earns the more satisfied he or she is with the entire relationship. A partner's income does not matter.[20] Satisfaction is predicated on *individual* economic success, rather than on their joint efforts.

Cohabiting men and husbands are alike in that they do not judge their happiness or financial well-being by how much their partners earn. Men are taught and have come to believe that they should not be financially dependent upon a woman. This belief is illustrated by a comment made in an interview with a fifty-three-year-old husband who has been married for thirty years:

> I think our daughter is married to a number one creep. She's out there working her fanny off and he's more or less retired from the active practice of making a living with some story about his need for artistic pursuits. I think she should kick him out, but I try and hold my tongue, although I wouldn't if I thought it would do any good. I think one of the lower things in the world is a man lying around the house letting his wife support him. Maybe I'm conservative but that isn't my idea of how to be a man or how to have a marriage.

Morris and Eva have lived together for four years. Morris, twenty-six, is a liquor distributor, and Eva, twenty-five, is a bookkeeper. Morris made it clear that Eva's salary is not their mainstay:

> Eva makes a good salary but we depend mostly on what I make. Which is the way I want it. I never want her to think she has to work, and she is thinking of taking some time off because she's working with a group of assholes. . . . She kids me sometimes, like why don't I

stay home and be a househusband, and she'll go out and take over. But she just does that to rile me. She knows I would never allow that and I know she wouldn't like it if I said that would be great. I wouldn't live off her. It's hard to imagine a man who would feel good living off a woman.

From interviews with men we came to believe that earning money is intimately bound up with a man's self-respect, and when he loses his self-respect, he begins to question how he feels about his life and his relationship.[21] Travis, a struggling twenty-six-year-old salesman, has been married for two years to Sissy, twenty-four, who teaches children with learning disabilities. This is Travis's second marriage. While Travis's salary is potentially higher than Sissy's, his take-home pay has been very inconsistent and this is troubling to him:

> I tend to brood if it's been a bad month, and there's really nothing Sissy can do to reassure me. She thinks because her salary can cover most of our monthly major expenses that I don't have to worry as much as I do. She personalizes everything; [she feels] that I'm really upset with her. Well, I'm really upset with myself. It is up to me to pull in the bigger paycheck around here and I don't want her paycheck to be important. . . . I don't want to have kids with a working wife. . . . I don't feel good about anything when I think I may be going under—not her, not myself, not anything.

David and Betty have been married three years. Both are twenty-five. They have one child, which puts additional financial strains on an already tight economic situation. David recounted severe conflict over income in the early days of their marriage:

> I don't care how much money you have. I don't care if you got Rockefeller's millions. You want to be happy? You need two of Rockefeller's millions. . . . The first six months, unequivocally, our worst problem was money. Just the sheer lack of it, the total overwhelming lack of it. . . . It was never that she said to me, "We don't have money and it's your fault," but it was always the underlying tension of never having enough. It wore on both of us, but more on me than on her.

David never questioned the logic that made him the provider and he took this responsibility very seriously.
Another husband, age twenty-six, told us:

> I started medical school and I found out that it wasn't for me. . . . Then I thought I would go to grad school, but I didn't, even though I took the GRE and did fairly well on them. . . . I was going back and forth and not earning any money and I was very disappointed in myself and I was a total drag to be around. . . . We were living together at the time and we both got into these long depressing dialogues about the relationship. . . . Most of this evaporated as soon as I knew what I wanted to do and all of it went away as soon as I went out and did it.

Mark, married seventeen years, expressed the same feeling. He is a self-employed landscape contractor, and his business has recently been cut back to less than full time because of economic recession in his community.

> I haven't been doing well lately because the landscape business is way down and I am real depressed when I can't handle all of our expenses. . . . We have never needed her paycheck before, it was just something she wanted to do and I thought it was okay if she wanted to work part time. But now we need that money and I feel sleazy every time I put her check in our joint account instead of letting her do whatever she wants with it. . . . I have had to see her in a new way which has been a plus for us, and I would say it would be in general a good thing for the relationship if I didn't feel so crummy about my business and worried about whether I was going to be able to continue in this line of work.

Even though it may not be his fault that he is not making much money, a husband may chastise himself for not being adequate in that role. Greg, forty, is a self-employed photographer. He has been married for four years to Wilma, thirty-nine, a successful TV anchorwoman. Both are in their second marriage. Greg's first wife had not worked. He told how he felt about being married to a successful working wife. At the time of the interview, Greg's business was not going well.

> I have always thought that I would be the primary breadwinner and even though I don't have to be, I can't get over the idea that I should be. . . . I am used to having everyone rely on me, and when they can't—even if they don't need to—it's very upsetting. I have a strong need to be independent—not to work for anyone else—to be able to have a successful business and make it on my own. If I can't do that I have a lot of trouble thinking I am being an adequate partner. . . . I don't mind her success, but I need my own. . . . I don't want to feel dependent, that there is a safety net out there. It's not really masculine. . . . When I see myself as less masculine, I see her as more self-sufficient and more masculine, which isn't so great. . . . It affects my sexual interest and the way I feel about the relationship.

A husband who feels as Greg does may be reassured by his wife that she understands his employment problems, but he may be unable to believe she does not think less of him. One wife, married thirty-five years, told us how delicate such a situation can be:

> You have to be careful not to step on their pride. He always jokingly says, "And who is the greatest?" and I always say, "You are," and it's a joke, but he needs it. . . . When he was out of work, we wouldn't play these games so much because he wasn't feeling great about himself. I also think—even though this is ridiculous—that he was afraid I wouldn't answer with the right answer. . . . It's very important for him to think of himself as a family man. And family

men live up to their responsibilities, and when he felt he wasn't living up to his responsibilities, I think he felt that we felt that way too.

Heterosexual women often understand the enormous importance of their partners' economic success and try to reassure them in every way possible. Some women take extreme measures to make their partners feel better. Alice, thirty, is a textile designer, who has been living with Gene, thirty-one, for three years. Her work has been much more successful than she had expected, while Gene, who is a set designer, has been unable to find steady employment. Alice is so worried about him that she does not mention what is going on in her professional life:

> I did not tell him about my last promotion. It would just depress him. Not that he wouldn't be happy for me, but it would make him feel like he wasn't keeping up. . . . I do things like tell him things that I bought cost less than they did so that he won't know how much more easily I can spend money than he can. It's lucky he doesn't know the real cost of some of the clothes I buy or things like that. . . . He is a very proud person and I have to watch it that I don't throw money around.

Gay men tell similar stories. Pete and Adam have lived together for eight years but Pete still worries that Adam's recent job problems are going to undermine their relationship. Pete, thirty-three, is a high-school teacher. Adam, thirty-five, was recently fired from his job with a brokerage firm, and his reaction has made Pete unsure of how to handle Adam's embarrassment:

> He is coming home with Tiffany candlesticks and saying, "No problem, it's not money, I can charge it." He is spending like this because he is saying to me that he isn't going to be worried about a little thing like getting fired, and to show me that he is economically confident and as good as the next person. . . . He is being pushier than usual because it is so important that I don't look like I have lost the tiniest bit of respect for him.

We have seen that heterosexual men are not happy when they have low or uncertain income. And they do not allow themselves to take comfort in their partners' ability to make money. One might think that gay men, too, would be unwilling to consider their partners' financial contribution as essential to the couple's well-being. Yet we find that gay men are indeed willing to take comfort in each other's earning power. Both men feel more secure with a high-earning partner.[22] This underscores the fact that it is the heterosexual man's inability to accept help from a *woman* that makes it difficult for the couple to act as a financial team. We think that one source of heterosexual men's ambition may be that they will not let themselves relax even if they have a partner with a high income. If they could take their partners' income into account, they might be able to strive less.[23]

On the other hand, in allowing themselves to take comfort in each

other's income, gay men do not lose the urge to earn. They are thus
able to build substantial incomes without having to spend any of it on
children or a nonworking partner,[24] and this surplus money that is not
needed for everyday expenses permits the purchase of luxury items. It
may be that some gay men are happier with their relationships when
they have money because they see other gay men living comfortably
and they want to do as well. Chuck and Jack have lived together for
sixteen years. Chuck, fifty-three, is a banker, and Jack, thirty-nine, is an
airline ticket agent. They live in an expensively refurbished home in a
city with a large gay community. Chuck said:

> What advantage does a gay male couple have? Money, money,
> money. Seriously, money is a big advantage. You have [two] big
> salaries. You can see what it's done to this town, everyone investing
> in real estate. You go look at a rehab building and I'll bet you fifty
> percent of the time the people who are doing it are a gay couple. . . .
> We are a lot better off together than we were separately. We have
> made investments ever since the first year and we are beginning to
> think of ourselves as a merger more than a marriage!

The catch-22 for gay men is that each appreciates a partner who
earns money, but if the partner is a success, he may become the more
powerful person in the relationship. There are two possible outcomes:
continuing resentment over who holds the reins, or a jostling for position as the less affluent partner is spurred on to increase his own
earnings.[25]
Lesbian couples are the only ones whose feelings about each other
are not affected when they are unhappy with the amount of money
coming in. Because women in our society have had fewer opportunities
to attain high-earning positions, many lesbians are used to having little
money and to living with partners who do not have big incomes.[26]
But although lesbians may be conscious of the fact that most
women they meet will not make a great deal of money, their satisfaction
with a less affluent way of life may have other causes. Many lesbians we
interviewed are all too aware of how money can function in a heterosexual relationship with the high earner receiving special privileges
and the low earner being subservient. They bend over backward to
avoid letting money have that kind of control over their lives. Lydia
and Jessie have lived together for five years. Lydia, twenty-six, is a
counselor, and Jessie, thirty-nine, is a nursing supervisor. Jessie said:

> Both of us had been married when we met. Lydia had been married
> eight years, a real child bride! She was a mess when I met her. She
> had been so browbeaten by her husband. He would give her shit for
> almost everything and his favorite trick was keeping her without any
> money. Everything went into the kitty and he controlled the kitty.
> My marriage was no bed of roses, but I can't believe some of the
> stuff *he* pulled. He would make her beg for grocery money! He
> would make her show him price tags of everything she bought

before she could take the tags off. And make her return things if he didn't like how much they cost. And they weren't poor either! She'd never ever get stepped on like that again, which is one reason I'm careful about money with her. I don't think she would ever want to have one account, for example. She doesn't want anything that even slightly resembles the way he used to yank her around. . . . It all suits me fine because I think keeping things separate is easier and fairer.

The desire among some lesbians to create a new set of values for dealing with money can be summed up in this response: "We may be unhappy about not having enough money, but that has nothing to do with the way we feel about each other."

It may also be true that when neither partner takes the role of provider in a relationship, there is less need for the other to take the primary role of consumer. Traditionally, in middle-class heterosexual marriages, the husband earned money and asked his wife to spend it. If they were poor, her task as a buyer might be to spend it wisely and frugally. If they were well-off, she might spend it with some fanfare. In either case, it was part of her role to become skilled at spending. We feel this is another part of the traditional homemaker role that some lesbians wish to avoid.

Men and women feel and act differently about money. To men it represents identity and power. To women, it is security and autonomy. These male-female differences are most obvious among our gay male and lesbian couples. The gay men are likely to equate power and money, but this is not true for lesbians; income does not give them the same feeling of control. Money is important for lesbians in the same way it is for the female cohabitors—it saves them from dependency. When we look at our heterosexual couples, we see that the meaning of money changes. Male and female emphases stay the same, but each person has to accommodate to a partner of the opposite sex. The men do not have a male partner to compete with, and the women do not have a female partner who wants an egalitarian relationship.

When we look at the female couples we see that they can find autonomy and security together. Each woman earns her own living and thus provides her own security. At present, since women tend to earn less than men, the decision to be without a man can involve being satisfied with a lower standard of living.

Gay men have potential conflict built into their relationships because if one man makes more money, he may attempt to control the relationship. His partner, being a man, is likely to resist. On the other hand, the couple's joint financial resources may give them a comfortable standard of living.

Among married couples the husband's provider role can get in the way of the wife's desire for autonomy. In a classic situation, she receives her security through him and simultaneously yields to his control. If she insists on autonomy, and he insists on control, their different attitudes toward money may have serious repercussions for the relationship.

On the surface it looks as if the cohabitors are well matched. The woman chooses autonomy over the security of being supported, and the man chooses the establishment of his own economic identity over the need to control his partner. This should make for a successful financial partnership, as long as the woman is *really* not going to resent the man for rejecting the provider role, and as long as the man is *really* happy to live with an independent woman who wants an equal say in the relationship. Since these couples are going against the established traditions for men and for women, and cannot isolate themselves in a same-sex couple, they face an intriguing social challenge.

# Money management

## A source of conflict

It comes as no surprise that couples disagree about how to spend their money. As single people, both partners were used to making decisions alone and were able to pursue their own self-interest. Once part of a couple, neither can enjoy such complete financial independence. At the very minimum, the couple will have to decide jointly on the kind of rent or mortgage encumbrance they can afford. They may start out with separate ideas and be challenged to compromise, and each person's private interest may have to be submerged in a decision that benefits the couple collectively. How couples make their financial decisions helps us understand how individual interests are negotiated.

It is particularly interesting to compare married couples with couples in other kinds of relationships. Husbands and wives are in an institution which, in its traditional format, has offered guidelines for money management, while other couples operate on an *ad hoc* basis. We wanted to find out whether the roles married couples have available to them minimize the potential for conflict or whether these roles have outlived their usefulness.

---

*Couples who fight about money argue more often about how it is to be spent than about how much they have.*

Our data show that couples argue more about how money is managed than about how much they have—and this holds true despite their actual income level.[1]

Money management can mean anything from making budgets and sticking to them (whether to save, spend, or invest) to deciding whether a sudden windfall should be spent on a charitable donation or an expensive vacation. Conflict can occur when partners have different views about how the money ought to be spent, or when they disagree on the process to be used in making a decision. One partner may want all decisions to be fully discussed and jointly reached while the other may feel it is his or her right to make a spending decision without

**CONFLICT OVER INCOME AND
OVER MONEY MANAGEMENT**

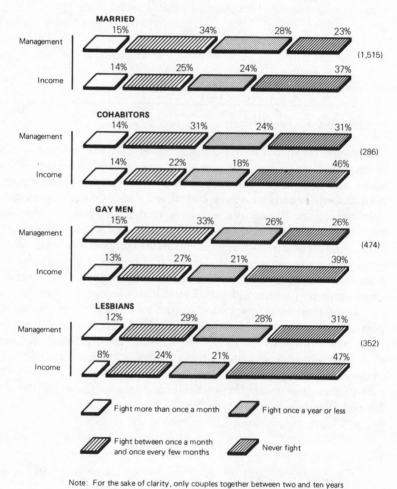

Note: For the sake of clarity, only couples together between two and ten years are presented.

Numbers in parentheses are the number of couples on which the percentages are based.

FIGURE    6

allowing any consultation. So, no matter how high a couple's income, there are still daily decisions to be made about spending it, leaving them much room for disagreement. Among couples with low incomes, money management surfaces more often as an issue because it is a daily and constant source of irritation. Although we may suspect that couples who find it nearly impossible to make ends meet are in fact arguing about income whenever the subject comes up, our data show that they themselves truly believe that the management of money is their main problem. This claim may also reflect their understanding, whether conscious or not, that it is more devastating to criticize a partner with a low income for the amount of money he or she brings in than to criticize his or her judgment about purchases.

Of course, when a fight is actually in progress, the participants may not be entirely clear themselves whether the process or their financial values are at issue: All they know is that they are furious.

*Married couples fight about money management more than all other kinds of couples.*

Sociologists might predict that couples who have already assigned one member to do the buying for the unit would have most spending decisions solved for them. Following this logic, married couples should have fewer conflicts since the traditional structure of marriage gives wives the responsibility for making household purchases. But our data show that just the opposite is true, and we think there are several aspects of marriage that make it more likely for spouses to fight over the management of money.

To start with, property and assets are usually commingled; hence partners have to consult with one another more about financial matters.[2] And even when married couples own property or objects that are clearly designated as individual belongings, it is hard to imagine a marriage where nothing important is owned in common. The longer a marriage endures, the more likely it is that the couple will incur shared debts, household furniture, and other substantial possessions, such as a car or a home. Deciding together how much to spend on a car, or what ·kind of car suits the taste of both, has more potential for conflict than if either spouse were to buy the car on his or her own.

Married couples are not the only ones who own property in common. But it seems to us that when couples who are not protected by the legal bonds of marriage buy property or other expensive items together, they do it only after they have reached a special understanding about the nature of their relationship and the financial rules they choose to abide by. As one gay man in a two-year relationship told us:

**CONFLICT OVER
MONEY MANAGEMENT**

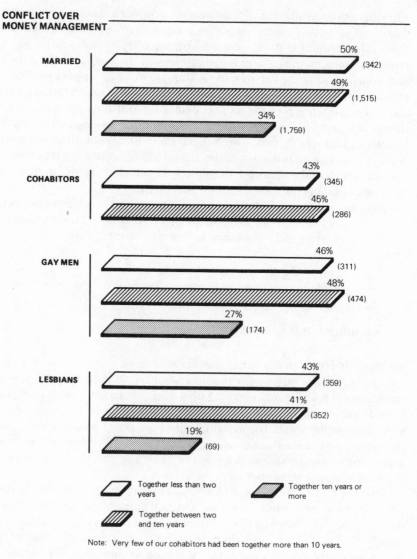

FIGURE    7

We just got over our major conflict. I did not want him to know my financial resources. And that was true not only for him, but for other people. . . . I felt that whatever we had should be together, but I hadn't really gone the whole route until we applied for the loan. I didn't know the interview for getting the loan would be so extensive. We had a long talk afterwards about the kind of trust we should be developing, and so I felt since this was going to be forever, that I should just relax and let him in on everything.

In traditional marriage, it is simply assumed that the couple will share almost everything, even if one or both partners is not really willing to do this. These couples are in a sense trapped by the rules of marriage, even though they continue to resist them.

Another source of conflict emerges from the wife's traditional role as buyer. In a typical scenario, where the wife has no income of her own, the husband gives his wife a sum of money to purchase both small and large items for the household. He has empowered her to act in the couple's behalf. He gives her great latitude, trusting her to do the best she can for them. He is freed from what he regards as onerous and tedious responsibilities, grateful that she is doing her job. Under this operating procedure, marriage provides the couple with ways of spending money that leave little room for conflict. A retired architect in his late sixties told us about his marriage of forty-four years:

> I don't think we have ever fought about money. No reason to. She controls it and does a damn fine job. I gave her my paycheck right from the start and she keeps our records and takes care of our expenses. Gives me an allowance. Very generous I might add. [He chuckles.]

Irwin, thirty-four, and Marcy, thirty-one, have been married eight years. Irwin owns a furniture store and Marcy is a bookkeeper. Irwin told us how comfortable he feels leaving financial matters to Marcy:

> It's very convenient to have a bookkeeper in the family. She comes into the office once a month and reconciles the books, tells me what money I have to spend, what to put away for taxes, the whole schmere. I never have to think about it. Anytime I've had to get somebody else to do it, it's never been done as well. She tried to retire the job a few times, but no one does it as well as her. So she does it and she takes care of everything at home too. . . . You know what they say about "I decide about Red China and she decides about everything else"? Well, it's true for us. She decides on everything and I just come and consult at the last minute. She went out, found this house, set everything up and called me in at the last minute. . . . I love it.

It is easy, however, for deviations from this procedure to cause conflict. The husband who gives his wife the authority to act as his agent may evaluate her performance and find it wanting. If he is critical of how she has spent their money, he may undermine her pride in her job. She may also be reminded of how little right she has to make independent decisions. Conflict may escalate if he then makes a purchase that she feels is outside the guidelines he has given *her* to work with. As one young wife told us:

> We've been fighting about money for a long time. Before we got married he would really piss money away on his hot rod. We always went to McDonald's and car racing. Every time he would race he

would change his oil and give the car a tune-up. . . . Then, when I would want to go to the movies or out someplace, I would have to tell him to get twenty dollars so we could go. So he'd take it out of his account and then, sure as shit, come Saturday night, man—that's the next day—this guy ain't got no money. And it was pretty much, "If we're going to get married, you're going to have to cut down on your car racing." Lots of fights like that, and after we got married it just carried right on.

When the wife complains—because it is her responsibility to be the buyer or because he has spent money more lavishly or indiscriminately than he would have wanted her to do—his response may create an argument. If he does not say he is sorry, but insists that he has the ultimate authority, the fight about spending may become a fight about the fundamental question of whether she has any power at all.

We suspect that when a wife learns that her husband does not really respect her judgment or when he fails to give her latitude to buy for the household and for herself, she may feel less compelled to be a "team player" in their marriage. Wives may grow antagonistic to such husbands and start to develop devious ways of running the finances the way they want to. One wife told us how she deals with her husband's anger over spending:

We fight about money. . . . When he sees the bills and how much is on the charge, he has a fucking shit-fit. You know, and I tell him, "Hey, I'm not walking around in Christian Dior." I mean, it's going to the electric company and Ma Bell, and all of this other bullshit, right? And you know, we have a fight because I get really insulted. . . . What's he so worried about? The guy is never wanting for cigarettes, for liquor, for gas, for clothes, for lunch, right? I mean, what does the guy need, right? I feel it's a personal insult when he starts yelling about how high the bills are. And yes, I do charge on them, but I have a legitimate alibi for every one of those charges. All right, so maybe once in a while I did buy myself something. So what? I'm not entitled to it? Fuck you if I'm not entitled to it. . . . So it's a drag, it's a fight.

This couple illustrates the kind of conflict that can arise when a husband does not trust or respect his wife's ability as a household manager. Things can be further complicated when each partner feels the other spends improperly on him- or herself. If the husband has the right to spend at his discretion, while his wife is accountable to him because anything she wants to buy for herself must come out of the household budget, conflict may occur.

In the interviews we observed two ways married couples with only a husband's income have been able to reduce this kind of conflict. Sometimes the husband gives his wife two allowances—one for all household needs and the other for herself. These couples believe that with a personal fund for which she is not accountable, and which is separate from money needed for the home, the wife is better equipped to perform her role as buyer and at the same time to maintain her personal dignity. In other cases a husband will turn all his income over to his wife. She then pays the bills and parcels out discretionary funds to both of them.

When both the husband and wife have incomes, it is still the wife who generally takes the buyer role, and the presumption usually exists that property is jointly owned.[3] We feel that these two factors remain a potential source of conflict. Because the wife now earns her own money, she expects to exercise more control, and her husband's attempt to compel her (as the buyer) to spend her money in ways he sees fit may meet with greater resistance. But even when a wife has relatively untrammeled use of her independent financial means, couples are not free from conflict: Because they are married, they cannot legally escape responsibility for one another's economic decisions; and custom dictates financial interdependence.

Finally, we think all married couples, whether they have one income or two, fight more about money simply because it is safe to do so. Couples who are contractually bound together can afford to express themselves in conflict. Other couples—cohabitors, gay men, and lesbians—fight somewhat less about money management not only because more of them lead separate financial lives[4] but also because they may be tempted to suppress any conflict that could threaten their relationships. The ideology of marriage helps a couple absorb a great deal without collapsing. Thus permanence and security permit greater conflict among married couples.

Some of our gay and lesbian couples, consciously or unconsciously, create financial arrangements that parallel those of married couples. They buy property together, make investments, and become so financially intertwined that it becomes difficult to tell whose money is whose, making it extremely complicated and costly ever to separate. The accumulated estate serves as a bond and makes it impossible to break up in the heat of the moment. We think these couples are getting the same trade-off as married couples: permanence but more room for conflict. Kevin and Jake have lived together for thirty-one years. Kevin, sixty-two, is a professional entertainer, and Jake, sixty, is Kevin's legal adviser and business manager. Theirs is a very volatile relationship, punctuated by occasional fights against a backdrop of constant bickering. When we asked Jake the secret of their long time together, he explained:

> Every couple of years we have an enormous fight and decide to break up. . . . The next morning we get the lawyers and start disentangling the business and figuring out how to go our separate ways. It takes so long that we always make up before the lawyers get very far. . . . It's hard to break up when you have been business partners as long as we have.

*Cohabiting couples are not very "liberated" about making spending decisions. When the woman has more influence than her partner, they quarrel.*

Couples who are living together have a fundamentally different orientation to money than do married couples. This is true even though individual couples have different reasons for being in a living-together arrangement.

For some, cohabitation is a form of trial marriage. They feel they are not ready for marriage or they believe that marriage is such a momentous decision that they want to proceed cautiously before making a commitment. They may be in love but feel they need more information and experience before deciding they are compatible enough for a lifetime match. Annette and Geoff are both twenty-seven and have been living together a little over a year. Annette is a photographer's model and Geoff is an assistant personnel director. Annette described her feelings about marriage:

> I am a serious sort of person and I would not have moved in with him if I didn't think we were planning a future together. When we first met, I think it was the first night, we had a long talk about what kind of person he was and I was. We went out for a long time before we had sex because he said that was the beginning of commitment for him and so we just got to know each other and develop our feelings. I was so impressed with that because I felt he had good values. . . . We talked about marriage the very first night we met. We both thought it was important and it was what you want to happen if you've got the right relationship. We've been spending some time to find out if we have the right relationship and if we're both sure we'll get married. If I'm not sure in another six months or so, then we'll have to cut bait.

Another woman, in a relationship for two years, expressed her desire to work toward a marriage that would not end in divorce:

> Marriage is forever—which makes you pretty cautious, you know. I am not setting myself up to have a divorce. I've waited a long time to make sure I know what I'm doing. Most of my friends are married and a lot of them are either divorced already or working on it. I think living together gives you the advantage of seeing if you've got what it takes to make a lifetime commitment, and if not you can bow out gracefully—or if not gracefully, then just get out however you can.

Until couples like these have made a pledge for the indefinite future, both partners find it more prudent not to accrue joint assets.[5] They feel it is safer to keep separate ownership clear so that, should the relationship break up, they know who owns what. These couples hold interdependence at arm's length until they decide to get married. Because marriage is their goal, they do not want the trappings of marriage until they have the real thing.

Shawn and Sybil have been living together for four years and are currently engaged to be married. Both are in their late thirties and both were married previously. Shawn is an accountant and Sybil works as a legal assistant. She told us how they tried not to own property together until they were sure they would marry:

> He was real adamant about not owning anything together. . . . Our big breakthrough came when we went antiquing and we saw two coverlets that we both liked and we decided to get one, but they were a pair and their value was as a pair. After we did that, it was a kind of a signal that we might be together and we started buying other things together. Of course we didn't buy this house together until we decided to get married. That was a big step for both of us and we would never have done it if we were just living together.

For other couples, cohabitation is an ideological statement about the rejection of the institution of marriage. These people may love one another and plan a life together but they do not want the law or tradition to define the structure of their relationship. Their ambition, if their relationship is successful, is to have a lifetime of cohabitation. Rod, a thirty-eight-year-old plumber has been living for three years with Yolanda, thirty-two, an aerobic-dance instructor. He described his feelings about marriage:

> Neither of us wants to get married. It's full of silly formalities and it doesn't apply to our lives. We're interested in each living our own life and not getting into one of society's weird trips. . . . When I got married before, I was into the idea of a permanent relationship and I got married because that was what you were supposed to do. But we were married then and not into the relationship because the relationship got lost along the way. So it was the legal thing that took over and we were in it even though we didn't like each other anymore. Finally it dawned on her and on me as well that we didn't have to stay married. . . . Once I got out of there I knew I didn't want to do that trip again. . . . Now this relationship might be permanent or it might not, but it's up to us, not some piece of paper.

Part of the ideology of cohabitation is that if the relationship ceases to be emotionally satisfying, it should be dissolved. Since the relationship is never completely permanent, it is hard for the partners to become financially interdependent. Laura and Dick have lived together for five years and are still adamant about preserving their financial independence:

> DICK: We could buy some furniture.
>
> LAURA: We couldn't buy furniture, because *we* can't own furniture.
>
> DICK: That's right.

LAURA: We could buy something we could split in two. We could buy . . . a horse.

DICK: You could buy the bottom . . .

LAURA: And you could buy the top!

DICK: I'll buy the chair and you buy the ottoman!

LAURA: We could do something like that.

A great many "ideological" cohabitors were previously married and turned sour on the institution of marriage at that time.[6] Some found the financial traditions of marriage especially alienating. And during their divorce proceedings they learned the danger of owning things in common. During a divorce, property that was bought together may be claimed to have "always" been the property of one spouse or the other. It is as if there has been a tag on each item in the household that says, "This belongs to us, but especially me." When there ceases to be an "us," all these tags are presented and a painful dialogue ensues about who bought what and who deserves the item more. This experience has made many cohabitors feel there is ultimately no such thing as joint property and they do not want to act as if there were. One man of forty-six was very clear about why he felt bitter after his divorce:

> We'd saved for many years to afford our house, and the cabin. It wasn't that I begrudged her her share of the house, and I went into negotiations expecting that she would want it until the children were out of school. But I wasn't prepared for her wanting everything. . . . I wasn't prepared for how vicious she was going to be. She was going to make me pay for leaving her one way or the other. . . . She did go right down to the wire and I finally settled out of court because I just couldn't stand the whole dirty process anymore. And like I was warned, she wore me down and she got way more than she deserved. . . . What really burns me is that I don't know if I'm ever going to be able to afford a house like that again and she gets it all just because she can play the tragically spurned housewife all alone in the world with her three children.

Their marital experiences also taught the women that there are costs associated with allowing themselves to become dependent on a man. Traditional marriage encourages the wife either to stay at home or to subordinate her career to her husband's. That may be satisfying to both partners if the marriage lasts a lifetime, but if it does not, the wife may learn the bitter lesson of how ill-prepared she is to maintain her life-style alone. There are many books and stories written by divorced women who have suffered because they sacrificed their careers or missed training that would have made them more employable. Such women are often determined never again to put themselves in this situation. Some see cohabitation as the only way to have a relationship and still preserve their own interests. Paulette has been living for seven years with Will. In the course of her interview we asked her about her earlier marriage. She replied:

> This story is so classic it's embarrassing. He was the young ambitious author and I was the humdrum worshiping wife. So I worked at a straight job and he got to do his thing because we both agreed that he was the brilliant one. I supported him so that he could go to Stanford Graduate School. . . . Sure enough, in his last year—not his first year mind you—he had this affair with someone he was in a class with. He was honest about it, I'll say that for him, but he also didn't return the tuition money. Breaking up was very painful for me, even more painful because I felt like such a fool. . . . I was a women's liberation joke. . . . He got to get ahead in his career and mine was not even started. . . . Now I pay serious attention to my work and while I'm supportive of everything Will wants to accomplish, it's up to him to accomplish it on his own. . . . I got used when I was with my husband, even if he didn't consciously mean to do it. And it's never going to happen again.

Another woman, now in a living-together arrangement, told us how adrift she felt after her divorce. Arlene, thirty-one years old, reported:

> The first thing I realized after my marriage fell apart is that I had never done my own taxes. It was the end of March and suddenly I was faced with the fact that I had never done them, didn't know anything about them. I panicked. . . . There were all kinds of discoveries. . . . Finding a job was incredibly hard. I hadn't really thought about what having a B.A. in English would look like to employers. They would take one look at me and say, "What have you been doing? Why should we take you seriously?" It was hard to find a good answer to give them. . . . It was the one big trauma and while I wanted to blame Guy for a lot of it I had to blame myself too. I'd bought into being a wife and housewife, and I just hadn't kept up. I would never put myself in that position again. My mother told me you always have to have a fallback position and I never really took it seriously. I was living in a two-hundred-fifty-thousand-dollar house. I wasn't thinking about the fact that I couldn't have paid for it. . . . With Scott I know what's mine and what's his and what I can do, as opposed to what he's doing. I'm not dependent on him except in so far as we both help each other out on small day-to-day things. I think it's better that way.

Men who have had previous marriages often told us that it was they who suffered more. If a husband had a wife who subordinated her life to his, he learned, when the marriage broke up, that he had to bear a responsibility that would endure beyond the divorce. If his wife was unable to earn money, he could expect to contribute to her support for a significant number of years. If he left one relationship and is paying large sums of money to his ex-wife, he may be leery of entering a new relationship with a woman who would be financially dependent on him.

In interviews, previously married men kept telling us they now insisted on living with a partner who could take care of herself. As one said:

> I don't ever want to be in the situation again where some woman expects me to set her up for life. It's like having another child. Except there are a lot fewer rewards. I don't want to be around the kind of woman anymore who thinks the world owes her a living. Fortunately Carol is a strong, independent person who has always been her own person and doesn't need me to run her life for her. . . . I wish I'd thought about these things a long time ago when I was in college. I would never have married Millie [his ex-wife].

When these men do move in with a woman, they generally insist that she contribute equally to the relationship. If she does not, they fight. Gloria and Cullen have been living together for four years and both are in their late thirties. Gloria has an administrative job that earns $21,000, while Cullen is a highly successful nuclear engineer with an income more than twice that size. Gloria described their struggles over money:

> I blow up at him when he accuses me of not having put much money in. It's easy for him because he makes so much more money than I do. . . . I sometimes have to wait until I get my paycheck again because I run out. I'm not being extravagant but this city eats up money. He gets a much higher percentage of my money than I get of his and while I agree with him that we both should pay for food and entertainment and things like that, I would also like him to acknowledge once in a while how hard it is for me to do.

There is little sign of the provider or protector role here. Cohabitation is a pay-as-you-go system and each partner's rights and privileges are based on what he or she contributes. The irony is that while both men and women insist that each partner's contribution to the household be as equal as possible, their ability to do so is hampered by the nature of the world of work. Most women cannot earn as much money as their male partners.[7] If a woman puts in an equal share, it may be a much larger percentage of her take-home pay than his—or such an amount may be completely out of her reach. If she does not contribute equally, they may both feel she is not living up to her side of the bargain. He feels that he is having to pay too much and this is precisely the kind of obligation he wants to avoid. The specter of her possible dependence can cast a pall on their entire relationship. The dependence may not be of their making, but the effect is nevertheless the same.

This adherence to equality is not always followed in other financial aspects of the relationship. At the same time that the man refuses to accept the mantle of provider and protector, he is willing to yield only a certain amount of control over financial decisions. We find that when the woman has greater influence over how money is spent (leisure activities and furniture buying), the couple faces more conflict. When the man has greater influence, or when the influence is equal, there is less turmoil.[8] Thus cohabitors have to juggle both traditional and non-traditional pressures, making money problems difficult to solve. We have ample evidence to show that this is quicksand for cohabiting couples. The women want to have equal financial responsibility and equal influence. The men are eager to have her share responsibility but are wary of her gaining too much influence.

---

*Among all four kinds of couples, partners who feel they have equal control over how money is spent have a more tranquil relationship.[9]*

---

In general we find that it is important for people in any kind of a relationship to feel they are participating equally in financial decisions.[10] There are, however, two ways to be equal. Couples can decide jointly on each item or they can agree that each person will go his or her own way and be individually responsible for personal purchases. In the interviews we found that the mere fact that a couple has very different ideas about how to spend money does not necessarily mean they have more conflict. If, however, in addition to having different views, at least one partner feels he or she cannot exert any control over spending, then we often observe anger and frustration.

Take the experience of Dale, forty, and Claudia, thirty-nine. They have been married for ten years. Dale, a high-school principal, has always been conservative about investments. Claudia has a master's degree in forestry and decided to open an environmental consulting firm. In order to do this, she needed a large amount of capital and the only collateral she had was their home. Dale was hesitant to use the house as collateral because he recognized that the business was a risky one. But after many discussions he decided it was the right thing to do. Her business prospered for a few years and then was hurt by an economic recession in the timber industry. She could not meet her loan commitments and the bank foreclosed on their home. While both of them were extremely unhappy, Dale did not blame Claudia. He told us he had been an equal partner in deciding what they should do as a couple.

Another married couple stands in sharp contrast. Amy and Dennis have been married for twenty-one years and both are in their early fifties. Amy is a homemaker, who is, in her own words, "driven to distraction" by Dennis's spending. Dennis is a successful salesman. He described an incident that occurred a few years ago:

Well, my philosophy is, make money and spend it. Lavishly. We ended up declaring bankruptcy out of the country. . . . I made a lot of money in Atlanta. We had a big house, maid, lived well, the kids went to the best parochial schools, and at the same time I was involved and worked hard for charities. I was doing what I liked. No one can stop me from doing what I like—spending money and enjoying it.

Amy has a somewhat different view:

We screwed ourselves financially very badly. You know the old story. Credit cards came in the mail. He had a very bright future so we started borrowing on his future. Then the financial thing fell down on our heads and so we decided to drop out. . . . We slept on the floor, brought our books and declared bankruptcy. For four years we were very happy.

But the same cycle has begun again. They have moved to a different city, and Amy is worried.

I've tried to tell him that the fact that he works so hard and makes so much money and runs around in a Cadillac and eats in the finest restaurants is his baby. I've tried to make him realize that me and the children are far more interested in him as a person than we are in the money he brings in or the trappings. But that seems to be unimportant to him, in spite of our dropping out and stretching ourselves. . . . It's an upward mobility problem with him and I want to go in the opposite direction 'cause having come from an upper-middle-class background, I could throw it all away. I could care less. I really think I'm honest about that.

But Dennis is not guided by Amy's concerns. They have different values on the subjects of income and spending. Amy's only choice—since she has little power in the relationship—is to complain bitterly and then give in. Witness this exchange when we interviewed the couple together:

AMY: Life-style is important. We've never discussed it, but as far as money goes, you like a big money thing and it's irrelevant to me.

DENNIS: Well, the problems we've had have something to do with me spending money like a drunken sailor. Where there is money to spend or not. I'll go and borrow and worry about it after I spend it. It doesn't bother me.

AMY: There is no way he could live in a cold-water flat on the Lower East Side. He would be just miserable.

DENNIS: We did in the islands. But there you don't have Regine's [a fancy disco]. You don't have Belmont [the local racetrack].

AMY: I think it's an ego thing you bolster yourself with, so that the world sees you a certain way. It's not the money that means so much to him. It's the image.

DENNIS: Like I said, I love the track. Last year I got my outfit to get me a Cadillac so that when I drive out there they remember me. I make sure they remember me. We went out there last week and it was jammed, but we got a table. Those silly little things are silly but I like it.

AMY: I wish I could spend our money in different ways.

DENNIS: I'm sure you would. And I agree, but not to the exclusion of getting out to the track. And I wouldn't enjoy that unless I can go there in style. If I don't have money but for one meal, I'll skip lunch and have dinner at The Four Seasons.

Dennis and Amy have a serious problem about managing money, but it is far from unique. While Amy, being the partner with fewer financial resources, is concerned and agitated, it is possible for the resentment to flow in the opposite direction. Consider, for example, the relationship between Valerie and Doris. This was one of the few lesbian couples we interviewed where there was a clear "butch" role (Doris was much more dominant and took on the roles characteristically associated with the husband) and a "femme" role (Valerie's behavior paralleled the wife's position). Doris expressed her frustration:

I'm supposed to do the heavy work around the household . . . supposed to be the big breadwinner. You know, bring home the fat paycheck and the wife will bring in the subordinate paycheck. *Well,* I wish to hell she would bring in more money.

Doris feels that Valerie does not understand what it takes to earn the kind of salary she does. She characterizes Valerie as seeing her as a bottomless fund of money and not understanding there must be limits:

I think Valerie is a little bit loose with money. I get a little bit irritated when she talks about buying a new car or something and I keep saying, "Look, think about it. You're a secretary and making fourteen thousand dollars a year. Can you afford a new car on fourteen thousand dollars a year?" Now I make more than that, I got into serious trouble once with credit cards—very serious to the point I had to move out of the state to get the hell out of the mess. . . . I don't think she appreciates the fact that there's a limit on my income even though it's thirty-two thousand or thirty thousand or whatever the hell it is. She's not sensitive to the basic dollar and cents of things.

Valerie and Doris's relationship, while quite different from Amy and Dennis's, reflects again that different attitudes about spending coupled with a lack of compromise can form the foundation for financial conflict.

Sam and Judy have been a couple for fifteen years, but only moved in together three years ago. Sam is an artist and Judy is a businesswoman. They have very different attitudes about how to spend money, and Sam has made their financial life precarious by making unilateral decisions. This makes Judy furious. As Sam expressed it:

People don't extend themselves the way I do. I'm used to living without any money because I bought something. I had to eat spaghetti for a year. Judy would never in a million years deprive herself like that. She'd want to know, "Where are your backups?" Well, I don't have any backups. We've come three times close to foreclosing on the whole thing because we didn't have the money to complete the building we started. And I think I'm beginning to learn what that means. Yes. But we argue all the time. She thinks she manages money better than I do. But look what I've done. . . . And, of course, Judy goes absolutely bananas every time I spend money on my car, 'cause she's paying money on the rent and then I don't have enough money for my share. But when this building is sold, she'll get back every dime. But my car is my car, and if she doesn't like it, she can lump it.

Judy, naturally enough, does not share this point of view:

There's never enough money. . . . I don't think he knows the first thing about budgeting or financing, and he gets upset when I say that, because he thinks he's a genius when it comes to money. There's no planning, nothing set aside. . . . The kind of training I have had . . . is that everything has a place. And also my parents were in business and very careful. But there was always money. And it bugs me that he doesn't have any money even though he's working. You know he thinks nothing of giving the kids money or spending the money on his kids [from his previous marriage]. But we can't go to a movie or we can't go out to dinner. It really irritates me.

Judy handles the situation with a policy that states the way she will and will not help:

I will not give him child-support money. I will not give him money for car repairs. We were in a car accident and he should have gotten rid of that car. He won't buy things for himself because he simply doesn't have the money. But he'll think nothing of spending some here or there. Me, if I have three dollars, I'll save it because soon that's twelve dollars and that's a theater ticket.

Or there are Ed and Norm, who have lived together for three years. Norm, thirty-two, is a clinical psychologist, and Ed, twenty-nine, sells real estate. Business has not been going well for Ed, and so he would like the couple to economize but Norm refuses. Norm controls the decisions because he has the greater resources. When we asked about money, Norm answered:

Problems about money? *Oh yes*, oh yes. That is, *yes*. I tend to spend more money than he does. It is a continual problem—probably will be a continual problem. Rightfully so. We don't have it—so I just extend my credit. . . . But then I did a conference and I earned enough to get *both* of us out of debt. In a matter of a week. I just have my ups and downs in life. But it is hard for him to adjust. I even understand his point of view. . . . Well, I have more purchasing power and I also have more power to get us into debt. Damned if you do, damned if you don't.

Ed complained:

We fight about what we can't afford . . . about running up bills. Buying another chest. *We don't need another chest.*

Another gay man, who has very little say about the purchases that are made, told us that money is a chronic source of strife in his relationship:

I was getting to the point where I didn't feel I owned anything. I didn't have a job and he had bought me a lot of things and I felt like a lot of things he purchased weren't mine. I just decided that I had to start owning things myself. We had quite a few arguments over that and I left for a few months.

Money management is a likely area of conflict for couples. It involves daily decision-making, which means that differences in financial values come to the surface. When we first began to investigate this topic, we thought that married couples would have the least conflict: The sharply defined provider and buyer roles ought to simplify decision-making. This did not turn out to be the case. Delegating buying to the wife, while efficient, does not always mitigate conflict. Wives want more autonomy than they usually have, and if husbands resist giving them more, hard feelings are stirred up. When married couples fight, the arguments arise out of the fact that each is intimately connected to the other's financial future—and so has the right to review all money decisions.[11] Nevertheless, unequal influence over money management persists and becomes the basis for much of their fighting.

Money management is accomplished with the least conflict when partners have an equal influence over decisions. If either partner is too dominating, conflict occurs. This is especially true when traditional roles are violated. It may be tedious for couples to create budgets together and decide jointly what to spend on everything from groceries to entertainment to clothes and even furniture. And it may not be possible for the two partners to do all their spending separately and not impinge on each other's decisions. When couples *do* take the time to share control over money management, they seem to have happier, calmer relationships.

# Pooling

## *A question of trust*

Couples have the choice of keeping their money as an individual resource or as part of a joint or pooled resource. From one point of view it is only natural for people to keep their money separate because human beings are territorial and grow up with a strong sense of what belongs to them. On the other hand, as one grows up, one is also taught to share, and adulthood requires the ability to leave total selfishness behind. Love itself is often defined as the desire to give to the other person and to be able to submerge one's own self-interest so that the couple's best interest can triumph.

However, there may be practical benefits to pooling at least some of the partners' assets. Some things that people want to buy require the participation of both earners. For example, a home, a large investment opportunity, or a child's college education may demand more than one income, and once acquired, the increasing value of the item over the years may profit both partners. Each person's life is enhanced and the impulse is to continue the partnership.

On the other hand, once the home has been bought, one partner may love it while the other may want to move, and there is no solution to this dilemma that pleases both partners. By joining their assets they have given up some ability to use their money as they wish. Many people are very aware of this possible state of affairs so even though they may deeply love their partners, they prefer to keep their money as separate as possible.

Some married couples do not have the option of deciding whether they will pool their income or assets. The law in some of the United States declares assets to be part of their community property. More important, married couples have traditional values to turn to for guidance on this matter, and tradition suggests joint property. Cohabiting couples, lesbians, and gay men have no such traditions and so they must resolve the question—to pool or not to pool—by themselves. We have interviewed couples who keep everything separate, and who claim that this is what has made their relationship a success. We have also talked with couples who totally merge their finances and insist that it is the source of their relationship's strength and durability. We wanted to know which of these views is more generally correct: Should couples keep their money separate or put it all together?

**ATTITUDES TOWARD POOLING**

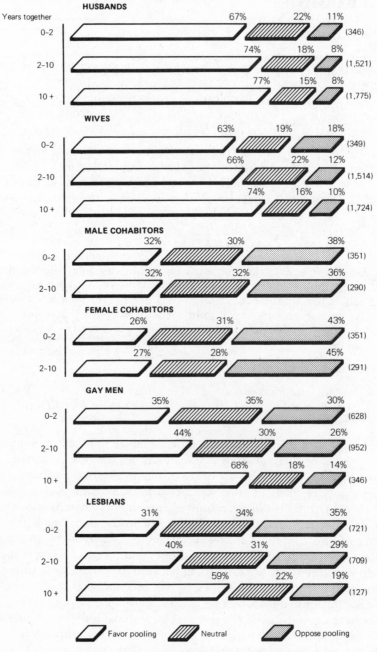

**HUSBANDS**

Years together

| 0-2 | 67% | 22% | 11% | (346) |
| 2-10 | 74% | 18% | 8% | (1,521) |
| 10 + | 77% | 15% | 8% | (1,775) |

**WIVES**

| 0-2 | 63% | 19% | 18% | (349) |
| 2-10 | 66% | 22% | 12% | (1,514) |
| 10 + | 74% | 16% | 10% | (1,724) |

**MALE COHABITORS**

| 0-2 | 32% | 30% | 38% | (351) |
| 2-10 | 32% | 32% | 36% | (290) |

**FEMALE COHABITORS**

| 0-2 | 26% | 31% | 43% | (351) |
| 2-10 | 27% | 28% | 45% | (291) |

**GAY MEN**

| 0-2 | 35% | 35% | 30% | (628) |
| 2-10 | 44% | 30% | 26% | (952) |
| 10 + | 68% | 18% | 14% | (346) |

**LESBIANS**

| 0-2 | 31% | 34% | 35% | (721) |
| 2-10 | 40% | 31% | 29% | (709) |
| 10 + | 59% | 22% | 19% | (127) |

Favor pooling   Neutral   Oppose pooling

Note: Very few of our cohabitors had been together more than 10 years.

Numbers in parentheses are the number of people on which the percentages are based.

FIGURE   8

*Married couples prefer to pool their money more than other kinds of couples do.[1]*

When people marry, both partners generally assume they will put some, if not all, of their assets together. Working wives or wives with high incomes want to pool just as much as do full-time homemakers. Wives of men who make modest incomes feel the same way as wives with high-earning husbands.[2] Once the mantle of marriage rests across the couple's shoulders, they are in it for better or for worse. Pooling is part of the package of marriage. In the interviews pooling seemed such a natural part of marriage to most of our couples that they could hardly imagine living any other way. Len, forty-eight, a newspaper editor, and Linda, forty-four, a part-time office worker at the same newspaper, have been married for twenty-four years in what looks like a very happy relationship. Their response to pooling is typical of couples of their generation. Len summarized:

> We have one checking account, one savings account. She handles everything—and beautifully, I might add. We take what we need and when we run out, we take less. I don't know what is her money and what is my money. It's our money. Otherwise it gets ridiculous. We don't divide up our children! Andrea isn't Linda's or mine; she's ours.

Linda had the same reaction:

> I'm not sure what you mean about separating our income. We've been married twenty-four years. How would we keep things separate?

In fact, it is difficult for married couples to avoid pooling. Since they think of themselves as a joint financial unit, if one partner hesitates to place the major part of his or her wealth into a common fund, questions are likely to arise about that person's commitment. We feel that is why the idea of a prenuptial agreement, whereby the engaged couple declares that property held prior to the marriage is not to be part of the couple's joint assets, is repugnant to many people and therefore very hard to execute without creating painful reactions. Prenuptial agreements are disturbing because they intimate both that it is not guaranteed that the marriage will last and that there should be individual rather than "team" control over all finances. Even if both partners agree to preserve their right to make independent financial decisions, the fact that this agreement has to be written into a legal document may make it difficult to insist that the relationship is based on mutual trust the way a marriage is supposed to be.

If marriage makes it difficult for couples to keep their finances separate, it is just as difficult for other kinds of couples to merge their finances, since no legal safeguards exist for couples who are not married.[3] If gay couples break up, no court is going to hear their dispute on the basis of a partner's spousal rights. They may draw up a contract, but if the courts look at it at all, it will be treated as a business understanding and not as a marriage. Since cohabitors and same-sex couples cannot count on the courts to help them divide up their property in the event they break up, pooling assets involves some risk for them. Another problem persists for all unmarried couples (cohabitors, gay men, and lesbians): Unless they want to go public about their style of life, they may be embarrassed to go into court to seek help with a property settlement. Thus a high level of trust is required for pooling among same-sex and cohabiting couples.

Just as it may be embarrassing for married couples to suggest ways of keeping finances separate, it can be sensitive for unmarried and same-sex couples to suggest pooling. The partner who suggests it faces having his or her honor doubted because he or she is asking for some control over the other's funds. The person who says no may appear selfish and mistrustful. If the suggestion to pool can be taken as a kind of "proposal to marry" by one partner, rejecting it may be interpreted as saying no to the long-term future of the relationship. If one partner has more money, it may be up to him or her to suggest pooling because the motives will be seen as pure. The poorer partner, however, may refuse so that his or her own motives will not be suspect. The fact that two people love each other and wish to spend a lifetime together may get lost in the attempt to maintain equality and trust in the relationship.

Unlike married couples, cohabitors have no difficulty understanding why we would ask whether they wanted to pool. Eric and Sandy are typical in their feelings on this matter. They are both forty and have lived together for four years. Both are employed full time, Eric as an airline technician and Sandy as a clerk-typist. Both were married previously, and this is the first living-together arrangement for either of them. They want it to be different from marriage and they feel their economic arrangement helps them. Eric answered our question about why they have stayed together:

> One of the things I think both of us would attribute as a strong factor in the success of our relationship is the fact that we're economically independent of each other. We make no decisions that involve joint finances and that simplifies life a great deal. We never have to worry about what the other is thinking about how we're spending money or not spending money or saving or whatever. I own this house and Sandy shares the expenses of it as if it were rent, and then we share food and utilities and all that sort of thing, but other than that, she has her possessions and I have mine.

Sandy emphasized the same reason for their success:

> We're a little strange from other couples . . . but everything is

separate. We pay for ourselves, the expectation being that I take him out for his birthday and he takes me out for mine.

Tony and Michelle have lived together for four years. They told us they are planning to get married, but that their period of living together has made them decide not to pool all their property. Tony is a lawyer and Michelle is a part-time paralegal worker. Even though they are planning to get married, they have still provided a way to make a tidy exit—just in case things do not work out. As Tony explained:

> I know it's cold-blooded and maybe it's the lawyer in me, but I want to be clear that the woman I live with is not going to be economically dependent. . . . Even if it turns out I bring in more money, it's important that she works too.

Perhaps the best contrast we can offer between the way married couples unconsciously assume a commingling of money and the way cohabitors assume separate finances comes from the following conversations. In part of the interview, couples were left alone with the tape recorder and asked to discuss how they would—together—spend six hundred dollars that they were to pretend we would give them. Caroline and Chris have been married for fifteen years. Caroline, forty, is a social worker, and Chris, forty-four, is a high-school sports coach:

> CAROLINE: I think we should spend it on ourselves.
>
> CHRIS: Okay, what do we need?
>
> CAROLINE: We have things we need. Let's spend it on something we both want, not just something one or the other wanted. . . . I've been thinking of something like airline tickets to Hawaii. You've been wanting to go to Maui. I think it would be nice for us.
>
> CHRIS: Okay, that's perfect. Sold.

This dialogue stands in sharp contrast to Mark and Susan's. They have been living together for almost two years. Mark is an electrician on construction sites and Susan is a musician:

> MARK: Okay, my mind is made up.
>
> SUSAN: Okay, let them leave the room first, though.
>
> MARK: I'm ready.
>
> SUSAN: Split it fifty-fifty, right?
>
> MARK: Exactly.
>
> SUSAN: We're finished.
>
> MARK: Same as always.
>
> SUSAN: Fifty-fifty.
>
> MARK: I'll spend at least two hundred dollars on photographic equipment . . . and probably pay off something to Visa. . . .
>
> SUSAN: And I'll spend mine my way. Very simple.

The gay men and lesbians are more diverse on the issue of pooling than either the married or cohabiting couples. They do not have a legal marriage to make pooling seem automatic, but neither are they generally like the cohabitors who are consciously designing their relationships to avoid the economic entanglements of marriage. When gay men and lesbians do not want to pool, they often feel very strongly about it. For example, Christine and Marilyn are in their mid-thirties and have lived together for two years. They both work in medical clinics and their economic arrangement does not include pooling. Christine described how it works:

> We handle money really well. We have definitely our own checking accounts which neither one of us ever dreams anyone else—the other person—would have two peeps about. 'Til we saw the questionnaires, I was amazed at the options they had in there. We have our autonomous checking and savings accounts that neither person can touch. We don't buy joint things. I wanted a lettuce dryer the week before we bought the house. And Marilyn said, "No, it's too expensive. We'd have to decide who got it later if we ever split up." This after we bought an eighty-thousand-dollar house! And we couldn't buy a fifteen-dollar lettuce dryer. But on principle she was right . . . if it's going to be expensive we talk about it. The only time we've ever had an argument about my money is this vacation because I wiped out my savings when we bought the house and had slowly been saving money and spent it all on the vacation. I got a cash advance on my MasterCharge which I wish I had never done. But we had to get away from our jobs. That was the only time she ever had a lot to say about what I was doing.

Marilyn outlined their financial understanding in the same way:

> We each pay for ourselves. Like we go out to eat or go to a movie. Sometimes we'll go to a movie and she goes, "Well, you still owe me a dollar 'cause I bought the ice cream cone on Saturday." And to us it's no big deal. It's just a way of keeping things fairly even. . . .
>     One reason I'm sensitive to this is that we had two women friends who used to be together, but they've split up now. One made fifteen thousand dollars and the other made twenty-two thousand dollars. And even though twenty-two thousand is not going to make someone wealthy, it's a lot more than fifteen thousand. And there was a lot of bitterness 'cause they pooled their money. We watched all that horrible stuff come out. And we decided we didn't want to be that unequal. And nor would we ever pool our money, so our [money] arguments aren't important to our relationship. 'Cause they're just picky.

When same-sex couples do decide to pool, they may be persuaded by a logic not unlike the one we hear from married couples. For example, Robert and Sol have lived together for four years. Robert, thirty-nine, owns a successful chain of beauty shops, and Sol, forty-seven, is a

TV producer. They live in a lavish home and commute to the city. Robert feels strongly about how to run the finances and he has convinced Sol he is right. Robert explained:

> I would never have a relationship where it is, "I owe you this and you owe me that." It's cut right down the middle. . . . If you're going to have a relationship with another male—or female for that matter—husband or wife, don't do this type of thing. It's degrading.

Robert makes it sound as though there is only one way for a couple to pool. Actually there are many ways. Couples can have small separate accounts of their own and put most of their income into a joint account; they can have large separate accounts of their own with only a minimal joint fund; or they can have absolutely no joint account, or absolutely no separate money. A couple may begin a relationship with the intention of keeping money separate, but find it too inconvenient to keep track of who paid for what. Or they may drift into more and more pooling in spite of their intention not to. For example, they may start taking vacations with a joint fund established for the trip. Or their home might need a new refrigerator, which benefits both partners, but which neither wants to own individually. If the couple has children, it may not make sense to them to tally each person's contribution to their welfare. Perhaps the most important issue in pooling is whether a couple's money becomes so commingled that the original contributor is unknown, or whether even joint accounts can be broken down by contributor. Couples who truly mix their funds may have the sense that their individual shares are obscured. This may be the case while the relationship lasts, but if it ends, the partners—with the help of a lawyer—can often remember how much they put in the pool and which objects in the home were bought with their own money.

---

*Among married couples and cohabitors, fewer women want to pool funds than do men.*

When husbands take on the provider role they take it for granted that their money will go into a fund for the couple's use. If their wives work, husbands often expect that this money will also go into the joint fund. Some husbands think it is perfectly all right for their wives to keep some money separate as "pin money," to spend it on child care or a housekeeping service, or to have a separate savings account for retirement. In some couples the wife keeps all her money and does not contribute at all to family expenses. As a rule, however, in marriage the presumption is not "your money and my money" but rather "our money."

HETEROSEXUAL MEN'S AND WOMEN'S ATTITUDES
TOWARD POOLING

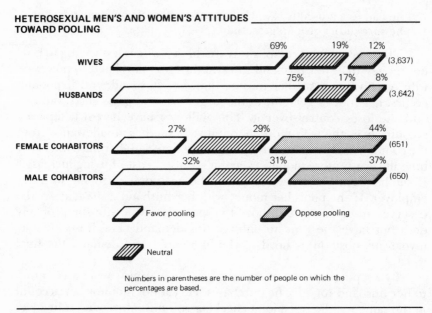

FIGURE    9

The couple's belief in the provider role can give marriage an interesting accounting system. While the husband views all or most of the money he makes as family money, the wife may think that the money she earns is outside the joint account. These wives are saying to their husbands, "Your money is our money, but my money is mine." If her husband does not agree that she has a right to keep some private funds separate to use as she likes, arguments may result. Todd and Mary have been married for twenty-three years and both are forty-two. Todd is the manager of an industrial plant and Mary is an executive secretary. She chronicled for us her desire to have her own separate funds and the struggle this created in her marriage:

In the first year or so I was willing to take on a very secondary role. But I wasn't satisfied. So somewhere along the line I started to get feisty. Took me a long time, I don't think it was until the second boy was in high school, but I started telling him that I wanted my own checking account and I wanted to keep some of my salary out of our joint account. Boy, he just hit the ceiling. . . . He was this very dominant male and he didn't feature having his wife operating without his blessing. He couldn't let me do that! I remember one night he was screaming at me that I was infected with women's lib or something like that and I was screaming back that he was a chauvinist son of a bitch. . . . It got so bad that year that we lived apart for almost a year. During that year I got even more independent, so when we got back together there were several things he had to get used to. . . . He gave in on most of my demands, but he sure didn't give up gracefully.

There are several reasons why we think a wife is less willing to pool her money than her husband is—and they are all related to power. A wife usually has a smaller income than her husband, and if pooling occurs, her money gets lost in the larger pot and gets called "ours"— and she loses control over it. The ability to have her own separate account gives the wife more autonomy. If she has an allowance from the couple's account, she may have to negotiate with her husband every time she wants more money, even if it is only a "cost-of-living increase." If she has kept her money separate, she need only negotiate with her employer. If she pools her money with her husband's, she may *say* she deserves an equal voice in how it is spent, but as a wife she probably does not have the rank to enforce this demand. The husband may invoke his position as head of the household and demand the final word.

By keeping her money separate, a wife may also avoid accounting to her husband for specific purchases. He cannot monitor her account in the same way he can a joint checking account. Moreover, if he gives her money every week, he knows exactly what she spends and when she runs out. If she can use her own earned money to pay for things she wants for herself, or for their children, or to buy a gift for him, she can avoid being beholden to him for money she has taken from their shared funds. As one wife said in her interview:

When I was married [before] I had to explain why and almost ask forgiveness for spending any money. And now that I've got my own financial situation and my own job, my own account and stuff, I know that I'm responsible for it and nobody else is. If I goof up, that's my problem. I don't have to rationalize or explain. I just do it.

A sizeable minority of our cohabitors favor pooling, but again, the men are more positive about it than the women. Such women feel strongly about the freedom it gives them. For example, Nola, a mid-wife, and John, a craftsman, have conducted their six-year living arrangement on the basis of strict economic separation. Nola explained her feelings about it:

He has a drawer for his silverware and I have a drawer for mine. Most of my income I just spend on me and most of his income he just spends on him. I don't have any say over him and he doesn't have any say over me. I'm still stuck about money. I think a couple should each have some money of their own. . . . I still think that even if they decide to pool their money, then they each should have some that they don't have to account for, that they can blow or do anything they want with.

What does it do to heterosexual couples when the woman has no discretionary money of her own? Writer Shulamith Firestone has discussed in *The Dialectic of Sex* that a woman who has little legitimate power in a relationship with a man must resort to manipulative and devious ways to achieve her ends, and consequently a dishonest relationship is created. Her reasoning implies that if a woman feels that her husband would not approve of her buying a new dress or giving an extravagant gift to their grandchild, she will probably find a way to do it anyhow. If she has her *own* money she can do it in a straightforward manner. If it is *their* money, she may be forced to be dishonest though she would prefer not to be. Maynard and Helena have been married for ten years and both are in their early sixties. Maynard owns a small but successful manufacturing company, and Helena is a homemaker. She told us about how she maintains some discretionary money:

> There is . . . a problem because he makes all the financial decisions and decides how all our money is handled and sometimes I have trouble getting . . . to do things that aren't stocks and bonds, investments you know. . . . So I withhold some of what I get each month and now I have quite a bit of money . . . just money to be frivolous with, you know? . . . So now Maynard doesn't know how much money I really have. I feel a little guilty about that but it's easier this way.

Another wife, also a homemaker, told of her "white lies":

> Nate is tightfisted. It's his most unflattering part of his personality. I don't try and meet him head-on. It's not that I don't think I can get my way; it's what I have to go through to do it. I don't like to see that part of him. So I'm more the politician. I skim a little off the top! . . . Oh, I'll tell him the groceries cost more than they did, or something like that. Nothing spectacular, but it gives me a little breathing room.

---

*Husbands and wives who do not believe that marriage should be forever are less willing to pool.*

In contemporary society there is no longer one text for marriage. There are now several variations on the traditional version. The variation a couple chooses when approaching marriage has important consequences. We have already begun to see the impact of the couple's belief in the provider role. We now need to consider another aspect of traditional marriage—*the expectation of its permanence.* Some couples feel that by marrying they have entered an institution premised on a lifetime commitment. These couples, whom we call "institutional," feel that their marriage may become unfulfilling, but they have entered into an unbreakable covenant and therefore they will persevere. A more recent view of marriage is found among couples we call "voluntary," who believe that while the institution may be important, it is not as important as how the partners feel about each other. For them marriage must justify itself on a daily basis. They believe that when a marriage has ceased to fulfill the partners' emotional needs, its continuation should be reevaluated. We gauged whether husbands and wives are institutional or voluntary by their agreement or disagreement with the following statements:

> Marriage is a lifetime relationship and should never be terminated except under extreme circumstances.

> Couples should try to make their relationship last a lifetime.

> A member of a couple that has been together a long time should not accept a job he or she wants in a distant city, if it means ending the relationship.[4]

We find that when married people have institutional attitudes toward marriage they are more likely to want to pool their money.[5]

**ATTITUDES TOWARD POOLING AND INSTITUTIONAL MARRIAGE**

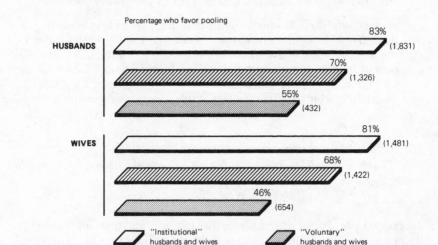

Percentage who favor pooling

HUSBANDS
83% (1,831)
70% (1,326)
55% (432)

WIVES
81% (1,481)
68% (1,422)
46% (654)

"Institutional" husbands and wives

"Voluntary" husbands and wives

Intermediate husbands & wives

Numbers in parentheses are the number of people on which the percentages are based.

FIGURE    10

Candy is thirty-seven and Zach is forty-six. They have been married for five years and it is the second marriage for each. Both work in social-service agencies. Candy never considered keeping her money separate:

> Either you are married or you are not. It's very simple. You either make a commitment or you don't. . . . Some of my friends made specific contracts about whose money was whose before they remarried again, which strikes me as setting up the end before you have tried to make it last forever. . . . My husband did not make a commitment to me in my first marriage even though I thought he did. I am not going to let that sour me. Whatever I bring into this marriage I share and I know Zachary feels the same way.

Another wife, in her second marriage, provides a sharp contrast to Candy. Because of unpleasant recollections of her divorce, she feels it will always be unsafe to pool her money:

> Usually when we go out, it's dutch treat. Since I work, he usually pays for himself and I pay for myself, except sometimes, he'll ask me out on a date and then it's his treat.

The high divorce rate is a national preoccupation. Only couples who are committed to the institution of marriage, not simply to each other, feel safe enough to be able to trust their resources to one another.

---

*The longer same-sex couples live together the more they want to pool incomes.*

Newlyweds want to pool as much as they ever will.[6] But gay men and lesbians must first get to know their partners and do not pool until they are convinced of the durability of the relationship.[7] The decision to marry implies that the couple, during courtship, has already resolved any ambivalences about staying together. Lesbian couples and gay male couples do not have such a symbolic demarcation. Initially they have only to decide whether to live together. But there is no institutional understanding that it symbolizes a lifetime commitment. So these couples can remain tentative about the relationship for a longer time. One partner may be quicker than the other to want it to be lasting, or neither partner may ever aspire to such an arrangement. The issue of permanence is something many same-sex couples discuss and negotiate over a period of time.

It is clear to us that learning how to deal with the question of pooling is an integral part of that process, a process guided by few established rules or understandings on how to proceed. William and

Mac have been together nine years. William, thirty-five, is a driving instructor, and Mac, forty-four, maître d' in a restaurant. William told us about their financial arrangements:

> We both assume this will go on forever. Unspokenly, we have agreed this relationship is bigger and stronger than any trauma that could happen. . . . We have life insurance for each other, . . . we can sign on each other's accounts. We have great faith in each other and it has grown over the years. . . . Eventually I will put his name on the lease. It took me awhile to feel at ease about that, but now it's just a formality, in case anything should happen to me.

Another gay man described how he and his partner gradually fell into pooling:

> When I was at school at Emory, I thought it would be embarrassing to him if we had a joint account. I didn't particularly want to do it either. But over time we have become more open and we are so involved in everything together that it doesn't make sense not to have joint accounts. . . . You forget who paid for something last and everything evens out eventually.

One lesbian in a four-year relationship made it clear that her hesitation to pool dissolved with time as she became more committed:

> In the beginning we had our struggles because she wanted to put down deposits in places that cost too much. . . . And she was thinking much more long-term than me 'cause I was thinking I didn't want to get into something I couldn't afford to get out of. . . . Now we put everything together except the money she inherited from her father, which we agree is personal and private. But everything else, like she has some income from some stocks, that goes to both of us. We might use it for my tuition if I go back to school. We figure we both want to get ahead and we will help each other. . . . That's one of the most satisfying aspects of this relationship, the fact that things are so flowing now.

---

*Cohabiting couples shy away from pooling if they doubt the durability of the relationship. Keeping their money separate makes it easier for the relationship to be impermanent.*

---

We find that cohabiting couples who expect to be together in the future and those who expect to marry express the desire to pool their resources.[8] Since the majority of cohabitors do not favor pooling, these facts say important things about pooling and commitment. When couples begin to pool their finances, it usually means they see a future for themselves. The more the couple pools, the greater the incentive to

**COHABITORS' COMMITMENT TO A FUTURE TOGETHER**
**AND THEIR ATTITUDES TOWARD POOLING**

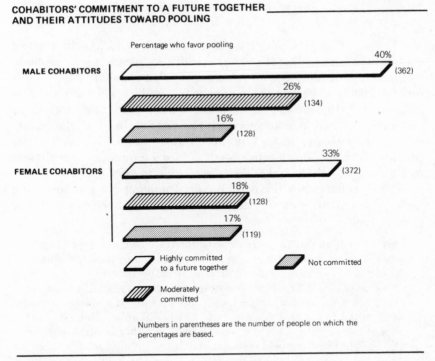

FIGURE 11

organize future financial dealings in the same way. As a "corporate" sense of the couple emerges, it becomes more difficult for the partners to think of themselves as unattached individuals. The complex structure of financial arrangements is a factor in keeping the couple together. Some couples may be very committed and still resist pooling on ideological grounds. We feel that not pooling in these cases may not hurt the couple, but gives them one less bond.

*Cohabitors who favor keeping money separate fight less.*

Cohabiting couples who reject the idea of pooling money have less conflict over income and over money arrangement.[9] Often they have consciously constructed their relationships to avoid precisely this kind of trouble. As one man told us:

We have arranged our finances to be as separate as they can be. If she wants to spend money or not to spend it or pay a bill or not pay a bill, she doesn't consult me. Same on my part. I'll tell you, I learned from my previous marriage to keep separate finances. I think it's a big plus in that we never have any money fights, money problems, money disputes.

Keeping money separate is associated with reducing the level of conflict over money; therefore, it is usually very pleasant for couples to maintain and preserve such a financial arrangement. But, unfortunately, while it lessens the potential for conflict, it is also a visible escape hatch. In practical terms, it keeps the relationship more easily dissoluble. Indeed, it may speed up the dissolution of a relationship that is in jeopardy, where another couple would find money ties providing the temporary cement—or at least a temporary impediment to a quick exit—that would allow the trouble to blow over.

Thus, cohabitors who avoid financial pooling are not bolstering their commitment. As a woman who has lived for five years with her partner told us:

> We keep all of our finances as separate as we can, like I own the mortgage on this house and make payments and whenever we get something (we have a rule about this) from his parents—like a fondue pot for Christmas—we just decide that if it's a gift to us and it comes from his side of the family, then it's his. If it comes from my side of the family, it's mine, even if it's to both of us. And when we bought something—like a stereo—well, I bought the turntable and he bought the loudspeakers and there is no question at all where that goes and we usually figure that out right away. It's a protective thing for both of us. I don't want to get hassled the way I did in my divorce or the way he was in his divorce. His wife ended up getting all his tools and camping equipment and stuff that she never uses because it was so bitter. He felt so bad that he didn't have the nerve to ask for them. He just wanted out. Now, after a couple of years, he feels it would be nice to have those things. . . . So, if that happens to us, we decide to split up, it seems to us that it will be easier to know what goes where.

We have seen how important an issue pooling is for couples. Some couples cannot fathom doing it, while others cannot imagine not doing it. Each kind of couple believes they have found the secret to a happy relationship. We are amazed to learn that both sides are right. Couples who favor pooling are no more and no less satisfied with their money management than those who insist on keeping money separate.[10] This is an area where different strategies for handling money work for different kinds of couples.

There does, however, seem to be a common natural history in the way couples come to pool money. It is a fundamental part of the commitment process. By looking at the cohabitors and same-sex couples, where there is no law or tradition to push them toward pooling, we are able to see that pooling begins when a couple senses that their relationship is going to last. Indeed, if we were going to use one major indicator to determine when these couples became solidified as a unit, it would be the point at which they joined their resources.

Same-sex and cohabiting couples offer a glimpse of what the future may hold for married couples. Unmarried couples have been wary of pooling because they are aware that relationships may not last. Today, married couples are coming to realize that the impermanence of "couple life" also applies to them. The divorce rate gives pause even to the most romantic, and makes it more likely that a couple will reevaluate the traditional concept of putting all their resources together. We think this is particularly true of the large number of people who have already been divorced and are entering a new relationship.

It is becoming more common to hear of American couples drafting prenuptial agreements to keep their property separate, and it may be that this is the wave of the future, that financial arrangements in marriage will come to resemble those we have seen among our cohabitors and same-sex couples. For once permanence cannot be guaranteed, a certain number of people will want to hedge their bets. Ironically, however, the very fact that a prenuptial agreement exists may make it harder for married couples to ease into pooling over time, and so their finances may actually remain more separate than those of couples outside the legal institution of marriage.

# Conclusion

All our couples face financial choices, which usually revolve around demands for equality and autonomy, or the sacrifice of one or both to achieve intimacy, trust, and interdependence. These last are critical for creating commitment, but may interfere with the individual rights of the partners. In traditional marriages, interdependence is usually achieved at the cost of the wife's autonomy and her participation on an equal basis in decision-making.

Heterosexual cohabitation and lesbian relationships are frequently constructed to avoid such inequality. Male cohabitors do not want dependent partners, and female cohabitors do not want to be dependent. Many lesbians stress the importance of independence and self-sufficiency for themselves as well as for their partners. These values help keep the partners on an equal footing, but if not much trust develops, an important stabilizing mechanism is missing from their lives. They avoid the difficult process of forging a bond that could support their relationship during troubled periods. Cohabitors and lesbians feel that in order to be *interdependent*, they must be *independent* first. They want to establish their individual strengths before they allow themselves to be vulnerable.

Marital interdependence evolves through a process of specific delegation designed to handle all facets of the couple's financial life—from earning to management. The marriage contract, rather than their time together, allows them to trust each other enough to work as a financial team. Cohabitors, striving to be independent, are reluctant to pool their resources. They avoid conflict but they also avoid the interdependence that pooling brings.

Married couples have a stake in each other's attitudes toward money and sometimes have to deal with divergent values about spending it. They occasionally fight if their personal sense of order and safety is to be maintained. Since they share their resources, they have to come to an accommodation. Because they have fewer worries that the marriage may end if they fight, they can mount some pitched battles. The marriage license can become a license to abuse. The institution remains intact, but over time, the partners may become less satisfied with it. Their lack of restraint can cost them dearly in terms of how they feel about their life together.

Gay men may have the hardest time of all. Unlike lesbians and cohabitors, their problem is not to move from an egalitarian to an interdependent relationship, but to move from a dominant/subordinate relationship to interdependence. Gay men can suffer when one partner has a larger income. Because earning power is a central part of a man's identity, having more money gives a man symbolic—and therefore real—advantages over his partner. This also happens in marriage; but there, although the husband's higher incomes gives him power, with it comes the responsibility to support his wife and family without rancor—and, ideally, without its being a reflection on his wife's adequacy as a person. Both husband and wife take pleasure in his ability to support them, whereas gay men are usually uncomfortable when being the provider or being provided for. Each man thinks he should be able to pull his own weight, but if one greatly surpasses the other, he may feel entitled to be dominant, leaving the other feeling inadequate.

All types of couples find it hard to put together the perfect package. Ideally, each partner would have an equal voice in decisions, each would trust the other to be fair, money in and of itself would not automatically give one partner power over the other, and men and women would not have such different values and roles in financial matters. But the reality of the situation is that money continues to be a provocative issue for couples, because trust, commitment, and the guarantee of permanence are the real issues.

We have made money issues sound so difficult. They are. But we hope we have not made them sound insoluble. Many of the couples in our study—in all four categories—had no complaints about the part money plays in their relationships. But couples frequently do not realize that even though they may not fight about them, their finances and the way they look upon them are shaping their future together. This is particularly true of couples who keep their resources separate. Bonds of all kinds supply strength in a relationship and these couples are removing one important tie keeping them together. There are many centrifugal forces that tug at relationships. To endure, couples need countervailing forces. One is financial interdependence. This binding force is not completely without its costs—so a universal solution to the problem of money does not seem to exist. Each couple must balance these factors in the way that is best for them.

# WORK

I N the past the world of paid employment had traditionally been thought to be comprised of men, whereas the household was considered women's domain.[1] It was the man's legal duty to support his wife and she in turn was obliged to take care of their home and family. But even with the most rigid division of responsibilities, men helped their wives with the housework, and women, particularly if the family owned farms or small businesses, gave the men a helping hand. Belief in the traditional male/female separation of work persisted, however, even if practice differed slightly.

Today, while many of our married couples still enthusiastically subscribe to the historic order of things, a new entity is clearly emerging: an egalitarian, two-paycheck couple. Both husband and wife work full time in the labor force and each contributes equally to the work that needs to be done in the house, including care of the children. Nevertheless, the force of the previous tradition still guides the behavior of most modern marriages. It is frequently difficult for us to separate what couples *think* is the nature of their work arrangement from what actually happens in their day-to-day lives. In these pages, we take a close look at the specific work roles our culture has assigned to the sexes—provider versus homemaker—so that we can discover what it really means when couples share them or decide to keep them separate.

Marriages in which the wife is employed offer a good opportunity to see whether having a job affects the amount of personal power a woman has and how much housework she does. We can see whether critics who blame the dissolution of family life on women's working are correct, or whether being employed outside the home, even attaining success and achievement, makes married life more satisfying for the wife as well as for her husband.

In cohabiting couples, both partners usually work. Do women in these relationships expect, as did their mothers, that their men will achieve greater success in the outside world than they? Or is it only wives who adhere to such a conventional belief since marriage brings with it the firmly established tradition of the man as provider and achiever? Do men in cohabiting relationships insist, as their fathers did, that their jobs are more important—thereby exempting themselves from many of the household duties? Or can they relinquish this position and divide the housework equally? The way cohabiting couples handle these issues helps us evaluate how strong an influence the institution of marriage has had on men's and women's attitudes toward work.

Same-sex couples offer additional insights into men's and women's attitudes toward work. Among our gay couples, keeping the relationship together in the face of career demands becomes the issue, not who has the right to work. These couples face a problem in allocating household duties since both men are not only busy in their jobs but disinclined to do what has always been considered women's work.

As women, the majority of lesbians have not been taught to derive a sense of self-worth from having a job. But any woman who seriously contemplates living her life unattached to a man quickly realizes that she needs to get a job in order to survive. When we see how lesbian couples both resemble and differ from heterosexual women who are employed, we gain a more precise sense of what happens when there is a man around the house. Does the presence of a man undermine a woman's commitment or ability to work? How do two employed women assign the task of housework?

Our observations and commentary on work and how it affects the lives of our couples come at a time when a great controversy is raging in our society about the nature of the family and the rights of women. Many people argue that all women, married or unmarried, have the right to equal employment and pay. At the same time, they hold steadfastly to the belief that the work that goes on inside the home is important as well as demanding and that men should therefore bear equal responsibility for it. Those who oppose these positions think that such sentiments will destroy the American family. They argue that taking the wife away from the crucial tasks of the home, particularly care of the children, erodes the authority of the husband and with it the established order.

We do not think that a single utopian vision of family life is likely to emerge from the debate. In our study we show the many different ways our couples coordinate work and home life and what happens when they do.

# Having a job

## *The desire for equality*

Most men cannot understand how working might be considered a privilege. From the time they are little boys, they know they are expected to
have a job, perhaps a career—at the very least, to make a living for
themselves. They also learn very early that someday they will marry
and become the provider/protector of their wives and children. As they
grow up, they orient themselves to adult life—from forming fantasies
of what they will become, to choosing courses in high school and college that will ready them for and determine their future jobs. Most will
join the labor force and try to succeed in it.

The place employment has occupied in women's lives is more ambiguous. Traditionally, from childhood they were steeped in the dream
of marrying a man who would take care of them. If middle-class
women entertained thoughts of a job or career of their own, it was
more often regarded as a choice, not a necessity. It never meant having
to bear the burden of supporting a family.

But as a girl grows up in present-day America, she may well be
forced to think of work differently from the way her mother's generation did. If she is poor, she may have to become part of the labor force
to help support her family. She may come to like working and develop
a commitment to it. Or she may still dream of finding a man who earns
a living that will enable her to quit. A girl who grows up with more
advantages may think of work as something she might enjoy. If she
goes to college, she acquires training that prepares her for a career. She
may plan to continue working even after she marries, taking time out
to raise children. This woman considers her work something she has
*chosen*—not something her husband expects. Only recently have some
women begun to plan a career in the same way men traditionally have.
But even these women expect to be able to devote themselves to their
careers at their own pace, not to become the primary financial support
of their families. To them, work is not their duty. Depending on their
husbands' attitude, it may not even be their right.[1]

In the past, when a woman married, she accepted her husband's
commitment to his job. Both she and her husband knew the marriage
could survive only if it was supportive of his career. Her right to work
was open to argument. The degree to which she could be ambitious,
the amount of time she could give to a job, even whether she could
apply for one, were issues a couple could disagree on.

Even though cohabiting couples have grown up with traditional
ideas about men and women working, because they are not married
they do not know quite what to expect of each other. Does a job that
profits only the individual and is not used for the couple's welfare make

it difficult to develop a feeling of togetherness? In the absence of tradition, does a man do what his father did and assume the role of provider? Will the two partners compete in work? Do women subordinate their career goals to their partner's, as their mothers did, even though it may not be in their best interest?

Gay men grew up knowing that someday they would work. Choosing to live with another man makes the provider role irrelevant. Among these couples, do both men vie for the privileges that role gives? Or does one man stop working and permit himself to be supported? Is work a central part of a gay man's identity as it always has been for a husband?

Lesbians know they must work. For some, this awareness came when they acknowledged they would not marry and would not be provided for. For others, it was part of an early commitment to independence. All women have an interest in the new issues lesbian couples are facing. For instance, how does one partner feel supporting the other when there is no precedent for the female provider in our society? How do lesbians reinterpret the age-old female tradition of doing the housework, when both women have jobs?

---

*There is a great division of opinion about whether wives should work. Among couples who disagree, there are more wives who want to work than husbands who want to let them.*

A large number of married couples feel that both partners should work, but a substantial minority of our husbands and wives believe there should be only one breadwinner in a marriage. This may come as a surprise when we consider that 52 percent of American women are now in the labor force. But many people continue to cherish the traditional family model—in particular, husbands. Claude, forty-eight, is a

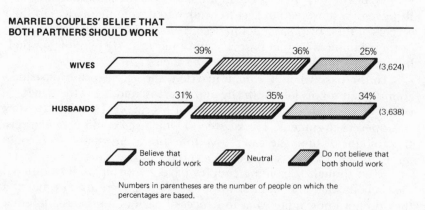

**MARRIED COUPLES' BELIEF THAT BOTH PARTNERS SHOULD WORK**

WIVES   39%   36%   25%   (3,624)

HUSBANDS   31%   35%   34%   (3,638)

Believe that both should work   Neutral   Do not believe that both should work

Numbers in parentheses are the number of people on which the percentages are based.

FIGURE   12

plastic surgeon. His wife, Annette, forty-one, works part time as a receptionist. They have been married nineteen years. Claude feels there are limits to how many hours Annette should work:

> I don't mind her having a part-time job, but she doesn't have time for a full-time job. . . . I am the breadwinner, she is the homemaker, and that is what we signed up for twenty years ago. . . . We do not make decisions around her work. My work supports us and we put that first. It is her responsibility to do her work well just as it is my responsibility to do my work well. . . . She takes care of our sons and I take care of everyone. It is part of her responsibility not to let her work interfere with her job at home. I don't mind her working as long as dinner is ready on time and the house is neat and clean. I think we deserve that, and so far it has worked out well.

Another husband, Lew, has strong feelings about working wives. He is forty, a realtor, and has been married to Shirley, thirty-eight, a full-time homemaker, for fifteen years. Lew said:

> Do you know what I think when I hear these guys who have wives that work while they have kids? That these guys have no respect for the family, and that those women have no respect for themselves or their husband. I don't think my wife should respect me if I can't make enough money for her to stay home and raise the kids and have some time for herself.

Both of these husbands voice an opinion we heard often from people we talked to: In some circumstances, it might be necessary for a wife to work, but certainly not when there are young children. Believing that wives should be able to work when they are mothers of small children is a far more liberal attitude than simply subscribing to the view that a wife should have the privilege of working.[2]

Even though a wife may be employed, it does not mean that her husband has wholeheartedly acknowledged her right to do so. Nelson, forty-three, is an insurance salesman. Muriel, forty-two, is a computer programmer. They have been married for eighteen years, and have no children. Nelson told us:

> I have always worked and I guess we have a rather traditional marriage from the standpoint that I expect to work and I am very happy to see her stay at home and do what she wants to do. And if she wants to work, okay, but I would rather see her join a club or something and just have a good time.

Not only do many husbands feel that a wife's first duty is to home and children; their wives frequently feel the same way. Bess, fifty, works part time as a checker at the local supermarket. Her husband, Tom, fifty-one, has recently been laid off as a steelworker. They have been married for twenty-eight years. Bess:

> We talked about [work] early in our life, especially after the kids

were born. I felt it was more important and we agreed that it was more important for Mom to be home when the kids came home from school. And it worked out that way and we were glad of it. I think it's a good decision. . . . The household tasks are my responsibility. They are mine because I am a housewife and I don't work outside. I think that is only fair. . . . Men's work is going out and working and women's work is working in the house. Tom probably helps me more than the average husband, but nothing he does not like doing. He doesn't *have* to do anything.

Another wife, twenty-one, a homemaker, repeated the same attitude. Married four years to Charlie, an electrician, Dee feels that being a full-time mother is essential if children are to be raised properly:

I think a woman is kidding herself if she thinks she can be a mother to small children and also have a job. The way I see those kids is that somebody else is bringing them up, and they don't get the kind of love and attention only a mother can give a child. . . . I'd like to work but I have to wait until the kids are in school full time. But even then, I think I should be back so that I give them their snacks and look at their schoolwork when they get out of school. . . . Children are my full-time work and I don't think there is anything more valuable that I can contribute to our family.

On the whole, however, wives tend to be more liberal on this issue than their husbands. Their desire to work can create significant tensions. Winston and Gail have been married little more than a year. He is twenty-one and works as a bank teller. She is twenty and works as an airline ticket agent. Soon after marrying, Gail discovered they disagreed about her working:

His expectation was that we would immediately start a family. My expectation was that we would do a family, but not for a while. I want to have a career first. He sees me getting more involved, not less, and he gets upset.

Another young couple, Bruce and Dianne, fight about Dianne's desire to work although she has never applied for a job during their four years of marriage. Dianne is twenty-two, and Bruce, a barber, is twenty-three. Dianne:

Sure I'd like to work because I worked after high school. Like a duck to water . . . They have asked me back because I was always one of their best employees. And every time they ask me, I ask him, and he is just not ready to have me be employed. We have some serious fights about it. . . . He comes from a very conservative background and his father would not think much of a son that had a wife that worked. So I have to argue through his whole background and not just him. We have had some good screamers about this one.

This issue is fairly common among young couples like these. Our data show that recently married couples argue more about whether a wife should work than couples who have been married for many years.[3] That does not mean that couples of longer duration have no conflict over this issue. Stan, forty, a veterinarian, has been married for eighteen years to Liza, thirty-seven. She works part time as a technician in an animal hospital and is also a part-time political volunteer. Liza told us about the conflicts that arise because of her work situation:

> He didn't mind me helping out with political campaigns, but when I started to have a real career—especially in his kind of area—we started having arguments about how healthy it is for the kids and why should I spend my time on anything else. . . . For my part, I am enjoying what I am doing and I think I am good at it, and I think I am getting better at it. I also think I'm more interesting because of it and I think he should feel that way too. . . . I think he is threatened at our relationship changing and I try and reassure him that things will just get better. I think I'm a much nicer, happier person these days, and I just have to show him that in terms he can see and not get defensive about.

Wade and Dorothy have been married for twenty years. She is forty-three and works part time as a computer consultant. Wade is a year older and owns an electrical contracting business. Dorothy:

> He and I agreed that I would go back to work after the children were older. I was ready a long time before Phil was in junior high, but I waited because that was our arrangement. . . . Now he is not so pleased about my having a job. He is particularly unhappy because I would like to buy into the partnership and he would like me to work less, not more. He would like to travel and have that time together now that he has the time, and I like to travel but I would much rather invest in having a serious job right now. He doesn't understand how seriously I take my job plans because we don't need the money and I wasn't like this when we got married. I was much more traditional and more supportive in a feminine sort of way. And he is not too comfortable with this. . . . We had a conflict recently where he got a cheap travel fare and wanted me to go with him on the spur of the moment. I couldn't because I was right in the middle of a project. We had a big fight and I ended up going, but I really resented having to go and he really resented the fact that I had put up any fuss at all.

There is also a small number of husbands who feel their wives should work, but the wives do not want to. Mary Jo, twenty-five, had worked, until recently, as an employment counselor. Her husband, Jim, twenty-eight, is a landscaper. When they married two years ago, Mary Jo left her job and has had no desire to return to it:

> He was just pushing at me and pushing at me to stay at work and I was resisting and I am still resisting. He doesn't know what it costs me emotionally to work. I don't want to go back and he is still pushing me to do it because we need the money and because he

doesn't understand how much I don't want to. It's a major source of conflict.

Another wife, Vicki, twenty-one, is not employed. She is expecting their first baby. Earl, twenty-three, is a fireman. Vicki feels belittled by Earl because she does not work:

> He used to insult me because I didn't have a job. He used to rub it in. He doesn't do that anymore, but he would try and make me feel guilty because he made the money and I didn't make any actual spendable money.

Lea, thirty-three, works in a day-care center, and her husband, Felix, thirty-five, is a TV cameraman. They have been married for twelve years. Felix:

> It takes so much money to make this boat float a month and I don't have enough by myself and she knew that before we were ever married. One of the things that we made sure was understood was that she was definitely going to have to work when we got married if we needed the money or if we were going to be a family unit. She knew she was going to have to work if we needed another salary. Sure, if I suddenly came into a different kind of job, I would be glad to let her stop. But that doesn't look like the way our lives are going to turn out.

Angie and Sid have also been married for twelve years. Sid, forty-five, is in the lumber-processing business. Angie, forty-one, works part time as a medical technician. She feels she has to work, given the present state of the economy:

> I pitch in during times like these. His industry has been terrible lately. We thought it would get better, but all our friends are going under. He doesn't feel great about it, but I can earn a lot of money, even working part time, and we just really need my help. . . . I think we both feel that that is what marriage is for—to have two people who can help out when it's necessary.

These women have entered the work force out of necessity, not personal choice. But work experience changes some women's outlook. While some wives we interviewed said they could not wait until they could afford to stop working, others told us they had learned to like earning money and having a position outside the home. Ned is fifty-five and owns a small carpet store. Sheila, also fifty-five, is a food-service manager at a university. They have been married for twenty-one years. Sheila was out of the work force during much of their marriage. She described what it was like to return:

> I went back to work about eight years ago, after our youngest child was in high school. I was a little hesitant because I had to do

everything better than everyone else. I had to go back and finish my degree and I was the only gray head in the class! I was terribly rusty and I dreaded and looked forward to every day. I didn't think I would get a job, but I did. Actually a very good one and I have been promoted twice since then. We are both rather pleased with my progress and we use my money for some things we might not have done or we would have had to think about for a long time. . . . I have enjoyed my contribution. I've enjoyed making money and I have started thinking of myself as a semi-ambitious person.

Rose and Loren have been married for fourteen years. Loren, fifty, is a transit police officer. Rose, forty-one, does interviewing for a social-work agency. She told us how she began her job:

I just did this, you know, for a little extra money that we needed, but it got to be a lot more fun than work. . . . He's been very supportive too. I was a little worried about that, but he's been great. He's very proud of me and now we are both interested in coming home and telling about the characters we have met during the day.

We should not forget that approximately 30 percent of our married couples feel that both partners should work. Each person feels a strong responsibility for the financial support of the household. Jay and Nancy, both twenty-six, have been married for two years. Jay is a lawyer and Nancy is a medical intern. Jay explained that careers were important to both of them:

We were both looking for someone who felt that work was very important in life. Neither one of us feels it's right for one person to have all the responsibility for a life-style and the other one to just sit back and clap or criticize. She may not earn as much as I do, but she contributes proportionately to what she is making, and that is almost equal as far as the necessities are concerned. . . . And then we both have control over our private spending, which is also important to both of us.

Another couple feels the same way. Peggy has been married to Bud for seven years. He is thirty-three, and she is thirty-four. Both are schoolteachers. Peggy said:

We earn approximately about the same amount of money and we contribute equally to the kitty. This is exactly the way we started out and it has always worked for us. I am not the kind of woman who feels like it's my right to be supported and I would feel very guilty if I couldn't support my part of the house. He has offered to do it all if I want to, for example, if we have a child, but I would just feel too guilty. I would much rather get good child-care and contribute to that equally, than suddenly just depend on him.

But some husbands urge their wives to work because they simply do not want a wife to be dependent on them. In the interviews, some husbands, who had enduring financial responsibilities to former wives, expressed anger at this arrangement or at what they felt they had lost in the divorce settlement. There was a "never again" quality to their descriptions of the current marriages: This would be different from the last one. Each partner was going to have to contribute and neither should be dependent. Joan and Don have been married once before.

> DON: I adopted my ex-wife's three kids, then we had two of our own . . . and then she wanted a divorce. . . . During the proceedings she decided that she needed this huge amount of money in order to take care of the kids. She needed the house . . . she needed everything. . . . She also didn't feel like she could work and she pretty near got her way on most of the things she asked for. . . . I have been saddled with more than I—more than Joan—can afford sometimes. Joan and I fight about it. She can't believe how stupid I was to get in a situation like that. . . . We set this up on a totally different basis. Joan doesn't expect a life from me—and I don't ask her to give up her life. She works and I support that. I work—and she supports me. Everything is fifty-fifty. I would never have it any other way again.

> JOAN: His wife took him to the cleaners. . . . He is hurt about it and I think he can't believe he set himself up for this. . . . When we first started dating he was screwed up about money. He made it very clear that everything was going to be dutch treat. . . . I didn't mind, I prefer it that way. But it was very clear to me that he'd been hurt and was overreacting. . . . Our relationship works because he knows I would never do that to him. I have my own work, I make my own way and he knows that's the kind of person I am.

Some husbands might enjoy the feeling that their wives are dependent upon them and the income they earn from their jobs. But such dependence can also create a sense of responsibility in the husbands. One husband of fifty told us about his confusion; he wonders whether he and his wife of twenty-one years did the right thing in choosing that she be a full-time homemaker.

> I worry about keeping enough life insurance, because I am not sure what would keep her and Dorrie in good shape if anything happened to me. . . . I feel bad sometimes that she has all these skills that haven't been developed because she's been at home and if something happened to me she wouldn't be able to go out and earn a decent living. . . . We have enjoyed our family life but I feel worried that she could not survive well without me. . . . Sometimes I worry that maybe we haven't done the best thing for her. I feel overwhelmed sometimes planning for the future.

Some husbands want their wives to work because they are affected by the women's movement and believe in egalitarian relationships. Others may merely wish to cast off the onerous burden of the provider role. For them it is a welcome relief to share responsibility for their children's education, for making mortgage payments, for supporting a comfortable life-style, or for accumulating investments to prepare for retirement. In either case, the provider role may be losing its sanctity.

*Many more cohabitors than married couples think both partners should work. But, once again, women feel more strongly about it.*

Cohabitors, particularly women, feel that both men and women should work.[4] In choosing not to marry, cohabiting women announce their willingness to be responsible for themselves financially. In fact, most cohabiting women are committed to doing their fair share. Cheryl and Grant have been living together for five years, both after unhappy marriages. Cheryl, thirty-three, works as an administrator for a municipal court. Grant, twenty-nine, is a paralegal specialist.

> CHERYL: He says, "If you want to stay home, stay home." But it's not financially possible, and besides, I would probably go crazy. I'm as necessary as he is to this household. The fact is [my job] is more important because I bring in more money than he does. I carry my load right down the line.

Another female cohabitor in her early forties feels that working and being able to be self-sufficient if necessary is essential for her relationship:

> Obviously, I could not buy this place on my own. [She gestures to their sumptuous home.] But I work and I do enough to show that I'm not here on a free ride and that I'm responsible for my part of

**MARRIED AND COHABITING COUPLES' BELIEF THAT**
**BOTH PARTNERS SHOULD WORK**

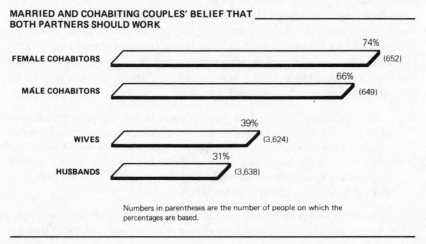

Numbers in parentheses are the number of people on which the
percentages are based.

FIGURE   13

the house. I don't want him ever to think that I can't leave and be on my own. . . . My husband used to make me thank him for every little luxury that we would have. . . . One reason I would say we broke up is that he didn't allow me to be an equal partner, have my own work and give me my space. I think one reason my partner and I do so well together is that he understands how important it is to me to contribute and to be taken seriously.

We have noted in our interviews that insistence on an equal economic partnership is common among older cohabiting women. They know how to support themselves and are fully aware of the benefits of working. Or they are like Marti, who suffered after the breakup of an earlier marriage because she had not established herself in the world of work. Marti is forty-four. She has been living for two years with Harry, who is forty-eight. She works in the copywriting section of an advertising agency. She described her return to work after her divorce:

Do you know what it's like coming back to work with a twenty-year-old B.A. in English? Madison Avenue is not exactly holding its breath waiting for you. . . . I worked at one of the most prestigious companies when I first got out of college, but they just glaze over those credentials. They want to know what you've been doing for the last fifteen years. Raising children does not impress them. I had to take a crummy job with a small company and I was relieved to get that. . . . I have worked very hard to be taken seriously again and I have just this last year gotten a job doing what I wanted to do. You can't take that long vacation and be welcomed back. I thought for a time there I would never be able to work again at what I wanted to do and I was miserably depressed.

Male cohabitors who hope to marry their partners—those in a trial marriage—are more willing to shoulder the financial burden of the relationship.[5] But we notice that as a rule male cohabitors reject the economic responsibilities they would have as husbands. They do not want to become the sole supporter or breadwinner. Rex, a college professor of forty-seven who has been living for almost eight years with Myra, twenty-nine, a cellist with the symphony, has a much better income than she. He voiced a strong opinion about not wanting to be obligated to support his partner:

I am very generous and I do pay for most of our life-style which is okay because I like to be generous. But I don't want to think I *have* to do anything because she is helpless, or because she won't work. I don't want to feel used and one reason Myra and I have done so well is that she carries her own weight and doesn't act like I owe her anything. What is given is given freely.

Anthony, thirty-five, is a biochemist. He has lived for two years with Anna, twenty-eight, assistant director of an art gallery. They expect to marry next year. Anthony likes Anna's independence—particularly her financial independence:

> She is the kind of opposite person I was looking for, one who doesn't need me to fulfill herself. She's quite capable on her own. So we sort of put our lives together and go in harmony. She's got her life and I've got my life. I am an independent person who likes to think and have my own ideas and she likes hers, and we put it together. . . . I don't want somebody clinging to me, dependent on me. I felt more secure in this, knowing that she has her own career and her own identity, and she can make her own way in the world. If we broke up I wouldn't want her to be economically dependent on me and I'm sure she wouldn't want to be.

Men who prefer that their female partners not go to work are ill suited for cohabitation. The woman resists and they fight over her right to work.[6] This conflict serves the relationship badly and they both wind up being dissatisfied with their life together.[7]

*The great majority of same-sex couples believe that both partners should work.*

Gay and lesbian couples believe that fairness dictates that both partners earn a living. They told us that except for the usual fantasies of a life of ease, they never thought of not working and never considered living with someone who did not work. Claudia, twenty-five, is a hairdresser, and Elizabeth, twenty-eight, works as a letter carrier. Claudia told us how much they see eye to eye about having jobs:

> We are very complementary to one another. We both like to work; we both like to keep the house clean; we both have the same values.

**GAY MEN'S AND LESBIANS' BELIEF THAT BOTH PARTNERS SHOULD WORK**

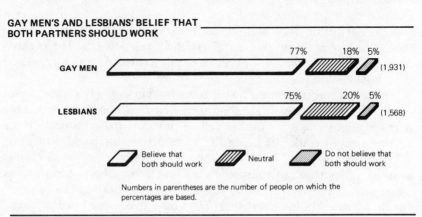

FIGURE   14

We respect each other because neither of us would ever be a burden. We are not dominant over one another: We take and we give, which means we contribute—emotionally and financially. I would never let her down by making her the only one who had to be the worker, and she would not do that to me. I wouldn't want to be with someone who would use someone like that and I also would never be that person.

Ian and Max have lived together for seven years. Ian, thirty, is a clerk in a drugstore and Max, fifty, owns a landscaping company. Ian pondered the possibility of not working:

I have had jobs of one sort or another since I was in eighth grade. Ideally, I can imagine being supported, but I know in real life I would just hate it. I have been bringing in money to my family and now I do my share with Max, and it's part of what I expect I have to do.

A lesbian couple told us how their belief in the notion of shared responsibility commits them to working. Belle, thirty-nine, is a legal assistant, and June, thirty-four, is a supervisor for the phone company. They have lived with one another for four years. June said:

I think we both feel pretty strongly that we both should work, even though we both would like not to. We both would like to stay at home and have the other one work! Not really. I don't think we would be happy that way. I think Belle would like a part-time job, but we can't afford that. It's our responsibility to each other to do our part and make sure we can afford to do the things that we want to do.

A very small percentage of our same-sex couples are not troubled by the idea of one wage earner. Fewer still (less than 1 percent) actually live in such a situation.[8] One example is Duncan, a man in his mid-forties. He and Avery have been living together for twenty-three years. Duncan stays at home, while Avery makes a very good living as a commercial airline pilot. Duncan feels that the best use of his time is to help create a life-style that supports their relationship. He regards Avery as "quite a catch," and Avery is happy to provide for Duncan and their household.

In a few interviews, we heard some lesbian and gay male couples say that under certain circumstances one partner need not work. One partner might leave his or her job to pursue further education, or partners might trade off being the wage earner for periods of time. When this happens, however, the homemaker role is absolutely avoided. They think of themselves as students or people temporarily unemployed. Lloyd, forty-four, is currently not working. His partner, Dutch, fifty, works in advertising. They have lived together for fifteen years. Lloyd actively resists the label of housewife because he stays at home:

We are just trying this little experiment to see how it works. Since I have stopped working, I have taken over some of the household things, but I *definitely* am not the housewife in this relationship. We both get very upset if anyone tries to insinuate that I'm taking over. I'm just helping us both out because he's breaking his ass uptown. I know some people think that I'm just sitting on my ass downtown, which isn't true. But I do have some extra time and I help out. When I go back to work, then it will be more equal, or maybe he will make up for lost time.

Although same-sex couples ascribe to the egalitarian view that both partners should work to contribute to the maintenance of the household, the reasons for such strong feelings give us a deeper insight into the special meaning of work for men and for women. For gay men, work is part of male self-respect. This was made clear in our interview with Drew, an unemployed waiter. He was very distressed about not working:

It really bothers me and I bitch about it all the time. I don't like being around the house and I spend most of my time either looking for a job or doing something that I think is useful. It bothers me more than it bothers him. He is really good about it. None of my other habits have changed and he knows I'm sensitive about it and so he lays off. He knows I'll get another job and I know I will, so there is nothing to get upset about—except that I do a little until it gets resolved.

Unlike heterosexual men, however, gay men do not feel obligated to support their partners. Only men in a relationship with a woman accept the duty to provide for their partners and children. On the contrary, in a gay relationship, each man is expected to work because this is part of what it means to be a man. These men embrace the need to work, but discard the provider role. Furthermore, like heterosexual men, they have no interest in living as a full-time homemaker; in addition, they do not think their partners should assume that role.[9] Thus housework has either to be shared or outside help has to be hired. Otherwise, one partner may feel he is relinquishing some of his maleness, and that is not an appealing prospect for most gay men.[10] Joshua and Gus have lived together a little over a year. Joshua, twenty-six, manages a retail paint store and Gus, twenty-nine, works part time as a hairdresser. Joshua:

I give Gus a bad time because he doesn't want to work. . . . I let him know I want him to work. When he's not working, it makes him more dependent on me and I don't like that. I like to know he can take care of himself. When he starts acting like he'd like me to take care of him, I start to think less of him.

Ozzie and Richard have been living together for nearly thirty-five years. Both are fifty-seven. Ozzie is a classical musician and Richard is a banker. They struggle, even after more than thirty years together, over Ozzie's work. Ozzie:

> I would really like to be home more and I'm always saying, "You could afford to support me." And I have a lot of our friends pushing him on this, but on the other hand, he won't go along with it and I never thought he would. I enjoy my work very much, but I would like to be at home more, but he won't allow it because I don't make much money that way and he gets mad because I'm not living up to my potential and he respects my work and he wants me to take advantage of more opportunities in it.

Richard would like Ozzie to be more assertive and is troubled by Ozzie's desire to stay home:

> I feel he should work more. I feel that he's not fulfilling his potential when he doesn't work as much as he could. I think he has more skills, new talents, and more salable qualities than he is using and pushing, and he'd be the first to admit it. I feel he's not aggressive, and in his business you have to be aggressive. He works a fair amount but if he worked a little bit harder, he could develop a lot more. So I keep at him.

For lesbians, work means the ability to avoid dependency and being cast in the stereotypical homemaker role. One lesbian, thirty-seven, related how she had had to get used to the concept of working in order to take care of herself:

> When I first realized I was gay, one of the things I was pissed off about was that a man wasn't going to take care of me and I had to figure out what I was going to do. . . . And I'd never been as career-oriented. . . . I always knew I was going to get married and have children, and maybe teach a couple of years, but I wouldn't have to support myself and be self-sufficient. . . . Since I've been with my partner, work has *become* an important value.

While they understood they would have to learn how to earn their own living, rarely did these women think they would have to support another person. Our culture simply does not prepare a woman to take the provider role upon herself. There are some segments of American society where heterosexual women are, by necessity, the sole support of themselves and their children. But only in rare instances do they take on that responsibility for a male partner. Lesbians do not expect to support another adult or be head of a family in the same way a husband expects to take on the position of breadwinner. A lesbian sees herself as a worker, not a provider or a dependent.[11]

The belief that both partners should work can change among same-sex couples when they have large incomes that make two wage earners unnecessary. They feel that one or the other partner should be able to take some time off to do other things. Alexis, a forty-one-year-old personnel manager, expressed such feelings:

I'd love to stop work, but then who wouldn't? You just do these things because you have to, because nobody is going to give you a living for free. If we could afford it, we'd both stop, or we'd take turns stopping. But so far, we haven't found a way to do that. . . . So we just choose jobs that make money and make it easier to have the kind of time we want together.

On the other hand, the lesbians, like the gay men, can find it difficult actually to stay at home when the chance occurs. Brigitte and Mattie had been trying to work out this issue when we interviewed them. They have been a couple for sixteen years. Brigitte, fifty-two, is trained as a nurse, but had just left her job when we spoke to her:

We have arguments about my work, about my ambivalence about having a full-time job. Mattie has been very understanding about my not wanting to work, and she says, "If you don't want to work, don't." I think she went through a period when it made her anxious that I wasn't working. First it was anxiety about money, but then she got more rational about that and I did too, because I was anxious about that. I still am, but in reality, I don't need to work because we have plenty of money, so we should recognize that and relax and make it easier for us to enjoy each other.

Brigitte's partner, Mattie, sixty, is a high-school principal. She interprets the problem slightly differently:

I think she has trouble not working. You know, in America, you are what you earn. Which is ridiculous, but then we all grew up under that. So she feels bad. . . . So I have to make sure that she knows that I love her, and I don't care what she does or if she is working or not. As long as we can afford it, I think she should do what she thinks is right and not what the world thinks is right.

---

*Married couples who disagree about the wife's right to work have less happy relationships.*[12]

Most working wives do so with the accord of their husbands, and husbands and wives decide together whether the woman will work full time or part time.[13] But when the couple fights about her working, the relationship is strained. Sometimes the fights stem from the husband's reaction to the effect the wife's full-time work has on the household. He considers the household to be her responsibility and is angry about her absence. Amelia, thirty-one, and Wayne, thirty-five, have been married four years. Amelia sells sportswear, and Wayne manages a fast-food restaurant. The way the house is kept is one of their major sources of conflict; it often leads to a quarrel about Amelia's work.

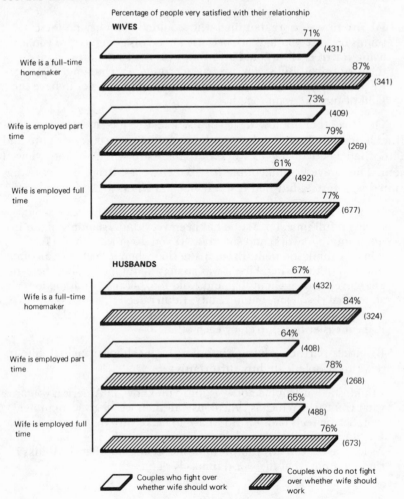

Percentage of people very satisfied with their relationship

**WIVES**

Wife is a full-time homemaker
71% (431)
87% (341)

Wife is employed part time
73% (409)
79% (269)

Wife is employed full time
61% (492)
77% (677)

**HUSBANDS**

Wife is a full-time homemaker
67% (432)
84% (324)

Wife is employed part time
64% (408)
78% (268)

Wife is employed full time
65% (488)
76% (673)

☐ Couples who fight over whether wife should work

▨ Couples who do not fight over whether wife should work

Note: In all of these couples, the husband is employed full time.

Numbers in parentheses are the number of couples on which the percentages are based.

FIGURE   15

WAYNE: This place is very small. It cannot take any clutter whatsoever. We have summit conference after summit conference about keeping it in shape, but the fact is that she is a slob. . . . When things get hot she finally digs up the defense of working hard and no time to take care of things. . . . My feeling is that if she can't manage to keep this place together and do her job then she should quit the damn job.

In another couple, the wife's recent return to work does not fit with the husband's sense of what their life ought to be. They have been married for nineteen years and both are in their early forties. The husband described his feelings:

> She thinks I am being very unreasonable about the limits I put on her work. But you have to see this in the context of the life we have made together. We have worked out things very well by her staying at home and raising our children and me bringing home the bacon. I find it odd now that she wants to go out and do somebody else's dirty work when she could stay at home and use the life we worked hard to put together. We argue about this about once a month, especially when she is grouchy because of something someone in the office said or did. I'll tell her again to quit and let me provide and she'll get huffy and unreasonable.

When the wife is a full-time homemaker and the couple fights about both partners working, it usually reflects her thwarted desire to be employed. Betty, fifty-seven, is a full-time homemaker, but prior to her marriage seven years ago to Aaron, she worked in an advertising firm. Aaron, sixty, works as a supervisor in an architectural office. Betty has not adjusted comfortably to being a homemaker:

> It was awful when we got married because right around that time he got fired from his old job. I stayed on working longer than he wanted me to because we had no choice. . . . I was perfectly happy to continue because I loved my job but he just couldn't stand having his wife work. As soon as he got another job . . . he put enormous pressure on me to quit work like I had said I would. I didn't want to, to tell you the truth, in the first place, and I resisted. He got very upset and very threatened and the whole first year was up and down, and sometimes I thought I had made a mistake. . . . I gave in and quit. It was so important to him—even though we have no children at home or anything like that. So I gave up, but every now and then it flares up again and we go at each other. . . . It's probably silly of me, but I thought it should be my choice and it wasn't.

We see another kind of conflict over the wife's desire to work in a couple in their late twenties. They have been married six years. Marta is a full-time homemaker and Lars is a groundskeeper for a city park system.

> MARTA: He has me on this pedestal—maybe I should say he needs to have me on this pedestal—where I am his wife and mother of his children and that's what I am. I don't need all of this. I would like to get out and do a little work and add a little to our bank account so we can travel. He gets quiet and angry when I try and discuss why this would be a benefit, and sometimes he just gets up and walks away. I think he thinks I am saying something about him, but I try and tell him I am only saying something about me and what I would like.

When the wife works part time, the fights may be about any number of topics—from the husband's feeling that the household suffers from her absence and that the significant additional income is no compensation to the wife's desire to increase her hours on the job and his reluctance to have her become more invested in employment outside the home. James and Rebecca have been married for seven years. James is forty-one and is a business consultant. Rebecca, thirty-five, is a part-time marketing research interviewer.

> JAMES: We love each other very much and we try to spend as much time together as we can. I only have certain times I can go do things because I am my business and when I am there, I have billable hours and when I am not, I do not. Therefore I do think she has to be ready when I am to take the time together when we have it and if she is tied up with her work it makes for an impossibility to get time off together.

James expressed a common feeling that a wife might work, but she should be prepared to subordinate her career to her husband's. We heard another version of this point of view in Burton, forty-five, an international-investment counselor. He has been married to Viola, forty-four, for twelve years. Viola works part time as a realtor.

> BURTON: It is simply a matter of promises made and promises kept. When I need her I think she should be available to help. She is the only wife in the office who grouses over entertaining clients and she was the only one of my friends' wives who couldn't come join us in Las Vegas. I felt she was getting her priorities mixed up. She works with a bunch of petty, unattractive people in a pretty revolting profession. I have trouble understanding why she spends the time, and if she quit tomorrow it would be fine with me.

Another husband resented his wife's part-time work for a different reason. Cy feels that Jenny's work is taking on a more and more central place in her life. They have been married for nine years and both are in their late twenties. Cy is an installer of computer hardware, and Jenny works part time selling soaps and other household products. Cy told us about their conflicts:

> She started selling these soap products which I thought was a good way to use up some spare time—especially since Sean goes to nursery school. . . . But you know, she's so much better than most of these ladies that they kept promoting her and giving her more responsibility and more territory. I think it's gone a little too far now because they want her to do more hours and be a trainer and I think it's gotten out of hand. She thinks it's great and we yell at each other occasionally about it.

Homemakers and wives who are employed part time have a harder time reaching an understanding with their husbands than fully employed wives: Our data show that they have a greater chance of conflict on this matter.[14] So, although a couple might try to compromise by having the wife work only part time, that does not necessarily mean an end to conflict.

---

*When a wife works, the couple fights more about how the children are being raised.*[15]

Conventional wisdom says that children grow up best by having their mothers at home, at least until the end of their preschool years. There have been studies that show this may not be true.[16] But the great majority of men and women do not believe it.[17] If a mother of young children is out in the labor force—as almost one half are—she may bring feelings of guilt to the job. One wife, married for two years, works as a teacher's assistant part time. She described how she feels being away from her baby:

> I feel bad when I have to leave her. Usually I will bend over backwards to try and spend as much time with her as I can, but I always feel that I'm not giving her enough time. . . . She's old enough now so that she will cling to me sometimes when I have to leave and that about breaks my heart.

Georgette, a legal secretary in her mid-thirties, has been married for three years. She has three children from a former marriage. She, too, is troubled by spending a lot of time away from them:

> I call them during my lunch hour and make noises to them over the phone at the babysitter's. The people in the office think I'm crazy, making baby noises over the phone. . . . But I feel sad about not being with them and I want them to remember that I am thinking about them. . . . Then I'll bring them things, too, or do something special on the weekends. . . . I think I am always making it up to them.

Another woman disclosed a feeling many employed mothers have, that no matter what else is happening at the job, the children are always vivid in her mind. Mavis is a traffic-court judge in her early forties. She has one child from a former marriage and is in a lesbian relationship.

> MAVIS: I hired someone to take care of him while I was at work. I interviewed a hundred people over the phone and four in person. They all sounded better than I did over the phone. In person, there was always something to worry about . . . but I finally chose someone. . . . I'm sure he is getting more attention from her than I would be giving him, but I feel guilty so much of the time, thinking it should be me with him. In between hearings, sometimes during

hearings, my mind keeps going back home, wondering if everything is all right.

Affluent mothers try to reduce their worry by hiring housekeepers or finding elite preschools with programs that promise to benefit the child. Parents of limited means have fewer ways to find child care they consider an adequate substitute for the mother. Children are indeed a potent factor in keeping wives out of the labor force.

We observe relatively little impulse to solve this problem by taking husbands out of the work force and putting them in the nursery. Almost none of our couples actually had the husband stay home to care for the children.[18] Fathers would help out with the children, but the primacy of the husband's work was almost inviolable. In our society, the presence of children is an occupational limit only to women. More than 60 percent of our husbands and wives feel that a mother of small children should not hold a job.[19] In our interviews they gave us two major reasons why it is important for women (rather than men) to stay home with the children. The first is that women "mother" better. A twenty-nine-year-old husband told us:

> There is no doubt that women are better mothers than men are. She is always telling me that I don't remember important things like birthdays or doctor's appointments, and she's right. She keeps a calendar in her head and she's always reminding me about something the kids have got to do or the kids need. I don't have a head for those things and it's built right into her.

Another husband, married for ten years, reiterated the same belief:

> If she wakes up in the middle of the night she screams for Patty, not for me. Which is fine. I understand that. Kids need their moms. More than their dads. Until they are older. Moms know how to make them feel better. It is a natural talent.

As a wife of thirty-four, in a thirteen-year marriage, told us:

> There's a little place in my mind that is always listening for one of the kids to cry. He's good about them, but he doesn't have that part of his mind that is dedicated to the kids. He might pick them up and play with them and forget to think if they've been changed or something important like that. . . . He forgets doctor's visits . . . shoes. . . . He loves 'em, but I just think men aren't as natural at it as women are. . . . I think it works to have him just play Poppa, you know? And me to play Momma. Of course I would go out too. He'd let me and I'd earn five dollars an hour, but what would that do? Just screw up my kids. I'd be out there earning nothing and they'd be learning things I didn't want them to learn. . . . I used to teach school and all the kids I saw with real problems were kids that had mothers who were working. I think it's fine for women to work, but I

think they shouldn't have kids. They're just being selfish, trying to have it all, and the kids show the lack of care.

Second, some couples pointed out that since one parent has to remain at home, it would be foolish for the woman—who is likely to earn less than her husband—to go to work. Allen and Kate have been married for seven years. They have a two-year-old daughter. Allen is an optometrist and Kate worked as a sign-language interpreter until she became pregnant.

ALLEN: We both agree that Jenny needs her mother at home. When she gets into school full time, then it will be different and we can afford to have Kate do whatever she wants to. But someone has to be at home with her and it makes sense for it to be Kate. I can earn more than forty thousand dollars a year if business is good, and she just was pulling in about sixteen thousand as an interpreter. So who's going to quit? Me, and live on her salary? And not do as good a job? We are doing it the only way it makes sense to us.

Another wife, contemplating going back to work as a part-time secretary, told us in her interview that it would not make financial sense:

He has a real good business going . . . with his friends. But it takes all of them spending a lot of time to keep it up. So I stay home with the baby and he comes home at lunch whenever he can to visit us. At first, I thought I would go back to part-time work as a Kelly Girl, so that we would have money for a few extras. But we have found that it's hard to get sitters just when I need them and it isn't worth it to hire somebody. I'd probably just break even. So economically it's best that I'm here and he's out there building up the business.

Not every married couple feels that mothers of young children should be banned from the labor force. Nearly a fifth of our married couples feel that good child rearing can be accomplished without the mother always being at home.[20] One wife, twenty-five, who has worked in retail sales, explained that her son receives the vital companionship he needs in preschool:

If it were up to me I'd go back to work tomorrow. It's been fun to stay at home, but I'm ready to get back to work. I miss the challenge of it. I miss my friends at work. I even miss having little things to tell him about people—you know, gossip, office politics, things like that. . . . He feels Owen is still too young. But he is more interested in his preschool friends than hanging around with Mom these days, so I think I should be going back to work sooner and he thinks it should be later. . . . It's too bad we argue about it. We are both interested in his welfare but we don't agree on what's best.

Another wife warned about what might happen to her relationship with her child if she were *not* able to work:

I don't think [a mother] staying at home climbing walls is good for a child. You know child abuse isn't working mothers. It's all those women who are taking out their frustrations on their child because that's who's home. I think what you need is quality time with your child—and quality time with yourself. One way I get quality time for myself is in my job, which I love. Jack worries sometimes because Cari has been in child care since she was four months old, but I know both she and I will profit from doing it this way.

In some cases, husbands are not dubious about alternate forms of child care. As one man, married for twenty-three years, told us:

We always thought it would be cheaper by the dozen and by God, we came pretty close. We had a lot of trouble with money, but then we had a lot of fun. I had a lot of fun, although maybe it wasn't always fair to her, being the only woman around six guys. . . . I would help a lot, especially during the years she was on night shift. . . . We did just fine, had a lot of good times. I never thought a woman had to stay at home all the time with kids, even a lot of kids. I think I do about as well as her and the older kids helped the younger ones. I think it's old-fashioned to insist that a woman doesn't talk to anyone but kids for ten years. . . . She's talented in her work. She has talents that have to be expressed.

Some couples are caught in a particularly difficult bind. Both husband and wife have to work because they need the money, but one or both feels it is injurious to their children. Seymour and Melody have been married for fourteen years. They have two girls, nine and twelve. Seymour is an economist with a small consulting business and Melody is a practical nurse. In his interview, Seymour expressed great concern about Melody's working while their children are young:

This has been a very difficult year. I have let my secretary go twice and then I hire her back when I get a job. . . . The worst of it is that Melody has had to go back to work when both of us feel she should be home with the children. We think these are important years and we are worried about the oldest one in particular. . . . We don't think they should spend too much time with TV and friends. We like to do a lot of family time. . . . But now I have to work weekends and sometimes nights and she is working every day and neither of us think that this is the best way to have a family. . . . It's not what I promised her. . . . As soon as we can go back to normal, she will quit her job and I will cut back on my hours.

There is some evidence that mothers will feel freer about going out to work in the future. In the 1970's and 1980's the number of working women with small children increased. This reflects a change in values. We find that cohabitors—both men and women—are more liberal on this issue than married couples.[21] More important, the young people in our study are more likely than their elders to favor work outside the home for women with small children.[22]

*Because working wives bring money into the household, their work helps equalize the balance of power in their marriages. Their work also brings them greater respect from their husbands.*

Each partner's relative income helps determine the balance of power in a marriage. In contrast to our other kinds of couples, married couples do not *assume* that both partners will have jobs. This means that some wives, either because they do not want to or are not allowed to work, do not have access to an important source of power, which would give them a more equal say in the marriage.[23] A wife who is not employed outside the home is at a disadvantage. But this is only partly because she earns no money. We think it is the simple fact that she has a job that gives a wife clout. Men respect paid employment outside the home more than they respect housework. Men's own self-respect is in part derived from their success in the world of work and while they may say they have as much respect for a wife who stays at home, they in fact do not.[24] Sheldon, a hospital administrator, is thirty-seven. He has been married to Dixie for five years, having lived with her for two years before marrying. Dixie is twenty-seven and works as a researcher in a medical laboratory. Sheldon's indirect feelings about full-time housewives are not atypical of many husbands:

**WIVES' EMPLOYMENT AND THE MARITAL BALANCE OF POWER**

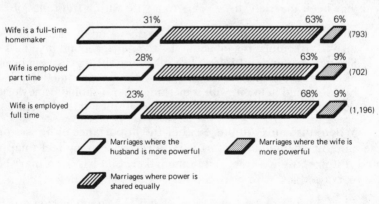

Wife is a full-time homemaker — 31%   63%   6%   (793)

Wife is employed part time — 28%   63%   9%   (702)

Wife is employed full time — 23%   68%   9%   (1,196)

Marriages where the husband is more powerful

Marriages where the wife is more powerful

Marriages where power is shared equally

Note:  In all these couples, the husband is employed full time.

Numbers in parentheses are the number of couples on which the percentages are based.

FIGURE    16

One of the things that makes us so happy with one another is that neither of us needs to cling to the other. She wouldn't want to be a poor housewife looking to me to provide for her all her needs and I wouldn't want to feel that I had to provide all of her intellectual stimulation. . . . We met working and that was one of our bases of respect for each other. Neither one of us would dream of staying at home, except, perhaps, for a special vacation.

We believe men respect work for a number of reasons. They esteem achievement for its own sake, even if it does not bring great wealth. They admire a person who does well in competition with others. They look favorably upon jobs that require skill and discipline, and they are sympathetic to the daily stresses of the work place, such as having an unreasonable employer or uncooperative fellow workers. While successfully running a household can demand great skill, husbands often do not have any appreciation for it. Hy and Lucy have been married for eight years. Lucy, twenty-nine, is a full-time homemaker. Hy, thirty-two, is a truck driver. Hy holds this opinion:

I do not think there is anything about women's work that is demanding. I just don't think it takes all that much to do it. . . . If I'm around the house and I feel like it, I can probably get it done in half the time it takes her to do it. I think she tries to mystify me with it. So I show her every once in a while just how easy it is to get it done. Then I tease her about what does she do with her day? Why does she try and tell me how busy she's been? . . . But I've stopped most of that now with the baby because I think that does take some time.

A similar attitude was expressed by a thirty-four-year-old husband who has been married three years to a wife with a full-time job:

She hates to clean houses that are too dirty, and this house gets very dirty. She complains a lot about it—too much about it if you ask me. She gets grumpy and I don't like it because she makes a big deal out of not much. . . . I get grumpy when I have to do something that's her work and help out with something when I should be at work doing my job. But I do it sometimes because I want to be a nice guy.

When husbands minimize either the importance of housework or the amount of time and effort it requires, wives may feel unappreciated. Eunice, twenty-nine, is a homemaker. She has been married for six years to Miles, who owns a bicycle shop. This is her reaction:

I just don't think he appreciates what it's like to go picking up after him. I agree that I don't want him doing anything because I don't like to see guys doing that sort of thing and I think he should do his job and I should do mine. . . . What I mind is that he doesn't make anything easier for me by not taking a little care about the way he lives in the house. I think he thinks it's part of my job to clean up whatever mess he makes. I would like a little more respect for what I do.

Not all husbands discount the importance of being a homemaker or the skills it takes to do it well. As one husband remarked:

> Oh, I think housework is terribly time-consuming, terribly boring, and probably infinitely demanding. That's why we hire someone so Janice doesn't have to do it. We help each other with the everyday things. She directs; I do what she tells me to do. I suppose I would like to be able to cook, but I have never gotten around to learning and she's so good at it. We both don't want to have to suffer while I train! Janice works hard at keeping this ship going and I certainly appreciate her efforts.

But even these husbands feel that the ability to hold a job commands greater respect.

Housework at one time was considered important by men because the skills women developed for the home, for example, sewing, weaving, gardening, and baking, required years of apprenticeship and not all women learned how to do them equally well. Women produced vitally important products for the life of the family, such as quilts, candles, preserves, and other articles that were not available in stores. As technology and retail marketing became more advanced, consumer items became easy to obtain from other sources. It became prestigious to have "store-bought" goods instead of those that were homemade. Modern homemaking accomplishments, such as gourmet cooking (one of our housewives calls herself part of "the Cuisinart generation") may inspire admiration and gratitude in husbands, but we think they do not confer the same degree of status they did a hundred years ago.

There is another way in which working may alter the balance of power between husband and wife. A woman employed outside the home may develop a sense of self-worth from her ability to make important decisions and from her interactions with employers and co-workers.[25] The demands of paid employment often push people to discover abilities they never knew they had. Once people develop self-confidence, they are not likely to want to give up such a new and rewarding sense of personal effectiveness when they come home from work. Husbands cannot unquestionably assert their decision-making ability when their wives have proof that their talents and wisdom are greatly appreciated elsewhere. As one wife, who oversees a large laboratory, told us:

> I think we share in the decision-making. I make decisions at the office from nine to five and I think it would be a little strange if I came home and was treated like a pussycat.

Her husband gives her respect and deference as a result of her success at work:

I am very proud of her. She was recently promoted and I would say
that in a few years, she may be making as much money as I am in my
business. Of course, . . . she wouldn't be making my gross amount,
but her take-home would be close to mine. . . . I think they recognize
her abilities because she is a very forceful person. . . . I rely on her
judgment on several decisions I've had to make in my work.

Freda and Jeb have been married more than thirty-five years. He
is sixty-three, and a professor of medicine. She is a sixty-year-old retired university administrator who still does some educational consulting. She reflected on the power she has lost since her retirement:

We don't get on as well as we used to when I was working because
then he used to listen to me more than he does now. He tends to
boss me around the way he tends to boss students. You know, when
he says something to his students, it's like an order. He starts that
with me. But when I was an administrator, I was the boss lady. When
he starts bossing me around, I don't like it; I remind him that I am
still working and I still get respect and he'd better give me some. He
does, but I have to remind him.

If a wife in a traditional marriage happens to be very forceful, she
may use this to her advantage and demand the right to work, over the
objections of an unwilling husband. If she succeeds, her power increases in the marriage. A wife married for thirty years told us:

I have always worked, even in the beginning of our marriage. I am
not the type to stay at home—never was, never will be. Even now, I
am officially retired but I am just as busy as I ever was because I am
talented and there is always some outfit that needs my skills. He
wasn't too happy about my working in the beginning, and he totally
can't understand why I want to do it now. He thinks that if he'd
made more money I wouldn't insist on working, but he's wrong
about that. It has nothing to do with how much money he makes.

There are, of course, couples who believe in equality between the
sexes, and so the men expect their wives to work and also to have equal
power in decision-making. These couples do not accept what they see
to be an old-fashioned set of beliefs that automatically grants greater
authority to the husband. Tyler and Hattie have been married for
twenty-two years. Hattie, forty-five, is a social worker, and Tyler, fifty-
two, is a toy designer. Hattie described how they look at things:

We both feel that since we're both helping financially we both do
work at home too. We have friends who say, "That's women's work,"
or, "That's men's work," but we don't feel that way. We decide
everything fifty-fifty, and it's always been that way. I do the cooking,
but he does the washing. I haven't cleaned the oven or mopped the
floor since I can't remember when. He takes care of that for me.
And then when it comes to something electrical in the house, like a
plug or something, I will do that. . . . It works out evenly in a lot of

things. Our lives look a lot like each other's so we need each other to sort things out.

Wives with full-time jobs have more power in their marriages than wives who work part time. We believe that in this society, part-time work is not as respected as full-time work. It is often paid on a lower scale than comparable full-time work. Part-time employees are taken less seriously by management, and they may not be treated as real colleagues by their co-workers. Many times these people are viewed as not being serious about having a career. If they are wives, what they do is often disregarded because they are thought to put their family ahead of their responsibilities to the job. Further, part-time work is often in a dead-end job; it is seldom seen as leading to further advancement.[26] In interviews we heard husbands with full-time jobs expressing a lack of respect for part-time work. They may give their wives some credit for their labor, but not much. Crosby, twenty-four, is a management trainee. He has been married three years to Elaine, also twenty-four, who works part time as a hotel receptionist. Crosby reflected:

> I don't care if she works. I think she has a good job, and until the kid is born I think it is fine if she wants to add something to her life. I don't want her to work after the baby is born and I think that will be the end of full-time work because we plan to have a rather large family. . . . I think it's nice that she enjoys doing something, but we don't rely on her having a job and I don't want to rely on it. We both agree that what she does is just a part-time thing—for extra money or for meeting people and that it is my work that will guide our decisions about where we are going to live. I am definitely the breadwinner and part-time work is a suitable support, but we don't overestimate its importance.

Even though a husband may not be aware that he disdains his wife's part-time employment, the message often comes through clearly to the wife. One example is Ruth, a twenty-nine-year-old part-time nurse:

> He never wants me to talk about my work. He doesn't credit my work with the same importance that he gives his work. It didn't start out being important but it's getting important. I don't need him to be wildly enthusiastic, but I need to feel that he knows what's going on in my life, and I want to be able to talk about the things that happened on the job. I think he is trying to show me that he would be glad if I didn't work at all, or that I'm not going to get any special privileges between us just because I'm hassled. . . . I don't think he sees me as someone who is in the same work situation he is.

It is not only husbands who may take a wife's part-time work less seriously. Some wives share the feeling that it is less important and therefore less deserving of recognition. Sharon is thirty-seven and works part time as a substitute teacher. Her husband of eighteen years, Gaston, is an accountant. This is Sharon's view of her work situation:

Since I am only working part time . . . I do have time to be a full-time housewife and I don't think it's fair to ask him to do much around the house if he is carrying the burden of such a consuming professional life. I make some allowances for when I am busy, but we both agree that my work is really quite flexible right now and so I should be responsible to make sure the household gets taken care of. It's hard to take my work as seriously as his when I'm not dedicating my whole day to it.

*Working wives still bear almost all the responsibility for housework.*

Working wives do less housework than homemakers, but they still do the vast bulk of what needs to be done.[27] Husbands of women who

**TIME SPENT ON HOUSEWORK AMONG MARRIED COUPLES**

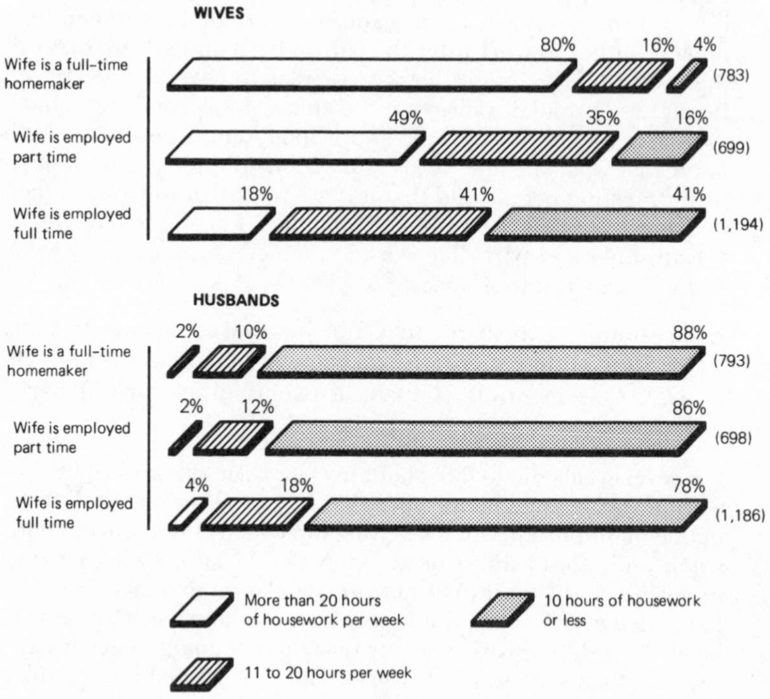

**WIVES**

| | | | |
|---|---|---|---|
| Wife is a full-time homemaker | 80% | 16% | 4% (783) |
| Wife is employed part time | 49% | 35% | 16% (699) |
| Wife is employed full time | 18% | 41% | 41% (1,194) |

**HUSBANDS**

| | | | |
|---|---|---|---|
| Wife is a full-time homemaker | 2% 10% | 88% (793) |
| Wife is employed part time | 2% 12% | 86% (698) |
| Wife is employed full time | 4% 18% | 78% (1,186) |

More than 20 hours of housework per week

10 hours of housework or less

11 to 20 hours per week

Note: In all these couples the husband is employed full time.

Numbers in parentheses are the number of couples on which the percentages are based.

FIGURE   17

work help out more than husbands of homemakers, but their contribution is not impressive. Even if a husband is unemployed, he does much less housework than a wife who puts in a forty-hour week.[28]

This is the case even among couples who profess egalitarian social ideals, including equal sharing of all the work that has to be done in the house. While these men do more housework than those who are in favor of a traditional division of labor between the sexes, they are still way behind their wives. On the questionnaires, we asked people how many hours a week they spent on household chores, such as cooking, laundry, and grocery shopping. The results were striking. While husbands might say they should share responsibility, when they broke it down to time actually spent and chores actually done, the idea of shared responsibility turned out to be a myth.[29]

**TIME SPENT ON HOUSEWORK AMONG MARRIED COUPLES IN WHICH BOTH ARE EMPLOYED FULL TIME AND BOTH FEEL STRONGLY THAT HOUSEWORK SHOULD BE SHARED EQUALLY**

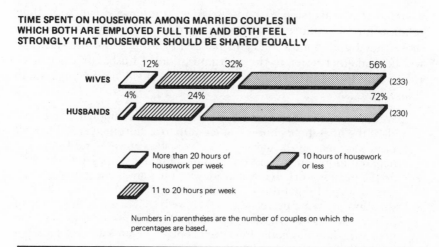

FIGURE   18

Recent social change has only moderately affected our married couples. In interviews working-class husbands were particularly vocal. They do not accept the fact that they should be equal partners in the house, hence they do little housework. They believe the house is rightly assigned to their wives and the advances of the women's movement have not altered their belief.

Among middle- and upper-middle-class couples, we find two patterns. One is the two-career couple in which the husband encourages his wife to invest herself in her work and contribute to their standard of living. She still does more housework than he, but some of the burden may be shifted to hired help.[30] The other is a couple in which only the husband works. He earns enough money so that his wife can either hire someone else to do housework and have her own time for family, friends, and charitable causes, or choose to do it herself because she feels it is her job.

There has been some recent interest by the media in men who voluntarily choose to stay home and take care of their house and family while their wives go out to work. Try as we might, however, we could not find a significant number of men who fit the description of "house-husband."[31]

---

*When husbands do a lot of housework, married couples have greater conflict.*

Married men's aversion to housework is so intense it can sour their relationship. The more housework they do, for whatever reason, the more they fight about it.[32] If this pattern continues into the future, it will be a major barrier to the reorganization of husbands' and wives' roles. One husband in his early forties described his feelings about housework:

> We have a very traditional labor pattern. Very traditional. She does all of the household chores—at least up to a short time ago. Then all I did was take out the garbage. . . . Now she's at work and I have to help out more, but I resist doing things I'm not supposed to do. I'll do the outside work, but the inside work has always been her territory and I don't think I should have to learn things that she has spent twenty years perfecting. . . . So we have got me in this mode of helper—which I don't like very much—but it is more necessary right now if the house is going to be well kept. . . . I am willing to make her life a little easier but I can't say I enjoy any of it.

Another husband of twenty-one saw his wife's handling of the housework and her suggestion that he do some of it himself as a factor that could break up their marriage:

> Our biggest arguments are about her being such a slob. I can't believe the things she will let go. She thinks I'm making a big deal out of nothing, but . . . I can't get used to her hair in the bathtub or no toilet paper when I go to the toilet or her clothes in a pile next to the shower. . . . We have screaming fights about it and she says if I want things different so bad, I should do them myself. Yeah, I'll do them myself over my dead body. She is going to have to shape up because I am not going to live like this and I don't think our kid should live like this. She is going to have to grow up.

*Cohabitation sets egalitarian standards for doing the housework, but women still do more of it than men do.[33]*

Cohabitors expect their partners to work. Each partner pledges to provide for him- or herself, or both count on contributing to the financial support of the household.[34] Since neither partner becomes the sole provider, we would expect that neither would become the housekeeper. And this proves true—but only up to a point. Cohabiting women certainly do less housework than working wives. But cohabiting men become no more involved with household duties than husbands.[35]

A few cohabiting women (3 percent) are full-time homemakers, and they do almost as much housework as wives who are not employed.[36] If they work part time, the cohabiting women do more housework than if they work full time.[37] We think that doing more housework is their way of providing their fair share. The same mechanism may operate, perhaps unconsciously, when a female cohabitor earns less than her partner. Unless she earns what her partner considers to be a reasonable salary, he may not take her contribution to the household seriously. So we find that even if she works full time, when she earns less than he does, she does more housework.[38] Since women in general earn less money in our society, cohabiting couples who unconsciously accept income as a basis for assigning household duties will more often than not hand over the greater burden of the housework to the woman.

**TIME SPENT ON HOUSEWORK AMONG
COHABITING AND MARRIED COUPLES**

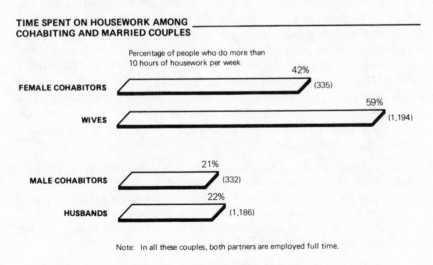

Percentage of people who do more than
10 hours of housework per week

FEMALE COHABITORS    42% (335)

WIVES    59% (1,194)

MALE COHABITORS    21% (332)

HUSBANDS    22% (1,186)

Note: In all these couples, both partners are employed full time.

Numbers in parentheses are the number of people on which the percentages are based.

FIGURE    19

But after all this has been said, when we look at cohabiting couples in which both partners work full time, *and* in which the woman earns at least as much as the man, she still does more than half of all the housework.[39] It seems to be a cultural given in America that growing up female makes housework something women do. Conversely, it seems to be a cultural given that growing up male in this country causes even liberal men to reject household tasks. In interviews these same men assured us they shared housework and were indispensable at home. However, when the men and women filled out their question- naires independently, the number of hours the men reported was much less than that of their female partners.

This inclination on the part of cohabiting men to sidestep house- work causes arguments between the partners. The more he pitches in, the more peaceful the relationship. The more he leaves for her to do, the less satisfied she becomes with the whole situation.[40]

---

*Like heterosexual couples, gay men and lesbians do more*

*housework if they are not fully employed.[41]*

Same-sex couples cannot assign housework on the basis of who is male and who is female. Even when we ask questions designed to find out who is more masculine or feminine, their answers do not relate to who does more housework.[42] Among gay male couples, neither partner is very likely to have been trained to do these tasks, and it is rare when one man wants to bear the entire burden of them.[43] As with our co- habitors, hours spent at work become a standard that determines how much time each man owes to doing housework. Lenny and Neal have lived together for thirty-one years. Both are retired. Lenny, sixty-one, had a career as a museum curator, and Neal, fifty-five, taught in a public school. Lenny said:

> Housework has never been a problem, just depended on who had the time. Now that we've both got the time, we both do it. Earlier, because [of our work schedules], he would get home earlier. So he would do all the yard maintenance while it was light out and get dinner ready and clean up a bit. We divided things according to what was fair but also who had the time off of work.

Another couple in their mid-thirties also base the housework re- sponsibility on the number of hours each partner puts in on his job. However, one partner was quick to remark that such an arrangement has the potential to be exploited unfairly:

> His job takes an awful amount of time and he has to put in a lot of hours. So naturally, since mine is just an eight-hour job, I do more of

**TIME SPENT ON HOUSEWORK AMONG GAY MEN AND LESBIANS**

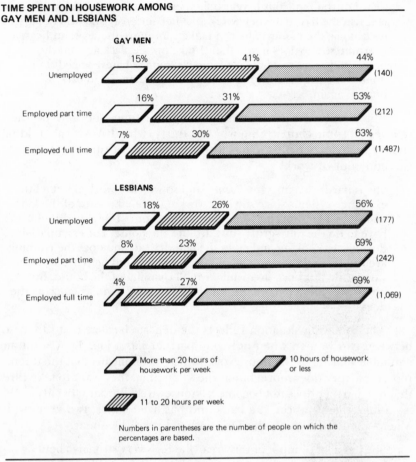

FIGURE 20

the housework. . . . Sometimes my hours are screwy—like late at night—and then he does more around here. But usually I have to do it. He does have a bit of spoiled-rotten-child attitude sometimes and he feels if he's working so hard he shouldn't have to do anything. I agree with him a little—he shouldn't have to do as much—but I make him do some of it.

Lesbians, on the average, do slightly less housework than gay men.[44] This may be because some of them are rejecting a role that has been symbolic of women's low status. Lesbians are especially careful to devise an equitable organization of household duties.

Corrine described how she and Lenore adjust their household chores to fit their work hours. She is twenty-seven and a telephone operator. Lenore, twenty-six, is a computer programmer. They have lived together five years.

Our tasks are pretty much divided by preference and ability . . . but it also depends on how much time either one of us is spending at our jobs. For the past couple years, she's been putting in overtime because she has to or they won't take her seriously and also because we can use the money. She can make a lot more money than I can at overtime so she does it and then I take up the slack around the house, doing more of the cooking, cleaning, whatever needs to be done. When she is working straight hours, then we go back to normal again.

But if only one partner is working full time, she may be then relieved of some chores. One woman, thirty, who drives a cab, told us about the arrangement she has with her partner of three years who is currently out of work:

She is hardly making any money and so we have worked out a little exchange system. Since she isn't working, she takes care of the kids and since I am working—and hard, long hours I might add—I don't have to do the nitty-gritty stuff around the house. For example, she does all the cooking and takes the laundry out and does the running around that takes time. I'll help on weekends and help her with the yard or do our once-in-a-while overall cleaning of the house. But unless she gets a job, we think I shouldn't have to do as much as she does.

The following situation reflects the delicate balance that can arise between two women when only one partner has a job. They want an equitable sharing of the housework, which often means that the unemployed partner does more, but at the same time, they want to take care that one partner does not become a "housewife." Barbara, twenty-nine, is an investment officer at a bank and has lived almost two years with Mae, a medical student. Barbara outlined their dilemma:

She has a lot of input in this area. She feels very strongly about having an equitable situation and I think that comes from her having lived with men and feeling taken advantage of in the past, so she definitely feels it ought to be equitable. It's easy to slip into something where she does more because I am the only one working full time and therefore she has to take some extra responsibility— but we see the dangers of that and we are keeping things in line so she doesn't get stuck with too much.

It is the recognition that a partner's unemployment is temporary or for a finite amount of time (as with a student) that allows the lesbians to live with an unequal division of the housework. One woman, thirty-five, in a twelve-year relationship, told us:

We are not into roles and we float in and out of each other's [responsibilities]. The only exception has been lately because she lost her job . . . and so she has been around the house lately. So she does a lot of the things we traditionally have done together because she is around to do them. . . . I feel somewhat guilty about that because we both should be doing it because nobody likes to do it, but we realize it's just for now, and when she gets a job, we'll go back to fifty-fifty.

We heard in interviews another reason why some lesbians reject housework. They feel they do not spend enough time together and they jealously guard what little they get. When they tell us about the importance of "quality time" together, they obviously are referring to precious hours they do not want to waste on chores. Susan and Deirdre have lived together six years and both are in their mid-thirties. Susan is a hairdresser and Deirdre is a waitress in a women's bar. Susan told us about their solution:

> We got to the point where we didn't think we were having enough quality time together. We would see each other only late at night after we were exhausted and tired. We would be irritable and it got so that we were wondering what we were getting from the relationship. It was made worse because on the weekend we would be rushing around with other things or we would take at least one day and clean the house. . . . We decided one way to remind ourselves about what we loved about each other was to tell the housework to go to hell and to not see friends that day and just spend it relaxing with each other.

Another lesbian couple, together ten years, repeated the same feeling:

> Recently we have just decided not to clean the house. We have a college girl come in and clean it once a week because we both hate it so much. We have better things to do with our time than spend it doing shit work. . . . It's worth money to have the time left over for ourselves.

---

*Both heterosexual and homosexual men feel that a successful partner should not have to do housework.*

If men feel their partners are doing very well in their work, they do not expect as much participation in mundane household matters. When a successful partner does do housework, he or she may get extra credit and be thought to do more than a fair share. A well-respected business executive who merely dusts on Saturday may be regarded by her husband as exceptionally giving, while a full-time homemaker keeping a ten-room house spotless might well be taken for granted. We feel that men tend to judge people, including their partners, by what they accomplish in the work world. They evaluate the importance of a person's time by its market value. We came to this conclusion from a number of interviews in which a man—gay or heterosexual—showed respect for his partner's work by saying that he felt that such a person should not be burdened with housework. Dorothy and Sherwin had been married only a few months when we interviewed them. Dorothy, thirty-one, is a stock analyst, and Sherwin, twenty-eight, manages a small radio station. Sherwin is proud of Dorothy's career and sees it as far too important to be jeopardized by time spent on housework:

> I don't want to see her assume the traditional female duties because she is also a business executive and we both have nine-to-five jobs and it would not be fair for one person to have two jobs. . . . I just don't think it would be fair for her to bring home the bacon and fry it too. . . . When you are busy and your career is important you aren't going to sacrifice it to housework. We let everything go— longer than we should—and save it for when the maid comes. I didn't marry her to have someone who passes out kisses and coffee. . . . We hire someone to do that sort of thing for us.

Ray and Mary Beth have been married for six years. Ray, thirty-six, is an engineer, and Mary Beth, thirty, works as an attorney. Ray also thinks that his wife should not have to be burdened with too much housework:

> We both hate housework intensely. She dislikes intensely housework and cooking so I do the vacuuming and cooking. . . . I do dishes and cook meals but she complains that she always has to ask me and that I am still not doing fifty percent. I think she always has work that she can do at night if she has the time. . . . I know she is coming up for a promotion in the next year or two and that she needs as much release from the house as possible so I try and give it to her even if it doesn't seem like it to her. . . . I am very aware of how much this promotion would mean to her and to us and I don't want to overburden her with unimportant things.

Rolf and Earl have lived together for nine years. Rolf, twenty-eight, is a waiter, and Earl, thirty-three, is an interior designer. Earl revealed why he thinks the effort he puts into his career entitles him to be freed from some household responsibilities:

> Our biggest arguments are about what I haven't done lately. He'll rave and rant, or just pout, about the things I promised to do around the house that haven't got done. . . . I am willing to help out when I can, but my career is not just nine to five and usually I either don't have the time or I'm so tired when I come home that the last thing I'm going to do is clean the kitchen floor. . . . We had this one discussion where he suggested I get up earlier in the morning to help clean up if I'm too tired at night. I blew up and told him that I was the one with the career here and it was my prospects and my salary that gave us his vacations and you just can't be a housewife and a success all at the same time. . . . He was hurt and I felt bad but

it is true. . . . He doesn't understand because he hasn't decided on anything yet and I am in the middle of my climb.

Most women do not exhibit special gratitude for housework done by a partner who has achieved professional success—although many heterosexual women expect little help around the house and are pleased with whatever their partners choose to do. But quite apart from all other considerations, compared to the men, not many of the women we interviewed—lesbian or heterosexual—thought of housework as demeaning. Women do not see a contradiction between being an executive and doing housework. Men do.

Why do so many wives want to work? They often face an unwelcoming job market, uncertain advancement, and generally lower pay than their husbands. Unless there are crucial financial needs, why do they not elect to stay home and let their husbands support them?

The answer is that work gives them more power, respect, and self-fulfillment. They gain status in the household. When a woman earns money, she acquires more of a voice in the decisions she and her husband make. If she makes a success of herself, she is not expected to do as much housework—a sure sign that she is elevated in her own and her husband's eyes.

It is clearer, then, why a husband might resist his wife's bid to work, even though it would financially benefit their household. When she gets a job, some of the classic and established rules of marriage become modified in ways he may not like. He may worry about her commitment to taking care of him and supporting his career. The more work-oriented he is, the more he may want her to be his helpmate, and the less he wants her to be his colleague.

The gay and lesbian couples show us what happens when historic expectations are absent from a relationship. Each partner is supposed to work and does. There is no assumption about the primacy of one partner's career, and if a conflict arises, it is negotiated between them. Neither job is automatically considered of secondary or of auxiliary importance. Fights may flare up over career issues, but rarely over who should work.

The same-sex couples profit in this instance by being guided by neither institution nor gender. However, they may have greater difficulty than married couples when confronted with such issues as relocating for one partner's job. Institutional guidelines make such a decision easier for married couples, although the wife's career advancement may be thwarted.

The years of learning how to be male or female have left their mark, and this is particularly evident when we find inequalities outside the context of marriage, as in the lives of the cohabitors. In fact, comparing the cohabitors to the gay men and lesbians makes it apparent that it is not just being outside the institution of marriage that gives equal status to both partners' work. The cohabitors and same-sex couples are all unmarried, but many female cohabitors still find themselves doing more of the household chores than their partners. And male cohabitors frequently respect women's work less than they do their own. At least in marriage the woman lives with a man who is morally committed to provide for her in exchange for restricting her work outside the home. Cohabiting women can suffer some of the same restrictions, yet do not gain the advantage of having a breadwinner. The fact that many female cohabitors accept terms that are clearly not to their advantage shows how difficult it is, even for women in unconventional living arrangements, to change the historic relationship between the sexes.

# Job satisfaction, ambition, and success

*The intrusion of work into the life of the couple*

Most people like to think that their partners will love them no matter what kind of work they do or how successful they become. Ideally, marriage or an intimate relationship functions as a refuge from the world of work—a place where each person is loved and admired for who he or she is, rather than for what he or she achieves. But some social thinkers hold to the view that modern society has become so judgmental that spouses and lovers now evaluate one another according to how well they do at their jobs. In his book *Haven in a Heartless World*, Christopher Lasch writes with bitterness that the working world has invaded family life and that personal relationships are no longer immune from being judged by its standards.[1] He goes on to say that unconditional love is no longer possible because partners and relationships are graded in the same way job performance is.

Is success on the job related to the way partners feel about each other? Are people who spend all day in a work environment appraising others for their skills and ability to produce able to put such measures aside when they return home? Can one partner be too successful and invoke competitive feelings in the person he or she lives with? Now that so many men and women are in the labor force we are eager to see how both sexes respond to a partner's success or lack of it in work. As work comes to dominate the time of so many American couples, do they know how to form emotional boundaries that keep it from affecting their personal lives?

*For employed wives, the happier they are with their job, the happier they are with their marriage.[2]*

We interpret this to mean that wives allow their relationships to affect their jobs and their jobs to affect their relationships. When things are not going well at work, they are likely to bring their concerns home, and when they feel upset with their husbands, it is difficult for it not to affect how they feel about work. As one wife in her fifties told us:

> I was very good at my job and I enjoyed it . . . but looking back on it, I also gloss over how hard it was to keep going when he and I were having problems, especially problems with our oldest daughter. We built our whole life around her and this took its toll on everything. There would be some mornings I would be at work and all I would be doing was thinking about if she [was doing all right]. . . . I would want to discuss these things with my husband, but he would be too tired in the morning and then he would say he was too tired at night and finally it was, "I don't want to talk about it because it produces too much tension." . . . I would be under a lot of tension myself and it was impossible for me to hide it from everyone. I had too many friends at the office, so that really became a very important emotional outlet for me as well as a professional one.

Stacey and Glenda have been married for six years. Stacey, thirty-two, is a music teacher, and Glenda, thirty, is a graphic artist. Glenda reported:

> When I have had a bad day I'm afraid I am grumpy and he's very good at getting me out of it by offering advice so that I don't ruin our whole evening. . . . I'm afraid I store up a lot of frustration and I am likely to take it out on him because I can't take it out on the people who deserve it. . . . He's very good about deflecting it and pointing out to me what I'm doing. . . . He never does the same thing back to me. I sometimes wish he would, so it would be tit for tat—but he rarely mentions anything but good news or maybe some office gossip. I have to dig to get information and he just has to watch me walk through the door and I unload on him.

From the questionnaires and interviews we get a picture of how intertwined work and home life can be for employed wives. When married couples fight about the wife's work, their conflict can compromise the pleasure she derives from her job as well as from her marriage.[3] Wives often want more time and attention from their husbands than they are able to get. Some seek stimulation in a job. We believe that when they work—and enjoy it—they indeed satisfy many of their needs. Consequently they can place fewer demands on their husbands and are more content with their marriage. We also feel that when they are happy in their marriage, they bring fewer anxieties and tensions to their job, hence the more able they are to enjoy it. As one wife, thirty-one, who works as a textile designer, told us:

> It's important to have at least one thing going well at a time. Because I can count on my marriage, I feel my energies are released for my work. It would be terrible if I had to worry about two things at once. But he is my support and my deep strength and having him there allows me to handle my day and get a lot accomplished. I don't think I could do what I do—or do it as well—if it wasn't for his support. He gets a great amount of pleasure from my being able to be in business and the fact that I enjoy it so much is something he can appreciate.

Thus we see that for wives, a good relationship and a good job can be mutually enhancing.

This does not seem to be as true for the other women. Many cohabiting women are in the process of defining their relationships so we think they are cautious about burdening them with worries from work. It is likely that they also take care to protect their work lives from the ups and downs of their private lives, and they do not wish to endanger the job in the event the relationship breaks up. They probably feel less free to allow a relationship to intrude into a work situation because their employers and co-workers may not consider cohabitation as serious an arrangement as marriage.

Much of what we think about female cohabitors we believe of lesbians as well. Lesbians may be inhibited even further from allowing a relationship to affect them on the job because they may have concealed its existence entirely and therefore be unable to display stress that comes from that quarter. Kathy and Liz have lived together for nine years. Kathy, forty, is a psychiatrist, and Liz, thirty-six, is a school psychologist. Liz told us:

> It's been tough at times. . . . Last year when she and I were going through a trial separation and it looked like we were going to break up—and she was living with another woman—I was in pain every day and I dreaded going to work and having to make light conversation. I kept thinking in my head that my whole life was cracking up but all I could do was look like nothing special was happening. I think that was a terrible strain on me and I know she experienced the same kind of thing later when she was going through tough times and she couldn't talk about it.

Another lesbian, in a six-year relationship, told us about having to hide her emotions at work:

> The absolute worst was one day I came in after being up all night crying because we were having another of our "should we stay together" conversations. My face was all blotchy and my eyes were puffy and several people tried to be nice, and asked me if anything was the matter. And I had to lie to them, 'cause I couldn't open up

then—after all those years—and I told them that a very close relative had died and so everyone gave me their condolences over that. . . . It was really shitty.

One lesbian, a hospital administrator, explained that she felt just as constrained about her private life even though she is not in the closet:

People know I'm gay but still I think that if I were going to bring up my issues when we were talking at the office, that some people wouldn't think it was in good taste.

Men try to segregate their emotional lives from their work lives. Historically, since men were expected to be the breadwinners, they could not allow themselves the luxury of letting their homelives influence how they did their jobs. This meant not letting their true feelings manifest themselves. For the most part, the world of work is not a therapeutic community. It teaches those who greatly invest themselves in it the absolute necessity of separating personal problems from the demands of the job. Those who learn this lesson well are likely to be rewarded professionally. We feel that when people orient themselves to their work and consider it essential for their survival, the more the division of the personal and the professional will occur.

---

*Husbands enjoy their work more than cohabiting men do.[4]*

What makes cohabiting men different from husbands? We think it is that cohabitors do not take the provider role as a central identity. Work may be important in their lives, but it is a source of personal accomplishment rather than an obligation to support a cherished partner. It could be argued that husbands have an extra burden because of the people dependent upon them, and that they should be more alienated from their work and worn down because of serious obligations. But we find that husbands actually enjoy their work more than cohabiting men do. We feel that providing for other people infuses their work with greater meaning, so that even a tedious job can reward them. Perhaps this is the truth behind the conventional wisdom frequently given to a young man—that marriage is good for him. The responsibilities of caring for a family may help him focus his efforts and cause him to be more serious about making himself a success. This may be part of the reason why many employers display a marked preference for married men.

*Gay men seem happier with their work if they are open about their sexual preference.*

There is a debate among psychologists, sociologists, and gay activists over whether it is psychologically harmful for gay people to keep their sexual preference a secret. In the interviews men told us about the compromises they had to make at work because they were "in the closet," and it seemed to us it diminished their satisfaction with their jobs. One reason a man chooses to stay in the closet is fear of losing his job or imperiling his relationship with his co-workers.[5] Being able to be open has distinct advantages—if a man survives the disclosure or has chosen a profession where his sexuality is not a concern to anyone. Dmitri and Walter have lived together for seventeen years. Dmitri is a nightclub singer and Walter is an executive for an automobile-manufacturing company. Dmitri told us how fortunate he is to have a job that allows him to admit that he is gay:

> We have a bone to pick over how "out" one or both of us should be. I am in the entertainment field and I picked that field because I refuse to live a lie, and I challenge anyone not to accept me for exactly who and what I am. . . . He is in the most conservative environment imaginable and he doesn't dare say anything about his home or me. . . . He can't take me to social events, whereas I take him to all of mine. . . . He gets upset with me because I am so open and I frankly think he suffers stress because of how he has to live. You'd think an employee of fourteen years' good work would not have to depend on such things to keep his job. . . . I think it is demoralizing for him and I would never never do such a thing.

Another gay man, who works as a flight attendant, has similar feelings:

> I have very lovely relations with the people I work with. I don't talk about being gay any more than they talk about their sexual needs, but everyone knows and I don't think anyone cares. . . . I suppose if I wanted a big promotion it might hurt me somewhere, but I don't think about that. . . . The price of pretending to be something I'm not is too high, and I have a much more pleasant day each day because I can let Andrew's name slip or mention that we are having people for dinner.

Gay men, like heterosexual men, do not want their private lives to affect their work. But some are keenly aware of the possible risk to their careers if their homosexuality is disclosed and this worry colors how at ease they can feel. In order to make exposure less likely, some may even create an imaginary heterosexual life. These men may hesitate to share casual banter with their co-workers for fear of saying something revealing, and co-workers, unaware of their sexual prefer-

ence, may unwittingly make jokes or derogatory remarks about homosexuals. If it were known that they were gay, they might be spared
these experiences.

If a lesbian is not open about her sexual preference, her satisfaction with her work seems to be affected less. Not only do lesbians prize
privacy more than our gay men, we think that people ask fewer questions about their personal lives.[6] A single woman, or a woman living
with another woman, is not as readily assumed to be homosexual and
so she is not likely to feel she has to give an account of her private life to
anyone. Sheila and Mia have been living together for seventeen years.
Sheila, forty-one, is head of neighborhood planning in a city government, and Mia, forty-three, is a dietician. Sheila believes strongly in the
virtues of being in the closet:

> No one asks about my private life and if someone did, I could give
> them a few leads to send them in the wrong direction and that would
> be that. . . . I don't see any reason to tell anyone anything. I don't
> think it's anyone else's business and I don't think it would help my
> work any. I have my friends and my private life and it works well to
> just let *those* people know. . . . You never know what people could
> use against you, or let fall even if they weren't meaning to. . . . I
> argue with her about this, because she would like to be more open,
> but I insist on discretion.

Another lesbian, fifty, an attorney in a federal agency, expressed
the same attitude:

> Lesbians of my age do not believe in all this rhetoric about coming
> out. The young gals do, because they think discrimination is
> something you can change. . . . Well, I don't, and furthermore, I
> think that people ought to be able to discriminate between who they
> want to be with and who they don't, at least on a personal basis. . . . I
> get along perfectly well with the people at work and that is based on
> professional business, which is fine. They respect my work and I
> respect theirs. There is no reason for them to have to evaluate me on
> other grounds.

---

*Wives, husbands, and cohabiting women are happier in their
relationships if their partners are successful in their jobs.
Male cohabitors are too competitive with their partners for
the women's success to enhance the relationship.*

Traditionally, a wife was assumed to take pleasure in her husband's
career as though it were her own. If her husband was successful, a wife
then considered herself successful. She would be treated in society on
the basis of her husband's accomplishments. We are not surprised to

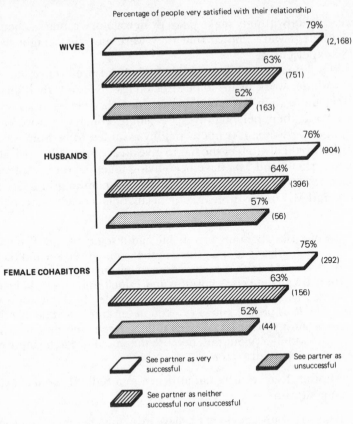

Percentage of people very satisfied with their relationship

**WIVES**
79% (2,168)
63% (751)
52% (163)

**HUSBANDS**
76% (904)
64% (396)
57% (56)

**FEMALE COHABITORS**
75% (292)
63% (156)
52% (44)

See partner as very successful

See partner as neither successful nor unsuccessful

See partner as unsuccessful

Note: In all these couples, the partner is employed full time.

Numbers in parentheses are the number of people on which the percentages are based.

FIGURE 21

find that this tradition still endures: When a wife has a successful husband she is more satisfied with her relationship.[7] We learned in interviews that when a wife feels that her husband is a success, she feels he is fulfilling the classic requirements of being a good spouse. He earns her respect as he has earned it in the outside world. She is pleased to be married to such a man and more content with their marriage. Alexandra and Whit have been married sixteen years. Alexandra, forty, is a homemaker, and Whit, forty-two, owns a plumbing-supply store. According to Alexandra:

> He has done better than I ever expected when we first started out. . . . All I wanted was security and a nice home, not having to worry about money, that sort of thing. . . . He has succeeded beyond my fantasies, and while it was not necessary for our marriage, I am

grateful for the ability to live as well as we do. . . . He may not have been a "catch" to my mother when we first married but I think she thinks of him as one now!

Another wife, married almost fifty years, expressed her pleasure about her husband's success as a building contractor:

> I always tell my children how lucky we are to have him. Particularly when I read in the paper about these men who desert their families, or don't work, or I hear about somebody not helping their kid with his education or, you know, deadbeat stuff. I tell them about what a good provider their father has been and how generous he is with them. . . . He has always worked very hard for a living and done a good job and I think he ought to be given credit for what he's accomplished for us.

It is not surprising that a wife is happier with her marriage when her husband is a success. What is surprising is that husbands feel the same way about their wives. Sociologists often imply that husbands do not derive any glory from a wife's success.[8] This is not generally true for the husbands in our study. Husbands with successful wives are happier with their marriages.[9] These are usually men who have chosen to be in a marriage where the woman is free to pursue her career fully, and neither partner is threatened at the prospect of sharing the provider role.[10] Milo and Estelle have been married for eighteen years. Milo, forty-one, is an engineer, and Estelle, thirty-nine, is an urban planner. Milo is proud of Estelle:

> Some of the guys in my company asked me if I was upset when she was promoted . . . last year. . . . I was shocked. Why would I be upset? Then I realized these guys would be upset if their wife started to get ahead and I began to wonder why, and I decided it must be because they are feeling crummy about themselves or are having some kind of trouble in the company. That's all I could think of. I was totally behind her working from the beginning—although I have to admit I was glad she waited till the kids were in kindergarten. . . . I want her to get as far as she wants to go. I think it helps us both out and it makes me proud of her.

Another married couple are both actors. They are in their mid-twenties and have been married less than two years. The husband takes pride in his wife's accomplishments:

> I respect her as an artist. I also respect the fact that she gets off her keister and gets out there and contributes to the mundane financial worries that we have. . . . I think the best thing that could happen is that we both make it and can arrange work together or help out each other's careers some of the time. . . . In the beginning, we worried that we might resent it if one of us got a call-back or got asked to read and the other didn't. But I think we are genuinely happy for one another when some good news happens. . . . We think as a team.

Women who are in living-together arrangements feel the same way wives do. Even without a marriage contract, they take pleasure in their partner's accomplishments.[11] But male cohabitors are not like the husbands: Their partner's success or lack of it does not affect the way they feel about the relationship.[12] We think this may have something to do with competitiveness between the two partners.[13] Phil and Judi have been living together for nine years. Phil, thirty-four, teaches sculpture, and Judi, thirty-one, is a painter. Judi described what she sees as Phil's competitiveness:

> Sometimes I feel like he is looking over my work looking for flaws. I don't always trust his criticisms. I think this is particularly true when he's feeling frustrated or blocked. If I think he is taking his frustrations out on me, I tell him so, and we can get into a pretty good row about it. . . . I sometimes wish we were doing work that was more different from one another than it is. Sometimes the collaboration is great and creative, but when he gets competitive, I get offended and then I get depressed.

Another male cohabitor, in his early twenties, complained to us about his relationship and his partner's success at work:

> She makes a lot more money than I do, which I must admit is touchy with us. . . . I would like her to cut back. I don't think we need the money so much, and we could use the time together. I think she is driven to work in ways that are not flattering to her.

It is ironic that male cohabitors hold to the belief that their partners should be independent—and they have partners who are eager to oblige—yet they are not happier when their partners have dramatically proved their ability to be self-reliant. Some male cohabitors are inclined to construe a partner's drive as competition with him, rather than dedication to her work.

---

*A working wife makes her husband more ambitious.[14]*

In our study we talked to many husbands who are not only happy that their wives work but derive great pleasure from their success. They do not, however, want their wives to take over the provider role. Instead, we feel a wife's accomplishments spur a husband to set higher goals for himself. He may not wish to do better than his wife, but he certainly does not want to do less well. Even most modern-day egalitarian husbands do not want to play a secondary role to their wives, either in their own eyes, their wives' eyes, or the eyes of the world. The wife of such a man may receive mixed messages. Her husband encourages her to achieve great things, but he is likely to become competitive if she begins to surpass what he has done.[15] Some competition is quite common, but if it becomes excessive the couple may start to take less pleasure in each other. We find that couples who say they suffer a lot of competition are less happy in their marriage.[16]

*Only gay men judge their success by comparing it to what their partners have achieved.*

All partners in all four kinds of couples feel successful when they earn a high income.[17] But only gay men feel even more successful if their partner's income is lower.[18] We believe that when men evaluate their success they look for someone to measure themselves against. The likely comparisons have traditionally been other men—co-workers, people in similar jobs, friends, or neighbors. Gay men have another man close to them—their partner—who can become a basis for comparison. Heterosexual men do not feel especially successful when their female partners make little money. They have not been accustomed to competing with women because it is difficult for women to achieve the same level of earning power as men do in our society.

Heterosexual women do not use their partner's success as a point of comparison. They are more likely to want him to succeed because his attainment will reflect favorably on them. While women no longer define themselves *only* by what their male partners have achieved, our society still categorizes a woman according to her husband's status. It is therefore impossible to imagine a heterosexual woman feeling better about herself if her partner is a failure, or earning little money. And finally, lesbians, like other women, have learned to want an accomplished partner.[19]

A man's sense of his worth is strongly affected by how he performs at work. He might like to compartmentalize his life, keeping the frustrations and setbacks of his job separate from his life at home, and to some extent he is able to do this. But work can intrude into his home environment in a number of subtle ways. For example, when he arrives home from work, he may very well be greeted by a partner who also works. And no matter how well he is doing in his career, his partner may be doing even better. He may think, as most people do, that he judges himself by the standards set by the marketplace. A promotion, a raise, or a special compliment from a supervisor are the clear and established signs of accomplishment. But these pleasures may be short-lived if he discovers that his own achievement pales in comparison to someone else's. In two-paycheck couples, the person he chooses to compare himself with may be his partner.

The American occupational structure has traditionally conspired to reduce the prospect of such competition between men and women. When women worked, they were employed in different occupations, almost always of a lower status, and they earned significantly lower wages. For example, a man might have begun work as a stockboy, but he could entertain the not too improbable dream of moving up. If a woman began as a clerk, she might be praised for doing her job well, but no one in the firm would mark her for a more responsible position. Now that women are more interested in and able to have careers, their mobility is not so impeded, and so there is a greater chance that both partners will have similar jobs with similar chances for success. Thus opportunities for comparison can present themselves, even among intimates, and gradually create tension in the relationship. A wife's success pleases her husband only if he is doing well himself. With a working wife, his home may become less of a haven and just another reminder of what he perceives to be his inadequacies.

We might have suspected that the tensions created by work would be magnified when both partners are men. Work is likely to be valued by both partners, both have access to similar kinds of jobs, and comparisons can be made more readily. We find, however, that while gay male couples do compete some of the time, their struggles are not worse than those of married couples with a successful working wife.[20] We think men grow more accustomed to competing with other men and they learn that sometimes they will lose. That is the nature of the game in the work place. When one gay man is more successful than his partner, he may gain some status. This may indeed cause competition in the relationship, but unlike the situation where the wife outdistances the husband, the less successful partner is not seen as having failed as a provider.

Lesbians may want their partners to be successful and ambitious, but they do not make invidious comparisons. Lesbians prize the same qualities in their partners that heterosexual women do. And they confront the same expectations from their partners that heterosexual men do. Yet, unlike heterosexual men, lesbians do not become competitive with a partner whose career is going well. This makes us think it is not women's working and achieving that causes problems between partners. Rather, the source is the difficulty men have in accepting female equality.

# Work versus the relationship

## The impact of priorities

Lord Byron wrote: "Man's love is of man's life a thing apart; / 'Tis woman's whole existence."[1] In contemporary society, however, many women and men might argue the point. And so we think it is useful to recognize that *some* men and *some* women are what we call "relationship-centered" while others put the greater part of their time and energy into other interests. We call this latter group "work-centered" although this term includes additional commitments, such as charitable works or an all-consuming hobby. We grouped people according to how they answered the following question:

> How much emotional energy do you . . . give your relationship, as compared to work and other outside activities?

Why do we make these distinctions? We believe that putting one's work first or putting one's partner first has a lot to do with the way a couple functions. More might be expected and asked of a partner who is recognized to be relationship-centered, while a partner who is work-centered may be let off the hook. We also wanted to know if it is important for both partners to share the same outlook (relationship-centered or work-centered), or if it is better if they do not.

We proceed from the assumption that few people intentionally structure their lives so that their relationship receives less attention than their work. But work sometimes takes. If one partner is the primary financial support of the couple, little explanation of time spent nine to five is necessary. Even if he or she spends time away from the household because work unconsciously provides the kind of psychological gratification that equals or even surpasses what is received at home, that fact never has to surface. The person can say, "I'm working for *us*," or, "I'm working because I have to," and may not consciously perceive any other motivation.

In American society, these responses are more often heard from husbands because they are usually the breadwinners. A traditional husband can pay less attention to the relationship because he knows he can rely on his wife to tend to the couple's emotional life. She is expected to be relationship-centered. Modern two-paycheck couples, married or not, have a dilemma. Neither partner may have time to take care of the relationship. If one employed partner is not really work-centered, he or she may try to reserve enough emotional energy to attend to the needs of the relationship, but this may be hard to accomplish when so many jobs require total commitment. A husband who takes a day off to stay home with his children because his wife cannot get away from her work may—as a result—be seen by his employer as not sufficiently ambitious to be promoted. This is the same attitude women have traditionally faced: Because they have always been presumed to be relationship-centered, they have not been taken seriously in the work world. The irony is that a woman who presents herself as committed solely to her work may be seen as a "failed woman" and hence a less worthy person. This, too, may undermine her professional advancement.

If a two-paycheck couple has no one who is taking responsibility for the emotional life of the relationship, they may be unaware their relationship is on "automatic pilot" and only notice when they hit turbulence. They may have been relying on the traditional pattern, assuming that things would take care of themselves because marriages are known to contain a built-in relationship guardian in the wife. But in relationships that do not have a traditional wife, the automatic caretaker of the relationship may be lost. Thus we are concerned to discover: Is it only tradition that makes one person the caretaker, and is there no caretaker without the wife's devotion to that role? Or do all women take on that role to some extent even if they have jobs or careers? Or does the more tender and understanding partner become the guardian, regardless of gender?

A related issue is how much time the relationship actually receives as opposed to how much time the couple thinks it *ought* to get. Does time together get lost in each partner's busy schedule? And if it does, how does that affect the relationship? We asked couples how often they have dinner together, how many evenings they spend with each other, whether they share hobbies, see movies, and enjoy friends together. Some people told us that they live very separate lives while others proved to be constant companions. But many, regardless of how much time they spend together, indicated that it was also important for them to have some *private* time. People frequently talked about the need for personal space. They wanted time not shared with their partner, accountable to no one. Psychoanalyst Erik Erikson wrote about the various stages of maturation and described one stage as a resolution of the tension between autonomy and intimacy.[2] Erikson felt individuals had to learn how to give up a part of themselves in order to become interdependent with someone else.

In some lives, work is the medium of autonomy. Modern life usually necessitates that the work environment be separate from one's home. Work in the industrialized world is now much more compartmentalized than in our ancestors' rural existence. On the farm, life and livelihood melded together. Today, with the evolution of occupations that require specific training and specific environments, work has become segregated from the rest of life. The home relationship is one sphere far removed from everything else. We feel modern work habits created the idea of time that is private and separate from one's partner. Now they have caused people to begin to think of time that is separate from one's partner even when they are away from their work environment. People have moved from seeing their lives as divided between work and their relationship to viewing it as divided into three parts: the relationship, work, and private time all to oneself. In contemporary relationships a crucial question couples confront is: How much time should be allotted to each other, and how much to oneself and outside commitments?

*Women and men who are compassionate, understanding,*
*and tender are more relationship-centered and less involved*
*in work and other interests.[3]*

All women, both heterosexual and homosexual, are more likely than
men to put their relationships before their work.[4] We also find that
among all the people in our study, irrespective of gender or sexual
preference, those who describe themselves as having "feminine" characteristics (tender, compassionate, and understanding) are more likely
to focus more of their energies on the relationship than on work.[5]

Psychologists and sociologists have assumed that women tend to
put their relationships before anything else and that this is biologically
determined or, at the very least, a consequence of having been taught
all their lives that the most important things in the world were their
partners and families.[6] But our data show that anyone who learns to be
tender, compassionate, and understanding will value a relationship
over other parts of life. What we call "feminine" characteristics are
more often present in women, but they are not *necessarily* found in

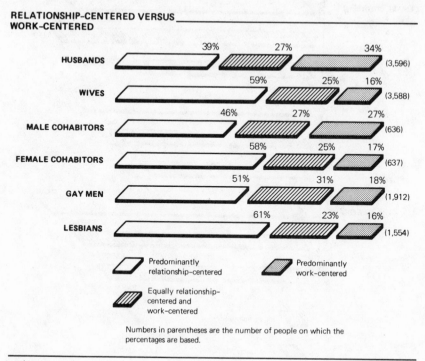

**RELATIONSHIP-CENTERED VERSUS**
**WORK-CENTERED**

|  | Predominantly relationship-centered | Equally relationship-centered and work-centered | Predominantly work-centered |  |
|---|---|---|---|---|
| HUSBANDS | 39% | 27% | 34% | (3,596) |
| WIVES | 59% | 25% | 16% | (3,588) |
| MALE COHABITORS | 46% | 27% | 27% | (636) |
| FEMALE COHABITORS | 58% | 25% | 17% | (637) |
| GAY MEN | 51% | 31% | 18% | (1,912) |
| LESBIANS | 61% | 23% | 16% | (1,554) |

Predominantly relationship-centered

Predominantly work-centered

Equally relationship-centered and work-centered

Numbers in parentheses are the number of people on which the percentages are based.

FIGURE    22

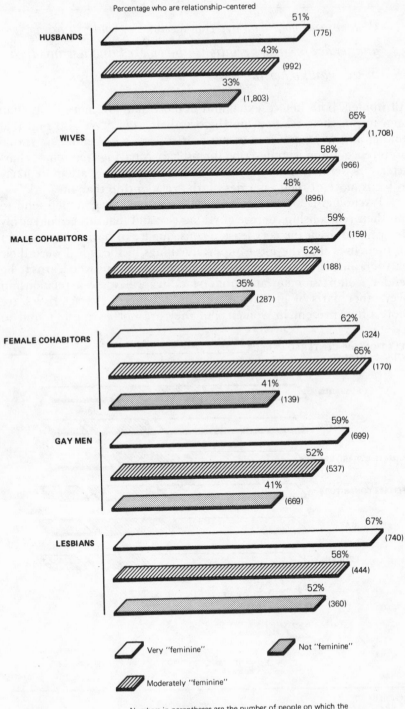

Percentage who are relationship-centered

**HUSBANDS**
51% (775)
43% (992)
33% (1,803)

**WIVES**
65% (1,708)
58% (966)
48% (896)

**MALE COHABITORS**
59% (159)
52% (188)
35% (287)

**FEMALE COHABITORS**
62% (324)
65% (170)
41% (139)

**GAY MEN**
59% (699)
52% (537)
41% (669)

**LESBIANS**
67% (740)
58% (444)
52% (360)

Very "feminine"    Not "feminine"

Moderately "feminine"

Numbers in parentheses are the number of people on which the
percentages are based.

FIGURE   23

women or *only* found in women.[7] It is good to take note of the number of work-centered women and the number of relationship-centered men we have in our study. When men develop feminine qualities, we find that they too center their emotions around their home life rather than the work place.[8] These qualities are precisely the ones that women have wanted their male partners to possess and many women have made it an issue that men should work to develop them.[9] Cohabiting men, in general, are more sympathetic than husbands to what the women's movement asks of them. We find in our data that these men see themselves as more "feminine" and are also more relationship-centered than husbands are.[10] Tammy and Leland have lived together for three years. Tammy, twenty-nine, is a literary agent, and Leland, thirty, is a business executive. Leland told us about the care he takes to make sure that his work does not take him away from his relationship:

> It is very important to me that she and I have enough time together.
> For a while there I was getting engulfed by what the company
> wanted from me and we were getting into this cycle where we only
> saw each other when we were too tired to care. We were getting very
> ordinary to one another and I was forgetting why we were in
> love. . . . We started talking about it and I decided to cut back, and
> she cut back some too, so that we didn't start to drift away from one
> another.

Another couple who have lived together for three years, are also careful not to allow work to overwhelm their lives. Howard, forty-two, works in a recording studio. Cheryl, twenty-nine, works in public relations. Even though his job is very high pressured, Howard still puts his relationship first:

> My father was never home and when we were growing up I always
> ` felt it was because we weren't quite good enough to capture his
> emotions. . . . I swore that when I got older and had a family that I
> was not going to get trapped by my work and all that male shit and
> not get to know my kids. . . . I have joint custody with my kids from
> my marriage and if Cheryl and I have kids it will be fifty percent or
> more on my part.

All of this does not mean that these male cohabitors have lost or given up any of their "masculinity." We find that they—as well as husbands who are relationship-centered—do not describe themselves as any less masculine (forceful, aggressive, or outgoing) than men who center their lives around work.[11]

Some husbands might actually wish to be more relationship-centered, but feel held back by their responsibilities as provider for the family. As one husband, married more than thirty years, told us:

> She complains sometimes that I'm not nice enough to her, that I
> don't think of her enough, forget birthdays, that sort of thing. And I

always apologize because I think there is some truth in that, but not because I don't love her or appreciate her. I am out there taking my lumps earning a living and a lot of times I don't have room to think about anything but earning a living. . . . Or sometimes I'm just sort of absentminded because I have to think about how we're going to get through the next pay period. . . . She understands, but I don't think she understands as much as she should . . . which may be partly my fault because I don't like to worry her all the time. . . . But I don't want her to think I don't love her. I just have to keep us economically afloat.

Duane, twenty-eight, is an auto worker, and his wife, Jeanine, twenty-three, is a part-time receptionist. They have been married four years. Duane feels he cannot afford the luxury of spending the kind of time with her that Jeanine would like:

I don't have time to sit around and be social with her girl friends, and boy, does she think I'm rude. . . . Sure I might like to take time out for gabbing—just like she does—but I don't have the time. I think my boss would love it if I said I can't work on Saturday because my wife wants me to visit with her girl friends. . . . We have some doozie of fights about what's important around here.

Because of the nature of the provider role, these men feel they cannot drain energy from their work or develop characteristics that they believe would undermine their ability to achieve.

Because men, in general, are less relationship-centered than women, we might suspect that an all-male couple would have no one to care for the relationship and the two partners would resemble roommates more than lovers. But individual gay men are on average more relationship-centered than husbands or even male cohabitors.[12] They describe themselves on the questionnaire as more tender, compassionate, and understanding ("feminine").[13] But as with heterosexual men with "feminine" characteristics, relationship-centered gay men are no less "masculine" than work-centered gay men; just as many characterized themselves as forceful, aggressive, and outgoing.[14]

---

*The majority of couples, heterosexual and homosexual, have at least one partner who is relationship-centered. Couples without a relationship-centered partner are less satisfied and less committed.*

---

Not all couples have two partners who both strike the same balance between relationship and work. In some couples both partners give most of their emotional energy to the relationship. In others both channel themselves toward their work. There are still others in which one partner attends to the relationship while the other emphasizes work. Traditional marriages were composed of this third type of couple. The man was supposed to think mostly of his work and the woman was supposed to think mostly of the relationship. In the past, sociologists, economists, and the average person felt that this kind of arrangement was best.[15]

At the same time, social scientists who study couples have argued that if the couple is to endure, they should see eye-to-eye on important values.[16] According to this view, two partners who invested themselves in their work would have more to talk about, and be more sympathetic to how work affects the other's life and their relationship. Similarly, when two partners were relationship-centered they would both be devoted to protecting their relationship from outside demands. Critics of this last perspective might contend that it might be all well and good for two partners to share a single vision, but if neither was relationship-centered, then the couple would be endangered because it possessed no caretaker.

We find, among all four types of couples, that the majority have either one or two relationship-centered partners. Among married couples we are not surprised to find a large number where the husband applies more of his energy to his job and the wife to the needs of the relationship. This is not true for *all* married couples. In one quarter of all the married couples in our study, both partners are relationship-centered, and in another 6 percent, there is no caretaker. We even find 13 percent in which partners have reversed the traditional roles: The wife dedicates herself to her job, and the husband focuses on the relationship.[17]

**RELATIONSHIP-CENTERED COUPLES, WORK-CENTERED COUPLES, AND MIXED COUPLES**

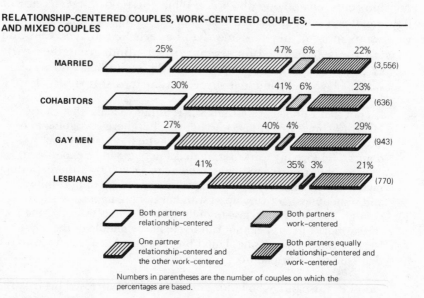

FIGURE 24

Cohabitors are not very different from the married couples. But there are more male cohabitors who are relationship-centered than there are husbands. This means there are fewer traditional couples in which the woman is the sole guardian of the relationship among the cohabitors.[18]

The gay and lesbian couples look very much like the heterosexual couples, in that there is a substantial number in which one partner is work-centered, while the other is the caretaker of the relationship. Since same-sex couples have no tradition of having one caretaker, it moves us to speculate why they should be so like the heterosexual couples. There may be something in the nature of attraction that includes a desire to live with a person who operates in a different sphere of interest from our own.[19] It may also be true that as a relationship deepens, specialization develops even if people start out similarly inclined. If one partner knows that the other is always looking after the couple's emotional well-being, then he or she may feel able to put more energy into work, secure in the knowledge that all is safe at home. The fact that there are such a great number of couples, heterosexual *and* homosexual, who show this kind of pattern indicates to us that this is one area in which many people prefer to be different, not similar.

We find that couples in which both partners are relationship-centered are the happiest and most committed of all those in our study. Couples with one partner of each type fall in between. And at the other extreme, couples in which neither partner is relationship-centered are the least happy and least committed of all.[20]

Married couples are most likely to have one partner who is relationship-centered and one who is not. While this is not always a cause of fighting, it can sometimes create turmoil within the marriage when the wife wants more of her husband than he feels he can give. Clay and Mindy have been married for seventeen years. Both are in their early forties. Mindy is a full-time homemaker who occasionally does volunteer work. Clay is a prominent surgeon. Clay took this view:

> It's not that I don't care. I think she is unfair to make that charge. My work comes first. I love my children, but there isn't going to be anything for them if I don't do my work the way it should be done. . . . I love my work; I have to if I'm going to be expert at it. I count on her to manage things at home so I can be out there, putting myself on the line. . . . My work gives us incredible opportunities and sometimes I get very upset with her not taking it seriously enough. She has come close to undermining things by not giving me the support I need. I cannot run home in the middle of the day because the dog is missing. I am upset about it, but she can't insist on that kind of participation.

Another husband, who holds down two jobs, expressed his frustration:

I am in a very competitive field and it takes whatever I have to get ahead in it. I am . . . working one job at one in the afternoon all day and then I teach till about nine at night. . . . So that means all I have is the mornings for myself, for anyone else. . . . I cannot use this time to do too much with the kids or be the second parent in the way she wants. I know this is very frustrating to her, but I didn't want kids too much in the first place for just this reason, and I did warn her that it was going to be hard for a while. . . . She doesn't understand how my life can be this busy. But she doesn't understand that two jobs is really two jobs and one of those jobs requires an endless amount of time. . . . She is just going to have to hold down the fort for a while.

The wife of such a man may agree that her primary duty is to their home and children, but she may still feel deprived. In order to cope with a meager amount of companionship from her husband, she may begin to deliberate about going to work as a release for her energies. This happened to Audrey. She is forty-two and has been married to Leo, forty-six, for twenty-one years. He is director of a nursing home and she now works as an editorial assistant in a publishing company. Audrey said:

My job is strictly subordinate to my other duties, but it turns out that the household has gotten easier to manage over the years and I have a lot of time left over. . . . When it got to the point where I was having to get imaginative about what to do—another cooking course, another exercise class—I decided that it was getting ridiculous. So I polished up my old B.A. and went out to see if anybody wanted to hire me. . . . I was so euphoric when I got hired . . . I couldn't wait to tell Leo. He was unflatteringly amazed. "Why did you want to go out and get a job?" he said. So I said, "Well, I was just tired of sitting around the house. If you have more time to give me, maybe I don't need to work." That shut him up.

At the time these traditional couples married, both partners often agreed that he would get a job and she would stay home. Neither realized that being home alone might not give her as much companionship as she wanted.

We think there is a subtle interaction between where people put their emotional energy (home versus work) and their commitment to their relationship. It is difficult for us to establish which is the cause and which is the effect. When a relationship fails, each partner may very well seek refuge in his or her work, and this is undoubtedly the pattern for many couples. We also think the reverse is often true: When two partners become so involved in their work that neither watches the relationship, even a relationship that started out on a firm footing may be undermined. We sometimes see evidence of this in our interviews. Some couples told us that they had found themselves moving toward separation and were able to resolve their problems by reducing the amount of time and energy one or both put into their jobs. For example, David and Abigail, married twenty-six years, told us what happened when David lost his job: It actually helped their relationship indirectly. David explained:

> I haven't worked since last March. . . . I'm looking forward in a few months to a . . . brand-new job. So my life has been different. . . . Before, I was so deeply involved in my job that I was going right and Abigail was going left, and when I was terminated in March of this year, they did me a favor because we were getting further and further apart, and we had to—and we did—get into counseling. So we made a hundred-and-eighty-degree turn and we love each other now, whereas a year ago we didn't because I was too involved in my job. Now we can sit and hold hands and say nothing and that's fine. We don't have to be out dancing or drinking or all this kind of garbage. We didn't have the money, and now we don't have the desire to do that sort of thing.

---

*Fighting about the intrusion of work into the relationship can undermine a couple's satisfaction.*

---

People's jobs are commonly seen as competing with time and energy that could be spent on the relationship and so they are very often a source of conflict. Heterosexual women are the angriest with their partners about the intrusion of work on their private time together.[21] If a woman accepts the idea of the man as breadwinner, or simply wants him to be a success, then part of the bargain is living with the great claims his work makes on him. On the one hand, it is commonly believed that if a man is to get ahead, he needs the freedom to dedicate himself to his work. On the other hand, many women know all too well that family life can be sabotaged by his work schedule and by the fact that his job may take precedence over her needs. As one wife, married thirty years, told us:

> When we first got married, the first six months of conflicts were all about getting him to take account of what I had planned for him at home. . . . He would come waltzing in an hour and a half late for dinner, or cancel an evening with friends, because he had to close a deal. . . . We would argue and argue . . . not because I didn't want him to make a living . . . but because I thought he had to be more considerate and that some things just could not be canceled at the last moment. . . . We solved it by starting dinner when he got home . . . and scheduling fewer evening commitments.

Another wife, married two years, explained how she and her husband had to change their life because their careers were taking a big toll on their marriage:

> We both are very serious and ambitious about our careers but we also have seen what a nonstop schedule can do to us. There was a while there where we were working different parts of the day and night and were not seeing each other at all. We made lunch dates, but the quality of time we had together was defeating the relationship. . . . We finally had a long talk about the general joylessness that had taken us over and we decided to bypass any jobs that made it impossible to have good, quality time together.

Couples reduce the bickering over the man's job in a number of ways. When a woman knows that her partner genuinely values time with her, she is less upset about his work because she takes comfort in the assurance that he would be with her if he could. But when a man says, "It is important that our relationship does not interfere with other important parts of my life," or, "There are times when I am with my friends and I do not want my partner along," or, "It is important to me that my partner spend some time without me," a woman may feel that he is intentionally denying her companionship.[22]

Wives do not just accept the intrusions their husbands' work creates. We find the arguments they have lessen wives' overall happiness or commitment.[23] The same is true for husbands. If a wife's job interferes with what her husband wants from their relationship, he may begin to question the viability of the marriage: Our data show that when married couples fight about the ways in which the wife's work intrudes upon the couple's life, the husband is less satisfied and less committed.[24]

Sometimes conflict flares up because the husband does not acknowledge the changes that will have to take place in the household. This is a common theme in interviews with husbands and wives. He may want the house to be as clean as it has always been, the children perfectly monitored, and his wife still available for leisure activities. He may be asking her to be a "superwoman," and not conscious of what that expectation may cost her. He may also be unaware that she needs to talk about her work. And even if he is aware, he may find her complaints about her job tiresome and upsetting. A husband may feel he suffers enough stress from his own work and therefore it is unfair of his wife to burden him with hers.

Among cohabitors and gay male couples, both partners want recognition and sympathy for the demands of their jobs. If the couple fights about work-related issues, the partners become less satisfied.[25] Lesbians confront the same opportunities for conflict and when arguments arise, they undermine their general satisfaction.[26]

*Among heterosexuals, young men have less desire for their partner's companionship than do young women, but the tables turn as the couple ages.*

Young heterosexual women are disappointed about the amount of time they get to spend with their partners.[27] During the excitement of courtship a man takes time away from his work and other interests to lavish it upon her. Courtship is usually a time for sharing activities, intense conversations, and emotional intimacy. The experience can confirm a woman's romantic hopes of what a companionate relationship will be like. But these women may be in for a disappointment. After their marriage, or when they move in together, men soon return to their previous routines, occupying themselves with the mundane but necessary task of making a living. Intense conversations and time alone together may become scarcer commodities for the couple.

As heterosexual women age, we think they adapt to spending less time with them and develop lives of their own. Perry and Renee have been married for thirty-five years. Renee, fifty-three, works in a religious bookstore, and Perry, fifty-five, is a city planner. Renee described how she developed her own interests during their marriage:

> The thing I resented most was the duck club. . . . He would go off every weekend in the season and go shoot and I would be absolutely stranded. . . . I tried once to go along but that was even worse. He would go off into the blind and it was wet and rainy and ugly and I would be stuck with the other wives and stuck with all the cooking when they brought the ducks in. I really resented losing all that time on the weekend after not having much time in the week. . . . There was also steelhead season and fly-fishing season. . . . Finally I got over my resentment. . . . After all, it was what made him happy, so I just developed hobbies of my own and I started work part time . . . which eventually led to this . . . so it all worked out quite well.

Sophia and Stavros have been living together for six years. Both are divorced. Stavros, thirty-six, is an importer, and Sophia, thirty-eight, is a dressmaker. Sophia described the difficulty she had in her former marriage because she had to get used to her husband's not being around:

> I am much more understanding about conflicting schedules these days. When I was first married, my ex-husband and I always fought about how much time he spent at work and with clients. I would sit home and wait for him and by the time he would get home I would be in a proper rage. . . . I never have any problems like that with Stavros. We go our own way. Perhaps too much, but I think it is very important to be able to give him his own time and for me to have my

own time. We are very informal, so if he has to stay late at work or take work home or whatever I really don't let it get to me. . . . We worked that out before we moved in together because both of us had experienced it as a problem when we were married [before].

As men get older their desire for time with their partners increases.[28] We believe this is because men become more secure in their jobs and better skilled at keeping them from intruding on their private lives. In the meantime, they have learned to depend on their partners' company. In fact, we find that husbands married for many years come to rely on their wives to provide their social life. They spend more evenings at home and they are more inclined to include her in all their leisure activities. They spend less time with their male friends, choosing instead to be at gatherings with other couples.[29] From the interviews, we heard from wives that they sometimes greet this turn of events unenthusiastically. They enjoy their husband's company, but they have become used to a lot of private time and do not want to lose it to his needs. We find that older women encourage their husbands to spend more time without them.[30] One wife of sixty-six told us about her husband of forty-four years:

I have to say that I would like more time by myself. . . . His needs are different from mine, and sometimes I would like him around and sometimes I just don't. . . . He can just feel alone even when I'm in the room, whereas I really need to be alone. He would prefer to do everything with me in the room. He doesn't even need to read alone, whereas I like to go off and really have some private time. . . . This has become much more intense ever since he retired because he wants to fill up all that time with me and I want time alone or I want to go over and see the children and do things for them. . . . I have been hoping that he will get active in one of these organizations or something because I am not going to be with him all the time.

Manfred and Emily have been married for thirty-three years. Both are fifty-two. Emily is a full-time homemaker and Manfred is a mechanic. Emily told us how surprised she was to realize that she now has too much of Manfred's company:

It's not like it used to be, I can tell you that. Used to be, I would have to call around trying to find out where he was and there were three or four places I would find him that I wasn't too happy about. . . . He did a lot of card playing and drinking and just spending time at the Democratic club. . . . Now he is just Mr. Homebody. He doesn't have too many friends anymore and he looks to me for what to do. I tell him to go out and look up these old buddies because I don't think he should be dependent on me all the time. I don't need him to be around all the time. . . . Whoever thought I'd be complaining about too much of Manfred?

*Young or old, lesbians cannot seem to find enough time together. Young or old, gay men are more satisfied with the amount of time they do have.*

Lesbian couples tend to be relationship-centered. At the same time, many lesbians believe that women should be able to take care of themselves and not be dependent on their partners. They are eager to succeed in their careers and encourage their partners to do the same.[31] However, they frequently discover that the demands of work and social life take them away from their partner much more than they would like. Lesbians are so relationship-centered that even though they profess a strong commitment to independence, they yearn for more time together.[32] Rochelle and Victoria have lived together for six years and both are in their late twenties. Rochelle is a stenographer and Victoria is a psychiatric nurse. Rochelle described their attempt to find a middle ground:

> I think it is important that I get to go out alone and that she doesn't feel like she has the right to be everywhere I am. I feel strongly that we should have separate friends and that we don't have to have friends as a couple. . . . I think my last lover would fuse her identity with mine and I found that very bad for her head and very bad for mine and this probably broke us up. . . . She gets upset about how strongly I feel that we need our separate space. She feels that we don't have enough time together as it is and she feels that we need to coordinate our lives more. I am very sympathetic and we sit down with our calendars every week to make sure we get enough time. It is hard to be together enough and so we make sure that at least one day a weekend we spend the whole day together and talk about our week and catch up. . . . It's not so hard to compromise with her because we are both in love with one another and it's just a question of putting together . . . our time.

Another woman, in a seventeen-year relationship, explained that she and her partner arrange to have time separate from one another, and yet they never feel they can be together enough:

> We have most of our time together, but then it's kind of like being in a room with someone and being totally comfortable and not have a word be said. . . . We share everything but we also know how to back away from each other so we both have private times, and private feelings. . . . Sometimes she will take a week of vacation one week and I will take a week of vacation another week, just to give ourselves a little room to grow, but not because we don't love each other and want to be with one another. We just know that we are individuals and that we need private time and we try to make space for that for one another. . . . We could be with each other one hundred hours

each and every day and not get bored, but we don't think that is good for our individuality. . . . So we never get enough of one another but we don't crowd each other either.

Gay men are quite like husbands: When they are young, they need a lot of personal freedom.[33] They may be absorbed in their careers or, because they are men, they may have had little practice at adapting their lives to spend a lot of time with a partner. However, unlike husbands, gay men are likely to have a partner who feels the same way. There is no female to feel upset because her needs for companionship exceed her partner's. Also, like husbands, as they get older, they settle down and develop a greater appreciation for more companionship. Palmer and Monty have lived together for almost eight years and both are forty-four. Palmer is a banker and Monty is a professional fund-raiser. Palmer commented:

> I think we barely have enough time together. I have modified my schedule so that we can have more time together even though it meant that I passed up a good career opportunity that would have meant more money and more prestige. . . . The reason I passed it up is that it also would have meant a stepped-up pace and that would have cut down on what little time we have now. I've gotten to a stage in my life where an additional title or an additional few dollars is not as important as what he and I have together. We want to be open to many things. We want the freedom to be spontaneous. We have such a good time when we are alone together just fixing things around the house or laughing at a late-night movie together. These are the things I want to preserve now—which is something I wouldn't have been smart enough to know twenty years ago.

Another couple have lived together for eleven years. Kazuo, forty-seven, teaches in a community college, and Tad, fifty-four, manages a record store. Their time together is very important to Tad:

> We are homebodies. We get up early so that we can have breakfast together and so we're not rushing around in the morning and miss that time to see each other. We'll have a long slow breakfast at about seven A.M. and talk about what the day looks like and what we're reading and what we think of it and errands and plans for the evening—a little bit of everything. When my day doesn't start like that, I feel deprived. . . . We've grown used to being each other's best friend. It's amazing that we never run out of things to talk about. . . . We even call each other at the office to tell something we forgot to mention. . . . I actually look forward to retirement so that we'll have more time together and we don't have to rush off anywhere.

*Same-sex couples build a life together by sharing more leisure activities than do heterosexual couples. This may have more serious consequences than either heterosexual or same-sex couples realize.*

Heterosexual men and women are more likely to go their separate ways for leisure activities than are lesbians or gay men. When they spend time on hobbies or go to spectator sports, they are more often alone or with their own friends. Russell and Paula have been married for fifteen years. Russell, forty, works as a technician in a TV studio, and Paula, thirty-eight, is a nurse's aide. Russell explained:

> I enjoy her company very much but there are certain things we do separately. I have these all-night card games maybe once a week, maybe once every two weeks. I wouldn't have her there. Too raunchy. It's just me and my friends and it's been a traditional thing for I don't know how many years. She has asked to come once or twice but I tell her that it's just off limits. Not that she wouldn't add a bit of class, but I think there are other things that she and I can do together. This one is just for the boys. Don't let it rub you the wrong way. You know, she has stuff she does just with her friends too. Nothing wrong with a little time off.

Russell emphasized that he sometimes needed to be in a setting that was not really appropriate for women. Another husband felt that there are certain activities that men can enjoy more than women:

> Probably sports are where she and I are going to get into the soup. I'm a member of an intramural program and I take it like a religious program. We are a very fine team which means we have to practice a lot and also means we always go into the playoffs and not just the regular season. This requires a lot of time, and from time to time she feels left out. . . . I just like being around people who understand the game. For example, I prefer to take my son [from a previous marriage] to games rather than Barbie. Barbie is always asking basic questions, or she won't get as gripped by the action as we will. So I prefer to be with someone who gets into it and yells and screams and acts as crazy as I do. I could go with Barbie but it really wouldn't be as much fun. So most of the time I don't. She mostly understands.

Same-sex couples are more likely to include their partners in leisure activities. Very often they share hobbies, belong to the same clubs, go to sports events, and socialize with friends together.[34]

Why do heterosexuals share fewer leisure activities with their partners? In our interviews, heterosexual men and women told us that problems arose when they wanted time to do things alone or with friends but not with their partners. They rejected any suggestion that they did not enjoy their partners' company and repeated what they had

## HAVING HOBBIES AND ATTENDING CLUB MEETINGS
## WITHOUT ONE'S PARTNER

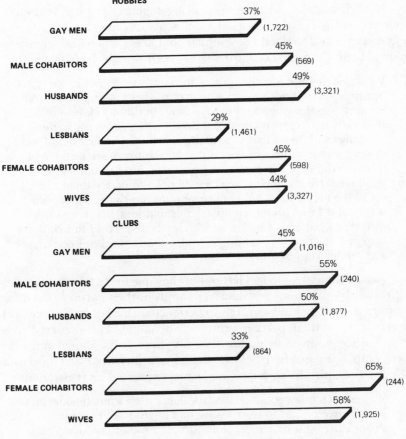

Percentage of people who have hobbies or attend club meetings, usually without their partners

**HOBBIES**

| | |
|---|---|
| GAY MEN | 37% (1,722) |
| MALE COHABITORS | 45% (569) |
| HUSBANDS | 49% (3,321) |
| LESBIANS | 29% (1,461) |
| FEMALE COHABITORS | 45% (598) |
| WIVES | 44% (3,327) |

**CLUBS**

| | |
|---|---|
| GAY MEN | 45% (1,016) |
| MALE COHABITORS | 55% (240) |
| HUSBANDS | 50% (1,877) |
| LESBIANS | 33% (864) |
| FEMALE COHABITORS | 65% (244) |
| WIVES | 58% (1,925) |

Numbers in parentheses are the number of people who have hobbies or who attend club meetings.

FIGURE   25

tried to explain to their partners—that they sometimes felt a need for the kind of camaraderie they could only experience with friends of the same sex. Colleen and Royce have been married seven years. Colleen, twenty-eight, is a homemaker, and Royce, thirty, owns an auto-body shop. Royce explained why Colleen mistrusts his reasons for needing time with male friends:

> We have this ongoing battle about a couple of my friends who she doesn't like. I know this is wacky, but she is jealous of them 'cause there are things I do with these guys that she isn't included in. . . . I think she thinks that the three of us go out and pick up women—

probably because we make cracks when we're together. But that's just part of fooling around. There's nothing going on, and I've told her that. These things we like to do together and it has nothing to do with her or other women.

Belinda and Lionel have been living together for five years and both are in their early thirties. Lionel is a surveyor and Belinda is a potter. Belinda described the conflicts that arose when she wanted to maintain the close relationships she has with women friends:

When we first got together one of the conflicts we had in the beginning was about my women's group. He didn't mind our one evening together for meetings. He thought that was fine—all politically correct, you know. But he got upset about my wanting to do things with them that I could do with him. The first time I went to see a movie with a girl friend that he wanted to see with me he went off the wall. It was okay if I see them, but just not on his time, you know. He was feeling rejected, like if I could see them when I could see him, I must not really love him. But this was a pattern I was in and I told him, even my friends told him, that it was a different need, that I had to be with my friends and I just couldn't stop just like that. . . . I think he understands now but I don't try and see his kind of movie without him!

Just as some people feel left out of their partner's leisure activities with other friends, some feel deprived simply by their partner's need for solitude. If they themselves rarely experience such a need, they may feel rejection when their partner prefers to be alone. This occurred in a couple who had been living together for three years. Daniel and Lori have both been married before. Daniel is a physician and Lori is a physical therapist. In our interview Daniel expressed his frustration:

We see each other so much at work that I need some time by myself. I might need it just to read a book or I might want to see my kids [from a previous marriage] or I just might want to be alone. She almost invariably feels rejected. We have arguments when she starts nagging me, which she doesn't see as nagging, which is another fight, that she would like to come along or she could just sit in the room and be quiet. Sometimes she'll drop by the office when I want to have a quiet lunch by myself and bring Chinese food or something. It's very nice, but it's too much. I feel she has to give me some room and understand that it is just something I need, and relax. Otherwise I will feel like I've got to get away from her, and it will have something to do with how I feel about the relationship.

Although it is common for men to want a "night out with the boys," and women to want "time with their girl friends," some people still worry that their partner's need to be with friends (of the same sex) really reflects flight from the relationship. One female cohabitor in her mid-thirties revealed to us the difficulty she has accepting her partner's reassurances that his time away from her is no cause for concern:

Our biggest fight in the beginning was ostensibly about his working nights but what it really was about was my insecurity. I wasn't sure he was through with his wife and I thought he was spending some of that time seeing her. Or even the kids, because I thought that might be a way she was trying to get him back. . . . He would reassure me that it was work, work, and nothing but work, but I didn't believe him for a long while.

The fact that gay people choose to share many of their leisure activities suggests to us that men and women do, in point of fact, have a need to be in activities with members of their own sex. It also makes us doubt that *everyone* needs to get away from his or her partner or that one's partner can *never* provide most of one's needs for companionship. Gay men and lesbians simply have an advantage in that their need for such camaraderie can be provided by their partners. Same-sex couples may share more leisure activities because certain kinds of recreation often appeal more to men or more to women. Thus heterosexuals are more likely to be drawn to different interests. It might also be true that men feel more comfortable in the company of other men and that women are more comfortable with women. Having had an entire lifetime of similar experiences makes communication easier and enables them to feel a kinship that is rare to find with someone of the opposite sex. Gay people can combine this need for friendship and their need for romantic love in one person, while heterosexuals lead more separate lives in their leisure time. As a result, partners who do not see each other during work time or spend a lot of playtime together may discover that much of their interaction is concerned with the mundane—and not very enjoyable—details of life. We also find that couples who spend less time together are less satisfied with their relationship and less committed to its future.[35] We believe that while unhappy couples may avoid one another's company, it is also the case that spending too much time away from each other, even when it is because of devotion to work or friends, can loosen the bonds which make the relationship precious and stable.

---

*Women want more time to themselves than men do.*

We asked three questions on the questionnaires to gauge how people felt about private time away from their partners. We asked respondents how strongly they agreed with the following statements:

It is important that our relationship does not interfere with other important parts of my life.
There are times when I am with my friends and I do not want my partner along.
It is important to me that my partner spend some time without me.

When we combined individual answers to all three questions, we found that on average women need more private time than men.[36] Since women are in general more relationship-centered than men, we were surprised by this result. It told us that even though women center their lives around their relationships, they feel a great need to get away occasionally to pursue personal interests. These may include spending time with friends, attending to one's parents or other relatives, taking care of household business, spending time at a hobby, or simply relaxing.[37]

In interviews, women in heterosexual relationships often told us they find their private time compromised by their partner's schedule. When he is not at work he may demand her presence for leisure activities. If she would like to use that time to see friends or kin, or to do personal errands, he may be unsympathetic. A man who sees himself as the breadwinner may feel he deserves to have his partner on call because his work leaves him so little free time. Hal and Eileen have been married for ten years. Hal, thirty-six, is a tax attorney, and Eileen, thirty-seven, is a travel agent. Hal thinks Eileen should be willing to adapt to his schedule:

> I have a couple of times in the year when I am completely busy, morning, noon and night. . . . After the fifteenth I am totally

**NEED FOR PRIVATE TIME AWAY FROM ONE'S PARTNER**

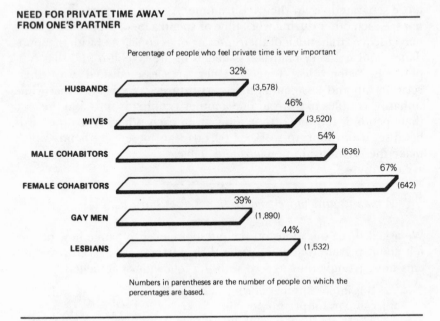

Percentage of people who feel private time is very important

| | |
|---|---|
| HUSBANDS | 32% (3,578) |
| WIVES | 46% (3,520) |
| MALE COHABITORS | 54% (636) |
| FEMALE COHABITORS | 67% (642) |
| GAY MEN | 39% (1,890) |
| LESBIANS | 44% (1,532) |

Numbers in parentheses are the number of people on which the percentages are based.

FIGURE   26

exhausted and I like to get away, I need to get away. . . . She doesn't have the same kind of schedule and she is in the kind of business where she feels she needs to be there all the time to show loyalty even if her work doesn't always require it. I feel she is in a ding-a-ling business to begin with, so maybe this isn't fair of me, but I think she has to understand a little more of what my needs are and what this marriage is about. She almost didn't come with me on vacation this year because she said she couldn't get away and I put my foot down. I only have so many natural breaks and if we don't take them, they're gone. If she can't take them with me, I'm not going to feel I have much of a wife.

In Hal and Eileen's case, the issue revolves around coordinating vacation time. For Chip and Penny the problem is coordinating their weekends and weekday schedules. Chip, twenty-seven, drives a delivery truck, and Penny, twenty-two, is a cosmetologist. They have been married for four years. Chip described their problems:

I am on the swing shift and that has us sleeping and working at different times. The only time we get the "right" time together is on the weekends, and sometimes they want her to work on weekends. Well, screw that. I'm not busting my ass to sit alone and babysit on weekends. We don't need the money that bad that we're going to mess up . . . my time off. . . . If I have to work extra time, that's different, because I get time and a half and it's worth it for us. Her working extra just ain't worth it, and I tell her she's cheating herself and cheating her family. Most of the time she gives me my point.

Working wives and female cohabitors may find it particularly difficult to get enough private time. What little time they have after work may be eaten up by the demands of the house and the children; their partners often request what is left. Some men understand that a woman who works full time may also need time for herself, but generally men are accustomed to having their partners manage the household and be their companions, so they may be ungracious when a woman wants to take time away from him for herself. Lucille and Hugh have been married for seventeen years. Lucille, forty-three, is a part-time student and homemaker, and Hugh, forty-seven, is a social worker. Hugh told us how Lucille decided to resign from her teaching job:

We have always done everything together. She is a real sport. Her work was getting in the way of our time together and I indicated that that did not sit well with me and she stopped, right then and there. . . . I consider the time a wife spends with her husband and family the most important job she has, and fortunately, she has always felt the same way. . . . Women who don't are going to have problems. That's where the divorce rate comes from. Men aren't going to stand for that very long.

A male cohabitor also told us that his need for his partner's company was not being met and it caused him to question their future together. Arnold is forty-four. He has been living with Francine, forty-three, for four years. She works in a radio studio, and he is a computer salesman.

> The first year we were really inseparable. We did just everything together. The second year it got more relaxed and we started branching out. The third year, we've taken different paths because Francine has gone back to work. She works part time and she spends a lot of time there we would have otherwise spent together. She's made friends at work and she spends some time with them after work or she goes early for coffee and chitchat. . . . We're sort of developing our own interests at different rates in different directions and I feel she's not there as much for me these days. I respect her doing her work and developing herself, but I think if this trend continues we'll probably end up splitting. I need someone who is around more.

---

*Cohabitors feel most strongly about having time away from their partners.*

Of all four kinds of couples, cohabitors have the clearest sense of a need for personal time. Not only do they consider it a central value in their lives, but their day-to-day activities reflect this belief. They are more likely to see friends separately, go to movies and other leisure activities separately—not even have dinner together. When we asked them whether they would like more time together, they were less apt to say yes than married couples.[39] This response, we feel, is rooted in a complex set of causes. Many cohabitors are tentative about their relationships: The partners may not have developed a commitment to each other, only in rare cases have they pooled their incomes or created joint property, and they have not subordinated their individual needs to their future together. This lack of focus on their life as a couple allows them to go their separate ways. Their belief in personal independence further encourages them to maintain separate lives. These factors combine to direct them away from the relationship, whereas developing a need for one another would sustain their commitment through bad as well as good times.

It is quite clear from our data that couples profit from having at least one partner who is the guardian of the relationship. Since women are usually relationship-centered, heterosexual men do not have to worry very much about taking on this responsibility. Some women are not relationship-centered, however, and unless they consciously know they are not, their chances of meeting a man who will take on the role of guardian of the relationship are slight. A woman may choose to be untraditional and put her work first, but that does not mean she does not want to live in a couple relationship. *Men* who are work-oriented will probably find a woman who will watch over the relationship so that it does not suffer too badly. But work-centered heterosexual women are clearly at a disadvantage. Relationship-centered women may be at a different kind of disadvantage because their sense of responsibility to their homes may make it harder to compete in the world of work.[40]

The only work-centered women who can easily find partners who will dedicate themselves to the emotional well-being of the relationship are lesbians. They are looking for a partner among a group where many women are relationship-centered. If gay men were as work-centered as heterosexual men, they would be at a serious disadvantage; there would be too few relationship-centered men to go around. We have no way of knowing how common it is among the general population of gay men to place work secondary to relationships. It may be that we did not see as many men who are work-oriented because they stay single. If it is as important as we think it is for couples to have at least one relationship-centered partner, then the gay men who have entered our study may be more likely to put their work second than gay men who have remained single. Thus they have a better chance than heterosexual women of finding someone who will take on the caretaker role.

One reason same-sex couples are so relationship-centered may be their capacity to spend their leisure time together. Being of the same gender provides them with a wealth of parallel experience; it allows them to be comrades, and their relationship is enhanced as they spend more time together. Heterosexual couples suffer somewhat by comparison and find it harder to discover common grounds of interest. One manifestation of this struggle is the mismatch between men's and women's desires for privacy. Men want more companionship when they are older, while women prefer their partners' company when they are young. Since this mismatch does not occur for our same-sex couples, this is a vivid example of how the differences between men and women can create barriers that even the most willing partners may find hard to overcome.

# Conclusion

The world of work is no longer the private world of men. While serious job discrimination against women still exists, the ratio of two-paycheck couples to single-breadwinner families is increasing. The problems gay and lesbian couples have had to face for years now confront the majority of heterosexual couples. Partners have to make a living, deal with competition, allocate housework, and then find time to be together. These challenges turn out to be formidable.

These couples face the dilemma of adjusting to life in a two-worker relationship, when most grew up in situations where only the man worked. And in a minority of couples women are not only working; they may be earning as much as or even more than their partners. As this trend continues, it will be unsettling to many men because money translates into power, and men are unaccustomed to yielding power to women.

Not only are men unused to having a partner with a high income, they are not familiar with women in prestigious jobs. They may take pleasure in a woman's success, but only as long as it does not challenge their own. Conflict is likely to increase unless men learn how to accept their partner's achievement without feeling threatened. Moreover, this competitiveness tends to occur in any couple in which there is at least one male partner. Thus we find that gay men match their own success against their partners', while lesbians do not.

There is a reverse side to this issue that may cause just as great a problem between partners. Men are used to having partners who expect them to be ambitious. And this fits with their own inclinations. The combined effect is to keep men deeply invested in their work. In heterosexual relationships this may thwart the woman's desire to have a partner who is a companion as well as a success at work. So the desire to have an ambitious partner may profit a couple financially, but may deprive it emotionally. A new question arises: How can couples create an atmosphere that is nurturing, and still allow both partners to be aggressive in their jobs? If one partner chooses not to work, this problem does not arise. However, some couples cannot afford the luxury of one partner staying at home, and even if they can, the woman may not be happy in her role as homemaker and wish to have outside employment. If both partners *do* work, the couple is faced with the question of who will be the custodian of the relationship.

At the present time, many women are employed, but most of the former wifely roles are still in place. Men are working and living with working women, but they resist changing the rules on which their alliance is based. When we look at housework and find that it is still the woman's job, even if she is working full time, we know that men still have not accepted women as true "partners." Housework—who does it and how it is divided—is a good barometer of how much further women have yet to go to achieve equality with men.

Finally, there is the issue of time together and how to find enough of it in modern relationships. Same-sex couples conserve more time because they share similar lives and interests and create a leisure world together. Gender roles work to the disadvantage of heterosexual couples because men and women have learned to like and need different activities. When this is added to the inclination of some people to want a good deal of private time (which many heterosexual women have learned to enjoy because their partners have been away at work), the couple may spend little time together.

In today's world, work and home life are more separate than ever, with work demanding much or all of a person's energy. The relationship may too easily become a secondary aspect of the individual's life. Work-centered people may not really want the relationship to go under, but if no one is serving as its advocate, the things that made a couple's life together special may be lost.

# SEX

HAVING sex is an act that is rarely devoid of larger meaning for a couple. It always says something about partners' feelings about each other, what kind of values they share, and the purpose of their relationship.

To understand how sex works in the lives of our couples, we devised several measures. Keeping a count of how many times who does what to whom is not very illuminating unless we know what each partner's expectations are and how well these expectations are being fulfilled. In addition, couples strike different bargains. Without understanding the nature of these bargains and how they are kept, our analysis of a couple's sex life would be pointless and superficial.

As sociologists we must also consider how couples use sex. Sex becomes an important instrument through which partners can influence each other: They use it to curry favor, to show displeasure, even to gain power in areas that have nothing to do with sex. And sex outside the relationship can also tell us a great deal about a couple, much more than simply the fact that it has happened. It shows us the circumstances that permit such an event to occur. It also reveals the amount of personal power that has accrued to a partner who can either open up the relationship or keep it closed.

In these pages we examine the ways in which sex fits into couples' lives. We consider how men and women who start a life together with different values develop the sexual style they ultimately adopt.

The first part deals with sex within a couple's relationship. We look at how often our couples have sex with each other to see whether the frequency of intimate physical contact influences the way they get along. While this is only one measure, it is a very significant one. We then turn to the more subtle ways in which couples relate through sex: By looking at who initiates the sexual act and who refuses, we come to see why partners take on different roles in the bedroom. We also examine various kinds of sexual acts to understand why performing them is important to the well-being of the relationship.

Sex, however, is not an isolated romantic haven. Good looks, money, religion, children—all the things that shape partners' behavior outside the bedroom—affect their behavior in bed. So, in the third part, we investigate these external factors and weigh their impact on our couples' sex lives.

Finally, we look at the degree to which one partner worries about the other's having sex with someone else. Couples have greatly varying views on the importance of monogamy and react in different ways to "betrayal" when it occurs. Studying sex outside the relationship helps us interpret the meaning of "loyalty" for couples and tells us whether sexual variety and commitment can co-exist.

# Physical contact

## *A major bond*

Two people become a couple in large measure to secure a trustworthy source of affection—emotional as well as physical. But they have other reasons as well. A couple relationship fulfills each partner's vital human needs, among them companionship, economic help, and children. Being a successful couple demands cooperation from both partners, two people frequently of different temperaments and wills. So the life of any couple is marked by conflict and accommodation, periods in which the partners pull apart followed by periods in which they come together. All couples create—usually without knowing it—bonds that help them to weather tensions. Physical contact—often sexual—is a major bond.

In these pages we are interested in how sex affects couples. Do partners need to be in constant physical communication to be happy? Can those who have little or no sex survive?

In our study more than twelve thousand people are represented. Each couple has a different profile and a different kind of bond. Some have a marriage contract; others do not. To some, sex is important; to others it is mundane. How does the sexual bond fit into the lives of each kind of couple? We can answer this question by finding out how often they have sex and how they feel about it.

*Sexual frequency depends very much on whether a couple is married, gay, lesbian, or living together.[1]*

Our data not only reveal fundamental differences among these four types of couples but also tell us how men differ from women and something about the unique nature of marriage.

The first thing we see in Figure 27 is that married couples are having more sex, more regularly than we might have expected. People have poked fun at marriage for "ruining" sex by making it humdrum. But Figure 27 shows that most married couples are having sex at least once a week. Even after ten years, 63 percent of our married couples have sex at least that often.

Not only does sex remain frequent for the majority of married couples, it rarely becomes truly infrequent. Figure 27 shows that only a small percentage have sex once a month or less. Even after ten years or more, only 15 percent have sex that seldom. Having sex reveals itself as a steady and continuous part of married life for both short- and long-term couples.

It is not, however, as energetic as sex among the cohabiting couples. Cohabitors outdistance married couples when we look at people who have sex three or more times a week. Cohabitation is generally regarded as a "sexier" living arrangement than marriage and if we measure only how many times a couple has sex, it is.[2] No matter how long they have been together, more cohabitors are having sex more often than married couples.

The big differences in Figure 27 emerge when we compare the heterosexual couples with the gay and lesbian couples. Gay men have sex more often in the early part of their relationship than any other type of couple. But after ten years, they have sex together far less frequently than married couples.

To understand gay men's sex lives we must realize that as a group they are much less monogamous than other couples.[3] Although interest in sex with their partners declines, interest in sex in general remains high. Sex with other men balances the declining sex with the partner. And in many cases this does not damage the relationship. We have come to see that gay men are very oriented to sexual expression in general, but as their relationships mature they rely less on sexuality as a focus for their commitment.[4]

Lesbians have sex less frequently by far than any other type of couple, and they do not have a compensating rate of sex outside the relationship.[5] The low frequency of sex at every stage of lesbians' relationships poses crucial questions about the nature of female sexuality. It could be argued that there is less frequent sex among lesbians because women are taught to be protective about their sexuality in our

## SEXUAL FREQUENCY

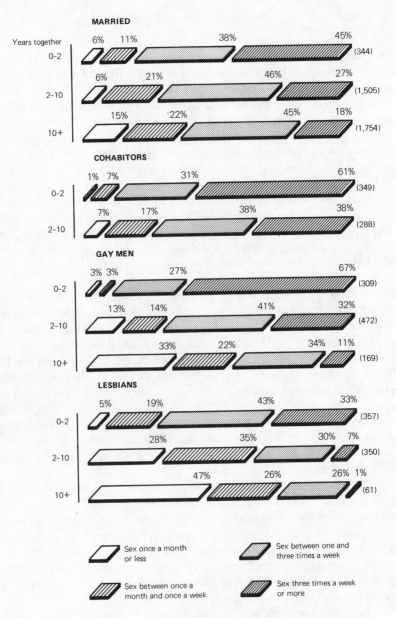

**MARRIED**

Years together

**COHABITORS**

**GAY MEN**

**LESBIANS**

Sex once a month or less

Sex between one and three times a week

Sex between once a month and once a week

Sex three times a week or more

Note: Very few of our cohabitors had been together more than 10 years.

Numbers in parentheses are the number of couples on which the percentages are based.

FIGURE 27

society; as a result they take longer to become sexually expressive. But our research shows that lesbians have a lower sexual frequency at every stage of a relationship, at every point in their lives.[6]

Do heterosexual women have a higher sexual frequency because of the presence of a male? History records men as having responsibility for being "the sexual aggressor" and women as the "purer" sex, whose virginity was kept until marriage and whose sexual appetite in marriage was not supposed to be excessive. Historically, female sexuality has been restrained because of the importance men place on legitimate offspring. Moreover, males were traditionally expected to father many children. This was assured by encouraging them to have strong sexual appetites. Impregnating women and being lustful were viewed as positive signs of masculinity.

Women entered marriage sexually uninitiated. After years of suppression they were expected to develop an appetite gradually under the guidance of their more worldly husbands. Even in modern times, while female appetite and freedom are allowed, it is still believed that the male has the stronger desire and ought to direct the couple's sex life.

Some readers would argue that what we are seeing among lesbian couples is the true nature of female sexuality: Without males to encourage sexual expression, lesbians reflect the level of sexual activity women really desire.[7] We think it would be misleading to use lesbians as an example of "true" female sexuality. Lesbians have been taught the same standards of appropriate female conduct as heterosexual women. Like heterosexual women, they unconsciously bring these standards into their relationships. So their sexual expression may be guided by their early training. We cannot know what the "true" level of sexual activity of men and women would be if they were not conditioned by social directives but behaved on pure "drives" or "appetites." Increased rates of female sexual activity since the 1960's confirm the impact of changing social values.

It is important to keep in mind that we are speaking here only of genital sexuality. From the interviews we learned that lesbians prize nongenital physical contact—cuddling, touching, hugging—probably more than other couples do. But more important, they are much more likely to consider these activities as ends in themselves, rather than as foreplay leading to genital sex. One lesbian explained that she preferred other kinds of intimacy to genital sex.

> Because of where I am, where my head is at, it's sort of like I've gotten into a thing where I felt when we only had a small amount of time to spend together, sometimes I would rather just spend it together, and I started feeling like all she wanted to do was be in bed, and I started feeling that that was taking away from everything else in our relationship. It snowballed into me feeling, like, well, I

don't even want that anymore if we can't talk and we can't do anything else together.

We believe that, like heterosexual women, lesbians need nongenital intimacy as much as—and, as it often turns out, more than—genital sex. Heterosexual women, having to adapt to male sexuality, come to view snuggling and touching as part of the pre-coital experience. While males want fondling to conclude with intercourse, many women would be just as happy to continue touching and holding for more extensive periods—sometimes never escalating to genital sexuality. Susan and Tom have been living together for two years. Susan, twenty-five, works as a veterinary assistant, and Tom, thirty-nine, is a veterinarian. When Susan seeks nongenital intimacy, she is often misunderstood.

> I initiate sex most of the time, maybe seventy percent. That's because I am not always serious. . . . Because sometimes I just want to cuddle or kiss and I don't always mean, "Keep going." . . . Sometimes he thinks I am initiating that and I am not. I just want to be close.

A wife in a twelve-year marriage told us:

> If I could design my own sex life, I would have uninterrupted, guaranteed uninterrupted time, say two hours. I've never had that. I would have two bodies, recently bathed. I'd talk a lot first. We'd have a lot of cuddling and holding and massage. I'd just proceed very tenderly and slowly. With permissions for interruptions in the process to be human and check out whether the other person is elongating the moment.

Since lesbian relationships do not take male sexuality into account, snuggling and touching become a major focus.

---

*The frequency of sex declines the longer couples stay together. Age can also have an impact.*

While the aging process takes its toll on sexual frequency, the process of living together for many years exerts a separate influence.[8] Even though a couple in a new relationship will have sex quite often, partners are still affected as the years pass and they become aware of their declining sexual activity. They naturally wonder how much is due to inevitable physical changes and how much is due to a waning interest in each other. While both things may be happening simultaneously, most couples find it impossible to separate these factors.

Most of the couples we interviewed felt that having sex less often was little cause for alarm. Our impression was that they rarely blamed their partners unless they were blaming them for other things. Most often, couples of all four types attributed it to lack of time, lack of physical energy, or simply to "being accustomed" to each other. Lila and Gino are a cohabiting couple who have been together for two years. She is a lawyer in her mid-twenties and he a radio announcer two years older. Previously, Gino was married for three years. They have sex about twice a week. Lila has given some thought to the change from the way things used to be.

> We used to have sex a lot more; in the first six months we were having sex five times a week at least, if not six. Maybe seven. After that it tapered off and I went through a hard time. I think he thought it was natural, but I was having a problem breaking off because I had this neurotic need for sex. But I've been able to deal with it. We've come down to twice a week. We're both busy and we're tired a lot and have different schedules and that's fine for both of us. I don't think either of us goes around sexually starved.

A recently married couple who had lived together for three years also expressed distress at the leveling off of their sexual activity. Darlene is in her late thirties and manager of a small business. Her husband, Burt, is a tax analyst. They have sexual relations about once a week and Darlene is not totally pleased.

> I would like it more often. When we're both not working, then frequency is more the way I'd like it to be. Although, frankly, I'm so tired I'm not really up for it either. Also if he's not in the mood, there is nothing he can do about it; whereas if I'm not in the mood, I can get in the mood. I don't usually say no as much. That's an issue of importance but not overwhelming importance. We're not both really sexed people. It's less than when we were first dating because we were making love two or three times a week. Now it's once a week. I think it's the pressure. I used to think he was less interested. Now I think just some of the mystique wore off. I would have been happy to continue at the pace we were handling . . . so most of the time I just say, "Okay, just store it up and it'll be more fun when it comes."

Karin and Nora, both schoolteachers, have been together almost four years and both are in their mid-thirties. Karin is upset that they have sex less than once a week. Nora, however, thinks that the change is natural.

> In the beginning it was five times a week, three times in one day. But it changed because the early adrenaline wore off. Karin took a trip for a month and when she came back we were both too busy because we were working sixteen-hour days. So we sort of settled down to your typical boring existence. [She laughs.]

John and Cathy, who have been married only a few years, do not get alarmed at occasional fluctuations in a relationship with high sexual frequency. Their marriage is the second for both. John, thirty-nine, is a meteorologist and Cathy, thirty-six, is an antiques dealer. John explains why it varies from month to month:

> We have sex about four or five times a week. Very often I'm tired, or sometimes she gets busy for several days. That's when we make appointments so that we get to sleep earlier, so there is time, because otherwise we begin to lose track. So we make sure we get it pulled back together. . . . Maybe once a week she doesn't want to, once a week I don't want to. It's mutual, random, varied. No set pattern, no set time. If she refuses I may be a little frustrated, but rarely. Sometimes I'm relieved because I'm just too tired. Sometimes just neutral. There is always tomorrow.
>
> It's declined. As a friend of mine used to tell me, if you took a piggy bank and put a nickel in for every time you had sex during the first year of your marriage, and then did it for the second year, you would have saved less and less money as the years went on. It's declined considerably, but for reasons of strength, not a lack of interest. We just get tired and preoccupied with things and pressures here and there. We used to make love every night and now we don't. But our relationship hasn't decreased. As I said, the spirit is willing, but the flesh is weak.

Of course, not all couples say they are too tired or busy or used to one another. With older couples we found that other reasons, specifically health, are given as the explanation. A couple who have been living together for more than seven years told us how physical changes produced a decline. Morton, fifty-six, is an industrial engineer, and Deborah, forty-eight, is a dental hygienist. The situation has been difficult for Deborah.

> Sometimes I get angry. When we were really much more sexually active you take sort of pride in the fact that you still enjoy each other so much. And then Morton started to be obsessive about his goddamn blood pressure. I think it made him age-conscious all of a sudden. Then you get sort of lazy. You fall into a pattern and the pattern has been established, and then I think, Well it's my fault too. Because, like, why am I paying bills at two o'clock in the morning instead of being in bed? It's the medication which produces this side effect. He really does not have an enormous amount of desire and now they've tried him out on different blood-pressure pills. I was beginning to feel like Poor Pitiful Pearl. So I would say we went from maybe two, three times a week, down to maybe a few times a month, and I think this year has been the least sexual of our whole relationship.

A similar tale is told by Barry and Kenneth, who have been together more than thirty-five years, but who have had no sex with each other for the past six years—ostensibly because Kenneth has had a series of heart attacks, but probably because Barry has lost the ability. Here is Kenneth's point of view:

Barry hasn't been well and since I have had my heart attacks, this has been one of the biggest problems, and I think I shall always bear it. He says, "You are sick."

I said, "Don't you think if I had a heart attack during sex that it would be a beautiful way to go?" I kid him along, but it doesn't do any good. The love is there, but there is no action. There hasn't been sexual relations for six years. None at all. I have been tempted many times to go out; after all, I am a human being, and I asked him about this once and I said, "My heart isn't all that bad." I made him confess to me that he couldn't. He was impotent. And I believe him because I have never caught him in even one tiny white lie. So this is the main problem in my life. We will never have sex again.

The couples we have quoted do not see the natural decline in sexual frequency as symptomatic of more basic problems in their over-all relationship. But that is not to say that having sex less often does not affect couples. Our data show that for some couples, sexual frequency matters more than they might realize.

---

*Both the quantity and the quality of sex are important to the well-being of the relationship for all types of couples.*

Our findings lead to the overwhelming conclusion that a good sex life is central to a good overall relationship. Couples who have sex frequently say they have a good sex life.[9] Moreover, infrequent sex is associated with conflict for everyone but gay men.[10] Married couples feel so strongly about having sex often that those who say they have it with their partner infrequently tend to be dissatisfied with their entire rela-tionship.[11] Indeed, this is true for all the men in our study. Sex is particularly important to gay men and male cohabitors, and they are less likely to be happy with their relationships when frequency is low. Lesbians and female cohabitors, however, do not feel less satisfied with their relationships when sex occurs infrequently.[12]

It is hard to know whether an unsatisfactory relationship leads to less frequent sexual activity and reduced sexual pleasure or whether the problems begin in the bedroom and eventually corrode the entire relationship. From our vantage point it looks as if other problems come into the bedroom and make it less likely that the couple will want to have sex together. The low frequency then becomes a source of dissat-isfaction in and of itself.

**SEXUAL FREQUENCY AND
QUALITY OF SEX LIFE**

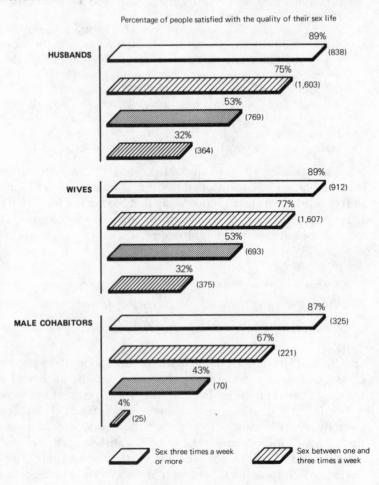

Percentage of people satisfied with the quality of their sex life

HUSBANDS
89% (838)
75% (1,603)
53% (769)
32% (364)

WIVES
89% (912)
77% (1,607)
53% (693)
32% (375)

MALE COHABITORS
87% (325)
67% (221)
43% (70)
4% (25)

Sex three times a week or more

Sex between one and three times a week

FIGURE 28

*When the nonsexual parts of couples' lives are going badly,
their sex life suffers.*

An unhappy sex life does not necessarily mean that a couple is sexually
incompatible. Their sexual relationship may be undermined by other
problems. Heterosexual couples who say they fight a lot about things
like housekeeping, income, expenditures, and whether or not both
partners should work are less happy with their sexual relationship.[13] It
does not matter what couples fight about. Any argument can sour the

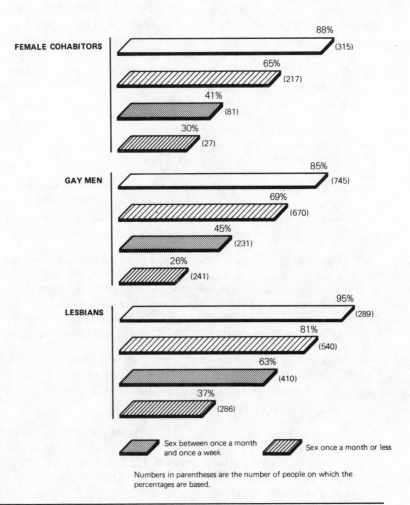

FEMALE COHABITORS
88% (315)
65% (217)
41% (81)
30% (27)

GAY MEN
85% (745)
69% (670)
45% (231)
26% (241)

LESBIANS
95% (289)
81% (540)
63% (410)
37% (286)

Sex between once a month and once a week

Sex once a month or less

Numbers in parentheses are the number of people on which the percentages are based.

sexual atmosphere, at least temporarily. Lyda and Barney have been married for five years. She is a homemaker of thirty-five, while he is an insurance broker of thirty-six. Lyda recalled an incident that upset her:

> I called him at the office because I really needed to talk to him. I was really down because I had just found out that my sister and her husband were separating. . . . He promised me he would come home early to talk, but he couldn't talk then because he had to be somewhere. . . . He showed up late and he couldn't understand why I was so furious. . . . Then he had the nerve to get mad at me because I didn't feel like making love with him that evening. He thinks things can be instantly made better and I should feel sexy. Well, that's just not the way I'm made.

Having dependent children in the home has a big impact on marital relationships, a particularly unhappy one on husbands. When we interviewed husbands with dependent children, they often complained about the effect children had on their sex lives. They often told us that the mere presence of children interferes with sex. It is the quality not the quantity of sex they find wanting, since the frequency of sex is unaffected by children.[14] Harold is a policeman, married ten years to Astrid, a homemaker. They are both in their early thirties. Harold gave a vivid example of how children get in the way:

> We don't make love until the kids go to sleep. Then it's "Be quiet" or "Don't make so much noise." She actually put her hand over my mouth once. I was so pissed off, I just lost it.

Disagreement over raising the children can also hurt the couple's sex life. Mel is a contractor, currently out of work. He has been married to Helen for twenty-two years and both are in their late forties. Helen is a part-time stenographer. Mel complained to us about the children.

> As soon as the children were born, I was more or less a second-class citizen. I would say something about their table manners—you know, discipline them like a father should—and she'd be up in arms defending them. I would lecture her about it, and she would admit she was wrong, but it would spoil it for the evening. I don't think sex was good until our youngest daughter got married.

Some husbands think their wives give too much affection to the children. Herm, a graduate student in his late twenties, described his wife, Toni, twenty-seven, who has stopped working as a receptionist in order to take care of their new baby:

> We are so tired, we just think of it too late to do anything about it. She is also tender, she tells me. But I am afraid that she is also less interested. It's been four months and she puts so much into the kid that I feel she's more maternal than sexy. I am waiting because I do feel that it will get better.

Another husband has become disenchanted with his wife and regrets what the children have done to their marriage:

> When I first married my wife, she was terrific. She had a figure on her that was like the brick shit house everyone is always talking about. After a while, she let herself go a bit, but it didn't change a lot until Michael was born. I'm telling you that everything changed with those kids. I love them, mind you, but my marriage was like I was second and those kids were always what we talked about. . . . I like spending time with them. But it's rarely quiet, and my wife and I disagree. I think she spoils them rotten and she thinks I have no patience and that I don't understand what it's like being home with them all the time, and yak, yak, yak.

Wives do not believe that it is the presence of children that causes sexual problems. For example, one wife married four years told us:

> We have gained much more from Todd's birth and our family situation than we anticipated. There have been some problems but they are not important. . . . Right now we have stresses from Joe's job and this has affected our sexual life as well. We are looking forward to a time when Joe is back at work full time, and when everything is normal I expect our sex life will be normal too. . . . Maybe Todd complicates our privacy a little, but I think our sex life is not affected very much by him.

Wives usually dismissed the impact of child rearing as a temporary sexual inconvenience or attributed their sexual problems to other factors, such as fatigue or sexual incompatibility. Anne is twenty-one, a homemaker and part-time student with a two-month-old daughter. She and Sean have been married nine months. He is twenty-two and works as a bank teller. Anne said:

> Jennifer has taken a lot of time away from us, the time that we normally spend doing things together or talking. It seems like maybe on a weekend when we would normally like to sleep in, or just have lazy sex, Jennifer wakes up and she needs to be fed. . . . We used to, for example, when we went to bed we would cuddle for a while, and now we just fall asleep in the most comfortable position just because we're tired. . . . But I'm sure that will pass as soon as Jennifer gets a little older. We're just going through a phase.

It may be that for mothers the rewards of having children are so great that the costs are not recognized. Or mothers may find it so threatening to think that children disrupt their sex lives that they will not consider it. However, we do not believe that motherhood is blinding women to the truth about their sex lives. Mothers accept the disruptions caused by children much more readily than fathers do. Women do not feel less satisfied sexually when they have children. This makes them very different from their husbands and can introduce a serious marital issue.

Sex functions as a complex bond in relationships. It is different for men and women, and how it works depends on circumstances and on individual expectations. But although sex is important for the happiness of couples, it is seldom their only bond. In fact, many couples in long-term relationships are quite satisfied with sex lives that could be considered only moderately active.

The institution of marriage allows sex to function as a bond when it occurs frequently. The institution can also preserve a married couple's relationship when the sex occurs infrequently. Cohabitors do not have the security of marriage or an assurance of a future together to cement their relationship, and so their sexuality plays a different role.

Sex becomes a more important bond. And so, if frequency is low, the relationship is bound to incur dissension.

Gay men and lesbians demonstrate that relationships can last even when the partners do not have sex very often. Some gay men come to de-emphasize sex with their partners and find unthreatening sexual outlets with other people. Both gay men and lesbians realize that many couples break up and so once they have found a compatible partner, they try hard to make accommodations in their sexual demands on each other.[15]

# Initiating and refusing

## The balance of power in the bedroom

Among heterosexual couples, men have traditionally been the sexual aggressors and women have traditionally waited for men to approach them. A woman might then be free to refuse, but a man was expected to be ever-ready. Nowadays, men and women are moving away from such narrow definitions of what "men must always do" and "women must never do." We might expect to have reached a time when the majority of our couples feel they can share the roles of initiator or refuser fairly evenly. Our evidence, however, strongly suggests that the old traditions are still alive.

When initiating sex, a partner is making something between a request and a demand: He or she may be invoking a right or seeking a special privilege. When refusing sex, a partner may be exercising an established prerogative or declining a sacred duty. The acts of initiating and refusing sex take on different meanings for different couples. These acts can tell us the degree of power or dependency each partner has, and the many ways in which partners use sex to control each other. By viewing requests and rejections in the bedroom, we get a unique perspective on the most basic aspects of a couple's life together.

---

*When having sex, many couples share initiation and refusal equally. Among heterosexuals, if either of these is not shared equally, men initiate and women refuse.*

In the 1980's, even though married couples are trying to share sexual responsibilities, initiation is still likely to be the husband's prerogative and refusal the wife's.[1]

Cohabitors, as a group, are very concerned about maintaining equality in their relationships. So we find that with them, initiation is

SEXUAL INITIATION

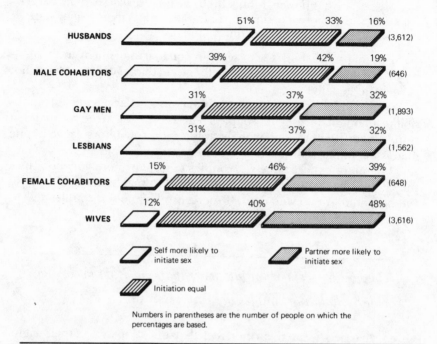

FIGURE   29

shared equally more often than with married couples. A good example is provided by Deanna and Chuck. At fifty and forty-three, they are older than most of our cohabiting couples. Both have adult children from previous marriages. Deanna was married for twenty-four years and Chuck for fifteen. They have lived together for three years and expect eventually to marry. Because of their age and their experience in other relationships, they have developed ways of approaching subjects that would be considered touchy by most couples. Chuck describes the give and take of their sexual communication:

> We have sex four times a week. Sometimes I initiate it; sometimes she does. Used to be more often for me. She's catching up. It must be because we're getting married. Yeah, a little self-confidence. I may start out unwilling sometimes, but with foreplay and desire and arousal, it changes. Sometimes she's tired or not feeling aroused and doesn't want to, but it doesn't bother me. I'm glad she's honest. I wouldn't want her in a position to do it just for me. That would turn me off. It can be a disappointment, but I think a better choice than to demand to be satisfied. I don't need a woman for that. But it doesn't happen very often that I'm not particularly interested. I think we're both equally interested.

Deanna's view is very much like Chuck's:

> We have sex four or five times a week. I initiate it less than he does.
> My sex drive is slower. I think his drive is more like six times a week
> and mine is more like three or four. So he starts more. I may start
> disinterested—but I never finish disinterested.

But many cohabitors who seek an equal arrangement in the bed-room are not succeeding very well; more than 50 percent do not participate equally.

The evidence clearly points to initiation as a largely male respon-sibility among heterosexual couples. This is especially true for married couples, but it shows up strongly among the cohabitors as well. The man is the initiator in more than twice as many couples as the woman.

We might expect same-sex couples to display more equality, since they do not have one man and one woman to play traditional roles in the bedroom. Yet fewer than 40 percent of same-sex couples tell us they initiate equally.

---

*Cohabiting women initiate more than wives. However, in older cohabiting couples the man resents it.*

Often, married women do not feel that initiating sex is their right. Cohabiting women, frequently the first to experiment with changing female roles, *do* initiate sex with their partners more than married women do. Seeking equality with men on all issues, they want an equal say in establishing how often the couple has sex. Denise is twenty-eight and has been living with Rudy for three years. He is a personnel agent, and she works repairing phones for a telephone company. Denise has strong feelings, some of which developed during her former marriage, about her "sexual rights."

> I may have had an unusual upbringing, but it never occurred to me
> that a man wouldn't let me be sexy. . . . That's why it took so long
> for me to pick up on the fact that whenever I suggested doing it, my
> husband was less passionate than when *he* suggested it. When I
> caught on, I was truly angry and upset. . . . I would never enter that
> kind of arrangement again. I have the same needs and moods as a
> man, and I am not going to let some chauvinist pig stifle them.

Older cohabiting women tell us they make the first move just as often as younger female cohabitors do. We found this very surprising: These women grew up during a time when there was a clear division between male and female sexual roles. By cohabiting rather than mar-rying, an older woman breaks with the traditions she was raised in and sets herself apart from her peers. She exhibits great independence in opting for an unconventional way of life. Considering the bold choice she has made, it makes sense that she takes up the role usually reserved for the man in the bedroom. Unfortunately, if she is living with a man of the same age, she may confront a serious problem. Older cohabiting men are still bound by traditional modes of sexual behavior and resent a woman's taking the initiative.[2] Gwen is fifty-four and has been living for less than a year with Ladd, who is fifty-three. Gwen has been a widow for six years after a marriage of twenty-seven years. Ladd was previously married for eighteen years. She works as a social worker, while Ladd is a manager for a small utility company. Gwen reported:

> I don't think Ladd would find it altogether feminine if I were to be too aggressive about what we do in bed. He is . . . of an older generation, where women don't use explicit language or swear or push themselves too much. Of course, he believes in being thoughtful to me, but I think it would insult him if I were to be the more sexually forward person. . . . He enjoys some interest and enthusiasm on my part (his wife was too much the other way), but being responsive is different from being overbearing. . . . I think some young women have forgotten that men need a certain gentle touch.

Ladd was more terse in his explanation:

> I do the asking. She does the responding. And she responds except for very rare occasions. When those happen, I am very considerate.

---

*Among heterosexual couples, a woman may hesitate to initiate sex when she fears her partner is feeling vulnerable.*

Some wives feel that husbands who insist on controlling the relationship do so out of insecurity. These men do not allow their spouses to take over the smallest area of male territory. Folk wisdom tells these wives to tread lightly on their husbands' egos. In our interviews, we heard from wives that when their husbands were having trouble at work or in some other area of their lives, the wives were more timid about making sexual advances. We think husbands become more proprietary about male prerogatives when other sources of prestige and power are disturbed.

This is an understandable pattern; men have traditionally had the right of sexual access to their wives. This right was even written into religious and civil law, and women were expected to be sexually available as part of their duty. But if men had the right to ask for—and expect—sex, they also had the *duty* to initiate it. To this day, men take this prescription very seriously. They often become angry when they ask for sex and their partners refuse. And they also feel guilty when they do not fulfill their duty to initiate sex.

From the interviews, we see that wives know implicitly when circumstances have made their husbands less secure; in turn they know they must be careful to reinforce their husbands' need to be in control. They frequently remark upon the delicacy of the issue of who starts sex. The inhibitions these women face are complex. They do not want to usurp what they know are historic male prerogatives and they fear bruising the male ego. Rita gave us a sense of the dilemma she faces. She is thirty-three, a caterer, and has been married to Angelo, thirty-eight, an out-of-work manager, for only a year. Although their relationship has a great degree of conflict, they express a strong commitment to each other. A major source of trouble is sex. They are both "very physical people," but Rita still feels she has to handle sexual matters very gingerly.

> Sex went from all the time to once a week or twice a week after three or four months. I became a given in his life and so he is no longer overwhelmed, and therefore his problems with business and with the apartment overwhelm him more. Whereas I think I have a greater capacity to separate things and say, "That's all back there."
>
> He tries to be very affectionate with me. The difficulty is that when he gets out of bed to watch a late movie, I feel totally abandoned. He doesn't feel this way. I suppose if I was the one to get out of bed for a late movie I wouldn't feel that way either. But it never is me. I wouldn't leave a bed to watch a late movie.
>
> I really don't know how to deal with it. At first, I felt honesty was everything. But now, I don't know. . . . There is this friend of mine and there is one thing she said: "Don't ever tell a man you are sexually displeased. Manipulate it the next time it comes up or say, sweetly, what you want." But I don't have that sweetness capacity. But she says that men's egos are frail. They can't deal with [honesty]. And I don't know if she's right or wrong.

Because of her concern for Angelo's feelings, Rita neither discusses sex nor feels she can initiate it. The matter is talked about in coded ways. This is frequently the way couples discuss the "undiscussable." But when it does come up, we see that both partners measure themselves against the traditions of male and female conduct. The following dialogue—their response to our asking what gives the most satisfaction in the relationship—is a prime example:

ANGELO: If I was going to answer for you, what would I say?

RITA: Yes.

ANGELO: Sex, for you. Not for me. It would be the time we spend together.

RITA: I'm just an animal.

ANGELO: That's it.

RITA: Thank you.

ANGELO: You're after my body. The first minute I walk through the door.

RITA: That's true, but it doesn't mean it's the *most* rewarding thing in the relationship.

ANGELO: [He snickers, as if to say, "Oh, yeah?"]

Comments like these in their interview with us were the closest this couple could come to an open discussion of their sexual needs and Rita's role as sexual aggressor. It is clear that Angelo's words serve as both reproach and warning: They remind Rita what is—and what is not—"appropriate" behavior for a wife in the bedroom.

Sometimes a husband will allude to patterns of initiation in a relationship in ways that subtly reveal his wife's self-restraint. In the case of one married couple in their late thirties, there is frequent sex and both partners feel it is important to please each other sexually. But what happens when the husband does not feel in a mood to make an approach?

I just lay back and enjoy it, that's all. I try and give her as much pleasure as I can. Maybe I feel a little performance pressure, but if I'm not feeling into it, and I don't want to, she never really pushes.

Wives frequently are afraid of "pushing it." Ellen, for example, has been married for five years and seems very happy. Her husband Larry, however, is several years younger than she, and she sees the age difference as something she has to balance carefully in their relationship. But both sound secure. Larry recently left a computer firm to open his own business, and Ellen is vice-president of a large corporation. They have sex about five times a week, but who makes the first move is an issue that requires a lot of tact, as Ellen indicates:

Well, after the initial period of passion started settling down, Larry wasn't quite so sure that women should take the initiative. So we would go back and forth. It is actually kind of funny. I would get some of the typical excuses women usually get: "I had too much to drink," "I have a headache"—a couple of those. And I said, "Hmm, this sounds familiar." . . .

So we deal with this issue very sensitively. It is much more sensitive than our issue about the dishes. I can remember a specific instance. It was when I was traveling. Right before I left I was making advances to Larry. He told me he felt like he was being used before I was going out of town. It is all so classical a situation in reverse! So on one hand we sort of laughed about it. But on the other hand, it was really there. I said, "I see your point." I knew it was a problem area for him so I just backed off.

As sexually egalitarian as the cohabiting woman can be, she, too, is careful about making requests for sex. Franklin and Cassie have been living together for a little more than a year. Both are nineteen, and Franklin works part time in a cannery. He has strong feelings about sex:

> I have this design in my head for what is going to happen and I don't want it messed up. . . . We were in bed and she was saying, "Do this lighter," or "Do this softer," and I just told her that I was making love to her and she was going to have to let me do it my own way. . . . You don't want to feel bossed around. . . . You don't want to be feeling like a machine.

Even if a male cohabitor encourages his partner to be sexually aggressive, she may still have to be cautious. Ron is thirty-seven, a production manager in graphic arts, and Trish is twenty-eight, a lawyer. They have lived together for two years in an uncertain relationship. Ron feels that Trish hesitates to initiate sex because she is insecure.

> I initiate most of the time, the reason being she has a real hang-up about being rejected sexually. If she catches me in a mood when I'm not interested, she's terribly hurt, and so as a result, she doesn't start anything.

Trish has another explanation:

> It is sort of an issue in that I don't initiate sex. I would always wait for him. And finally he said, "Look, I'm not going to initiate sex all the time," and I would give him the argument: "Oh, men say they want women to initiate sex, but really when it happens they're, like, 'I have a headache tonight, honey.'" So in my mind there was a reason not to initiate it because it threatened him. Even now I'm perfectly willing to say, in a joking sort of way: "Do you want to fool around tonight?" Almost like we make fun of it. And that's to ease my feeling about the fact that if I were really making a serious sexual advance, I think it would bother him.

Another couple who live together, Bill and Christina, aged twenty-eight and twenty-two, do not share equally in the task of starting sex— but for a very different reason. Their problems do not arise out of fear of rejection, but have a lot to do with something we hear about more often from young cohabiting women than from young wives: too little sex and what to do about it. When the man always takes the lead, his sexual appetite is the only one that has to be directly satisfied (although he may feel it his duty to suggest sex because of what he perceives to be his partner's need). Part of the male role means living up to the image of a man with a substantial sexual appetite, certainly greater than his female partner's. This image is unlikely to be challenged when he is the sole initiator, even though his partner's fulfillment may not be achieved. As the woman initiates more, the issue of her having the bigger appetite emerges and with it a challenge to the man's sense of worth. Bill and Christina's case is not uncommon. Bill feels his occasional lack of interest in sex is due to overwork and exhaustion. What is interesting here is that it is only *his* fatigue that determines whether they have sex. Bill is a physical therapist and Christina is a nurse. Both work long and grueling hours, yet Bill is the only one whose desire for sex is affected by tiredness.

> Listen, sometimes I'm going on three or four hours of sleep, and she'll approach me for a little affection, and I'm just looking at going and jumping in bed and falling asleep. And that has led to some arguments. Like, she'll get up sometimes in the morning and be a very difficult person. She'll jump at you for no reason at all. . . . I'd like to have more of a sexual relationship, but it's been so difficult for two years. Previous to living together we were very, very active and then I started school and our relationship sexually has diminished.

Christina has become less assertive about her sexual needs.

> In the beginning I would put pressure, sexually too. I would say, "When are we going to make love?" And I realized that it was just no good for him. Because he would get very anxious; he would pace the house and I'd wait. . . . So I let loose, let go on all those pressures that I put on him and I was saying, "Whenever you have time for me, fine." And maybe I bottled up a lot, but I think I helped him in a lot of ways. . . . I put the pressures on him that I did because we don't have sex often enough, as we did before. In the beginning it was every night till like one or two. One night a week then was really bad, very upsetting for me because I love it so much, and I would get down on him about it and then he in turn would have sex less because he'd worry about it more. . . . Now, with less pressure, he's not unwilling, but he might just be sleeping in bed and I look at him, and I'll go, "Oh, boy, I'd like to have him now." Yeah, right, necrophilia!

Bill suggests that Christina's sexual desires come from "neurotic insecurity":

> Oh, yeah, sure, that's our real problem. She was worried she was becoming less attractive to me, which she wasn't, but you know sometimes I just can't convey that to her. Sometimes she just gets a little overbearing about it, to the point that I just don't want to hear it anymore, because I really feel that she's trying to look under the blankets when the answer is right on top. And I feel that once I finish school and we have a more normal life together, I think sexually we'll be more compatible than we have been over the past couple of years.

Saying no to men when they ask for sex is one of the rights of women, partly because of the image society has ascribed to them of being the "less sexual sex." When a woman refuses sex, a man can interpret it as a sign of her smaller appetite, not a rejection of him. When a woman takes the initiative, she wants her partner to be glad she asked and have him eager to oblige. If he refuses, she is likely to think he is uninterested in *her* rather than uninterested in having sex. A woman who has been living with a man for ten years told us:

> He has a wall that he puts up that I feel like I can't penetrate. Sexually I can't even attempt to because I feel so vulnerable about it. So if he backs off in a little bit of a way, it affects our relationship. I feel rejected very easily and that doesn't help.

It is clear that both married and cohabiting couples share many of the same strains over who initiates sex. Problems arise because these couples feel restricted in what they are allowed to do by virtue of their being men or women. Lesbians and gay men do not have two sets of expectations to determine their behavior. Is it then easier for them to coordinate their sexual desires?

---

*Same-sex couples have their own problems over*
*who initiates sex.*

In heterosexual couples, initiating sex is usually left to men. Should we therefore expect lesbians to be uncomfortable with taking the lead? And find gay men ready and able? Our interviews tell us that this is the case. We feel that many lesbians are not comfortable in the role of sexual aggressor and it is a major reason why they have sex less often than other kinds of couples. One woman describes the difficulties she and her partner have:

> The problem is that I want more than she does. And she feels guilty about wanting less. Recently, we've been to a counselor to talk about it. I think we've come to a point of deciding that *we* probably are not going to be able to solve it . . . that we've gone around in circles long enough.

Another couple, Sally and Rhoda, are at an impasse because of their different perspectives on sex. Rhoda is twenty-seven and Sally a few years younger. Both administer social welfare programs. They have been together five years. Sally said:

> I generally initiate by asking. It's always been an issue that I would choose sex more often than her. So now I'm more discreet. I edit how much I ask in order not to get rejected as much. Also, she sometimes says no, but more often than not she says yes. But then I don't ask all the time.

If Sally were a traditional heterosexual man, she would not hesitate to ask, because it would be both her right and her duty to do so. Nor would she be so hurt when refused.

Another real consideration for lesbian couples is their disdain for conventional male and female role playing. Over and over again they tell us in the interviews that one partner resents "always being responsible" for initiating. The other partner then feels pressured because she would like sex to "evolve more spontaneously." For this to happen, however, both women would have to want to be, and learn how to become, the initiator. For example, Rosemary and Nina have been together for seven years. Rosemary, twenty-eight, owns a beauty salon and Nina, thirty-two, is in school full time, working on an M.B.A. Rosemary resents the burden of being the aggressor.

> I think I initiate about ninety percent of the time, and that is one of
> our continuing arguments. . . . I want to be approached just as much
> as she does, and I don't think it's fair that if I don't start anything,
> nothing gets started. . . . She agrees with me in principle and she
> rarely refuses, but I don't see any changes. I think she got used to
> that kind of role when she was married, but that was a long time ago
> and she can't use that as an excuse. I feel a little oppressed by it.

While Rosemary feels that their problem is Nina's inability to share the responsibility for sex, in another couple, the problem arises because one partner resents the other's excessively active role. Polly and Claire have been together for eleven years; they have sex about once a month. Polly, forty-six, teaches in a community college, and Claire, fifty, is a nurse. Polly explained how she has learned to initiate less often:

> We have sexual problems when she doesn't have an orgasm and gets
> very excited and upset. She will cry. This has sort of disappeared
> now because I let her begin things and I don't try and pressure her.
> For a while she was extremely tense, and I kept saying, "It doesn't
> matter. It doesn't matter if it doesn't happen. We've had an
> enjoyable time. Why do you have to do this? There's nothing
> wrong." But we have gotten around the tension and stress by my
> staying back and letting her pick the time and place and have the
> right feelings ready.

One lesbian who works as a psychotherapist, and has many lesbian clients, has given a great deal of thought to the problem of sexual initiation. When we interviewed her she gave us some of her thinking on the matter:

> Women have a hesitancy to initiate. My forthrightness makes sex
> happen. They don't ask; they wait. All that "boy asking them to
> dance" stuff. It's not all right for women to ask for things for
> themselves. . . . Sometimes I have gotten these messages from my
> partner. It's very subtle. Subtly to imply I am too intense. If you're
> the only person asking, you get to feel pretty weird. I ask, "What do

*you* want," and they say, "Whatever you want." So I start to pull back on asking for what I want. . . .

What the women's movement has done is make women even more uptight and self-conscious about their bodies and what they want. There are even more "shoulds" piled on top of the old ones. A lot of women feel that they should not feel too passionate, too intense. . . . It's male, dominating, and I think it's a crock of shit. . . . They mistake passion for violence. I was walking once on the beach with my lover and we had just had a very passionate time, and she said that our sex was so violent, and I said that wasn't violence, it was passion. And she was so relieved. She said, "Okay, I feel so much better." It wasn't violent; it was intense. You can express yourself powerfully without domination, without putting someone down. That's why lesbian sex is so gentle and soft-fluffy. They are afraid of passion. It is not politically correct.

What happens when both partners are male? They both feel free to be the initiator.[3] This may account, in part, for gay couples' frequent sex in their early years together. But we think having two initiators in a couple can create problems. Initiating symbolizes maleness and dominance; therefore double initiation, which goes unnoticed in the romantic beginning of the relationship, can escalate into competition—not to prove who can provide greater satisfaction but to demonstrate to the other who is running the show. In reaction to being pushed, one partner may begin to refuse, exerting his own method of control. He then places himself in the same situation as traditional heterosexual women: By using his veto, he strikes back at his male partner's attempt to define the terms of their sexual relationship. This may trigger a rapid decline in the couple's sex life, because a gay man, unlike a heterosexual woman, is not compelled out of "duty" to respond to his partner's sexual desire. Gay couples may attribute the fact that they have sex less often to a diminished sexual attraction for each other, but sometimes it may actually reflect the fact that each partner is reading the same male script.

As one gay man told us:

I don't want sex enough, according to him. He would like me to be more aggressive. But sometimes I'm just beat and I don't feel like having sex. . . . Of course, if Paul Newman or John Travolta walked through the door, I'd say, "Hi." . . . However, at the beginning of our relationship I was a bit more so. . . . I used to be more dominant, but he would turn me off because he felt so uncomfortable about [receiving anal intercourse], and although we never articulated it, it embedded itself as a memory that he felt he wouldn't be able to satisfy me, so we'd better not start. So in a sense he trained me not to be as dominant or as insistent as I might have been. So now, in a sense, the seesaw has changed direction and I have to remind him occasionally that I've gotten used to his not wanting it and now I don't want it so much.

Because men are expected to be sexually interested at all times, initiation becomes more tentative when there is a likelihood of a rebuff. The would-be aggressor fears being personally rejected. Prescott and Bill have been together for twenty-four years. One is a lawyer and the other an editor in a publishing house. Prescott expressed the delicacy of initiation:

> We have learned very quickly that in making an advance and the other person is not interested or feeling interested, you can tell. You have good antennae so you can tell if it is a genuine reaction, and if not, we spare ourselves the ignominy of pushing for what is not available.

Bill's perspective is the same:

> You've got to know Prescott. It's very bad to initiate with him. He's got to be *very* receptive or he's not receptive at all. In most cases I initiate. And if he's not interested, oh, well, he'll be here tomorrow. . . . There's no use forcing the situation. Neither person is going to enjoy it.

---

*In lesbian and gay male couples, it is the more emotionally expressive partner who initiates sex.*

While initiating sex in heterosexual couples is usually the man's role, we find it is not an intrinsically "masculine" act. On the contrary, among lesbians it is the more emotionally expressive partner who introduces and maintains the couple's sex life. The initiator is the woman who is more likely to begin to talk about what is troubling the couple when there is tension, and the one who is more able to give her partner a spontaneous hug or kiss when something good happens.[4] These kinds of behavior are ordinarily associated with women, and in our heterosexual couples the female partners perform them more than the men.[5]

We find among gay men, too, that the more emotionally expressive partner is more often the sexual aggressor.[6] This brings up a crucial question: Is it also the more emotionally expressive partner in a heterosexual couple who is more often the initiator during sex?

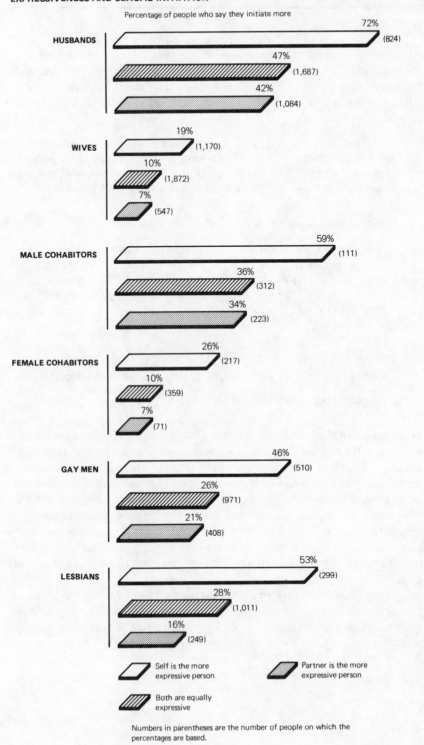

EXPRESSIVENESS AND SEXUAL INITIATION

Percentage of people who say they initiate more

**HUSBANDS**
72% (824)
47% (1,687)
42% (1,084)

**WIVES**
19% (1,170)
10% (1,872)
7% (547)

**MALE COHABITORS**
59% (111)
36% (312)
34% (223)

**FEMALE COHABITORS**
26% (217)
10% (359)
7% (71)

**GAY MEN**
46% (510)
26% (971)
21% (408)

**LESBIANS**
53% (299)
28% (1,011)
16% (249)

Self is the more expressive person

Partner is the more expressive person

Both are equally expressive

Numbers in parentheses are the number of people on which the percentages are based.

FIGURE    30

*In married and cohabiting couples, the more emotionally expressive a partner is, the more he or she initiates sex.*

Even though it has been the man's right and duty to initiate sex, heterosexual men are actually more sexually aggressive when they display the "feminine virtue" of expressiveness.[7] It is also true that heterosexual women who are more emotionally expressive initiate more.[8] Expressive men and women are comfortable with making the first move because they are sensitive about how to approach a partner. Their success encourages more attempts and soon they inherit the role.

Overall, expressiveness seems to be an important quality in a relationship. The expressive partner, ever mindful of the other person's feelings, is also less likely to refuse sex. This is true for all men and women, heterosexual and homosexual.[9]

*The more powerful partner is more likely to refuse sex.*

According to conventional wisdom, men are more aggressive sexually because they like sex better, and women reject it more because they are less interested. At first glance, our data seem to support this view. Heterosexual women tell us they are much more likely to veto sex than their lovers or husands are. This dovetails with the data that heterosexual men are more likely to take the initiative. But we think that something more symbolic is going on here: The act of refusal is one way a person may achieve power; it is also a way he or she may exhibit power already possessed.

We find that among cohabitors, when the woman is more powerful she is also more likely to refuse sex; when the man is more powerful, he tends to refuse.[10] We find the same pattern among lesbians.[11] Among gay men we find that the person who gains the upper hand in the relationship by being less in love is more likely to refuse to have sex.[12] That is also true for the married couples.[13] When a person refuses sex, he or she can become a force to be reckoned with. The initiator becomes more clearly the supplicant and may have to comply with his or her partner's wishes. As one husband told us:

> She has traditionally used sex as a lot of women use it on occasion. Not vindictively, but as a weapon, you know. As a legitimate weapon to get something, to reward something. And this new idea that sex is different from love makes it a more legitimate weapon. "Ah ha! This is a weapon I can use differently than I anticipated before."

## EXPRESSIVENESS AND SEXUAL REFUSAL

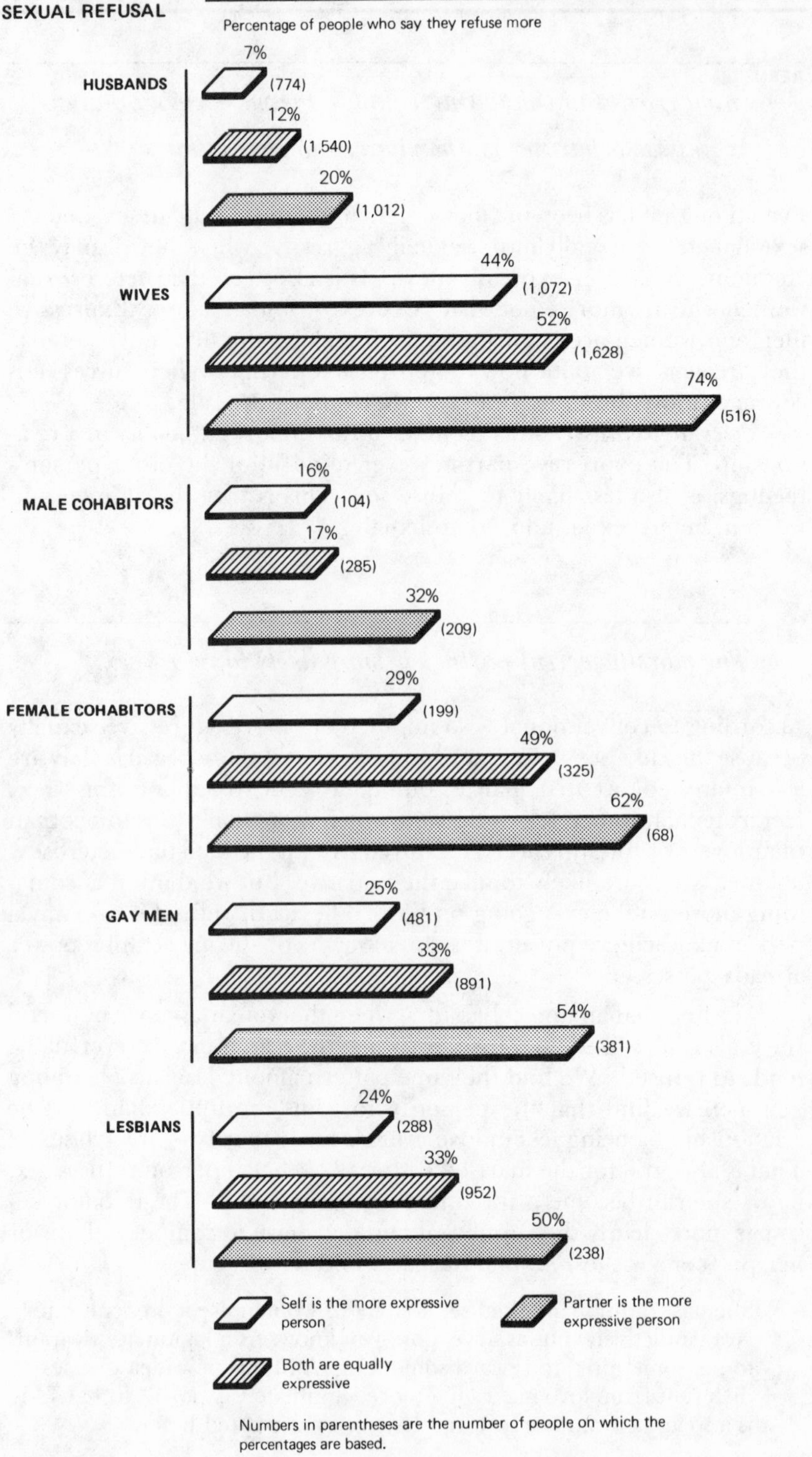

Percentage of people who say they refuse more
HUSBANDS
7%
(774)
12%
(1,540)
20%
(1,012)
WIVES
44%
(1,072)
52%
(1,628)
74%
(516)
MALE COHABITORS
16%
(104)
17%
(285)
32%
(209)
FEMALE COHABITORS
29%
(199)
49%
(325)
62%
(68)
GAY MEN
25%
(481)
33%
(891)
54%
(381)
LESBIANS
24%
(288)
33%
(952)
50%
(238)
Self is the more expressive person
Partner is the more expressive person
Both are equally expressive
Numbers in parentheses are the number of people on which the percentages are based.


FIGURE 31

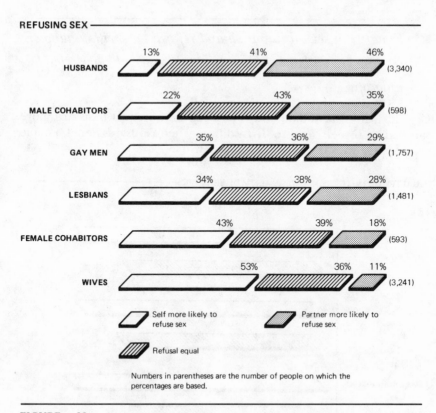

REFUSING SEX

**HUSBANDS**  13%  41%  46%  (3,340)

**MALE COHABITORS**  22%  43%  35%  (598)

**GAY MEN**  35%  36%  29%  (1,757)

**LESBIANS**  34%  38%  28%  (1,481)

**FEMALE COHABITORS**  43%  39%  18%  (593)

**WIVES**  53%  36%  11%  (3,241)

Self more likely to refuse sex

Partner more likely to refuse sex

Refusal equal

Numbers in parentheses are the number of people on which the percentages are based.

FIGURE   32

On the other hand, not everyone is in a position to get away with refusing. For example, a wife who is afraid her husband will go elsewhere may not refuse even if she would like to. She would have to feel truly strong and secure before she would refuse often.

Men, by recognizing as legitimate a woman's right to refuse, increase her power to control scarce goods. We believe that women's right to refuse has evolved hand in hand with the conventional belief that women have a weaker sex drive. It may be that it has been in their best interest to suppress sexual desire in order to become less dependent on sex, and therefore more powerful. Perhaps, then, the idea that women have fewer sexual needs has evolved as a counterbalance to their weaker position in their relationships.

Same-sex couples do not have a power imbalance based on gender. Nevertheless, sexual refusal works in the same way for them.

*Equality in sexual initiation and refusal goes with a happier sex life. Going beyond equality to role-reversal makes couples unhappy.*

Couples who can initiate and refuse sex on an equal basis are more satisfied with their sex life. In addition, when refusal is equal, people are happier with the relationship as a whole.[14]

**EQUALITY OF INITIATION AND QUALITY OF SEX LIFE** —————————————

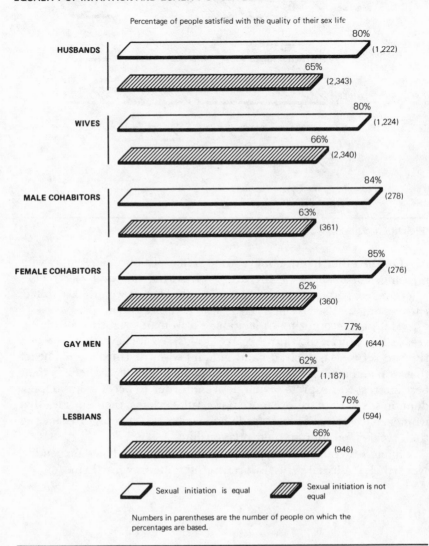

Percentage of people satisfied with the quality of their sex life

HUSBANDS
80% (1,222)
65% (2,343)

WIVES
80% (1,224)
66% (2,340)

MALE COHABITORS
84% (278)
63% (361)

FEMALE COHABITORS
85% (276)
62% (360)

GAY MEN
77% (644)
62% (1,187)

LESBIANS
76% (594)
66% (946)

Sexual initiation is equal

Sexual initiation is not equal

Numbers in parentheses are the number of people on which the percentages are based.

FIGURE    33

**EQUALITY OF REFUSAL AND
QUALITY OF SEX LIFE**

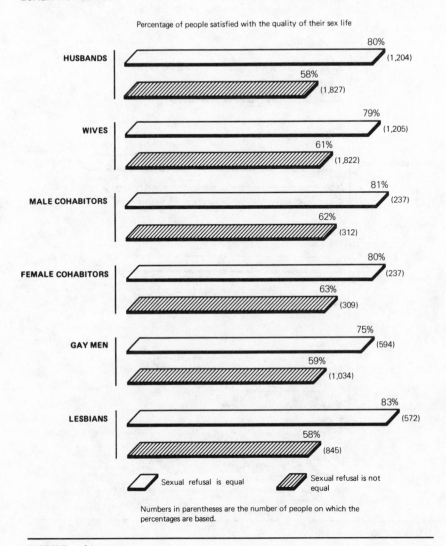

Percentage of people satisfied with the quality of their sex life

HUSBANDS    80% (1,204)    58% (1,827)

WIVES    79% (1,205)    61% (1,822)

MALE COHABITORS    81% (237)    62% (312)

FEMALE COHABITORS    80% (237)    63% (309)

GAY MEN    75% (594)    59% (1,034)

LESBIANS    83% (572)    58% (845)

Sexual refusal is equal          Sexual refusal is not equal

Numbers in parentheses are the number of people on which the percentages are based.

FIGURE    34

Moreover, for all kinds of couples, when both partners refuse equally, they have more frequent sex.[15] Such equality means that the partners share control over their sex life, so that neither feels anger at the other's "excessive" lack of interest and neither feels guilty when he or she is sexually unavailable. As a consequence, a couple is happier in their relationship.

But from our interviews with heterosexual couples, we see clearly that when they go beyond equality to a point of role-reversal (where the woman initiates and the man refuses), the partners become troubled.[16]

## EQUALITY OF REFUSAL AND SEXUAL FREQUENCY

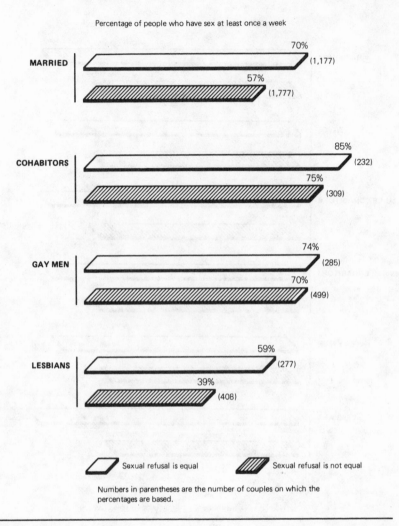

Percentage of people who have sex at least once a week

FIGURE   35

Greta, twenty-seven, is a graduate student in art history, and William, thirty, is doing graduate work in economics. They have been living together almost two years. Greta said:

> We were lying in bed on Sunday morning and I was feeling really like having sex. We were talking and it was nice and relaxed, and so I reached over and started to touch his penis. He withdrew from me real sharply and angrily and moved to the other side of the bed. He said, "You never give up, do you?" I was embarrassed and angry. . . . So even if I feel like it, I wait until he gives all the signals.

Equality in sex is a delicate and elusive balancing act. As a couple teeters from the point of absolute equality, they are most likely to fall back on traditional roles, the male initiating and the woman refusing. But some couples teeter in the other direction, the woman becoming more of an aggressor and the man the reticent partner. The momentum that brought them to equality has overshot the mark and they arrive at a reversal of roles. It is here that the images of the husband "abdicating his maleness" or the wife "becoming the man of the family" begin to crop up. It is here that the partners begin to hold traditional roles up to one another as tests that are being failed. This overshooting of the mark in the pursuit of equality is easy to do. Sexual equality is a kind of rebellion from the status quo, but a small one, with few risks. Switching sexual roles, however, is a much greater departure, and one that has more troubling consequences for the couple.

When, on the questionnaires, we asked a couple which of them initiates sex more and which refuses more, we were asking them to summarize very subtle behavior. When partners have sex, they may be less interested in how it begins than in what actually happens. They may become preoccupied with the technical aspects of sex rather than with its meaning. As researchers, we were interested in sex acts because they reflect important themes in a couple's relationship: power, control, submission, maleness, femaleness, sharing, selfishness. We were eager to know why couples prefer certain sexual acts, why some make them happy and others make them feel uncomfortable. We wanted to discover if men and women have different needs and aims when they have sex and whether these contain the seeds of sexual incompatibility.

We chose to study sex acts that are common in heterosexual relationships and common in homosexual relationships.[17] The homosexual acts may be unfamiliar to the heterosexual reader. We discuss them because they occur in and illuminate couples' relationships.

---

*Kissing occurs usually, though not always, when couples have sex. It is most consistently present among lesbians, and least present among gay men.*

Kissing may seem the most innocent of sexual acts, but in many ways it is the height of intimacy. Many people told us they could not imagine the intimacy of sex if the intimate act of kissing was not part of it. This is particularly true for women. As one wife explained:

> Kissing is sensual, and it's an orifice where a connection can be made. And I also like the taste. I like tongues. There is never a time I don't want to kiss.

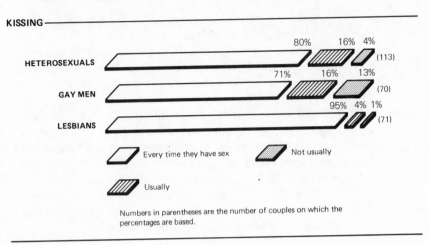

KISSING

|  | | 80% | 16% | 4% |
| HETEROSEXUALS | | | | (113) |

71% 16% 13%

GAY MEN (70)

95% 4% 1%

LESBIANS (71)

▱ Every time they have sex    ▨ Not usually

▨ Usually

Numbers in parentheses are the number of couples on which the percentages are based.

FIGURE    36

It is interesting that some couples do not kiss every time they have sex. We find that people kiss less during sex when they feel somewhat removed emotionally but still want a physical release. And couples who are feeling a lot of tension over matters that have nothing to do with sex or affection (money or work, for example) kiss less often when they have sex.[18] One wife was saddened when we asked about kissing, and told us why:

> Kissing is equally important to both of us. . . . But it's sort of been a lost art to us both. But we are rebirthing it, rediscovering it. How could you not like it? It's one of the few things we share in exactly the same way. . . . I've thought about getting back to it. I miss it. It's very erotic and I miss it. . . . We kiss about fifty percent of the time when we make love and it's always prior to the culmination of intercourse. . . . I think when you're in a marriage as long as mine, every four or five years require effort to get back to kissing. It is still very erotic, but a kiss is more than a kiss and somehow it gets lost. We've been aware since our sixteenth anniversary to consciously try to kiss each other more. In a recent bout of lovemaking, we had a prelude of kissing and nothing else, and it was just as erotic as anything ever done to me. But we hadn't done that in so long.

Couples with one man and one woman kiss less than couples with two women, and couples with two men kiss least of all. Men seem more able to enjoy sex as a physical experience, even when some of the emotional properties are missing. One gay man, in a non-monogamous relationship of one year, gave an example of how he could have sex with someone without kissing:

> I would be self-conscious kissing someone I was tricking with [having an uninvolved sexual experience] because it was too intimate, too tender. That was because I knew Jeff [his partner] would not like me

to be that tender with someone else. Occasionally with a trick, I have not wanted to kiss but I would do other things.

---

*Intercourse is a more essential part of having sex for heterosexual women than for heterosexual men.*

Heterosexual men have been accused of being obsessed with intercourse to the exclusion of all other sexual acts. While it is true that most heterosexual couples have intercourse when they have sex,[19] and that men desire and initiate sex more often than women,[20] intercourse is not always the preferred form of sexual expression for men. The stereotype of a man pressuring his partner for intercourse, and the woman in turn de-emphasizing it, may be misleading. When we look at what makes heterosexual couples contented with their sex life as well as satisfied with their entire relationship, we discover that intercourse is just one sexual act among others that heterosexual men enjoy—but a central ingredient in women's happiness.[21] One husband told us:

> Ninety percent of the time when we make love, it includes intercourse. It doesn't bother me when it doesn't include it. In fact, that's often great because I'm tired, or I've gotten off some other way.

We have no reason to think that women achieve greater happiness from intercourse because it is more physically satisfying.[22] We think women prefer it because of what it means to them. Intercourse requires the equal participation of both partners more than any other sexual act. Neither partner only "gives" or only "receives." Hence, women feel a shared intimacy during intercourse they may not feel during other sexual acts. Mitzi is a forty-one-year-old free-lance photographer. She explained how she felt about having intercourse with her forty-one-year-old husband, Curt, who is a physician:

> Intercourse is great. We tend to both come that way, fully, totally, a good way to end our lovely task. . . . I love intercourse because it's the time we communicate the best. We communicate best because it doesn't require my husband to talk. Most American males raised in the fifties—and every decade before—are not allowed to emote— which is communication—talking. American males are effectively verbally castrated. I hope my sons will be part of a generation of males who can express feelings. Intercourse is the emitting of emotion, and I think males only allow themselves to emit this emotion when they are in ecstasy. So for my husband, it is a real freedom. He's finally allowed to let go, to communicate: "I'm happy. I'm having a good time. Oh, boy. Wow." These emotions are usually

bridled in American males over the age of thirty-five. I think it's the best way he and I communicate. It's an expression of the whole body.

Women may also feel that their male partners will not be as satisfied any other way. In their effort to please them, heterosexual women may eventually measure the success of their sex lives by the frequency of intercourse. As one wife analyzed it:

> Intercourse is . . . important for men because they have less permission to acknowledge the emotional-spiritual part of sex.

A woman may be aware of her partner's arousal and assume that his first and immediate desire is for intercourse. If he does not want it, and prefers to have sex another way, she may feel slighted.

In his role as sexual initiator, the male partner establishes how much intercourse there will be in the couple's sex life. Therefore, unless she rebuffs his sexual advances, he is having as much intercourse as he wants. Women may veto having sex, but once they accept, it is tacitly understood that it will include intercourse. But there are other sex acts that bring diversity to a couple's sex life which men cannot introduce as easily. It is these which are more important than intercourse for heterosexual men's sexual satisfaction.

---

*Heterosexual couples with traditional sexual values limit their sexual behavior to intercourse in the "missionary position."*

This position, with the man in a symbolically more dominant role, also requires him to expend more physical effort than his partner. Her flexibility is constrained; hence, the man establishes the pace and content of their sexual behavior. Men and women who hold traditional values about sex are more likely to reject any positions that require the woman to be more physically active or more in control than the man. As one wife described it:

> I am on top maybe ten percent of the time. . . . I like being on the bottom. It feels better. . . . We always finish up in the traditional missionary position. Those missionaries knew something. It was less physical work for the woman. I like to avoid all that physical work.

Couples with more avant-garde sexual values, those who advocate sex without love, do create a more diverse package of ways to have sex. They are more likely to engage in oral sex and to have intercourse with the woman on top.[23] Ira has been married to Jayne for nine years. He is an accountant and she works in an investment firm. Both are in their mid-thirties. Ira prides himself on being sexually uninhibited.

In my other relationship, this woman had an incredibly strong preference for being on the bottom and being real traditional. I tried to break her of that. I find that position gets boring and each position has its own little benefits. Also, the switching of positions, multiple positions, all prolong the act for a more substantial period of time. So you can go on an hour or more. Builds up your stamina, kind of like working out. . . . I like novelty of sensation. . . . Variety is very important to me. You get bored. You lose interest. If it's so satisfactory, if you know what you'll get, how to handle it, if there are no surprises, it just isn't that great. . . . I like making love on kitchen tables, in the shower. My perfect sexual scenario is the unexpected scenario. The place least likely. We recently made love in the back seat of our car at the drive-in. It was just wonderful.

Once intercourse becomes one of several sexual choices available to a couple, it is no longer a "required" part of every sexual session. For example, couples who have more oral sex have less intercourse.[24]

---

*The less power a heterosexual woman has in her relationship, the more likely it is that the couple's intercourse will be performed in the missionary position.*

The partner on top during intercourse has greater freedom of movement and is better able to direct the event. These may both be thought of as traditional male prerogatives. For many of our couples, the woman sometimes assumes the "male" position. This happens more in couples where the man does not completely dominate the relationship and where the partners share power more equally.[25] In these couples, the man does not always feel compelled to be in control, and his partner feels freer to try another position if she wants to. Mitchell is a physicist of thirty-nine. He has been married to Cara, a teacher, for two years after having lived with her for almost six. He described their positions during intercourse:

She's on top between one half and sixty percent of the time. I introduced it initially. I don't know if she does it for herself or for me. . . . During dating periods with other women, I used to think women felt they had power when they were up there, so it was an easy form of giving them something they thought mattered to them which didn't matter at all to me. They felt sexually equal, which was fine with me. Some had never been on top in sex, which was a surprise to me.

A young wife described her feelings about sexual positions:

> I am on top quite often. I suppose a man could think a woman has control on top and so he has lost it. But my husband doesn't, I don't think. . . . I love to be on top, but I don't really consider that intercourse. I feel very different about that. I can come that way, so it's an accommodation to me. . . . Intercourse with the *man* on top is the most mechanical type of sex and the most available to a man, so they opt for it rather than other variations. They just do what they do, reach orgasm, and turn on the TV. . . . It allows less attention to be paid to the woman. I feel used when my partner has no awareness of my sexual plateau. That's no fun.

As a heterosexual woman acquires power in her relationship, her partner is more likely to respect her sexual preferences. When the woman does not always defer to a man's judgment, and when she has an equal say in the couple's decision-making, sex is more likely to include the man touching her to orgasm.[26] She also feels more comfortable about letting him know what she wants. In couples where the woman is less powerful, it takes longer for the man to learn to be sensitive to her needs. Our data show that men touch their women to orgasm more regularly in couples who have been together many years.[27] Hollis and Millie have been married for thirty-one years. Hollis is an unemployed salesman and Millie works part time in retail inventory. Hollis has become more attentive to Millie's sexual needs.

> I don't think it's a physical thing, but she is not able to become excited during intercourse, and to, well, reach orgasm. . . . That is one thing that used to be no problem for me at all. Well, wham, bam, thank you, ma'am. But it has always been a problem with her. . . . I play with her, talk to her, and help her to get an orgasm because it is no more than fair.

*When heterosexual women are attractive, they have more varied sex lives.*

Our data show that attractive women (as judged by themselves and their partner) are more likely to be on top during intercourse,[28] and to receive and perform oral sex. This may be an indicator of the sexual power that attractiveness provides women. It may also affirm the fact that attractive women arouse men's sexual fantasies more often. A very attractive wife in her late thirties said she enjoyed being on top during intercourse, but she had one reservation:

> Sometimes it's voyeuristic for him. Some men love to see their women in that position, and if it's that that's going on, I don't like it.

Another wife made a similar observation:

> He might be fantasizing when he's lying [there] and I'm on top doing all the work, it's so pleasing to him.

That attractive women have a more varied sex life may indicate that the self-esteem they gain by being good-looking allows them to be less inhibited during sex. Then, too, women who find themselves attended to in so many ways may work harder to maintain their looks.

---

*Heterosexual men who receive oral sex are happier with their sex lives and with their relationships in general.[29] Men who perform oral sex are also happier.[30]*

It is easy to understand why men like to receive oral sex. They learn very early in life that their genitals are a source of great pleasure. And post-Freudian society accepts the idea that a penis is valued by both men and women. Men often think their genitals should be the main focus of the couple's sex life. They do not expect or want their partners to find them unappealing or untouchable. So men think of fellatio as a very appropriate part of sex with their partners. Should their partners be squeamish about it, the men are likely to be displeased.[31] As one thirty-six-year-old husband put it:

> Oral sex is very important to me. I enjoy the sensation so much. I've never liked dealing with female inhibitions against it. . . . I like a combination of intercourse and oral sex. But for pure physical pleasure, oral sex is better. . . . I think oral sex is a bit less intimate because you're not face-to-face, kissing. But it is more exciting in a peak physical sense.

Some heterosexual men also enjoy fellatio because they feel it is a reflection of their partners' love and willingness to please. As one husband of forty described it:

> When she gives me oral sex, I view it as an expression of her feelings for me. It's something she would not choose to do except for her feelings for me. . . . She is trying to say something about our relationship, but she's not doing it for self-gratification. I think she is feeling love towards me.

Less clear is why *performing* oral sex is also very important for a heterosexual man's sex life. This is an act designed for the physical pleasure of his partner rather than the direct stimulation of his own body. Certainly part of his pleasure comes from his partner's appreciation. We feel this is especially true in the 1980's, when a man's sexual prowess is often measured by his ability to bring a woman to orgasm. As one husband explained:

> The whole process makes me feel good about myself. I take serious pride in being a good lover and satisfying my partner, giving her pleasure. . . . I enjoy being the recipient [of oral sex] and I also enjoy giving it. The "tonguer" and the "tonguee" . . . I don't feel degraded going down on her and she shouldn't either.

Performing oral sex may also be pragmatic for the man because in exciting the woman, he causes their sex to be all the more passionate.

We believe, however, there is another reason. Performing oral sex is psychologically exciting for men. For human beings, sex is not merely the rubbing together of body parts. It is an act endowed with rich associations. Themes of control, abandon, romance, sacrifice, domination, submission, or worship may be felt by a person during sex. For example, one husband described his feelings about cunnilingus:

> When I'm going down on her, I feel like I'm controlling her, especially the closer she gets to orgasm. I like to get her close, then back off. I like to play. It's a pretty vulnerable point. . . . She's less in control. I think she appreciates it that I work to heighten the intensity of her orgasm. And I enjoy that as well.

Each person may conjure up a different feeling or fantasy and may choose not to convey it to his or her partner. One wife, in describing cunnilingus, made it clear that *both* partners can feel in control.

> I think he likes it so much . . . because it's the only time he controls me. That has some heavy connotations, but it's probably true. . . . I do feel powerful when he does it. I feel quite powerful. I feel domineering when he's going down on me. Sort of the Amazon mentality—all-powerful woman, real woman—sort of sensation.

The power of the mind explains why, as in oral sex, a person can be very excited although not directly stimulated. Dean, aged twenty-nine and married less than a year, spoke about the element of fantasy in his sex life:

> Sometimes I fantasize. Usually it's when I have trouble keeping my mind on what we're doing. When I'm bored, I use it as a crutch. Usually it's about other experiences I have had, usually the more kinky things I've done. If you . . . are not that close to orgasm, you can focus on a wild sexual experience . . . and it seems to help.

We think men who like oral sex possess a vivid sexual curiosity. They do not want habit to dull the art of lovemaking; hence, they constantly stimulate their sexual imagination by having sex in a variety of ways. Such a man is likely to have intercourse with the woman on top and to be preoccupied with his partner's beauty.[32] His sexual imagination is stirred by visual stimuli. Because of his capacity for mental stimulation, the world becomes a very erotic place for him.[33]

A great many men consider cunnilingus an erotic and exciting sex act, not a "dirty" or obligatory part of foreplay. There are many anti-female jokes to the effect that men should avoid oral sex, but the truth is that many men are aroused by the image of their partners' genitals, and claim their relationships are enhanced by such activities.

This does not mean that the negative jokes are not an indication of real male ambivalence about female genitals. A minority of men we interviewed found them unattractive and unerotic. These men will not perform oral sex, even if it means not receiving fellatio in return. Others who occasionally perform oral sex still retain some negative feelings about women's genitals. One husband who enjoys oral sex told us about the denigrating stories he had heard as a young man:

> All men tell each other—my father told me—that blond women never smell.

Another husband illustrated how he had rid himself of negative feelings:

> Doing oral sex is sexually exciting. . . . I like the appearance and the smell. I never had other feelings except when I was young, before I'd done it. Then I had anal cleanliness sorts of feelings. I knew where the urethra was and I had fears from toilet training about leakage, you know, getting urine on the toilet seat. So I felt fastidious about it. Cleanliness values . . . made it an unattractive thought. But that was before I had any experience. Now I find it very attractive and I find the smell exciting. . . . I've heard misogynist males—my roommate in college used the word *cunt* to mean the ugliest thing in the world. But he was a very strange person.

There is more at work here. We think some men do not initiate oral sex because they fear their partners would be put off and they do not want to offend. Others feel that fellatio is not a "nice" sexual practice, and therefore unsuitable for women they respect. They feel women would be "servicing" them, a concept they dislike. A few men told us they had no moral or aesthetic qualms about receiving oral sex, but they felt it was not masculine to be "passive" in bed with a woman.

*Oral sex is not necessary for heterosexual women's sexual satisfaction.*

Women who perform or receive oral sex are no happier than those who do not.[34] We think the meaning of oral sex is different for men and women. While many women may enjoy fellatio, others see it as a form of submissiveness, even degradation. If her male partner is too directing, this may take away her sense that sex is an act between equals. A man may prefer to specify that he wants oral sex, thereby putting his partner in the position of acceding to his request. As a consequence, she may perceive his behavior as selfish and insensitive to her right to proceed according to her wishes. Her impulse to please may be blocked by his coercion. Evelyn is a wife of thirty-one. She explained her feelings about oral sex:

> I've never initiated it. I want it, but I always wait. But my partner does it frequently and predictably. I wouldn't ask; I'm not skilled at asking. . . . We almost always have oral sex. He might ask me to begin. I've known men that would pull your head down. I never do well with that. He always makes a verbal request. . . . Sometimes I don't mind if he comes in my mouth. It means a lot to him. When you come to realize it means a lot to them, you want to do it. Maybe it's power to some men, but I think it's intimacy.

When we asked another wife how oral sex is initiated in her marriage, we touched her sense of humor:

> We never talk about me going down on him. It just evolves. Would you call it his suggestion to me that he starts waving it toward my face? With a hundred-dollar bill attached to it? I call it friendly persuasion.

We feel that heterosexual women prefer that fellatio be freely given, not demanded. In cunnilingus, the male partner is not as likely to perceive the act as symbolizing sexual obedience, because he is apt to be the more powerful partner.

Women may also shy away from performing oral sex because, historically, the canons of female decorum permitted a minimum of sexual abandon. While modern sex education is trying to teach children that sex is not "dirty," we feel that some ambivalence about genitalia still lingers. Wives seldom talked about these feelings in the interviews; they were clearly uncomfortable with the discussion. One wife who does engage in oral sex did tell us, however:

> His genitals don't attract me in and of itself. It's who's attached to genitalia that I care about. Who owns it, who's wearing it. . . . I like going down on him. It makes him feel good, truly good. I don't find it unpleasant. I don't say I wish I could do it all the time. I don't equate it with a sale at Bloomingdale's. That I could do all the time. But it's not like going to the dentist either. It's between two extremes. Closer to Bloomingdale's than to the dentist.

We feel that vestiges of former sexual taboos may also inhibit women from enjoying cunnilingus. Some women have learned to be self-conscious about their genitals and are embarrassed to allow a man the kind of intimacy oral sex entails. Even a woman who escapes negative feelings about her own body may still be uneasy receiving oral sex. A wife who has learned to enjoy her husband's performance of oral sex described her feelings about her genitals:

> While we have oral sex, I sometimes worry if he's worried I'm going to go to the bathroom or get my period right there. . . . I like his genitals. I don't worry about his liking mine. If I do worry I think of it as my own projection of self-loathing, rather than his. Early on, there was this feeling of mine that you could tell the level of experience a man had by the fewer fears that he passes on to you and you pick up. . . . Of course, I had feelings about loathing my genitals when I was younger. I got them from my mother, the Catholic church, the Girl Scouts of America, and every piece of literature I ever read—*Fear of Flying.* I just decided that I would let go of it. It wasn't my relationship that did it. I just got over it.

If her partner performs cunnilingus, a woman may view it as submissive on his part and feel it is unseemly for him. Some women who do perceive that their partners have no other motive than to give them pleasure are still uncomfortable with the practice. Most women are in the habit of catering to men—serving them food, picking up after them—rather than the other way around. These roles are seldom reversed, but when they are—for example, when a woman is ill and must be cared for, or when she is served breakfast on Mother's Day—she may feel awkward and be unable to enjoy the experience unselfconsciously.

There is also the issue of reciprocity. A woman might be more comfortable receiving oral sex if she knew she could return the same kind of pleasure. But reciprocity may be hampered by whatever dislike she may feel toward performing fellatio herself. Overall, our women do not perform oral sex on men as often as men perform it on them.[35]

A number of women in our study are not ambivalent about oral sex. These are the sexually liberated women who like oral sex and who find it neither embarrassing nor demeaning. One wife, a successful businesswoman, described her feelings:

> I find oral sex very satisfying. It brings me to orgasm. Sex doesn't hurt when we do it orally. Other ways I can come, but it often crosses the threshold from pleasure to pain. If he's not gentle, it'll hurt. I like oral sex very much because it is extremely intimate and I'm moved by it as an act of intimacy. . . . If oral sex is successful, neither of us is thinking regular thoughts. He's into a different thinking mode, a different level of consciousness. . . . I suspend worry. . . . I'm not in present time. I'm in space outside of it. . . . You let go of everything other than the act.

Another wife explained her favorable feelings toward oral sex:

> It almost always starts with him going down on me, then me going down on him, and then he may do it more to me . . . prior to

## ORAL SEX

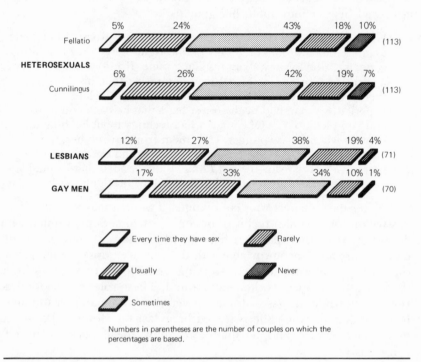

FIGURE    37

intercourse. Two to one in favor of me. Being the "eatee." I think I require more revving up. I'm a little slower to get started. . . . When he's going down on me, I think about words, a litany of erotic words. . . . I encourage him to go down on me. . . . I think it is the best thing in the world. For me it is the most erotic act. I'm surprised at how much I enjoy it. I can say to him that I'm not interested in sex tonight, but that's the way to change my mind. It feels warm, so good, and he's so good at it and he enjoys it so much. Which is why I enjoy it. He never made me feel bad about myself. He really wants to do it even more than I want it.

These women think of oral sex in more egalitarian terms, and do not bring to it any associations of dominance or submission. A few told us they enjoy it because their partners enjoy it so much, thereby making them feel sexually powerful. They believe that men expect sexual intercourse but appreciate oral sex. For example one wife said:

Sometimes when I'm going down on him . . . I feel powerful. . . . He likes it so much—that's where the power comes from. I'm exerting power. I'm rewarding him. The giving of pleasure is a powerful position and the giving of oral sex is a real, real gift of pleasure.

A husband explained that he views fellatio as a selfless act on his wife's part.

> I usually initiate intercourse. I view intercourse as a sharing of pleasure. I get pleasure out of doing it and I know she gets pleasure. I'm less clear about what she gets out of fellatio. . . . She does it just to give pleasure to me.

Because there are so many meanings that heterosexual women can attach to cunnilingus and to fellatio, their willingness to engage in oral sex varies greatly. For some, there are no obstacles; for others, it is inconceivable; and for most, it is a source of ambivalence. Because of this diversity, we find that *on average,* oral sex neither contributes to nor detracts from the quality of these women's sex lives.

---

*The more often lesbians have oral sex, the happier they are with their sex life and with their relationship.*

The more oral sex lesbian couples perform and receive, the happier they are and the less they fight about sex.[36] In this regard, they stand in sharp contrast to the heterosexual women. We found no evidence that performing oral sex has any connotation of obedience or subjugation for lesbians. Most of them believe in the right of each partner to participate and be gratified equally in sex. As a woman of thirty-six told us:

> I like giving and receiving oral sex. It feels very special when we do it mutually. I feel like when my partner chooses to love someone that way, it is a very intimate thing to do. It is much more intimate than manual. It is like a gift. . . . I was once involved with a woman I was incredibly sexually attracted to. . . . She wanted to make love to me all the time, but rarely wanted me to make love to her. After a while it was very hollow. . . . I never felt I could give back. It wasn't an intellectual response, but a spiritual emptiness without the reciprocity.

Another lesbian expressed a similar feeling:

> I would not like to be kept from reciprocating. I wouldn't be attracted to someone like that. I would be hurt that she wouldn't allow me to live out my sexuality, make my feelings clear to her. That's part of my sexual enjoyment. . . . I am very interested in an equally giving-and-receiving kind of relationship.

Even when heterosexuals strongly share these same values, it is easier for them to fall into patterns where the men behave one way and the women another.

In our study, the majority of lesbians who have oral sex receive and perform it equally.[37] Only a small minority do not reciprocate, and these tend to be from working-class backgrounds.[38] These women prefer to divide up sexual roles, but they do this as a matter of sexual style. This does not mean that one woman usually assumes a masculine role and the other a feminine role in the relationship.[39] In fact, the more feminine both women are, the more they perform and receive oral sex.[40]

We feel there are other reasons that lesbians are less inhibited about oral sex than heterosexual women are. Heterosexual women sometimes worry that their partners either do not like, or are ambivalent about, female genitals. They frequently think that men apply exacting standards in evaluating women's bodies. Lesbians assume their partners are less judgmental and more accepting of female genitals because they are women. In the past decade, lesbians and heterosexual feminists have written many articles and books to counter the negative feelings women have about their bodies, in particular their genitals.[41] There is an assumption among many lesbians, even if it occasionally proves false, that because a woman is a lesbian she will find female genitals appealing. A lesbian of thirty-three spoke of her experience with other lesbians and their feelings about women's bodies:

> Gay women are very much into each other's genitals. They're very comfortable with and attracted to women's genitals, worshiping iris flowers, et cetera. Not only accepting, but truly appreciative of women's genitals and bodies. My feeling about my body and my genitals has significantly been enhanced by my experience with women. Lesbians are really into women's bodies, all parts.

Jacqueline, a lesbian in her mid-thirties, explained why lesbians are accepting of women's looks and bodies:

> Among lesbians you don't have the cultural stuff about women's bodies. You're coming from the same place about your bodies. You don't have the one-up one-down stuff. You have the same bodies. You have the same acculturation as women. You have a whole starting place for having fun. . . . I have a friend who is very cute. She is very small up top. She has a small waist and small breasts, but she has an enormous ass. I mean an *enormous* ass. Her lover calls her the Great White Hope. She says, "I want to grab your big ass." She wouldn't mind if she lost some weight, but she loves her big ass because it is hers. . . . It's a whole theme through the whole women's movement. Women reclaiming their bodies. How do my genitals work? What is stimulating to me? What can I do with my body? It's part of a whole spectrum of women exploring their bodies.

*Even though lesbians who have oral sex are happier, it is not usual sexual behavior for the majority.*

Since lesbians have grown up learning society's restrictive guidelines governing female sexuality, we feel their sex lives may be affected in many unconscious ways. While they seek to celebrate their femaleness, we have evidence that lingering taboos prevent their enjoyment of oral sex. Some lesbians do not like to have it performed on them because of extreme fastidiousness or shyness, or because all sexual intimacy embarrasses them. For example, one lesbian we interviewed mentioned that another woman's genitals repelled her because she disliked the smell. In general, few of the lesbians we interviewed had negative things to say about oral sex, but a much larger number claimed they knew *other* women who had such feelings. One woman felt very strongly about other lesbians' hesitation:

> It was very surprising to me to learn that some women do not like oral sex. . . . A gay woman might not like it because it would have something to do with it being too earthy, too musty, and too musky. Almost a kind of vulnerability. You plunge into a kind of darkness, both physical and spiritual. It is very vulnerable to both people. . . . When someone I was with seemed not to feel comfortable with it, or when I talked to other women about it, I sometimes got the feeling: I wonder if they think it isn't nice. With all the liberalism around, it's hard to get a straight answer. . . . It might be just bodies. It's real close to where you go to the bathroom. I have asked women about it, but I just can't get an answer.

Even though only 39 percent of our lesbian couples have oral sex frequently, very few say they never do it at all. This means they do sometimes overcome any negative feelings they may have. If at least one partner is aggressive enough to initiate oral sex, it is more likely to occur. Self-confidence and leadership in the bedroom are not taught or encouraged in women. Hence, unless one partner reeducates herself, or both do, oral sex will be suggested infrequently and thus remain sporadic, even if it is enjoyed when it does happen.

We have also learned how important reciprocity is to lesbians, in all aspects of their relationship. Thus, if one partner feels comfortable initiating and performing oral sex, she may not want to assume that role all the time. If her partner enjoys it, but refuses to reciprocate, the initiator may become resentful and back off. And a woman who is always the recipient of oral sex may feel guilty about not reciprocating. Unlike heterosexual men, who are willing to take the initiative all or most of the time, lesbians will sacrifice frequent performance of a well-enjoyed sexual act if it is maintained by only one partner. Neither woman may want to have a sexual relationship that appears to mimic male-female sexual patterns.[42]

These patterns are changing. Younger lesbians, who tend to reject stereotyped ideas of female sexuality, demonstrate their new freedom by having more oral sex.[43] We also note that as lesbians gain more sexual experience, they overcome their inhibitions and become more aggressive about defining and acting on their sexual needs. As lesbians become less sexually naïve, they become more comfortable with oral sex and perform it more often.[44]

---

*Oral sex is important for gay men's satisfaction. But it is only one of several ways of having sex that produce a happy sex life.*

Oral sex is a very common and accepted sex act among gay men.[45] The more oral sex gay men receive and perform, the more satisfied they are with their sex lives.[46] Additionally, the more anal sex they receive and perform, the more they touch each other to orgasm, and the more they rub against each other to achieve orgasm, the more likely they are to be sexually satisfied with each other.[47] We conclude, therefore, that the more varied a sexual repertoire gay men have, and the less inhibited they are, the more pleased they are with their sexual relationship. As one gay may put it:

> I would expect from a lover a tolerance for any act, kissing, going down, fucking, being fucked. Anything he wouldn't do would be a stumbling block.

---

*In spite of how common oral sex is in gay men's lives, it has the potential to be disruptive. This is often avoided by reciprocation and by the equal commitment of both partners.*

Like heterosexual men, gay men enjoy oral sex and want it in their relationships. But they prefer it to occur in a context of equal and mutual exchange. We think that if only one man performs it, he may worry that he appears submissive. Communication between the two partners does not always solve the problem. When two people have sex, it is often difficult for one to know what the other is thinking. While one man may feel powerful, aggressive, and dominating when he is performing oral sex, the other may also see himself in a commanding, rather than receiving, role. One man may see it as an act of love, the other as an act of homage. An example of this occurs in a gay male couple who have been together seven years. The older partner usually performs oral sex on the younger, who is widely admired for his good looks and well-developed body. The older partner sees performing oral sex as an act of love and a source of great arousal. His partner feels differently:

> I don't think we are similar in intensity towards each other. I think there is usually a lover and a lovee. And, I think . . . a giver and a taker. . . . I'm trying to figure out if the person you live with should turn you on, sexually, you know, all the time or part of the time. Or if love is deeper than that. You know, he doesn't turn me on. Unfortunately, most of my life has been spent not being turned on. I was always turning somebody else on, with a fantasy or something like that. . . . [In this relationship] I wanted a worshiper and he wanted a god.

If one man is almost always the partner who performs oral sex, and the other almost always receives, the loving meaning of the act may be eclipsed by the fact that it is one-sided. In moments of passion a man may want to submit to his partner in order to give him pleasure. However, if this scenario is repeated too often, the behavior may be perceived as self-debasing. Over time, the partner who at first gladly performed oral sex may feel used and abused. "Why am I always the one who does it?" he may ask. "I thought that's what you wanted to do," his partner may reply.

The frequency of oral sex may decrease unless this issue is resolved in one of two ways. The first occurs when both men are convinced that they are equally committed to the relationship.[48] This reassurance allows one-sided performance of oral sex without conflict, because each partner knows he is loved and respected, and assertions of power are not feared. The other way gay men de-escalate tension, we feel, is to have reciprocal oral sex.[49] For example, many partners report having oral sex simultaneously, and perhaps this helps avoid any sense of unfairness. In interviews some men have told us that they try to make sure, over time, that neither person performs or receives more than the other. One man may like to perform oral sex more, but holds back and waits for the other to do his part. The other may make an extra effort to please his partner and thereby keep the relationship on an equal footing. Imbalance in performing oral sex is avoided and the couple is happier with their sex life.[50]

*Among gay men, anal sex is less common than oral sex.[51] It can bring up sensitive issues of dominance and reciprocity.*

Many heterosexuals find the idea of anal intercourse extremely unappealing, and heterosexual men find it hard to conceive of being penetrated as pleasurable. Among heterosexuals, all images of intercourse, including anal intercourse, portray the person who penetrates as more male than the person who is penetrated. In men's prisons, where heterosexuals often engage in homosexual acts, the man who is penetrated is stigmatized and looked down upon as female, while the man who penetrates is seen as exercising a male prerogative.[52]

Some of the gay men we interviewed recognize the gender imagery that is possible in anal intercourse and accept it in their relationship, while others are troubled by such imagery, which they believe to be widespread in the gay world. Otis is forty-five and works in a post office, and Jon is thirty-five and is a librarian. They have been together three years. Jon says:

> I interpret anal intercourse as being a feminine piece. That doesn't happen between us very much because I don't like it. He doesn't like it either. I've tried, but I have a problem with it because of pain, and I don't like the way he acts when he is on top. . . . We try not to divide up our sexuality as male-female, so our sex ends up being oral or masturbation or anything else but anal sex. . . . He has more the psychology or philosophy . . . of being more into the macho role than me. And I can't come through the other role because I don't like the bottom. We've had to work on this a long time, because he was really into a strong butch macho role when he met me, and it's taken to this point for him to even out. . . .
>
> Most of our gay friends don't know what in hell goes on in bed between Otis and me. Many people know Otis as being very, very butch in the sense that he never liked to do anything but fuck. They don't know me at all, and I think that at times I come on very butch myself, and that really confuses them. So they're out there wondering, because we're both pretty private.

It is our impression from the interviews that most of the male couples, however, generally reject any male-female image of anal intercourse in their relationship, even though some acknowledge that issues of control can become part of this form of sex. One partner, in a couple where both men perform and receive anal sex, put it this way:

> The person who is on top is in much more control, so any kind of fantasies of being in control or controlling the other are just perfect there. It is to some extent what I act out. The top and bottom are different. On top, you get the feeling of being active and more forceful, aggressive. These are great feelings. It is a real charge to be

on top and seeing them get a lot out of it, and it is an excitement to know that physically you can control them. . . . You can see them go nuts at the same time you're feeling good. . . .

I enjoy being bottom, too, because it feels good to be physically dominated. . . . There was a time that my partner always wanted to be the top. When he did that as an element of control, I realized that was the only method of control open to him in the relationship. I'm much more dominant, so he needed something to be dominant about. Only thing available to him was sex. I'm sort of strong or self-satisfied with myself as a person. I don't accept stereotypical dichotomies. I know I can do both [be on top and bottom], so I don't feel the need to prove that I can do both. There was a phase when my former lover was only a bottom, and that bothered me because it seemed to be verging on roles in his mind. And I didn't like that.

In this interview we were told that the dynamics of the couple's sexual roles "counterbalanced" the pattern of dominance elsewhere in the relationship. We find a different pattern in a couple trying to stay together after a stormy first year. Seth is twenty-seven and is a management trainee for a bank. Kelly is thirty-six and a lighting designer for a small theatrical company. Early in their courtship they developed a pattern where Kelly always performed anal sex on Seth. Seth described how things changed and how their sex came to mirror their relationship:

At the time it was happening I couldn't understand. With Kelly it became more and more apparent that it was symbolic for him. Symbolic of being dominated sexually. When we first met he put everything he had into my life. And who Kelly was, was lost in all that. I told him I didn't want to get to know him well because I found that what was happening [sexually] was real exciting and I wanted it to last. It became more and more apparent that I liked being top and he liked being on bottom, and it switched in subtle ways. This was happening as Kelly was becoming more and more submerged in my life. At first I just wanted to be bottom and he wanted to be top. It was just a chemical thing between us. But it was the opposite of what we really are. The fantasies of domination in Kelly's background are real strong. To me it just seemed like a part of men having sex together.

Anal sex presents a complex array of symbols for gay men. It varies from couple to couple, and yet the ideas of masculinity and femininity, or of dominance and submission, come through in many of their accounts. When we look at the overall patterns, our couples fall into three groups: those who have anal sex rarely or never (30 percent), those who have it regularly with the partners reciprocating (27 percent), and those who have it regularly with only one of the men being the penetrator (43 percent).

It takes gay men time to learn to accept penetration. One of the difficulties is avoiding being thought of as female or of thinking of oneself as female. It takes some time in the gay community to get over heterosexual definitions. We find that the more sexually experienced a gay man is, the more likely he is to accept penetration.[53]

---

*Among gay male couples, the partner who performs anal sex is no more "masculine" or powerful than the partner who receives it.[54]*

While it is true that the man who penetrates is no more "masculine" than his partner (forceful, aggressive, and outgoing), he may have certain behavior patterns that would cause the outside observer to think of him as more male—he is less emotionally expressive than his partner, he feels he is more rational than emotional in his dealings with problems, and he tends to keep his feelings to himself.[55] This "strong, silent type," however, is not necessarily in control of the relationship. For example, he may be more inclined to give in to his partner when they have an argument.[56] The fact is that, for both partners, anal intercourse is associated with being masculine: In couples where both partners are forceful, outgoing, and aggressive, there is more anal sex.[57]

Sex does not just "happen." Partners negotiate what they do and do not want. Factors such as gender or a partner's power in the relationship may determine the kinds of sexual acts that take place. Among heterosexual couples, the content of sexual behavior in the relationship is guided by gender. Men direct the couple's sexual life and women modify what happens by what they choose to accept. Sometimes this arrangement works well. At other times, male and female desires are very different, and the tacit understandings do not permit the woman to communicate her sexual needs. Same-sex couples face different problems. Their sexual needs may be similar to those of heterosexual couples, but they have no ready-made guidelines that define who does what to whom during sex.

We have seen that each kind of couple has its own problems in learning to be sexually compatible. Sexual compatibility, after all, is what all their physical and emotional efforts are aimed at accomplishing. But there are no quick and easy formulas. Only the couples themselves can say if their sex lives are what they wish them to be. We asked people how sexually compatible they were, and when we tabulated the answers, we found that more heterosexual men rate their relationships as compatible than anyone else does. The female partners, however, rate the same relationships as less compatible.[58] Since men are usually so much in control of the couple's sex life, this difference is not a surprise.

A remark made by a forty-year-old wife reflects this essential difference between women and men:

> Even if I wasn't feeling particularly good about him at the time, I would make love to him. I'm a woman; women accommodate. Even the more enlightened woman knows she has to. Sometimes I figure his needs are greater than mine, and the act of giving is rewarding in and of itself. He wouldn't know I wasn't interested or really there—unless he cared to—and most men don't care to. . . . I don't think he would do it for me. And I don't think I'd be interested in lovemaking if I wasn't feeling good about the relationship at the moment. But for men, it's different. I think they learn this distancing because of the way we raise them, our expectations of them, the performance standards we subject them to.

More lesbian couples rate their relationships as sexually compatible than heterosexual women do. While lesbians encounter many sexual problems, we feel their insistence on reciprocity and mutuality enables them to consider their sex lives compatible even if they are not fully satisfied. Gay men place less emphasis on sexual compatibility than do lesbians. This is convenient, because they are the least sexually compatible of all our couples. Gay men are often very experienced sexually when they enter a relationship. From the interviews, we get the impression that they have developed specific tastes which they are reluctant to yield or to compromise in order to please their partners. Instead they frequently go outside the relationship for sex. As their relationship matures, they concentrate on preserving its emotional dimensions.[59] They cease to worry about finding a partner who is a perfect choice sexually. Like the lesbians, they come to feel that the relationship is more important than its sexual limitations.

# Beauty, competitiveness, and possessiveness

*The influence of factors outside the bedroom*

A couple is made up of two people who construct a "reality" all their own. But from the outside world come influences beyond their control. That world sets standards by which they try to get a sense of how well their relationship is going. And not surprisingly, partners often seek advice and counsel from other people because they are "too close to the issue to evaluate it," and they cannot rely on each other to provide an unbiased assessment. Every couple is fundamentally dependent on others for objective feedback about themselves and their relationship.

One of the easiest kinds of feedback to acquire concerns an individual's physical worth. Like it or not, looks are an instantly available measure of a person's value in our society, and this seems especially true for heterosexual women. This culture has created a demanding standard; people either measure up or they do not. Moreover, the steps they can take to meet this standard are limited. Within the couple's closed environment it is difficult to get a reliable sense of one's physical worth, so partners may seek an independent judgment from the outside world. If the response is good, one partner can return home with a restored sense of physical value—and then make new demands on the other because of what he or she now "deserves." If the outside world reacts less favorably, a partner comes back humbled, feeling very fortunate to have such an irreplaceable companion and wanting to try harder to please this other person who "deserves the best."

It is difficult for a couple to admit that physical beauty is an important force that intrudes on their lives. People prefer to evaluate themselves—and to be evaluated—on things they have worked for and achieved, not on the roll of the dice at birth. But if a partner works at becoming beautiful (exercises, develops great talent in grooming), he or she may then gain approval for making an attractive appearance. If one partner is naturally beautiful or handsome, might it actually be painful for the less good-looking partner to accept that fact generously? Jealousy and competitiveness might begin to interfere in the relationship.

Social scientists have not devoted much study to the impact of physical appearance on an established relationship.[1] Since most scholars overvalue the power of the mind, they tend to denigrate or even ignore the power of the body.

Nonetheless, it is an undeniable fact that humans are physical creatures and the way they "wear themselves" profoundly influences their experience in life. Researchers have found that people who are considered beautiful are chosen over their less attractive peers at school, at work, and in the social world.[2] What we find in our study is that the power granted by beauty affects every couple, both in how they interact with each other and how they deal with the wider world.

---

*Marriage and commitment do not free couples from the tyranny of beauty.*

Physical attractiveness is an important motivating factor in bringing couples together in the first place. We believe that people assume that as their relationship progresses, their looks will become just one of many bonds between them—indeed, that they *expect* looks to become less important. A wife assumes her husband will still love her if he sees her in the morning without makeup. If her husband puts on a few extra pounds, it is not grounds for divorce. These are the expectations and hopes of all couples. But our questionnaires reveal that the appeal of beauty endures long after courtship. For all kinds of couples, except lesbians, people who find their partners attractive say they have a better sex life.[3] In fact, they are happier with their overall relationship.[4] Joe's marriage did *not* last and he places much of the blame on his wife's lack of attention to her appearance. He is a salesman in his late twenties, talking here about his ex-wife:

> I think she forgot about being my lover. She got fat. She wouldn't listen to my complaints about that at all. She stopped dying her hair, and I got off on her being blond, and she did not look for my physical self. I think she was actually relieved when I wouldn't start something. . . . I put up with that horse manure for six years, if you can believe that. Not anymore!

Most wives, however, are keenly aware of the importance to their husbands of their looks. Faith is a homemaker of thirty-nine, and Gerry is a city manager of the same age. They have been married fifteen years. Faith knows Gerry cares how she looks:

> I don't think I am naturally attractive . . . but I take care of myself. I think he would be disappointed in me if I didn't. In fact, if I gain a few pounds, he will kid me by pinching my waist or my thigh. He's kidding, but he's also telling me to go to the gym. . . . It's worth the work. I need to feel good about myself, and believe me, I wouldn't get to first base with him if he wasn't proud of my appearance.

Continual evaluation of one's partner's appearance does not end at the marriage altar. All the same, looks have an even greater impact on cohabitors. A cohabiting male is likely to be more committed to his partner if she is attractive.[5] And good-looking cohabiting women have more sex.[6] Of all the couples we talked to, cohabitors place the greatest premium on each other's looks.[7] Elliott, twenty-four, is a fashion designer, and Patty, twenty-two, is a clothing buyer. They have been living together for three years. Their concern about each other's looks is only partly related to their work. Patty told us:

> I don't really care about the way Elliott looks, except if he weren't taking care of himself or something like that. But I do get pleasure out of the way he dresses, and the way he comes across. I think he has a "presence."

Elliott feels the same way:

> [Attractiveness] is very important in the fashion industry. People expect designers to have glamorous lives. . . . We were invited to this fantastic villa in the Caribbean as part of a promotion. I was very glad that Patty was beautiful. You really had to play a part there, if

**HAVING A PHYSICALLY ATTRACTIVE PARTNER AND QUALITY OF SEX LIFE**

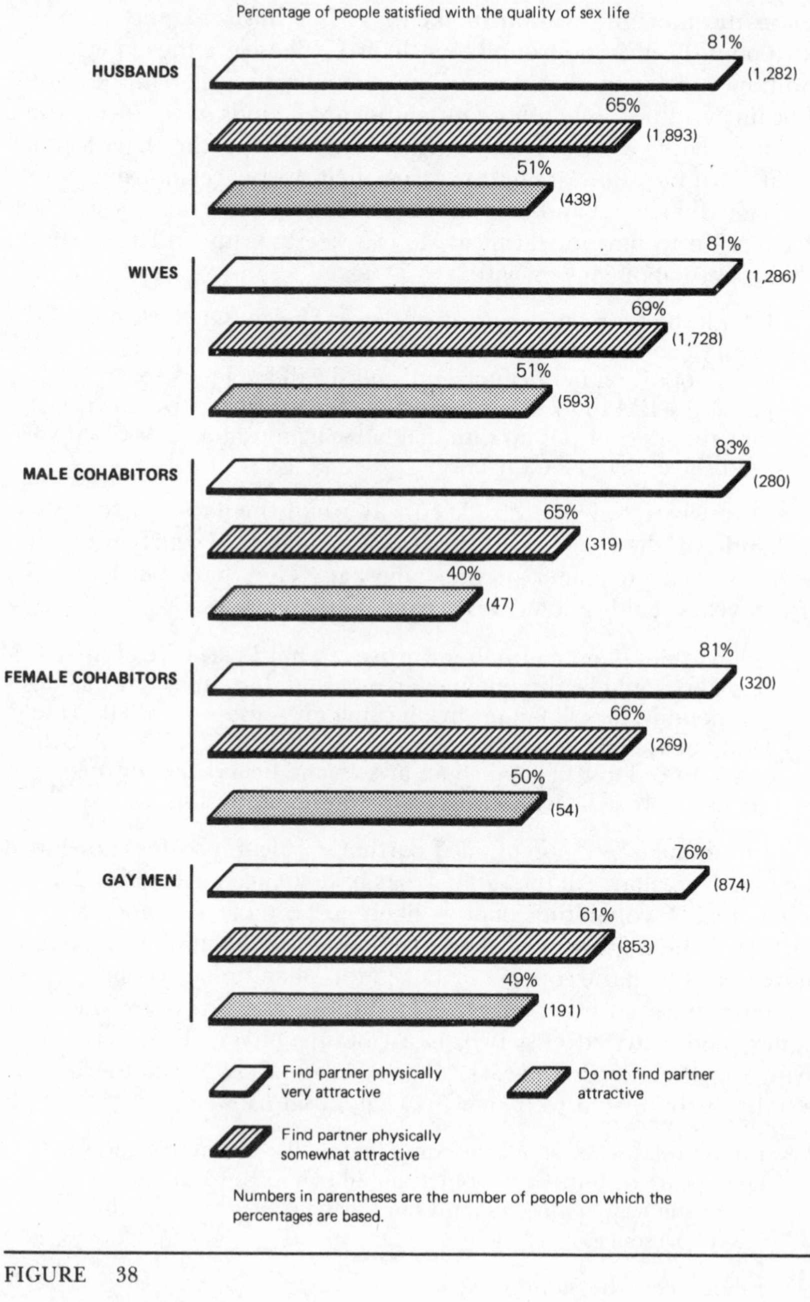

Percentage of people satisfied with the quality of sex life

**HUSBANDS**
81%
(1,282)
65%
(1,893)
51%
(439)

**WIVES**
81%
(1,286)
69%
(1,728)
51%
(593)

**MALE COHABITORS**
83%
(280)
65%
(319)
40%
(47)

**FEMALE COHABITORS**
81%
(320)
66%
(269)
50%
(54)

**GAY MEN**
76%
(874)
61%
(853)
49%
(191)

Find partner physically very attractive

Find partner physically somewhat attractive

Do not find partner attractive

Numbers in parentheses are the number of people on which the percentages are based.

FIGURE   38

IMPORTANCE OF PARTNER'S
PHYSICAL ATTRACTIVENESS

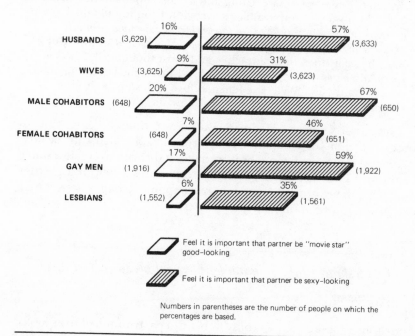

HUSBANDS (3,629) 16% 57% (3,633)

WIVES (3,625) 9% 31% (3,623)

MALE COHABITORS (648) 20% 67% (650)

FEMALE COHABITORS (648) 7% 46% (651)

GAY MEN (1,916) 17% 59% (1,922)

LESBIANS (1,552) 6% 35% (1,561)

Feel it is important that partner be "movie star" good-looking

Feel it is important that partner be sexy-looking

Numbers in parentheses are the number of people on which the percentages are based.

FIGURE    39

you know what I mean. I don't want to sound like that's the most important thing to me, or the reason that I love her or anything, but quite honestly, if she were not beautiful, it would be awkward for both of us. I would bet she feels the same way about me.

Gay men, being male, also desire beauty in a partner. Peter tried to build a relationship with Russ on the basis of other characteristics. Peter is a very handsome insurance broker of forty. He has been living for nine years with Russ, thirty-five, who works as a ferry operator. Peter fell in love with Russ because he enjoyed his personality even though he felt him to be only "somewhat attractive . . . nothing devastating . . . not especially sexy." For nine years they have had a relationship that both describe as "very close, happy, and without strife." In many ways they are a perfect couple. Or, rather, we should say *were* a perfect couple. Six months after our interview, Peter met Louis, found him more handsome, and announced to Russ that he was leaving. After we learned of their breakup, we reread their interview to see if we could tell why. We discovered a clue in Peter's past. Before meeting Russ, he had lived with a man he did not think was handsome. He described how that relationship ended:

I met somebody else and . . . this was a very exciting person, a very dynamic, gorgeous, very exciting and excitable person that turned out to be absolutely impossible to live with. I found out and . . . many times wondered [*Why*] *in the world you gave up a relatively comfortable relationship for one with an incredible amount of strife.* But he was physically incredibly attractive and I just thought: *Well, this is reason to end the other relationship.* And so I just came bounding home one day and said, "Well, I've fallen in love with somebody else. Good-bye." Oh, it was cruel, just really awful.

The pattern was repeated with Russ. Even though Peter wants to choose a partner for compatibility, he remains obsessed with beauty.

We feel that a fixation on beauty makes it difficult to create a stable relationship. Each partner will readily respond to a new and prettier face. Unless the existing relationship rests upon a stronger base, it may crumble when a tempting situation arises.

---

*Only lesbian couples do not let physical beauty affect their happiness.*

Of our four types of couples, only lesbians have triumphed over looks. Whether a lesbian is physically beautiful or not, her partner's sexual fulfillment, her happiness, and her belief that the relationship will last are equally unaffected.[8] Time and again gay women have told us that conventional standards of female beauty ultimately do not matter to them, and when we examine the way their relationships work, we find this is generally true. Beverly, thirty-six, and Marsha, thirty-eight, have been together for seventeen years. Beverly is an associate dean at a university, and Marsha is an obstetrician. Beverly's view is common among lesbians:

I think she is beautiful inside and outside. But I don't really care who else thinks she's beautiful, or if she's beautiful in society's eyes. . . . What is important is who the person is, and not a lot of standards that were composed by some copywriter for *Playboy*. I could really care less about that stuff.

While some lesbians respond to the dictates of fashion, many inhabit a culture scornful of what they consider male standards of female attractiveness, which they reject as indicators of women's worth. They have no desire to attract men, nor any purpose for doing so.

*When heterosexual men and women are very attractive, they*
*resent it when their partners receive more attention from*
*others than they do.*

Because this society is preoccupied with beauty, looks help to establish a person's worth. When the world judges a person beautiful, he or she feels more valuable. We feel that beautiful people become accustomed to the power that derives from their looks, and do not want to lose it. This can generate competitiveness between partners. Our study shows that the more attractive heterosexuals are, the more they compete with their partners and resent the attention paid their partners by others.[9] If at a party one partner of a couple is fawned over and treated as more sexually attractive, the less complimented person may feel slighted. We find that people who are vain about their appearance do not like being ignored, and will compete even with their partners for attention from others. But these people are unusual; most of our heterosexuals do not vie with their partners in this area.[10]

We think that most shun this rivalry because of the basic fact that women and men are physically different from each other. Men and women never compete in the same beauty pageant. They are judged by such different standards of physical attractiveness that they would never be put in competition with one another. It is hard to imagine complimenting a woman on her broad shoulders or admiring a man

**COMPETITIVENESS OVER**
**SEXUAL ATTRACTIVENESS**

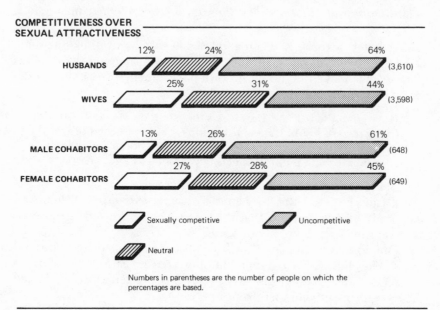

Numbers in parentheses are the number of people on which the
percentages are based.

FIGURE    40

for his hourglass figure. Miss America does not win because the judges find her ruggedly handsome.

When we asked heterosexual couples in the interviews to say which of them was better-looking, most men and women found it impossible to make comparisons. They simply did not know how to answer. For example, Bernice, forty, works in a department store and has been married three years to Harold, forty, who owns a small printshop. Bernice said:

> I think we're about equal. Maybe I get a little more attention because I'm more the life-of-the-party kind of person. But if you were trying just to go by looks, I think it would be impossible to compare us. I don't know; I've never thought about it. I really don't think you can compare men and women.

And Harold felt the same way:

> I think we're about equal. . . . To tell you the truth, I don't know how to judge how attractive I am, or any man. It's been proved. Every time Bernice asks me to fix up this single lady friend of hers, I am always accused of describing the guy [I suggest] wrong. I told her I thought the guy was good-looking. She thought he was terrible. I wasn't lying. I thought he *was* good-looking. I just don't think men and women see each other in the same ways.

---

*Same-sex couples may compete with each other for the attention of others. When they do, it causes conflict.*

Unlike heterosexuals, gay men and lesbians may be rivals for the same admirers. When a gay man goes to a party, flirtations aimed at his partner may make him doubt his own handsomeness. As a thirty-one-year-old dancer told us:

> If we go to the bar and Derek gets the attention of every trick I'm trying to zero in on, I know I shouldn't, but I get pissed off for the whole evening. . . . I get pissed off even if he doesn't want the attention. I don't mind if he gets one, as long as I get one.

Being judged less attractive than one's partner by the outside world can create serious problems for same-sex couples. When gay men and lesbians perceive that their partners are treated as more attractive, they fight more about sex.[11]

One extreme version of such conflict is illustrated by Clara and Doris. They have been together almost two years. Clara, twenty-four, is a college student, and Doris, twenty-three, is a baker. Doris explained their problem with competitiveness:

> I'm jealous. I'm jealous when she gets more attention, because then I

feel less powerful. . . . We're really competitive—where we want to look better than the other person, we want to sound better than the other person, we want a better job, want to do everything better. . . . If we go somewhere and I am basically ignored, I feel so bad that I am angry with her. It isn't fair, but I just can't relate well under those circumstances. Things have to be equal, or I have to feel somewhat ahead.

A couple is continually being reminded of its solidarity—or lack of it—by the possibility of other people's interest in one of the partners. When couples view this interest as a potential threat to their continued existence, they may become defensive and therefore possessive. One person may try to control his or her partner's opportunities to meet other people. But possessiveness, and its expression, varies greatly from one couple type to another. Some people worry about any kind of attention a partner may receive; others worry only about sexual contact. Still others can tolerate non-monogamy as long as their partners remain emotionally uninvolved. Some people are so unpossessive that they can even permit a full-fledged affair and remain confident the relationship will survive.

---

*Men are less possessive than women because they are more*
*powerful.*

When we asked people how troubled they would be if their partners had sex with someone else, we were surprised to learn that women are a bit more possessive than men.[12] We had reasoned from the common stereotypes of males and females: A man loathes being "cuckolded" and considers his woman his "property." A woman forgives her man's wandering eye because it is a "natural" part of the male drive.

We think heterosexual women are more possessive than men because they are more vulnerable and financially dependent. Even after the gains of the women's movement, it is still difficult for the average American woman to earn as much money as a man or to see herself as an independent force in the world. Most women still grow up believing they need a man to take care of them and their children. We find possessiveness especially common among heterosexual women who are frightened of making a new life for themselves if their partners should leave them.[13]

Even though heterosexual men are somewhat less possessive than women, we should recall that it is still a very common emotion. In the interviews, men told us about times when they felt possessive. For example, a married schoolteacher described his feelings:

POSSESSIVENESS

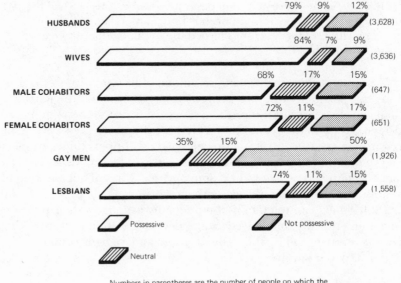

FIGURE   41

There was a party with some of her old boyfriends and I didn't want her to go there alone. I said, "It's not that I don't trust you. I don't want to do that. I just want to be there." I was very hostile and I went to the party with a big chip on my shoulder, and someone almost knocked it off. If anybody just looks at her, I establish my territory.

Even in same-sex couples, where no traditions give one partner authority over the other, possessiveness operates in much the same way it does in heterosexual couples. We find that among lesbians and gay men, just as we saw among the heterosexual women, when people are scared of living without their partners, they are more possessive.[14] This suggests to us that it is not being female that makes a person sexually possessive, but rather being afraid to be on one's own.

*Women, more than men, have needed to be in love to have sex. This has made them more possessive.*

On the questionnaire, we asked how people felt about sex without love. Wives are more likely to disapprove than husbands, and lesbians are much less in favor of it than are gay men.[15] The female cohabitors, however, are different in that they disapprove only slightly more than their partners. They are living in sexual relationships with men to whom they are not married. Having taken such an unconventional step, they are unwilling to condemn untraditional sexual behavior. In some cases this means they are more liberal than their partners. Lorna has been living with Jorge for one year. They are both in their early thirties. Lorna works as a practical nurse and Jorge drives a cab. Lorna feels that sex and love should go together, but she can understand how one may operate without the other.

> We discussed those things on the first night we had together. We both had the same basic feeling. I think we will be faithful to one another and if something ever came to an overwhelming degree, we would discuss it and say, "I really want to spend the night with so-and-so." But we equally understand that could be the end of the intimate relationship. He feels very strongly about that. I feel less strongly. I believe in passing fancies more. He has more of a romantic notion.

Jorge does indeed feel more strongly:

> We have an understanding. As far as I know, we are both loyal people. And it would be a totally negative thing if either one of us

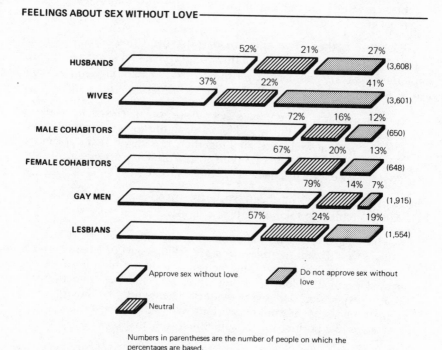

FEELINGS ABOUT SEX WITHOUT LOVE

HUSBANDS 52% 21% 27% (3,608)
WIVES 37% 22% 41% (3,601)
MALE COHABITORS 72% 16% 12% (650)
FEMALE COHABITORS 67% 20% 13% (648)
GAY MEN 79% 14% 7% (1,915)
LESBIANS 57% 24% 19% (1,554)

Approve sex without love       Do not approve sex without love

Neutral

Numbers in parentheses are the number of people on which the percentages are based.

FIGURE   42

had a relationship outside of our own. I've told Lorna that if I ever found out that she was disloyal—and that is how I would interpret it—I would pack my clothes and leave.

Women have traditionally been taught to be cautious about men who wanted to have sex before marriage. Even contemporary women who believe in premarital sex acknowledge possible pitfalls in their new sexual freedom. A man might not call for another date, or he might speak ill behind her back after a sexual encounter. A woman thus fears having sex without first being assured of the man's love, or at least of his respect. We also think that wives want to believe their husbands loved them the first time they had sex together. A wife would like to see her husband as "different" from other men, and their sexual relationship as sacred. She feels he can be trusted not to engage in casual sexual conquests. But since she cannot imagine him having sex with someone else for callous reasons, she then fears their relationship is in grave danger at the first hint of another woman; it means the beginning of love for another and the end of love for her. Gloria, a homemaker who has been married ten years, explained to us how sullied she would feel if her husband, Pat, were to have sex with someone else:

> Before marriage we discussed monogamy and we both wholeheartedly agree about how important it is. I don't believe in cheating and he doesn't believe in cheating. And that's what it would be—cheating someone out of love and trust. It would make a mockery of marriage.

Francine is thirty-five and breeds pure-bred dogs. She has been married thirteen years to Greg, a thirty-eight-year-old lawyer. Francine explained that she could not continue to see her marriage in the same way if her husband were to have sex with someone else.

> If Greg ever was going to have sex outside our marriage, he would end [the marriage], I'm sure. He is a straight shooter. It would mean the end of what we had created together. It is very difficult for me to even imagine. . . . I don't think he would do it to hurt me. He would do it because we had failed each other in some way.

Anne-Marie, who has been living for three years with Brian, feels he is too romantic to take outside sex lightly.

> We have agreed that we will not have sex with anyone else. I don't think I would want to, unless we were falling apart or I felt he didn't love me anymore. I don't think he would want to unless it was the same kind of situation. . . . I don't think he could have something that was "just sex." He is very tenderhearted, and if he did something sexual, it would be serious. We both try hard not to put ourselves in a position where something romantic could happen.

For many women, monogamy is so elemental a symbol of trust that any kind of outside sex would destroy the relationship. Gertrude is sixty-eight. She and Jerome have been married for almost fifty years. He is a retired stockbroker, and she is active in supporting the arts. When we asked Gertrude about extramarital sex, she replied:

> I have trouble understanding how people can have a sexual act before marriage, and I really don't understand someone who would destroy the trust of a marriage by violating the meaning of marriage. I don't understand why someone would get married if they were not going to be monogamous. For me, that is the part of the commitment you make. . . . And sex is not just an act within it [marriage]. It is a rededication of two people to each other and a very precious, trusting exchange.

Heterosexual men have traditionally learned it is important to be sexually experienced before marriage. Experimentation was supposed to be conducted with someone other than one's future wife, in a context free from love or commitment. A history of "recreational sex" could enhance a reputation unless a man went overboard. When he married it was assumed he would put his sexual adventures behind him.

But most men retain the belief that it is possible to have sex without implication of commitment. Even if they remain monogamous, they maintain the capacity to distinguish love from lust. As one husband, married for nine years, told us:

> Our idea is that we are married to one another. But it's always been my belief that sex and love are two different things. For a man, sex is a physical thing and it can be as impersonal and as casual as shaking somebody's hand or eating a sandwich.

Many a man assured us that his relationship would survive an outside "fling." Such men are so certain that they can enjoy sex without romantic entanglement, they assume that if the "worst" happened and their partners were "unfaithful," they, too, could put sex in its proper perspective and not endanger the relationship. We think some men are less possessive than women, in part, because they do not really expect women to be non-monogamous, and they misjudge women's capacity for sex without love.

Some heterosexual men may not be very concerned about their partners' having sex outside the relationship. But given what we have learned about women's sexual values, if a woman was non-monogamous we would expect it not to be casual. We feel that if men are cavalier about this possibility, they take a chance on the future of their relationships. On the other hand, heterosexual women are more concerned about their partners' straying. But in the light of men's ability to separate casual sex from love, a non-monogamous episode is not necessarily serious. And so, we feel, the women are safer than they imagine.

The gay men are the least possessive of our couples, and the most able to separate sex from love. This is no coincidence. It is common for them to have sex outside the relationship, and both men usually expect it to have very little emotional content. One gay man described for us his feelings about two kinds of sex:

> I make a distinction between love and having sex. Making love, you get into the person you're with, rather than just do it for the body or the cock or whatever. The latter, that's just plain sex. . . . I have never felt the involvements were anything more than what they were—either trying to get a threesome going or just my one-on-one with someone else. I'm not having a dual marriage or being a bigamist. . . . It's never entered my mind to leave him. . . . It's always a secondary thing.

His partner explained how important it is to preserve the sense of their relationship as sexually special:

> I mentioned to him, that in order for us to have a healthy relationship, that we ought not to impose heterosexual mores on our relationship, and that I would understand that he would be attracted and that he simply could not go without, and he should go and not feel guilty and have a physical relationship with someone else. I would not feel badly at all. I would only begin to feel badly if there was going to be a great amour or great emotional involvement. But if it's just a physical thing, go and do it. Because if you're going to be attracted to these individuals, you're going to start resenting me after a while if you don't have sexual release. . . .
> As for me, if I get cruised on the way home, I might do it. As long as it doesn't take any time from me and him. On the other hand, I'm more careful than I used to be. I have never contracted a venereal disease, but nowadays it's rampant and I'm a little afraid. . . . He is allergic to certain wonder drugs and I'd be terribly upset if I contracted something and transferred it to him and he would have a difficult time. . . .
> I think we've solved any jealousy problems. I don't care with whom he shares his body as long as he doesn't share his mind or soul. You know the French prostitutes have a wonderful attitude. They do their bodies, but they save their lips for their lovers, you see. As he saves his mind and heart for me, and he doesn't give his body that much, and neither do I. . . . I will not do it with somebody I know. . . . I don't like to have sex with people whose name I even know. It's the back room for me. Totally anonymous. If they ask me for my telephone number, my erection goes right down. I'm really not interested in having a conversation with them. I have a beautiful life and I don't want to complicate it.

Gay men do not live with women, so they do not have to adjust to women's sexual values. When a gay man understands casual sex for himself, he understands it for his partner.

Lesbians are not like gay men. As women, they usually have trouble with casual sex. However, because many lesbians feel they should be less bound by female sexual values, they are not as possessive as the wives in our study. Marguerite and Barbara are currently unemployed. They live with Marguerite's child. Marguerite is monogamous, while Barbara is not. She describes their situation:

Marguerite always told me she wasn't a jealous person. . . . And I said, "Well, I'm not jealous either." But I am. And she found out she is too. I had a brief affair with a woman who is twenty-nine. . . . She is a very attractive flight attendant. Marguerite said, "I know how much you love me and everything." Because this woman was beautiful and traveled all over the world and made good money. And it was real interesting, because what it did was make me appreciate my relationship with Marguerite more. . . . She'll tell me she won't do anything, but I say, "It's okay if you do." I don't expect to come home from a trip and be replaced.

The rejection of possessiveness often has ideological overtones among lesbians. Marguerite and Barbara succeed in being unpossessive, but they are exceptional. Thelma is fifty-five and is bureau chief of a federal agency. Meg is forty-seven and is assistant director of a private social agency. When we interviewed them, Thelma and Meg were getting back together again after Meg had had an affair. Thelma reported:

She got involved with a woman in her office. It was the first time she responded to someone . . . so I encouraged it. I thought it was good for her because I don't believe that one person can meet all of anyone's needs. In fact, when they began to have a sexual relationship, I even encouraged that. . . . But then I got caught in my emotions . . . my head no longer being in control. I knew what I wanted to think, but my emotions and ideology were not the same. . . . I started to feel excluded. At that point I just flipped out and that drove us into a crisis and into therapy. . . . I still think I'm more likely to have an affair. But then I don't think we could go through all that trauma again. So here I am the one who is more likely, with the realization that in eight years, I haven't, by choice. So that must say something about our relationship and who I really am. I play with the idea, but I can't imagine it really happening.

Meg stated her view on the matter:

The interesting thing is that she does not believe in monogamy and has been monogamous, and I do believe in monogamy and I have not been. She felt it was important that I would say she could have an affair and I would still love her. And I said, "I can't do that psychologically." And she pushed and pushed and said she couldn't have a relationship without that freedom. So I finally gave in and said yes. But it was not a real yes from my heart. I knew psychologically I couldn't do that. . . . And ultimately we find that it is best for me not to, and she makes the choice not to.

Like most heterosexual women, the majority of lesbians cannot separate sex from love. When actually called upon not to be possessive, they frequently do not succeed.

---

*For all types of couples, possessiveness escalates when one partner fears the other might have a meaningful affair.*

Even though some people in each of our types of couples can accept a partner's having sex outside the relationship, this does not mean they could tolerate a significant affair.[16] When we asked people how upset they would be if their partners had a meaningful affair, we found the men possessive and the women somewhat more so. Even heterosexual women who face with equanimity the possibility of a partner's casual sex feel threatened by the thought of his becoming emotionally involved with another woman. We think they know what it would mean if they themselves were involved with someone, and they project their feelings onto their partners. They believe that two intense romantic relationships cannot co-exist and that one would have to go.

Charles and Peggy have been married twelve years. He is forty-five and she two years younger. They own a small grocery store which they manage together. When we interviewed them, Peggy told us about an affair Charles had had a few years earlier:

> I found a letter from her in his pocket. I felt rotten searching his pockets, but I was sure something was going on, and he would jump all over me when I would suggest that this girl was doing more than just shopping in the store. . . . So eventually I found a letter that made me sick to my stomach. I told him he was throwing away everything he had. And he had the nerve to try and say that this had nothing to do with us. . . . I went as far as talking with a lawyer and we separated. . . . He stopped seeing her, but it will take me a long time to get over this.

The lesbians we interviewed were troubled at the thought of an affair. Helen and Mona have been together four years. Helen, a political consultant in her late thirties, spoke about the difference between sex outside the relationship and a meaningful affair:

> We said if you were going outside the relationship for confidential sex just because you wanted a fuck, that was fine. If you were going, you should be discreet and that way you would know it was just a fuck and the other person would never find out. If they found out, obviously there was something going on that you needed them to know—which immediately says that it wasn't just a fuck. If you were going outside the relationship, then your first responsibility was to deal with the relationship.

**POSSESSIVENESS AT THE PROSPECT OF PARTNER'S NON-MONOGAMY_____
AND AT THE PROSPECT OF A MEANINGFUL AFFAIR**

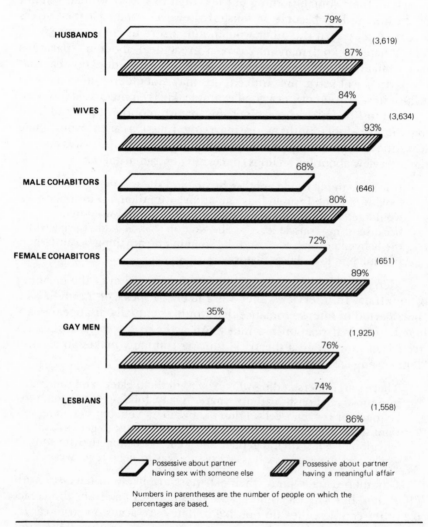

FIGURE   43

Mona, a junior-high-school teacher in her early forties, feels even more strongly:

> I'm supposed to agree to [non-monogamy] but I don't think I could accept it. . . . If she has to run out and get that from someone else, that's not saying much about what she thinks of this relationship. It's one thing if it's for sex, but another if something serious is going on there. And I don't really like the thought of either.

We also feel that women—both heterosexual and homosexual—understand the psychology of the "other woman." If one's partner offers another woman nothing but sex, then the other woman will not be encouraged to become serious. If, however, one's partner offers love, that may turn the other woman into a serious competitor.

A heterosexual man may care a great deal about his partner's having an affair, but his concern may be reduced if he does not fear that his partner will leave him. Indeed, this may embolden him to have an affair himself. Jules offers a good example. He is eighteen and has been married to Roxanne, who is nineteen, for two months. They had lived together for eight months before marrying. Jules is a cargo loader, while Roxanne is a homemaker. She is five months pregnant. Jules was open in the interview about his feelings concerning extramarital sex:

> If it came to me laying another broad, and she was that good-looking, I think I would [have an affair] even though Roxanne would get very very insanely jealous. But in a way I wouldn't, because of my conscience. . . . She wouldn't. She couldn't leave with the baby almost here . . . and she wouldn't do anything because she's too much in love. Put it that way.

Men are also likely to have a different conception of the meaning of an affair. In interviews, they were likely to speak of an affair as a short period of intense romance that would eventually disappear, leaving the original relationship intact. An actor in his early thirties reflected on how life in a theatrical touring company makes an affair a "limited engagement":

> There's an understanding when you're in the theater. You can get into those relationship affairs where, "Okay, folks, we're all going to be together for ten weeks. I don't know about you, but I'm going to want to get laid, and you're probably going to want to get laid, so why don't we just do it together, and we'll just be together for ten weeks and that's it." . . . It is a very safe way to sleep together.

Gay men usually know their partners are likely to have sex with other men, but when it comes to the possibility of an affair, they react like other couples; they do not like it. They are accustomed to casual outside sex, but emotional involvements are quite another thing, and they fear losing their partners. Troy, thirty-eight, and Stephen, forty-three, have been together for four years. Troy is a manager in a public agency and Stephen is a dentist. They have an easy understanding about sex with others, but Stephen explains how the understanding keeps things safe:

> We only have three-ways and four-ways because I don't want him doing anything when I'm not there. . . . I could probably tolerate him going to the baths or something crude like that, as long as he never got to know anyone. I think it is very important that we save

our hearts for one another. . . . In three-ways, we are sharing everything. I think that is a good way not to let anyone in between us.

Gay men are certainly unhappy at the prospect of their partners' having a serious affair, but they are not as troubled as the husbands. Because gay men have so much casual sex, it is inevitable that some serious romance will intrude. Two strangers may have sex with every intention of keeping it impersonal, but they may be surprised to discover they like each other. This is the way affairs begin. One man in a long-term relationship told us how it was almost ended by an affair:

We had one big problem that almost broke us up on our tenth anniversary. We had not been communicating well. . . . We went to the baths and I met someone at the baths who fell head over heels in love with me. Which was fantastic for my ego. And he was following me on the phone, wherever we went. He paid for my trip back to the Midwest and he wanted me in the worst way to be his lover. And I was very intrigued, someone coming on so strong to me after so many years. . . . I thought I was going to leave [my partner] and I told him so and went through an awful lot of crying and discussing and arguing and everything else. . . . I said, "I really do love you. I really want to stay with you. . . . If you're willing to go through counseling, so am I." So we did. Here we are.

A serious affair can break up the original couple. But if the couple does survive it, a new commitment and security may be forged. The longer the couple goes on, the more likely it is that they will come to regard any outside sex as passing fancies.[17]

Although lesbians do not like affairs, they, too, become less concerned about non-monogamy with time.[18] In interviews with lesbians who had been together for many years, we often heard that a good relationship is hard to find and that not even an affair could shatter their commitment to it. As one woman in a non-monogamous relationship explained:

We reassure each other a lot, not an inordinate sickening amount, but as time goes on, we know how much we mean to each other, and that we would like to pass our old age together. There's so much more than sex. You spend forty hours a week working, and similar amounts sleeping and doing laundry and all the mundane things that you have to do, and enjoy that time together. To lose my mind over seeing her with someone else in a secondary fashion is not worth losing what we have.

*Possessiveness has nothing to do with commitment, except for wives.*

Couples sometimes take perverse delight in each other's possessiveness. An assumption is being made, equating the partner's possessiveness with degree of emotional attachment. A very territorial partner may be thought to be deeply in love and devoted to the relationship. A partner who shows no sign of jealousy must not truly care. If one's partner is overbearing, it may be resented; but if the partner shows no sign of possessiveness, one feels unloved. However, our data tell us that these feelings do not reflect the true situation. Whatever makes some people less possessive than others, it is not a lack of commitment to the relationship.

People may test their partners' real feelings by attempting to arouse jealousy. There are several ways in which we feel they can be misled. For example, a wife seeking confirmation of her worth to her husband and assurance of his steadfastness may flirt with another man at a party, hoping to get a rise from her husband. If he reacts in the way she wants, she may relax, believing he is committed to her. However, our data tell us that he may or may *not* be committed in this case. What she may in fact be observing is his need for control over her actions. These women would be surprised if their husbands were to leave them, since they have relied on scenes like this to define the state of their marriage.

A lesbian trying to provoke a possessive reaction from her partner may be upset when none ensues. Believing her partner does not care about the relationship, she may then seriously pursue another woman. She may have been mistaken about her partner's lack of commitment and have therefore jeopardized her relationship unnecessarily.

Or consider the following scenario: a gay man would like his partner to be possessive, and so he threatens to have a love affair. The partner still does not react with jealousy, but calls his bluff. Even though the first man has received permission, he does not genuinely want to get involved. In failing to carry his threat through, he has inadvertently informed both himself and his partner how completely attached he is to the relationship. The partner has no need to fear any threat from outside—which gives him additional power.

The exceptions are the wives. Our data show that when they are not possessive it means they are less likely to feel the relationship has much of a future.[19] Such a wife is not attached enough to be concerned if her husband has an affair. In this case the man may misunderstand why she is unpossessive. He may feel she has liberal sexual values or trusts him not to get involved. But in reality she does not expect their relationship to last. Why is this true only of wives? We believe it is

within the nature of the institution of marriage for wives to be possessive about their husbands, and that when a wife has ceased to believe
her marriage will be permanent, her motivation to be possessive is
diminished.

---

*Husbands and wives who view marriage as a "lifetime
contract" are more possessive than other married couples.*

Some husbands and wives feel that no matter how good or bad a
marriage is, it is an indissoluble lifetime contract. We have called these
people "institutionally married." One of the clauses of their tacit contract states that both spouses will be forever faithful. This makes them
feel secure,[20] but it also causes them to be very possessive.[21] If a spouse
had sex outside the relationship, a serious crisis would be provoked.
The contract upon which the marriage is based would be invalidated.
Institutional husbands and wives are possessive because no matter how
they resolved this crisis, their entire belief system would have been
shattered.

Nowadays married couples tend to be less "institutional" and more
"voluntary." Voluntarily married couples believe that marriages should
last only so long as the spouses remain happy and care for each other.
They are less possessive, not because they love each other less but
because they feel people should stay in a relationship from choice
rather than obligation.

Every couple has to deal with the risk of an outside affair luring a
partner away. Institutional husbands and wives control that risk by
clamping down on the partners' freedom. Since voluntary marriages
are based on a certain amount of freedom, some risk is implicit.

We now see how attractiveness influences the lives of men and
women. We think that even when beauty is not particularly important
to people, a couple is more likely to prosper if both partners are equally
attractive than if one partner is far more alluring. If one partner lets
his or her looks go, then the balance between the two may become
unstable: One is reaping compliments from the outside world while the
other goes unnoticed by it. The less attractive partner may become
territorially defensive—not letting the other out alone, behaving in a
manner defensive (and offensive) to suspected interlopers, or growing
obsessive about his or her ability to command attention from other
people.

Gay and lesbian couples face the biggest problems because both
partners can be judged by identical standards of physical attractiveness.
Less competition is likely between heterosexual partners, who evaluate

each other according to different standards. One way some gay and lesbian couples can—and sometimes do—avoid the pitfalls of being measured by the same yardstick is to adopt different ideals of physical attractiveness. Each partner may have a very different "look"—for example, a pair in which one man is tall and the other short. It is true that many lesbian and gay couples shun role playing because they regard it as an undesirable parody of heterosexual roles. Nonetheless, by invoking these conventional images—for example, a lesbian who is very feminine in appearance (the "femme") with a very boyish or masculine partner (the "butch")—they may succeed in defusing some competitiveness.

Everyone seeks admiration from the outside world, and one way to achieve it is to identify with a partner who is much admired. A person can take great pride in having a handsome or accomplished partner. It redounds to one's own worth: Someone who is able to attract such a person must be very desirable. If one's partner remains a "good catch" over the years, a couple's relationship may be strengthened because each continues to receive the reflected glory of the other. At the same time, we learn from our data that if one partner feels unattractive in comparison with the other, insecurity, territoriality, and other negative emotions may develop. No one wants to be the brown wren sharing the nest with a bird of paradise.

It is clear that standards of beauty bring tension to our couples' lives: On the one hand, there are the gratifications that come from having an attractive partner, and on the other hand, the insecurities that grow when a partner is too attractive. Popular songs and private fantasies are filled with yearning for a beautiful mate, but the experiences of our couples tell us that there can easily be too much of a good thing. When it comes to physical appearance, a fairly equal balance between partners seems to be the best and most salutary arrangement.

Our data show that women worry more about losing their partners than men do and therefore are more possessive. Heterosexual women do not fully understand male sexual psychology. Consequently, they view the possibility of their partners' having outside sex as a commentary on—and a threat to—their relationships. Men feel more secure, but they, too, have an incomplete understanding of female sexual psychology. They do not recognize how significant it is for a woman, particularly a wife, to have sex with someone else. We think that heterosexual men might become almost as possessive as heterosexual women if they had a keener sense of what sex means to women. Conversely, women might become less possessive if they knew how casually many men view outside sex.

But no matter how well each gender comes to appreciate the other, we feel women will continue to be more possessive as long as they remain more dependent, as long as their status in society makes them more vulnerable in the event of separation. It is easy not to be possessive when one is more secure and more in charge—and this is true in both heterosexual and homosexual relationships. Not being possessive says little about a partner's ability to love or about his or her other qualities. Rather, a partner who is not possessive has the upper hand, and knows it.

# Non-monogamy

## The diverse alternatives

We have purposely chosen the word *non-monogamy* when we write about sex outside a couple's relationship. We would prefer to use a less clumsy word, but this is the only word that is morally neutral: It neither condemns nor condones. We need a word that merely describes; therefore, we have intentionally omitted expressions like *cheating, infidelity,* and *adultery,* except when the couples we interview use them to express the way they feel.

A substantial minority of the heterosexual couples in our study have had sex outside their relationships. Whether it occurs by mutual consent or through the purposeful design of one partner, such an act cannot but affect the relationship. The consequences of outside sex therefore warrant careful analysis.

For some of our couples, particularly gay men, non-monogamy is a way of life. Accordingly, we need to understand precisely how it works in order to gauge its impact on the happiness of these couples and the durability of their relationships.

We would not do justice to this important topic, however, if we discussed nothing but the frequency of its actual occurrence among heterosexual and homosexual couples. Non-monogamy touches the lives of all couples. Even if they are in fact monogamous, they wonder about it—what it would be like, and what it would do to their relationships. They worry about sexual competition and may suspect their partners of deceiving them. Even if they feel secure, couples often have family and friends who are not monogamous and they are uncertain about how to judge such conduct.

Moreover, if the so-called sexual revolution really implies that more couples in the future will have sex outside their relationships, then we need a better understanding of the behavior of couples who are not monogamous today in order to get an idea of what lies ahead.

Non-monogamy conjures up different images for different people. Much depends on the observer's values. For some, it may seem a lark: an adventure, a treat with little or no bearing on the primary relationship. To others, it may sound the death knell of a relationship:

the end of trust, love, commitment, and loyalty. What non-monogamy means and how it is interpreted depends a great deal on whether a person is male or female. Men and women exhibit wide divergence in their views on sex, romance, adventure, and commitment. Therefore, when we understand non-monogamy, we gain additional insight into the priorities and sensibilities of both sexes.

Finally, partners who have experienced what they consider a sexual trespass are often at a loss to know what it means for their relationship. Examining the circumstances of non-monogamy in many relationships gives us more insight into the possible meaning of a given couple's experience. For many, an act of non-monogamy is the ultimate betrayal. A partner who has always been honest and honorable risks losing his or her partner's trust forever by a single indiscretion. Once the foundation has been rocked, the relationship may be forever changed.

Couples who have established a non-monogamous relationship, on the other hand, demonstrate that it is possible to create rules that help partners isolate sex with others from their feelings about each other— if they have to and believe they should. This is impossible for traditional couples to imagine, but our data show great variation in the sexual "laws" couples legislate.

We devote a lot of space to non-monogamy because it occupies a lot of space in our couples' imaginations. Also, if it happens, it need occur only once to be a crystallizing event for a relationship. It provides us with insight into rule making and rule breaking and the complex reasons why sexual exclusivity is sacred to so many couples.

---

### Most suspicion of non-monogamy is justified.

The vast majority of people learn about it sooner or later if their partner has had sex outside the relationship.[1] There is really very little unfounded suspicion.

In interviews a husband often told us that his wife's fears of non-monogamy were based on the reputation men have for indulging in extramarital sex. For example, Neil and Virginia, a newly married couple, are monogamous. Neil is twenty-seven, assistant manager of a retail store, and Virginia is twenty-four, a homemaker. Although Neil is monogamous, Virginia worries that eventually he will slip. Neil told us:

> We've had discussions about it. Virginia feels that I must always be totally, from here to the day I die, true to her, loyal to her. We've watched a number of shows on TV where the plot is along those lines, and she gets very upset watching it because I am not as upset as she is when the story involves a man cheating on his wife. She

**ANY INSTANCE(S) OF NON-MONOGAMY AMONG PEOPLE WHOSE PARTNERS BELIEVE THEM TO HAVE BEEN NON-MONOGAMOUS**

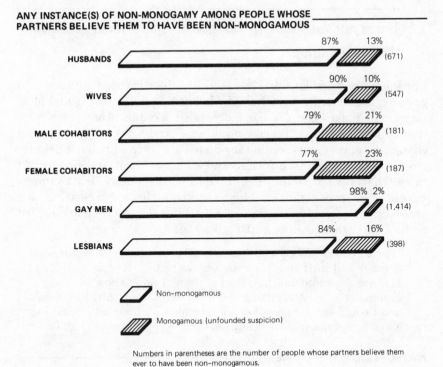

FIGURE 44

feels that this is an indication that I am not going to be loyal to her. Well, that is ridiculous. Now, I do have to say I don't know what my feelings are going to be ten years from now. I have to swear in blood that I'm going to be truly loyal to her. I have no intention of not being loyal to her, but it is hard to believe that something won't happen. . . . I love her, so when and if it does happen, I will have to make sure it's something very, very private.

Many gay men do not care if their partners are monogamous. If a gay man is monogamous, he is such a rare phenomenon, he may have difficulty making himself believed. Clarence and Daniel, both fifty-six, have been together thirty-two years. Clarence is an actor and Daniel teaches law. Because Clarence is often touring, he has become blasé about the possibility of Daniel having sex with someone else.

Because of our constant separation, I don't overlook the fact it's entirely possible that he might have a sexual relationship while I'm gone. But if he does, I know it's not going to mean anything and I don't want to know about it. I think he feels the same way. It's not supposed to happen between us, but we both know it is not impossible. After all, we weren't born yesterday.

*Wives and husbands are the most deceptive about sex outside their relationship.*

Cohabitors and lesbians are less secretive than married couples, and gay men are the least secretive. The interesting point here is that marriage itself makes couples more deceptive. Couples who marry have traditionally sworn to "forsake all others," and it is rare that couples change the agreement, even if they do not always live up to it.[2] Because most non-monogamous husbands and wives have broken their contract rather than revised it, they are forced into dishonesty. For example, Ernest is a forty-eight-year-old technician. He and Felicia, a dog groomer, have been married seven years. It is the second marriage for each. Two years ago Ernest had a brief affair:

> We had this neighbor who I used to talk to when I would throw the garbage and stuff away. She was very attractive, very nice, and, you know, it grew into a flirting kind of thing. I don't know why, but eventually we started talking about personal things. She was divorced and I could see she knew her way around. . . . I started fantasizing about her and it just got really clear that we were going to go for

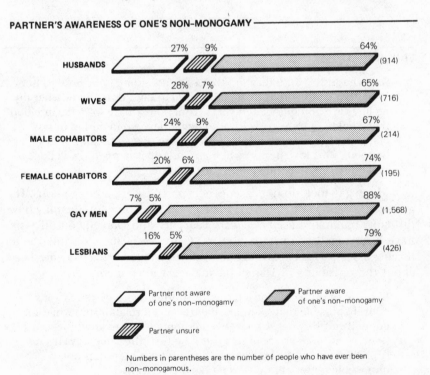

PARTNER'S AWARENESS OF ONE'S NON-MONOGAMY

HUSBANDS — 27% / 9% / 64% (914)

WIVES — 28% / 7% / 65% (716)

MALE COHABITORS — 24% / 9% / 67% (214)

FEMALE COHABITORS — 20% / 6% / 74% (195)

GAY MEN — 7% / 5% / 88% (1,568)

LESBIANS — 16% / 5% / 79% (426)

Partner not aware of one's non-monogamy

Partner aware of one's non-monogamy

Partner unsure

Numbers in parentheses are the number of people who have ever been non-monogamous.

FIGURE 45

each other. . . . I kept putting it off because it was so close to home and I was scared silly that Felicia would find out. That would just destroy her. So I waited until she was out of town and until I was sure Ellen [the neighbor] was the kind of person I could trust. When you have a wife and two kids, you can't just go do the first thing you want to do.

From the interviews we have the impression that a wife is likely to be more suspicious when she cannot account for her husband's time. Myrtle and Wayne have been married for sixteen years. It is the second marriage for both. Myrtle is fifty-six, a homemaker; Wayne, who is five years younger, does consulting work which causes him to travel often. Myrtle expressed her concerns about her husband's faithfulness:

I worry about him when he is away. . . . I know this is a little crazy-causing, especially since you'd think I'd be used to it by now. And I am, but I'm not. He needs a lot of flattering and I think he gets it mostly from flirting with friends and office girls, and I don't think he has ever been unfaithful, but I'm not absolutely sure. . . . I think I worry about it more than I used to. Before, I think I filled all his needs for flattery and now I'm a little less thoughtful. . . . I don't think anything serious would happen, but I have to be honest. If I am so secure, why do I worry so much?

It seemed to us that husbands are less suspicious of wives, particularly when the wives are full-time homemakers. There have been countless dirty jokes about the frustrated housewife's affair with the hapless milkman. We feel these jokes are a smug commentary on the scarcity of the men whom full-time homemakers have customarily been expected to meet. Compared to women employed outside the home, they do not encounter many men whom their husbands do not know. Furthermore, if a wife spends most of her time at home, her husband assumes she would not let a stranger enter the house they share. And if she did, he is confident the visitor would be noticed by a neighbor or friend who would tell him. Wives would probably feel the same way about their husbands if men were home much of the day, but they seldom are. Perhaps one of the reasons husbands have traditionally tried to stop their wives from getting jobs is their fear that sexual involvement with other men would follow.

---

*Monogamy is a strongly held moral ideal, even when it is not always adhered to.*

In spite of all the worry about "infidelity," the personal standard most people hold for themselves is monogamy.[3] But the ideal and what people can live up to are two different things. More people told us they would like to be monogamous than have actually succeeded in being so.

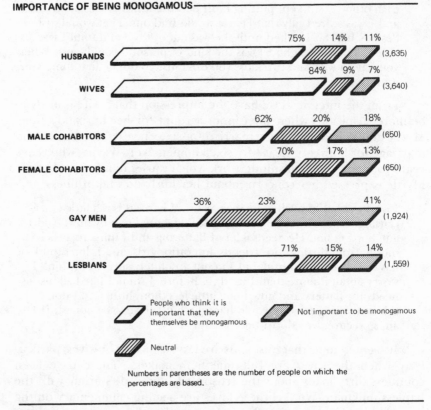

IMPORTANCE OF BEING MONOGAMOUS

HUSBANDS  75%  14%  11%  (3,635)

WIVES  84%  9%  7%  (3,640)

MALE COHABITORS  62%  20%  18%  (650)

FEMALE COHABITORS  70%  17%  13%  (650)

GAY MEN  36%  23%  41%  (1,924)

LESBIANS  71%  15%  14%  (1,559)

People who think it is important that they themselves be monogamous

Not important to be monogamous

Neutral

Numbers in parentheses are the number of people on which the percentages are based.

FIGURE   46

Fewer women have sex outside their relationships than men do. But among heterosexuals, the difference between the two is smaller than we would have expected. It is when we compare how many partners men and women have had outside of the relationship that a greater disparity emerges.[4] Wives who have been non-monogamous have usually had only a few outside partners. Non-monogamous husbands have had more. Female cohabitors look almost exactly like the wives, but male cohabitors have somewhat fewer partners than husbands.[5] The lesbians have fewer outside partners than all the other groups, and the gay men seek more variety; they seldom stop with a few outside partners. In sum, non-monogamous women have fewer partners than non-monogamous men.

*A couple can never be completely sure that their relationship will remain monogamous.*

Ten years of monogamy does not mean the eleventh is safe. Sex outside the relationship can occur at any point, and both new and well-

## ANY INSTANCE(S) OF NON-MONOGAMY SINCE BEGINNING OF RELATIONSHIP

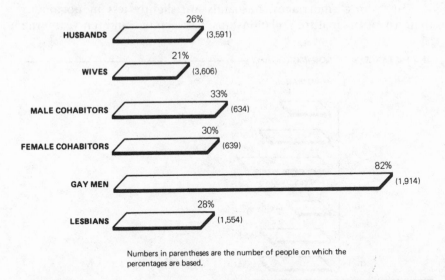

HUSBANDS 26% (3,591)

WIVES 21% (3,606)

MALE COHABITORS 33% (634)

FEMALE COHABITORS 30% (639)

GAY MEN 82% (1,914)

LESBIANS 28% (1,554)

Numbers in parentheses are the number of people on which the percentages are based.

FIGURE 47

## NUMBER OF OUTSIDE SEX PARTNERS

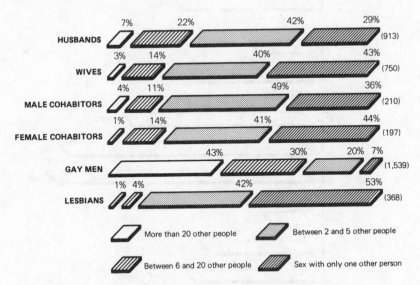

HUSBANDS 7% 22% 42% 29% (913)

WIVES 3% 14% 40% 43% (750)

MALE COHABITORS 4% 11% 49% 36% (210)

FEMALE COHABITORS 1% 14% 41% 44% (197)

GAY MEN 43% 30% 20% 7% (1,539)

LESBIANS 1% 4% 42% 53% (368)

More than 20 other people

Between 2 and 5 other people

Between 6 and 20 other people

Sex with only one other person

Note: This figure deals only with people who ever had sex outside their relationship. Among gay men and lesbians, these percentages represent only sex partners of the same gender.

Numbers in parentheses are the number of people who have ever had non-monogamous sex.

FIGURE 48

established relationships are at risk.[6] However, our four kinds of couples look very different from one another.

In "young" marriages, husbands are slightly less monogamous than wives. In "mature" relationships (between two and ten years) the

**ANY INSTANCE(S) OF NON-MONOGAMY**

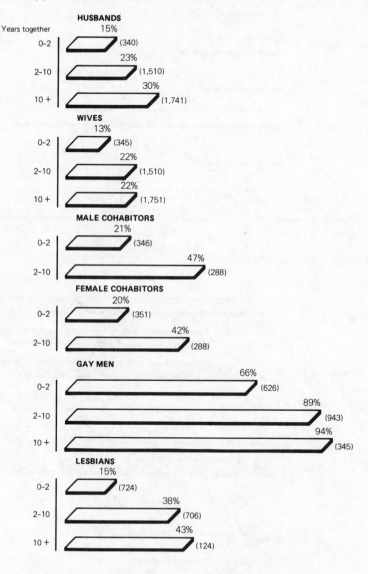

Note: Very few of our cohabitors had been together more than 10 years.

Numbers in parentheses are the number of people on which the percentages are based.

FIGURE   49

gap is wider. The early years of cohabitors' relationships are less monogamous than those of married couples. The difference is even more
dramatic in established relationships. Over 40 percent of our cohabitors in the two- to ten-year category have had sex with someone else.
After a couple of years, some of our cohabitors marry, and the ones
who do not are more likely to favor a sexually open relationship.[7]

Sex outside their relationships occurs within the first two years for
most gay men. But these years are like a honeymoon; as the relationship goes on, virtually all gay men have other sexual partners.[8] The
lesbians in "young" relationships resemble the wives, but in established
relationships look more like the female cohabitors. Why have so many
of our lesbians and female cohabitors in "mature" relationships been
non-monogamous, when women prize sexual fidelity so much? The
cohabitors and lesbians have no legal contract forbidding outside sex.
And in the interviews, some of these women told us that monogamy is
an element of the marital institution they wish to avoid.

We also think that even when lesbians disapprove of non-monogamy, the refusal of many women to separate sex from love can lead
them into unanticipated sexual experiences. Close friendships with
other women may become erotic. Instead of sexual attraction leading
to non-monogamy, it is emotional attraction that transforms the friendship into an affair. From the interviews we get the impression that this
occurs because lesbians often have tight-knit friendship groups
founded on relationships of a passionately loyal nature.

We also believe that women's high expectations for their relationships can open the door to non-monogamy. Every couple has to survive
the transition from early euphoria to the routine of everyday life.
Women prize romance, and when there are two women in a couple, the
transition may be all the more troubling. In interviews, some women
told us that they went outside the relationship to regain the excitement
they had lost. We feel that when there are other bonds to replace
romance—such as children or a joint business—the couple may withstand outside lures. When the couple has little but romance to hold
them together, the relationship may end.

---

*One act of non-monogamy does not mean a partner has
embarked on a "career" of infidelity.*

We asked our respondents if they had recently (within the past year)
had sex with someone other than their partners. The number of affirmative answers was substantially smaller than the number of those who
said they had had an outside encounter *at some time* during their relationship. Most people fear that once a partner has stepped outside the
relationship he or she can never be trusted again. Or they wonder, if

**ANY INSTANCE(S) OF NON-MONOGAMY EVER, AND IN PAST YEAR——**

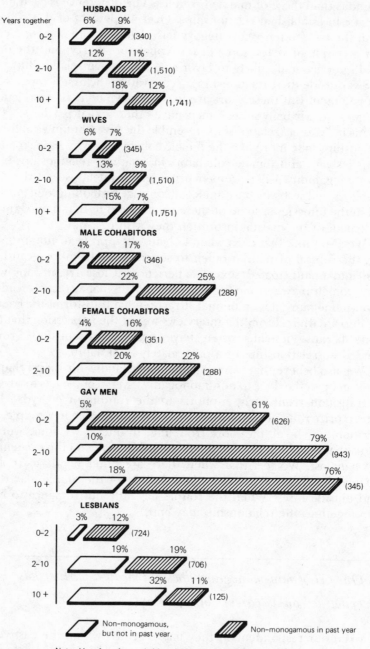

**HUSBANDS**

| Years together | | |
|---|---|---|
| 0–2 | 6% / 9% | (340) |
| 2–10 | 12% / 11% | (1,510) |
| 10 + | 18% / 12% | (1,741) |

**WIVES**

| | | |
|---|---|---|
| 0–2 | 6% / 7% | (345) |
| 2–10 | 13% / 9% | (1,510) |
| 10 + | 15% / 7% | (1,751) |

**MALE COHABITORS**

| | | |
|---|---|---|
| 0–2 | 4% / 17% | (346) |
| 2–10 | 22% / 25% | (288) |

**FEMALE COHABITORS**

| | | |
|---|---|---|
| 0–2 | 4% / 16% | (351) |
| 2–10 | 20% / 22% | (288) |

**GAY MEN**

| | | |
|---|---|---|
| 0–2 | 5% / 61% | (626) |
| 2–10 | 10% / 79% | (943) |
| 10 + | 18% / 76% | (345) |

**LESBIANS**

| | | |
|---|---|---|
| 0–2 | 3% / 12% | (724) |
| 2–10 | 19% / 19% | (706) |
| 10 + | 32% / 11% | (125) |

▱ Non-monogamous, but not in past year.   ▨ Non-monogamous in past year

Note: Very few of our cohabitors had been together more than 10 years.

Numbers in parentheses are the number of people on which the percentages are based.

FIGURE   50

the outside involvement is their own, whether they will be able to re-strict themselves to their partners in the future. We cannot predict what choice a specific individual may make. But many people do not go on to make a habit of non-monogamy.

For lesbians, sex outside the relationship is often an isolated event; one outside sexual experience or affair may occur and never be re-peated.[9] The turmoil aroused by the act may prompt the women to reevaluate the terms of their relationship and recommit themselves to monogamy. One lesbian whose partner had had an affair told us:

> Non-monogamy used to come up a lot. She wanted freedom because she had had it. . . . I think I always wanted to be monogamous. There was a point at which I was willing to accept her not being monogamous. Now I think it would be hard. Now I don't think I could accept it. We have discussions about it twice a year. We both, after a couple of years, decided it should be monogamous.

In another lesbian couple, the person who had sex outside the relationship decided once was enough. Vanessa, twenty-three, and Emma, twenty-four, have been together for two years. Vanessa works as a clerk in a shipping company and Emma is a teacher. Vanessa said:

> I had an affair in March. The shit really hit the fan for sure. We just about broke up over that one. It was a woman from the team. Emma felt very strongly that monogamy is the way to go. And I feel committed to her. But always wondered what it would be like to do it with another woman. Had a lot of questions and feelings like I'd like to do some exploring and be a little freer. I felt real shitty about myself when I was having this affair. I only slept with this woman twice and I just couldn't handle it. It really bothered me. It didn't seem right. I was not fair. It was a real nasty thing to do. I'm glad I did it, because I think it was something I needed to do, something I had to experience. But I'm not going to do it again.

Wives, too, commonly had only one outside sexual experience. One wife of twenty-two, who has been married for two years, described her experience with extramarital sex:

> I was resisting the thought of being married—underline *married*. I was restless. . . . There really is no excuse. I used having an affair as a way of expressing my worry about what I had committed myself to. . . . I consider it an unhealthy thing to have done and I selfishly put a lot on the line for very little. He doesn't know, and he's not going to know about it. It won't happen again, I'm sure.

Another reason for a wife's having just one extramarital experi-ence is simply to satisfy her curiosity. Sandra and Jock have been married nineteen years. Jock is a bookkeeper of forty, and Sandra is a librarian of thirty-eight. Sandra has always been monogamous, and yet her curiosity makes her keep open the possibility of sex with an-other man:

I have not told Jock this, but I would hate to think that I would die knowing only one man. Just out of curiosity . . . I have never wanted to do anything that would threaten Jock or our marriage in any way. So I have thought about it, but I have never been in a situation where I have been tempted, and if I was ever tempted, I—God, it would have to be just perfect and right. So that I am just putting it on the back burner. . . . Faced with an actual choice, it may not be worth it to me. But the curiosity is there.

Many husbands have similar feelings, but there are more of them for whom extramarital sex becomes a repeated pattern. One husband loves his wife of many years, but still justified the woman he calls his mistress:

I am in this [marriage] to the finish, you know. I come from a strong Christian background, and I didn't do this to walk away from it. I love my family and I love my wife . . . and I feel bad about Mary Ann [his lover] 'cause I know it isn't fair to her either. . . . But giving it up would just kill me. I would have to find somebody else.

Many a male cohabitor has sex with someone other than his partner early in the relationship but chooses not to repeat it. As time goes on these men become more committed to the relationship and more faithful. Josh and Beth had been living together for ten months when we interviewed them. They were married a month later. Josh, thirty, is a lawyer, and Beth, twenty-nine, works in a municipal government. Josh said:

Being married is a lot different from living together because we will both try a lot harder. . . . When we first met, I didn't want to promise anything. I told her what I did was my business, what she did was her business. That had some disastrous results. I had sex with another woman—as much for my freedom as for anything else—and she was very upset and left for a while. I realized that if I were serious about this relationship, it couldn't tolerate that kind of conduct. So that was the only time it happened.

Fewer female cohabitors have ever had sex outside the relationship, but when they do, they are about as likely as the men to continue. For example, one woman of twenty-five told us:

I plan on having someone in [while he's away]. This is very idealistic, of course, and we'll see if it works. At least in my mind, I think I can have a sexual fling with someone and not disturb my relationship.

The only couples who adopt non-monogamy as a way of life are the gay men. Cliff and Rob have been together seven years. Cliff, twenty-seven, is a bank auditor, and Rob, thirty, works as a voice teacher. Cliff explained to us how outside sexual experiences are woven into their life:

I think that was one of the absolutely very first things, almost on the same night we agreed that we were in love with each other. The next sentence out of our mouth was: "But I don't want to be monogamous." . . . Yet, as it worked out, the first couple of months we were together, we were pretty monogamous, mostly 'cause we were afraid of jealousy. And then after a while I found out that he has been going out with other people. Then that broke the barrier, and we just decided: "Well, we may not like it, but realistically, we are going to be going out with other people frequently, and so, come what may, we'll have to deal with it one way or another." And so it was always agreed upon, right from the very first night we knew we were going to be a couple. It was always very explicit.

---

*A woman's non-monogamy is more likely to be an affair than is a man's.*

Men are less monogamous than women and they have more partners. What they do not have are as many emotional attachments.[10] Our data show that both men and women are able to have uninvolved sex outside their relationships. However, even those who believe in the right to a sexual dalliance generally feel they must have something more than a solely physical experience. One wife contemplating extramarital sex in the form of couple "swinging" told us:

You know, I don't really give a shit who knows what. It doesn't bother me. I'll tell the fucking Pope. That's the way I feel. I think strongly about an idea and it's my idea and I believe in it and I don't give a shit who hears it. . . . We're still looking. We got to find a couple who is desirable to both of us. The man is different. He can fuck anything, because they just do it to screw. But the woman has to be turned on. I don't know about all women, but I would say the majority need to be turned on. If this person isn't going to strike you a little just by looking at him, then forget it, man. You're a dud in bed. He sprang one man on me and there was just no way. He just introduced the idea about three years ago and then it was like "whoa." This is life in the fast lane, right? But I knew that man would do not just one thing for me.

From the interviews we get the definite impression that in outside sex, men more often search for variety while women prefer a special relationship. Lesbians underscore this female quality. Those together for more than ten years are more likely to have had an affair than anyone in the study except gay men. Gay men's sex with other men is based on the premise that it will be kept fairly impersonal, and it almost always is. Nevertheless, because they meet so many people, by the sheer law of averages a one-night stand will sometimes turn into an affair.

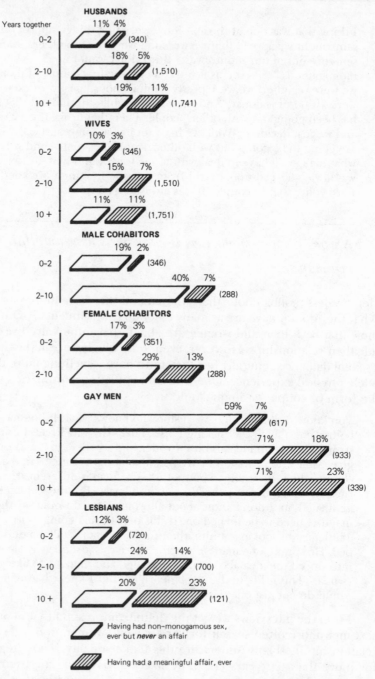

**HUSBANDS**

Years together

11% 4%
0–2 (340)

18% 5%
2–10 (1,510)

19% 11%
10 + (1,741)

**WIVES**

10% 3%
0–2 (345)

15% 7%
2–10 (1,510)

11% 11%
10 + (1,751)

**MALE COHABITORS**

19% 2%
0–2 (346)

40% 7%
2–10 (288)

**FEMALE COHABITORS**

17% 3%
0–2 (351)

29% 13%
2–10 (288)

**GAY MEN**

59% 7%
0–2 (617)

71% 18%
2–10 (933)

71% 23%
10 + (339)

**LESBIANS**

12% 3%
0–2 (720)

24% 14%
2–10 (700)

20% 23%
10 + (121)

Having had non-monogamous sex, ever but *never* an affair

Having had a meaningful affair, ever

Note: Very few of our cohabitors had been together more than 10 years.

Numbers in parentheses are the number of people on which the percentages are based.

FIGURE 51

Many cohabitors have outside sex, especially those who have lived together more than a few years. But relatively few of those outside experiences are affairs. Cohabitation is a fragile arrangement. These couples can live with their partners' having casual sex, but the idea of an outside emotional involvement makes them question why they are together in the first place.

---

*Couples who live "separate" lives have more opportunity to be non-monogamous, and they are.*

Some couples see each other only when they kiss good-bye at the door in the morning and when they crawl into bed after an exhausting day's work. Others are constant companions. Some of these people are frustrated by their circumstances; others have designed them. Being "separate," whether couples want to be or not, opens the possibility of sex outside the relationship. When the opportunity is presented, it is more likely to be seized.[11] For example, Hans, a regional computer-sales representative of forty-two, has lived for twenty years with Fritz, forty-six, who is a chef. Hans often finds himself between appointments with nothing to do for a few hours. He told us that he takes these moments to visit baths or public restrooms to have impersonal sex. He reasons that this is an efficient use of his time because it gives him "sexual variety" without sacrificing any of his time with Fritz.

Among all four kinds of couples, it is people who are separate because of a passionately held value about personal independence who are more committed to non-monogamy as part of their personal philosophy.[12] But it is only among gay men and lesbians that belief in personal independence translates into non-monogamous behavior.[13]

Lesbians and gay men show us that the opportunity for outside sex is not enough; people need the appropriate values if they are to take advantage of it. Some gay people live in a world where all their friends and neighbors are gay—even their work associates. For others, their partners are the only other gay people they ever see. We thought that couples who live in a largely gay environment would have greater exposure to sexual temptation. We were half right. It is true for men. Those who live in "gay ghettos," such as the Castro neighborhood in San Francisco or New York's Greenwich Village, are more likely to be non-monogamous and to have a greater number of partners than are more isolated gay men.[14] This is not true for lesbians. Whether or not they spend time in lesbian organizations or live in a gay neighborhood is unimportant. It all depends on a woman's values. Even in a completely gay world, lesbians can be monogamous.[15]

*Young women today are more "liberated" about*

*non-monogamy.*

The facts are very clear. Young wives, cohabiting women, and lesbians are more likely to have sex outside their relationships.[16] More of these young women have adopted the idea of a "sexual revolution," and have changed their minds about monogamy. Sylvia, a twenty-four-year-old student, has been married for three years to Walter, who is a photographer. She feels good about not being monogamous.

> I have a roving eye and sometimes I give in to it. . . . If it's time that doesn't take away from Walter's and my time, I'll let it happen. I consider myself a very sexual person, and I need an adventure from time to time. And I think he does too. But that's all it is—fun and a little bit of an ego thrill.

Pauline, twenty-nine, and Bart, thirty-five, have been living together for two years. He is a truck driver, and she works in a day-care center. Both were married before and have children from their marriages. Pauline feels that "sexual freedom" is part of personal freedom.

> That's one of the freedoms we give each other and it works out fine. We believe in a life without games . . . or mind trips . . . or tests. We don't need to tell each other or explain anything. This is just our individual life which is separate from our other life. I don't owe him and he doesn't owe me anything except what we decide is important to keep the relationship happy. . . . I can't imagine only having sex with one man for the rest of my life. I don't think he can believe in that either. This doesn't mean outside events are always happening. It just means we have that right and we can use it occasionally.

When we interviewed older women, many had never even considered the possibility of outside sex, much less engaged in it. Ethel is fifty-nine and has been married to Edmund, sixty-two, for two years. They met through their church after their previous spouses had died. She works in the advertising department of a newspaper, and he is a state legislator. When we interviewed Ethel, she was clearly uncomfortable even discussing extramarital sex.

> I have been in two happy marriages. My first husband and I never discussed such an issue because it would have embarrassed us both and been totally unnecessary. When he died, I did not have a personal relationship again until I met Edmund. We never discussed it. I don't think people our age and generation think it's a topic of discussion.

Younger women are more interested in non-monogamy now. But we do not know if this will continue. It is possible that we are seeing the first wave of a new female sexuality; it is also possible that younger women will have a limited romance with non-monogamy and then return to more traditional female patterns.

---

*Being the partner who "loves less" gives power in the relationship and makes non-monogamy more likely.*[17]

Power is the ability to enforce one's will even over the objections of others. Where does power come from? The less "needy" a person is, the more power he or she has. This was recognized more than forty years ago by sociologist Willard Waller, who wrote about the "principle of less interest."[18] According to this principle, the person who loves less in a relationship has the upper hand because the other person will work harder and suffer more rather than let the relationship break up. This partner's greater commitment hands power to the person who cares less. When we evaluated our interview data, it seemed to us that when a partner was the less committed person, he or she was also more likely to be non-monogamous.[19] On the other hand, the more committed partner is too much in love and prizes the relationship too highly to look at other people.

If the more committed partner were able to go outside the relationship, it might restore a balance of power to the couple. The other might not feel so irreplaceable if forced to recognize that the person with whom he or she was living had other alternatives. Even pretending to be willing to go outside the relationship can reaffirm the other person's commitment. Jerry and Skip have been together almost five years. Jerry, thirty-eight, is a personnel manager in a state licensing department, and Skip, forty-three, is a radiologist. When we asked Jerry how permanent he felt the relationship to be, he told us something he did not want Skip to know:

> I think I would not want him to know that I would probably sacrifice a lot to continue the relationship . . . because I think that would create a false sense of security in Skip. It may make him think that he could do anything, wouldn't have to be concerned with his actions, and I don't want him to feel that way.

A wife may also feel less powerful in a marriage where there are dependent children. We feel that these wives sometimes think the costs of being left are so great that they have no choice but to tolerate their husbands' extramarital sex. Cynthia and Irving have been married for thirteen years. Cynthia is a homemaker and Irving is in management with a large clothing store. They have three children under the age of ten. Cynthia said:

> I wonder from day to day. I don't know if it's worth it just to stay on.

Because many times I've said to myself: *Am I happy?* And I say to myself: *I don't know if I'm happy or it's just everything's fallen into a routine.* You become a system. Everything's automatic. It comes to you automatically. You can wake up in the morning, do your chores, until you're dependent on one another. And that's what it comes down to, you're dependent on one another. . . . His cheating just provides me with an excuse. . . . I'm afraid to take a chance on my own, because, as I have said, [I have] no great background. I have no profession behind me. Maybe if it was years back and I had something going for me, I would definitely not be in this relationship today. . . . And yet, I say to myself: *Maybe when the girls get a little older I can get a little more independent and try my wings and fly a little bit.* But I've been afraid.

A wife who decides to be non-monogamous may feel it more necessary to conceal this activity if she has children. Maureen has been married to Frank for seventeen years and both are unhappy. Maureen is a homemaker of thirty-nine. They have two children, ages thirteen and seven. Frank is forty-three and employed in a small delivery business. Maureen has channeled most of her sexual feelings elsewhere, but Frank does not know it. Even though love is absent, Maureen wants the relationship to continue.

It started about three years ago. We were at a dance and there was a guy in the crowd that I always thought was a nice guy. And he was the best dresser—not just the best-looking—well, maybe he is, but looks are not that important. He was the nicest, and we were dancing, and he sort of cuddled up or held me in such a way, and said that he would like to have lunch sometime. It surprised me, but I said, "Yeah." But then he told me to call him or he was going to call me. I was very upset about the idea of how to work it out, and I thought at the time it was wrong. But I wasn't caring for Frank's feelings. . . . I agreed to meet him and I got a babysitter and now I see him almost every day of the week. . . .

Most of the time Frank doesn't ask. Once or twice it would come up and he would ask what I do with my time. Well, my answer is that I do a lot of things. I see people, I go shopping and strolling, and that ends his questions. . . . I really do not know how he would react if he knew. It's so hard to predict. I know him so well, and I keep saying, *Well, he doesn't give a damn about me. Why should he even get upset?* Then I think, *Well, he's going to think, "Damn it, I've been gypped. She's been going out these years, and I could be doing that myself."* And yet I don't think he's the type. . . . I don't have any plans. I haven't got a job that will take care of me or our children. If I confronted him with this, he might say we should go to hell. He might leave us high and dry.

Power, we feel, can encourage people to be non-monogamous. But the paradox of power is that "to use it is to lose it."[20] What non-monogamous partners do not realize is that their "infidelity" may make the relationship less appealing to the other. When a relationship loses its desirability, it loses its ability to command allegiance, and the other person is then freer to pursue other relationships or to exert his or her own power, since the emotional cost of such actions is reduced.

*Couples who attend church or synagogue are not more monogamous than those who do not.*

It is commonly believed that religious people have more conservative values, particularly when it comes to sex, and more conservative sexual behavior. This is half right. We asked all our couples how often they attend church or synagogue. Sociologists use this question to measure how religious people are. Although we recognize that some people may never attend church and yet be very spiritual, this question has proved to be the best way to show which people take the values of their particular religion seriously.

We find that those who attend church or synagogue regularly are much more conservative when it comes to what they believe about sex. They feel that sex and love are inseparable, they oppose "pornography," and when they are heterosexual, they do not favor equal rights for homosexuals.[21] But at the same time, there is very little difference between religious and nonreligious people when it comes to how they act. They have the same amount of sex. They are just as satisfied. They have no more and no less conflict about sex. And they are just as traditional about the woman's right to initiate it.[22]

But perhaps the most startling finding is that religious people are as non-monogamous as anyone else.[23] However attached people may be to religious institutions, they do not seem to be insulated from the temptations of the flesh.

*All non-monogamy is not the same. Some is "cheating," and some occurs in an "open relationship."*

Francine du Plessix Gray has made a statement about honesty and non-monogamy:

> I believe that both the discipline of fidelity and a measured use of the untruth offer more alternatives for the future than the brutal sincerity of open marriage.[24]

She feels that spouses should aim for monogamy, and failing that, they should be discreet, thereby protecting their feelings and their partners' as well. This has been the traditional form that "infidelity" has taken in our society. However, there have been small numbers of people at various points in history—sometimes called free-thinkers, or libertines or radicals, or people committed to free love—who felt that it was worse to lie than to perform the act itself. More recently a number of psychologists, sociologists, and popular writers have recommended "open marriage."[25] An open marriage is a relationship in which everything is discussed and an understanding is reached that both partners consent to extramarital sex.

We asked all our couples if they had an understanding allowing sex outside their relationship.[26] Only a minority of our couples said yes, except for the gay men. Almost two thirds of our gay men are in open relationships.[27]

We should note that in a number of couples, the two partners do not agree on whether they have an open relationship. This is frequently apparent in the interviews, for example, in the marriage of Cal and Alberta. Cal is forty-one and works as an insurance executive, and Alberta is forty and a homemaker. They have been married for thirteen years. It was apparent from their interviews that they had discussed the subject of extramarital sex, but they came away from their discussions with different perceptions. Cal reported:

> I suddenly found myself not wanting to be monogamous. . . . I believe that if I was very discreet and didn't do anything serious, that she could live through it. So it might be sometime that extreme discretion might allow an experiment.

This is Alberta's view of their understanding:

> He was the one who was wondering whether he wanted to be monogamous. . . . It would never be something I would want to do. . . . We talked about it and we didn't actually resolve it except that he knows I would never countenance such a thing. I trust him. . . . I am sure we understand each other. . . . We have a very happy, stable marriage. We spend almost all our time together. . . . I think these are just mid-forties passing fancies.

When we reread our interviews with another couple, Diane and Bruce, it struck us that when it came to a shared understanding about extramarital sex, they seemed not to be in the same marriage. Diane is a homemaker of twenty-four, and Bruce an electrician of twenty-six. They have been married for five years. Bruce's view:

> Sure we have an understanding. It's: "You do what you want. Never go back to the same one." See, that's where it's going to screw your mind up, to go back the second time to the same person.

DIANE's: We've never spoken about cheating, but neither of us believe in it. I don't think I'd ever forgive him. I don't think I'd be able to. I don't know. I haven't met up with that situation.

---

*Couples with an understanding about outside sex do not always avail themselves of it. Couples with no understanding are not always safe.*

Some people have "cheated" on their partners in the last year. But the number who have had outside sex without permission is small except for the gay men, where 43 percent of those without an understanding have done it anyway. No other type of couple comes close to this figure, but the male cohabitors are the closest. They do not have the gay men's sexual opportunities, but neither do they have the husbands' constraints.

There are a great many couples who tell us they have an open relationship, but have not taken advantage of it. The gay men seldom fail to exploit their permitted opportunities. The other couples with understandings often reject the idea of monogamy but never have to put their beliefs to the test, because neither partner actually goes outside the relationship. For example, one lesbian told us:

> What we say and what we do are sometimes two different things.
> Most people say it's monogamous and it isn't. We say it isn't and it is.

Carmen, who has lived with Jan for seven years also reflects this pattern:

> The big question for me was always, to her: "If I slept with someone, would you still love me?" Because at the outset the threat had been if I ever slept with anyone else, that was the end. And finally she agreed with me and reluctantly said yes, I could sleep with other people. But I learned in the therapy process that her head said yes, but her emotions didn't.

Other couples who have tried to put their beliefs into action have had such unhappy results that they now shy away from non-monogamy. We heard this most often in our interviews with cohabitors and lesbians.

Theodore, twenty-nine, and Eugenia, twenty-five, have lived together for nine months. She works in an art gallery, and he is a writer. Non-monogamy has not worked well for them, according to Theodore:

> We found out that it's so sticky and so heartrending if one of us does have a sexual relationship with someone else that neither of us is going out of our way to encourage it. In fact, sometimes I take large

**NON-MONOGAMY IN PAST YEAR,
WITH AND WITHOUT AN UNDERSTANDING**

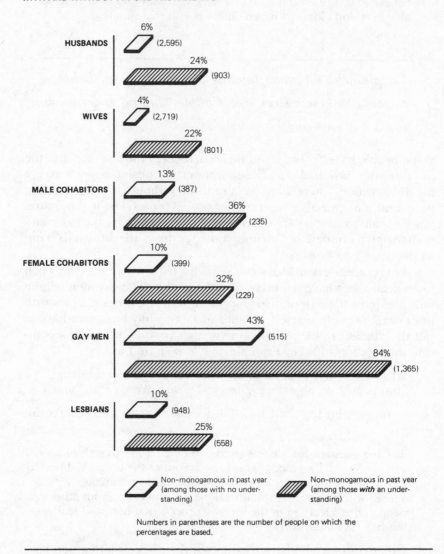

FIGURE   52

steps out of my way to avoid it. . . . The prospect of my just having
sex with only one woman for the rest of my life seems somehow
mildly depressing to me. But for the sake of what works best for
each of us right now in our relationship, it's de facto monogamous.
Maybe at some future date, when we're totally secure with each other
and with our own selves and we're not insecure either about
ourselves or how the other person feels, and we're totally accepting,
no matter what, then maybe other possibilities might be entertained.
But for now it's monogamous.

Carol and Sarah have lived together for five years. Carol is twenty-seven and manages a bookstore; Sarah is twenty-five and a graduate student. Sarah said:

> I think we are basically agreed that we don't have the right to say a
> person should not have another sexual experience if our relationship
> is getting the attention it deserves. . . . On the other hand, I am a
> jealous-type person and when her ex-lover needed a place to stay
> and stayed here, it was a bad scene. She was nuzzling at her and I
> walked into the kitchen once and they were kissing. I just about
> threw her out of the house. So we've made an agreement that we are
> going to put that possibility out of the relationship for a while until
> we can understand our feelings and not have them work against us.

---

*A successful open relationship has built-in rules, whether or*
*not the couple realizes it.*

An open relationship does not mean that anything goes. Even though some couples claim their understanding has no restrictions, we never interviewed a couple who did not describe some definite boundaries. Some couples devise rules that keep their daily life from being disrupted—for example, never being late for dinner, not spending money on someone else, or not bringing home a sexually transmitted disease. Others establish rules of discretion—for example, not letting the children, relatives, or neighbors know. The most important rules provide emotional safeguards—for example, never seeing the same person twice, never giving out a phone number, never having sex in the couple's bed, or never with a mutual friend. Sex outside the relationship is potentially very disruptive. It triggers people's insecurities and fears. Traditional marriages have dealt with this by ruling out non-monogamy. Couples who engage in open relationships formulate rules to guide their behavior, to make outside sex very predictable and orderly. These rules remind the partners that their relationship comes first and anything else must take second place.

What is forbidden to one couple may be permitted to another. Fred and Wes, who have been together for fifteen years, have a very explicit and detailed contract, even though they say they do not. Fred, age fifty-two, is headwaiter in a hotel restaurant, and Wes, fifty-five, is a stage manager. They are both very pleased with their relationship and well adapted to its sexual freedom, as Fred described it:

> Yes, we have an understanding. . . . The only thing we understand is
> that either of us can do what we want. The only thing is that if we go
> out together, we always come home together. That is the only rule
> we have. . . . I am not upset when we go out and he is cruising or
> being cruised, or carrying on. That doesn't bother me, but it would

bother me very much if I had to come home alone. So it never happens. . . . We knew from the start that it would not be a monogamous relationship. . . . That is the way we did it. . . . Some things have developed. We have to tell the other one about it so they will be the first to know. We agreed that we don't bring people to the house for sex. If we've met somebody and have had sex with them a few times, dated them, whatever, sometimes we bring them to the house to meet the other person. The other is fully aware of what has transpired up to this point. People we meet, if they sort of come to us after the first encounter and want to make more of the situation— which isn't going to happen—we always tell people that we have lovers and that our lover is understanding. . . .

There was jealousy in the beginning, but not now. It was a lot to ask somebody to go through. It took a lot to realize that no matter how exciting these escapades were, the person we loved was the one we came home to at night. We both found out that these people, no matter how beautiful or sexually exciting, were not a threat to our relationship. We know what we want and where we are going and how we are going to get there, and these people don't fit into it. It never has been a problem. Wes has had affairs and so have I, and we have met each other's affairs, and we have had three-ways and most of our friends have become our friends through these kinds of meetings. The sex stops and they just become part of our friendship circle.

Mike and Brad have been together for eleven years. Mike is thirty-seven and works as a probation officer; Brad is the same age and manager of a charitable agency. Brad explained to us how "natural" it is for gay male couples to have a non-monogamous understanding:

We still quarrel about sex with other people. He accepts my behavior, but he still worries and comes down on me if I see someone more than once, or if I give anybody my telephone number. . . . Sometimes I get furious with him. He should know by now that we are better off than ninety percent of other men. We are in love and we have things worked out. Being gay is being nonexclusive. I don't know anyone who doesn't ever trick. If they say they don't, they're lying, or there's something wrong with them, or they are still in the honeymoon stage. I promise that I won't bring anyone to our bed, that I won't have an affair, that I won't fall in love, that he doesn't have to come to the city on the nights I go in. But he's going to have to accept that gay men—and especially this gay man—are not monogamous. . . . Can you believe we have this dialogue after eleven years?

Daryl and Sally came to an understanding after Daryl confronted Sally with his "infidelity." They were in the eighth year of marriage. Daryl, a geologist of thirty-two, had always chafed at the idea of sexual restrictions and ultimately convinced his wife, a homemaker of thirty-three, that sex, when he was out of town at conventions or on field trips, would not hurt their relationship. Daryl told us:

You should have seen her. Crying and "How could you?" and generally making me feel like a shit. She knew I loved her. She knew I wasn't just fooling around in this marriage. I just couldn't believe she really thought that just because I had gotten it on with some girl that the entire marriage was flawed. . . . So I asked her if she loved me and she said she did. And I said if this really wasn't at least possibly separated from our relationship under some circumstances. And she finally said yes. But I don't think she believed me until it came up for her too. She met this guy when she was out of town, and he was kind of an asshole—I think he was a plastic surgeon—but he was good-looking and she was bored and you know how it is. And she made this confession which was half guilty and half "Look what I did." . . . And so we still say, "Go out there and screw your head off," but it's understood that a little casual screwing just doesn't mean more than a little casual screwing.

Another wife added her thoughts about the precautions she feels couples must take if they are to be non-monogamous:

We're pretty open. So what if you have an affair? As long as it didn't hurt anybody and you benefited personally, it would be okay. I've always believed it from the day I got married, only I didn't believe it as much as I do now. . . . Now, if you're going to start neglecting your husband or your children, then NO, but if no one's neglected . . .

Lowell and Cleo have been a couple for five years, the first three of which they lived together; for the past two years they have been married. Cleo, twenty-four, works part time as a receptionist in a physician's office, while Lowell, thirty-five, drives a truck. Cleo described their understanding about sex with other people:

It's an informal understanding, but we have rules. The major one is no secrecy from each other, but making sure that nothing happens in front of the kids. . . . We also stay away from close straight [conventional] friends of the other. For some reason that bothers both of us. For instance, if one of his friends makes a pass at me or one of my friends makes a pass at him, that's off limits, because there's too many games—and it might get too public. It's threatening in a number of ways. We try and be discreet and our rules help us keep our private life private.

Some couples feel most comfortable with their understanding when they are kept in the dark about details. There may be a simple verbal recognition that something has occurred, or no outward acknowledgment at all. Others react differently, feeling very threatened by what happens in their absence, and having a greater sense of control if they are present for all sexual encounters. These couples often develop a system in which some or all of their non-monogamy occurs in "three-ways" or "threesomes." Indeed, for some gay men, "prowling together" is a hobby of considerable importance which actually becomes a significant bond in their relationship. For example, we received a letter from a couple who have been together for ten years. Arnold is a professor and Edgar is an advertising executive. In their letter Edgar described some of their recent activities:

> Yesterday Edgar and I were walking down the beach and we spotted this man we had been courting. We hurried and joined him and spent a wonderful afternoon together. We invited him to the house and fixed dinner. Then he spent the night and we had a great time. We had been working on that one for months.

Three-ways are a common arrangement among gay men. For example, Pierre and Randolph have been together for six years. Pierre, twenty-nine, is a professional athlete, and Randolph, forty-six, is a salesman. Pierre told us how they coordinate their non-monogamy and some of the complications that can crop up:

> Let's face it. I'm the attraction here. They come to worship my perfect body. [He laughs.] Seriously, I do get a lot of attention and Randolph used to go nuts about it. We'd go to a bar and I would get cruised and cruised and then cruised some more, and Randolph would get really jealous. . . . Worse than that, he'd get down, you know what I mean? . . . So we got in the habit of: "You take one, you get both." And that worked out well, because we have, uh, different things to offer. I don't know how to put this, but Randolph is a lot sexier undressed than in a bar. . . . We get a charge when we're doing a number on someone who thinks they've died and gone to heaven. . . . Occasionally it gets rough, like someone ignores Randolph and he gets down. This is pretty rare though, and usually we enjoy it. It is about the only way we have sex with other people. We keep tabs on each other.

Three-ways are often a form of protection. They can take the potential for romance out of sex by creating a less intimate situation. If two people are never alone together, it is easier to ensure that one's partner will not get into emotional trouble.

In interviews, we encountered only a few married couples who have something approaching three-ways as part of their non-monogamy arrangement. One of these couples, Irene and Douglas, have been together for twenty-one years in a marriage with very little conflict. Irene, forty-five, is a speech pathologist, while Douglas, fifty-three, sells automobile parts. Douglas described how their understanding has evolved over the past eight years:

> It started with us talking about it, because of reading some letters from [a sex magazine]. We were reading some letters . . . and we were talking about them. Right after that, one of our friends came to visit and we ended up with a threesome. . . . That was the first. But Irene has a steady boyfriend now. I don't have a steady girl friend. I

used to have, until she remarried. I haven't found anybody again that interests me. . . . [Irene's] boyfriend and I are real good friends.

Irene gave more details about their arrangement:

We both are free to have other sexual partners. I do have a boyfriend. I've had one for six years. Other people do not understand this, but in a way it brings us closer together. We know that there is no one who will take each other away from us. But that doesn't mean that other people can't be attracted to us. Now I don't mean that I could just jump in bed with any guy. I have to know him; I have to like him. Douglas has to know him and like him. Douglas and my boyfriend are very close friends. And it works out beautifully! . . . I understand that a very small percentage of married people who try to be non-monogamous can work it out. . . . And a lot of people think younger people do this, but not people our age. . . . Well, if we find someone that we care for—it's not just someone that we see and want to jump in bed with—someone that we know and we like, we're both free to have sex with them here if the children aren't here. We can bring them here. It can't be just anybody. Usually both of us know the person. Sometimes three of us are together—not in a heterosexual and homosexual way. I just get all the benefits when two guys and I are together. . . . We realize that you can be attracted to somebody else and still love each other.

Douglas added a summary:

There's no jealousy between us either. . . . We know what each other does. Matter of fact, I can walk into the house and I can tell whether her boyfriend's been here or not. . . . Just from the way she looks. It's a glow!

Irene and Douglas's marriage is unusual in that their understanding is predicated on the durability and intimacy of the outside sexual relationships, rather than on a strict standard of noninvolvement. At the same time, they believe in the absolute primacy of their marriage.

Another, rather rare, way heterosexual couples keep tabs on their partners is by "swinging" or "mate swapping." Unlike threesomes, each person may have his or her own partner and they may have sex in private once everyone has met and approval has been given. It is such a departure from the traditional notion of marriage or heterosexual love that it usually takes a long time before the couple evolves an understanding that permits this particular form of experimentation. One wife described their decision-making process:

We decided no sex outside of marriage unless the other guy is there. We've got to keep it balanced. We've got to get into swapping because he's sneaky. . . . We haven't quite gotten into it yet. We got into talking about it. We're trying to find the correct people. We're not one to call up ads. You don't know what you get. We're looking to swapping with friends. But our friends are, well, not at that point yet. So what can I tell you? Come back later and I'll tell you how we're doing.

Swinging couples expect that their relationship will remain stable and durable. Swinging is seen as a solution to the problem of sexual boredom, or as an acknowledgment that commitment to marriage should not mean that one's partner is the last lover one will ever know. Almost never will a couple say that these understandings have been made because their relationship is intolerable or they want to bring it to an end. Some couples, however, do start non-monogamous understandings because sex is so bad inside the relationship that they feel they must have outside sex. Carl and Ella have been married eleven years. Ella owns a small publishing business and Carl is head of a municipal agency. They have two children. They are very dissatisfied with their sex life. Their despair has driven them to agree to non-monogamy, as Ella explained:

> We had a real good time, but sex was still shitty . . . and at that time one of my old boyfriends came back and I saw him and I made love with him. And Carl knew, but it was okay with him because he knew I need that physical satisfaction. So he wanted me to have it to make me happy, but on the other hand it was pissing him off. . . . I just wasn't being satisfied because I really liked Carl and I found that I wanted to go out and play the field and see if what I had at home was really what I wanted. And sure enough it was, but just the sexual thing wasn't there. And so I went out and did that a whole lot. . . . And sex was still shitty. He had other affairs and that worked out, so it was like sex between us was bad, but for me and another man it was good and for him and other women it was good. . . . I think that if Carl and I could ever get a good sexual relationship going, I wouldn't have affairs. But I guess there's always a trade-off. . . .
>
> Now we got some problems from this pattern and we got to break it to save what we got. We're really working at it. I want it to be permanent and he wants it to be permanent. I'd like to grow old with him. . . . So right now we just make some rules to protect ourselves. . . . The only thing he says is to be discreet for his work and for it not to hurt him. He can have an affair and I can have an affair if I want to, but we just keep it under our hats. . . . We don't do it when he's coming home or in front of the kids, or with his best friend. We say, "Use your head." . . . I know he's having affairs, but he's acting as he said he would. Right now I talk big, but I've gotten real jealous. I think it would be great for him to get his confidence up, but I don't think I could handle it if it got to be more than sex.

In spite of all the talk about "sexual revolution," the heterosexual world is far from embracing outside sex as an uncomplicated event. Openly non-monogamous married and cohabiting couples often feel they are thought of as bizarre or immoral by the rest of their world.

They have to work out their sex lives in opposition to the rest of society. They may have an understanding with each other, but they usually keep it secret from friends, children, and people at work.

---

*Of all the rules people make in their sexual understandings, the one they emphasize most is keeping sex casual. To do this, they need the ability to "trick."*

A major difference between male and female non-monogamy is illustrated by lesbians and gay men. While lesbians' sexual partners are very rarely strangers or women whom they meet just for sex, gay men commonly have sex with strangers.[28] We call the capacity to enjoy such experiences the "trick mentality." A trick, in the language of gay men, is a sexual adventure.[29] The other man is called a trick to show that the adventure has been entirely sexual and impersonal. Last names, or sometimes even first names, do not have to be exchanged. In some places where sex is at its most impersonal (for example, gay steam baths) a man may never get a good look at his trick's face. Two men meet because of physical attraction, have sex, and then go home to their partners.

What we have referred to as the trick mentality is more than a state of mind. It is a social institution within the gay male world. It takes place in designated areas, like pickup bars, baths, and public restrooms. It also has unwritten rules that every person entering these places understands. Even among unattached gay men, a tricking situation is an encapsulated erotic event and rarely leads to the beginning of a romantic relationship.

The existence of so many cruising places can make it hard to be monogamous in the gay male world. But the trick mentality allows many men to have sex without emotional involvement. This is why gay male couples can tolerate very high rates of non-monogamy. Some gay men also protect their relationships by having as tricks the kind of people they would not choose as lifetime partners. Alex, a TV reporter, told us:

> I don't have to date some dumb but beautiful man so that I can have sex with him. I can find Mr. Lovely, for an hour, and save dinner for someone I really want to talk to!

Another gay man supports this point:

> I get perverse pleasure—maybe it's perverse—of seeing the people he has gone with. . . . I just absolutely am flying when I see the numbers he's gone with and know that he comes home to me. . . .

But he doesn't particularly like the numbers I've gone with, 'cause he thinks I don't pick anyone worthy of him, who is his equal. But I'm not looking for his equal; I'm looking for something else.

There are few social barriers in gay sexual meeting places. A man can have sex with someone who may not speak the same language, much less share the same interests. This makes serious emotional closeness even less likely.

A minority of gay men are monogamous. For these men, the trick mentality is foreign; they might understand it as an abstraction, but it has no personal meaning for them. Living in a world where casual sex and non-monogamy are taken for granted is often a source of great consternation for them. They feel it odd that they must justify their belief in "old-fashioned" values. They often blame the gay world for not supporting their desire for sexual exclusiveness. Their dilemma is particularly poignant when only one partner in a couple feels this way. Craig, twenty-seven, is a graduate student in molecular biology, and Marcus, twenty-five, is a librarian. They have been together for four years. Craig feels "trapped" in a world whose values he does not want to accept. He wrote to us about recent developments:

We've just celebrated our fourth anniversary. . . . I almost didn't make it to this fourth anniversary, since Marcus had a meaningful affair last fall and I almost called our relationship off. Funny, but I discovered that I can't tolerate infidelity. I've read lots of books on it and I've considered the subject endlessly. I've tried to see the perniciousness of jealousy and possessiveness and to overcome the insecurity and dependence on which these feelings are supposedly based. But it came down to trying to change the way I felt, and ultimately I didn't think I wanted to change the way I felt. Relationships are the center of my life, and I expect a lot of my primary relationship. Love, support, respect, honesty, and communication with more intensity than in any other of my relationships with friends or family. So I read some modern literature on affairs, and saw that it basically urged recognition of the individuality of one's mate and a tolerance of his freedom—that is, his pursuance of orgasms—as well as willingness to appear oblivious to any affairs. That is, no questions, no prying, no communicating about this "beautiful but private part" of one's lover's life. It all sounded very convenient to me, but not exactly in accordance with the joy of mutual exploration and self-revelation which I associate with romantic love. Growing together appeals to me. Growing apart doesn't. And despite my romantic inclinations, I don't have much tolerance for people who haven't decided what they want but nevertheless commit themselves to relationships and then "just can't help themselves" when an opportunity to "grow"—that is, screw—comes along. That's not romance; it's puerile irresponsibility and lack of consideration. . . . Anyway, Marcus and I are trying to work

out our difficulties. . . . Our initial involvement grew out of the fear
that we were the only gay men willing to commit ourselves to a
relationship, and we had better hang onto that despite our marked
differences. . . . Actually we were just young and unable to cope with
the pressure of wanting to belong to our subculture, but not wanting
to . . . champion a subculture of sybaritic clones.

Ironically for Craig and Marcus, they intentionally live in a city
where gay life is highly tolerated. Craig did not know, when they
moved there, what we have learned in our study: The more enmeshed
in the center of the gay world, the more likely men are to be non-
monogamous.

Lesbian bars do not perform the same social function as gay bars.
Women often go to them to socialize with their partners, with other
couples, or with a group of friends. It is not clear who is with a partner
or who is single—or if the single woman is "on the prowl." Friendship
groups, organized clubs, and social events are other settings where
lesbians can meet potential partners, but none is conducive to tricking.
We have been told that in many lesbian circles, a woman who has a
reputation for sexual "promiscuity" (liking casual sex) is someone to
avoid. Like heterosexual women, most lesbians want to feel that a sexual relationship is special, and they will be wary of a woman who might
make them feel like a trick. They prefer settings that encourage romance or friendship.

In the heterosexual world, the only analogies to gay meeting places
are singles bars. Prostitutes are used by men almost exclusively. Heterosexual singles bars are available to both men and women, but they
are not exactly the same as gay pickup places. In gay bars, men meet as
erotic equals. There is no tradition of a double standard. Because only
men go to gay bars, the man who accepts a sexual advance is never seen
as "cheaper" than the man who has made the advance. In heterosexual
bars, the double standard still endures and therefore shades the meaning of a proposition. Even if a man would not denigrate a woman for
saying yes, she cannot be sure of that. And there is often a problem of
mixed signals. Some of the men are hoping for quick and casual sex,
but many of the women are looking for someone to date. If a heterosexual woman made herself available for a one-night stand, her male
partner might—like a gay man in a similar situation—think of her as a
trick. Unlike gay men, however, heterosexual men have a hard time
thinking of themselves as someone else's trick.

It is difficult to translate the idea of tricking into the female
idiom—either lesbian or heterosexual. While some may seek and enjoy
one-night stands and even go through a period of having many sex
partners, it is rare that a woman wants this to be a consistent part of her
life. It is almost unheard of for a woman to have sex with someone
whose name she does not know or whose face she has not seen.

Lesbians and heterosexual women rarely trick. Heterosexual men can, but seldom do.[30] Why? We think it is because their sexual habits are constrained and retrained by the presence of a female partner with habits specific to her gender—as well as by the institution of marriage and all it implies. Since most female partners do not understand tricking for themselves or their loved ones, they seldom consent to a non-monogamous understanding. Without the protection of a trick mentality, such an understanding would create emotional risk. Heterosexual men who are intrigued by casual sex may refrain from it because they have agreed to their partner's terms. Additionally, most of the women men meet—for example, neighbors and co-workers—are not interested in tricking.

---

*Non-monogamy tells us about heterosexual couples' feelings about the future of their relationships.*

It is widely believed that with a truly happy relationship, partners would not be "driven" to non-monogamy. Another piece of folk wisdom is that partners go outside for sex when there is too little of it at home. We find that heterosexual couples who are monogamous have neither more nor less sex than those who are not.[31] Some might say that it is not the amount of sex, but its quality that keeps partners from straying. This also turns out to be untrue. Monogamous and non-monogamous heterosexual men and women are on average equally pleased with their sex lives together.[32] Another possibility exists: that partners are non-monogamous because they are fundamentally unhappy with the relationship. There is no evidence for this contention.[33] Heterosexuals who have non-monogamous sex are on average as happy with their relationships as monogamous people. But they are *not* as certain that their relationships will last.[34] These facts tell us two important things. First, most heterosexuals are not propelled into non-monogamy by bad feelings about their relationships. Second, for most heterosexuals, non-monogamy is associated with less commitment to a future together.

*Non-monogamous lesbians are less satisfied with the sex in their relationships and less committed to the relationships' future.[35]*

When lesbians are non-monogamous, the relationship seems not to be going well. Our impression from interviews is that problems within a lesbian relationship, particularly an unhappy sex life, make the women more likely to become involved with someone else. We also feel that once she has become involved with someone else, she starts to doubt if she wants to remain with her partner.

This is a finding of some import, because one of the issues we often heard lesbians discuss was their feeling that monogamy ought to be rejected as a sexist institution. But we also heard that the attempt to put this belief into action often causes problems for both partners. Sunshine, a twenty-nine-year-old therapist in a lesbian counseling center, told us:

> Right from the beginning it was a problem. She [her partner, Suzanne] was involved with other women. She didn't feel . . . it had to affect our relationship, which I thought was bullshit. But I was also having personal conflict because politically I believed it was okay for a person to be involved with more than one person at once. I'd read all the good stuff and thought that was what you should do. But I couldn't handle it. I hated it when it was her birthday and I wanted to spend time with her and her other two lovers were there. I just wanted to kill, you know. [She gives a slight laugh.]

*Gay male relationships adapt well to outside sex, but this can replace sex between the partners.*

Outside sex is not related to gay men's overall happiness or their commitment to the relationship.[36] However, they have less sex together and are less pleased with their sex life together.[37] This may reflect an extreme version of the trick mentality. We think some men become so accustomed to associating sex with new partners and novel experiences, they fail to be aroused by someone with whom they are familiar. Nevertheless, the nonsexual gratification derived from their relationship is enough to keep them committed to it.

Some of this pattern may be changing because of a significant event: the discovery of a terrible disease, probably transmitted sexually, which non-monogamous gay men run a particular risk of contracting. It is called AIDS (auto-immune deficiency syndrome) and, while heterosexual as well as homosexual people are among its victims, it has hit gay men particularly hard. Because it is often lethal, it has frightened many gay men and considerably reduced the desirability of tricking. AIDS may have a long-term impact on the number of outside partners a gay man has sex with, unless the spread of the disease is checked or a cure is found.[38]

The evidence from our couples makes it clear that outside sex can manifest itself in a number of different ways. The act may be a solitary event never to be repeated, or it may be one incident in a long career of non-monogamy. It may be done in secret, suspected but not acknowledged by the monogamous partner, or it may be fully agreed upon by both members of a couple. It may be a simple sexual adventure that does not compete with a partner's primary relationship, or it may be a deeply meaningful act that does intrude upon the life of a couple.

When one or both partners decide to go outside the relationship, the couple's life is altered even if both persons adapt well to the change. The shape of the couple's adaptation depends on which kind of non-monogamy they "specialize" in.

Married couples have the rules and sanctified nature of the institution of marriage to guide them. Traditionally, their contract forbids extramarital sex; they risk invalidating the entire contract when they break this rule. Having promised to be faithful, married partners raise doubts about their essential loyalty if they bargain for outside sex. Therefore, cheating is the kind of non-monogamy most married couples choose; rarely do they agree to an understanding. Only a small number of married couples radically revise the rules of marriage to make room for an open or swinging relationship. Husbands and wives may indulge their curiosity or succumb to a moment of romantic temptation, but they will nevertheless continue to regard these acts as out of bounds.

Cohabiting couples have no marriage contract. Furthermore, many are trying to revise and reform traditional marital customs, even though they have no precise or defined idea as to the kind of institution they would substitute. These couples are more likely than married couples to have an understanding, and outside partners. But they also tend to differentiate between romantic and casual sex. An emotional alternative to their relationship is potentially just as powerful an attachment as what they already have. Therefore, when a real threat is perceived, liberal attitudes may break down.

Married and cohabiting couples share one important element that makes outside sex less likely: Both contain one female partner. Even female cohabitors, who are sexually more avant-garde, tend to want sex with their partners to be as exclusive as possible. They may seek outside experiences in their youth, or endure them when they feel powerless to object, but in point of fact they do not want to share their partners with other people.

Heterosexual men are less monogamous than heterosexual women as a component of their traditional gender role. Men are conditioned to find outside sex more appealing, yet their ability to seal off such experiences emotionally means these encounters are of diminished significance. They also have the famous double standard on their side.

Many people feel that this standard is moribund in present-day society, but it remains very much alive—in subtle ways. Individuals may claim to have put the double standard behind them and they may be perfectly correct from their own point of view. What they fail to realize, however, is that the double standard is not merely part of an individual's personal psychology. It is also part of the entire fabric of society and as such is inescapable.

Some heterosexual women demand the same sexual freedom as men. They also succeed in liberating themselves from self-recrimination and guilt. Yet their non-monogamous behavior is in fact judged by a different standard. Accordingly, when they act on their beliefs, they are treated differently from men by the people around them.

The general female preference for monogamy is most obvious among the lesbians. They do not do well with outside involvements. Lesbians live in a world that espouses two sets of contradictory values. One ideology rejects monogamy because it is a symbol of men's traditional control of women. Another prizes traditional "female virtues" and rejects "male values." Not surprisingly, therefore, lesbians prefer sex to take place in a context of warmth, affection, and respect, not to be a purely physical experience. It is easy to understand why they commit themselves ideologically to sexual freedom but find it difficult to put into practice. Women are neither instructed nor experienced in the art of casual sex; having sex with someone requires liking or loving the other person. Outside sex, if it occurs, is usually romantic, not casual, and frequently provokes a crisis of trust between the two women in the relationship. Lesbian couples can survive non-monogamy, especially if it happens in a solid relationship, but rarely does it become part of their lives.

Gay men can make non-monogamy part of everyday life. They have no trouble incorporating casual sex into their relationships. Since their partner is male, they are not called on to honor the female preference for monogamy. However, in enduring relationships, gay couples evolve understandings and generate rules that protect their primary bond. Many of these men eventually have frequent and regular outside sex and although their relationships remain intact, they are likely to make love to each other less often.

The ability to trick, to create special rules of conduct, and to thrive in a non-monogamous culture demonstrates to us that outside sex is a "normal" part of the life of many gay male couples. Heterosexual couples who want to stay together and yet have sex with others may seek to work out the kind of arrangement gay males have. But the women in these couples are not as disposed to tricking and it is difficult to find the same culture of friends to support the activity. Thus gay men are more successful in maintaining such a life-style.

We regard such success, however, as a two-edged sword. Gay male couples who wish to be monogamous find it difficult to escape a culture that encourages sexual variety. The monogamous gay couple faces the same difficulties confronted by non-monogamous heterosexual or lesbian couples: Each is out of step with the world in which they live.

Non-monogamy tells us about appetites, but also about the breaking of rules and the patching up of relationships. Not all couples have the skills or strength to survive a breach of faith or a clash of ideologies. Some, however, do. Not all monogamy displays purity of desire and stability, and not all non-monogamy is venal in origin or intent. This is a complicated aspect of human behavior. It changes over time within a single relationship, throughout a couple's history.

# Conclusion

There is no doubt that being a man or being a woman shapes a person's sexual opportunities and choices. We have seen that women, in general, are the keepers of fidelity. Sexual compatibility is important to them because they want sex to stay within the relationship, to function as a strong emotional, as well as physical, bond. Men, in general, are less confined to the emotional side of sex, and are more likely to seek sexual variety. But men who have female partners are attuned to the female preferences for monogamy and do not go outside the relationship as much as they otherwise might. Heterosexual men are primarily monogamous. They adjust to this restriction by designing their sex life with their partners to accommodate their idea of sufficient and diverse sex.

In these pages we make generalizations about *men* as a group and *women* as a group: Our data have compelled us to see that men and women represent two very different and distinct modes of behavior. But our writing is based on statistical analyses that focus attention on broad patterns and central tendencies, and do not account for the behavior of each individual. A particular man may be an ardent believer in the sanctity of monogamy, and a particular woman may be wildly non-monogamous. That man is no less "male," nor the woman less "female," than any other person, merely because neither fits the statistical mold. For every pattern we describe, we leave out alternative patterns that occur infrequently. But these eventually accumulate to affect the lives of many people: It is a rare individual indeed who reflects the statistical average in every aspect of his or her life.

But the extraordinary diversity in our couples' lives should not invalidate the inescapable message in the data—the continuity of male behavior and the continuity of female behavior. Husbands and male cohabitors are more like gay men than they are like wives or female cohabitors. Lesbians are more like heterosexual women than either is like gay or heterosexual men. What do these gender uniformities tell us that could help guide couples in building their relationships? How do the differences between men and women help heterosexual couples, and where do they create problems? When does sameness serve gay and lesbian couples well, and when not so well? When should couples try to compromise for the sake of tranquillity, and when should they take advantage of their small differences in order to organize their lives more successfully? Answers to these questions lie in the details that we have presented. From these details, some overall patterns emerge.

Ideally, if sexual frequency and satisfaction are going to be high, partners in all types of couples should share equal responsibility for initiating and refusing sex. This is difficult for the married and cohabiting couples because tradition frowns on female initiative as well as on the male's right to refuse. Heterosexual couples, however, have another avenue to a satisfactory sex life: If they are willing to accept the more traditional model of sexual interaction—one based on male leadership—they will continue to have sex often, largely because the man takes his role seriously. It will be particularly often if the traditional standard is tempered so that the woman is allowed, or allows herself, to participate by being accessible or by offering encouragements. Thus, couples who share sexual privileges—*and* couples where the male assumes all the responsibility—can have a satisfying sex life. The snag in heterosexual relationships occurs when the couple assigns sexual responsibilities in ways that go against each sex's prior training. If women take most of the initiative and men are sexually coy, then both frequency and satisfaction suffer. Few couples can avoid being affected to some extent by society's strictures.

Lesbians are caught betwixt and between. Neither partner is fully comfortable with sexual aggressiveness nor with the belief that one partner ought to dominate. If each woman could adopt an active role in sexual matters, their activity would be greater. If one woman could be assigned the active role without provoking the other's resentment, sexual frequency would increase. But one or the other strategy would have to be agreed upon. Otherwise, each woman's response to the aggressive role—distaste—results in an inactivity that makes sex less frequent than lesbians like.

Gay men confront the dilemma of too much similarity in their sexual approach. They both claim the right to initiate sex, which can result in competition between the two partners. Each wants to be the initiator because it confirms his male identity. If one man prevails in this competition and takes the lead most of the time, it does not work well for either of them. The one who is doing the accepting or refusing takes on a role he may resent. The one who always takes the lead suffers from being rejected some of the time. He would be able to understand this better if his partner were a woman, because she would supposedly have a lower sexual appetite, but when his partner is a man, the refusal is perceived as more personal. Gay men who wish to avoid competition and traditional role playing work out a sensitive ratio of initiation and refusal so that neither partner can be accused of dominating the sexual relationship and thereby causing dissension.

Sexual competitiveness for the admiration of others is always a possibility when partners can be evaluated by the same physical standard. Heterosexual couples seldom suffer from sexual rivalry because they operate in two different marketplaces, with two different sets of standards. This is not true for most gay and lesbian couples: If they are similar in appearance and aspire to the same physical standards, they may be reminded of their failings by their partner's successes.

In bed, heterosexual couples suffer from having "male only" and "female only" prescriptions, and from the different meanings they attach to the same act. For example, oral sex can be seen as "controlling" or "servicing"—depending on whether the male or female is performing it. The similarities within gay and lesbian couples help them somewhat here, but because so much heterosexual imagery invades certain sexual acts—imagery of power and dominance—differences can be created or imagined even when none exist. Since many sex acts are seen as more male or more female, same-sex couples face the dilemma of how to enjoy these acts within the constraints their sameness creates. When the same sexual acts are performed equally by both partners, and some form of reciprocity is maintained, sexual satisfaction is likely to be higher and there will be less conflict. But this is not true for all kinds of sexual expression. Indeed, for some sexual behavior, the more the partners are the same, the more frequent the occurrence: For example, the more feminine both lesbians are, the more oral sex they enjoy, and the more masculine both gay men are, the more anal sex they have.

Finally, the fact that men and women have different attitudes toward non-monogamy does not serve the heterosexual couples well. Female values predominate, but men and women do not understand each other's feelings about sex without love and what an experience outside the relationship might mean. Similarity of outlook generally helps gay male couples. Each partner can understand the other's need for sexual variety. Similarity of outlook helps the lesbians when both realize the dangers posed by non-monogamy. Each woman can understand how sex with someone else can lead to a deeper involvement.

Both partners may have decided that monogamy was unimportant and, indeed, an invention of men in order to control female sexuality. Still, if one or both begins to fall in love with someone else, their mutual willingness to understand their own and their partner's emotional vulnerability may help them reevaluate their feelings about non-monogamy as an option.

When a couple consists of one male and one female, partners take over different spheres of the sexual relationship and thus competition and ambiguity are minimized. But empathy may be superficial or absent. Same-sex couples understand each other better and share similar sexual goals, but roadblocks may arise when neither partner wants to take on behavior that seems inappropriate to his or her gender. In heterosexual couples, gender imagery has attributed to one partner greater appetite, greater license, and at the same time greater responsibility. These constraints do not serve a couple well: Women often feel restrained and not in control of their own experience, and men feel pressed to perform. Men are expected to be sexually more aggressive because they are thought to have greater desires than women. By following the male prescription to be more aggressive, and the female requirement to be more passive, couples help to perpetuate the assumption of different sexual needs in men and women.

If all of this sounds as if nothing is changing, then it is somewhat misleading—but only somewhat. There *are* new men and new women, among both heterosexual and homosexual couples, who are dealing with sexual responsibilities in new ways, and trying to modify the traditions that their maleness and femaleness bring to their relationships: But they are fewer than we might expect. It is particularly difficult for the new heterosexual woman, who often finds her partner less "liberated" than she—or he—thought he was. Cohabiting couples and younger married couples come closer to blurring the boundaries between male and female as they learn to share sexual roles. However, when partners go beyond sharing to role reversal, there is still a backlash of dissatisfaction and conflict.

Lesbians still find it hard to get over traditional inhibitions about female sexuality and to revise customary sexual values. Some "new lesbians," rejecting all the old patterns, have abandoned monogamy. But it is difficult to find partners who feel the same way, and the desire to free themselves from past roles does not necessarily imply emotional readiness for the actual event.

There are fewer new gay men than new lesbians or new heterosexual men and women. Beyond resisting the model of monogamous heterosexual marriage, the majority of our gay men are not self-consciously involved in a movement to change existing sexual values. The issues most important to them involve their relationships—negotiating power and respect between two competing males. They are trying to rid themselves of the stigma that still attaches to some of the acts they perform, and like all gay people, they are involved in learning how to feel good about themselves in a society that condemns them. But beyond these important concerns, their feelings about sex have failed to propel most gay men into new political consciousness.

All of our men and women, however, work hard to come to some kind of sexual arrangement. Sexual compatibility, even among people of the same sex, is never automatic. Putting body parts together is the easiest element of a couple's sexual life. Communicating needs, respecting differences, and discovering how to compromise and change are more difficult.

# Epilogue: Who Broke Up–and Why

**E**IGHTEEN months after we surveyed our couples, we sent short questionnaires to about half of them to find out if they were still together. If they were not, we asked what had happened and whether one or both partners had wanted the relationship to end. Cohabitors were also asked if they had married in the interim. We analyzed our findings in the light of how long the couples had been together when we first surveyed them.[1] Some of the results are surprising, while others were expected. We did not anticipate great changes among the married couples and indeed we find that only a small percentage broke up. We were interested to note that among couples in their first two years, cohabitors, gay men and lesbians had approximately equal likelihood of breaking up. When we look back at their original questionnaires, the three groups were also approximately equal in their expectation of staying together.[2] We are surprised to learn that the lesbians had the highest breakup rate of all our couples. We have been told in interviews by gay men and lesbians alike that they believe lesbians to have more stable relationships than gay men. Moreover, since women are more likely to be relationship-centered, and since we have found that being relationship-centered is associated with couples' happiness, we would have expected a lower breakup rate for lesbians than for gay men or cohabitors.

To shed light on the breakup patterns, we must first look at the factors that influenced each kind of couple to break up. In this book we look at the impact of money, work, and sex only, but we are aware that there may be other influences.

**COUPLES WHO BROKE UP** ————————————————————————

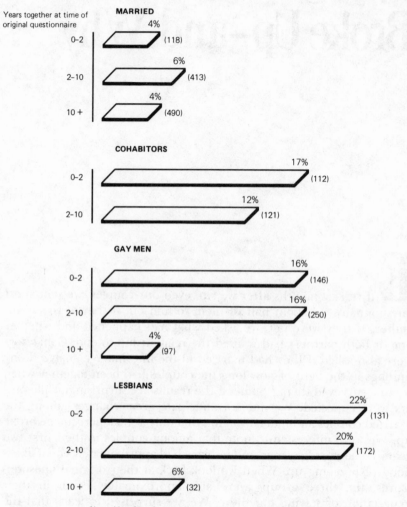

Years together at time of
original questionnaire

**MARRIED**

0-2    4%    (118)

2-10    6%    (413)

10 +    4%    (490)

**COHABITORS**

0-2    17%    (112)

2-10    12%    (121)

**GAY MEN**

0-2    16%    (146)

2-10    16%    (250)

10 +    4%    (97)

**LESBIANS**

0-2    22%    (131)

2-10    20%    (172)

10 +    6%    (32)

Note:  Very few of our cohabitors had been together more than 10 years.

Numbers in parentheses are the number of couples on which the
percentages are based.

FIGURE    53

# Money

*Money management.* Except for the cohabitors, all couples who told us in their original questionnaires that they argued a lot about how money was managed were less likely to be together when we contacted them eighteen months later. Among our married couples, fights about money management were hardest on couples in the early part of their marriage.[3] It is in the early years of the relationship that married couples have to come to terms with each other's spending habits and find a way to coordinate their financial values and styles. This is a critical period of discovery. If the same conflicts emerge later on, the marriage has proved durable enough to withstand the turmoil.[4]

Gay men's and lesbians' relationships can be disrupted at almost any time when they begin to quarrel about money management.[5] Even established couples are more likely to break up when this problem is chronic. It seems to take some same-sex couples longer to discover that they cannot resolve their differences. This may be in part because it takes some same-sex couples longer to feel certain that the relationship is going to last. So more of them may not have to come to grips with differences between partners' financial values until they have lived together for several years.

*Pooling.* Cohabitors are not endangered by fighting over money management, but they, as well as the gay men and lesbians, are more likely to break up when they choose not to pool their money. Failure to pool often indicates that couples have not given up their independence and may never have visualized the relationship as lasting into the indefinite future.[6] Not pooling is associated with breakups among gay men in the early years of their relationship.[7] In contrast, pooling seems to affect lesbians at any stage in the relationship.[8] Pooling, however, is not important in predicting marital dissolution.[9] The decision to marry and the legal realities of marriage are binding enough that pooling is not necessary to make the couple financially interdependent.

*Economic dependence.* Economic themes relating to female interdependence and dependency are associated with breaking up among married, cohabiting, and lesbian couples. We find that the likelihood of a marriage surviving its early years is related to whether or not the wife feels she has the financial resources to leave.[10] It may seem unconscionably cynical to say that wives stay in marriages because they cannot support themselves outside them, but our data show there is some validity to this. We think many unhappy wives stay married because they could not maintain a decent standard of living alone. Women who can support themselves can afford to have higher expectations for their marriages beyond financial security, and because they are more self-sufficient, they can leave if these are not met.

It may also be true that these are women who have not committed themselves to the idea of making their marriages survive at any cost. Wives in marriages of less than two years who had told us it was important for them to be self-sufficient were less likely to be still with their partners when they completed the follow-up questionnaires.[11] These were women who made it clear that it was important for them to be able to take care of themselves. This gave them two advantages. First, a self-sufficient woman knows that she can make it on her own. Second, she knows that this capacity to leave actually gives her more power and influence over how the relationship will be structured.

For cohabiting women a major reason they desire self-sufficiency is that they want to remain an equal partner. If they have equal influence in spending decisions, they and their partners are more likely to stay together.[12]

Dependency is a critical issue for lesbians. Women who saw themselves and their partners as strong and self-sufficient were less likely to break up than those who saw themselves or their partners as dependent and not forceful.[13] Our data have told us that lesbians hold up, as the ideal relationship, one where two strong women come together in total equality. If both women are strong, but one woman is significantly stronger, then the important equality rule is undermined. For example, we find that lesbians in established relationships who have unequal incomes or unequal influence over spending are more likely to break up.[14] We thought such a power imbalance might be so uncomfortable for both women that both advantaged and disadvantaged partners would wish to leave. We find, however, that the more powerful partner was more likely to precipitate the breakup.[15]

*Fighting about income.* Fighting and unhappiness about level of income seem to contribute to breakups only among same-sex couples.[16] We are surprised to find lesbians susceptible to this issue. We saw that income is important to gay men. Lesbians, however, appeared relatively nonmaterialistic. In the first questionnaires and interviews, those who told us they were unhappy over income did not report less commitment to their partners. They did not suspect that being unhappy with the amount of money coming in might be putting their relationship in jeopardy.

Amount of income did not have the same kind of effect on the heterosexual couples.[17] We believe that since married couples are supposed to succeed or fail as a unit, husbands and wives see a low income as a mutual problem rather than as one partner's transgression against the other. By this reasoning, cohabitors might be supposed to be in the same boat with the gay men and lesbians. But we feel that those cohabitors who fight over income do so because they are progressing toward seeing themselves as having *mutual* problems. This kind of fight happens because they no longer anticipate breaking up.

# Work

*Impact of jobs.* In all four types of couples, unhappiness and conflict over the way jobs intrude into the relationship are often associated with a couple's breakup. Among heterosexual couples, it is primarily the woman's job that is at issue. We find that when a husband gets upset about his wife's job, even in established relationships, the marriage is more likely to fail. The wife's dissatisfaction with her husband's job seems to be critical only among newlyweds.[18] At the beginning of the relationship a wife may not accept the demands that her husband's job places on the marriage, and if he does not change his habits, she may leave. In a more established marriage, an unhappy wife may have accepted this as one of the ways in which wives must compromise and has probably found activities, friendships, or work of her own to compensate for her husband's absence. Husbands do not seem to make the same kinds of adjustments. Even after many years of marriage, a husband who is angry about disruptions caused by his wife's work does not accept it as an inevitable part of their marriage. In a new relationship conflict may address the question of whether or not a woman should work at all. We find that fewer of the married couples survived if in their early years they fought about the wife's right to work.[19]

Among the cohabitors we find, once again, that if the man is unhappy about his partner's job, the relationship is more likely to break up.[20] These findings reflect a difficult dilemma for cohabitors. Both partners want the woman to work and not to be dependent on the man. We think, however, that when her work interferes with some of the man's expectations about the benefits a relationship should bring, the bond becomes unstable. While the man may be more than pleased to see her out in the work force helping to support their household, he may not be so ready to bear the costs of her efforts. By expecting her to work but giving no quarter for the demands of her work, he is asking her to be "superwoman," and few women can comply.

Gay men and lesbians who had argued about work were less likely to be together when they filled out the follow-up questionnaires.[21]

*Ambition.* Ambition plays an important part in the breakup of all four kinds of relationships. Gay men and lesbians have a similar profile: The more ambitious partner, and the one who gives more time to his or her work, is more likely to leave the relationship.[22]

When husbands and male cohabitors are not ambitious, their relationships are less likely to last beyond the first few years.[23] Heterosexual women want their male partners to be ambitious. If the man indicates that being successful is unimportant, his parnter may see him as less worthy. A husband feels just the opposite about his wife. Her lack of ambition does not seem to bother him. On the contrary, we find that new marriages where the wife is ambitious are less stable.[24] It is not that an ambitious wife necessarily grows dissatisfied with her marriage or seeks greener pastures. Rather, it is her husband who does not want to live with such an ambitious or successful woman. Among married couples who have broken up, we find that the more ambitious the wife, the more likely that the husband wanted the relationship to end.[25]

*Housework.* Working for wages is not the only kind of work with the potential for dividing couples. Among both married and cohabiting couples, housework is a source of conflict. We find that new marriages are more likely to fail when the husband feels his wife does not do her fair share of the household tasks. This is also true for cohabiting men at early stages of their relationship.[26]

This means that a woman cannot be perceived as doing less housework than her partner wants her to do without jeopardizing the relationship. However, a man, who is unlikely to be doing even half the work, can be perceived as doing less than his fair share without affecting the couple's durability. It is difficult for women to achieve an equal division of housework and still preserve the relationship.

*Time together.* In all four kinds of couples, we find that those who spend a lot of time away from each other—take separate vacations, have separate friends, dine apart frequently—have a lower survival rate.[27] This is true of married couples only in the beginning years, but for the others, it holds true for established relationships as well. Couples may lead separate lives because they value autonomy and reject accountability, and do not wish to operate as a couple all the time. For other couples the desire to be apart reflects incompatibilities which they may not consciously acknowledge. In either case, spending too much time apart is a hallmark of couples who do not stay together.

# Sex

*Fighting about sex.* Among all four kinds of couples, dissatisfaction and fighting about sexual difficulties is associated with a breakup.[28] They may be fighting about any one of a number of specific issues, including how much sex they are having together. However, we do not find any direct association between how *much* sex a couple has and how long they stay together.[29] People who have sex infrequently are just as likely to have a long-lasting relationship as those who have sex often.

It may also be that some of this unhappiness about sex is really unhappiness with the quality of affection that is displayed between the partners. We find that in marriages and cohabiting relationships a man's ability to be tender and expressive is important in keeping the couple together—and this is especially true at the beginning.[30]

*Physical attractiveness.* An important part of male sexuality is the value men place on physical attractiveness. And we find that men's emphasis on the physical attributes of their partners—and of themselves—affects the stability of their relationships. When husbands and male cohabitors place great emphasis on having a good-looking partner, their relationships are less likely to survive past the first few years.[31] It may be that these men to whom looks are so important find the grass is always greener elsewhere. We also find that the better-looking partner is the one who is more likely to leave. We believe they feel they have opportunities for finding another partner, and so they are more likely to do so.[32]

*Non-monogamy.* All four kinds of couples were less likely to survive if they had told us on their original questionnaires that they had had sex outside their relationships within the preceding year. Husbands and wives who had had extramarital sex were more likely to break up, whether it happened at the beginning of the marriage or after many years.[33] In marriage, non-monogamy is such a trespass that even those in established relationships do not shut their eyes to it.

This is also true for lesbian couples. We find that those who have experienced non-monogamy are more likely to break up.[34] But this is not because the monogamous woman dismisses her errant partner. We find instead that the woman who has had outside sex is more likely to choose to terminate the relationship.[35] It is likely that she has fallen in love with someone else and cannot treat the new person as someone auxiliary to her existing relationship. There is a pattern quite like this among heterosexual couples who break up. When it is the woman who has been non-monogamous she is also the one who is more likely to leave the relationship.[36] These data confirm to us that women have difficulty engaging in casual sex—or they have sex outside their relationship only when they are looking for a way to get out of it.

In the early years of their relationships, monogamous gay men have a better chance of survival.[37] If they are non-monogamous after they have established a strong bond, it does not seem to have any great impact on them. But even gay men—with all of their capacity for impersonal sex—need some time to feel secure and to create trust. We also feel that they need the first several years to find out if they agree on how sexually open their relationship will be. If they cannot come up with a mutually satisfying philosophy, they are more apt to break up. In this beginning period gay men do not know how strong their bonds are nor can they always be certain of how impersonal outside sex really is. Indeed, we find that when these men have meaningful affairs in their first few years, they are more likely to break up. If they have an affair once their relationship is established, it need not bring the relationship to an end.[38]

Non-monogamy is also destructive in the early stages of a cohabiting arrangement. If the male partner has outside sex in the first few years, the relationship is likely to end.[39]

*Open relationships.* In some couples non-monogamy is either tacitly or explicitly permitted. A partner may indicate that he or she is not possessive and allow the other to do as he or she wishes. Or a couple may work out specific rules under which non-monogamy can take place. In either case such couples, except for the gay men, have a higher "mortality" than couples who do not give any permission.[40] By giving permission, partners open up the relationship to risk. This does not affect the gay men very much because they have the trick mentality; they can separate sex from emotional attachment. Everyone else, no matter what his or her principles, has a greater chance of getting involved with the new person or becoming disenchanted with the old.

*Living in the gay world.* The world in which gay men live is a highly sexual one. The idea of going to a gay bar or other meeting place and finding someone for casual sex is a common theme in the gay male culture. In fact, many of our couples met under these conditions.[41] But meeting in these kinds of places may not always serve the goals of creating a permanent relationship. Since men go to bars often to find someone to trick with, and make choices there primarily on the basis of physical attraction, they may have little else in common. There is little reason that they would be from the same social class or have the same interests. We find that the gay couples who filled out the original questionnaires reflect this difficulty of meeting someone of similar background. More than other kinds of couples, they differ from each other in educational background.[42] This is more serious than it sounds because the gay men who broke up eighteen months after their first questionnaires tended to be those whose educational backgrounds were ill-matched.[43]

The gay world also has an impact on lesbian couples. We find that when lesbians in established relationships are involved in gay and lesbian organizations and live in the "gay ghetto," they are less likely to remain together.[44] We think that with constant exposure to eligible women in circumstances where love and respect can emerge, it is more likely that one or both partners will become involved with someone else. When a couple is more isolated they can create their private reality and they are freer from temptation.

# Which cohabitors married

Cohabitors who marry tend to make the decision in their first few years together. Some people begin cohabitation as a trial marriage and as soon as they learn enough about each other, they marry or break up. Others fall more deeply in love and marriage no longer seems like something they wish to avoid. A third group are those truly dedicated to cohabitation as a way of life. These couples reveal themselves to each other—even if their views have not been explicitly stated—by staying together for several years without marrying. And the longer they stay together, the less likely their eventual marriage becomes.[45]

The cohabitors who do get married look very different from those who simply continue to live together. On the whole they are a traditional group of people. They have more traditional ideas about the roles of men and women in society, and they are not avant-garde about their own relationships.[46] They want to spend more time with one another.[47] They are more possessive and do not have an open relation-

**COHABITORS 18 MONTHS LATER**

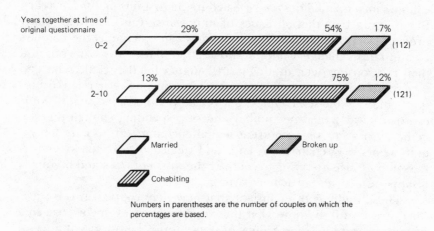

FIGURE   54

ship.[48] They are likely to put their money and resources together from the very beginning.[49]

They also see each other in flattering ways; each sees the other as "a catch." The men feel their partner is sexy, they are happier with their sex life, and they report having sex more often than couples who remain cohabitors.[50] Both the men and the women remark on their partners' ambition and success in the world of work.[51]

We have given only the bare details of why relationships ended and who left whom. They do not show the heartbreak that one or both partners felt or the anger between two partners who have grown estranged. In the interviews, some people described how a previous relationship had ended, and rarely did they talk about it with no sadness, hostility, or regrets. The end of a relationship, even when it is a relief, is almost always a profound disappointment. It is common for the partner who brought an end to the relationship to feel guilty—or at least sorry not to have foreseen the elements that would ultimately spell disaster. The person who is left faces the loss of self-esteem, as well as the loss of the other, and so the emotions involved may be even more devastating.

People often ask, "Why couldn't I have avoided all this pain, and gotten out of my relationship early on?" It is true that many of a couple's incompatibilities are revealed in the first few months or years. But it is not true that all issues of importance can be settled. Many problems become chronic and new ones can emerge as the couple's circumstances change. Couples who weathered the early years can find their relationship deteriorating just when they felt they could relax and take comfort in its strength. The risk is lower in long-term relationships (particularly same-sex couples) but breakup is not impossible. People can drift away from one another and stop spending enough time together. An affair or an outside sexual encounter can occur. Job requirements may change the kind and quality of a couple's time. A person may give up trying to conquer the world of work and become a disappointment to his or her partner.

These findings offer insight that may help couples in two ways. First, it is useful to know what the common areas of discord are so a couple can explore their values on these topics before moving in together. Second, it is important to notice that the dynamics of the people involved are more crucial than any particular issue. Couples tend to break apart when they get out of sync. We might have imagined that the person with more power and control would be content with the relationship. But we have evidence that power is not to everyone's taste. Among the lesbian couples, the person more likely to leave is the more powerful partner, the more forceful and aggressive person, the person who does less housework.[52] Lesbians seem not to like to be too much in control. Indeed, we conclude that women in general do not like to feel superior to their partners. A woman prefers equality and she needs to respect her partner if the relationship is going to last.

Gay men also struggle with the question of dominance. In the case of gay couples, however, the partner who leaves may have had either *more* or *fewer* advantages. If he feels dominated and controlled, he wants to spare himself further subjugation. So a gay man is likely to leave when he is the less powerful person—less well educated, less forceful and aggressive, or with a lower income.[53] On the other hand, a gay man may also pull out if he is younger (an advantage in the gay world), more self-sufficient, more ambitious, or better-looking.[54] Once the relationship gets out of balance, it is more vulnerable.

Maintaining equality is also very important to cohabiting couples. We find that when power and commitment are not equal, such a relationship is more likely to break up.[55] Only married couples do not rely on equality to hold them together.[56]

Money, work, and sex are all parts of couples' lives that can cause their relationships to end. But they fit into a larger picture.

As we look at what broke couples up, we are most impressed by the differences between the four kinds of couples. We notice that married couples differ in many ways from all the others, and we are impressed that although men and women have the same kind of experience, they may interpret it differently and it may affect their relationships in different ways. Therefore, in the next chapter we wish to draw some conclusions about what makes the four couple types so different and about the similarities and differences between men and women that shape their relationships.

# Conclusion

WE did this study because we, like many others in this country, were becoming increasingly aware that relationships in general and marriage in particular were in flux, that they seemed to be getting more fragile, and that we were witnessing social change that needed to be understood. We wanted to know if the institution of our past—marriage—would be the institution of the future. We wanted to know whether any intimate relationship could meet modern challenges, be satisfying, and last for a lifetime.

What do we mean by *institution*? An institution is a way of life that is very resistant to change. People know about it; they can describe it; and they have spent a lifetime learning how to react to it. The *idea* of marriage is larger than any individual marriage. The *role* of husband or wife is greater than any individual who takes on that role.

Institutions set up standards and practices that let people fall neatly into niches, giving them roles and rules of conduct that help interaction proceed smoothly. Each relationship does not have to deal with the same problem as if it has never occurred before. Trust can be assumed because of the nature of the rules. This is illustrated by one of the major differences between marriage and cohabitation: Marriage has no need for the kind of financial bookkeeping so common among cohabitors because the rules help keep people together and help make for an orderly exit if the relationship ends. Bookkeeping is alienating. It implies the possibility of a breakup or suggests that partners will not do their share unless watched, or that the relationship has to be fifty-fifty and that anything else is a bad bargain.

At the present time, marriage is an institution that seems to be in danger of collapse. We understand it in its pure form. Indeed, every schoolchild understands what marriage is supposed to be like. Ask a young child to explain marriage and he or she can tell its essential parts: that there are a husband and wife, and eventually a mommy and a daddy, that it entails a ceremony, and that the two people live together for the rest of their lives. The child knows just as well as the adult that there are marriages that do not look like this. He may have seen his own parents divorce. But he will not describe real life when he describes marriage—he will describe the "ideal type." The question is, Is that ideal type disappearing because of the exceptions to it? Is marriage becoming less an institution because of the prevalence of divorce, because of new roles for husbands and wives, and because society is debating what relationships are and should be? Are there now different types of marriage, and if so, does that strengthen the institution or weaken it? Moreover, if institutionalization is intrinsically good—if it gives shape to a relationship so that partners know what to expect of one another and can predict what their future together will be like—is this something that our other three kinds of couples should aim for? Indeed, do any of these three already have institutional aspects to their relationships?

# Types of relationship

In looking at marriage in the last part of the twentieth century, we see that there are different marital forms. At one end of the continuum there is traditional marriage, with the man working outside the home and having unquestioned authority, the woman a homemaker, and no possibility of divorce. At the other end of the continuum are the most experimental forms of marriage.

It may be that this continuum will start to break off into little clusters, each a different kind of marriage. We may see, for example, that "voluntary marriage" will take on a recognizable profile. These are the marriages that last only while the couple is in love. Based as they are on "happiness" and "compatibility," they may be expected to be less stable than relationships grounded in a presumption of permanence. Such marriages might be seen as requiring special contracts, renewable every year or every five years. Partners would anticipate the fact that their high expectations made permanence improbable. If voluntary marriage became an institution people would say, "I'm entering into a voluntary marriage," to their friends and their friends would immediately know this was different from any other form of marriage. For example, economic arrangements might be quite specific and separate.

The question is, however, Does voluntary marriage simply create a new form of marriage, or does it have deeper implications? Does the mere concept of voluntary marriage undermine the institution so thoroughly that even the most traditional of vows lose their effect, thereby bringing the permanence of the marital institution, its most critical aspect, into question?

Another modern variation may be cohabitation as a "trial marriage." Trial marriages, as we have seen, are quite conservative and it might be said that they are exactly like marriage except that the couple has not yet made the final decision. But trial marriage is really quite different from the *institution* of marriage. It is not the mere anticipation of marriage but the actual experience of it that shapes people's lives. A woman who intends to quit her job will not do so until the marriage has occurred. No children will be born until their future can be assured by the safeguards of marriage. While trial marriage may be the nonmarital form closest to marriage (because it presumes an eventual lifetime commitment), it is still not marriage.

Traditionalists see voluntary marriage and trial marriage as truly threatening alternatives because they *seem* to be supportive of the institution while in fact they are not. Allowing such variation erodes the historic nature of marriage. And society does not sit by complaisantly and allow its institutions to change radically. Those who champion voluntary marriage and argue that what modern society needs is many different forms of intimate life-style are ignoring the fact that such a development would be a revolutionary one.

There have already been revisions in the concept of marriage that may prove shattering. Society now questions whether husbands should have absolute authority. Soon it may be taken for granted that the working wife will be a financial partner, sharing even the man's provider role. This gives a woman more power because many of the justifications for the couple's division of labor were predicated on one person, the male, directing the relationship because his work made survival possible. If he is no longer the provider, he may lose his legitimacy as ultimate decision-maker. Other decisions, such as who chooses where they will live become problematic. (We are already, for example, seeing one outcome of such a situation, wherein couples commute rather than live together because each partner values his or her job and neither will compromise success by moving to the other person's location. Changes such as these do not simply modify the institution; they alter the very meaning of marriage so drastically that it may cease to be an institution in the way we have always known it. We are not arguing that these changes should not occur. We are merely saying that if and when they do, the institution may fail and need to be reconstructed according to a different model.

What about other kinds of couples? It could be argued that cohabitors who plan never to marry are attempting to create a new institution.

The whole idea behind lifetime cohabitation is that people who love each other can create a bond that does not need the state's participation and can be durable and satisfying. But relationships are both public and private. It is difficult to create an institution without support from society and this society still recognizes only marriage as an institution.

Furthermore, to be an institution, cohabitation would have to have a predictable shape, and at present cohabitation takes too many forms. The fact that two partners often have very different concepts of what cohabitation means is evidence that it is not yet institutionalized. It is not recognized as a stable *form* by law or society; it is seen as a *situation* which may change at any moment. Its lack of predictability and the absence of clear understandings about what the relationship means to the participants themselves make establishing the institution of cohabitation very difficult.

Before cohabitation can become an institution, its properties must be clear to any schoolchild. It must be seen as legitimate. Both partners must have the same level of commitment (or lack thereof) to the future. At the present time, we think that because there are so many possible permutations of cohabitation, partners may have trouble being sure they both want the same things out of the relationship. There is often no basis for trust, no mutual cooperation, and no ability to plan.

Currently, cohabitation as a way of life is unstable. Cohabitors may be dismayed by this because they feel their love is enough and that all it takes to create a way of life is two people who see eye to eye. But they do not take into account the importance of society's reactions and how poorly society is equipped to accommodate them. For example, parents may not want to acknowledge a cohabitor's partner as a family member. Even if they want to be welcoming, they may be unsure of what to expect of such a person; they may not know how to act toward him or her. One symptom of this confused state of affairs is that cohabitation has been widely discussed and openly practiced for the past fifteen years, and yet we still do not have a term the two people can use for one another. Couples who want to create an institution should be aware of what an awesome task they have taken on. It is very hard to anticipate the results when one tries to create a new tradition and it is very hard to maintain one's resolve in the face of an unsupportive society. After all, it has taken a long time for Western marriage to evolve the features that it has. Institutions are not made or redesigned overnight.

Moreover, we think it will be hard for cohabitation to become an institution while the traditional model of marriage still exists. As long as marriage retains its image as the highest form of commitment, it acts as a lure to cohabiting couples who want to prove their love for each other. So they are likely either to get married or to break up once their commitment falters. If cohabitation is to be a unique institution, it must be perceived as different from marriage, and marriage cannot be allowed to be seen as a better or next step in the relationship. But, the establishment of cohabitation as a lifetime alternative to marriage is an implied criticism of the latter, and hence is likely to be resisted by government and society in an attempt to defend the concept of matrimony. Society accepts cohabitation now only because it is thought of as a phase in a person's life. It is not understood as challenging the legitimacy of marriage.

Do same-sex couples exist as an institution? Certainly not in the general community. Neither schoolchildren nor heterosexual adults can explain accurately how such couples function. Furthermore, because of the general antipathy toward homosexuality in American society, gay men and lesbians are not encouraged to be open about their sexual preference or about their relationships. Hence they are seldom extended such commonplace courtesies as having a partner invited to an office party or to a retirement banquet. Even heterosexuals who might like to welcome a gay friend's partner may not know how to go about doing so.

Are same-sex couples an institution within the gay and lesbian community? At present, we think not. There is a general fear in both gay and lesbian circles that relationships are unlikely to last. Long-lasting relationships are seen as quite special. They are unexpected, and therefore newly formed couples are not treated as though they will remain together for fifty years. People are less likely to ask, "How's Jerry?" and more likely to say, "Are you still with your lover?" This is particularly true for gay men. But it happens with both men and women, and when a couple is not treated as inviolate, the less likely it is that the partners will see themselves that way.

We might expect that the existence of a gay culture would help the development of "couple" status. A community could offer the support of public opinion, the reinforcement of a relationship by friends, and censure of a person who treats his or her partner badly or dissolves a well-thought-of partnership. Conventions could be established and a couple who violated them would have an awareness that they might be headed for trouble. Role models would be present to show that relationships can last, and more important, to show how.

The problem with gay male culture is that much of it is organized around singlehood or maintaining one's sexual marketability. Meeting places like bars and baths promote casual sex rather than couple activities. The problem with the lesbian world is quite different. Women are often in tight-knit friendship groups where friends and acquaintances spend so much intimate time together that, it seems to us, opportunities arise for respect and companionship to turn into love and a meaningful affair. Thus, gay men imperil their relationships because of the availability of a singles market that draws men out of their relationships; lesbians are in jeopardy because of opportunities to fall in love. We have found that when gay women are involved in the gay world, they break up more, not less. If couplehood were an institution, participation in the gay world would not be detrimental; it would be supportive.

What would give institutional status to gay relationships? They would not need to look like marriage or to have the same rules as marriage. But they would have to have some predictable elements so that couples could agree on their obligations. Ideally there might be a public witness to the couple's vows to one another, perhaps even a ceremony. The couple might want to be legally joined by the state and have reciprocal legal responsibilities that would make it emotionally and financially harder to break up. Sometimes gay men and lesbians have put each other in their wills; sometimes one has adopted the other. These are attempts to give the relationship stronger ties than the couple's private promises to one another.

The chance to marry legally, however, is denied to gay people. We think the courts, as agents of the broader society, have resisted same-sex petitions to wed, partly because of anti-homosexual precedents and prejudices and partly because it would be the most fundamental change ever made to the institution of marriage. The judiciary understands that if gay people were allowed to marry, it would help institutionalize their relationships; the courts do not want to do this. Nor do they want to create parallel institutions to marriage. Just as the courts once enforced laws that forbade blacks and whites to marry because white America feared an interracial society, so they also prohibit gay marriage, fearing that it would in some way encourage homosexuality. Courts are by nature conservative; they enforce the status quo and resist change. They do not want to redefine marriage.

This is very upsetting to many gay people, but they should also remember that there are some minuses to balance the pluses institutions provide. For one thing, when relationships become institutions, this reduces pluralism. There becomes only one model of how to live as a couple. In addition, the more the couple is extolled, the more the single person is excluded. At present, the fluidity of couple status in the gay community makes it easier to be a single gay man or lesbian than it is to be a single heterosexual person. Institutional standing for same-sex couples may reduce some of the freedom the gay community offers.

A more important drawback is that the institution of marriage, at least until now, has been organized around inequality, and attempts to change this framework have not yet been very successful. The traditional married couples in our study often laid their solid foundation on roles that stabilized the relationship but gave the woman some of the less pleasant responsibilities, such as housework, and assigned her duties, such as the buyer role. If tasks were allotted on the basis of efficiency or affinity, we would expect that married couples could reassign household chores and have the institution remain as durable as ever.

We have found, however, that when roles are reversed, with men doing housework and women taking over as provider, couples become dreadfully unhappy. Even couples who willingly try to change traditional male and female behavior have difficulty doing so. They must not only go against everything they have learned and develop new skills, but they have to resist the negative reaction of society. Thus we have learned that while the institution is bigger than the individuals within it, it may not be bigger than the assignment of roles by gender.

# Gender

Gender has been a second theme running through this study. We have described many differences among the four types of couples, but we have also observed that heterosexual men have traits in common with homosexual men, and this is also true of heterosexual and homosexual women. It has been clear that a person's gender affects what he or she desires in a relationship and how he or she behaves in one. It is equally clear that the way people expect their partners to behave depends on whether the partner is male or female; thus gender requirements set the stage for how individuals will interact as a couple.

An extremely important effect of having one male and one female in heterosexual couples is that each gender is automatically assigned certain duties and privileges. A couple does not have to think about how the house is going to be cleaned or money is going to be earned, if they depend on tradition to guide the male's efforts in one direction and the female's in another. All this is taken for granted except when people are trying to reject tradition or when they have no gender differences to guide them. Then the true complexity of running a household and running a relationship become evident. Each element of the couple's life—from cooking a meal to initiating sex to writing Christmas cards—becomes a potential point of debate. Both may want to take on a responsibility or neither may be so inclined. Both may have been trained to do certain things, or neither may know anything about them. For heterosexual couples, gender provides a shortcut and avoids the decision-making process.

With this enormous advantage comes two enormous disadvantages. First, while the heterosexual model offers more stability and certainty, it inhibits change, innovation, and *choice* regarding roles and tasks. Second, the heterosexual model, which provides so much efficiency, is predicated on the man's being the dominant partner. Giving one person the final say guarantees less argument about the organization of the relationship—as long as neither partner sees this as unfair.

Historically the man's authority was questioned by neither the man nor the woman. But today, the right of men to have authority over women is widely debated and it is not as clear what the internal organization of the relationship will be. Same-sex couples cannot, obviously, rely on gender to guide their decisions about who will do what in the relationship. But they do not have the inequality that gender builds into heterosexual relationships. Some individual gay male or lesbian couples may not have equality, but that is either the happenstance of that individual relationship or perhaps the result of modeling their relationship on marriage. It is not thrust upon them as part of the nature of their relationship. Same-sex couples who wish to build a relationship based on equality are a step ahead of heterosexual couples, but the price they pay is the lack of traditions or guidelines.

When asked how they came to organize their relationship the way they do, same-sex couples usually refer to trial and error, both partners minimizing the number of tasks they hate doing, or say they had to discover which partner was more talented in one area or another. If heterosexual couples today wish to avoid the hierarchy that gender places on them and to escape from adherence to notions of "men's work" and "women's work," they often arrange their lives so that each performs the jobs he or she prefers or to which he or she is better suited. They do not fully realize, however, that growing up male or female shapes one's preferences and one's skills, so choosing tasks on the basis of personal preference still brings them within the traditional framework.

What is there about men's and women's roles that enhances relationships, and what is there that undermines them? What are the properties of gender that men and women prize in their relationships, and which do they wish to discard? Among the heterosexuals we find that men are still invested in their work and treat it as a major focus of their lives. The provider role, however, is in jeopardy. Husbands are still in the work force supporting their families, but many are now joined by their wives who help carry financial responsibility. Many husbands told us in the interviews that they no longer wish to be totally responsible for a partner's economic well-being. Looking at the cohabitors, we can see that when relationships between men and women are less scripted, men can, and indeed do, cast off that responsibility. Their ambition to achieve, however, is not diminished even though they are no longer the sole support of their partners. The world of work has not lost its allure for men, even though a major reason for conquering it is disappearing. It is too important a source of respect for them. What may be lessening, however, is their ability to use their responsibilities to family or relationship as a rationale for devoting themselves to work. In the future a man's excessive attachment to his work may be viewed as selfish rather than selfless.

There is another reason why work is an important part of a man's self-image. For most married couples, it is still the man's work that remains sacrosanct. His superior earning power means it is in the couple's best interest to make choices that will support his presence in the work world. It is interesting that even when the couple shares the provider responsibility, the husband's career will probably continue to be put first. This is extremely important for gender hierarchy. This assures that he will remain a dominant force in the relationship.

His work gives him a great deal of influence. Historically, a husband's influence came from the fact of his being male and therefore the head of the household. While there is a residue of this kind of authority left, it seems to us that it is fast disappearing and that it is being shored up by a man's achievements. Thus men may be even more attached to their work because they now derive their influence from how well they do as well as from who they are.

When the husband was making the only money the couple had, it was traditional for the wife to make his life at home as comfortable as possible. Since his labor was synonymous with the couple's welfare, doing things for him was doing something for the whole family. Men learned to be indulged without feeling particularly selfish. They learned to make decisions without consulting the rest of the family because of their authority and the importance of their comforts. They felt it was their due to be taken care of in return for the burdens they carried. They became accustomed to doing no housework unless they wished to be magnanimous, and it was unquestionably their right to have their sexual needs and desires shape the couple's sex life. Although times are changing, it is still difficult for men to give up these privileges. The assumption that they should be indulged shapes the lives of heterosexual men, both married and cohabitors. Men are starting to give up the costs of being male, but they are moving much more slowly in giving up benefits that were their due in an earlier age.

Women in relationships with men increasingly see employment as part of their self-image, although this does not yet include taking on the provider role. We believe that this role is still foreign to most of them. They wish to work, but not as the primary support of the family. Further, while some women in our study are "work-centered," it remains a minority. We think that most employed women continue to value their role as companion and caretaker. Women in the study seem to want respect for both roles and are seeking a way to perform them both successfully. They also want to preserve part of men's traditional commitment to the world of work: They still want their partners to achieve. When they enter the world of work, they do not want him to leave. Women want to look up to, or at least directly across at, their male partner if they are to respect him.

Women, like men, want to be admired for their success at their jobs. Men, however, are more likely to see their own work as more important and the woman's work as auxiliary. This is partly because she generally earns less money, but it may also reflect the belief that her work is more voluntary or done more for her self-fulfillment than for the couple's welfare. In established married couples, if the woman wanted to quit working, if it were financially feasible, her husband would probably acquiesce. If the man wanted to quit working, it would be considered a central change in the relationship. There is still some residue of the provider role, and in a man any reluctance to work would be seen as abandoning his responsibilities.

Cohabiting men and women feel that neither should be responsible for the other's economic welfare and so they are more likely to see the woman's work as a duty rather than as a choice. Cohabiting men and women do not give the woman or the man a provider role. They are likely to invoke the rule of doing one's fair share. Cohabiting women seem pleased to be as self-sufficient as possible and to contribute to the financial needs of the relationship, but their desire for equality is often stymied by the fact that women still do not earn as much as men. The woman with a high income may easily do her fair share and more, but in general, cohabiting women are struggling to keep up with their partners. Until women earn as much as men, even cohabiting women would like to base their financial participation on what they can afford. These women have rejected most aspects of traditional female subordination and they do not like to be in a less than equal position in the relationship. But while some cohabiting men subscribe to an equitable arrangement of splitting expenses, many prefer absolutely equal contribution. This is frustrating to a woman because it puts her at a disadvantage and gives her less influence. The fact that the woman brings in less income keeps the couple from operating along egalitarian lines, and it is a reminder to her that she is in a second-class position. There are of course more traditional cohabitors, those intending to marry, who are not as taken up with the idea of equality, but most cohabiting women want respect for their ability to pay their own way. It seems to us that this may be evidence that dependency, financial or otherwise, will eventually cease to be such a large part of the female role.

Furthermore, it seems likely that women will press for some changes in men's roles. Women, in exchange for sharing financial responsibilities, want more help with burdensome chores, and in most of the areas we have studied, would like to move closer to equality. They do not want to dominate their men any more than men want to be dominated. But they want enough power so that they can have their desires considered and so the relationship does not always operate on their partner's terms. This may be accomplished as work plays a more important role in their lives and, by making them less dependent, moves the relationship more toward equal decision-making.

The gay men, like the heterosexual men, derive much of their self-esteem from the world of work and the ability to make a good income. As men, they expect to work. Because they have a male partner, they expect him to work as well. The provider role lapses because it is really suitable only in a heterosexual context. Men do not expect to provide for other men. They ask of their partners the same things they ask of themselves: ambition, earning power, and initiative. This can create a problem for the internal dynamics of couples where one man clearly does better in the world of work than the other or where one man is clearly more powerful than the other. Men do not do well in such relationships. The more dominant man finds it difficult to respect his partner and not punish him for being less successful or for not being forceful and aggressive. The man who is less powerful may have trouble staying in a relationship where he is unable to see himself as an equal. A man might like to cook or keep house, or be less invested in his work, but if these things bring him less respect or power from his partner—as they may well do—this is likely to be disturbing to all but a small proportion of gay men. Relaxing some of the demands of the male role seems to be less of a problem than assuming roles that have traditionally been held by women.

It seemed to us that, at least in some ways, lesbians also find the female role demeaning and wish to change it. Like the other women, they still value being companions and they still want their relationships to be at the center of their lives. These are parts of the traditional female role that they continue to prize. But while we spoke to lesbians who had relationships where one woman supported the other or where one was content to be clearly subordinate, our overwhelming impression is that most lesbians, young or old, affluent or poor, wish to avoid being dependent or having a dependent partner. There is a strong emphasis on being able to take care of oneself. If, for example, one woman seemed to need a lot of help making decisions or was clearly glad to be supported, the more dominant partner was usually unhappy about it. Lesbians are vigilant for signs of weakness or lack of initiative in themselves or in their partners. They want their partners to be ambitious and to enter the world of work, and they are careful to divide evenly the tasks like housework that remind them of women's subordinate status in heterosexual relationships. They do not want a partner to dominate them, and just like heterosexual women, they have no desire to dominate. As we saw when we looked at the data on who broke up, the woman who was in a more dominant role was the woman more likely to leave the relationship. Lesbians are in a double bind: On the one hand, they want a great deal of attention and communication from a partner. On the other hand, they do not want a partner who is so relationship-centered that she has no ambition or attachment to work. Lesbians want an intense home life, but they also want a strong, ambitious, and independent partner. They want to give a great deal, but only if their partner gives as much. They demand a lot, but not more than they can return in kind. They do not want to be provider, but neither do they wish to be provided for.

This gives us a clue to why lesbians have such a high breakup rate. They are the vanguard in changing women's roles in the 1980's. They have many conflicting desires in their relationships, none of which can be solved by reverting to the traditional female role. Both partners are rejecting the comfortable supported position that women have been trained for in favor of being a full and equal partner in a relationship. This endangers their desire to place their relationship at the center of their lives and their need for emotional intensity because it means that both women need to be equally ambitious outside the relationship. Moreover, they are at the same time moving away from male traits that they feel provide inequality. They do not wish to dominate in their relationship or take too much initiative. They know that if they do, their partner may actually relax into what they see as a traditional female dependency, and this they refuse to allow. Thus lesbians are rejecting almost all available gender directives at once.

The lesbians are trying to carve out a new female role. This is an exceptionally difficult challenge and it is a testimony to their persistence that so many of their relationships do thrive. We think that one reason some are successful is because lesbians still retain women's desire for closeness and nurturance. Most are still relationship-centered and are willing to put time and effort into working out their problems and being attentive to their partner's emotional needs.

We have tried to describe some of the major issues that will be confronting couples in this decade and perhaps for far longer. Institutions evolve slowly and change slowly. Gender roles are entrenched, and they are difficult to change even when they are no longer satisfying. We hope that after seeing where the conflicts and successes lie, couples will be more aware of where the directives imposed by gender serve them well and where they serve them badly.

We have focused a great deal of attention on the problems couples face, their sources of conflict, and the factors that stand in the way of their contentment. These are the issues that challenged us as sociologists and these are the issues we felt that couples would most want to understand. What we have not shown is why so many couples can face up to extremely difficult problems and yet endure and be happy. We have been impressed with the energy that human beings are willing to put out to conquer problems against great odds, to make compromises, and to achieve enough satisfaction to stay and work things out. We have tried to stress the reasons why some kinds of couples face greater hurdles than others. We hope that while drawing attention to the conflicts that can erode a couple's relationship, we have also offered insights into what can make them stronger. Many of the problems we have discussed have no easy solution, and this is particularly true because a couple does not live in a vacuum. The modern world in which they are trying to create a life together is full of complexities. There are demands made of men and women by virtue of their gender that they may resist because they see them as an affront to their individual values—only to find it difficult to invoke new, better, and fairer guidelines. People may avoid marriage because of the inequalities built into its traditional design only to find that there are pitfalls in not having rules and regulations and social recognition.

Looking at marriage and its alternatives, we see advantages both in the institution and in nonmarital forms. As we look at the impact of being male or female, we see no evidence that historic gender-role traditions and restrictions help solve *all* issues for couples. We believe that the time for orthodoxy is past. Neither, however, do we reject the idea that gender differences may be valuable for a couple in certain areas of their life together. Gay couples face problems that arise from "sameness" of gender; these give us an indication of where it might be wise for partners to be different. Heterosexuals face problems that arise from their "differentness"; these give us guidance about where it might be better for two partners to be more alike.

There is, of course, no perfect composite picture that will fit every couple's needs. But we hope that the findings of this study will help a couple identify roles and develop understandings that will help make their relationship satisfactory and long-lasting. As the institution of marriage loses its predictability for heterosexuals, and while homosexual couples have no institution to enter, each couple will have to establish guidelines for making gender work for, not against, the possibility of a lifetime relationship.

# COUPLES' LIVES

D URING the course of this study three hundred couples were interviewed. Each couple has a story to relate: When both partners tell us about the relationship from its beginnings, so much is revealed about their lives, their aspirations and their quarrels, their successes and failures, that we feel we know these two people well. And ideally, we would wish to discuss each couple's history, in all its rich detail.

But that is impossible. If we presented the full stories of even one quarter of the couples we have interviewed, there would be no room to explore the larger trends and patterns that give us insights into the dynamics of couple life. Even if we omitted the larger picture, we would still need more than one book to do justice to all their lives; and some of these couples deserve a book of their own.

So, we have found a way to make peace with our limits by introducing twenty couples whom we found particularly interesting or moving, and who helped to illuminate some of the ways in which money, sex, and work shape the nature of their relationships. These couples are not "representative," either of couples in general or of couples in this study. Rather, they are people who reveal a variety of approaches to issues all couples confront, in different economic classes, in various stages of life, and with diverse goals. Some are contented. Some are not.

The criteria we used to select them, other than those we mention in the introduction, were simple. We chose a given couple if, after reading their interviews, we felt we really understood them, comprehended why they were happy or unhappy, and could in turn provide insights about why their union might or might not endure. To protect their anonymity, we have slightly altered the ages, places, and occupations of our couples, keeping these details as close as possible to the original facts; and some anecdotes have been switched from one couple to another, similar one. The result is true to the couples' lives, but sufficiently masked that their privacy is preserved.

With these limitations, the next chapters explore the lives of five couples in each of our four kinds of relationships.

# Five Married Couples

## Lisa and Albert

We chose this couple because they are committed and happy despite serious economic and personal difficulties. Their relationship is centered around children, and in their case, this arrangement strengthens their household and increases their pleasure in each other. This is a first marriage for both. They would not have considered living together before marrying. They are traditional in their roles and in their financial arrangements. Each of them has separate spheres of responsibility.

Their home is a small, very plain house in an area comprised of similar dwellings, outside the city. Some of the houses are built of brick, most are wood, and all seem to have come to life in the 1950's. None is expensive and many are rented. The neighborhood is tidy: Each small front lawn is well tended, some of them brightened by flowers. It looks like a neighborhood where people value what they have and try to preserve it.

Albert and Lisa's house is largely indistinguishable from the rest, although they are a little luckier than most in their front-yard tree, which enhances the modest facade. Inside the two-bedroom, one-story house, the furnishings are simple and inexpensive, but the rooms are neat and there are attractive framed prints on the walls. One bedroom is full of children's toys and though a few more are scattered on the floor of the living room, the overall effect is one of fastidious care.

Lisa greeted us at the door, Albert behind her. A couple in their early twenties, both are quite attractive. Albert works as a machinist on an assembly line in a huge plant while Lisa stays home with their two-year-old son, Roland. She is three months pregnant and they are redoing the second bedroom to accommodate their growing family. The couple apologized for the temporary disorder, though we didn't see anything we could call messy.

Albert and Lisa have been married three and a half years. They met about five years ago at a friend's birthday party.

> ALBERT: It was funny. I was about half drunk and she was sitting on the floor by the fireplace with nobody sitting next to her. I kind of walked up and said, "Is this seat taken?" Real corny. I liked her right off. She got up and left the party and wouldn't come back till I was gone. . . . She just didn't like me.

Lisa corroborated his account:

> He was drunk off his behind, and I'm not a drinker. He was too forward. He kept bugging me. He wouldn't leave me alone. He wanted to sit by me and talk and he couldn't talk a straight conversation.

This was not an auspicious beginning. Albert tried a different approach a week later that piqued Lisa's interest, but her initial reasons for seeing him could hardly be called magnanimous.

> LISA: He sent me flowers. . . . And he kept going back to my girl friend and asking questions about me. . . . She'd say, "Albert wants to know this and that." And I started getting more curious and I thought, *Well, I've been hurt a lot by this other guy. Albert's got a good job. He's making good money. Why don't I do what they've done to me. I'm going to go out with him. He likes to dance. He likes to do the same things I like to do. I might as well go out with him and get a few free dinners and stuff. Have a good time anyway. What could it hurt? Better than sitting home.* That was my first reason for going out with him.

But even so, she firmly stated her conditions:

> LISA: I decided to let him come to my apartment and talk for a while. I told him I'd consider going out with him only if he didn't drink. As long as he was not drunk, I would go out.

They started dating. He would show up at her door with a steak and potatoes and cook dinner. Or take her for a drive. They would go out just to look at newfallen snow together. Lisa began to thaw.

> LISA: At first it was just for something to do. But then as I got to know him I found out that he was really a very sensitive guy and he cared. He wasn't like most of the guys I'd gone out with. They were out to get a good time. They come home and they want to take you to bed. Well, Albert didn't. I didn't kiss him for more than a month after we started dating. But you know, he didn't try anything. He was real polite. Just really good to me. That made me feel really good. I didn't feel pressured, so I could relax. Right from the start I was myself. I didn't have to impress him. . . . We were both

ourselves. We talked openly and got to know each other first. That to me was more important than anything. . . . The last guy I had dated wouldn't date me anymore because I wouldn't go to bed with him. I was kind of down on guys.

Their relationship grew.

LISA: We have this little joke going that Albert chased me until I caught him. . . . I wasn't that interested at first and I let him know. . . . In a couple of ways I was quite mean to him as far as things I said. . . . I just told him right from the start that we could have a good time but not to expect anything. . . . If I didn't like something, I just said it in a blunt way. And then it was only a couple of months that all of a sudden I woke up one day and I realized I had more feelings for this guy. And I actually fell in love with him before he probably realized that he was in love with me. And I told him.

Both sets of parents approved of the idea of marriage.

ALBERT: We were at a dance. My dad came back from dancing with her. I made some comment about: "Be nice to her. It might be your future daughter-in-law."
　　That was a mistake. They got overencouraging. I finally had to say something. They were telling me how good she was for me. She was straightening me out because I was going out drinking too much. I got a drunk-driving ticket. . . . I was on the way downhill and she kind of pulled me out of it, so they were telling me how good she was for me. And that kind of clouded my feelings, because I didn't know whether I loved her because they *said* I should love her or whether it was really me. I finally had to tell them to butt out and quit telling me how good she was.
　　As far as her family: The night her parents met me, which was about three days after our first date, they told her to get married.

LISA: When he met my parents for the first time—the next time I talked to my mom she told me that they thought there might be a wedding pretty soon, and I told her she was crazy. They'd met the guy once and I don't even know the guy that well. You can't start saying things like that. Every other guy I'd brought home, she'd warned me: "Well, if you guys got married, there would be problems because of this or that." And this time it was the opposite, and it threw me.

It was just a matter of months before both Lisa and Albert were serious. They did not, however, consider living together. The only thing they thought of was marriage.

ALBERT: We talked about it, but both of us felt that it wasn't us. We just didn't, even though we had some people comment, "Why get married? Why don't you live together first and try it out?" We were both raised that you don't do that. We won't condemn anybody for it, but we won't do it.

LISA: I like to write poems sometimes. And I wanted to write him a poem that told him I valued our friendship. I started writing that, but I couldn't come up with it. I kept coming up with another poem. It was about love and it was about marriage. It started me thinking and I realized that I was going to marry him one day. I decided to tell him that. I told him, "I am not trying to pressure you or anything, but I happen to be in love with you and I'm going to marry you some day, whenever you're ready, and you just let me know whenever the time comes. Till then I won't bug you." . . . About three months after that, he proposed to me and it shocked the hell out of me.

They had a big church wedding and moved into the house where they presently live. There were no large-scale arguments in the beginning, only a few misunderstandings.

ALBERT: Our first major argument was that I fell asleep on the couch and she argued with me for about a half hour, but I was asleep. When she finally discovered I was asleep, she felt kind of silly.

LISA: We never had any really big serious arguments. If there has ever been any problem, we end up talking about it. . . . But right after we were married, there were some things that bothered me that we have gotten resolved. He had this habit of walking in the house and turning the TV on, whether he got home at two A.M. or ten that night. And he'd fall asleep on the couch and I'd have to turn the TV off. . . .

He was asleep for our first fight, during which I was yelling and very mad at him because he wouldn't come to bed. I didn't get married to go to bed alone, and I'd gotten up about four times, and he said, "Yeah, I'll be there," and even sat up on the couch. But he was asleep.

Life is relatively trouble-free for the couple these days. The household revolves mostly around the baby—when his parents can find time. Albert is working very hard to support his family and that means long hours. Lisa's pregnancy complicates matters.

LISA: He works seven to three, which is good hours. For a while there, though, he had to work nights part of the time, days part of the time, graveyard part of the time. That was really rough on him. . . . So that took all his time for a while and was really rough on us. . . .

Sometimes I'd like to have a little more time with him. It's just, like, I'm pregnant again and I've been really really sick except for the first week or so. So I've been going to bed really early. We have time, but I haven't been able to spend it with him as much as I'd like 'cause I haven't felt well.

The time they do have is spent happily, as a family.

ALBERT: We are no longer a couple. We are a family. There is the three of us and soon to be the four of us. . . . He [Roland, the baby] and I have developed quite a relationship between the two of us. When we decided to have a baby, we decided that the baby was going to be part of our lives and we wouldn't shut him out. We'd include the baby in it.

Albert has been an enthusiastic participant in parenthood from the start, even before Roland was born.

ALBERT: This baby added to our marriage, made it stronger. While she was pregnant we went to baby classes and learned breathing techniques. I got some real participation in it. I was with her during the labor and timed her contractions. Was with her in the labor room and the delivery room. Then I got to cut the cord—the umbilical cord. And just going through the experience together strengthened our relationship.

Lisa feels the same way, and as a father, Albert delights her.

LISA: I like it when Albert is home to play with Roland. I love to watch the two of them play. That to me is more excitement than anything.

At the start of her pregnancy, Lisa was irritable and touchy, but Albert's understanding helped to carry them through.

LISA: The first three months of my pregnancy with Roland, we had a lot of problems. Not anything specific, but he would look at me and I'd cry. He'd say something and I'd disagree with him. I was always disagreeing with him and then he'd say, "It's okay. I understand. You're pregnant." And I'd get mad at him because he was blaming everything on me being pregnant. I was just totally gone emotionally.

That lasted about three months. . . . He was really good. He called the doctor at one point and said, "What can I do to help?" The doctor said it was just normal. "There's nothing you can do. Just be patient." And I tried my best, and I couldn't control it.

Once we were through that stage, we were all right.

The birth of the baby, Lisa agrees, was a wonderful experience.

LISA: It brought us closer than ever. We had a natural childbirth. Albert was just fantastic. I was in labor twenty-nine hours. I wouldn't dilate but I was in labor. We didn't get any sleep. We did everything we were supposed to do. Albert took care of all the timing of the contractions, everything. The only thing I did was concentrate on my breathing and relaxation during the contractions. We'd go to the doctor and [Albert would] have to answer the questions because he knew all the stuff. All I did was concentrate. He did everything, and he got me bouillon to drink because when you're in labor you're not supposed to eat. He would fix all that stuff for me.

He would just baby me, pamper me, take care of me. . . . It was just neat.

Of course new problems arose:

LISA: When Roland was born I was forced to ask for help. I wasn't just taking care of Albert anymore; I was taking care of Roland too. And it was not *my* child—it was *our* child, and it was time for [Albert] to start helping. His life changed dramatically. He would change diapers too—not just me. He could put him to bed. He could pick him up. He couldn't feed him, 'cause I was nursing. He could burp him. He could get a bottle of juice or something. He could pick up the kitchen for me 'cause I didn't have time or couldn't do it that day or whatever. It was just a time when I had to ask for more help. In that way we were closer, because we shared more as far as the work goes.

The addition to their family meant a change in their division of household responsibilities. Lisa and Albert had agreed that the home would be totally her responsibility. Albert thought that was a lot.

ALBERT: I work eight hours a day, which is nothing compared to a housewife. She is happy to be a housewife and stay home and take care of the kids. . . . When we decided to have children and started trying, I made quite a firm statement that I felt children need a mother at home—or a father, depending on how you look at it these days. We're both traditional—you know, the mother is the housewife. She won't work outside until our kids are in school.

To Lisa, that is the natural order of things. Asking Albert's help was a temporary expedient.

LISA: I grew up where my mom stayed at home and my mom did the housework, and to me, being married was being able to take care of my husband. Albert has always helped when I needed him. He's never been one who wanted a spotless house, thank God. It's never mattered to him if things aren't exactly right. I do my best and he appreciates and helps when he can.

But it's just my view of marriage. My job as a wife is what I've looked forward to, even though sometimes I hate it. . . . But the house and the kids are my full-time job. It's both our choice. It's what we wanted. . . . He's not really responsible for housework. Just basically put his dirty clothes in the hamper, if he will. Takes the garbage out. He doesn't really have to do anything if he doesn't want to. . . . Now, because I'm pregnant, I have to ask him to help me with some things. I hate doing that to him but sometimes it works out that way.

It has not proven too taxing for Albert, who also finds time to help out with the baby.

ALBERT: Most of the time, he makes our evenings a little fuller. We feel close just playing with him and watching him grow and teaching him things. Some nights it's miserable. The last couple of weeks he's had a cold and it's been just miserable. There's been tension there when I come home after working all day and she's had a rough day. He was upset, and just like you see in the movies, there have been a couple of times when there were rash statements made because we were all tired and upset.

Each partner makes an effort to alleviate any pressure the other may be under.

LISA: Sometimes he'd be crying a lot and I'd need a break. So I say, "You take him." I'd go walk around the block or something, or the yard, just to get out of the house for a minute. By sharing the responsibility, it helped a lot. Albert would agree with that. It's his responsibility too. I wouldn't just shove Roland on him every time he walked through the door, but when I needed a break he would take over.

They also talk things out together.

ALBERT: We always find time to sit down and discuss any feelings we have. We've discussed in length, several times, about—when we see how other parents discipline their children, we discuss our feelings on it and how we would like to discipline ours. We always keep saying that we hope that it works the way we plan for it to work. . . . We both have our opinions, and I know a couple of times she's done some things that I didn't feel were right. And I've done some things that she didn't feel were right. But whenever it happens, we just come right out and tell the other person we didn't think it was right and we talk about it. We talk a lot.

They don't always agree on Roland's future upbringing.

ALBERT: Well, fighting is one thing we've discussed. She doesn't feel the kid should fight. I feel that if he ever starts a fight, God help him, but if somebody else starts a fight, I'm going to teach him how to finish it. She doesn't feel I should teach him. She figures he would learn. But I never learned. I always got beat up. I don't want that to happen to my son.

LISA: There's been a lot of little things. One of the things that we're discussing now is, is he spoiled? Am I spoiling him? Is Albert spoiling him? . . . We haven't decided on that yet.

But they do agree that there are minor, if somewhat troubling, issues.

ALBERT: It's all really fun. Even a little loss of privacy. He's not big enough to intrude on anything major. Although you can't go sit in the bathroom or attempt to go without him knocking on the door. . . . But we're fine, and I'm looking forward to the next one. . . . My personal opinion is that a pregnant woman is about the most beautiful woman in the world. . . . As far as the joys, I didn't realize the joy a child could bring. I always enjoyed children. This house gets more kids on Halloween than any other house in the neighborhood. The joy of watching your own grow and learn is more than I ever dreamed of.

LISA: I knew there were going to be problems. I knew it was going to be fun. I love kids. I just totally love them. I wish I could afford more than just a couple. The joy is much more than I ever expected. The pain is sometimes more too. It's just totally intensified all around. You can daydream as much as you want but it's a reality that you just can't imagine.

If it were up to Lisa, she would have more children. But there are other considerations:

LISA: We both knew that we wanted at least two children and possibly more. I would like more kids than him. But we'll probably end up only having two because of financial situations. I never thought I'd ever say that, but at least we both want at least two. As far as more, it will just depend on our finances in the future.

Another aspect of the boon that Roland has been to their marriage is expressed by Lisa:

LISA: It helps, because I just love to be real close and just cuddle. Well, Albert doesn't particularly like that. Before Roland was born I had a tendency to hug him too much, because I just wanted to be close to him and cuddle. I think since Roland's been born, it's kind of given me somebody else to cuddle with and get that feeling out with. So when Albert and I get together, we can cuddle, but I don't need it constantly. Albert basically needs a little room, and now I am able to give it to him without it affecting me.

It is obvious that the baby brings them joy, but he also represents a financial burden. The couple is committed to Lisa's staying at home because, as Albert says, "We decided we didn't want our baby brought up by babysitters." That makes them a one-paycheck family in a time when many wives are joining the work force from sheer economic necessity. Lisa nursed longer than she wanted to in order to keep the food bill down, and the whole extended family has been called upon to chip in.

ALBERT: We don't buy him any clothes because we get our brother's old clothes. The only new thing we bought him was shoes.

LISA: Most of the stuff we got for him before he was born was all from garage sales, and that reduces prices, and a lot of it was from other people and free. We have always used that kind of planning.

But even the best planning, and sacrifice, cannot solve all their financial problems.

ALBERT: We have money worries all the time. Money has been very tight this last winter. We had to think about each thing and whether we could buy it or not. Or don't go to the doctor now, because we might have to go for something serious. I have been working two jobs off and on when I had to. Things were, and are still, very tight.

Lisa's special efforts probably spell the difference in keeping them from the kind of money-management difficulties many of our low-income couples have.

ALBERT: In this society, you can't get by without money. Lisa takes care of it for us. She's kind of the penny pincher and I spend it more at whim. Without her, we wouldn't have savings 'cause I can't save. So she's in charge.

LISA: We have problems. For example, I don't like this house anymore, but we're not sure if we can go looking for a bigger place. If things don't go well, it'll just have to be a remodel. . . .
And we have some differences. I moved out of my parents' house before I could afford it, so I learned how to budget the hard way. Albert never moved out of his parents' house. He owed them a lot of money for back rent, which we have mostly paid back, but we still owe them some money. I pretty much take care of this.
He spends more than I think is necessary. He doesn't control it. So we have to stop quite often and discuss our budget and where did all this money go to. "Why are you broke? Where did it go to? If it went to good causes, I can find ten dollars more. If it didn't, tough." I decide: "We need this for this. We need this for that. That leaves this much money left over. I'd like to leave it there for this purpose. If you really think it's that important, tell me why and we'll discuss it some more." . . . That's the way we work it out.

Both of them are very pleased with their successes. They often pointed out to us how much they talk things over, and with what balance.

LISA: I think we are equal. It depends. If I have a strong feeling towards something, I usually get my way. If he has a strong feeling towards something, he usually gets his way. So far we haven't hit anything there's been indecision on. I guess usually we would get his way unless I have a strong disagreement. If it's important, I'll really fight for it. But if it's not a big deal, I might as well go his way. . . .
We talk about everything, no matter how little it is. Everything.

Lisa and Albert have had to surmount other difficulties. Albert's mother started intruding her opinions much more than either her son or his wife felt comfortable with. Albert had to tell her just how and when her intervention would be welcome, and there were many touchy moments until that got settled. He was adamant, however, that his mother respect his family life, and Lisa appreciated his support. It took a while, but now they spend a good deal of time, most of it pleasant, with both families.
There is one serious issue they are working on:

LISA: Albert has a drinking problem. Shortly after Roland was born, it was getting worse—not due to Roland, but to getting together with friends and stuff. He would go fishing and come home really drunk.

And pass out. I try very hard not to fight with him when he's drunk, because he's not going to remember anyway. We had several instances of this. We discussed it and we talked about it.

Nothing really came of it, and finally the last time it happened, it made me very upset. I just told him that something had to be done. We made a little agreement that he felt he could control his drinking. I told him, "I hope you can, but you are an alcoholic. You admitted to that. I understand. But why don't we make a little agreement that as long as you keep it under control, fine. But the next time we have any problems, we start going to an organization for help. I'm going to start getting some information."

There hasn't been any problem since then. He has his occasional drinks. A few times, more than I thought he should. But nothing bad. . . . I have to admit, I do expect worse some day. One of these days we're going to end up going and getting professional help. But right now, we're at a happy medium. He's happy. I'm happy. And until that time comes, we'll just thank God it's happening this way.

Albert admits he has a problem, but acknowledges that his wife "is straightening me out." We asked Lisa if she thought Albert's drinking could harm their marriage.

LISA: The only way I would ever leave him is if it looked like he might hurt me or the kids. And then it would be just in terms of getting him help. In my opinion, divorce is out of the question. I didn't get married to get divorced. And as long as you think divorce is a possibility, it is. As long as I don't think it's a possibility, it isn't. . . . We got married for ever and ever. If it was going to be a temporary thing, we would have lived together. But we wanted a permanent thing. This is permanent.

Lisa and Albert are "institutionals." They are devoted to each other. Fights are rare, and both of them told us it has never taken them more than ten minutes to resolve an argument.

LISA: What will generally happen if I get mad—I do not want to get mad and say things that are mean. If I get mad, I clam up and say, "Give me ten minutes." I go into another room or I walk outside. I told him a long time ago: "If I walk out on you, I'm not walking out on you. I just need a little time. I'm sorting things out." I take a deep breath and go back into the same room. One person shuts up while the other talks, and vice versa. We try very hard not to interrupt each other.

ALBERT: We don't decide who is right or wrong. Because whether we still feel we're right or we've decided we're wrong has no bearing. We're each entitled to an opinion. We get things understood. We come to a decision. I kinda live by the rule that you don't go to bed mad at your husband or wife. . . .

Our relationship is based on trust. This might sound a little weird, but we're friends before we're lovers. That's the whole basis of our relationship. If a guy is a friend and you get mad at him, you tell him. You say, "I think that was really a stupid thing you did." You owe him that.

They are lovers as well. Both of them express satisfaction with their sex life, even though it has slacked off temporarily with Lisa's not feeling very well. Usually they have sex at least once a week, and though they are traditional in other realms, both of them feel that either is as likely as the other to initiate sex. At one point, Lisa worried that she was asking for sex too much. She began to think "that he didn't want me much anymore." But that was during a period when Albert was under a lot of pressure at work. When he talked about it with her, they were able to survive that difficult period, and sex has not been a problem since.

Sex is a special and intimate act for them. They are strongly monogamous. Albert says, "There's no indecision on that, because we are both married to each other and we are each other's sexual partner for life." Lisa's only real complaint is that she'd like a little more affection. This is a common unfulfilled desire we hear again and again from wives.

> LISA: I sometimes wish he'd do a little more. I'm the type of person who likes to hug and kiss and just really be loose. And sometimes it seems that I initiate too much, as far as just holding hands or being close. Sometimes I'd like him to just come over to me and say, "Hey, come here. Give me a hug." He does sometimes, but sometimes I just wish he would a little bit more. But it's not serious.

They had sex before they got married and it was a pleasurable experience for both. Lisa was terrified nonetheless.

> LISA: It was very special, but I was scared that I might never see him again. It had turned out that way before. I was so scared. I cared about him by then and I didn't want to lose him, and I didn't know if it was the right thing to do.

In retrospect, it did not harm their relationship but marked the beginning of their commitment to each other. But Lisa wishes her life before Albert had been different so that it would have been even *more* special.

> LISA: I always wished that I could have given my husband my virginity. But I lost that before and there was nothing I could do about it. . . . I've been hurt by it a lot. I wanted Albert as bad as he wanted me, but I was scared at the same time that something was going to happen again. I wanted it to be special. That night I didn't know if I'd ever see him again. But he was special.

They place a lot of trust in one another. Eagerly, they let us know what pleased them most about their relationship:

ALBERT: I'm happiest about the son we have made sleeping in the other room. Our son has been about the greatest joy to this marriage.

LISA: He's added everything—happiness. Not that we weren't happy before, but it's just put a new dimension on it.

ALBERT: Put a new story in the house of happiness, I guess you could say.

LISA: I think you would also say we're happy because we're comfortable. I never have to worry. I could do the most dumb thing in the world and he's still going to love me. . . . It has helped a lot that we were made to have kids.

What is their advice to other couples? They have quite a bit:

ALBERT: Be friends before you're lovers.

LISA: Be friends when you are lovers. Talk a lot.

ALBERT: Yeah, communicate . . .

LISA: And listen.

ALBERT: And even more than that, learn little things about the other person that maybe you don't have words for, but you can tell by an action.

LISA: Or that special gleam in your eye! [She laughs.]

ALBERT: Or a glow. Like when we got married. I knew she was thrilled to death. She made her wedding dress. And I made sure I didn't see her in her wedding dress until she was walking down the aisle. As soon as I saw her, we were still thirty feet apart but she knew how I felt just by looking at me.

LISA: I'll never forget that look. In fact I felt sorry for my dad in a way, 'cause he was holding real tight to me and I only had eyes for Albert.

ALBERT: And it was like that with the baby too. When he was born, she couldn't talk but she could communicate with her eyes. There was so much communication and love between us. It has to be there, because if it wasn't I couldn't have gone through what I had to go through in her giving birth to that baby. . . . So it's body language, and eyes, and talking—and whatever you got, you use.

After a couple of hours with Albert and Lisa, we could not help but think in corny phrases like *true love*. Albert himself says that their love is deeper than anything he has ever known.

ALBERT: Before we got married, I decided in my own head that . . . if for some reason we could not have intercourse—like if something was wrong with her or something was wrong with me—would I still want to marry her even though there was no sex involved? And when I could answer that question "yes," I was then ready to marry her. I still feel the same way.

LISA: And I always think, "How can I make him happy?" And I always try.

No one can predict with certainty the future of any couple, but we left the interview feeling truly positive about Albert and Lisa. In this case, parenthood has strengthened an already strong commitment. Even so, children are not the heart of it. As Lisa says:

A child is part of both of us and is a greater bond. But a relationship is either going to last or it's not. We will last through anything. The baby is just the icing on the cake.

This couple embodies the traditional vows of institutional marriage. While many of our couples have dropped some or all of the parts of the marriage contract, Albert and Lisa consciously embrace them. From what we can see, it has been to their benefit.


# Wendy and Christopher

These aggressive young professionals, overwhelmed by job demands and by their own ambition, were chosen as representative of those modern couples who have little time for each other because they are engrossed in their careers. Lack of time, fatigue, and competition all take their toll on the marriage.

Wendy and Christopher live in a small apartment in a luxury high-rise on the edge of a very expensive neighborhood. The larger units in the building are inhabited by people who have "made it," and the smaller places are occupied by those who are on their way. There are many young professionals who make good incomes and work very hard to meet expensive rents. Wendy and Christopher fit right in.

Wendy met us at the door, wearing a beautifully tailored outfit that she had worn to the office that day. She is twenty-seven, short and very attractive, with curly dark hair. Christopher, thirty, was inside. He is tall, fair, and more reserved than Wendy. He walks with a slight limp as a consequence of an injury he suffered in Vietnam. They have been married one year.

They met briefly as undergraduates at the same New England college but lost track of each other until they both worked as summer clerks in a New York law firm, which subsequently offered them both full-time employment after their graduation from law school. That precipitated their first crisis. The firm did not know how serious their relationship was and preferred not to employ husband and wife teams. They had to decide which of them would accept the offer.

This was their first taste of how their careers could cause them problems. Up to that point, it had been a happy fact that they were both law students, working for the same firm, facing the same challenges. They had courted all summer, staying mostly at Wendy's apartment, working together, just having a good time when they were not busy at the office. Christopher was down in the city only for the summer and had to go back to New England to finish his last year of law school. At first they thought theirs was only a summer romance.

> CHRISTOPHER: We had very deep feelings. First about our occupation and talking about our livelihood and vocation, and soon there were deep emotional feelings too. I thought she was a sexually attractive person too. . . . But neither of us were looking to become involved in any long-term liaison. We were really wrapped up in our work. At that point we viewed ourselves in this apex of mobility and freedom, and neither one of us wanted to limit that in any fashion. We did not categorize ourselves; we did not plan for the future. It was day-to-day, and as such, was just great. We enjoyed being with each other each and every moment.

Furthermore, Christopher's awareness of his imminent departure made him feel uncertain.

> CHRISTOPHER: I had reached a stage of cynicism. I was going back to school, and I knew from past experience that absence does not necessarily make the heart grow fonder. So I couldn't predict. There is a Victorian kind of love where people pine their hearts away for years and years away from each other and are still in love with an image, and I had no desire to do that.

Meanwhile, Wendy was feeling a bit less uncertain than Christopher. She had picked him out right from the beginning.

> WENDY: I first saw him and thought he was attractive. I sort of remembered him from college. And then I read his resumé. . . . It struck me, *This is a person who fits my idea of a perfect mate.* Later, emotional things were important, but my head reached that point before my heart did.

It was Wendy who proposed that they marry. They corresponded and talked to each other on the telephone all year, visited back and forth on weekends, and when Christopher made up his mind to come back to New York, they reached a decision. They weighed the idea of living together, but considered the alternative "more appropriate."

> WENDY: We thought marriage best because of the profession. We didn't want the partners going, "Hmmm, living in sin . . ." We weren't averse to getting married, so we said, "Why not?"

Christopher was just as practical:

CHRISTOPHER: I remember when Wendy first raised it. I was kind of surprised but evaluated it and decided, *Yeah, it might be prudent.* I didn't really want to get married. I didn't see any need for it, but I think people take the route of least resistance, and this was the route of least resistance to us. It was almost a cost-benefit analysis.

So they married, but they did not realize what career choices lay ahead, what struggles over their differences. The first big issue was the job: how to decide who would take the offer in the firm and who would go out into the job market.

CHRISTOPHER: We both agonized over who should go where. . . . Both of us liked the firm we were working for. We dealt with the conflict in a good rational way, but there were conflicts of interest that were just not reconcilable. If both of us had kept wanting it, there is no question that it would have torn us apart. So we agonized and then in addition had to deal with the mechanics of getting the other person a job. . . . It worked out that I went with the firm we both worked at, and Wendy went to another firm, and in retrospect it worked out fantastic. We made a rational decision about whose needs would be met by that firm and whose needs would be met by another type of firm, and we concluded that my firm was better for my specialty than hers. . . . So she went out on the market.

But the job market was less open to her than to him. That in itself created problems.

CHRISTOPHER: It was hard. You tried to be sensitive to the other person's feelings, so you tread softly, and then you can be oversolicitous and that can be destructive too. You don't get the facts on the table. Wendy went out and interviewed and the offers just weren't coming in. . . . I had the better selling resumé, so I took the train down and got another job that was just as good, so then we both had offers. But then she finally got an offer from a firm that was a very good offer and acceptable.

WENDY: It was hard for me. . . . I had a really tough time, even though I had the credentials and I was very high in my class. Of course I was selective, and here I have this golden offer that I can't take and I still didn't have anything else, and I was in a real panic. So he came down and interviewed and immediately got another offer— which is disgusting.
    So then we had options, but he really didn't want to take that other offer. Then finally I got this great offer with a very good corporate firm—much better than his firm in corporate law. But it was difficult because he didn't understand why I was having so much trouble getting an offer, until he realized it was happening to all my woman friends and he could see what a rat race New York was.

There was considerable competition between them. They both wanted to work in the best firm possible. They expected a lot from each other, and each of them wanted to do at least as well as the other.

Furthermore, they had different views on how they wanted to approach the law.

WENDY: We started having some problems when we were studying for the bar. Christopher's attitude toward school was very casual. He's awfully bright, and he would just read a book and wing his way and fake it. I'm a much more serious student. I tend to work at it and go to class because I like class. He hated class. I like class. To me, that's more fun than reading a book—to interact with other students and professors. He hated it. He would sit in the back and grumble and get up and leave. He could never understand why I would go to class or do my homework. He was annoyed with my study habits and I was annoyed with him interfering with my study habits. It was the same way when we were studying for the bar review. I would want to go to the class to discuss the reading. He would skip the reading as well as the class. I would get lost and get behind. He only needed to study at the last minute. . . .

Today, I think I take work more seriously than he does too. I bring homework home more than he does. It's in my head, bothering me. I'll wake up thinking, *Oh, I should have called somebody,* or, *I should have done this, and I don't think he does that, and he knows that I do.* . . . Then I'll get depressed on Sunday nights thinking about all that's waiting for me on Monday, and then he has to put up with my fading mood. . . . He will say, "If it's so bad, quit." So then we fight about who gets to quit first and support the other one. So I know he wouldn't want me to quit first, because that would preclude him from quitting. So he puts up with it.

Now that they work at different firms, job pressure is no longer a joint problem for them to share. Each of them suffers individual tensions at work. It was particularly bad at the beginning:

CHRISTOPHER: I was perhaps insensitive, in that she encountered an entirely new institution whereas I went back to the old familiar institution and I knew exactly what my job would be. I fitted right in. There were no adjustment problems. She had to learn an entirely new institution, all the people—find out who had the power, find out what you have to do to get along. And in the early period it was tough and I was a bit insensitive to that. She perceived a bit of inequity from our joint decision. And after a while that evened out, and our work load is now about the same. . . . The jealousy thing is probably switched. I'm more jealous of her than vice versa. Whereas she was initially the one that kind of suffered, and she was probably jealous of my position.

Work issues continue to pervade the relationship, however. It is hard for them not to bring their moods home from the office. They wrangle about what each of them has to do for the other's career, about what kind of work each of them should be doing, even about working at all.

Both of them talked separately about each and all of these issues. Christopher attributes their moodiness to a sort of freshman nerves:

CHRISTOPHER: We're both fairly new to the profession. We evaluate it on almost a daily basis. Whether we should continue or not . . . Then one of us comes home in a good mood, bubbling over about what he did that day, and the other comes home in a depressed or bad mood, pissed off at the profession. And a conflict arises and that can pervade everything.

WENDY: Oh, working long hours or working weekends, it gets to you. Recently we both had our first trial, and when he was having his I had to put up with his nerves and all his opening arguments and his cross-examination. And when I had mine, he had to put up with me being incredibly anxious—nervous state, and fairly obnoxious I'm sure. . . .

And then I have to travel sometimes. I get the definite impression he doesn't like it. So there will be sarcastic remarks about the hours I'm putting in, and in fact, I hear from some of his friends that he talks to them about the long hours I work. And it is irritating to me that he is bitching about it to someone else.

The moodiness may be directly caused by fatigue and lack of time together, which in turn results from the demands of their careers.

WENDY: We have been making an effort to get home, so it's been better. But occasionally he's involved in a big trial and he'll have to stay downtown, or he'll come home and change and eat and go back down and stay until eleven. And I will have worked until seven three nights that week, and that night I can come home at a reasonable hour, like six o'clock, and here I am sitting here, having to have listened to him bitching when I come home late the three previous nights. And so now I'm free and he's busy to eleven. And I think, like: *Why does this have to happen on my one good night?* You know there's a reason and you shouldn't get mad, but you can't control it.

Even when we do spend our time together—and we spend all our nonworking time together—much of that is spent being very tired, eating, or sleeping, and the actual time we have any energy together seems to be fairly limited.

With so much work, so little time together, and so little of that time relaxed, social obligations to their firms are sometimes an issue. Neither of them likes going to official business functions, and Wendy feels that Christopher is sometimes derelict in this area.

WENDY: Whenever there is a party—a firm party—well, he'll have a class or something and I'll go to the party alone. This weekend there was *his* firm's party, and we always go to his firm's party and fight about going to mine. I feel that it's important that I go with him to his—sort of a wifely duty—and also because I clerked with some of those people. Whereas he doesn't feel any obligation at all to go with me to mine. In fact, there's this one woman who met Christopher at the bar convention that, because he never showed up at any of the parties, she thought he was a myth and that we had broken up and I wasn't really married!

Christopher sees his avoidance of such duties differently:

CHRISTOPHER: In the last few months we've established that we keep impositions down to an absolute minimum for the other spouse on firm-related activities. It has to be a very important function for the spouse before the other person would have to go. I attempt to avoid traditional stereotypes, and whose function it is to go along, and the spouse has to come along, and that sort of thing. We have applied this equally.

There is also general anger between them about the law itself. While they enjoy their work, and both seem to be getting approval and encouragement from their firms, they are not really sure if the law is what they want forever. Sometimes they argue about "who would get to quit first."

CHRISTOPHER: I don't know how serious this is, but I think both of us would like not to work. And whether or not one of us would not work is a different issue, but both of us would like to work less—like getting into careers that are less demanding and provide more personal time. It comes up, as to who would be able to do that and would be allowed the luxury of being fired first.

Wendy agrees that they both would like to do a little less, but neither seems to want to support the other. It goes further for Wendy. She feels some ambitions are going unfulfilled, particularly Christopher's.

WENDY: I've always wanted to write junk fiction. I've read enough and I'm sure I can do a better job at it. He wants to, too, but neither one of us is doing anything about it now. I have trouble with it because I'm not sure it's a worthwhile occupation, whereas Christopher, I think, has fairly high aspirations to write something serious. Every once in a while he'll start off on these big research projects. He'll go to the library and read books and start, and then it kind of fades. And that is really annoying to me, because he sits around and complains about being bored and not challenged and wanting to write something, and then he doesn't do anything. I think he could. I think he would be good at whatever he wrote. He's awfully bright, and if he's unhappy, why doesn't he do that? . . .
    When we were first going together, he was telling me that he always thought that I would end up doing great things, and here I was always thinking that *he* was going to end up doing great things. I guess that's one of our major conflicts—that is, who is going to do the great things? Because the other person is always pushing. One person pushes and both persons push, and neither one is doing great things.

She hopes that Christopher will change.

WENDY: I have been thinking about it lately, about how important it is to me that he do these great things that I envisioned him capable of doing. And then I think, *Is it fair of me to put that kind of expectation on him when he really doesn't want to do it?* I've talked to one very close friend of ours about both our feelings, and she was saying, "Give him a couple of years." . . . He needs . . . experimentation. But he'll get bored and go do it.

But Wendy is ambitious and it is hard for her to wait. And she is unhappy with Christopher's attitude about work.

WENDY: We both feel some dissatisfaction with the law—a little disappointed in it. And my reaction is: "Well, we should figure out what we want to do and be interesting, and set our goals as high as we like and then start out to achieve those goals."
Christopher's reaction is: "Ah, hell, it's just a job, and all jobs are obnoxious. You can't obtain happiness through a job, and if you think you can achieve any great things, you're silly. There's a surplus of talent, and don't bother." It's a defeatest thing, and I'm trying to think of how to improve the situation.

Wendy feels Christopher does not rise to meet life's opportunities as she would wish. She has ambitions for him, and he is not living up to them.

WENDY: A friend of his was running in an election and Christopher got involved with helping run the campaign. And then he backed out because he didn't want to lower himself and become a part of this. . . . And to me that was an irritation. Here he has all those ideas and all these ambitions and then, when it comes down to doing something, it stops. . . . At some point I'm going to get tired of hearing great things and seeing nothing.

Work is their biggest field of dissension, but really, when one looks over their history, it seems as though they lock horns on almost every issue imaginable. Competing, negotiating their differences, actually started on their honeymoon.

WENDY: We had different concepts of how our time should be spent. . . . My idea was to go to a few places and spend a considerable amount of time in each. . . . You know, get a flavor of the way people live. Christopher's idea was to hit twenty-three different capital cities. We ended up, I thought, with a compromise. I wanted to go to France and he wanted to go to England and so we were supposed to go to both. But we ended up going to Scotland, Ireland, Spain, Austria, Germany, Greece, Italy. . . . I wanted a restful and cultural experience and he wanted an overview.
It's like how we read. I read very slowly. And he does a brief overview. It's classic. And he walks very fast. I spent all of Europe at least twenty feet behind him. . . . I got fairly tired. . . . The last half of the trip was not fun, although I do have fond memories of all those places. But the first month I came back, people would ask how was the trip and I would say, "Terrible." It was a bad start for the marriage.

*Some* areas are relatively free of strife. For example, since they both make very good salaries, each person can buy what he or she needs. They keep their money separately and finances are rarely at issue. They can clash, however, over joint purchases for the house. The choice of a blender provoked heavy discussion. Christopher insisted that Wendy not simply go out and buy one. They thought it a major victory that they waited until they could shop for it together.

In fact, joint decision-making is largely difficult because they have not yet learned how to live as a couple. Hence, small issues assume great symbolic importance.

WENDY: Early on we would have problems with decision-making, but we are getting better now. I would do things without telling or asking Christopher. . . . I would eat the last bagel—that was a big problem! We had a big fight over the last bagel—which was technically his— and who had eaten how many bagels. It was a classic example of only thinking of myself and not the fact that somebody else was in the apartment and that they have some kind of rights. . . . But that's a lot less now.

Fortunately, housework is not too big an issue.

CHRISTOPHER: We don't make a plan. When somebody is in the mood, they do it. We share. . . . I tend to get stuck with mechanical types of things even though I'm not very gifted there. We have consciously tried to allocate car repair equally. And Wendy is an experienced cook, so she will tend to cook more often. Easy things we split right down the middle. But she will cook gingerbread on weekends and things like that. She is a better seamstress. But we split cleaning the house, and clothes washing and ironing falls equally. Fortunately we both have about the same dirt threshold, so we both just start doing things when they need to be done.

Wendy concurs. But, she says, more subtle issues emerge after the household tasks are done. She suspects Christopher has a less generous motive:

WENDY: One of the reasons he's very good about helping around the house is that I want to get a housekeeper or a maid or something to come in once or twice a week, and he's fairly set against that. And he knows that if things get out of hand, there will be need for some help, so he has to stay in there and help out.

Wendy does not really appreciate Christopher's contribution to "male" tasks. Here, again, he has not met her standards.

WENDY: Christopher tries, but he's not my father. My father could do anything. One day Christopher announced that he was going to put up some hooks in the bedroom to hang things on, and asked me to come in and see the hooks he put up. He had nailed in the wall.

Horrible. *This is going to be good,* I thought. I pulled the nails out—
and insulted him by pulling the nails out—and I went and got hooks
and put them in.

Now he has helped out, though. He pries open the windows that
are stuck. He does those areas, and I don't mind unless he's screwing
it up, and then I step in.

Because almost everything has to be negotiated as to relative
power, control, ambition, and mutual respect, certain other issues, by
mutual consent, lie semi-dormant. For example, Wendy is actually
more religious than she admits to Christopher.

WENDY: He's always assumed that I'm an atheist, which I'm not, and
I have some fairly strong religious feelings which I don't openly
share. . . . I don't make an issue of it, but I think it has kind of
discouraged me from pursuing my religious beliefs—which is
unfortunate, and I'm going to do something about it someday. . . .
We occasionally have disagreements about it. He, for example,
might be saying something very derogatory about Krishna religious
movement, or Christ and Christian believers, and I would disagree. I
will say, "I do believe in Christ and in God," and he will be amazed,
like it's the first time it's come up. He doesn't seem to understand.

Christopher does understand the difference between them, but
doesn't think it is important.

CHRISTOPHER: When we met, we were past the stage of wondering
whether God existed. . . . We just didn't do a lot of delving into basic
philosophical assumptions. We both had a similar life-view. Wendy
may think I am more cynical, and I think she has reserved a more
private area of her belief system that she is not going to let me
intrude upon. I really don't know whether she believes in God or
not. I think she believes in some kind of pervading spirit. I think we
both see this area as highly individual. . . . We did have a church
wedding, but that was more my idea than hers.

There are some other minor frictions: Christopher is not as "social" as Wendy and it bothers her. She does not like his taste in clothes,
but he will brook no interference with his choices. Wendy has gained
about fifteen pounds since they first met, and Christopher disapproves.
She is not happy about it either, but feels too overwhelmed by her life
right now to work at losing weight. She feels she will lose it eventually.
Christopher would like "eventually" to come sooner than she has
promised.

Perhaps more important than *what* they argue about is *how* they
argue. Wendy's comment about their mode of discussion was one
heard more often from lawyers' wives than from fellow lawyers; nonetheless, it is apparently not uncommon in the profession.

WENDY: Feelings of competitiveness have surfaced, and it became
identifiable where every once in a while I would say something and

he would do a devil's advocate sort of thing—you know, attacking it when I wasn't trying to get into an argument or a discussion about it. I was just talking about it, and he would attack me and I would defend myself and then it would go on. . . . And I'd go, "Wait a minute, I don't even feel like arguing—why am I doing this?"

And it kept happening, until finally I told him that I didn't like doing it and I thought it was competitive and I didn't feel like being competitive all the time. And I wanted to talk sometimes, and I wanted to say dumb things without being jumped on. And to knock it off. And it happens on and off. I think it's tapering off now. I'd say, "You're doing it," and he'd say, "Sorry." So it's better now. If it starts, we cut it off.

All of these issues—competition, high expectations, job anxiety, fatigue from work, and lack of understanding of some important needs of the other person—combine to affect their sex life in negative ways. For one thing, Wendy would like Christopher to change the way he demonstrates affection for her.

WENDY: I wish he wouldn't tickle me. I mean, to him that is an expression of affection, and I find it quite obnoxious. He does a few things I think are obnoxious. And I tell him, and he thinks they're cute and that I really like them—and I really don't.

The outcome of all this conflict is that they make love once a week, which both of them consider too seldom. Wendy admits she's the one who keeps their sex life suppressed.

WENDY: We've gone through a long hassle since we've started working, and I must say my attitude towards sex has changed— which has not been good. I come home really tired and I find that I can't concentrate at all on sex, and one has to do that to get anything out of it. . . . It's really been difficult for me and difficult for him. I feel badly that I have responded so little. He is the only one who starts things and I turn him down a great deal also. I mean, it's getting to the point that he doesn't expect much anymore after we go through several months of this. Though we've gotten better about it lately. . . . It's funny: I started out more interested, but it's really Christopher now.

Christopher is not pleased with so much refusal.

CHRISTOPHER: I wouldn't characterize it as a major conflict, but it's a kind of traditional male/female breakdown. I would like to have intercourse more often and we have a difference of opinion on frequency. We do, however, have many shared beliefs and shared patterns of living, so it's not an important thing overall.

He feels that the problem arises mainly from their disparate sleeping patterns.

CHRISTOPHER: We have a difference in sleeping habits, which

doesn't help. I like to stay up later and she likes to go to bed early. Wendy gets tired at night and so she prefers to have intercourse in the morning. Well, I'm sleepy as hell in the morning and I would just as soon sleep at that point. . . . So we have a sexual interest cycle, and when you're working during the week and you really get tired, you have to preserve your sanity by getting maximum sleep. So she'll prefer to wait for the weekend. Then sometimes the mood just doesn't match.

This is a big change from their early days.

CHRISTOPHER: It's disappointing to me, in the sense—initially in our relationship we had sex quite often, and it was a very dynamic, fun part of our relationship. And it has changed. I would have preferred that it stayed dynamic. . . . We would have intercourse every night. . . . Now it isn't dynamic; it's kind of almost instinctual. Oh, I don't know. It's just more planned and artificial.

And there are other factors to blame:

CHRISTOPHER: It's work. It's a less playful environment than being students. It's a more dreary, drudgery-oriented type of existence, and that tends to reduce our playfulness. And as we spend more time with the other person, the romantic Victorian essence of sex leaves. It becomes more physiological. . . . It takes extraordinary efforts to make it interesting and varied and exciting, and the extraordinary efforts aren't always there on behalf of both people.

    I guess I also think there is a basic psychological difference between the two of us. How much is shaped by perceptions of others' work and other things I just don't know. It may be male or female or just us.

Wendy assents to most of Christopher's analysis:

WENDY: It's changes in life-style, changes in how you expend your energy. Being an attorney preempted a lot of my emotional energy. . . . Also, it's usually brought up to me when I'm going to sleep or fading fast, and we go to bed and he sees me dropping off and he'll make some sarcastic remarks. And I either respond or I decide not to dignify his attack by responding. And then that gets bad for a while and then goes on for a week or so, and then we talk about it when it gets bad enough.

According to Wendy, neither partner has ever considered non-monogamy and they have no understandings between them about sex outside the marriage. Christopher, however, has a somewhat different version:

CHRISTOPHER: I think there is an understanding that circumstances may arise that would be forgiven and would fit into the parameters of a monogamous relationship. For example, a wild fling in a faraway city with a romantic person that bounces in and out of someone's life just for that short reconnoiter—and I think that that is within the parameters of a monogamous relationship.

In the joint interview we asked them what makes them happiest.

CHRISTOPHER: Well, I'll take a stab at it. I would suggest that the most happiness and satisfaction comes from our amazing amount of synchronization and harmony in the way we view the world and the way we view life in general, and that reflects itself by minimizing conflicts and maximizing areas of agreement. We seem to keep the hassles of life, in regard to our personal relationship, at a minimum. And that sync of ideas is amazing, and almost required for stubborn, independent people like us.

While listening to this, Wendy is knocking on wood.

WENDY: Yeah. Well, it's true that we actually get along very well, considering our potential for not getting along well, and that's nice. To me, I would say that perhaps I get the most happiness from doing things together, like the weekend when we actually do things together and we're not just sitting back and watching. That feels really neat, and I feel really close when we do that.

   It is true that we do share a lot of similar goals and dreams, and we're still both finding a lot of them. We get along really well, and although we can be awesome, we are both fairly mellow in habits of living, and living is easy. There's just never a time when I don't want to go home—avoid going home—and I know that there are marriages like that.

We asked them what they had learned and would want to pass on to other couples:

CHRISTOPHER: I read this observation by some people doing a study which struck me as important . . . that perhaps couples get along better by recognizing certain spheres of privacy and not just by saying more communication is the answer. I think our relationship is special because we both respect certain spheres of privacy. I think there is a kind of marking off the areas you kind of retain as your own. It makes for a kind of personal integrity.

WENDY: I'm not sure I agree. Sometimes I find that when we start doing things by ourselves—you doing your thing and I doing my thing—that we draw really apart and become less tolerant of each other.

CHRISTOPHER: Yes, but I think there is also the joint recognition that too much inquiry into the other person's life is counterproductive. Don't you think so?

WENDY: Well, I don't know. One thing I would say is that if two people are two professionals that haven't worked together, I would warn them that there is going to be a strain. And I don't think the marriage is going to be a typical marriage and they just really have to prepare to work that out. It's not easy, and you have to decide if your career is really important and your marriage is going to suffer, and you have to decide which is the most important thing. If your marriage is most important, then you have to control your career and not let it eat you up. You really have to be aware of both all the time and keep a grip on them both and it is a real juggling act. And I'm just beginning to see how I've been tossed around. You really have to try, because it just doesn't happen magically.


*Epilogue:* For all of Christopher's assurances that any trials of his life with Wendy were subordinate to the satisfactions, and for all of Wendy's determination to sort out her work and her marriage, within a year after we interviewed them, they had gone their separate ways.

We called Christopher in Chicago, where he had recently moved, and told him we wanted to explore the reasons for the marriage's dissolution, but he refused to discuss it. "I wish I knew why we broke up," he said.

Wendy, on the other hand, was more willing to talk to us, and we made an appointment for a conference call.

She remembered the original interview very well and recalled thinking that she had not really listened to Christopher's answers to our questions. She wondered why she had been so inattentive. At that time, it had been hard for her to remember exactly what it was that had brought them together.

Now, she felt that a good part of their infatuation with each other could be ascribed to their shared ambitions in writing. But nothing came of that interest. Christopher grew cynical, she said. But, she added, if truth be told, their differences probably existed even before their marriage, though she had not wanted to acknowledge them. She had simply decided it was time she married.

WENDY: I pushed for marriage. He was bright and unusual, and I thought it was a rare opportunity. I thought, *You don't run into people like this.* I thought it was important to marry. I didn't think we had such a great relationship, but I thought if we got married we'd have to work on it and that would make us tie it up. It's an embarrassing admission. . . . In fact, I wasn't initially attracted to him. Only after knowing him as a clerk did I get interested in him. And I had this fear that that lack of attraction would come home to roost. And it did.

There were personality conflicts as well.

WENDY: I had a queasy feeling before the marriage. There were signs. When we were studying for the bar, he became critical of me in ways he hadn't been before. *Whoa! Where did this come from? I don't need this.* We had discussions about it before the marriage. He'd say, "That's the way I am." It didn't get settled.

But they did get married, and Wendy says she became so accustomed to Christopher's ways that she no longer noticed. But friends did:

WENDY: I didn't realize when we got married that he was going to be so antisocial. We had someone over for dinner after we were married, and usually when I would do this, Chris would not be involved because he didn't like company. But this night he helped with dinner and was nice. Later, my friend—after the divorce—remembered that night and said, "Why didn't you take that chicken and shove it down his throat? He said such terrible things to you!" I didn't remember that at all. I was so used to him that I thought it was a fairly pleasant evening.

Wendy said she was not aware of how badly they were getting along because she was so immersed in her first year of practice. Her firm had "an aggressive sink-or-swim attitude" and she wanted to swim. Meanwhile, Chris's firm was granting him much more leeway and fewer responsibilities, so he was not nearly as overburdened. This complicated matters. Wendy was overwhelmed by the immense responsibility she had to bear, but Chris, frustrated by the lesser responsibility he was given, was unsympathetic.

WENDY: He'd be writing memos and I'd be closing deals for thirty million dollars. I was trying to survive. I wasn't paying attention to what was going on at home. Every now and then I would think, *Something real sick is going on here,* but I had no energy. He was unsympathetic to me and I was unsympathetic to him. He'd come home and read. I'd come home and die. No one was watching the marriage.

Things started to fall apart.

WENDY: We got to the point where we just weren't talking. We had nothing to say to one another. I started to realize how unhappy I was and I said we should separate. . . . I told him to move out. He said, "I don't have any place to go. I won't move." So I became pretty shitty—to the point where he wanted to go.

There was a trial separation. They agreed to try to work things out, but Christopher failed to live up to that agreement. Wendy is still angry about that. She thinks that as soon as Christopher left, he emotionally sealed himself off forever. In about six months he sought to file for divorce. Wendy was surprised, but acquiesced.

WENDY: It was out of the blue. He said filing fees were going to go up. We could save money by doing it now. And so we did.

Her emotional reaction to the end of the marriage surprised her.

WENDY: I didn't think I had a whole lot of feeling about it. I was in trial with another attorney and the judge was going to let us go, and then in fifteen minutes I had to go down and finalize the divorce. I almost threw up. I turned green. One of my co-counsels helped me and gave me moral support. She bought me a drink afterwards. It wasn't painless, but it was quick. I was surprised to find out I still had feelings.

She looks back at the marriage with a great deal of regret.

WENDY: I wasted time and energy and got very little out of it. I wasted significant years. I'm angry that I tried so little and he tried so little.

She also misses the advantages of marriage, finding that the life of a single corporate lawyer has problems of its own.

WENDY: I have some very old-fashioned clients. They are shocked I don't have children. What if they knew I was divorced? . . .
    Being a single woman is strange in a law firm. It's a man's world. It is much safer to be married. . . . For example . . . dirty old men crawl out of the woodwork. There were blatant things and opportunities and snide comments. It is safer to have a boyfriend.

Now that she is alone and reflecting on her marriage, she has managed to evaluate what that period meant, and what she wants to change in her life. First and foremost is her career, and the problems it poses to a relationship.

WENDY: I was working all the time. I would be here all day, and entertain clients, and go to sleep, and do it again. . . . Now I have started working less. I decided to work only eight hours a day. I am trying not to have the firm the only thing in my life. My real goal now is trying to be a person I like. If I can do that and practice law . . . great. But it is important to me to be a person first.

She is interested in men again. How has the failure of her marriage affected that aspect of her life?

WENDY: I don't want relationship goals anymore. No expectations. I just want to appreciate it. If something good comes along, it will come, but in its own good time.

But she feels guilty.

WENDY: I forced a marriage that wasn't ready. I felt responsible because I really got us into this in the first place.

We asked her what the main issues were in her marriage. She immediately cited work, and the toll it took on their psyches and their sex life.

WENDY: In the beginning of the relationship I dominated it. He was naïve about a whole lot of things. I would say what we would do. . . . I was running things. Then he moved here permanently, and he wanted to start directing things. It was a change in power.

Now she is trying to avoid these conflicts. Learning gradually how to know men, she is seeking companionate relationships. She resists some of the office competition.

Divorce has changed Wendy. She tells others that if they have any doubts, they should not marry. She thinks living together is not the same as marriage because, as she discovered, the commitment needed for marriage is very different: Expectations of and projections for the other person increase once that commitment is made. Attorneys, in particular, she would advise not to get married until they have practiced at least one year. It's just too tough. Wendy says couples need to be prepared to work at their relationships, not just at their jobs.

This is good advice. Couples who are working hard would understandably prefer not to have to expend more energy at home, but a relationship—at least a "voluntary" marriage like this one—cannot survive that kind of neglect. Furthermore, ambitious people like Christopher and Wendy tend to be ambitious for their partners as well as for themselves. These expectations, untempered by much exposure to the difficulty of doing everything one is supposed to do, lead to disillusion. The person one marries does not manifest all the golden qualities he or she is imagined to have. Christopher and Wendy would criticize each other for not being what they were presumed to be and, rather than supporting each other, would demonstrate their own insecurities by competing with each other for supremacy at work or in pursuit of other ambitions.

Neither one of them listened to the "subtext" of their relationship, or tried to understand what all the carping was about. They ignored their emotions. After their courtship they never made a romantic partnership, and they could not maintain a commitment.

# George and Margo

George and Margo are a couple who have accommodated their lives to constant conflict. They voice their dissatisfactions loudly and often. Margo stays at home with their children, but unlike many women in this kind of marriage, she insists on absolute equality in decision-making. Discontented with many aspects of their relationship, they are nevertheless an "institutional married" couple. This is a lifetime relationship.

George and Margo live in what might be termed a rough neighborhood. The city's attempt to "rehabilitate" it by planting palm trees and installing decorative streetlights has had only slight effect on the overall atmosphere. One notices an unusual number of police cars around, and many unemployed men hanging out in the numerous bars on the street or standing in doorways. Teenaged boys walk down the street in twos and threes, and occasional larger groups, wearing club jackets embroidered with names like The X-Rateds. We were glad it was not dark yet.

The couple's apartment is in a small, grim-looking building that resembles all the others around it. Litter bedecks the entranceway, and the stairways are dark and musty, filled with the smells of yesterday's cooking. George and Margo's apartment faces the street, however, and the light and fresh air afford a welcome respite from the claustrophobic journey to their door. The apartment is inexpensively but brightly decorated, and the rooms are pleasant. They have lived here since their first son was born seven years ago, but recently have been seeking the means to buy a house.

George hopes that can happen when he gets a degree from night school and can change jobs. He now works as a forklift operator, but he will be starting his second year of junior college in the next few months. He is thirty-one and Margo is twenty-nine, and they have been married for nine years.

Both met us at the door. Margo is tall and might be described as the "blonde bombshell type." She is very pretty, with almost platinum hair which she wears long. George is about her height, a little overweight, less striking. He was still in his work clothes.

They have known each other virtually since childhood. When he was sixteen and she was fourteen, they started to go steady. They stayed together throughout high school, breaking up when George joined the Marines. When he came back at twenty-one, they started seeing each other again.

GEORGE: I didn't write her at all. I was writing to another girl. But when I got out I didn't go see the other girl. I just happened to run into Margo 'cause she was in the neighborhood, and we started dating again, and then I became serious. Up to that time I had never been serious, and I only found out later that she was.

It was Margo, says George, who started things up again.

GEORGE: I was more mature than when I had left, and she really took an interest in me. She aggressed me in a way I can't put a finger on. She bought me clothes, you know, like a shirt or something. It was different. I didn't know what the hell it was, you know. It was like getting hit with a thunderbolt. I had never been in love before. I didn't know what to call it. I didn't quite know what it was. Prior to this, if she had wanted to date someone else or show someone else attention, it wouldn't have bothered me. You know, lackadaisical— "If you don't need me, I don't need you." But then I found out that I had very strong feelings about her, so it dawned on me that I must be in love with her.

Margo says that her entire family set their collective cap for George:

> MARGO: I saw him and I liked him. He looked nice. My family adored him. My family loved him. I'm telling you, if there are ideal in-laws for a man, mine are for George. They'd mortgage the house for him, I swear to God. They like him. Even from age fourteen when we first met . . . they encouraged it. George was a sweet, nice fellow. And I went out with some doozies.

The beginning, however, as George indicated, was tempestuous.

> MARGO: I would break up with him on Friday night; and then on Sunday—that being such a turndown day—I'd call him up and we'd be friends again. Then we'd be engaged for a week again. Then we'd break up. I guess it was too much.

At first they just "hung out with the gang."

> MARGO: We watched TV and I'd fall asleep, and my mother would wake me up at eleven and then George would go home. Monday through Thursday. Then Friday night we'd go to the Doggie Diner. Saturday we'd go car racing. A heavy schedule. We did this every week—don't laugh. Like, in the sixties that's all it was. It was good, though. We had good times, definitely. He was into hot rods and I was into hot rods, too.

But the relationship was not proceeding fast enough for Margo. She would break the engagement because she felt George wasn't serious enough. There were many ups and downs.

> GEORGE: We were going out about a year and a half, and engaged the last six months. We broke the engagement because Margo didn't think we were getting married fast enough, and she wanted to see other people, even though I didn't want to see other people.
>
> But once we broke up I saw a few for maybe two or three months. . . . I was back, you know, in the meantime, to my old rascal self—you know, *love 'em and leave 'em* kind of attitude. . . . At the time, my idea about fallin' in love was that it was a drag, you know, because you had all these feelings that were hard to cope with. Like, *What if she wants to do this and you have to put up with that?* Like, I was immune to getting dumped on, but with most girls—so what? I could just walk away from it.
>
> But with Margo, it was a whole different ball game. Feelings that I never had before, and I just didn't know how to handle them. And she could just manipulate me all over the place, like a puppet. I knew she was winning me more each and every day.

George was really serious about her. He sold his car to buy her an engagement ring, and Margo, knowing how much the car meant to him, was touched. But it was not enough to keep the engagement together. Margo wanted George to make the final commitment. Things started to fall apart.

GEORGE: Margo started seeing some fellow at work. She didn't want me to know it, and although she said it wasn't serious—this was still when we were engaged, so of course I found out—and I broke the engagement. And odd as it may seem, she didn't want the engagement broken. You know, she wanted her cake and eat it too. Now this is the type of thing I would expect from me—you know, I'm the male; I am supposed to do this, right? She's the one, and it brings up all these ideas in my head like: *Is she going to be true after we're married?*—you know. Here she is, engaged to me and running around. I get out of this situation, because you can't trust them.

So I broke up with her, but I hadn't counted on the fact that I was in love with her, and it's a hard thing to deal with. Here she is going out, and I'm in love with her. And I'm thinking about what to do. I kept feeling that under all this, Margo was this true-blue American girl, and this aberration was just a quirk in her personality, and that she would see the light eventually—which she did. Maybe it was to spite me because I had treated her lackadaisically earlier. So it was tit for tat.

They broke up and patched it up four times. George kept trying different techniques to bring Margo around.

GEORGE: I would confront her, but I found that was no way to handle her. I found the iron fist is no way to handle Margo. Her father tried, and if he hit her, she would look at him and laugh at him. You know: "Hit me again." So I changed my tactics. . . . I would punish her the only way that was effective: break the engagement. . . .

Then we would run into each other for the next couple of months with other people. And she was with some shaggy-raggy-looking hippie character, no one to get jealous about—the guy was a zero. And to make matters better for me—I mean, every dog has his day—I'm with this good-looking girl. . . . And I would not normally dance, but since she was there, I started to dance with this other girl. Really rub her face in it. So it was my night, every dog has his day, and when I see her three weeks later she brought this incident up. . . . We got back together.

But not before a spectacular event:

GEORGE: Her folks had rented a room [for a wedding reception] on one occasion and put a deposit down another time, and we were driving them nuts. It's on again, off again. One day, Margo—she's got this temper, you would think she was Italian or something—she's mad. She goes in the bathroom and she says she's going to flush the engagement ring, one and a quarter carats, down the toilet. I don't know why it didn't go down—she flushed it about fifteen seconds.

She says, "Oh, my God." It was eight hundred dollars at the time. "I just flushed eight hundred dollars down the toilet."

I was outside the bathroom at the time. She had the door locked. I thought to myself: *She's just nutty enough, she just might.*

I hear her say, "I'm flushing this ring down the toilet." Then I hear a WHOOSH. So I hit the bathroom door and it's a flush-panel door. Those things are like paper. Bang, break it. There she was with her hand down the toilet bowl. She finally came up with it.

There were lots of doors broken. We'd put decals up so her parents wouldn't see the holes. It was a rocky, rocky romance.

Margo remembers it too:

MARGO: Oh yeah, our engagement was the pits. I almost flushed my engagement ring. I flushed it, and then I realized what I had done and he was coming in like The Hulk. And I put my hand in the toilet and it was just hanging out in the bottom. Visions of going to the mayor to dig out the sewers were in my head: *What am I going to do? This guy just spent all of his car parts, motors, transmissions—I mean mag wheels; I mean heavy stuff—to buy an engagement ring. I mean, this is as bad as selling his* Popular Hot Rod *magazines.* Really. That's the kind of fights we'd have.

Does this sound as if the marriage was going to get off to a rosy start? No. And it did not. They fought then, and—as we shall see—they have never really stopped.

MARGO: We fought about everything. We fought about money. Who was going to handle it. . . . We were both working then, and good money too. If he didn't give me the money, then fuck him then. I have the money to pay bills with and do what I have to do, and pretty soon he would get tired of me paying the bills and me paying for everything. He was pissing money away and I was working just as hard as he did. He came around pretty quickly.

George remembers other problems:

GEORGE: Let's see, a major one is that she is a night person and I'm a day person. She's party, party, party. Where I'll crap out at eleven or twelve.

But Margo insists these differences were minor. The major issue was her husband's attitude.

MARGO: My husband comes from a very very macho macho family. They think that women are for shit. And so when George got married he thought this was the way to treat a wife. And I said no. . . . His specific phrase was: "I am the master." Doesn't that blow your mind? . . .

I said, "Fuck you, baby. There ain't no master here. And if you don't like it, just take a walk." As much as I cared for him, I was not going to take that. Hey, this guy was really foul. He thought this was the way to do it.

But he came around. He's been excellent to me.

A certain amount of negotiating was required to establish equality.

MARGO: He used to go out with the guys at night. I didn't like that at all. It was three o'clock in the morning. I would wait up for him and give him a hard time. And he'd be bombed when he'd come in and I'd say, "Hey, this shit doesn't float. This is not nice. If you go out, I'm going to get in my car right after you and I'm going to be out there." And he decided: *I don't want her to go out, and if I don't want her to go out, I'd better get my ass home.*

Or they would quarrel over where their money was to go:

MARGO: There was so much macho bullshit to break down. Like I wanted a dishwasher. He'd say, "What the fuck you need a dishwasher for? Do the dishes by hand. Everyone else does. You're only a woman, so sit down and shut up."

But things are really a lot different now. George pitches in and helps with the housework and, according to Margo, is in many ways a model husband.

MARGO: George is out to make me happy, you know. If something really brings me down, and is really a total drag, he'll help me out. And I'll do the same. He hates to go shopping, so I wouldn't make him do it. He hasn't bought a pair of shoes in ten years. I buy all of his clothes. He doesn't go shopping, for food or otherwise, unless he's in desperate need of a cupcake.
 The only thing we go buy together that is food is a hamburger at Doggie Diner. We do that together. It's a sin to go into Doggie Diner alone. He proposed to me in Doggie Diner, I want you to know.

George may pitch in, and Margo may actually have the control she thinks she has, but George's attitude remains that there is a leader and a follower.

GEORGE: You know she's the established homemaker. I'm established as the breadwinner, the head of the house. There's gotta be. There's only one ball in front of the rack. I'm it. She's the one immediately behind it. She's at my heels.

Nevertheless, he will help.

GEORGE: Once in a blue moon I'll vacuum. Actually I'll do anything she asks me. If we're having company and we're pressed for time. If she asks me to clean the dishes, I'll clean the dishes. If she asks me to clean the bathtub, I'll clean the bathtub. I don't think there's anything in the house that's women's work that's demeaning for me to do. This is my home as well as her home. But traditionally she does it all.

He has changed in this respect. When Margo had a job, he admits, he wasn't too helpful. If she ever went back to work, he says, they would split the housework fifty-fifty.
 It is not too likely that she soon will, however. Their sons are seven

and three, and both parents feel it is best for them to have their mother at home.

> GEORGE: I didn't want her to work because my mother didn't work. I was very happy to have my mother at home when I came home from school. That was a positive thing, to know my mother was handy. Margo's mother worked when she was growing up and I think it pushed Margo to grow up too fast. She missed out on a lot.

Still, there are pressures that might provoke George to reconsider.

> GEORGE: In the past year or so I've been thinking maybe she should go to work. But it makes me feel like a rat. It's only because inflation is killing us. It's so hard—but I don't know, when I think about the effect on the boys. So maybe not for another couple of years anyway.

When George brings the issue up, a pitched battle always ensues. Margo will not hear of a regular job while her children are small. She would be glad to work as a cocktail waitress at night, but George won't hear of that.

In general, they both think the children have been a plus and a "good thing" for their relationship. But it was difficult in the beginning.

> MARGO: Well Brian had colic for five months. That's enough to drive anybody buggy. There was tension—you know, walking the floors together, terrible nights that we just all wanted to die. The relationship was altered. He was supposed to bring us joy and we had nothing but tears.
>
> But once he got off that and was a nice normal baby that didn't cry, then it was nice. We really got into him, and I think it definitely enriched the relationship.

George can enumerate many rewards that their first son's birth brought them. For instance, their roles became more defined, with one partner working and the other at home.

> GEORGE: It was a good thing that came along and made a good thing better. Margo was already a good housewife and companion and so she became a good mother. It was like another feather in her cap. . . . She is a very doting mother. I didn't have to change diapers. I changed them once in a while, but she's the type of mother who didn't want the child to sit in a wet diaper for two seconds.
>
> I told her early: "Don't expect me to get up when the baby wakes up in the middle of the night."
>
> "Oooooh," is her first reaction.
>
> I say, "Listen, I need eight hours of sleep to get up and go to work. You know that."
>
> She says yes. Yes, I'm the one who goes out and earns money for the house, and I need my sleep. "Fine," was her attitude, and that's the way it went.

Margo thinks there has been one unfortunate side effect:

MARGO: It was all great, except for our sexual relationship. That
went—shit, man—out the window practically. We were living in
small quarters. We were all sleeping in one bedroom. So we're all
together. . . . That was when Brian was up to two. . . . Then he
turned three and it was even worse. Doors became a problem.
Coming in in the middle of the night was a problem. Now we have a
door with a lock. . . . Also, to tell you the truth, I was sort of distant
from George anyhow. I was very much into Brian and that
complicated things.

George remembers that period too.

GEORGE: Yeah, we finally put a door on our bedroom and a lock on
the door. I think if Brian had walked in, Margo would have handled
it superbly, but the fear of it she handles miserably. That fear of
being discovered by her son doing, quote, "that dirty thing," sex.
You should be able to say, "We're doing something married people
do. It's okay. Pick up whatever you want and be on your way." But
that's not the way it is. Margo is always worried about privacy.

Margo did not mind the extra work that having children in the
house entails. She felt it was only fair that she tended to all the boys'
needs.

MARGO: I took care of everything. George never gave them a bath
and I never let him get up in the middle of the night to feed them. I
felt it wasn't his place to do it. He's got to get up for work. . . . It was
an act of love, and he was glad that I was considerate enough of him.

The boys are almost totally Margo's property.

MARGO: I am with the children most of the time, and what I say
goes. He is like a treat to them and they'll walk all over him. I'm
telling you, when I go out at night all hell breaks loose. The kids are
up till eleven o'clock. All they say is, "Daddy," and they get it. And
here Brian's got school the next day. But on the other hand, they
don't get a bath, and if they didn't talk they probably wouldn't get
fed. Not because he doesn't love them, but because he's not
programmed to do it. So he pretty much knows that what I'm doing
works and he leaves well enough alone. I tell him: "Don't ever
interfere. I'm going to rear them the way I think is best and they are
going to listen to me." He's not with them enough to listen to him. I
love them too much to make them into brats.

Apart from sex, the only other activity of their parents that the
boys inhibit is one of their chief pastimes: fighting.

MARGO: Well, it affects us because we can't have a decent fight. You
know, you're afraid the kids are going to hear something they
shouldn't, something said in anger. I guess it's a good thing, but I

feel stifled. On Saturday nights they're not here and then we fight like crazy. Practically every Saturday night.

Their favorite fights are about money. They fight about George being a homebody, and Margo wanting to party. They fight about George not spending enough time on Sundays with the children. They fight about how to raise them—but they both consider them a strong support of their marriage.

MARGO: Sure, we fight a lot, but still—because of the children, you know—you are really sewn together. They're part of both of you. We both knew that I have a short fuse, and we were glad to have them to make us work on things. I mean, I'm the kind of person— well, I broke this fish tank once, with the fish and the water in it. Flung a plate at it. I kicked his windshield in. So you know, we needed something to cement this marriage. And they did, definitely. Kids are the clincher. Of course if the relationship is not there to begin with, then, boy, if you're sewn together you're in a heap of trouble, but fortunately I'm not that way now.

Margo needs the fighting, wants the fighting, feels it clears the air between them. George hates it, avoids it, and tries to stop it. Both George and Margo think their different styles derive from their particular family backgrounds.

GEORGE: I come from a very argumentative family. My father *talks* five or six times louder than necessary, in his normal tone of voice. That is how he speaks. . . . I tell him not to raise his voice and he says he's not raising his voice. . . . I come from a home where there's a lot of tension. So I don't like to argue, you know. I like it nice and quiet.
    Now, Margo, she comes from a nice and quiet home. She likes excitement. She grew up in this home where Mom looked like Donna Reed and Dad looked like Robert Young and they were perfect. And me, I would look at these kind of programs and say, "Jesus, is my family screwed up. Boy, if that's what a typical American family is like, I live in a nut house. This is an insane asylum. Nobody is normal here." Everyone is screaming and arguing all the time. My father doesn't go to work in a suit. He goes in work clothes.
    So I want it nice and quiet and sedate and Margo, from this nice home, wants action, plays the stereo all the way up. . . . She tried to make me fight and I won't buy it. She needs me to argue with. If I don't, she'll yell at the children. Then I jump on her back for yelling at the kids. I don't want her yelling at anybody.

MARGO: I usually introduce the fighting. But sometimes I just get so frustrated that I've got to have a good fight. He had come from a family that has always fought, day and night, middle of the night, every time you turn around. And I mean outrageous knock-down, drag-out fights. So when the boy got married, he does not want to fight. We have had those big ones only three times. We have, however, daily disagreements. I may say, "Fuck you." He'll say,

"Drop dead." . . . I usually introduce the fights because I need it to clear the air. Like: "You're a slob, man. Pick up your socks. You throw 'em next to the hamper, you goddamn pig, man. . . ." It makes an impact.

We have short fights. I'll scream and yell and rant and rave. I break his possessions, but it really isn't worth it. The day I busted his windshield, the next day he had a job and he handed me seventy-five dollars from the job. And he said, "Now, my dear, you can go get me a new windshield." And I had to pay seventy-five dollars for the windshield. So I really didn't gain. We had a ten-gallon tank and I busted it. He graduated to a twenty-gallon. So it cost me more money in the end. So, I figured breaking things is not my bag, right? So I don't break things anymore.

I have a truck-driver mouth and I scream. I don't give a shit who hears. And again, he says, "Keep it to a dull roar." He won't fight back mostly. I fight with myself. I'm better off in the mirror.

How do these fights get resolved?

MARGO: I will sulk for three or four days. If I really want to make a point—are you ready for this? you're going to love this—I go on strike. I don't do wash. I don't cook. No screws. No talking to. Nothing. It works. Then, I washed his shorts with fiberglass drapes. Those little things, they stick to him. But then I didn't have the heart to let him wear it. . . . But if it's a long fight, I don't give in, and he gives in to me because he knows I'm right. If I think I'm wrong, or if I think it's not that important, that there's better things to fight about than this bullshit, then I'll make up with him. I send him a dirty note in his lunch. . . .

After we make up I can get anything. I can tell him I want a new car. It's easier to get a new car than a new dress because he's a workaholic, day and night. So it's easier to aim high, ten-thousand-dollar car. God, it's a breeze.

When she is pouting, George will leave her alone (he says he "likes the solitude every once in a while") and of course that exasperates Margo all the more. But eventually one or the other will make up and life will return to normal, until the next time. "Normal" conversation, however, is always barbed, and colorful.

This is the way George and Margo resolved an imaginary problem we posed for them: They had to decide how they would spend $600 if we gave it to them. The following gives a sense of their everyday style:

GEORGE: First, a hundred dollars for a night on the town—dinner, theater. Then we're going to get a hundred dollars and put a windshield in my car, and the final hundred we put an interior in my car. Then we get four tires for Margo's car, and a hundred dollars for food.

MARGO: I love it. Is that great or is that great?

GEORGE: It was her idea for the tires. Mine for the windshield and interior. The food and the night on the town were her idea.

MARGO: But he agrees with them, so it's all right.

GEORGE: Yeah, you got to think fast. I had to think fast to get my two hundred bucks out of there.

MARGO: Oh, you lying sack of shit, man.

GEORGE: Well, I get half the food and night on the town. . . .

MARGO: Oh, fuck off, man. How about the tires to make my car that you bought me look better?

GEORGE: Listen, motormouth, you got two hundred bucks for the car before I could think of anything.

MARGO: All right, all right. Moving right along . . .

GEORGE: Boom. Two hundred dollars for the tires.

MARGO: Well, shit, look at them.

GEORGE: Well, look at my windshield.

MARGO: Well, okay. [To the interviewers]: Are you going to give us the six hundred bucks?

They do go after each other. But oddly enough by many people's standards, they do not view this rough and tumble as their real problem. By Margo's lights, the real problem is the kind of attention—or lack of it—that George gives her, and that may be the source of some of the hostility she exhibits toward him in conversation. They have begun counseling to try to understand what is going on and what they can do about it.

MARGO: I don't feel that he's giving me much, that he is being honest and open with me as much as I would like him to be. He's a very unemotional person, and I'm at a stage in my life where I need a little bit more emotional involvement. Not that I need reassurance. But I need nice gestures, nice things, nice words, a nice place to take me to. Something that he would do on his own, instead of me always planning where we go on our anniversary. . . .

And trying to break this father image he's got, because his father, of course, never showed any emotion. . . . So George didn't know which way to go. He tried to do what his father did, and when it didn't work, the poor guy was up shit creek without a canoe. He says, "What the hell do I do now?" So I try to show him a little niceness. I mean, I come from a family where they fight about who gets to do the dirty work. And my father brings boxes of candy on Valentine's Day. . . . He's making her happy with what she wants and needs. They're still together for thirty-some years. Now, I know George is capable of this because I have seen bits and pieces of it, and I want to get it all out. I mean, I'm married nine years and it's not all out yet.

Margo provides an example of how shut out she feels:

MARGO: Today I pulled in at lunchtime to bring him his lunch. I pulled into the place right near where he works. And right there is a real nice plaque saying what good work he does. I freaked out. I said, "Now, that's great. When did you get it? Today?"

He says, "No, I got it about two weeks ago."

I said, "Oh, man, you're a fuck. You didn't tell me."

And he says, "Oh, I forgot." You know, a little thing to him . . .

Margo is really upset by George's inattention, his lack of sensitivity.

MARGO: He doesn't give me enough emotional and mental stimulation when he comes home from work. Now, you know, I know he works hard all day. But you know, I'm with a seven-year-old and a three-year-old all day. I need something. And I can't go to work because of this tie. And there's only so much sewing and cooking and business you can do. You need a little something else. . . . I think about, *Hey, what the fuck am I doing all this bullshit for?* I'm not getting the rewards I need for cooking, cleaning, bullshitting, whatever. I know I do have it better than a lot of other wives—he doesn't beat me, or he isn't an alcoholic or gambles all the money—but still, there's got to be a better way.

George really does not see what the problem is.

GEORGE: I am trying to find out what is going on. I don't have any problem or doubts, but I do because Margo has this feeling that I don't share as much with her as she does with me. . . . That's why we're going to a counselor. We've been going nine months, and I still don't have the faintest idea of what she's talking about. She feels I have been much closer to her in the past and she wants that feeling back, and she says she doesn't have it now. I don't see changing an ounce. I feel fine about her. But she is disillusioned, and I wish I could tell you what it is, and then I would change it for her and make her a bit happier. . . .

Now the counselor says that Margo expects me to fulfill her. She expects her fulfillment out of life from me. And the counselor says, "Uh uh. No one can fulfill somebody else completely. They can help, but not completely." So he says to Margo: "You got to find yourself something. You got to supplement what George gives you to be a happier person."

And Margo bristles at that idea. That causes tension in the room 'cause I'll say, "Why don't you listen to him and give it a try?" She flatly refused to consider that as a possibility. She claims in the past I have fulfilled her completely and she wants me to do it again. She says this over and over, and that's where it stands now. . . . It's all very elusive. Nothing you can nail down. She says she shouldn't have to tell me. I tell her on more than one occasion: "Tell me what it is and I'm perfectly willing to do it." Nothing specific back. That's why it's such a mystery to me.

George does have a theory:

GEORGE: You know what I think it is? The old seven-year itch. You know: "You're so used to me. I'm so used to you." You get up every morning; you put the same four heaping teaspoons in the coffee pot . . . Mondays, Wednesdays, Fridays. Paper's there every morning. Blah, blah, blah. Life is a drag at times. What are you going to do?

I think she thinks I should do something about it. I guess I could. One night I come home without any clothes on. There's a little excitement for one day. Then I guess the next day I could have a car accident. You know, do something each and every day to make it a little different for her. Call her from the hospital and tell her I'm just about to die: "I love you." And then miraculously recover. You know, show my devotion each and every day. Jesus.

George thinks the counselor has created more arguments than he has provided solutions.

GEORGE: They didn't think I would go to counseling, but being interested in psychology, I jumped at it. The counselor said, "Don't be surprised if he does." . . . But it gets hairy there. One day they'll be both shooting at me—you know, both of them. . . . But I can take it. I've got tough skin. I don't get crazy. Margo, on the other hand— she can dish it out but she can't take it. . . . 'Cause I can push her button in a certain way, and she knows how to aggravate me. When I push her buttons, she gets upset. Which I do intentionally, and hard, at times. I mean, let's get some reaction and see what happens. So the counselor has caused arguments in the past six months, the best ones, the biggest ones, the strongest ones.

Margo gets back at him in other ways. For example, this scenario:

MARGO: Tonight he was showing me on the roof—we have a mother bird who's got a little bird's nest in there, and you hear them going chirp chirp. So he says, "Oh, Margo, look at the mother bird. She's bringing something home."

And I says, "Get the bastards out of my house."

He says, "Oh, Margo, they're little babies. . . ."

I said, "I don't give a fuck. I don't want them."

So he's looking at me. He can't believe this and he's saying, "Little baby chick."

I said, "I don't give a fuck how big they are." So I figured, *All right, he's trying to get togetherness*, but I go over and I said, "I think tomorrow I'll plug it up." And he got mad. . . . I said to the cat: "Max, Max, look. Here are the birds."

He says, "You're mean."

Another recurring source of friction, though a less important one, is his family. George admits that his failure to confront the issue has aggravated the situation. It was Margo who stepped in and made things bearable.

GEORGE: My father is an alcoholic. And the way I was dealing with it was ignoring it and ignoring him. Punishing him: "I'm not going to talk to you and I'm not going to do nothing."

And Margo says, "You're being foolish. This is not solving the problem. This is your father, and you love your father, and yet on the same hand, you have to stay away from him, and you know that's not the way you feel about him." So Margo was instrumental in making me aware of Al-Anon. You know, opening my eyes to the fact it's an illness, et cetera. How to deal with it.

As a wife, Margo thought it her duty to bring some order to his relationship with his family. She describes her feelings about his family and hers.

MARGO: Two weeks after Brian was born, his mother wanted to move in with us. And ninety-five percent of our everyday fights are about her. They live close to us. There is no escape.

Now, I'm extremely family-oriented. I could not see me living thousands of miles from my parents, even though growing up as a teenager I had no use for them. I mean, they were just people who gave me a roof and fed me, bought me some clothes, paid my car insurance. But after I got married I realized that, wow, parents are not just for that. They live just down the Peninsula. So what I try to do is enjoy my parents now. They're going out now and bopping around and staying out till six and doing this and that. . . . They're really living. And I really dig it. They're having a good time. Kids are grown and married. But I know they haven't many more years, and I feel like a lot of years have been missed, so I wouldn't want to be more than a stone's throw away from them. . . .

But George's family is another thing. A month ago when his father was drinking, he was really violent. And I said, "You know, you really got to do something with him." Thank God for Al-Anon, AA, and everything. Because even though he's sick and an alcoholic, he's still his father. . . . And I said, "There's got to be a better way." And I had seen one of the commercials on TV, and I figured, *Well, fuck it, I'll call them and see what they got to say.* . . .

Also it was the counselor, 'cause I said, "His fucking father is going to bust up our marriage for sure." Because I'm respectful and everything, but I can't be respectful to someone who is going to verbally abuse me. I'll tell you where the fuck to get off. I'll punch you out—father or no father. You know, everyone can only take so much. . . . And it was getting so that even when he wasn't drinking, George would have nothing to do with him. And it annoyed me. So the counselor also gave me some literature. And I called and we went. They even provided a babysitter. And we started to see his father in a different light.

Margo also blames George's father for what she considers George's worst traits and for his misconceptions about women and marriage. So sometimes they get into fights. Even at the best of times, George's father cannot understand what is going on in their marriage.

MARGO: George's father . . . has no use for women. Absolutely. He thinks of me as a measly little scrunge. And when George says,

"Margo doesn't like this," or I'd never go for that, his father says, "What? So what if Margo doesn't like it?"

When he told his father that we were going to a counselor, wow! They were sitting in a bar one day and George told him. And he says, "What seems to be the trouble?" He got scared, like a marriage counselor is one step before divorce, even though we don't really have marital problems like some people. So he says, like: "Tell me all about it, son, and I'll straighten it out."

And George says, "It's our family."

And his father says, "Yeah. You know, the carburetor you put in my car really works good."

George told me about it. He's never seen his father shut up so fast in his life. And that's where George comes from. It's a battle of the sexes.

Some of their general marital problems are also present in their sex life. They have sex about once a week, usually at George's initiation. George thinks their sex life is fine, although he admits it is a bit "humdrum." But he thinks that is just the way married sex gets. Occasionally he asks Margo for a little more direction.

GEORGE: Only recently have we gotten down to brass tacks about our sex life. I said to Margo: "You have to tell me what you want. I'm not a female. I don't have the foggiest idea what's going on in your body." If you want to know what to do, you've got to be a very, very observant person, or you've got to ask. So recently I asked: "How does it feel?" And only recently have I found out that Margo doesn't like [some of the things I do]. Something I took for granted, that this is where you start, and she told me this is not where you start. You start somewhere else. So I said, "We've been married for nine years. When did you expect me to figure this out?" For another girl, this might be the exact place to start.

If the truth be known, it doesn't much matter to Margo where he starts, or *if* he starts. Most of the time she is uninterested. Generally, when he asks, she accepts, but she is not initially enthusiastic. While their sex life includes a lot of variety, she is essentially dissatisfied with the quality.

MARGO: When it's good, it's good. When it's bad, it's bad. But . . . he's very, very rough. He's like, *Wham bam, thank you, ma'am.* And I have to be—like hundreds of other women, I have to be coaxed and romanced and—I mean, come on, sweep me off my feet. And face it: You do good by me, I'll do good by you—right? And sometimes it's just very, very harsh and rough and, you know, it tends to bring you down. And it tends to not be something to look forward to. . . . You know, even though the outcome is good, the warm-up is what you need to make you look forward to it. Going into it right now, cold turkey, it turns you off.

Margo considers it a problem but not a crucial one. Sexual satisfaction and commitment are not related to each other in this marriage, as they are in most others.

> MARGO: It's very important, because when sex is good in a marriage, it's only ten percent of the marriage, but when it's bad, it's ninety percent. I don't want it to get there. . . . We're past the point of breaking up our marriage. It could never break up our marriage, because we've come to understand that we are together not just for sex. . . . We care for each other. So it's not a problem, just a drag.

George thinks sex has slowed down and become unimportant to Margo because of habit. Margo is not so sure:

> MARGO: I think it's age and I think it's body change. . . . I slowly petered out and aged with him. And he has put on some weight and gone through a body change too. So maybe it's all the changes.

We felt that many values and rules of behavior were in transition for this couple. For example, George is going back to school and loves it. He tried earlier to complete his education, but Margo resented its preemption of his evenings. So he stopped. But he has begun again: first, because he loves it, loves every class he has taken, and really feels he has an aptitude for his studies, and second, because it is part of his larger plan for himself.

> GEORGE: I enjoy what I do, but I'd like the option in ten years, if I'm tired of getting my hands dirty and working hard physically—which I enjoy now—that I'll have an option. This is something that I've told Margo, and she doesn't buy it. But I want to go on and finish college and just blast through four years there. Then they have a graduate school over there, and I'd just steam through. I could see me going four years at night—but Margo is a big roadblock, and so we'll accommodate to what is necessary. But I am prepared for a battle.

George is afraid that Margo sees his return to school as a threat.

> GEORGE: I get the feeling sometimes that Margo is afraid that I'll educate her out of my heart. I think that's wrong. She's not interested in education at all. I came from a family that stressed it a great deal. I wasn't ready until I came out of the Marines, but now that I'm ready, I'm really ready.

The couple does feel their marriage is very strong. When we asked George what made him happiest about the relationship, he said it was just Margo. In response to the same question, Margo said she couldn't "quite put her finger on it," but that it is a good relationship.

We asked them what advice they would give to other couples. George mentioned the importance of "give and take—and give more than you take." And, he said, marriage can be "rough."

Margo, never missing a shot, said, "Be good to him and he'll be good to you—and don't tell him everything. And always keep an ace in the hole."

George looked at her and said, "Oh, baloney."

It seemed a fitting exchange to end the interview. George and Margo, hanging together, but hanging tough.

They are there for the duration—but they are going to make each other pay for whatever inadequacies they perceive in each other or in the relationship. Margo's main needs are for more communication, affection, and consideration. George gets about what he wants and has genuine trouble understanding Margo's complaints. Margo has already turned to her children to make up for some of the missing emotional content of her marriage, and may do more of it in the future. She also uses conflict to keep the relationship emotionally engaging. It is a high price to pay for supplementary attention, but she is unlikely to get it otherwise. George is growing more ambitious, and his work and school plans may take him even further away from the kind of contact Margo craves. Whatever they do, they are committed to each other as a family and as a marriage, and it is likely they will stay together.

# Keith and Jean

We selected this couple because they represented many of the elements of traditional, lifetime marriage. Keith has his own business; Jean is a homemaker. They respect each other, and are as devoted to the family they have raised in the thirty years they have been married as they are to each other. Now they are looking forward to being alone again as their children grow up.

Their home is a classic saltbox, beautifully proportioned and painted, but the most arresting thing about it is its site: four lots in the middle of the city. Old trees tower around it, and the lawns are meticulously maintained. It presents a striking contrast: an unassuming house set on a mansion-size plot of land. It is clear that the house has been here a long time and that the owners have preferred to keep it as they originally bought it rather than to build a grander residence as the land went up in value.

The occupants, like their home, are charming, hospitable, and unpretentious. Both come from "old families" with old money. Keith is fifty-eight and Jean is fifty-three. Keith is president of a large corporation formerly headed by his father, founded by his grandfather. Jean is the daughter of a successful painter whose father was a world-renowned artist. She has been a homemaker and mother for their entire marriage. They have three children: a son who has gone into his father's corporation, another son who is a sculptor, and a daughter about to enter an Ivy League college.

They greeted us warmly, Jean with freshly made oatmeal cookies from her kitchen. Keith, clipping some roses from his garden, exhibited them to us with obvious pride. We were immediately made to feel at home and the feeling lasted throughout our interview.

Keith and Jean began a long and happy courtship thirty-four years ago, during her college days.

> KEITH: It was . . . at a house party, as an extra man. That means that my roommate knew Jean, and he was invited to a house party and asked if he knew anybody else to bring along. It was at her summer place. . . . We all headed for the Grange Hall Dance, and I enjoy dancing and so does she, and I guess we enjoyed each other that evening. And that aroused my interest in her, I guess, without knowing her feelings. I had a delightful weekend.

Jean remembers that first meeting just as vividly:

> JEAN: I was going with somebody else, but we needed extra men 'cause we had other girls. So I invited him and his fraternity brother, and they came. He sailed in on his sailboat . . . and he threw a case of beer on the sand in front of me, and I was doing handstands to show off to him. I hate beer with a passion, but I didn't hate him.

Keith's feelings about Jean were platonic at first.

> KEITH: I would say my first impression was that she was just a lot of fun. And very vivacious. I guess the word sexy is not—well, I just didn't think in those kinds of terms.

Jean did not think in those terms either, but to her the meeting was more significant.

> JEAN: It must have been love at first sight, because after that weekend was over, I remember telling my cousin who stayed with me at the beach that that was the man I'd spend the rest of my life with. Like to dance with him all my life too. But it was to take a couple of years.

They both returned to more purposeful pursuits in the fall, she to college and he to his job. They exchanged a few letters during the year and met again the next summer.

> JEAN: That summer I really liked him and he liked me, but he never let me know he liked me as much as I thought I liked him. And I didn't dare make the first step. . . . I remember driving around his house hoping he'd . . . look out the window. I was old-fashioned enough, waiting for him to ask me out or say he's coming up by sailboat. But I would certainly try to make myself seen if I were in town, or "accidentally" go down the street where he lived in the car—you know, driving slowly. . . .

Then I got offered this job to be a governess in another state, and he encouraged me to take that job. And I was really mad at him because I wanted to be closer to him.

As it happened, Keith had his own reasons for urging her to take the job.

KEITH: I encouraged her because I thought it would be a good experience for her. And also because I was getting interested in her. If a gal was away I could write to her—which I guess I did about once a week—and we'd find out if it was a good relationship or not. It would be a good way of checking it. I wanted the gal I would marry to have a skill, experience at some kind of job, and the confidence you get from that.

But Jean was unaware of these promising motives, and was worried. She dreamed about him constantly, missing him.

JEAN: I had this dream about him. It wasn't a sexual thing. It was marvelous. I would have liked to have been with him all the time. But he didn't let his feelings be known. He was already . . . known as a confirmed bachelor. I had no way of knowing how interested his feelings were. I think he liked me very much, and he was trying to find out why he could like me so much and nothing was wrong with me. He was going slow and easy to see how a girl could be in his eyes perfect. I only know this from what he's told me since. At the time I didn't realize it.

When Jean came home, Keith proposed. Her acceptance delighted them both, and the engaged couple started spending a lot more time together. He would sail down to see her at her family's summer place and stay overnight in a guest room.

KEITH: I guess we would say, without making a real issue about it, that we saw that we have a very similar background, knew similar people, and that that carried through several generations. Her grandparents knew my grandparents. Later on, one of my uncles married one of her relatives. You can say it's a small world or you can say perhaps we had a mutual response based on a mutual background. So we had good rapport because we were so much on the same wavelength.

Keith used the time of their engagement to get to know more about Jean.

KEITH: I decided that one should have all kinds of different experiences before you tie up with somebody. If you just have a Saturday night date instead of going sailing or going driving or going walking on the beach, you couldn't really tell enough. I know I tried all kinds of varieties for dates and ideas, and I guess I had a good time at the lot of them and she did too. So I guess that's when the light flashed.

At first they kept their engagement a secret. After a few months Keith went with Jean to her parents' house, "brought a bottle of bourbon and mixed them a good drink" and announced their plans. They were married in early fall. First they traveled, then settled down for a few years to being just a couple, before deciding to have a family. Though people kept repeating to them the old cliché about the first year, their experience refuted it.

JEAN: Everyone warned us, kept saying to us: "You wait. The first year is the hardest." We kept waiting.

KEITH: Our first year was wonderful. We used to sit down at night at the dinner table over coffee . . . and chew the fat for an hour or so. It was wonderful. I know my sister said, "Just wait until the first fight." But we just had a hell of a good time. We're still having a hell of a good time.

Except for the very early years, much of their largely contented traditional life together has been organized around the concept of family.

JEAN: Well, you're almost too young to understand it, but when you marry, you marry a family. And so a lot of decisions have to be tempered by the family, or so we thought. So there was struggle sometimes, not between me and Keith, but because we always had to consider our mothers and our children.
    Both of our mothers became widows, and were strong people. They're both gone now, but we'd get criticism or flak from one or the other. So making decisions was harder then, because I was very sensitive to trying not to hurt anybody's feelings, although we stood up for what we wanted.

The family had its opinions on how Keith and Jean should live.

JEAN: They thought we should have a baby instantly, nine months after you're married. And we said, "No way!" So we had to resolve things between the mothers. But it did bother me personally 'cause a girl has more of an emotional conscience about things. And my mother always taught me to do things this way and that way, and I didn't want to do those things that way in my own home, so I didn't. But then she'd appear and I'd say, *Oh, boy, I'd better do it her way*. But we got through that.

While they have enjoyed their children enormously, they are looking forward to the time when their youngest child is in college so that they can spend much more time alone. Keith has had some difficulty lately in empathizing with his youngest daughter, but child psychology and caretaking are Jean's area, so she takes the responsibility of interpreting the children's behavior for him.

KEITH: If I say to her privately, "Why does Janice do that?" and so forth, she explains it to me. Jean is really the expert, because I didn't know anything about kids and she . . . has taught me what I know. So I'll keep quiet, realizing that it will take care of itself when [Janice] grows older, or she's going through some kind of phase and breaking away from family restraints. Which is good, but it's always the pulling apart which is difficult.

Jean is also in charge of the household, and Keith thinks that makes sense.

KEITH: It's just logical, because she hates the lawn, so I do the heavy gardening. She does the more delicate gardening. I take care of the cars, et cetera. She does a hell of a good job on buying food and handling it. I eat anything, but she likes food more than I, so she spoils me and I enjoy her good efforts. And the kids' teeth and braces and that kind of thing. I hear about it, but she takes care of it.

Keith knows Jean doesn't love doing housework, but a neat house is important to her.

KEITH: She groans and does it. It's just like all of us, I guess. Housework is dull, and like Frank Lloyd Wright once said: "I don't have time or any money except for the luxuries of life." But there are certain things we have to do, and she is more concerned about it than I am. I say, "The house looks fine," and she says, "Well, it looks messy." I guess her New England conscience comes to the fore. Well, you have to look at it: because it's her office, if you will, like a man's office, and you're more concerned if it's your own.

Jean believes that Keith does help out and that ultimately there is a lot of sharing.

JEAN: It isn't as if he doesn't do any of the household work, but the majority of the time I do all the things. But obviously, each of us can do the other's things. I can do repairs and he can do cooking and laundry as well as I can. We never gave it any thought. I was brought up that way, and he was brought up his way, and we just do those ways and never worry about it.

Much of this division of responsibility was established at the very beginning of their relationship. Jean has always been in charge of the children and the upkeep of their home, and Keith has always been very involved in and loved his job. Both believe in family and marriage, and despite Keith's habit of working long and arduous hours, they have always made time for each other. At first they wanted a big family, but they settled for three.

KEITH: Well, I wanted to have ten kids, and I always jokingly said I'd have ten kids, but I realize you have to have a farm or something for that and people to take care of it. And when you live in the city it's pretty hard to handle ten kids and educate them up right. So I ended up with three happily.

Jean remembers those early child-raising days as wearing but wonderful.

JEAN: When you're nursing three- or four-month-old children, you just sort of live from day to day until they sleep through. As far as my feelings toward Keith, or times together, the quality was great but the frequency was less. . . . But he was a great father. He was a super marvelous father, just darling with the babies. Children are such an enriching experience. It was neat to look upon a little someone you created together. I'd have to say you feel closer. It's an extra bond. . . . You've got a family, a baby you two have created, and he's part of you and you're part of him. And you see yourself in this child. And it gives you a permanent stake in the earth.

They took Red Cross parenting classes together and Keith involved himself in his children's infant years. But he became too busy at work to keep it up through all the childhood stages, and Jean took over.

KEITH: She knew I wasn't excited about running around to PTA, dancing lessons, et cetera. So she'd cover for me. Provide some of our point of view by going to the meetings herself. I didn't want to go to Boy Scouts. Even though it is important. The kids were in Scouts and got some good value out of it, but it was just a part of growing up. I was not as involved in it as some fathers. But I did teach them how to sail and I have boats and a workshop. We'd always have a pile of junk around and I showed them how to make anything they wanted to. I showed them how to handle tools, and they'd make all kinds of things out of neat junk.

They accepted the drawbacks of parenthood as readily as they embraced its rewards.

JEAN: Nope, not as much privacy as we had before. Not as much time to do adult things alone together unless we went out of the house, got a sitter, and went and did something. You know—like going out for dinner, which we don't do very often, so it's always a treat. . . . When you decide to have children, you have to realize what it entails, so you don't resent them. You accept the less time you have together. Because now you're a family. But on our part, that was a conscious decision that we wanted. We had four years together, which was super. And then this is what we wanted. We were very lucky that we've had that. We wanted them then. More than anything.

Jean finds motherhood a most rewarding vocation.

JEAN: I'm the mother. Taking care of the kids' needs. That's what being a mother is. I mean, he's working every day. So, obviously, I'm here and we each have our hours. But I love it. I enjoy it. I'm proud of it. I think it's great to be a mother. It's one way to pass the culture on . . . to be a good mother and do your best and bring up a good citizen. And it takes a lot of work—a hell of a lot of work.

Keith offered her the chance to escape the household, but she didn't want it.

KEITH: I told her once when she was groaning about housework that I would be very happy if she wanted to get a job . . . but she's been offered a job teaching and she turned it down because she felt that her priority was raising the kids and being home when they got home from school. And I agreed with her. And I also think she's maintained a good balance of not being on top of the kids every minute, but being available and seeing that things were taken care of.

They are in accord on how to treat the children.

KEITH: We're very good at being on the same wavelength with the kids. In other words, they can't go to one person to get one answer and then go to the other and get the other answer. Discipline *per se* is rare. I may occasionally put my foot down, but usually if we get a chance to talk about things ahead of time, we're going to handle it.

Even the best of marriages has its dissensions, but they both share in the decision-making process.

JEAN: We don't disagree very much. He'd probably like to live on a boat. I can't do that because I get seasick. But at this point in life, we don't disagree. We just sort of laugh over it. I've told him to go get another girl and go live on a boat! [She laughs.] . . .
But we really never fight. We never go to bed mad. We never go to bed angry. We learned never to do that. . . . We had a little thing last week. He bought a convertible as an investment and I thought it was a little screwy. And I thought, *Well, what can I go out and spend money on?* But that's not a real disagreement. I laughed and thought, *Well, wonderful, he has a new toy.*

Keith seconds her:

KEITH: I told her when we got married: "I won't try and change you, and you don't try and change me." 'Cause we agreed that people don't change that way. And we agreed to that, and secondly—well, as a sidelight—I can look at pretty girls and you can look at good-looking men. There's no problem on that. After all, it would be a dirty trick if someone didn't like it.
Oh, yeah, we also agreed that we'd take turns being mad. I suggested that if we were both mad at the same time, it would be more difficult. I suppose we've done that a couple of times. . . . We don't quarrel. I don't know what you gain. If you want to blow off steam, we take turns blowing that off to each other. If you're mad at the world or something, it's nice to have someone you can talk to. More than to argue or fight with. . . .
We may disagree, but basically we respect what each one wants.

She may say, "That's absolutely crazy," but she says, "I know you want it, so I'm glad you bought it." She might want something I think is ridiculous. But I say, "If it gives you pleasure, why not?" We like the other person to make themself happy.

They do not, however, concur on everything. Jean is more religious than Keith, who prefers to work on boats. So Jean took the children to Sunday school and church while Keith worked around the house. Sometimes they vote for different political candidates; they do not always approve of each other's purchases. But these differences do not faze them. They like to collaborate.

KEITH: I know it sounds ridiculous, but I can get a lot of pleasure out of trading off ideas together and seeing if we can't pull a problem apart and look at it more thoroughly. She's got some very good ideas that I might not think of, and I have some good ideas too. And I think it is an interesting relationship when you can chew on those ideas together.

Keith thinks Jean is a great emotional partner.

Keith: She's marvelous. She's a little warmhearted pussycat.

He also thinks they do well together sexually. They satisfy each other. Non-monogamy has never been an issue, although both admit to noticing attractive people. They have intercourse about once a week, and signs of physical affection in between are numerous. Their sex life has, to Keith, a dynamic quality.

KEITH: It's a learning relationship that gets better as we learn more.

Jean agrees, and while she thinks Keith is more interested in sex than she is, she is very happy with their sex life. While he initiates sex most of the time (she says 65 percent of the time; he says 90 percent), this does not reflect any significant unwillingness on her part. Keith would change that ratio a bit if he could.

KEITH: She claims to be an old-fashioned girl, so it's a man's job to initiate it. However, I'm trying to teach her that that's not necessarily the case anymore. So I probably initiate, but she doesn't discourage it.

Keith feels he is ready whenever she wants him, but admits that sometimes he may not have understood her signals. He has, in fact, asked for more "signals clarification." Jean is occasionally disappointed when Keith is not in the mood for sex and she is, but she handles that with good humor.

JEAN: Oh, you just say, "Oh, nuts." You know—you stop and think, and you figure, *He's either had a busy day or there's a multitude of reasons.* And earlier in our marriage he used to get pouty at me. Oh, darn. Oh, well. And I learned you should count to ten and be grateful for what you got and not fuss over one time. You get a longer-range view.

They are so pleased with all aspects of their relationship that in the joint interview we were curious about which gave them the most satisfaction. They provided these responses:

JEAN: Just being with him.

KEITH: Knowing each other and coming home to somebody I like.

JEAN: *Being* with him.

KEITH: I tell her she's brilliant.

Why do they think they have been so extraordinarily successful?

KEITH: I think our marriage is stronger because our background is so similar and we have such a commonality of experience.

JEAN: Yes. We started right out with understanding about what we were talking about.

KEITH: Makes it sound dull, doesn't it?

JEAN: On the contrary. Because I believe you have a far better chance to move forward in a relationship if you start out on more or less an even keel. You understand the family, and you marry a family when you get married. And you just understand so much more than if you were marrying someone from, say, Pakistan, or another culture.

KEITH: And we enjoy people. We enjoy the same people. We entertain together and Jean makes it perfect.

What is their advice? We suspected what they would say.

JEAN: To like each other. . . . To be able to talk.

KEITH: And be friends. That's Jean's favorite word.

JEAN: And give—give more than fifty percent.

KEITH: Yes. Fifty-one percent!

JEAN: Fifty-one percent!

That does seem to get to the core of their relationship. They like each other very much. Their individual jobs, in the household and in the outside world, are very different but are given equal status. Each is the other's partner and confidant. They have felt comfortable and sure about each other from the beginning, and they have shown each other the utmost courtesy, whether that means being nice to one's in-laws or taking pleasure in the other person's interests and acquisitions. They have paid attention to their emotional and sexual needs. Each of them has kept the other happy by giving 51 percent.

# Jack and Henrietta

This is a two-paycheck couple who integrate work and home lives successfully. After a slow, careful courtship, they lived together for six months before marrying. Time is at a premium for them, but they spend whatever leisure hours they have with each other and in church-related activities. They are supportive rather than competitive, ever willing to sacrifice for each other. They choose untraditional roles in the management of finances.

Jack and Henrietta live in one of the nondescript apartment buildings that mushroomed a few years after World War II. The space is difficult to make interesting: square rooms, low ceilings, exactly the same as every other unit in the building. The couple has made it more inviting by lining the walls with books and by choosing bright and cheerful colors. It is very neat and clean. We got the sense that neither of them spends much time in the public spaces, and they do not.

Jack is a twenty-eight-year-old sales representative. He is tall, dark, intense-looking, with a well-manicured beard. Thin but wiry, he looks as if he works out or engages in sports in his spare time.

Henrietta, who is two years older, is short and sharp-featured. One would not call her pretty, but she is so intense and animated that she seems very attractive after brief acquaintance. She is a research geologist doing post-doctoral work at the university on a prestigious grant from a national foundation. When we interviewed them they had been married just a little over one year. It is a first marriage for her, not him. They do not now have children.

When they met, Jack had been married for two years, and the marriage was deteriorating at the time. Henrietta had joined his kayaking club, where she got to know him in a platonic way, and shortly after he broke off with his wife he asked Henrietta for a date. She was delighted. She found him a nice, open, friendly person, and besides, she had just moved to the city and was lonely.

> HENRIETTA: I had zero friends here. I'd been going through a long period—I think it especially happens to women who are in professions. . . . In college I had just assumed the right man would come along and then, as I got past twenty-five, I started to panic—you know, this is never going to happen. And then after a while—especially in the last years—I finally realized that it wouldn't matter all that much, that I would like very much to be in a relationship with someone, but if it never happened I could still survive quite well. I was financially independent. I could have a job for the rest of my life and support myself, so that I was in a good place to meet people, but I in no way felt I desperately needed him.

Although neither Jack nor Henrietta was particularly "desperate," their relationship quickly grew serious. Their first date was followed by a second in the same week. Henrietta got scared:

HENRIETTA: I was just here for professional business. . . . I hadn't planned to meet anyone. It sort of took me by surprise, and I have to admit I was afraid of it. I mean, for so long you think that's what you want, and then when it actually gets closer to reality, you begin to wonder, and so . . . I was debating about it and afraid of it . . . and I moved back from it. . . .
We tried right from the beginning to be very open with one another and discuss everything, and I felt he was pressuring me too much and he felt that I was closing him out. And in talking, I realized that he was right, that he wasn't so much pressuring me as I was looking for reasons to find fault and maybe break up, because it was getting serious and scaring me. And I realized I should reevaluate.

She had been afraid before, during her adolescent and college dating days, but this feeling was new.

HENRIETTA: My love had an edge of fear to it. But different from before. Before, it was: *Is he going to like me?* I think I am a person who is family-oriented and relationship-oriented, so I always wanted a relationship and to be married. . . . There were times when there was someone and I desperately wanted to be in love with that person, but I was afraid they weren't going to love me. Looking back, I don't think that was a love situation. More of an *If I'm lucky, they'll take me.* I didn't feel that way with Jack. It was more examining my own feelings, rather than his.

Both Jack and Henrietta recognized a specific turning point.

HENRIETTA: I know exactly when it was, because he had asked me over to his place for supper. And he played a tape for me and it was an old tape of his grandfather, who had died and who he had really loved as a kid. And this was one of the first times I had really seen an interaction of him with someone else. . . . I could see a part of him I had never seen before, a very caring side that I had felt was there, but things had been going too fast to see it. . . . It was like I had broken down a wall and saw him, and liked what I saw. And I thought, *Wow! This guy's someone I always hoped I would meet.*

That clinched it for Henrietta. Jack had been falling in love slowly, but he was sure of his choice before she was. He took a different approach.

JACK: At that point, falling in love was not something that happened to me. Eyes meeting and hearts thumping is physical, not love. I was physically attracted to her, but then it was: *Great, where do we go from here?* Where we went was to be good friends and realizing that she had a lot of similar interests. When we get away from work, we still have an awful lot in common. We just talked and became very good friends and found we had similar moral convictions. It was amazing to me, in fact, that we did, and so we developed a certain sense of respect, and then I fell in love with her.

Jack knew Henrietta would take longer to reach that point, in part because of her moral convictions.

JACK: She had a strong, perhaps stronger desire than I did to get into a relationship, but she was more hesitant too. Because at that time, Henrietta, as far as I know, had been a very strong Christian. And total commitment, to her, means an awful lot. So there was the fear of getting into something too soon.

They began to spend several nights a week together. Then one day, Henrietta sent Jack a card telling him how much she loved him. Jack said, "It was probably more intense than anything anybody's ever said to me before," and after that he started to think of this as a permanent relationship. They decided to marry.

JACK: I can picture the exact moment perfectly in my mind. I'm a pretty sensitive person and that is probably why I'm a good salesman. I can tell what a person is thinking by body language, et cetera. I said, "Gee, I've been seeing little Henriettas all week."
And she said, "Yeah, I've been seeing little Jacks all week."
So then we knew we were going to get married.

Still, Henrietta was glad they had a few months to live together before the wedding.

HENRIETTA: There's definitely a lot of things you're never going to learn about a person until you live with them, and that's besides the things like sex, because you can sleep with someone without living with them. But it's the nitty-gritty of who's going to make a bigger mess at breakfast and who's going to clean it up, and who's going to spend three hours in the shower if the other one's late for work, and these type of things. I can tell you we've got a lot more adjusted to each other than when we first started living together. It was a kind of safeguard before making the total commitment. It was only a couple months, but it still gave us the time to say, "This isn't going to work. We'd better drop it now before it's too late." Of course that didn't happen.

Henrietta was a little worried about what her parents would say when she told them. After all, she had not known Jack very long, and since her family lived out of town, they had never even met him. But they were delighted.

HENRIETTA: They were glad about it. My father had given up hope on me quite a few years ago—that I was going to get married—so he was very glad. And I'd hear from my sisters how excited he was about the wedding.

Meeting his family also helped to reenforce Henrietta's love for Jack. She liked them very much.

HENRIETTA: I had good feelings about him when I met his family. His background seemed very similar to mine, and I knew that he would fit in well with my family—which I think really helps when you're building a relationship. Especially if you're close to your family, which I am, and he's close to his parents too.

They had a church wedding, went on a wonderful honeymoon, and set up housekeeping in Henrietta's apartment. The first six months—as well as subsequent months—were relatively easy. Jack could not recall any difficulties; Henrietta said that those they did have were inconsequential.

HENRIETTA: No big problems. Little ones. We had decided early on that we would tell each other when we were upset with what the other one was doing. And even though it might be painful—'cause no one really enjoys conflict (although some people seem to, neither of us do)—so we got things out in the open before they would fester. We'd have a blowup, and it may mean an hour or so of both of us feeling really bad and getting it out and choking on the words and stuff, but in the end we would come away feeling a lot better about it and making up. We've gotten better about it too.

They spend most of their free time together. While they enjoy being with other people, they also like a lot of quiet time, so with work and other responsibilities—they are both very active in their church—they constantly feel the need for more hours for all the many things they would like to do. Time is a genuine problem, but neither of them sees much change in sight.

JACK: I don't see any pattern in our marriage. We have so many commitments. And a lot of our leisure time is involved in the church. It certainly comes down to a lot more than us. Both of us are on too many committees. We have a dinner party we've been trying to put together for months. . . . We are overwhelmed, so there's no typical pattern. I'm wondering if there will ever be one.

HENRIETTA: The only way that we could have more time together would be if we cut out of our work somewhat, and I think we both care enough about our work not to want to do that. So even though we would like to be together more often, I guess we're trying to be realistic about it and say, "Okay, this is the life-style we've chosen."

Indeed, both are very engaged in their careers, doing well, and achieving their goals, supporting each other every step of the way. Jack is an ardent defender of Henrietta's career and, in truth, would not have it any other way.

JACK: I don't think I could stand a wife who was always sitting home with the kids and getting frustrated. . . . That was a major problem with my first marriage. I think her having a career is very important. Henrietta is looking for a professorship somewhere, and before we even got married I said, "Yeah, wherever you can find one—as long as I can tolerate the place, we'll move there."

He also respects the impact work has on their personal life:

JACK: I do wish we had more time together. I have enough time by myself, simply because I work—my whole business is me. Henrietta works with a lot of people, and there's a lot of people taking up her time coming up and asking her questions: "How do I do this? How do I do that?" So she often needs time to be alone in the evening, usually just about the time it would be nice for me to be home with her together. She needs a bit more of that than she gets. We work that out. She has no qualms about me getting together with friends during those times and doing things.

He definitely knows when and why to leave her alone, and he does it without resentment.

JACK: When she's at work she gets into it, and that's it. You talk to her at lab and she's a whole different person than when you talk to her at home, because her mind's on her work. It's set more [in a] pattern, and if it's interrupted she'll snap at you. That's because she's intensely concentrating. So I try not to call her or expect her to call me unless it's something important.

This aspect of their relationship—their mutual respect for the place work occupies in their lives—is particularly important to Henrietta. She was not certain she could find a man like Jack.

HENRIETTA: This was the one thing that I found the hardest to believe in Jack: that I was the type of woman he wanted. That he did not want someone who was going to be home all day because he found that type of person usually not very mentally challenging, and he preferred someone who had more to do and who would bring mental stimulation into the home. And I thought, *Yeah, I've heard this before.* And usually it's not really what they mean. But he did. And so that meant a lot to me, in the fact that I was not going to have to give up an essential part of me for this relationship, that I could be what I wanted to be and still have a relationship.

If Jack's attitude had been more conventional, no relationship would have been possible.

HENRIETTA: I'm not the kind of woman who could be a housewife and mother. It would drive me up the wall. I do want to be a mother, and I do want to be a wife, but I need an outside activity, and I think I'll be better at both if I have time away. Twenty-four-hours-a-day, seven-days-a-week companionship is not my type of thing, and I don't think it's his either. And so it's nice that we have our work and our times apart, as well as our times together.

Henrietta and Jack consider themselves a very egalitarian couple, with equal power to influence each other in major and minor things. Henrietta admits, however, that her career needs are less flexible than Jack's right now, and tend predominantly to influence some of their choices.

HENRIETTA: I think there are areas he has more influence and areas where I have more. The biggest area I have more influence in these days is that I'm looking for a job. He told me before we got married—and it was a very important thing to me—that he was willing to move to wherever I could get a job. So in that sort of thing, he was probably giving in more than I have, but I certainly won't accept a job without finding out if that was a place he really wanted to live.

The only imbalance in the general equilibrium is money. Because Jack works on commission, it is hard for them to project and maintain a budget. Then, too, Henrietta presently earns more than Jack does, although he thinks that will change.

JACK: I made more gross. Net, I made less. This year, so far, she's made more money than I have. Give me two more months, I'll make a lot more than she has. . . . She has a better job, in the sense that pay is certainly more steady, and is recognized as being more intellectually demanding than mine. But I think each of us weigh each other's jobs as equally important, and always have.

He does acknowledge that his working on commission causes them worry.

JACK: I'm a commission salesman, and time is money. She gets her check every month, but with me—I had zero income this last month because I had some charges back against some commissions that balanced out the renewal commissions coming in. And the big thing that had been going on all summer was one large deal. It's been submitted for a month, and the company came back and said we had all the wrong forms, and there's something like sixty people—we have to go back out and do everything all over again. And this kind of thing causes strong concern.

They started out in marriage with widely divergent balance sheets, and that fact determines the use of their income.

JACK: We keep separate accounts. Money is kept separate. Henrietta has a large amount of savings and I have a large amount of debts . . . including some alimony to my former wife . . . so most of my money comes right to the debt reduction, and we're living off her income.

Henrietta is perhaps a little more affected by the situation than Jack is.

HENRIETTA: The hardest thing has been the money situation. I came into the relationship with savings and he came in with debt. And I'm making more money, and so the idea was that in the beginning we'd live off my salary and put his salary toward debt reduction. And that hasn't always worked simply, because, since he's self-employed, sometimes there's no money and then it gets tight. And I feel uncomfortable with this, and I guess it's been three years since I've had to worry about monetary things. . . . And he was feeling insecure about the fact that things weren't going well, and so it was a hard issue to bring up.

Yet we have dealt with things, and I think we've dealt with them fairly well. Money doesn't resolve itself, but we've come away from it feeling we know the other person a little better and that at least we've come to an agreement for a while.

They try to share all responsibilities, including such mundane tasks as cleaning the house. In fact, there is a certain amount of "role reversal" when necessary.

JACK: I cooked dinner tonight; she took out the garbage earlier. I usually end up cooking dinner, simply because it works out like that. I have from four-thirty to six-thirty free almost always. Simply more convenient. Henrietta tends to do the dishes more than I do. I tend to do the laundry more than she does because I've got five dress shirts and I've got to have a clean shirt every day. We both clean about equally.

And in the traditionally male jobs?

JACK: If it were some kind of mechanical adjustment I would attempt to do it myself, but she got involved. I would bite my tongue and let her try. . . . She's got this attitude of *let me try,* so I shut up and let her find out for herself rather than tell her. . . . If something goes wrong with her car, she'll try and fix it, especially if it isn't near the engine. Recently she tried, but her license plate fell off. But I don't comment, and just let her figure it out, because she wants that feeling of accomplishment. . . . The only thing is that I have a tendency to drive, and if I don't sense that she wants to drive, she will eventually snap and say, "Let me drive." And I do.

Their shared responsibility for the housework was important to Henrietta.

JACK: She has mentioned that she's very glad about the way it's worked out. She tells a story, for example, about a guy that she went out with a couple of times going over to her place for dinner. He plopped on the couch to read the paper while she cooked two steaks he brought over, and that was the last time she saw him.

Henrietta's version of this incident is identical to Jack's. She is very pleased that he does so much in their home.

HENRIETTA: We're traditional in some things, but when I start talking to other people about their marriages that I know, we're not.

I get upset if I have to do more than fifty percent of the work, and everybody else [of her women friends] thinks it's super if they have to do only ninety-five percent. And I say, "You've got to be kidding. Why do you put up with that? You know, I'm working full time too. I shouldn't have to do more than half of the work when I get home. So I guess we're not traditional, but this shouldn't make us renegades either. Why should helping each other mean we are social outcasts?

They feel they are becoming more and more of a team. One thing that draws them together is their work in a Protestant church, and many of their leisure activities and friends result from that connection. Jack had not attended church in fifteen years when he met Henrietta, but he liked becoming involved again.

In addition, they have begun to achieve a mutually satisfactory way of dealing with any problems that arise.

JACK: We don't yell but, boy, there's a lot of tension and restrained yelling. There was one point one month, I had a very low income and very large bills came up, so I didn't say anything to her because I didn't want to worry her about them and my business. I didn't say anything, but she knew something was wrong because I was worrying. And I think the thing that hurt her most was that I didn't say anything to her. And that hurt her quite a bit, and she wanted me not to keep things back. And it got to tears and everything, and we talked about it.

They recognized the importance of talking things over.

HENRIETTA: We decided early on to be very open with one another, and we developed this pattern early on that we would not lay guilt trips on each other. You know: "Why are you doing this to me? Don't you love me anymore?" Et cetera. Instead of: "Is this a critical part of your personality? This irritates me. Will I have to learn to live with it?" Et cetera. . . . I think we've managed pretty well. I think we're ready for the pressures we get from work and from moving and things like that.

There is no name-calling, and fights are usually made up within an hour.

HENRIETTA: Well, if something does happen, it starts out with one or the other saying something the other does not like, and getting a little defensive, and you can feel tension and we get angry. There's never anything said about *you rotten person* or something like that. It's always: "I don't like it when you do this," or, "You make me feel bad because of this." We get pretty emotional sometimes—sometimes I cry, sometimes he cries, sometimes we both cry, but usually when we see how bad the other is dealing with it, we tend to try and comfort each other through it too. So it's conflicting and comforting that ends up with us realizing how much we care for each other.

They are very affectionate and demonstrative with each other.

They have sex almost every day, and both are very pleased with their sex life. Generally unrestricted in their choice of positions, they feel relaxed with each other in bed. Everything is satisfactory, although Henrietta is not sure if she has orgasms.

HENRIETTA: I've always found it difficult to know. I always enjoy it, and sometimes I feel it more intensely than others, but I guess I'm not too sure exactly what orgasm is. It's a little harder for a woman to be able to define it than for a man. Well, maybe not—maybe I'm sexually naïve enough that I don't know about that, but I do get pleasure from it and sometimes I get more than others. It's always enjoyable.

While this ambiguity would be distressing to some women, as well as to their partners, it upsets neither Jack nor Henrietta. They feel so good with each other, so certain that they have the emotional wherewithal to deal with any problem that might arise.

When we asked them what gave them the most satisfaction about their relationship, they both cited the quality of their conversation and the amount of communication.

JACK: We talk. She's as crazy as I am.

HENRIETTA: We are really close. We are good friends. I think we share about everything. Maybe not everything, because I'm sure there are little secret parts to both of us, but most of it is shared.

JACK: Oh, yeah? What?

HENRIETTA: I'm sure there's something.

They also take pleasure in the "fit" of their two personalities.

HENRIETTA: This is the most stressless relationship I have ever been in—not that I've been in too many, but I think it is our mark so far.

Their advice to others is to follow a model that has served them: Talk, talk, and talk some more.

JACK: Talk and be open.

HENRIETTA: When things bother us, we get them out right away. We don't like painful moments, but it won't get any less painful if you don't address things.

JACK: Yes, it's no benefit to stew on it, think it over, let it eat at you. Get it over with and go on.

Jack and Henrietta are working toward an equal partnership. They are a career couple who believe strongly in their work but just as strongly in each other. It is inspiring to see them work at integrating their desire for achievement with their need for communication.

They also illustrate the ways in which traditional and untraditional elements can coexist in a relationship. In some senses they are unconventional. They keep finances separate. She does "male" tasks and he does many household jobs that society has earmarked for women. And he is willing to relocate for her career. However, they are also religious, monogamous, and "institutional" about their marriage. Each puts the other first, and both intend to create a family and a home to last a lifetime. Debt causes them difficulties, as does the prospect of moving for Henrietta's job, but they compromise and extend themselves for each other. It is a young marriage, but an ambitious and loving one.

# Five Cohabiting Couples

## Abbey and Biff

Abbey and Biff are two young cohabitors who are very serious about their relationship. They are protective of it in a world—the theater world—which allows more sexual freedom and more instability than they would like. We chose them to represent young couples totally immersed in a profession in which competition for success can easily threaten a relationship. Abbey and Biff are a modern couple, leading unconventional lives, yet determined to make their relationship work.

They live in a one-bedroom apartment on the third floor of a converted brownstone in a changing neighborhood. Some of the buildings in the block are being lovingly restored to their former elegance. Others still have broken doors, unlit hallways, and a pervasive rooming-house atmosphere. Abbey and Biff's building is in the latter stage but work has begun to make it more habitable. In the meantime it looks unwelcoming, with exposed lights in the hallway and padlocks on some of the apartment doors. After a steep climb up to their apartment, the interior proved pleasant. The rooms are very chic, with an exposed-brick fireplace in the cozy, well-decorated living room, and a spacious, attractive bedroom. The kitchen is almost nonexistent and one has to wedge oneself into the bathroom, but Biff and Abbey consider the apartment a "steal at the price" and are delighted and grateful to have it.

Abbey and Biff are both actors. They have other jobs to support their careers: Abbey works at a clothing store when she doesn't have a part and Biff works either in production or at the box office. Recently he took a job in an advertising agency writing copy because they need

395

the income. But he doesn't plan to do it very long. Both partners are willing to sacrifice to stay in the theater.

Abbey is a tall, thin, attractive blue-eyed redhead of twenty-seven. Biff is thirty-one, dark, of medium height, and also very good-looking. They have been going together for three years, ever since they met "on the road" in a repertory production of *Romeo and Juliet,* and have actually lived together for two years. Neither had cohabited with anyone before, but Biff was married once—for a short time.

They met during the first cast meeting. They talked afterward about the play director, and since Abbey had worked at this theater and for the same director before, Biff asked her for all the information she could give him. He was very impressed with her. He was also ready to meet someone special.

> BIFF: It was very lonely at the time. I had come off a lot of very screwed-up relationships . . . very short things, very crazy. A lot of not really one-night stands, but extended one-night-stand kinds of things, and I had been married a number of years before that. It just happened. We really hit it off.

It was also a very physical first impression:

> BIFF: That first night I found her very sexy. It was warm. . . . It was a turn-on.

But most of all, their work and their disappointments with other people brought them together.

> BIFF: We knew from the first we were going to have a good friendship. The question was where it was going to go. She had someone who was returning to the company to work and she wasn't sure how she felt about that. . . . She also knew we were importing an actress from New York who he would immediately start having a thing with. He would chase this actress immediately—and she was right on both counts. . . . We trusted each other a lot, an awful lot. . . .
>    The first twenty-four hours were emotional. Then it got passionate and there wasn't time to let down and talk about what we were doing. . . . We didn't see an awful lot of each other except at two, three, or four in the morning. Sometimes we'd rehearse different schedules and between us cover twenty-two hours every day.

Abbey was just as taken with Biff—if not more.

> ABBEY: I remember him being totally unlike anyone else . . . this big guy coming . . . to a country-hick place. I was at a point where I was disillusioned with men, and I was ready to swear off them and just deal with them for a while. I had decided to stop looking for someone because I had not been successful at any kind of permanent

relationship with anyone over the past two years . . . but I needed somebody. . . .

I was impressed with him because he was very businesslike and mature compared to all the guys I had spent time with or worked with—from a totally different league.

Her first attraction was more intellectual and emotional:

ABBEY: I didn't walk in the room and think, *Aha, I'm going to have an affair with this man,* or *This is my dream come true.* . . . I remember talking and he was saying, "God, you're the first person I've been able to communicate with that's intelligent and seems to know what's going on in this group." . . . I remember feeling the same way: *My God, there's some hope, somebody intelligent is coming in.*

They had sex within two days. They lived separately but saw each other a few hours offstage every day. It was exciting, and working together was wonderful. About halfway through the show's run, Biff suggested they move in together.

ABBEY: I was doubtful because I had never had anybody that wanted to move in with me . . . that wanted to spend every night. . . . It was so new, so remarkable that I was very doubtful that it was going to continue. It was too good to be true. Whereas Biff just assumed it would happen.

They were both satisfied with their salaries and felt as if they had a lot of money. They ate out, talking in bars after performances with the rest of the cast, and sometimes wondering if they would ever get time alone. It was emotionally intense, and they decided they were in love.

ABBEY: I definitely thought it was love. I was swept off my feet. I had never had anything work like that before. This was a first time. . . . In fact, I remember it was during a heated discussion with the producer about the score, when the producer said, "Did you hear what he just said?" And I said no, and he said, "Biff just asked you to marry him." And I said, "Oh, I'll have to think about it." We were just joking, but after the producer left, I remembered Biff sitting down and saying: "I really mean it. I know it's early . . ." So I think very early in the game we were very serious.

BIFF: I was fairly confident that we were doing very well for one another. I was very excited and I still am intrigued by how well we seem to do together. . . . We don't fight. We are very open with one another. It seems like there really isn't anything we don't deal with . . . not stress it or hide it or disguise it as something else. I found that very exciting. I wanted a relationship, a continuing relationship with Abbey. I knew that it was growing and getting stronger all the time.

Friends, for all kinds of reasons, encouraged the relationship.

ABBEY: I think everybody thought it was terrific. I had enough ex-boyfriends in the company that had been rats to me that I think they were all thrilled that I had found somebody who was finally interested. I had slept with at least three of the guys on the road. It wasn't weird because I had become friends with all of them and I think all of them were thrilled that finally they didn't have to worry about it, whether I was going to go after them. I will admit, in my time I would get desperate enough for attention that I would run after guys.

The project they shared ended, and they had to decide what to do next. Biff wanted to go to New York because that's where he needed to be for his profession—and he had to decide if he wanted Abbey to go with him.

BIFF: I had made the decision that I was coming back to New York City, and I knew that working in the performing arts and being on the road makes strange bedfellows, and so I had to ask myself some questions . . . and I brought them up to her.

But Biff knew that being in New York was not going to be as idyllic as their road trip and he wanted Abbey to know that.

BIFF: The pressures were going to be different: not being able to make things happen, a great deal of frustration, countless meetings, having to spend money and no money coming in. . . . I have an incredible temper, too, at times, and frustration will make me yell, scream, and carry on. It didn't take her long to just ignore it all. It was a freedom between the two of us I had never found before.

Biff decided he wanted Abbey with him, and she was enthusiastic. At the same time, Biff felt that if Abbey came to New York it would put their relationship in jeopardy.

BIFF: I felt if I got to New York I could find work. I wanted Abbey to come with me and I told her I thought it was necessary for her to leave Kansas City. . . .
I told her that I thought if she came back to New York with me, I ran the risk of her discovering things about herself that would make her want to leave me eventually. I don't know if she agrees with me. . . . I just felt that after a few years in New York, being who she was—her personality, character, independence, intelligence, and ambition—she would get sophisticated very fast. I think in some respects that's happening, but I think she enjoys it a great deal and it's strengthening our relationship. I love it.

In the beginning, they thought of getting married. Abbey didn't think it was a good idea. Now Biff agrees.

BIFF: We talked about it. . . . There were and are moments when I think, *Shit, why don't we just get married. This is ridiculous.*
Unfortunately, at this point in time there are almost more arguments

not to get married, in terms of logical arguments. It would not help us economically—not that that should be a motivation—but it would hurt. . . . She's going to go away this summer for ten weeks and I'll be traveling all summer. . . . It just doesn't seem necessary. . . .

But I do recall asking Abbey: "Will you marry me? I'd like to get married," and she being smart enough to say, "You don't have to do that right now. Be cool."

Abbey's hesitation was prompted by some of the economic facts of Biff's life, and by her observation of other couples.

ABBEY: Biff proposed—but he also made a stipulation very early . . . that he has a lot of debts, so there were a lot of things to clear up before it [marriage] could ever happen. I knew things wouldn't change in a couple of months. If the stipulation hadn't been there, I probably would have said yes. . . .

And I also felt people should live together first. . . . There was this couple we knew and they got together about the time we did, and they married and divorced in nine months. I think her parents pushed her into marriage.

So Biff and Abbey moved to New York. Abbey had to leave a good job at a local theater, but her contacts landed her a nontheatrical job in New York and helpful introductions to "showcases" (nonpaying productions off-off Broadway, where actors hope that influential people in the theatrical community will see them perform). Biff wasn't so lucky. When he was out of work, the stress affected both of them. Finally Biff got part-time work and small acting parts, and things calmed down.

But work still complicates their life. It organizes their time, their feelings, their pleasures, and their frustrations. It defines their relationship.

BIFF: It's really hard to separate work from personal life. . . . We actually just went through a period when we got on each other's nerves a lot because we were both working from eight in the morning until midnight every night and not seeing each other. That means weekdays, weekends, and that got on our nerves. We came to the conclusion one day that we've got to be real careful. . . . We're both so heavily committed that a whole web of things that we enjoy doing together—cooking, spending time reading, and talking about things we read—all that web breaks down and starts to deteriorate. All of a sudden it's McDonald's and on the run, and you don't want to come home because it means a pile of dirty laundry. We strive to keep a sense of order and structure in our day-to-day lives because it makes us both happier. When that starts to break down, things get a little tense.

Time. Time to see each other. Time to have free time. Time to remember what the other wants. Sufficient time: the great need of two young people with careers and ambitions. Both of them are aware of the problem—but at the moment they can only try to keep it from getting out of hand. They accept the conditions of their lives.

> ABBEY: He's been working with this theater company and a lot of times he would be over there every evening. And there were two months that he overlapped with another job, and there were lots of times I never saw him. There was a week or so where I would leave in the morning and he would be asleep; I would get back at six and he would be gone; I would leave at eleven to go to the theater and work until three. Meanwhile he would come home and go to bed. We literally for five solid days did not see each other awake. We'd wait for just one weekend . . . and then something would come up for that to.

Abbey is not overly concerned about the problem. She believes they can handle it because they share the same aspirations and therefore understand that their work demands enormous sacrifices.

> ABBEY: One reason we get along so well is that we are both busy and we don't get on each other's case a lot. It's not a problem, because he's in the theater. If he had a regular nine-to-five job, then it might be.

Biff agrees:

> BIFF: We've established a certain SOP—standard operating procedure. . . . The girl that I married could never have dealt with it. I may call Abbey at three in the afternoon and say, "I'm going to be at the theater at six to take care of some things. I should be home by seven, seven-thirty"—and not get home till midnight. I may not remember to call, whatever—it doesn't bother Abbey. But my ex-wife would have killed me for that or tracked me down by three-ten. That's what I meant when I said we had a partnership here. We both understand the business, and we operate within it, without consulting each other very much. . . .
>
> I have friends who have problems. One has a structured job and the wife doesn't, and they can't keep the relationship. We seem very adaptable.

Even in different jobs and with separate hours, their professional lives are somehow intertwined. Sometimes the theatrical community seems very small.

They often feel as if they are fighting the city.

> BIFF: I think New York is a real bitch town. Abbey and I are good friends and that has helped both of us surmount it. . . . I think we do very well . . . basically because we . . . help each other a great deal.
>
> There are just more things to decide that affect both of us. Abbey has access to professional information that I need, that I couldn't get any other way. . . . If she has a bad day it affects me too. . . . So, we have to harmonize. We interact so much. I call her much more about work than I do about groceries.

They both feel their ambition is salutary, and that neither should hold the other back.

BIFF: I think both of us are very much committed to allowing the other person to pursue their career as actively and ambitiously as they can. Within reason—not taxing the relationship where both of us are out there killing ourselves sixteen hours a day, seven days a week.

Abbey has gotten a good part in a touring company this summer and they both feel she should take it. But Biff is nervous about it, and worried about their future. Moreover, she would earn only enough to meet expenses, so it is all the more urgent that Biff take this "straight" job in advertising to contribute to their livelihood while she is on the road.

BIFF: So many issues . . . Will she work when she comes back from the tour? I'm not hostile or upset that I'm taking this very straight job. I've just decided it's going to be fun . . . or I'm not going to do it very long. I've done this before. The first year we were here it got so bad that I had to wait on tables. This summer it's gonna cost everything she gets paid for her to live there. So I'll just deal with it.

So far they have kept professional jealousy and competition down to a minimum. But they do see this as a peril of being in the same profession.

BIFF: No problem, but I keep wondering if we're heading for one. It isn't good for us to work at the same theater. That causes strain— when I can't provide things that are needed or run interference for her. She wanted to fight about it, but said, "I can't get angry with you because I love you and live with you." But that's not good for the work, so I think it's good to stay separate. I don't want the personal. I want a professional working relationship.

Abbey does not much care what Biff does as long as it makes him happy. But that's easier said than done because he wants accomplishment. He is ambitious and he wants to contribute his monetary "fair share." Abbey has managed their financial life and that has presented problems.

ABBEY: I make most of the financial decisions. I have sort of been the keeper of the budget ever since we've been together. I'm usually the one who has the steadier income, although last year we were both making a steady paycheck for the whole year, but it all went into my account and I paid the bills. I am the one who has credit cards and has made the credit history, and the phone is in my name. So, as far as financial decisions, I tend to have the final say. . . .

It is a problem when things are insecure. When he's between jobs and he's not sure . . . he's contributing as much financially. I think Biff comes from a background where the man is supposed to be the breadwinner, and if he's not contributing like that, it's not right. . . . I'm convinced that Biff is going to be very successful financially. I don't know if we'll ever be rich, but I'm convinced he is going to be very good at whatever he is into.

She does worry if he will be able to achieve his ultimate goal: to direct.

ABBEY: I think I have more self-confidence about myself and my career because . . . he has chosen a career that is so much more difficult. . . . He wants to be a director in the theater and there's never a way to be a surefire success at that.

All their big issues revolve around work. It pulls them apart and also brings them together. But they, too, have everyday problems that plague other couples. They share the housework and have had a few fights about her housekeeping—which was nonexistent.

ABBEY: There were some problems when we first moved to an apartment, based on the fact that I was a real slob. . . . It took me two years to understand that it was nice to do the dishes right after a meal.

They have untraditional talents, and divide the labor in the home according to their time and abilities rather than on customary male/female lines. This was accentuated when Biff wasn't working.

ABBEY: I generally do the dishes but it depends who is busiest and who has projects. . . . When he was unemployed and I was working, he did them all the time. At first I just wouldn't do it and he would do it all. He would housekeep and pick up behind me and I would just let him scream at me.

But even when both are working, each of them will handle jobs that are usually considered appropriate to the other's gender.

ABBEY: I will do the electrical repairs around here because I learned how to do it at the theater and Biff doesn't like to fool with that. And I'll do some carpentry things, although he tries to horn in on that. I wish he would let me do one project without him coming up and saying, "Let me do it." Normally I'll let him.

Biff has difficulty allowing for Abbey's aptitude in conventionally male areas.

ABBEY: We repainted the bathroom a couple of weeks ago. I had originally put up all the towel racks, so I was re-putting them up and he said, "Let me help you," and I said, "Fine." I knew the holes had to go in at weird angles and very slowly. He was working on one of those I had been doing, and I knew if you went very slowly the screws would go in eventually. His screwdriver kept slipping and he just blew up and said, "Why couldn't you do this right?"

I screamed back at him: "If you'd just let me do it myself you wouldn't have this problem."

He just left—we knew at that point he should just leave. I just took it down and went and got the drill and redid it myself and put it back up. It took me twenty minutes and it blew over.

Biff recognizes that he is more accustomed to traditional roles, so both are trying to strike a balance between the way he'd like things to be done and the way they actually tend to get done. He is also learning to like it.

BIFF: One real factor is time. The other is my traditionalism. It's her kitchen. She's gotten into gourmet food: Chinese, Italian. And now if she leaves a big pile of dishes, I'll just start doing them, with the kind of feeling that I'm making an investment in the relationship. We want to help each other. . . . Things get based on what's to be done and who's there to do it. . . . If she's working all the time in a show, then I might do everything. We buy our freedom hiring people whenever we can. . . .

I think we are more traditional than we used to be. I think our parents are models. Those traditional models were extremely satisfactory for both of us when we were growing up. . . . We're falling into those same models to some degree.

That doesn't bother Abbey. Things have balanced out fairly equally and she doesn't feel at all downtrodden. Furthermore, she would look upon full-time housework as a vacation—at least for a while.

ABBEY: I have never had the women's lib type of rebellion. If somebody told me I was going to get to stay home for a year and be a housekeeper, I would love it.

They regard every aspect of their life together as important. Money is kept separate, but they have a joint account as well which both contribute to and Abbey dispenses. Biff doesn't like to manage money, so she sets the couple's budget.

They are still working out family relations, complicated by their different religious backgrounds.

ABBEY: He gets along great with my family. Every time we go visit them . . . it's a treat. . . . I don't think I will ever get along with his parents like he gets along with mine . . . because his parents still have problems that I'm not Protestant. My parents don't care. . . . We've never fought about it because he knows that I'm more than willing to try. . . . If his parents said, "You will never see this girl again" . . . it would not keep him from being here.

The religious differences do, however, present obstacles to their future.

BIFF: I'm Baptist. I have very, very strong feelings about it. I haven't been in a church in I-don't-even-think how many years, but that's beside the point. When Abbey moved to New York she started looking around for a Catholic church to become affiliated with, and she asked me if I would have a problem if she joined a church. I really had to think about that and I concluded, no, I didn't have a problem. . . .

I refuse to let that be a problem in my life. I don't know how we'd deal with that in terms of children—we've never really discussed it. I don't know how Abbey would like her children to be raised, but I know how I want mine to be raised. We'll cross that bridge when we come to it.

ABBEY: I belong to a Catholic church and I'm a member, whereas he's Baptist but very inactively. The only argument is the marriage question. I think part of the reason we're not married is, first, 'cause he's been married, but also because my parents would like . . . a nice wedding with a nice dress in a Catholic church, with a wedding cake and a reception and the relatives and all the bullshit. . . .

I know myself I do not want to go to the justice of the peace on the corner. I want to have a white dress and walk down the aisle. . . . We've discussed it and I've said I don't need to have a huge wedding, but I want that and he said, "Fine." We still haven't dealt with the fact that he once said: "I will never get married in a Catholic church!" . . . It's not a big deal; we could have it in a park somewhere or in somebody's back lawn. . . .

I don't know what's going to happen when there are children. . . . We are both intelligent and mature enough to deal with it when it happens.

They have flare-ups, but they are not big fights. Everything is discussed and usually resolved within a few hours. Occasionally a little melodrama is introduced. They both mentioned that they "love to throw things." But neither one feels there is residual tension in the relationship. Biff says, "I'm afraid, in that respect, we probably have what I would call a perfect relationship." Biff feels the world is tough enough—why upset each other?

BIFF: The relationship is so rich it can withstand the outside world. . . . I'm just saying we've come through a number of things together . . . and it sure made it a hell of a lot saner doing it together. Coming through those kind of confrontations, you find out there's only so much the system or world can do to you. The rest you do to yourself. We don't allow ourselves to do that to ourselves very much. Life just goes too fast.

They are affectionate with each other—although Abbey is more satisfied than Biff.

ABBEY: I think it's terrific. I can't imagine anyone being more appreciative and more open about his affection. I've never seen anyone else who is as much.

BIFF: It is not my ideal, but it works better than anything I imagined. . . . I suppose we go through whole days when maybe not even a peck on the cheek. It's not that we're thinking about things, it's just that it doesn't happen.

They have sex three or four times a week, sometimes more sporadically. There are personal and medical reasons.

BIFF: We go through periods where we don't have sex together for three, four, five days at a time. . . . Two reasons: One is medical. We both have herpes. Every once in a while it just happens. The other is sometimes one of us doesn't feel like it and the other one understands. We don't spend time worrying about it or thinking that it is a sign of something Freudian.

ABBEY: It hasn't changed much but it's more sporadic . . . because of herpes. . . . If anybody has sores there's no sex. . . . That's weeks at a time. . . . Sometimes it will be just because we're too tired, and then all of a sudden we'll spend hours a night every night for a long time.

Even with medical problems and restrictions, they are content with their sex life. Biff is slightly more aggressive, and occasionally worries if he is really pleasing Abbey.

BIFF: I wonder if I satisfy her sometimes. I suppose I do all those cliché things to ask, to find out: "Did you come? Is it okay?" But I don't dwell on it.

In the abstract, Biff is against jealousy, but sometimes he is prey to it. When we talked to him, he was considering the question of non-monogamy during Abbey's proposed ten-week absence on tour. He wants to be monogamous.

BIFF: There have been times when I've been jealous—we're talking about people here, aren't we? In the profession we're in, it happens a lot. I remember being jealous of time Abbey would spend with a particular person. . . .
   We talked about her going away for ten weeks. . . . I said, "I really don't know whether I want to say to you I won't mess around with someone else while you're gone. I don't think I should, but who knows what I'll do?" We talked about it and we'll probably talk about it some more. I don't know what we'll do. . . .
   We probably have an undiscussed arrangement in which we will be faithful to each other. And it affects us both equally. I don't know how I feel about that, but I wouldn't want to hurt Abbey in any way. . . . We'll probably be faithful while she's gone. Because I don't want to live with cheating on her or running the risk of her finding out. . . . The risk is not worth the potential loss.

Abbey has a slightly different understanding of Biff's feelings, but she, too, thinks their relationship will be monogamous.

ABBEY: We've discussed it. I have not slept with anyone else since I met Biff. But from the beginning he made it clear that he didn't totally believe in being faithful to one person. Intellectually, I am of the opinion that one should be able to experiment outside without jeopardizing the relationship . . . but I don't know if I am ever going to want or need it. I'm not at all interested now. . . . I was out of town for a week once and saw some old boyfriends, and I was not at all tempted. I don't get aroused by anyone else but Biff since I met him.

Biff and Abbey seem increasingly close, and Biff is learning to trust his feelings about Abbey. But he still finds it hard to believe in the notion of permanence. Abbey views the relationship as a "trial marriage"; Biff sees it as less defined than that. While there is no one he'd rather be with than Abbey, and they are spending more and more of their precious free time together, Biff is still insecure about the future, because his marriage—particularly the end of it—was traumatic for him.

BIFF: We were both too young. We didn't know what we were doing. I loved her very dearly—I love her still today. Abbey knows it. She turned me on, but we just couldn't live together. . . . We had to go through so much goddamned pain . . . but it probably was a valuable experience. It opened up perspectives on how to really think about another person. . . .
      She threw me out. . . . I did everything she wanted and I put her on a pedestal and it was ridiculous. It suffocated her. It stopped me from doing the career I wanted to do and she was the one who . . . was ultimately courageous enough to say, "This has got to stop. We're killing each other. Now get the hell out of here, whether you want to leave or not."

Biff remembers many painful moments, but he does think he has come away from the marriage with heightened insight.

BIFF: We were competitive. Abbey and I are not. There was a lot of ego-stomping in that marriage. . . . My first wife was a real nut crusher. She could really do it, but what did I know?
      It was extremely painful. It was ego shattering for me. I felt I had been let out on a limb and then had it sawed off behind me. . . . I felt I had been betrayed. . . . When I got married, I had made a commitment and my wife betrayed that commitment. It made it very hard for me. I trust Abbey, but there has not been a woman that I have been involved with up to Abbey that I felt I could trust. . . .
      But the relationship I have with Abbey has truth to it. . . . There's some genuine sharing. I wanted to possess my wife and I learned a lot in that not working out. I do not possess a desire to possess Abbey. . . . She is a person, I'm a person, and we have a complementary relationship that works. And we can build something together and build individually as well. It's healthier. . . . I learned a

lot more about the job of living and sharing a relationship with somebody else. It really doesn't have a whole hell of a lot to do with love. Love helps—but it is not the answer to making all that happen.

When Biff and Abbey are together they agree that they feel lucky to have each other and that they love each other very much. They differ a bit on the definition of the relationship. Biff is pleased "that we are held together by desire, not outside pressure," while Abbey considers them "sort of married." They advise other couples to be patient with each other, but Biff feels that the most important thing is to know yourself well.

> BIFF: You've got to be willing to understand that you don't know all about yourself, and that part of the relationship is to help let the other person help you find out. . . . Being committed to being in love is not enough. You've got to be happy with what you're committed to. You've got to be working towards something, or the relationship won't be working toward something. That, communication, and patience.

This couple really seems to want their relationship to last. They consider all the modern alternatives, yet choose very few of them. Abbey would like to get married and eventually raise a family. Biff would like to as well, but is dubious of the permanence of marriage. They are liberal about sex, ambition, and household jobs. But ultimately they guard their relationship from other suitors, make sure they are not totally overwhelmed by their careers, and recognize the importance of their home environment. They believe in some of the traditional concepts that bind: their families, their religions, the possibility of children. But they have to struggle to build toward these goals, because their careers are so taxing. Nonetheless, the future looks promising.

# Paul and Jane

Paul and Jane exemplify some of the attitudes and goals of older cohabiting couples. These are people who have been loath to marry because of past experiences which they consider failures. Jane and Paul have tried to protect themselves financially and emotionally by consenting to a contract (in this case, a verbal agreement), by pursuing and rewarding independence, and by keeping finances separate. They are learning to relax their defenses and are beginning once again to consider a lifetime relationship. People who have lived conventional lives can change—radically—and be content. These previously married people have altered all the rules they grew up with.

Paul and Jane live in a big frame house just outside the city limits. The white clapboard house, probably built in the early 1900's, has a porch that nearly encircles it. Paul and Jane were on the porch arranging pots of flowering plants when we arrived. The effect of all the red and pink flowers against the white background was lovely. Jane was flattered by our response and presented a bouquet. Paul took us out back to display his own project, a vegetable garden. He is gray-haired, thin, and looks somewhat younger than his sixty years. Jane's hair is perfectly white, and at fifty-four, she is a bit plumper. They looked the very picture of people who have lived together all their lives. They have not, however. They are cohabitors and have lived in Jane's home, part of a settlement from her previous marriage, for almost seven years.

Paul is an electrician and thinking about retiring. Jane has been an architectural secretary for twenty-five years and she, too, is starting to plan for retirement. Their work and personal lives have been very different. They might never have met had they not attended adult education classes to fill up their lonely free evenings. Jane was recovering from the end of her thirteen-year marriage; Paul, divorced for the second time a year earlier, was dating but felt unfulfilled by his partners. Believing that he was incapable of a successful relationship, he wanted to avoid serious involvements. When he met Jane he took pains to outline the emotional limits he had set for himself.

> PAUL: Well, we met in this class and it wasn't a big group . . . and before the class was over, we went out and had dinner together . . . and, well, it was kind of interesting. I didn't intend to let anything serious happen out of it. I don't know what her intentions were, but mine were certainly not to let anything get out of hand. But that's the way it went.

He was dating someone else at the time and reflecting on his marriages: what he had done wrong, why he had chosen unwisely. The other woman, Martina, was trying to get a commitment from him. This pressure was relieved when he chose Jane.

At the time, Jane's life bore little resemblance to Paul's.

> JANE: At that point I was very much aware of being alone, because I was recently divorced, and paid attention to any men that were around. . . . I had been very unhappy but I was beginning to get to the point where I was . . . getting over the business of being single and being able to enjoy it.

Once they began to date, they saw each other steadily. They slept together after two dates. They enjoyed each other—but neither called it love.

> JANE: It was a comfortable relationship. . . . I didn't think much in

terms of love. . . . I wasn't ready for thinking in those terms. . . . I never felt madly in love. But I became very attached, very dependent on the relationship.

PAUL: Oh, golly. Love. You're asking a guy that's sixty years old, using the term of love. That meant so much different when this guy was twenty years, you know. Love to me now is a sense of value. . . . I used to think love was this passionate feeling I had. Well, now it's something else again. I had previously told women that I loved them. When I got together with Jane, I found it hard to do. And I still find it hard to say.

They did feel emotionally drawn to each other, however, and Paul suggested they move in together.

JANE: He was the one who suggested it. And he was the one who suggested that we try it for six months. I had to go on a trip . . . so he moved in to take care of the house and take care of the animals and things. It happened to work out rather neatly. I needed him at that point. . . . We were both equally enthusiastic—and we were both equally cautious.

They were cautious in every way. Paul determined they should begin their relationship logically and with agreed-upon stipulations.

PAUL: We started out and decided to try it for six months and see how it went together. Then we could always renew our agreement at the end of six months—which we've done fourteen times now. . . .
    We set ground rules. . . . We had to decide first which place we were gonna stay at, mine or hers, and there wasn't room in mine for all her stuff so we stayed here. We had financial arrangements, promises for complete openness. . . . Almost nothing has changed, except we added one little thing that said if either of us decided to break it off—which had to come at the end of a six-month period—we wouldn't go right up to the twenty-first of the month and say: "Hah! Goodbye, I'm gone!" We would give thirty days' notice.

Paul believes in the contract, its logic and its power to bind:

PAUL: It's important. If after two months you have a real big hassle and you decide . . . *Ah, the heck with this, I want out,* well, okay, but you must put up with it for another four months, and leave with honor. But then, if it was just a minor thing by the time the four months have gone by, chances are it can heal over.
    I didn't want to agree to a year. You can't know the feeling I had after having had this history of failures behind me. By God, I didn't want to get involved with another failure. But you can't get involved with a winner either unless you keep trying. . . . So I figured you couldn't tell for sure what it would be like living with a person until you live with them. And in six months' time, you sure as hell can tell. So that's why I picked six months, not a year. Jeez, imagine a year of hell, if you didn't need to.

You see, a contract to me is—I don't know if the word to use is *sacred,* but a contract to me is—by God, it's, I guess *sacred* is the thing to say. For me to break the contract, God, it tears me up. I give my word and my word's my contract. . . . I guess it was Robert Service who said: "A promise made is a debt unpaid."

Jane also believes in the contract. We both take it seriously. We're still on six-month contracts. But it has worked out well enough that we think of it somewhat more seriously as a long-term relationship. . . . We still have our agreement and to give thirty days' notice so the other person can get ready for it. But if it ever came to that, we would both take the six-month deadline seriously. If we got mad at each other in the first month of the newest contract, we would both feel obligated to stick out for the other five months.

Now they celebrate the day they renewed their contract as their anniversary.

PAUL: It's not a formal ceremony. We picked the equinox date so it'd be easy to remember, the first day of spring and first day of fall. We are both very much aware of it. It's kind of like a meek celebration, but we don't throw a party. . . .

And I will do things, slyly sometimes—like one time I put a notice in the paper, something to the effect that: "This date of our sixth contract, I'm finding it more difficult to keep from telling you I love you." Things like that.

Things started nicely between them and continue so. Still, those first few contracts brought much stress. Jane had an adult child by her previous marriage and Paul had two from his first marriage. There were some resentments and misunderstandings.

JANE: Well, neither of us is wildly fond of the other one's children but . . . it's not a source of any great conflict. . . . In the beginning my daughter was jealous. Someone was replacing her father, of whom she was fond. And she was not in such a good place herself. She was young. She tended to be snooty about it.

She didn't show her face for two months. I told her I was going to the hospital and I never heard one word from her for two solid months. Not even a phone call or a note. And she was used to dropping in periodically on a weekend. . . . I think she didn't like Paul very well and I don't think she approved of her mother behaving like that. . . . But things are fine now.

Paul's son and daughter are more conspiratorial. They approved of his dating and abetted his relationship with Jane.

Both Jane and Paul were encouraged by the early days of their relationship. They tried to avoid the sore spots that were still sensitive from previous attachments. Jane insisted that Paul call her if he was going to be late from work, because her last husband had stood her up all the time.

JANE: I had a lot of insecurities about "What time are you coming home?" I don't care what time, but if you say a specific time, then either come or call. He had to get used to that. But he got very good at it. He understood it was a real problem: the business of coming home and expecting somebody, and then sitting around and waiting hours and hours and they don't show and don't call. I couldn't deal with it, and so he's considerate.

Time has proved their compatibility. They synchronize their activities (she is active in local politics; he spends time at sports and with his children) and they spend most weekends together, sometimes with family. They talk a lot.

PAUL: We may be somewhat different from average people in that, my God, we talk over everything that bugs us. And nothing left to chew over that bugs us. Seems to me, if there's one thing that makes it work out well, that's the thing bigger than anything else.

Even so, they don't feel they have enough time together. Both work long full days, and they complain about their stresses at work. Jane feels work puts "pressure" on their relationship.

JANE: I would like our relationship to have more leisure to it, instead of a lot of outside pressure. Time to stay at home and to do things, and to go out and do things. Not enough time. One of the signs of approaching old age is that we feel time is running out.

PAUL: I think work takes too much time away from us. I'm trying to convince my boss of that! No luck. He sort of hinted that if I didn't like it, I could lump it. . . . I tried to tell him I don't need all the money I'm making. I can do fine on four days a week, but he doesn't want it that way.

They adjust, like most people: They put up with the situation and plan for better days. Household work is something they *can* control, however, and they do. *Very* equally. Or they assign chores to someone else.

PAUL: This is an E.R.A. household. She cooks, because she is an excellent cook and likes to cook and I hate to cook. If I were living by myself, I would eat almost anything raw . . . and consequently I'm a good salad maker. So I make salad. People rave about it! . . . Detergents bother her, so to keep her hands out of the dishwater, I do the dishes. . . . Someone comes in once every two weeks and gives the place a good housecleaning, and the rest of the time we each try and be a little bit neat. . . . We both grocery-shop. She doesn't like to do it alone, so I go along to keep her company most of the time. This I don't particularly like, but, well, I can put up with that.

JANE: Well, work around the house is easy. He does most of it! He doesn't like to cook even more than he doesn't like to do dishes, so that worked out very lucky. . . . The cleaning lady had been coming long before he was here. . . . He launders more because I hate the basement. We each pretty much have our own chores. We help each other when it seems easy or necessary or both, and cooperate as much as we can. . . .

We both had the feeling, since we both worked, that we should equally share in the regular routine day-to-day work.

Paul is very proud that they share equally in the management of the house.

PAUL: Jane is political and she isn't gonna take that doggone backseat role that women have traditionally taken. . . . She pretty much lets you know she expects to be treated like an equal. And she doesn't ask for any quarter. She doesn't expect to give any and she doesn't expect to ask for any. . . . I think that's fair, the way it should be. I think women have been the underdog in the past and it isn't right. There's no reason for it except I think generally they were physically weaker than men, and men put it over on 'em in the past. . . . Your father did it, so you do it—that sort of generation thing.

This is a new style of behavior for Paul. His other relationships were "traditional."

PAUL: No one else ever let me know that she wanted it this way. You know, lots of these women find strength in weakness. Like those women in Florida trying to defeat the Equal Rights Amendment. They know they'll lose more than they'll gain.

They prize their independence and, like most of our cohabitors, make it the most consistent theme of their relationship. *Everything* is equal. Some things, like money, are also separate.

PAUL: We have separate accounts and we each have our own stuff. We have an agreement that I pay so much a month toward the house and we split our grocery purchases. Jane is the bookkeeper and she tells me how much to write a check for at the end of the month.

Despite this orderly arrangement, money remains their number one area of disagreement. Keeping things equal, while still getting to do what you want to do, is a common problem among non-pooling cohabitors.

JANE: We are both free to spend money, without consulting. . . . We have mild disagreements about it. . . . Our major disagreement comes because he's something of a tightwad and just hates spending money on some things I enjoy spending money on, particularly clothing and eating in restaurants, which he hates. We get some rather hostile feelings about that issue sometimes. We work it out . . . sometimes my way, sometimes his. It comes up about once a week.

Paul recognizes the difficulty and acknowledges some of Jane's points:

PAUL: The thing we disagree most on is on spending money. I'm much more apt to pinch a dollar . . . like for example, I don't like to go to a damn restaurant where I gotta pay fifteen dollars or so for a dinner. I think it's a rip-off and she doesn't mind it. She tries to work it out by going to restaurants with somebody else. She'd be much more in favor of an expensive vacation, but again I'm the old tightwad, see, the old "hoot-mon" thing going on. But she's prevailed, and we've taken an expensive vacation, and after it's been all over, I really dug it. . . . A year later you forget about the price. You got the best thing you could get.

Their disagreements about money are kept to a minimum because Paul respects and trusts Jane and believes she will be fair with him.

PAUL: Jane is a very unusual person in that she is so goddamn fair, she's got scruples to the extreme. She wouldn't pick up a dollar if she thought it was somebody else's.

Now that they are getting older, they both worry about how to maintain the independence they admire in each other.

PAUL: We are quite independent from each other, yet we are also dependent on each other in certain ways. Jane has interests I don't have, and I have certain interests she doesn't have. But there is a little matter of physical dependency that's come up gradually in the past year or so. My hearing has gotten worse, and I am depending on her ears. . . . Her eyes have gotten worse in the past year, so she's depending on me more for eyes. So I drive her sometimes, especially at night, and she very often uses the telephone for me. . . .

I'm much more aware now that I feel more responsibility for taking her places because of her eyesight. And that rubs me a little, because one of the things I particularly found attractive in Jane was her independence, and I like a person to be independent.

He doesn't want to be dependent either.

PAUL: You know, I'm sixty years old. I've got to be considering retirement—before-I-get-kicked-out sort of thing. And yet I don't feel—as long as I'm physically able to keep going, I don't want one hundred percent retirement. I think it'd kill me.

Jane feels the same way.

JANE: We never talk about ending the relationship. He's more inclined to talk about not wanting to be a burden on me. . . . We talk about retirement. But we haven't made final decisions about what retirement really means. . . . Right now there's no reason why both of us shouldn't work. I would not want to be financially dependent on him by staying home and not working when he was, and I was able to work.

They may fret a bit over something, but they rarely argue and disagreements are usually over quickly.

JANE: We discuss things back and forth, back and forth. . . . Often it happens on the way to work and of course it is terminated very abruptly when we get there, because I have to go. It's a very convenient way to end it, because by the time we see each other again, we're no longer tense and irritable. . . . We don't stay mad.

We compromise. Nobody wins. I mean, if one person loses, we both lose anyway. So we don't try to win.

So we compromise. If I want him to go somewhere he's not enthused about, it's sort of: "If I go with you there, you'll go with me to the other place." Or, "If you want me to go with you to that game, then you take me out to dinner first."

They have learned to be good negotiators and are both pleased with the results of their give-and-take. But they have not moved toward marriage. In this respect, they are true "ideological" cohabitors.

PAUL: I think Jane could talk me into marriage sooner than I could talk her. But I still have a lot of reservations. We know the pros and cons. Financially, with the income we both make, if we'd have been married last year it would have cost us forty-two hundred dollars more! . . .

Now, though, as we approach retirement, it's going to be more advantageous to be married. Her union benefits and my union benefits . . . We both get spouse medical benefits if we marry.

We get some advantages, but I don't know. This was not a trial to see whether we would want to get married. After all, what would be our reason for getting married at that time or this time? What's the reason? Why do people get married? They get married so they can live together. Hell, we're living together. We don't have to get married to do it. When I was a kid you had to get married—not anymore.

But Paul is adamant about Jane's status as a partner. He will tolerate no disrespect to her because of their unconventional living arrangement.

PAUL: I would not let anybody treat us in any way inferior to the being-married treatment. Like a couple of weeks ago they had a retirement dinner for one of the employees that I work with, and Jane was invited with me the same way other fellows' wives were invited. If they hadn't of invited her, and cut her out, I'd a told 'em what to do with their invitation. They know we're living together and, by God, they're gonna treat us as equal to any other married couple.

Part of Paul and Jane's antagonism to marriage evolves from their rejection of the rules of monogamy. It is Paul's belief that possessiveness would be antithetical to their relationship.

PAUL: I don't believe, if you really love someone, you can feel jealousy. It's alien to love, even though I didn't think this way as a kid.

If someone were making a big play for her, it hopefully would make her feel like a very valuable person and that's a good feeling to have. I should get mad because they're giving her a good feeling? I mean it's crazy.

They are free, but each feels some restraint.

JANE: Either of us is free to do pretty much what he or she wants to. We tend to be monogamous . . . but there's no pressure to do so. We're just free to do it if the other person is comfortable with it.

Paul considers honesty their most important rule. Their understanding is based on mutual consideration, trust, and openness.

PAUL: We just gotta be honest with one another. The traditional fella says—and I'll quote one of the fellas I work with—"There's no sin in cheatin' on your wife. The only sin is if she finds out about it." And it's a one-way role, of course. To me, the sin, if we could call it a sin, would be if one of us was hiding it from the other. If I had a sexual fling and I was concealing it, I would feel guilt. And I would feel guilt if I were having a good time with someone else and wasn't able to give her a good time too. I would be stealing something from her.

Their sex life has slowed down. They have sex about once a week, but they impute the change to different causes. Paul thinks it's his fault because he's older, because he's so "goddamned tired from my work," and also because he feels he's been less "horny." Jane thinks it is mostly psychological. She is unconcerned, however; he still wants sex more than she does and she is satisfied with their sex life together. Neither one refuses the other, although Paul says he will not initiate sex unless she acts very interested. He says he knows she'd "go along with it" but prefers that she "really want it." As for initiation, he says it's difficult to tell.

PAUL: Who really knows who initiates it? A little play is made and a little play comes back. Maybe more often than not I take the first aggressive step towards it. But before that, there may be some subtle invitation or something.

They are both proud of being able to take care of themselves and relieved to have escaped past marriages that each found debilitating. In Paul's case, his second marriage was a misjudged search for affection. His first wife was a fine woman who didn't like sex or physical affection of any kind. She refused his overtures constantly and he felt like a "sex fiend." So when he met a woman who was, in his words, a "sexpot," he "completely overlooked everything else." And that was a mistake; he and his second wife had very little in common. By the time he met Jane he had realized he needed both sexual compatibility and sound personal attributes.

Jane was escaping an abusive marriage. Her husband kept other women behind her back, took advantage of her financially, was dishonest—and, ultimately, rejecting. She was very hurt and felt safer if she stayed as independent as possible. Only after seven years together can either Paul or Jane start to take real pleasure in their true "partnership."

PAUL: I find satisfaction now in the fact that the whole is much greater than the sum of its parts. The partnership is much greater than either of us alone.

Jane draws comfort from their absence of conflict; Paul is reassured by the feeling he has for her.

PAUL: I often get a very high feeling, being with Jane. How can you describe a feeling, for God's sake? Like—it's a high. It's a great feeling that, dammit, everything's just right.

And Paul believes that at last he can trust his feelings.

PAUL: We've had years of experience. Good and bad. How can a young couple make a good choice with no experience behind them? Honest to God, that's amazing. We have had experience.

Finally, they both feel that living together without marriage gives their relationship a special advantage.

PAUL: We always know we'll be together because we want to be together and not because any law says we've got to be. That's a big thing, I think.
JANE: Thank you. I would have said that if you hadn't.

They both give great credit to their contract and would like to see other cohabiting couples adopt a similar arrangement.

PAUL: A young couple did come to us for advice, and sort of interviewed us to set something up for themselves. And they almost did like we, except they wrote their contract out and put a lot of details in it. And then they paid absolutely no attention to their contract when they busted up. These were people who didn't know how to honor a contract.

Paul and Jane were full of advice for others—especially Paul. Jane felt that strength came from communication. Paul thought it important not to be misled by sexual infatuation. And important not to marry, at least not for a while. The consequence of breaking a lifetime promise was too great a burden of guilt. Finally, much to Jane's delight, he cautioned all men to treat their partners as equals.

PAUL: Remember that people are equal. The old chauvinist crap is not just old-fashioned, it is false. Nobody is superior because he happens to be male.
JANE: Statements like that will get you everywhere.

Jane and Paul are ideological cohabitors inching toward marriage as time, trust, and convenience nudge them. They are learning to need and depend on each other, even as each grants to the other real and symbolic freedoms and responsibilities. Jane needs and appreciates Paul's respect for her independence and equality; Paul can love her because his sexual needs are not ignored or restricted and because he knows she is equipped to take care of herself. These are two people scarred by past relationships but healing in the unaccustomed warmth of good treatment. Independence in financial affairs, competence at earning a living, and sexual leeway have not in this case pushed the couple apart, but rather have allowed them to grow together. The needs of aging have encouraged tenderness, consideration, even dependency. If marriage does happen, it will come as a natural outgrowth of their feelings for each other and not as the trap or convention they both fear.

# Rick and Bonnie

Cohabiting couples are often young; therefore many of their professional and personal plans are still developing. They are unwilling to commit to each other because they don't really know what they want for themselves. Bonnie and Rick demonstrate the difficulty of making plans when life is in a state of flux.

They also illustrate the dynamics of unbalanced commitment—when one partner is manifestly more in love, more attached than the other. Ideological statements about independence cannot hide the fact that it is easy to grant freedom to one's partner when one is not sure about the relationship.

Bonnie and Rick live in an old building that in their eyes has a lot of personality. Their parents consider it a tumbledown wreck. It is wood frame, with balconies that run across each unit to the next, so that one can walk the entire length of the building and see the back of each of the twenty apartments. The balconies extend over the water on pilings which are probably not as rickety as they look. The apartments are tiny but are considered a great find by people (usually in their twenties and thirties) who clamor to live there. There is a certain group spirit about the place. During the summer everyone gathers on the dock and all the occupants become a community.

Bonnie is twenty-five and Rick is twenty-seven. They have been living together at the "Hacienda" for two years. Neither has ever been married. They are both extremely attractive—Rick might even be described as dazzling. He is of medium height with very blond hair and pale-blue eyes and he flashes an engaging smile. Bonnie might almost be the negative of his photograph. She is about his height, but with dark hair and dark eyes. He is manager of an import-export firm and also has credits toward a master's degree in business. She works as a technician at a hospital and has applied to several medical schools for the coming fall.

They met while working at a restaurant in Aspen during a summer break from school. Their first attraction was physical.

RICK: The first thing I was attracted to were her eyes. Brown eyes. That did it right there.

BONNIE: Oh, I just thought he was real handsome. It was really funny because I was trying to be real low-key, and all the women I worked with knew and they were all kidding me about it. And he did not know. I thought I was being so obvious, but I was playing it so cool that he thought I wasn't interested in him at all. Finally he sort of said something about going out and then dropped it. . . . I finally took the ball into my own hands and I asked him if he would like to go out for a drink, and he said yes. It was a long weekend, and three days later we went back to work together.

For both it was a "rapid beginning." As Bonnie puts it, "a delicate combination of love and lust." Rick was lonely, but Bonnie believes it happened because she wasn't looking for "just anyone."

BONNIE: I spent a long time without a mate or a serious relationship. . . . About a month before that, I had a bad experience and I sort of resolved: *Man, I don't need men. Forget it. I'm going to be a strong woman on my own.* And of course, when you're not looking, you get along just fine. And he did not come on real strong. He was just a person that I felt I had a lot in common with. He was real interesting to me . . . easygoing . . . fun to be with, and I knew it was something real special. He just wasn't a one-night stand.

They started spending all their time together. They both felt serious immediately—which scared them enough to take precautions against moving ahead too quickly.

BONNIE: After about three weeks we talked about living together, and we thought: *This is just too fast and we can't do this.* And we said, Okay, let's have a week and don't mention it, and give time to think about it and not feel pressure. And at the end of the week, we had rented a place and signed a lease for six months.

Rick remembers that their decision to live together was based on many practical considerations.

RICK: It was real quick. . . . In a lot of ways it seemed to be almost convenient timing. We both needed a place to live; we seemed to like each other quite a bit, more than usual; we were together a lot daily, getting along on a day-to-day basis. . . . It seemed like a good thing to try. So we did. . . .
There were other things too. We'd both come from a time of not having had someone to care about for a while and then found someone we really cared about and felt mutual closeness to. It would

be more lucrative—we both felt that we would be getting as much as we were giving. We didn't feel something was going to be taken away from one another.

They felt they were in love, but they wanted to proceed cautiously:

RICK: We both thought, *This is a nice situation with a lot of satisfaction to be gained.* But we didn't think long-term. I try not to think that way. I don't quite know why—that I have to defend myself against something. . . .

Nonetheless, they were wrapped up in each other. Their days together were so intense that they didn't even see friends.

BONNIE: We told each other we loved each other in a couple of weeks. . . . We were laying in bed talking, real rational almost, on how we were feeling and what was happening. . . . We were scared, but real positive and wonderful.

The first six months were fairly easy. Bonnie's parents disapproved of her living with someone she was not married to, but did not give her a hard time. Both sets of friends approved the match. But since neither had lived with anyone before, they both had adjustments to make—especially Rick:

RICK: A lot of it was just being forced to consider someone else and their needs on a day-to-day basis, whether it be staying up late drinking or having the dishes done at a certain time, or just two people being forced to be in the same space for a large part of the time and having no one else to balance or rotate the tension. . . . I was an only child and started to live alone a long time ago, and started to get used to and very confident of being male. And so it was difficult for me to have someone around physically. And that, I would have to deal with.

Now, it's too little time together, rather than too much, that poses a problem. As a couple, they live a "separate," as opposed to a "companionate," life.

BONNIE: I probably spend the smallest amount of my time with him. We actually have to have dates—schedule our time together. We both have a lot of things going on and we make a real conscious effort to have friends outside our relationship. . . . So, I see him in the morning; I see him in the evening when I eat dinner. Of what I call my playtime, [it is] maybe a third or a half. . . . I feel very pressured. I feel like I don't have enough time for anything or anybody.

Even though their free time is precious, individual plans still take precedence over their plans as a couple.

BONNIE: I'd like to go to Europe next year before I go off to medical school. And I think we travel very well and he speaks many languages—but he is adamantly against it. He doesn't like to travel with me. And I get really hurt. He really likes to travel alone. He thinks you are more open to meeting people, and I can understand that, but, gee, how can you go off to Europe for six months without me? How could you really have a good time without me being there? He says he'd suffer through it somehow.

There is little struggle for control between them. Rick allows Bonnie as much leadership as she wants.

RICK: I don't think of relationships in terms of male dominance. I appreciate someone taking charge. . . .
Sometimes you don't feel like making decisions. You'd just as soon come home and say, "Wow, we're going to do this and that." That's fine with me. There's no concern with who's in a position of power.

They contribute approximately the same amount of money to their joint bank account and are generally unconcerned about spending decisions. They are not as casual about housework.

BONNIE: This is one of the few areas we have fights about. I really like to yell and scream it out. Rick is kind of a stoic Northern European, and I get annoyed because he won't fight with me. And the only thing we fight about, nine out of ten times, is housework. It usually happens five days before my period—raging hormones—and I want to take it out on somebody.
The case is just in terms of a dirt-tolerance level. This is a fairly small place. I am very tidy and he isn't, and I really believe he doesn't see that there are cobwebs in the corner or that the stove is turning brown. . . . If I say something like: "The bathroom is so dirty that I'm afraid of getting a social disease," he'll say, "Oh, fine," and he'll be willing to clean it. So we have a little pattern: . . . we decide to do it on a day we're both here, and if I cleaned the fridge last time he'll do it this time. But he doesn't notice the way I do. And I get uptight that he doesn't, and he thinks I'm just too uptight on the subject.

Rick is consistent in his notion that work should be equitably apportioned and feels he does his share, if not more. But not according to traditional male/female assignments.

RICK: We sat and talked about how to avoid traditional roles. Having seen mothers strapped into the kitchen, and trying to avoid that and the influences it produced . . . it was a very conscious effort. . . .
Our only problem is that she gets obsessed with doing things right now rather than having it done tomorrow, but otherwise we alternate. I cook, especially if there's company. It's fifty-fifty on laundry, and she's a better mechanic than I am. She can adjust the valves of the Fiat, et cetera, so I just let her do it.

Rick's reaction to conflict is to withdraw and Bonnie's is to confront it head-on. They quarrel very little—largely because Rick will do almost anything to avoid a fight.

RICK: Bonnie usually initiates some kind of argument because she is feistier than I am. I am more laissez-faire. I'd just as soon keep things on an even plane and not get too upset about things. She would initiate through verbal attacks about something I did not do that should have been done. I'll say, "I had something else to do," or, "You missed it," or, "I did it."

We go from the particulars to generalities—"Well, you never do it when I want to do it"—and from that into discussion or an accusatory phrase where we both level at one another. And we try and zap each other psychologically: "Well, you are this way."

"No, no, you always try to say that because *you* are."

There is never any yelling or throwing things. Eventually I will storm off, leaving the apartment, to kind of cool off. I don't like to get too emotional. She does. She doesn't get any satisfaction out of it. I won't fight . . . and I think that makes her madder. So, at times I use it as a tool. At times I just don't want to be bothered. . . .

Sometimes I just try and cool it down and say, "What are we talking about? Is it really that important?" . . . We're hardly ever mad for more than half an hour. There has never been any bickering that goes on to, say, maybe the next day. We go our separate ways and come back and everything will be okay. . . .

Sometimes I think our relationship suffers from too much tranquillity and never any attempt to stir things up. And a lot of disagreement comes from that. We start with a real issue and it'll be resolved by affection, like: "Come on" . . . and we'll touch and bring it closer—not two people on sides of the room, but actually sit and talk and touch each other. And it goes away.

Bonnie feels they don't argue *enough,* and when they do, they adopt *his* style.

BONNIE: We hardly ever have arguments. When we do, Rick always discusses things gradually and rationally and I have to use the same means. If there is an out-and-out argument, I usually pick it because I am in a testing mood and I want to pick a fight. Usually I say something real nasty to goad him into a really hot verbal feud.

I'll say something like: "I'm not here to be your maid," and he'll have to rise to defend himself. We knock heads for a while and we have fun making up. . . .

I love to fight. I would just as soon throw a few pots and pans around and I'll feel fine. But it makes him feel uncomfortable, so he'll work it out by saying, "I'm sorry. It was a real bummer." He'll be the bigger of the two and come forward and apologize.

It genuinely upsets Rick to argue. The day after, he says, he feels "melancholy," as if he has a "hangover." Bonnie is in better spirits, but it takes him some time to shake off the effects of any confrontation. He starts to worry about their "different makeups" and her "abrasiveness." She manages to be upset about only the issue at hand.

Their personality differences emerge when she is with his friends.

> RICK: Sometimes I get a little uneasy. Bonnie is real brash. It's not that I think she should be very coy and unassuming; it's just that people sometimes have trouble relating to her when they first get to know her. . . . I'm real gregarious, get along with people very well, and to see her putting people off immediately and having trouble relating bothers me at times. I think she could be more thoughtful, more diplomatic at times, but she maintains that's the way she is and that's the way it goes. . . . No real big deal, but it does bother me at times.

Rick may be particularly sensitive to Bonnie's manner with people because he has known most of his close friends since grade school or junior high. He has a close-knit group of male friends, some of whom Bonnie has found uninteresting, even unpleasant. Naturally he is affected by what they think of her, as well as by her opinion of them.

There is also the question of how their social life with others will be conducted. Right now, they have very different jobs, and when they come home they need different things from each other.

> RICK: She might seem to get a little sore at me because I am more introspective and don't mind sitting at home reading. I work in an office and I see people all day. I have a lot of friends—customers who come in, and we chat over products, et cetera. That kind of takes care of my social life in a way. But she works in a place where she doesn't socialize that much, and she'd like to do more together and outside. And we don't do it.

Day-to-day work issues come up, but the big concern is the development of Bonnie's career and what it means for the continuation of their life as a couple. Bonnie is applying to medical schools and it looks as if they are coming to a genuine emotional crossroads.

> BONNIE: In the last few months a major thing has come into the picture, which is that I'm applying to medical school next year. . . .
> There is no given that Rick will come with me. I was going through this arduous process of trying to figure where I can go and what I'm going to do. He was very encouraging, but he never said, "Why don't you try and apply to U.C.L.A?" for example, "because I would like to try living in the L.A. area." He didn't give me any input. And if he had given me some, I would have tried hard to work it out with him rather than to forge ahead on my own. . . . He wouldn't have any voice in the decision. And that was upsetting me. His response is that it is real difficult for him right now to decide at this point in his life what he wants to be doing a year from now. . . .
> I have to choose now. I could be just fat, happy, and complacent. I know that I would not be happy to do that, and I've been talking about going to medical school for the past three years.

And if I'm going to do it, I feel I have to now . . . but it hurts me to think I might have to move away from Rick. It's hard.

Rick still doesn't know what he wants to do.

RICK: She wants to go to medical school, probably in the fall, and I don't know if I want to go. It's difficult for me to talk about. It's like planning in advance, and I don't know how to do it. It's very abstract and it's very difficult.

The possibility of Bonnie's move has brought the question of their future more sharply into focus—and made Bonnie tense and uncertain.

BONNIE: Sometimes I think, *Damn it, don't you love me? How can you love me thousands of miles away? How can you survive?* And I think to a degree it's not that he doesn't love me; it's an indication that he's a very independent person and he doesn't need anybody for his happiness. Obviously he is happy or he would have left. I guess I'll just have to accept it: That's the way he is.

The proposed move has forced both of them to examine their personal goals. Bonnie wonders if Rick is capable of committing himself to a relationship.

BONNIE: I think he has some questions in his mind if he really belongs in this kind of relationship. We discussed this recently, that in his mind he kind of lives with his suitcase packed. And it's a mental thing, but he liked to think he has that kind of freedom. Both of his sisters have married the men they lived with, and it's kind of a joke that Rick is still the free agent. And he likes that.

Bonnie was a free agent herself for a while, but she loves Rick enough to consider marriage, if he wanted it.

BONNIE: At one point of life I was adamantly against. At this point of my life, I don't care. I think we're as married as a lot of married people. But now it would be okay for me to be married. It would not be okay with Rick.

She has radically modified her views:

BONNIE: I was a very political feminist: open marriages, liberal marriages. It was an institution, like church and state, and oppressive to women. But I stopped that mind-set. I might as well face it: The relationship I have is pretty married, although not being married. I do think we would live a little differently if we were married. I think society defines you in terms of your label.

I guess I'm really upset over couple-ism. I get really upset when people say, "We like our eggs over easy." You could say: "Harold and Jane both like their eggs over easy," but then it's two individuals. I think that's very important for me to maintain.

Rick knows that the question of marriage looms in the background, but it doesn't tempt him. Nor does he think Bonnie is pressuring him.

RICK: Once in a while we go to weddings. It's painfully obvious that we're not married. But it's not like she's tugging on my shoulder saying, "Gee, we could be like that."

But he does acknowledge that he may not be ready for the kind of relationship Bonnie wants.

RICK: We've recently had to sound out each other about what our commitments are. . . . We don't seem to be on the same level—whether our relationship or our work is the most important. We don't discuss the future that much. It's so sensitive . . . I back away from discussion even when she thinks I shouldn't. It probably would be better if we discussed it more, but I prefer things to be an even succession of events. And to discuss our relationship would dig up things. I think I'm a coward about it at times. . . . I read some survey where it said married couples only talk about things about twenty-eight minutes of a week. In view of that, I think we do plenty of talking.

Occasionally, he will air his doubts about their relationship to a close friend.

RICK: I'll sometimes talk with a close male friend. Sometimes I think I might like better living alone and seeing several other women at the same time. . . . I spout off to friends—just letting off steam, not necessarily my real desires or wants. They say, "Oh, yeah, a living-together relationship isn't easy, let's have another beer."

This ambivalence, combined with their ideological commitment to independence, is reflected in their sex life. They have an understanding that non-monogamy is acceptable. Rick supports this view, yet he is monogamous. It is unclear whether Bonnie really does believe in non-monogamy, yet she has been non-monogamous in this relationship. Rick believes in the *idea* of non-monogamy despite a basically monogamous personality. He is against possessiveness even when that belief works to his disadvantage.

RICK: I took Swedish for a while, and the Swedish word for jealousy is translated as "black sickness"—and that sums it up for me. It's really negative. So I make an effort to get away from it.
I'm totally monogamous. In the abstract, we say that monogamy is not something we're really suited to. We should be able to have relationships with other people that might enrich yourself and our relationship together. We agree on that. When it came down to the real day-to-day—a sexual relationship with someone else while still carrying on here—ahem, it could be tough to handle. It's better in the abstract.

BONNIE: I had this nice affair this summer. . . . We talked about it. "What do you think if I do this?" And, "Do you want to sleep with him?" And, "Yes, I think I'd like to, and how do you feel about that?" . . .

He was totally nonthreatened, and his attitude, in a nutshell, was: "If you're loving and you're good to me, and the quality of our relationship doesn't diminish, then I can't ask any more of you."

But very different motives underlie Bonnie's feelings about non-monogamy. Rick may be able to tolerate it because his commitment isn't firm; Bonnie, on the other hand, approves of it in part theoretically, and in part because she needs non-monogamy to keep from feeling too dependent on a person who isn't forthcoming with the kind of commitment she wants.

BONNIE: The affair was real good for my ego. . . . Several months before I had this affair, Rick and I had a discussion about our relationship, and I think I was the one who started to think it was a long-term monogamous relationship. Rick said it wasn't, and he pointed out to me that he wouldn't be, and that I should not be thinking of it in those terms. It was then I realized that I needed to do something so that I would not be quite so dependent on him. That he was not totally dependent on me, and that I shouldn't be on him, for my own mental health. Maybe it was a way of proving to myself that I had my own life.

Bonnie admits that she would be jealous if Rick were non-monogamous. She says she is a bit mystified at his complaisance.

None of this seems to affect their everyday life or their sex life. They have sex about once a week and they feel that while they initiate sex almost equally, it is Rick who is more interested more of the time. Bonnie thinks work, or lack of time and a general lack of energy, accounts for the decline in their sex life. They both say that sex together is almost always satisfying.

In fact, when Rick and Bonnie talk about themselves as a couple they sound generally happy with the relationship. Rick likes Bonnie's "self-confidence and her affection and her love," and Bonnie thinks Rick is "fun to be around," and looks forward to the time she spends with him.

BONNIE: It's also great that Rick is a real secure person, not a typical male. He is not threatened, not possessive, and a real . . . leveling force . . . and able to interject humor.

They agreed on their best common attribute:

BONNIE: Communication is the most important thing in my life. . . . I can say anything to Rick. And, hopefully, listen to anything. We talk things out and I don't have to apologize for anything stupid. . . . There's a real feeling of openness.

RICK: Yes. It's just something we do. . . . A natural flow of chemistry and interchange . . . It was an intangible thing that moved us together.

*Epilogue:* Communication and chemistry were not enough to save this couple's relationship. Even as we interviewed them we sensed the tenuousness of their bond. Rick had never fully invested in the relationship: He wanted it only for the here and now. Bonnie loved him more than he loved her, and try as she might, she could not inspire possessiveness or attachment in him.

This relationship might have lasted longer if Bonnie did not have ambitious career plans. We learned on our follow-up questionnaire from Bonnie that she had moved in order to attend medical school and Rick had decided not to go with her. The relationship ended then. It was probably for the best, because Bonnie could not get the love she needed from Rick, yet we felt her anguish. At the end of her original interview she had anticipated the loss of Rick:

BONNIE: I give it until May. If I could, I'd spend a much longer time with him. I can't envision not being with him. But it's not realistic. I'll come to terms with it. I'll be real intellectual about it, but emotionally it will be really devastating.

# Stewart and Adrienne

There are couples who, by mutual consent, are in a "trial marriage." In this case, the man has never been married, and the woman is divorced after one marriage. We selected Stewart and Adrienne because they adhere to a rigid "separates" ideology: equal economic responsibility, separate finances, and separate time. They also have very negative feelings about the institution of marriage. Nonetheless, they are moving, grudgingly, toward taking part in the institution they claim to dislike and reject.

We drove up a private drive in a particularly lovely suburban development. The house at the top was made of wood and stone and seemed to spread over two lots. The design was architecturally interesting: the house several stories high in some sections and only one story in others. It looked as if Stewart and Adrienne were its first occupants.

This impression was strengthened when we went inside. The furnishings were spare and Adrienne apologized: They had just moved in and were not yet settled. She still wore the clothes she had worn to work. At twenty-nine, she is tall, trim, and "dressed for success" in a three-piece business suit for her job as a junior executive in a large corporation. Stewart, thirty-two, had come home earlier and had had time to change out of his suit, loosen his tie, and make drinks and coffee for the four of us. He is of medium height, also conservatively well-dressed, and works as a partner in a large accounting firm. While we set up the tape recorder, they fed and tended to their three cats.

They met two years ago when a mutual friend referred Adrienne to Stewart for help with her taxes. She was going through her divorce at the time and needed special advice on the forms.

They were immediately attracted to each other—Adrienne was so excited she spilled her drink all over her tax sheets. They talked and talked and began dating right away.

It was a great feeling for Adrienne. Her marriage of eight years had been deteriorating for a long time and she had "gone through hell" trying to save it. With great difficulty she had decided to divorce and was just starting to go out with men again. She was ready to care for a new person, but a little skittish about becoming too involved. Her marriage had broken up because of her husband's extramarital sexual adventures and she was still feeling hurt and defensive.

Stewart, too, was defensive, but for different reasons:

STEWART: I may have been unconsciously looking for someone to couple with . . . but my pattern is to have close and intense short-lived relationships. On a couple of occasions she called me and I felt a little intruded on, and that was kind of an important time. . . . It was late at night, maybe a month after we met. I was in bed and she freaked me out about something with her last relationship. . . . She needed someone to be there and she asked me to come over. And I didn't really feel like being bothered, but she meant enough to me that I said okay, and one of the things she said was that she loved me. And it kind of freaked me out. I felt crowded by it. . . . I didn't say that at the time, but I think I probably got a little bit more reserved for a period of time.

In the beginning they did many things together: movies, outings, dinner—in general having fun. It took a week for Stewart to respond to Adrienne's first declaration of love. In retrospect, he is glad she pushed the issue.

STEWART: I had a pattern where I didn't expect a lot from the people I was seeing and I didn't want them to expect much of me. . . . Adrienne made it clear from the outset that she had expectations. . . . So I had to reassess my style with Adrienne and I think it was a good thing.

After six months a handsome apartment became available, and Stewart proposed they live together. Soon they were seeing other single friends less and were spending more time together. When they moved in, Stewart made it clear that theirs was "not a premarriage arrangement." Adrienne didn't like that, but she accepted it. Stewart relented and said it would be a "trial marriage, not premarriage"—that is, no guarantees.

> STEWART: At the time I thought I wouldn't want to get married except if we're going to have children—that would be the only reason for marriage.

Even marriage would be thought of as "trial." Like so many male cohabitors we interviewed, Stewart said he "refused to think in terms of a permanent relationship." He just wanted to enjoy what he had on a day-to-day basis. Permanence was too improbable to plan or hope for.

The first six months brought arguments about personal territory and money.

> ADRIENNE: We disagree a lot about money. And how to deal with our finances. I have a lot of hang-ups about money and so does he. I don't want him to think that he is supporting me at all, and he is afraid that he will have to support somebody. And so we always make things incredibly equal. But he makes about twice as much money as I do. . . . It's the only really tense thing between us.

Everything to do with money was and is calculated very carefully, which was emotionally upsetting.

> ADRIENNE: I just hated him saying to me: "You owe me so much." Or me having to go to him and say, "Well, I paid the water bill and you owe me half." I hate that. And Stewart gets it all down on paper. And if I buy something for the house it goes down that I bought that particular item. If he bought it, and if it was something we bought together, it goes down that way. I just thought it was so unemotional to put everything down in numbers on paper like this, and I found it really hard to deal with.
>
> And yet I totally agree with him, because when I split up my apartment with this woman I was living with, we had a terrible time figuring out whose things were whose. She had a bunch of my stuff. And so I think it makes sense to put it all down, and yet I had trouble doing it.
>
> So we finally came to the conclusion that the rent and monthly bills that come in, we'd write checks for them and pay half. And then the food and so forth, we put money in a kitty . . . every payday. And he pays a little more than I do because he eats more. And it worked out all right.

This problem continues even now, not only over everyday expenses but also because of payments for the house.

> ADRIENNE: It comes up every once in a while. In buying this house, all the money was from him and his family. And I had very little money in savings and my family is not helping me out. So sometimes we talk about it as our house, but I think of it as his house.

The house and what it represents, emotionally and financially, have become the focus of Stewart's ambivalence about interdependence and Adrienne's uneasiness about the disparity in their economic resources.

STEWART: It is hard for me to deal with community property. . . . It is hard for me to feel interdependent, even though we are getting more intertwined. . . . But what is mine is mine and what is Adrienne's is hers. Where the common goals are the same it isn't important whether I put in for both, but I am not going to spend money that I earned for something Adrienne wants unless I want it too.

We hold this house as joint tenancy with rights of survivorship: She gets it if I die; I get it if she dies. I put . . . all the money in the down payment. . . . I feel I have to get credit for that if it ever has to be split up. My business or pragmatic or cold-blooded self is very uncomfortable for Adrienne. But I think we have to be clear.

She earns less money than I do. She earns a very decent salary and she is not someone who would take advantage of me or not pay her own way, and I think it is upsetting to her because she does pay her way and feels like I am accusing her of trying to take advantage of me in some way. . . . I had very strong feelings about not wanting the woman I live with to be economically dependent, and I think some of that is based on what I saw in my parents' relationship and how economically dependent it was. What I think I see it did to their relationship . . . I don't like that kind of being taken for granted and expectations of things. I don't want it to be a built-in role that I support Adrienne.

Adrienne understands him, and wants to contribute her fair share. But she finds it hard to do so and is therefore frustrated. Buying the house seemed to spotlight her lesser contribution.

ADRIENNE: When we first talked about the house I was going to attempt to put a third of the money down. . . . because we figured that was proportionally fair, given our salaries . . . but I had very little savings. I was going to borrow from my parents and that caused problems, because I didn't want to compromise myself to get money from my parents. So I couldn't put anything down. . . . And I felt, because I wasn't putting any money down, I couldn't voice an opinion. . . .

Oh, God, did we talk about it. And we got an agreement where I would have some say because he wouldn't have done this alone. . . . I will make a third of the monthly payments and we are going to have a promissory note between the two of us, and if the house ever gets sold, a third of the house is mine and I will pay him a third of the down payment out of the profit of the house.

But it is nonetheless difficult for Adrienne to overcome the emotional aspect of Stewart's financial rules. She genuinely desires to be economically independent and she would like Stewart to understand that.

> ADRIENNE: I have trouble with the "I owe you—you owe me." . . . It's like all we are is a business partnership.
>
> I hate it—and I'm the one more likely to get taken advantage of. . . . I hate the fact that somebody might owe me money and so I'll pay for things. And Stewart is exactly the opposite; he doesn't want to have to pay for one thing more than what he has decided to pay for. Although he is very generous, it doesn't come out that way. . . .
>
> I think he has realized that every woman in the world isn't going to be his mother dependent on his father. Totally, for everything. That there are women now who have their own careers and their own money. And he is not going to get stuck supporting someone and have that . . . burden. . . . He has come a bit more to the middle.

The couple tries to "share" in all realms of their life. They consult each other on almost every decision. They check with each other before making commitments, purchases, or plans. If they have trouble agreeing on something, they work out their difference with a game of skill and chance: They play Scrabble, and the winner gets to decide what they do.

They apportion the housework evenly. They sat down and consciously divided things up according to who hated to do what, making sure that neither had too many truly odious tasks.

Stewart cooks all the weekday breakfasts. Adrienne cooks weekend breakfasts. They do weekday dinners together and she cooks for company because she likes to. Stewart makes a serious effort to do precisely his half.

> STEWART: I try hard to do my share and no less than half a percent more. I don't want to do more than my share. Whereas Adrienne doesn't mind filling in the slack. . . . We complement each other.

Their relationship works for them but is never without some conflict. Stewart believes in conflict.

> STEWART: I enjoy disagreeing. . . . I might even cop to the fact that when we haven't disagreed about anything for a while, I will often find things to disagree about. Just because I enjoy the process of disagreeing. But I honestly don't think Adrienne and I disagree strongly about any important issues. Maybe whether or not to have children, but we're not discussing that now.

Stewart feels it is important to talk everything out, and he believes it essential always to tell the truth.

> STEWART: Adrienne might tell a little lie and I would not say anything or exactly what I felt. . . . Being honest or dishonest is very important to me. . . . I am a confrontive type of person. Adrienne is not and I try and push her to be confrontive. . . . Sometimes that is uncomfortable. . . .

Adrienne, I feel, takes the position that all I ever talk about is how I feel—me, me, me. . . . I'll take the position that until you talk about that, there is no way to talk about how we feel about anything. It is real important to me that if there are two people there, two points of view get expressed. . . . It is a vital thing that I know how she feels about something. A lot of times Adrienne will deny having a feeling about something, and when we talk about it, it will come out that it hadn't reached the scale that she wanted to take a position on it. And I'll get uptight because I feel that everything is important enough.

Adrienne feels that even though Stewart's style of communication is not her style, it is a valuable one and benefits their relationship.

ADRIENNE: When I was married before, I did not know how to fight. . . . If a disagreement came up and it got hot, it would be dropped. I couldn't deal with the emotional part. . . .

When Stewart and I first started to disagree, Stewart would actually force me to fight. . . . He would bring it out and he wouldn't let me say, "Oh, I'm not going to discuss it." . . . I would get to the point where I was yelling and screaming. But it is so much better because I get it out.

Among the points they have yet to resolve are their obligations to family and friends.

STEWART: I don't want her family to think of me as family. I really want them to like me and to have affection for me, but I don't want them to take me for granted either. . . . Her parents stayed with us on a trip, and that was okay although it made me a little nervous. But her mother brought a kitten that wasn't quite house-trained, and I said, "I can't deal with that," and I left. . . . This is sort of a symbolic thing but was how I felt. . . . It bothered them a little that I left.

I set limits with my own family, and maybe Adrienne has learned something about setting limits.

Adrienne understands and accepts Stewart's feelings.

ADRIENNE: There were a number of birthdays in his family this month. And I wouldn't send any birthday cards. And I knew they were coming up, but I wasn't going to take it on myself because it is his family. . . . I think that was wise. . . . His parents asked him why he didn't send a card, and he dealt with it on his own. No one looked to me for it and I'm glad they didn't.

They do see his friends more than they see hers, but it has not caused contention. He prefers his friends to hers, and she doesn't fight him.

Sometimes a few of his old friends include old girl friends. Though at first Adrienne was jealous, as her relationship with Stewart stabilized she became less worried. But both of them can be jealous and possessive—even though Stewart feels they ought not to be.

> STEWART: I have said, "I'm not going to tell you that I'm not going to be sexually involved with anyone because of our relationship. I may not tell you about it, but I want you to know that when I have to make a decision, I want to make that decision because of how I feel—not because of how you feel." . . .
>
> Adrienne doesn't talk about her attraction to other people and I don't about mine, but somehow mine get talked about and hers don't. . . . I don't want her to feel like I couldn't be jealous or that I want her to act out any other relationships with other men. I want to keep it ambiguous. I am not sure how to explain it. . . . I don't want to decide that I am never going to have a sexual involvement with a woman besides Adrienne for the rest of my life . . . and yet at the same time I feel that our relationship is understood to be monogamous. . . . I don't think it is a good idea if I were to get sexually involved with another woman.

Part of Stewart's ambivalence comes from past experience. He encouraged his last important girl friend to "find out what sex with other people was about." She did, and he really "freaked out."

His ambivalence has not gone unnoticed by Adrienne; she has called him on it.

> ADRIENNE: He told me, if I was going to see a lover or whatever, that he did not want to know about it. . . . And he went away and thought about it and realized that he was lying to himself. That he would not want me to do that.

Adrienne has no ambivalences. She wants a monogamous relationship:

> ADRIENNE: We talk about that a lot. And I feel it's very important. After everything that I have been through, and the way society is, and the way I have seen people, and things I have tried, when it comes right down to it . . . I don't believe I can deal with infidelity, and I told him that. . . . You go through the philosophical discussion—oh, one night it might happen, but when we get down to it emotionally we know it would be hard to deal with. . . .
>
> We sort of came to an agreement that right now neither of us has any interest—and we both feel it is not good, and yet neither one of us will take the stand and say that we will never do that. It is not a promise that we made to one another that we know it is very important to the other not to. . . . I do tell him that I would be absolutely furious if I ever found out that it happened. And I might even leave.

Still, Stewart keeps the discussion open-ended. He thinks there's some benefit to that, an additional modicum of control.

> STEWART: I was sort of expecting the "don't count on me not to have

any." And yet I didn't want the kind of understanding that later, if she were to decide to want to, she could turn around and say: "You told me it didn't matter to you." . . . I didn't want things I saw early in the relationship to come back and haunt me. So I have modified some of them. . . . Sometimes I say them not because I feel them but because they give me some kind of leverage in a particular situation.

They enjoy their sexual relationship. They seemed especially pleased when we asked about the affection in their relationship.

STEWART: I love it. I really find it nourishing and it brings out a part in me I couldn't have developed on my own.

ADRIENNE: Oh, fantastic. I couldn't ask for anything better. And I have something to compare it to.

Adrienne feels that her marriage suffered most of all from a lack of affection.

ADRIENNE: I wasn't going to compromise on that again. I need to be hugged and held and I need to feel that warmth. And I gave that up when I got married. To the point where I would go and hug my husband and he would just stand there, rigid, until I was done. . . . I don't think I could ever give that up again.

For Stewart and Adrienne, sex is very satisfying. They slept together the first night they dated—something Adrienne had never done before. She surprised herself and thought, *He must be pretty special if I would do that.*

They have sex about once a week, according to Adrienne; two to three times a week, according to Stewart. He initiates sex most of the time. Stewart says they're working on that; he'd like it to be equal.

STEWART: I would like her to feel more comfortable with initiating— as long as I could feel comfortable with expressing a reason not to have it. We are trying to get to the point where Adrienne can initiate it and not feel torn apart if I don't feel like having sex then. And I don't feel pushed.

Stewart doesn't often have to face refusal. It bothers him when it happens—but he feels it is an important "right" for Adrienne.

STEWART: It bothers me at the time, but I have the feeling that I want that right—not to have sex if I don't feel like it. And I feel if I have that right, she has that right. So it bothers me, but not in terms of the relationship—just in terms of not getting what I want at the time I want it.

Sex is mostly reciprocal, except that Stewart doesn't like playing what he calls "the passive role."

STEWART: It has to do with receiving, as opposed to giving, pleasure—with being in control, giving up control.

Both say their sex life has diminished in frequency since they met. Both blame the decline on work, fatigue, and day-to-day tensions. It doesn't worry either of them.

> STEWART: If it is on weekends and we decide to make time, then we do, but sometimes in the rush of things that is hard. . . . If you were able—if work hours were different—if you were able to get home for a siesta in the afternoon . . . it would be a lot more frequent. . . . But lots of times, by the time we go to bed we are ready to go to sleep.

And also, as Stewart says:

> STEWART: The early stuff is based on fantasy. And when you know someone, there isn't the same fantasy about whether they are going to be receptive to you or not, how you are going to feel about that, and when that issue is removed, then you are left with how you feel about having sex.

Stewart and Adrienne feel very good about each other. Even with all their rules and demands for separateness, they are planning to marry.

In the beginning, when Adrienne pressed for some kind of definition of their relationship, Stewart tensed and said it was "working now. As long as it works, fine." This affected Adrienne, but she was able to relax about it for a while.

> ADRIENNE: Stewart, since we first met, was very verbal against marriage. And even though my first marriage didn't work, I didn't think getting married was an awful thing. But I wasn't ready to get married again. So it wasn't too important.

But their attachment grew, and while Stewart didn't really change his opinion of marriage—or even his belief in the possibility of marriage—he did ask Adrienne to be his "legal lady." They set the date and planned a small party, to be held a few months after our interview. Stewart is happy about their decision and his family is even happier.

> STEWART: Well, my brother approved—sort of a "misery loves company" attitude. . . . And I remember my mother—when we recently told her we decided to get married, and a big, icy veneer dropped away from her and she almost cried, and said to Adrienne: "I just start to like them and they are not there anymore." Until we made this decision I don't think they thought it was different from other relationships.

But Stewart still hasn't changed his mind about marriage as an institution:

> STEWART: One of the things I am concerned with, about being married, is a feeling that people have more of a tendency to take the other person for granted in making decisions about what the couple

is going to do . . . and I don't want our relationship to change—our independence to change.

Stewart feels so strongly about independence that he is trying to circumvent as many traditional marital customs as possible.

STEWART: Adrienne is going to take her maiden name when we get married. I said to her: "There are enough Mrs. W's in my family"— my mother, et cetera—and I would rather that she took her maiden name. She doesn't like the idea much, but she has sort of gotten into the idea of taking it back. . . .

It might look like I'm going into this marriage dragging, but I am not. . . . I just want to play it my way. . . . I don't want to be transformed into a marriage relationship. . . . Marriages are set up for society, not for the people in them. . . . I don't want to become "married" . . . that kind of couple.

By that I mean I don't want to feel Adrienne has tied her wagon to me, and for this to reflect a sense of permanence. That, for me, would involve taking the person for granted: i.e., the person will always be there; therefore you don't have to consider that person's feelings. . . . I want something that will strengthen us, make it more difficult to split because our goals are getting long-range. But I still want it to be Adrienne and I struggling over things each of us feels. . . . I don't want to get lost in the concept of marriage, or a couple.

Children, naturally enough, threaten his sense of independence. And he doesn't feel ready for them. Adrienne does want them but has put aside her initial panic about time passing her by.

ADRIENNE: Last year it seemed like all my friends were having babies. And I was approaching thirty and thinking, *My God, I'm not married. Pretty soon I'm not going to be able to have children.* . . . Fortunately, Stewart has come around to the point where he thinks it's definitely possible. But not now.

Once again, Stewart's fear of losing independence surfaces:

STEWART: If the issue of children becomes active, we will have to discuss . . . work . . . I don't want to support Adrienne. That might change but, for example, if she wants to go back to school, I know she can do it through her company. I would not encourage her to do it any other way. I don't want her to take time off, understanding that I am going to support the unit unless we have some kind of agreement that at some point it would work the other way.

Someone who considers personal freedom and independence less paramount a value than this couple does may wonder how their relationship can endure. But Adrienne and Stewart do not doubt the validity of their design. Adrienne gets great satisfaction from Stewart's affection and from the constant conversation they have about everything. She is glad they have lived together, because she feels it gave them "the ability to work out differences without feeling totally hooked and without bringing families in. . . . It gives you more breathing room." In Stewart's view, it has given them a chance to get to know each other without pressure. Now he feels that their chances are good, and that even the changes they will experience will work for, not against, them. At least, he wants "to try it."

Adrienne and Stewart are two people who, because of their personal histories, are afraid of being taken advantage of rather than loved. Stewart in particular fears a loss of identity, fears he might be used, fused, and become "a couple." He has put Adrienne to some severe tests to determine that it is he, and not security, that she desires. Adrienne, in her previous marriage, worked to put her husband through school, only to find that he felt he had not known enough women and that he was being repeatedly non-monogamous. She was starved for affection, felt betrayed and used, and was more than ready for a relationship in which each partner was expected to take care only of himself or herself. As long as she felt loved, talked to, and appreciated, Stewart's were terms she could understand.

For all their talk of independence, these are two people who love each other. Stewart usually seems, after much intimidation of Adrienne, to come around to satisfying her most important demands: for example, fidelity.

This is a relationship of great mutual collaboration, paradoxically based on the principle of separateness.

# Lauren and Blair

This is a couple betwixt and between. They have been together for seven years and are still trying to define their relationship. We chose them because they are struggling with the idea of commitment while running a complex household. Unlike the other cohabitors we have described, they have children living with them, two daughters from the woman's previous marriage. Thus, child rearing is added to the usual cohabitor issues of finances, monogamy, and equality of roles.

Lauren and Blair live in a pleasant 1950's rambler in a suburban neighborhood adjacent to a large eastern city. The house, with a yellow brick exterior and striped awnings on the windows, is on a large corner lot. What looks medium-sized from without turns out to be surprisingly large within. A master bedroom, two smaller bedrooms, and spacious public rooms occupy the first floor. Below are a large "daylight basement" and "rec room" and two more bedrooms. The two children—

Dina, thirteen, and Jessica, fifteen—live downstairs, and Lauren and Blair use the upstairs bedrooms as studies.

Lauren, thirty-nine, is a speech pathologist in the city school system and Blair, thirty-eight, is a social worker in the same system. They met while working at the same school. Both are tall, slim, and nice-looking, and their first impressions of each other were more than favorable.

> BLAIR: I was impressed . . . by the way she was able to verbalize feelings and attitudes about education and social relationships. I was impressed with her insight . . . and I thought she was a handsome-looking woman.

> LAUREN: I just thought he was a fox, and then I found out he was married and decided that was too bad.

Lauren saw Blair daily. They'd meet for coffee after work and talk about personal and professional matters. Lauren did not want to become involved with a married man, but they spent more and more time together.

Blair was not trying to avoid a sexual relationship. His marriage of five years was rocky, and he had already had one affair. He was unhappy with his wife and disillusioned with marriage as an institution.

> BLAIR: I was dissatisfied being married 'cause I didn't like that contract. . . . The overriding feeling of commitment was something I really didn't want. . . . And my wife was not a person I would want to spend the rest of my life with. She's a wonderful person and I like her a lot, but I'm not interested in spending a whole lot of time with her. We had fairly basic conflicts . . . and I think I just got married out of a sense of commitment to family—societal expectations. . . . My wife was a homebody. I wanted more freedom.

One night, after an evening out with colleagues, Blair and Lauren had sex together. Things quickly got serious.

> LAUREN: He walked in Monday morning and said, "I'm not playing games." I thought he might say, "I'm sorry about Friday night." I almost hoped that, because the idea of getting involved with an attached person was not my cup of tea. But this was no game. He moved in here ten days later and hasn't left since.

They were in love, inseparable at the start. They talked and talked, if not in person, then on paper.

> LAUREN: When we weren't together, we were writing—it was totally sickening stuff—to each other, incredibly long love letters. We were always talking about what was happening.

The outrage expressed by Blair's wife, their families, and the school served to draw them closer.

BLAIR: My parents would drop innuendos and wouldn't meet Lauren for over a year. I would be over there and be conscious of wanting to talk about Lauren, wanting to ease the path in . . . and my father would sit back and say, "Lauren? She's thirty-two? Thirty-four? Couple of kids? Divorced?" And it was clear he was voicing his disappoval, but he would never come out and say it. My mom would not say anything. My sisters . . . told me I was crazy. . . . I didn't see most of my friends, because most of those I had were friends of me and my wife.

LAUREN: Obviously his wife did not want him to leave her. His sister called over here—I think after he'd been here just a few days, and his wife had gone to his family and said: "Blair has left me and he is living with a woman." And his sister—I don't know how she ever got the number—but she called here and asked to talk to Blair and said, "You come home now. We want to talk to you." And they sat him down and said, "What in the hell is going on?"

Caught up in the maelstrom that whirled around them, Lauren and Blair were reacting rather than planning. Blair hadn't really thought about moving in—it just happened.

BLAIR: What had happened was: I had come for a couple of days and stayed. So then there was kind of the next decision which needed to be made, which was: "I think I have to go home and get some more clothes." So I remember that day as being an incredibly intensive emotional day, 'cause I knew then what I was really doing—which was moving out of my marriage. I knew at that point I was making a commitment.

I went home with every intention of packing my stuff and sitting down with my wife and telling her that I'm getting out for a while. At that point, it was still "a while." I didn't know whether I was going to get divorced or what, but I knew that I had to break off that relationship for a while to see what was going on here. And so I went home, packed . . . She didn't show up. The script read like a B-grade movie, and it started raining and there was no waiting around, so I hopped in the car and left. And got back here, and it was clear then—almost unspoken—that I was going to be here for a while.

Lauren's nearness was a great solace to Blair, helping him to cope with his feelings of guilt.

BLAIR: What I knew was going on for sure was that I was splitting with my wife, and that was very traumatic. And my wife didn't accept it well, was hurt terribly by it, and I had a lot of guilt about that. And this was like a refuge . . . a way to get away from it with somebody who supported me. [The psychologist] Carl Rogers would have been proud. Unconditional positive regard just flowed all the time and it was a really nice place to be.

They were both aware that such tempestuous beginnings tend to blow themselves out, so they made no promises to each other. After some time, still together, their belief in the relationship grew.

LAUREN: Obviously we talked a lot about it. We were just sure it was love, but we both said: As neat as this is, it probably isn't going to last very long so, and that was our understanding for months. In fact, at . . . three years we were still sort of operating on that basis, long past the time when it was obvious we were going to be together for quite a while. We just sort of said, *This is the neatest thing that has ever happened to me. I place no limits on it. It may be over tomorrow and I'm not going to worry about it. I'm just going to enjoy it for what it gives right now.* And love was used every other word.

Not just their personal lives were disrupted at the beginning. The whole school knew.

LAUREN: I think that at the time it all seemed real terrible, real harassing and menacing. But the other thing that happened is that it really drove us together. The principal at our school . . . called us in and tried to talk to us, and in fact that following summer they transferred me. . . . It was the height of gossip for a bunch of people, and this other teacher at the school called and chewed me out and what did I think I was doing? But the idea that there were people in opposition to it made us feel a sense of—that we had something to fight for.

On the whole, the first year together went very well. But Lauren was used to a lot more privacy than Blair was, and it took her a while to adjust. She never mentioned it to Blair, however.

LAUREN: Blair didn't find this out until quite a bit later, but after about three months . . . I was feeling really suffocated in the relationship. I would write about it. I never told him but I wrote [in my diary]: "I am feeling strangled and suffocated. I have no time to myself." I didn't do anything about it. I didn't attempt to get time away. It was probably more than anything a reaction to the relationship I had had previous, where I could never get him to spend even half the time with me that I wanted him to. And here was somebody who wanted to be with me all the time, and as much as that felt good, I just started to feel inundated.

A greater problem arose when their school, embarrassed by the fact of Lauren and Blair's relationship, transferred Lauren. Blair quit in protest and the financial and emotional repercussions were severe. At first, neither Blair nor Lauren coped well with the reversal of customary roles. But eventually they did confront, and solve, the dilemma.

LAUREN: In the beginning, for the first several months, it was—God, whatever you want, I'll be died and gone to heaven—we were just so up in the clouds over it. Then we had one really bad year. He quit his job in the city because they transferred me, and they wouldn't give him a transfer and they wouldn't give him an appropriate job. It was really a bad year.

And he was home all that year and he became really dependent on me. If I would call and say, "I'm having a drink with friends," he'd say, "What time are you coming home? Well, gee, I made a special dinner." The relationship just got totally out of whack. He had never experienced anything like it, and I was pretty unused to it.

It was only bad for six or seven months, and we didn't realize it. And then we thought about it and screamed about it and tried to figure what to do about it, and he finally got a job, even though it was out of his profession, selling cars. He got himself out of the house and went out and started doing something.

It was a really difficult problem for two people that were as love-stricken as we were, to deal with something as basic as dependency and jealousy and all of that. And the fact that we dealt with it—and it got better almost . . . as soon as he started doing some things—and that we got over that was just incredible. And we began to believe, well, shoot, this is not only just a romance; this relationship can do stuff. Probably what has been the neatest thing for me is that he is willing to work on the relationship.

Blair knows that Lauren sometimes worries about doing more than her "fair share," and he was well aware that his unemployment hurt their relationship. But he feels that they have no money problems now. They keep everything separate.

BLAIR: It's her house. And she makes those kinds of decisions. She will usually ask me, but it's clear that ultimately it's hers. We maintain very separate financial records. The money I make is mine. The money she makes is hers. We have some arrangements that we work out in that regard, but I essentially make all the decisions about what I do with my money. She makes all the decisions about what she does with hers. Those are two really distinct areas.

Lauren is in accord. But she is still concerned about keeping finances straight, and equal.

LAUREN: We keep all of our finances as separate as we can—like, I own the mortgage on this house and make the payments. . . . We have a rule that when we get something from . . . friends, we just decide that if it's an *us* gift and it comes from my friends, it's mine, even if it's to both of us. And when we buy something, like we bought a stereo, I bought the amp and the turntable and he bought the speakers, and there is no question at all where that goes. Usually we try to figure that out right away—which some people think we are strange doing that, but it's a protective thing for us. I don't want to have the hassle that my divorce was, or his was.

She hasn't forgotten the period when she supported Blair. She felt used, and she doesn't want that to happen again.

LAUREN: The conflict is . . . I don't like to talk about money. I'd just as soon really not even deal with anything financial, and at first—the first few couple of years—he just lived here. And really it was just like if nobody lived here, because I just paid all the bills and everything. And it took a long time for me to finally say, "Hey, I don't think this is fair. I think you ought to be contributing something." And I don't think he was working then. He was on unemployment. It took me long enough to finally say something. . . . I think we went that whole year of him being unemployed before I ever finally said that that was bugging me.

Then he finally got a job and figured out what he could pay and then paid that. And how we have it arranged is that rather than him paying, like, one quarter of the house payment (we figure . . . the house is mine and I'd be making payments on it whatever, so . . . we forget that; he doesn't pay that), what he pays is a quarter of the food bill . . . and a quarter of the lights. . . . We figured it out a couple of years ago, and finally a few months ago I said we probably ought to figure that out again because of inflation and everything. . . . I don't feel I am getting ahead.

On the other hand . . . I just don't even like to deal with it. Basically, when it comes to money issues, I sandbag and I don't want to talk about it. And then I start gathering feelings about it before I ever bring it up, and then when it does come out it's really a hairy issue—so we have some conflicts over that.

As for housework, Blair told us their plan was to share it equally.

BLAIR: We consciously attempt to divide that. I still have the sense that she probably does a little bit more, or what traditionally would be considered woman's work. She does all the cooking—almost all the cooking. She does all the sewing. I do all the laundry. I shop equally. We clean house equally—she cleans house a little bit more than I do—actually it's probably fairly even. I have a sense, for some reason or other, that she probably does a little bit more. Maybe . . . we have just finished summer, where she's home all summer, so she does a lot more than I do now. But when we are both working it's pretty equal.

Even if she does perhaps do a little bit more, Lauren is thrilled. No other man in her life ever helped out as much.

LAUREN: I do most of the cooking, although he does some of it, but he does all the laundry and I think that's traditionally a woman's. Mostly because he'd rather: He's quicker and better at doing the laundry, and I'm quicker and better at cooking, and it's mostly an organizational thing. We just get it done. . . . I just love having somebody be responsible. I guess most of the men I have been involved with, my husband and my ex-boyfriend, were terribly sloppy, and I was always picking up their stuff and putting it away. And Blair does a lot of that.

Apart from money, the only issue that causes them real conflict is the children. Blair loves her kids and shares in their upbringing. He misses them when they visit their father on alternate weekends, and likes to include them in home activities as much as possible. He "parents" them a lot—goes to PTA meetings, takes them to their father's house, shops for them—but he is not their biological father and he thinks that limits his participation. He and Lauren diverge over who should discipline the children, and how.

BLAIR: That's a real gray area. We aren't satisfied with the way it's going in terms of our relationship with the kids. I tend to do more disciplining because the system that we are on sort of lends itself to that. I am also very picky and I notice when things aren't the way they are supposed to be. Lauren tends not to notice it as often, so when I notice it I make a note of it. So it sort of sets me up to be a little more of the disciplinarian, or the heavy, than Lauren. She's more the nurturer of them and I am more of the disciplinarian. That is not as we would have it, but it is the way it is right now. So that is something that we . . . have been working on.

Blair criticizes Lauren for not sticking to her own rules. But Lauren isn't sure she wants to be too strict or too consistent.

LAUREN: I think another conflict that we have that maybe comes up four times a year, or six times a year—every couple of months, maybe—is him wanting me to be more consistent with the girls. We'll set up a rule and I won't enforce it to the letter. I'm too lax and . . . like, we'll say, "If you don't rinse your dishes before you put them in the dishwasher, you [have to do some housework]." And I won't bother to check to see if they have done that, and he will, and then he ends up feeling like the bad guy 'cause he's following the rule and I'm not. . . . Or, if Jessica doesn't get her Spanish done, then she can't go to the dance Friday night, and the dance will come around and I'll want to let her go. And he knows that the reason I want to let them go is because I want my daughter to go to the dance. I know . . . it will be better for her to realize that if she doesn't get her Spanish done she can't go to the dance. The consistency in that is far better for her than a single given dance. But I have a really hard time following through on that, and he would, I know, like me to be more consistent. And that's a conflict.

They are consciously working on ways to handle this dispute and others. Lauren described one successful innovation:

LAUREN: Family Powwow. We have a Family Powwow. All the decisions about how our family is run are made there, which includes the kids.

The four members of the family get together at least once a week to discuss the week's events, plan for the next, and consider problems and solutions. Blair and Lauren also plan a separate weekly meeting for themselves.

LAUREN: We finally decided. We had kind of talked about it before for maybe a year about having meetings, just the two of us and sort of formalized, and evaluating our progress and what we were doing. . . . Maybe once a week or every ten days we should go out, sit down—and he had some really organized things to suggest about how each of us should bring up at least one positive thing and one negative thing and a solution for the negative thing, so that we would keep track. 'Cause I guess I started saying: "You don't give me enough specific feedback. You say, 'I love you,' but I don't know what specifically you love and I would like it to be more specific." It kind of started from that, and so about once every ten days we go to a restaurant and then just sit down and talk.

But Blair is still not as open as Lauren would like; sometimes they have arguments about it.

BLAIR: The major one that is an ongoing one is when one or the other of us have the sense that the other is not dealing out-front with our feelings—and usually that is me. I tend to be more of the sandbagger. I hold it in. I'm not as demonstrative or as out-front as Lauren. Lauren is incredibly out-front about all her feelings . . . and often when we have conflicts it is Lauren confronting me with: "I don't think you are being honest about how you feel about this issue."

These days, Lauren feels, most points get aired and reach some kind of resolution.

LAUREN: Once it comes out, we never quit till it's over if that means staying up all night. I think the latest is about three o'clock in the morning once. What always amazes me is that I don't feel insecure bringing anything up that bothers me, 'cause we can always work it out. It's just beginning it and then saying what you really think.

In most other matters, they have few problems. They have a lot of shared interests, especially athletic ones: They fish, play baseball, swim, snorkle, and play tennis together. Occasionally Blair feels a certain malaise. He would like to have a few male confidants to share some of these activities with. And he is a little bored with the predictability of their leisure time together.

Perhaps it was this kind of feeling that opened up the subject of sexual nonexclusivity. Sex inside the relationship has always been pleasing to them, although now, at once a week, they have sex quite a bit less than they used to. But it was not any complaint about their sex life that accounted for Blair's two brief sexual adventures. Both Lauren and Blair speak well of the level of affection and intimacy within their relationship. Sex is available whenever either one wants it, and so are hugs and kisses.

LAUREN: We seem to have, not cycles but, well, peaks—like sometimes I'll feel really interested in sex a lot and sometimes he will, and usually if either one of us is, it's real easy to get the other one interested. . . . We kiss and pet a lot and sometimes that leads to intercourse. Sometimes it doesn't. We talked about it some time ago, about being in the low part of our sexual cycle. I mean, there are just times when it won't occur to me. I feel really close to him and everything, but it won't occur to me. . . . I feel like hugging or something, but I don't really feel like screwing, and sometimes I feel really high sex drive or something. And I don't know if sex drive really exists, but it seems to feel like it sometimes, and then other times . . . not much.

Whatever the reason for Blair's sex with other women, Lauren found non-monogamy a painful experience.

LAUREN: We had a bad time with that for a while, because we attempted for a while to have a really open relationship, where he would go to sleep with his wife again and I could sleep with who I wanted. And it was just a disaster. We ended up in this incredible intellectual discussion that went—well, it just makes me feel yuch. And we finally agreed that—we almost immediately agreed that we both felt yuch, and that it was not going to work for us. I guess we both attempt to take care of the relationship so that other possible relationships aren't a threat to the kind that we have. We have agreed on an exclusive intimacy.

Now they have an understanding that anything "premeditated" would have to be discussed.

BLAIR: We agreed to sort of write it off, if it may be a one-time sort of thing that may happen as a result of getting really stoned sometimes. . . . And that's the only situation we wouldn't need to know about it. If one or the other of us has decided, *It's something I am interested in doing,* we have made a commitment to discuss that interest with the other before it is consummated, and the appropriate steps will have to be taken at that point—which may mean that we will have to break for a while.

They are trying to maintain a good, fair, and honest relationship, but they do not see it as a trial marriage. Lauren wants never to marry again.

LAUREN: I just feel very strong that I would never marry anybody again for any reason other than money or health. It would have to be something pretty tricky. There would have to be something specific. I can't imagine what it would be, other than all of a sudden it would be an incredible tax break or something like that. Other than that, I would never marry anybody.

As much as Lauren loves Blair, she, like many cohabitors, has trouble believing in permanence. Nor does she wish to be truly dependent on anyone again. She does hedge, saying the relationship *could* last, even if she doesn't count on it.

LAUREN: I still don't think of it as permanent, because so many things have happened to me. I have moved from relationship to relationship. I could see myself out of this. . . . I mean, something could happen. I don't know. He could meet somebody else and I could meet somebody else. He could die. I could die. I don't know. I mean, there just are a whole bunch of things like that.

But about a year ago, I guess, I began to see that I could also foresee us being together for the rest of our lives and retiring. We've talked about it—I don't know when. It just sort of gradually crept in about when the kids are old enough, when they are in college, when they are out of the house, then we'll sell this and get a condominium, and then we will be gone every summer and visit a different country, and a whole bunch of things like that. At first I was very reluctant to ever even think about that, let alone discuss it. I was more comfortable thinking about just me, myself, and what I want to do when I am retired.

Both Lauren and Blair were previously married to people they cared for, under conditions they didn't. Lauren, in rejecting marriage, recalls the marriage she left. She wanted freedom, equality, unconventionality, and her husband fought her on all of them.

LAUREN: The issues were: I wanted an equal relationship. He did not. He wanted it very traditional. . . . I wanted intimacies with other people. . . . I wanted to go to school, and although he supported that verbally, he was just terribly frustrated and jealous. I didn't understand it as that, at the time that he'd say, "Yes, go to business school," and then when I'd come home he'd say, "Well, who did you see? and what did you do? and that's a bunch of crap that you are learning." You name it, it was a problem.

It shaped her views on marriage.

LAUREN: I went through three years of psychotherapy thinking I was crazy for not being happy. . . . I just wasn't the same person he married, and dealing with all of that was just incredibly painful. It was awful, and because of that I'm sure I don't need psychotherapy to tell me that that affects why I don't ever want to marry anybody again.

It shaped her views on independence:

LAUREN: It definitely affects me in terms of wanting my life and my self straight. . . . I know if Blair were to walk out and get hit by a truck, I would be devastated but I would be okay. I would make it, and I'd raise my kids and I'd still have things to do, and I lost all of that in marriage. I was either tormented or I was tormenting.

Blair, too, feels he has made of this relationship a deliberate contrast to his marriage.

BLAIR: I learned a lot from it. I grew, I actualized more as a human being, and that gives me more to offer to this one. Lauren and I specifically said, "Do you have other interests? Pursue them." That means if you want to go hunting every weekend, go. If you want to get involved in other kinds of interests outside of work and home, you are free to do that. Neither one of us intend to get married. Neither one of us intend to have any children. . . . And we have tried to make an ongoing commitment to talk openly about problems as they occur rather than sandbagging. . . . I am making a much more conscious effort to deal with that now as a result of what happened with my ex-wife, 'cause I think a lot of it had to do with the fact that I sandbagged for a long time, and never been out-front with it, and then when I really decided it was time to get out-front with it, it was too late. It had become too intense and I just wanted out.

At this point both Blair and Lauren are pleased with what they have worked out together. Lauren believes it works because "we are so much alike . . . and such good friends." Blair concurs, pointing out how many activities they enjoy together. He thinks the key elements are "dealing openly and honestly with conflict" and "allowing each other space." While Lauren agrees, she adds that a lot of their success is due to luck, and to being independent. They both stress independence:

BLAIR: The best thing we have talked about, an attitude that we really share, is that the best relationships probably are made by people who don't really need them, just want them; don't have to have it, but since it's around I'm sure going to take advantage of it.

LAUREN: If you ever need me, we're going to be in trouble.

BLAIR: Right. Right.

*Epilogue*: Two years later, Blair and Lauren are still involved, but maintain separate homes. Living together got in the way of plans and people they wished to explore. Yet they are, in their own way, still attached. Their future is in limbo.

These two share a philosophy that makes commitment difficult. What is the glue in a relationship when both cohabitors find any kind of interdependence unnecessary, even threatening? This kind of couple does not want the kinds of entanglements that occur when people are creating a future together. Mutual responsibility is so onerous that each person eschews the emotional and financial advantages of marriage in order to achieve freedom, equality, and unaccountability to the other's needs or expectations. The woman escapes from the bonds of conventionality, but she also loses the man's commitment. The women say they don't need such emotional support—but sometimes that seems to us a reaction to past disappointment. Men escape from economic support, and being partly responsible for another person's life, and then say it is a relief. But again, when these things are totally rejected, the individual often seems disconnected, still searching for emotional sustenance. In the most extreme couples, the fear of being in love, and loved, is almost palpable. Some of our cohabitors have obviously been so hurt in past relationships that it will take them a long time before they can be trusting or interdependent in a relationship again—if, indeed, they can ever be.

# Five Lesbian Couples

## Marion and Grace

We chose this couple because of their emphasis on communication, honesty, and emotional warmth. These are women who had no previous lesbian experience but who felt that women might make up for the emotional deficits they experienced in marriage. They typify a traditional, egalitarian, companionate relationship based on emotional rather than sexual attraction. Like many older lesbian couples, they are "closeted" about being a couple and present themselves to the world as roommates.

Almost all of our interviews took place in the couples' homes. Occasionally, however, couples would worry about their anonymity. If gay men or lesbians were very private and secret, they worried that our presence might expose them. Sometimes they wanted to meet us away from their home before they placed their trust in us. Sometimes they had children at home and could not speak freely. Marion and Grace had all these reasons, so they insisted on coming to see us in our office.

When they walked into the project office, our first impression was that they were sisters. They wore their hair in similar styles, were about the same shape (*roly-poly* was the word they used), and were both dressed in flowered blouses and dark pants, with small gold earrings and the same style of eyeglasses. They had identical gold watches on their left wrists and each wore a wedding band. Both of them were all smiles, with a gentle, happy way about them. We wondered if they had grown up together, but they had different accents and had come from different parts of the United States. They were madly, devotedly in love.

Marion is fifty-three and Grace is fifty-one. They have lived together for three and one half years. Financially they aren't very well off. Although they both have good jobs on a factory assembly line, they don't earn much money. Neither one completed her college education. Given that they both prefer jobs that require manual labor rather than sitting behind a desk, it might sound as if they look "masculine," but they don't. They look like grandmothers—which they are. Both have adult children and some of those children have children as well. When Marion and Grace met, they were both married—each for more than twenty-five years.

How did they meet?

MARION: Well, we met by mail. I wanted to meet a woman for a long time and I'd been really unhappy in my marriage for about fifteen years and I was afraid to get a divorce. Because my parents were alive, and that—really, I just couldn't do that to them. So, after they died I kind of felt freer, but I still didn't really get a divorce. And I saw one of these mailing lists in *Ms.* magazine. It was like a pen-pal mailing list with names on it that I sent in a dollar for. . . . That was all I had in mind, really. And I found her. She was so honest in her description: She said she was fat, forty, and frustrated, and I thought, *Everybody else is giving flowery descriptions, but there's honesty. That's what I want.* And we just started corresponding, friendly and kind of opening up little by little.

Grace wrote in to the magazine because she was unhappy in her marriage and in fact had never really been in love with her husband. She said it was a good marriage, but it had never satisfied her emotionally. Toward the end it had become very bad, and she was aggressively seeking a way out.

GRACE: I'm a mail-order pickup. It would take a book to tell you all about my life. I have always been a lesbian. My earliest memories are loving women and I've never related that way to boys or men. But I decided very early in life to try all the straight paths and play all the roles and play all the games that are supposed to be fulfilling for women and see if I couldn't find enough fulfillment for myself that way, because I couldn't see any way for me to live as a lesbian in the South. Not that I knew much about lesbianism. I just liked the idea of closeness. So I married and went through the whole ritual of having children, and I did all that because I wanted to. . . . I liked my husband; we had good times together and we were good friends . . . but I never felt that I needed him and I was not in love with him in the romantic sense, and so he and I grew apart. . . . So as I watched the relationship go down the tube, I began to look around women's magazines for some possible bits of help. I began to read *Ms.* magazine. Especially the ads in the back.

Grace found a service that put women in touch with one another in the back of the magazine where the ads were listed. She said, "All I wanted was somebody to just talk honestly to, about me as I had actually felt all through the years. There was a large portion of me that was unused . . . and it was the center portion of me."

So Marion saw Grace's ad and wrote. Grace explained how it all began:

> GRACE: We just clicked right away, and I think the first thing she said to me was, "I think I found a soulmate." . . . We wrote letters, thick and fast and furiously, and we exhausted all the possibilities of words between us by three months. . . . She wanted to meet me. I didn't have any way of going there so she borrowed money on her credit union and flew down to Tennessee and we met there.
>
> We were both open, completely honest, as honest as we knew how to from the start. This was one relationship where I wanted everything to be comfortable and right and open and not fakey in any way. It was such a treat. I met her at the plane and we just loved each other already from the way we had gotten into each other's heads. So we went straight to the motel and had a fantastic honeymoon. When she caught the plane to go, I knew there was absolutely no way in hell that I could adjust to living as I had been living.
>
> I told her I was coming here. I just told my parents and my husband that I wanted to go.

The meeting between Marion and Grace was the first lesbian experience—indeed the only sexual experience—either woman ever had outside of her marriage. It was instant love, and within a few months they were living together. They have been together about three and a half years and it would be hard to find a more loving, more committed, more consensual relationship. Marion describes them as "The Bobbsey Twins." Grace put it this way:

> GRACE: I could honestly believe in reincarnation. We think so much alike and we have so much in common and we do these dumb things like get the same clothes on. We buy the same things. We bought each other the same valentine at different stores at different times, and we'll give each other valentines and they're identical. We go out and buy the same groceries, not having discussed what we wanted ahead of time. . . . We'll shop at the same places and drift into each other. We drive up nose to nose in the same parking lots at the same moments.

Nobody knows about Marion and Grace. They live a quiet, closeted life because they don't think their children or friends would understand. This is a cause of great sadness to both women, but they are resigned. In essence, they don't feel they pay too high a price for their happiness. Even keeping their relationship secret isn't too much of a problem. As Marion says, "I just say she's sharing my house, and people don't seem to think too much of two little old ladies sharing a house." They just wish they could be honest.

The rest of their life together is very much to their liking. They *never* quarrel.

> GRACE: We've never had an argument. And we've never been angry with one another. I hurt her feelings once with a misunderstanding. . . . I went to a bar with a friend and Marion didn't understand and thought I'd lied to her. She cried the first part of the night and I cried the second part of the night.

Marion cannot think of any real conflicts either. Reaching a bit, she came up with this:

> MARION: Well, the only thing we argue about is vitamins. For two years now she's been trying to cram vitamins down me. And that doesn't sound like much, but that's the only one and she's forever after me. . . . I know she's right, but I just hate to take pills. She's always thinking of my well-being.

They both work long days, and they try to spend as much of their leisure time together as they can. Their house is busy, busier than they would like, with Marion's children visiting and grandchildren running around at least once or twice a week. Their real preference is to be mostly alone together, going to a movie or out to dinner or driving around the state. They never give up a chance to be in each other's company.

Decision-making is easy. Grace agrees to anything Marion wants, and Marion tries to make Grace less giving. Tasks are equally shared, with some specialization. Marion does most of the light housekeeping, partly because she likes to and partly because she has been ill. Marion says that Grace insists on doing the hard work.

> MARION: She does the heavy work. Especially since I've been sick. In fact, if I start to do it she'll come over and take it away from me and forcibly make me stop. It's a protective thing, but she was this way even before I was sick, so it's just natural. She's strong and she likes to do heavy things. She doesn't like to do little dumb things.

But they don't feel this division of housework is indicative of male-female role playing in the relationship. They feel more alike than different. Both have strong emotions, although Marion is lighthearted.

> MARION: We laugh about it. She will laugh and say, "Well I guess I'm the femme today," but we really aren't into role playing at all. Perhaps I would be more like the femme role, because I feel she's more sheltering. But she's still feminine. Oh, she's very feminine. . . .
>
> If we see couples into butch-femme relationships, we go, "Oh, yick!"

> GRACE: Perhaps I'm a little butchier than she is and she's a little femmer. We both cook. I'm more of a breakfast cook and she's more of a dinner cook. But tomorrow night I'm going to bake a cake and put up preserves. For most things . . . it's just who has the energy.

I'm more independent and a little pushier and more aggressive, more outspoken and more self-assertive. More traits that are, quote, "masculine." But mostly because my father taught me to cultivate autonomy and I think I've done a fair job of it.

We do have friends that are much more into it. The older ones especially. We laugh because some of them will address me as "the butch" because I'm taller and therefore I'm supposed to be butchier. We went to some club meeting and they wanted Marion to come along as a femme and go sit by the fireplace with the other femmies. We just laughed and laughed. Of course we did it, but it was hard to do it with a straight face.

Seriously, though, I don't want to be a male and I don't cultivate masculinity. I like autonomy and I don't like to have people wait on me and I despise the clinging-vine role. I never did much of that. So we treat that other stuff as a joke, because both of us love to be women and we've been women to the hilt and we've enjoyed it thoroughly.

Egalitarianism and consideration are the themes of their relationship. They keep their money separate because both find it works best that way. But each is in the other's will and insurance policies. They feel too many couples argue about money, so they help each other out—but from their own separate accounts.

They have only three sources of sadness. First, they would like to be more open to their children. One sister did find out, and an ugly scene ensued. They don't want to go through that again, so they keep as quiet as they can. Second, Grace would like to spend more time with her children—but the first problem complicates the second. They are adult now and don't have as much time for her as she would like. Finally, most worrisome, Grace fears for Marion's health. Marion has had surgery for cancer. She is on chemotherapy and frequently doesn't feel well.

What impressed us most about this couple was their cheeriness and good spirits. They are so much in love, and have been since their first letters. Marion marvels at it:

MARION: We first told each other we loved each other after we had been writing. I remember writing her and I said, "Is it possible to fall in love with someone through the mail?" And I said, "It's unbelievable." So it first entered my head in writing.

GRACE: I was really crazy about her by three months. . . . It was because we were already into each other's heads, so we felt like sisters, friends, lovers already. By the time we met, I knew that I wanted to spend the rest of my life with her. . . .

I think Marion loves me as much as she can love me and I love her as much as I can love. I've never loved anybody as much as I love her. And that's obvious. I left everything that was secure and comfortable and familiar and family and friends to come here, so that's how much I wanted to live with her. . . . All I really want to do is be with her. . . . We're together forever.

Sex is an expression of feeling for them. They are resolutely monogamous, although at one time they tried to be liberal and said they would understand if something else happened. But they really didn't mean it.

> MARION: We talked about it when we first got together. I said it wouldn't bother me any. I felt secure in our relationship. And then, since then we've both changed our ideas and said no. . . . We both decided that we didn't think it was such a good idea. It never happened. We were going to be broad-minded, but we don't feel . . . that we could allow that closeness with somebody else.

They have sex about once a month now. There is no conflict about it. Sex now is, as Marion puts it, "comfortable." Grace talked about its meaning:

> GRACE: It's not that important a thing. The thing that is important is the togetherness of our heads and the side-by-sideness of our bodies, and the sex is just a side issue really. . . . Sex is just an outgrowth of tenderness.

Sex is also less frequent because Marion does not feel well much of the time. Grace treats her delicately and does not want to make demands. She says Marion knows she is always ready and will be there for her if Marion has enough energy. She also feels they would be having less sex in any event.

> GRACE: Well, usually the honeymoon is very wild and sexy, and gradually you taper off because you get more used to it or something like that. I don't quite understand it but I think that a lot of lesbians get less and less sexy and more and more satisfied with other aspects of the relationship as time goes on.

They share almost everything. What do they withhold? Marion would like a little more privacy—but she doesn't say that to Grace because she doesn't want to hurt her feelings. Grace doesn't tell Marion how much she worries about her. She talks to close friends about that, not to Marion.

The things they like about each other mostly revolve around how close they are emotionally and how much better their lives are now. Grace compares life with Marion to her marriage:

> GRACE: There was so much missing in that relationship that it gave me a standard of comparison to use, so I know when I'm having a ball. Sitting by my husband's side was so empty, and sitting by Marion's side is so full, regardless of whether a word is said. It's because of intellectual rapport. My husband would agree with anything or pretend to listen, but sex was what he was interested in. You could talk to him about anything and he'd say, "Yeah, yeah, yeah," and "That's interesting," and "That's very right," and so on, and he wasn't thinking about it at all. So I stopped trying to communicate with him.

In the joint interview, when we talked to the two women together, Marion and Grace described how they got along and what made their relationship work:

GRACE: It's the equalness and the freedom. I've never felt so totally committed and I've never known an equality in sharing.

MARION: And I've no pressure on me to do things that I want to do for her, nice things. It's easy. Most of our decisions just arrive and often we'll make the same decision. Just not knowing even. We think alike.

GRACE: We even went out and bought the same damned bag of ice.

MARION: The same ice bag at different stores one day.

GRACE: We're at the point now so we say, "I'm going to buy so and so; don't you do it too."

MARION: We do—this is so typical. This is just ridiculous. We are happy. I can talk to her about anything and I've never been able to do that with another person in my whole life. And she's not critical or judgmental.

GRACE: And I love you unconditionally. . . . I think it's the fantastic contrast between such a sense of total freedom and yet such a complete commitment. It's really a dichotomy in a way, but it's harmonious.

And there are no roles to play. And therefore nothing is expected of you, so you're free to make the relationship what you want it to be. So you can take advantage of that if you want to.

MARION: In my marriage I had so many have-to's. The have-to's piled up so bad that I was just so frustrated I thought I would go ape sometimes. This is expected of you; you have to do this; you have to do that. There wasn't any time left over for me.

Marion and Grace feel they have learned a lot, and they had advice for other couples, gay or heterosexual. Marion thought that money should be kept separate and that people should give each other "a little space." Grace agrees:

GRACE: Don't lean. Don't clutch. Loving includes letting go. It has to be what's freely given. What I think makes a relationship good is to keep it free, where nothing is demanded, nothing is expected. What you offer each other is what you want to give. Like it says in *The Prophet*, it should be like two oak trees with your branches intertwined.

These women never felt as if their husbands *knew* them. They needed the kind of warmth, display of affection, and perspective on life that they felt women rather than men possess. They had successful marriages by any external yardstick, marriages of long duration, homes, and families, but they felt emotionally barren and searched for another woman who could understand.

Marion and Grace wanted female attributes in a partner. They didn't want a hierarchy of authority; they didn't want "roles," and they needed empathy and companionship. Sex was, and is, an expression of love rather than an intense physical need for either woman. They feel completed by each other in a way they have never felt before.

# Rachel and Bea

We selected this middle-income professional couple as an example of a long-term, high-conflict relationship that has survived despite emotional tumult. One partner dominates; the other fights back. There are religious and cultural differences. They have different ways of expressing emotion. Their sexual incompatibilities were a causative factor in one partner's having an affair and in the temporary dissolution of their relationship. They are back together, learning how to redefine their sex life and living with a non-monogamous agreement.

It was a steep uphill walk to Rachel and Bea's home in an attractive Southern California suburban neighborhood. Their house looked as if it might lose its tenuous grip on the precipitous lot if there were a heavy rain. Since there were many houses on similar lots around it, and some of them appeared to have been there for more than half a century, we decided it must be safe. Still, with many houses supported on stilts and others with very elaborate foundations, one had the feeling of climbing up to a bird's aerie.

The house, all wood and very handsome, incorporated such details as window seats and heavy beams. Most of the wood was dark, and the house itself would have been rather gloomy except for some modifications made by the present owners. Several bay windows and a couple of skylights welcomed in the light. The house ultimately felt cozy rather than claustrophobic.

The owners are Rachel, forty-one, and Bea, forty-six. They have lived here for ten of their sixteen years as a couple, and have filled the rooms with tasteful, expensive furnishings. There is a certain precision to their arrangement: nothing out of place. Both partners take enormous pride in their home and are in the process of adding another room.

Our welcome was not entirely cordial. The two had been quarreling before we arrived and the dispute continued throughout the afternoon. Rachel, a tall, dark, attractive woman with sharp features, met us at the door and immediately made it clear that she considered our arrival a burden. She did not disguise her disapproval of the fact that one of us was a man, even though he would be interviewing Bea, not

Rachel. Bea, with light-brown hair and a sort of "California girl" look to her, did not seem to be irritated. She looked quieter than Rachel, and she was.

We were somewhat reluctant to proceed with partners who were less than enthusiastic, but Rachel insisted on it. She felt it was "politically important" for them to be represented in our study. But her negative attitude spilled over onto Bea, and it was some time before Bea could relax during her individual interview; then, when we brought the couple together for a joint interview, she became very tense again. It was obvious that Bea took her cue from Rachel.

Both women have graduate degrees and both are professionals. Rachel is a former college teacher who had just begun a career in business and Bea is an accountant. Rachel held part-time positions during most of their relationship so she could take care of her daughter, and Bea had worked to support the family. Nevertheless, both women were manifestly strong, career-oriented women. But while Bea protested that it was not so, a casual observer would have called Rachel the controlling partner.

They met as undergraduates and became friends, confiding in each other about their emerging sexual preference. Although they did not go out together in those days, they formed a strong tie and kept in touch even after they had gone their separate ways, settling three thousand miles apart.

They bumped into each other several years later by chance. By this time Rachel was married and had just given birth to her daughter, Lynne; Bea was dating both men and women. They were both visiting a mutual friend on the East Coast.

> RACHEL: It's a great story actually. So here we are in Vermont and I'm with my husband and child, and she can't figure out how I've gone from where I was . . . to be married to this very straight person with this child and everything. . . . And the one line that made her think that all was not initially as she thought it was, was talking about movies. . . . She said, "*Thérèse and Isabelle* is playing at the neighborhood theater." . . . And I said, "Have you seen *The Fox?*" [Both films are love stories about two women.] And she said no, she heard it was really awful. And I asked why and she said because it wasn't very believable, 'cause the relationship between the two women was so much more meaningful than the relationship between the man and the woman. And without thinking about who else was around, I responded, "Isn't that the way it is?" And that's all I said, but on the basis of that, she started to think that maybe I hadn't changed all that much.

Rachel had to go out to the West Coast on business a month later and she phoned Bea while she was there. They met, talked, and immediately became seriously involved. Within hours they were confessing their love for each other. Rachel persuaded Bea to come back to the

East Coast, get a job there, and continue to see her while Rachel remained married.

It was a mess. First Bea moved in with Rachel and her husband and they undertook a clandestine affair. Relations became strained and Bea looked for a place of her own. But it did not work out as planned.

RACHEL: Bea found an apartment and she was supposed to be moving into it. This is a classic story. It was a block and a half away from us. Ned and I walked over there 'cause he was going to change the locks on the door, and we walked into the apartment and he said, "Gee, this is a nice apartment. I wouldn't mind living here." And I said, "Why don't you?" And that's how it was decided that Ned would move out. It was supposed to be a trial separation in which I figured out what I wanted to do. Obviously things between us had deteriorated.

The separation put a strain on all three people. Bea and Rachel were in love but there were violent mood swings. Rachel was worried about what this relationship had become:

RACHEL: First I saw this as a wild, passionate affair for a month, and it never occurred to me for the first three weeks that it would have implications for the rest of my life. When I saw her in California I really felt that I would go back and have some more children and be a middle-class wife. . . . That's how I saw myself and in some ways still do.

But I wasn't satisfied by my marriage. . . . I was being married to this relatively successful, incredibly bright, nice man. . . . I bought the package . . . but it wasn't enough. . . . Both of us knew my needs were not being met in the relationship.

Neither of us wanted this to happen. She didn't want to break up this happy home. She didn't want responsibility. She wanted it to be that I made the choice independent of wanting her. And I said I can't do this alone. Later on I made her responsible for my having made that choice and it was a heavy burden.

We had a confrontation. Ned said, "Either you get rid of Bea right now or I'm gonna divorce you." . . . I went home and had this sleepless, horrible night, and said, "Okay, Bea, let's do it. Let's go to California." At which point she started this craziness about: "Okay, we'll go, but we'll redefine our relationship and see other people." It was bizarre. I'm gonna make this huge commitment, leave my husband, and she's defining the relationship! I said, "Obviously you can't make a commitment to me. You can go back home and decide." So I sent her back and tried again with Ned.

I wanted her to swear to me that we'd be together forever, and she would say, "What does that mean? How can I say that?" I was so scared to be on my own. I wanted a commitment. I wanted her to swear that I would never be alone. I knew Ned would never abandon me, and I wanted a *forever* from her before I was willing to give up this forever. So she, of course, said, "What difference does it mean if I say those words? What does it mean?" . . . It wasn't enough.

So Bea went back to the West Coast, and Rachel tried to make her marriage work. A few.months later Rachel, too, left for the West Coast. The beginning years were stormy.

RACHEL: I hated her because I had lost all of my security and she had made me do this thing in a moment of weakness. She had taken me away from everything. Why couldn't we have stayed in Washington, where at least I would have had my friends and my apartment? But to give up everything at once and be thrown into this situation was really awful. We knew almost no gay people. . . . It was a really isolated, horrible time.

I was hysterical. She didn't have a job. I was sure we were gonna starve. I was just very frightened and we fought a lot.

At the same time Bea was not sure about what she had gotten herself into:

BEA: Once I got back to California and with my own friends and in a safe environment, I wasn't sure anymore if I wanted to go through with this or not. We went through this cooling-off period and then heating up again, but by the time it was over we were committed.

Somehow they stayed together through two apparently torturous years and committed themselves to the relationship. But from their recital, it is hard to believe that their association could have lasted this long. While there is no end to their affection and respect for each other, theirs is still an emotionally volatile union, with clashes about almost every important subject.

Both agree that the major differences between them are emotional and cultural.

BEA: The biggest thing is that we are from totally different worlds and totally different backgrounds. I am a WASP, from a small town in Oregon. And she is a Jew from Chicago. And, God, I couldn't think of a bigger difference. So that our approaches are different. Mine's apt to be passive and manipulative. Hers is confrontive and manipulative. You have no question about what's being requested, right? You will do this and you won't do that.

And the whole emphasis on food. I come from a family where you get your pork chop and that's what you had for dinner. She comes from a family where you have five-course meals, and dinner is the important thing of that day.

And there's cultural things. Like, I don't know about the things that go on in the East . . . and that puts me at a disadvantage in terms of decisions. Knowing those sorts of things sort of puts her in a leadership role.

Bea feels that others get a distorted picture of their relationship.

BEA: Because of her background, people coming to the relationship might think of her as a real bitch. Maybe that's not the appropriate word . . . but at least *dominant person*. And that I seemed real submissive. But that isn't true. . . . People of her [background] would know her strengths and weaknesses. But you come to California, and you have the same person, and everyone sees her as dominant. And that is a burden, because I am not this poor weak person that's being dominated. It's just that she's a foreigner in California.

Nevertheless, there is some evidence that Rachel uses that very "foreignness" to alter Bea's behavior.

BEA: We go out to lunch at this Italian restaurant. I don't know if this is cultural, but this is how I grew up. I ordered a glass of milk right with my Italian lunch. Rachel practically hit the roof. You don't order milk, first of all, because it's not couth . . . but that didn't occur to me. It's like putting mayonnaise on your roast beef sandwich, right? She'd curl up and die right on the spot, just watching anybody do it. But to think *I* would do it!

So, okay, so I went along. What did I care? I gave up milk. I never drank it again. I haven't drunk it since then. She is someone I care about. If she wants that, okay. . . . Milk's not that important.

Rachel agrees that the differences in their backgrounds and temperaments are a source of contention.

RACHEL: Being Jewish is real important to me and it's become more and more important to me. . . . I meet with a group of Jewish lesbians and it's just been incredibly important. And it is a way of making Bea an outsider. And Lynne [Rachel's daughter] and I are both Jewish chauvinists of the worst order. . . .

It's less religious and more cultural. It bothers Bea that I am a pushy Chicago Jew and that Lynne is like me and that I reward her for it. . . .

I am a Jewish elitist. . . . I want perfection in every area. . . . I want to make love with the person who makes love best. . . . I want to go to the Dodgers games with people who know all about baseball. I want to go to the opera with somebody who is really into it. I want to eat in restaurants with people who know food. And I have my separate friends for each activity.

Rachel also recognizes that her temperament gives her the edge in decision-making.

RACHEL: I have an advantage because what happens is that I put energy into whatever is gonna happen, and because I take charge, then it is almost de facto my decision. . . . I'm willing to negotiate, but if she doesn't have a position . . .

I have a position on everything, and it works out then that I'm gonna fill the vacuum. And on the other hand, I give her such a bad time about a decision she makes that interferes with my plans that she is reluctant to do it. It's not just her problem. It is the dynamic between us. And I will certainly cop to that!

This has modified:

RACHEL: I have less influence these days over decisions that only affect Bea. . . . I was used to intruding on every area of her life, from what she wore to when she brushed her teeth—or whatever there was.

Both women have gotten a little more independent—but there is no doubt that Rachel gets her way most of the time. Take housework:

RACHEL: How do we divide tasks? I do the things I want to do and she does everything that's left.

Bea feels the situation has changed, has "evened out." She lets Rachel direct the household and it doesn't bother her very much. They share most chores that the maid does not do, and although they both insist there are "no roles" in the relationship, their division of labor does seem to parallel the apportionment of wifely and husbandly duties.

BEA: Rachel hates housework but she does all the cooking. And she does the laundry. Because she's more skilled in these things than I am. I do the other household things like cleaning and ironing and stuff like that. She does all the buying too. So I empty the garbage and do the dishes. Although I'm getting Lynne to do more . . . I used to mow the lawn. . . . I know more about household repairs and stuff. Rachel wouldn't have any idea about how to do it, although I'm sure she could learn. But usually she'll bully me into them.

Rachel has gripes about this: not so much about the division of labor as about the onus of responsibility.

RACHEL: There are times that I really feel put upon. I do feel she abdicates a lot of responsibility. And part of it is my problem. I have said, "This is my domain and you are not to come into my kitchen." But I do feel she could take more initiative. Why does she come home and think that dinner is going to be on the table? Why does she never come in and say, "Is there anything I can do?" That is not a phrase I have heard from her. Why can't she come in and see the table isn't set and do it? She can get the dishes out as easily as I can. She just assumes, and I am the great martyr—so that if I walk in from work at quarter to six and I know she will be home at six-thirty I will kill myself to have dinner on the table in time.

But when it comes to Lynne, they participate almost equally in taking care of her and in loving her. Bea has known her since she was a baby, and considers herself one of Lynne's parents.

BEA: I drive the car pools. She takes care of anything to do with Hebrew school. If it has anything to do with music, I take care of it. . . . She might buy her clothes but we have joint responsibility. The only difference might be that she has more of a life plan for Lynne than I do. In that sense she's more her mother. She knows what she wants for her, what she wants her to be and know. I don't have that clear a vision.

Both women care enormously about Lynne, so that differences of opinion about her behavior and development can become severe.

BEA: Rachel tends to be autocratic with her and I tend to be laissez-faire. . . . She's more tied into Lynne's dependency and is conservative, so while she might tell her what to wear, I might say it's time she got her own clothes. We get into fights about that.

But overall Bea tries to be sympathetic and encouraging to Rachel's plans for Lynne. In fact, because it is so important to Rachel that Lynne grow up in a Jewish home, Bea has converted to Judaism.

BEA: I am very supportive of Lynne going to Hebrew school. I go to all the Jewish holiday services and stuff. We never go to Methodist church, which is what I was raised in. For anything religious, we go to the temple. I go to the temple for all the holidays. I go to all the bar mitzvahs and bat mitzvahs and, you know, I'm pretty much in there. Rachel is adamant about Lynne going to Hebrew school because she feels that living in Southern California, the whole thing of being Jewish is lost if you don't make an effort. So, I'm pretty supportive of that.

If they have largely made peace about Lynne, they have not been so successful in some other major areas of their life. They would attribute any discord to their divergent backgrounds, but it is also true that one of them is basically private, a quiet and controlled personality, and the other is gregarious, open, and volatile. This is reflected in one of their primary sources of conflict: their social life. Rachel likes to be surrounded by friends, while Bea is happiest when they are alone. Bea, characteristically, mentions it in passing—but Rachel is very upset about Bea's style.

RACHEL: I would say that this is our major battle through all our years together. I think of spending time with Bea as spending time with friends, and Bea says, "That's not spending time with me." . . . I am very social. I love entertaining and being entertained. I have a lot of friends and my favorite activity would be having Bea with a group of women and playing charades. Having both Bea and playing charades is one of my ideal dream nights. Spending a long quiet evening talking to Bea is no longer my favorite activity. I think Bea would say that's something she would like more of, and misses and resents and regrets that it's not a priority for me.

Their debate about what constitutes meaningful time together is part of a larger argument about the type of affection they get from each other.

RACHEL: This is a source of incredible pain and conflict. I can't imagine it will ever be resolved. What all our issues are involved in is that I think she's a withholding bitch. Our sexual needs and interests are totally different. It's just not a successful part of our relationship, to say the least. In the old days, when I was more dependent on her, then I used to cry and scream and say, "How can you be so cold and withholding?" Now I don't care. I deal with it in different ways. But that has been *the* issue between us.

It is certainly the issue that seems to arouse much of their dissension and disharmony, and includes within its scope both the emotional nature and the sexual expression of the couple. Bea feels it is a soluble problem that perhaps originated with her:

BEA: I think we are closer to working this out than we have ever been. . . . I guess I lost interest . . . or maybe it was part of my natural inconsistency. But it made her feel very unhappy and rejected, and she became involved with other people . . . and, of course, that's always a potentially dangerous situation, because once you're out there fooling around, you know, you might be apt to find someone who would be more of a threat. . . .

I wasn't prepared to deal with our problems, so I had no objection to her doing this, because it was easier for her to do that than to deal with whatever it was that was going on between us. Until [the affair] happened and we separated. Since we've been together we've reaffirmed our emotional ties and have vaguely committed ourselves to working out this sexual thing.

Rachel is less hopeful, more angry, and the affair that happened was only the beginning of an entirely different way of handling her relationship with Bea.

RACHEL: When we finished our questionnaires we looked at them. No one would believe that we had really filled them out independently because the consensus was so incredible and our knowledge of each other is so amazing. . . . But if you look at our sex questions you'll understand a lot. Sex is the most important thing in my life. And it is not important to Bea. That has enormous implications for how we live our lives. So [non-monogamy] is my condition for our contract.

It was an issue from the first, but it took Rachel a while to analyze it.

RACHEL: In the beginning I thought it was my problem. I had very little sexual experience and I let Bea define the sex between us. It took me a long time to realize that's not how it needed to be. I was monogamous for five years before I had a sexual relationship with another woman—which is a long time to make do on so very little. I have a lot of resentment.

What is it about their sex life that is so unsatisfactory and makes Rachel non-monogamous?

RACHEL: How do I feel about the way she gives affection? On a scale of ten, I'd say minus six. I am a very huggy, kissy, touchy person, not just in sexual terms. Bea is a very non-touchy person. It is hard for me to believe that I am with her. . . . We can go days without touching one another. We sleep in the same bed every night. We can go nights without having any physical contact.

Rachel never initiates sex, however.

RACHEL: What's happened to me is I have become very turned off. I am not interested in having sex with Bea. After years of being rejected, and also the quality of the lovemaking, I'm not very interested in having sex with her. So now it's Bea who can complain—the roles have been reversed. That's where we are. . . . She still is very concerned about working it out. I don't believe we'll work it out. I believe there is such a thing as sexual compatibility. I know now that Bea and I like very different things. I think she ought to be sleeping with a man. . . .

You know, I was thinking the other night that here I am in the same position I was with my husband: When I do it, it's not terrible, it's not painful, I don't find it repulsive, but it's such a different experience than making love with a lover. It's not just that it isn't as good as something special; it's not even as good as a run-of-the-mill lover. It's amazing we've been together for so long and she still doesn't know how to touch me.

One important concern is oral sex.

RACHEL: The big issue is that Bea doesn't like oral sex. And that was true the first night we went to bed. And I didn't know what it meant then, but I sure did after a while. And that has been our fight from day one.

Rachel sees in them two opposing sexual models:

RACHEL: We are very different kinds of lovers. Bea is in the heterosexual model of being very orgasm-oriented and you do this thing and you have one orgasm and you go to sleep. And I am from the school of the seven hours of making love and having forty-seven orgasms and a lot of touching and very soft lovemaking. You can get better and more conscious of meeting one another's needs, but I am never gonna get what I want and that's clear. Sure . . . I get orgasms—I mean, that's why it took me so long to understand what was wrong, because it seemed all right 'cause we always had orgasms. So what!

They have sex about once a week—which is amazing when you consider how conflicted it is for both of them. One thing Rachel does not want to do is "talk about it":

RACHEL: I am a process person, but maybe on a scale of one to ten, I am a ten and Bea is a thirty-seven. And I got tired of that. After this many years I am tired of it. I don't want to talk about the same old shit anymore. How many times do you have to have the same old conversation?

So now they handle it by having a non-monogamous relationship. Or at least Rachel does. While Bea has not been entirely monogamous, it is clear that this is a nonnegotiable demand from Rachel, and Bea agrees because she has no choice.

But because they do love each other, there are rules.

> RACHEL: I will never agree to a monogamous relationship. But it was agreed that there are rules about who the women are and when I will see them. . . . I am at home every night. The only time I spent the night with my lover has been when Bea has been out of town. Everyone knows that I am in a primary relationship and that's my first concern, and that I will do anything to accommodate Bea.

The idea was: no mutual friends, and nothing serious. But once something that started out casually got more emotionally involved. Rachel fell madly in love with another woman; it was a passionate, sexual affair, and it ended with Bea leaving the house. Bea kept up her relationship with Lynne, but she refused to watch Rachel fall in love with someone else. It lasted for about half a year and then, when Bea herself got involved with someone else, Rachel panicked. When it came down to really losing Bea, she could not do it. She and Bea went into therapy together and Rachel gave up what she still calls her "great romance." She left it while she was still in love with the other woman, and recalling it obviously gives her great pain.

It's been two years since Rachel and Bea got back together. Now Rachel has lovers, but they are not emotionally important to her, and she and Bea have a new rule: not to tell each other what is going on sexually in their lives. They decided it was too painful to know. Both women bear scars: Rachel feels her loss and Bea has to live with the fact that Rachel was willing to leave her.

> RACHEL: We had a commitment and we were planning a life together. I threw that out. I said, "I found another person and if I can make it with her I'm gonna do it." That was the betrayal of everything that Bea and I ever were to one another. It's a long time to make that one up. Bea doesn't trust me in some ways and with reason. I made the choice to go back to her for the notion of family and stability and security and continuity. But I know that experience changed my life and I can no longer say that I know I'm going to be with Bea forever.

Bea is not open about whatever doubts she may have. It was hard to get her to level with us in the interview. She made these events sound less devastating, and it is hard to tell if she simply underestimates their importance, or if Rachel's fears are still not enough to shake up this deeply involved relationship. Perhaps nothing is—because these partners already quarrel so frequently that if they can survive their combat, they must have something binding them together that is stronger than conventional provocations to separation. When they fight, they fight.

BEA: We never end an argument. Fighting is one of the things we do. We've had some doozies. All night screaming at each other. . . . It could start about anything—you know, an argument at dinner on if you're going to have a second helping or not. Anything could trigger it. For example, she could ask me to do some minor thing and I would go into a long thing about feeling sorry for myself and I don't have time and that kind of thing.

We will say incredible things. We don't care what we say. I think an outsider would find it awful unless you're into the school of screaming. There's nothing we wouldn't say to each other. No insult. I mean it, like an Italian family—that's the prototype. We even hit each other. But we have cut back on that because it's a waste of energies and destructive.

Rachel corroborates Bea's description, and tells why she thinks she usually wins:

RACHEL: Because I will fight to the death. I don't dislike anything—I love or hate. . . . I'm usually gonna win 'cause I will feel more strongly. Actually, I don't win the argument—because Bea will win the argument—but I will get my way. She is very persuasive, but I am a bully. I will usually prevail if I force it sufficiently long. I mean I am a very oppressive person if I am in that mind-set.

Rachel told us about a typical skirmish:

RACHEL: Well, I am a screamer and a yeller. And both of us are hysterics. There is no subtlety in our disagreements. Bea will come in and say something, and I'll start screaming at her and she'll start screaming back, and she'll start crying and I'll slam out of the house. It's real easy.

I'm much more provocative and I have a much worse temper than she does. But she can be bitchy and disgusting and snotty, and then I get into that too. So I'd give us equal responsibility.

It is hard for them to get out of these battles. They openly, and quite bitterly, acknowledged their styles of combat during part of our joint interview. We had asked them to solve some hypothetical problems we gave them, and wondered if their decision-making process was the same they would have used in real life:

RACHEL: No, it would be noisier.

BEA: I would be screaming.

RACHEL: Or Bea would be crying, or I would be crying and Bea would be screaming. Now, of course, Bea doesn't scream. She would be that cold, icy, disgusting WASP person that I hate.

BEA: No, I scream plenty.

RACHEL: But you'd also be the cold, disgusting WASP person that I hate.

What holds this couple together? There is so much that tears them apart. Their sexual incompatibility, their level of conflict, their background differences, all would seem to indicate they would not have stayed together this long. And there are other problems as well: Rachel hates Bea's family (who have not accepted her) and is as nasty to them as she can be. Bea is a private person and would like to be more closeted; Rachel will have none of it. Rachel is more social than Bea. She is judgmental and not above publicly humiliating Bea when Bea doesn't meet her "standards" of knowledge or manners. They have different attitudes about raising children. Bea is jealous and uncertain of Rachel's commitment.

What balances this list of negatives? An overwhelming mutual need for security and stability, and a belief that they have grown together in so many ways that to disentangle the knot of their association would be not only difficult but frightening. When asked what they like about their relationship, Bea responded:

> BEA: I think the best part of our relationship was pointed out to us so marvelously when we filled out the questionnaire. And later compared our responses and we saw how incredibly alike we are and how well we know each other and what a marvelous sense we have, even when it was not self-serving. We were very aware of our strengths and weaknesses and one another's strengths and weaknesses. And we have the same perspective, the same values. And I can always count on Rachel.

Bea also acknowledges that the emotional latitude they give each other brings a sense of security:

> BEA: We allow one another those extreme feelings, and I think that's one of the important things about our being together. That we no longer have to be on good behavior, and all those social expectations went down the tubes and we allow one another to be crazy.

Through it all, each declares her confidence in the other:

> BEA: It's important to have someone who is always on your side. Even in those areas where we are worlds apart . . . I think there is a sense that we would kill for one another. Sure, we might fuck one another over . . .
>
> RACHEL: But no one else better.

Their bond calls to mind the image of trial by fire: the bond that goes through the inferno and comes out strong.

> RACHEL: One of the most reassuring and wonderful things about my relationship with Bea is how we care about one another. I don't know if we will be together forever but I know she will be important in my life forever, that I love her and think she is the best person in the

world. And one of the signs of that caring is how we will never leave one another in a state of anxiety or pain. . . . We will have a fight and she will drive off in the car, and she will call me in ten minutes and ask, "Are you okay?" Both of us will always do that. . . . There are some terrible dilemmas, but I do believe in the process and the caring and the concern we have for one another.

Rachel is going through a process of reevaluation now. She is in therapy with a woman she respects, and is trying to chart the direction of her relationship with Bea, and to figure out what she owes both to the relationship and to herself.

RACHEL: I realized this year that I could spend the rest of my life with Bea but thinking that I had given up this great love of my life and that I had settled for whatever this is 'cause it's convenient. . . . And I could punish her either overtly or covertly, because we're together and she's not this other woman. . . . Or else I could focus on those reasons why I am with Bea and what she provides in my life that makes me make this choice. And there's a whole lot of difference in how I live my life depending on which of those viewpoints I take.

Bea does not seem to share Rachel's view that the relationship is at a crossroads. She is less emotionally torn inherently, and she has faith in the longevity of her commitment. She blames some of their conflict on the very nature of being a couple, and a lesbian couple at that. In fact, while both women think women are more suited to each other as partners than a man and a woman (because they believe that women are more sensitive and caring and because "women together have a process and that gives them more chances for working things through"), they also think their relationship illustrates what may be a key issue for other lesbian couples:

BEA: There may be a disadvantage that comes from the sameness. . . . That is, there has to be a balance, because it seems to me that there is a kind of intensity that comes from being with the same sex. . . .
RACHEL: Yeah, like getting into an argument and not being able to get out of it. . . . With men there is sometimes a kind of a distance and it helps create this balance between heterosexuals. But there is not the intensity. So maybe you opt either for the intensity or the distance, but you can't get both.

This was one of the most conflicted and intense relationships we encountered. Though its future was unpredictable, it was not unhopeful. Two years later, Rachel and Bea were still together. Their conflict did not make them happy—but it did serve to create a kind of bond.

They are unusual in that they are more or less consensually nonmonogamous. Rachel seems able to discriminate between secondary lovers and her primary relationship, and thus is more similar to gay males than to most other lesbians. Given the level of sexual dissatisfaction still present in their relationship, this may have been a necessary adaptation for survival.

They still fight about everything. They are, in sociological language, "conflict-habituated." It is part of who they are together. They are bound up together in an intimate, furious, but also loving drama that may go on forever.

# Anita and Freddie

Anita and Freddie exemplify a conservative lesbian couple who have modeled their relationship on heterosexual roles. Freddie works long hours, and like many of our heterosexual men, she uses her work to justify a limited participation in maintaining the home. A number of activities, including money management, are also arranged along traditional heterosexual lines. In spite of severe dissatisfaction with their sex life, Anita and Freddie are a committed, long-term couple.

They live in a modest bungalow in an urban neighborhood. They have a small, nicely kept yard with a wood fence. The house, somewhat older than the others around it, bespeaks tidiness and economy. This is a blue-collar neighborhood, and there is nothing to signal that the people who live in this house differ at all from the occupants of any other house on the block. Anita and Freddie do have a lot in common with their neighbors. Like many people in their area, they both work at a large department store. Anita is a clerk in the shipping office and Freddie works in the warehouse moving heavy boxes. In their forties, conventional, they believe in long-term relationships, and have lived together nineteen years. If they were not lesbians there would be nothing to distinguish them from most of the couples in their neighborhood. They live a low-key life and feel that they "fit in," and are accepted and respected by their neighbors and co-workers at the department store.

Freddie characterizes Anita as "a girl out of the nineteen-fifties." It is an apt description. Her teased blond hair is piled high on her head in a bouffant coiffure, and her long nails are meticulously glossed with dark-red polish. She wears a lot of makeup, artfully applied, and her clothes are mostly in pastel shades. She was once a hairdresser. It is immediately obvious that she takes great pride in her appearance.

Freddie, on the other hand, takes a lot of pride in *not* caring about her appearance. This is one of the couple's areas of "discussion." Fred-

die would be called masculine by most who meet her. She is about five
foot seven, and at 165 pounds is not fat but solid and big-looking. She
cuts her hair very short, never wears skirts, and thinks of herself as a
"butch."

They met in a gay bar. Freddie was very enthusiastic from the
start.

> FREDDIE: I was here on vacation from North Carolina and staying
> with a friend. We were sitting at a table at this bar making
> composites of different people we liked and making up our own
> persons. And I'm sitting at a table and Anita started walking up the
> aisle part, and she only glanced at me a second but the response
> between the two of us was the same. We just knew we had to know
> each other, one way or another. And that is how we met. Anita went
> to the bathroom and came out and said hello to a friend that was
> there that she knew I knew. I'm sitting there going, like, you know,
> waving my hand, saying, "Introduce me, introduce me."
>
> So Anita pulled a chair from way over there to way over here by
> me, and the first thing she said was, "Gee, I think you're cute." And
> I'd never had anyone say that to me before—you know, just off the
> wall—and I said the same thing to her. And she asked me what my
> sign was. She was into signs and astrology a long time ago, and I told
> her Libra and, well, that's it. She didn't want anything to do with
> me—plus I was with somebody. And then she got up to leave and
> she said, "I'll be sitting down there in the corner. If you want to
> dance, you can come down and ask me to dance."
>
> I went and sat up on the stage, right near where she was sitting,
> so I could see her. And we just sat and looked at each other for the
> longest time. And I thought she was going to leave, but she was just
> coming up on the stage to sit with us. And it just started from there.

Anita was intrigued, but a little slower in her approach.

> ANITA: We met in a bar, which is a horrible thing. I thought she was
> a fun-loving type of person. . . . We had a common bond because we
> were both initially from Indianapolis. I was very impressed with her.
> She had a good sense of humor and I enjoyed talking to her. So I
> was very impressed with her at the initial point. . . .
>
> But no, it wasn't love at first sight. I would say it was more a very
> practical, down-to-earth approach. It was after knowing her for
> about two months or so that I decided I wanted to settle down with
> her. It was a very practical way of looking at things. It wasn't a very
> passionate *we're madly in love, let's run off somewhere*. It wasn't like I was
> head over heels in love with her. I thought she and I would make
> compatible partners. And it's turned out really well. I wasn't wrong.

Anita and Freddie started to spend all their time together. But first
they negotiated Freddie's dress and behavior. Anita was concerned
about Freddie's masculinity.

> ANITA: When I met Freddie she wore men's clothes and she had

bleached blond hair and had a flattop. I was very much a part of the gay life then. You were either butch or femme. We reflected that. But I never really felt comfortable with the extremely butch-type girls. They never sat well with me. And they don't now. Freddie ran with a crowd oriented in that direction. It took me a while to make her realize that you didn't have to do that. I think I finally rattled her one day when I told her that if I wanted a man I could have a man. I want a woman who acts like a woman and who looks like a woman. Since then, that has been something that she could relate to. So now, while granted other gay people can look at us and tell who is who, we don't do everything butch-femme in the relationship.

Freddie talked about those early days:

FREDDIE: The type of people I ran around with were into role playing. Either you are the aggressive or athletic, or the other—the other is domestic and does all the cooking and that sort of thing. When we met I wore a flattop and nothing but men's clothes. So it was quite an adjustment for her because she didn't want to live with someone like that. After about a month living together it was first: "Maybe you ought to change your hair style," and this sort of thing. She said, "We are two women in love and I want you to act like a woman." It was quite an adjustment for me. I realized that Anita was more mature than me, so I have tried.

The couple had a difficult beginning. They had money problems. In addition, Freddie had been running around a lot—and liking it. She was accustomed to feeling sexually adventurous and Anita was worried about her fidelity. Their first fights were about money management (Freddie likes to spend; Anita likes to save) and personal freedom. Freddie thought Anita wanted a parent, not a partner.

FREDDIE: I feel that she has become much less of a dependent person than in the early stages. She talked love in the early stages but I think she was expressing a lot of dependency. It was more of: "I need a human being with me, and you're available, sweetheart, so you're number one on my list." But I think she's gotten over that. 'Cause I frequently force the issue—which is a risky business, because one of these days she may become too independent. So I've gone slow in that direction. But anyhow, one part of what she was feeling initially was not love. She was feeling a very strong need— financially, physical—and I was the candidate to fill it.

It wasn't until later that we had a relationship. I see her more as a person now, and she sees me more than somebody who flashes in your life and has all these needs and is using you to get what they want. She's made some tremendous sacrifices. She puts up with me, for one thing. That's a tremendous sacrifice right there. She's a very sensitive person. She's a very generous person. Love, to me, is something that has taken time. It takes time to know and it takes time to grow together and to appreciate each other and to respect each other's differences. I'm a basically selfish person. So for me to love her is—like I say, it's taken a lot of effort. But it's a very nice experience.

After confronting issues of commitment and the way each spent money, the couple settled down quickly and contentedly. Now they share their lunch hours and eat dinner together almost every night. They have a few close friends—mostly gay—with whom they socialize.

Their lives are not without conflict, however. These women take strong positions about their relationship—which, over the years, has led to some strife, though they have never once separated or, indeed, doubted that theirs was a solid relationship. There has been friction over household tasks, sex, and Freddie's social life with her co-workers as well as her drinking.

Anita is resigned about the housework.

ANITA: I do everything. Sometimes she puts the garbage cans out on Tuesday and sometimes she forgets that. She does help me clean if she's home. But then again, if she's only got one day out of a weekend free, we're not going to spend it cleaning house. If I've got the time on a Saturday and she's working, I'll clean. Or it doesn't get cleaned. She helps when I really push.

Freddie's lack of concern about the house occasionally exasperates Anita.

ANITA: I consider my home—our home—more important than a lot of things. I really like a home and being a homebody and having a nice home and having it clean with decent furniture. Freddie doesn't agree with that one hundred percent, and I have trouble relating to that. Like, I want to make new drapes and she doesn't understand the need for new drapes. And if somebody is coming over, I would like all the ashtrays cleaned and she can't understand why. I think it's because she's had a crummy background. Her mother did everything. Her mother never worked. And maybe Freddie just took it for granted. She's very absentminded about things. Little etiquette things which can get on my nerves. We argue about that.

Freddie has things the way she wants them and that is the way they are going to stay—as they have for nineteen years.

FREDDIE: Around here, Anita does the women's chores and then she does the other chores too. I hate to keep bringing it up, but the amount of time I spend at work, I am not that available for household chores. And when I get time here, the last thing I want to do is spend it cleaning house. I have an aversion to cleaning house like you can't believe. So Anita does most of the work. If I have a whole weekend off, which is very rare, I'll help out. I enjoy doing it with her only because I'm doing it with her. In my house, on my own, I would not do it, or pay somebody. . . .

What will I do? I won't clean bathrooms. I figure they will clean themselves because they are full of water all day long. I will vacuum only because we have so many dogs. You can get a sense of satisfaction vacuuming. You can notice a change immediately. We have agreed that when we get a new house I will have my own bathroom. Then I have the option of keeping it clean or not keeping it clean.

Housework is a significant instance of the different roles Freddie and Anita assume. Freddie has a masculine self-image, and both women recognize that although they are not completely stereotyped, they do parallel the traditional male/female heterosexual roles:

FREDDIE: I don't intellectually agree with the butch-femme business, but I think there is some truth to it. I obviously am the butch. Your butch stereotype, for example, does not do housework. I fit that beautifully because I hate the damn stuff. And not because it's woman's work but because I don't think it should be anybody's work, male or female, butch or femme.

She looks more feminine visually. She is probably much more strikingly feminine and makes a point of wearing makeup. She does the cooking. Traditionally femmes do the cooking. She does all the sewing and household stuff. She's a skilled seamstress. I said *seamstress*, instead of *tailor*. If I'd said *tailor*, she would have been butch. I'm not interested in that. I'm beggin' her for my own computer for Christmas so I can sit down there and get the old racetrack system down to a science.

I like being a butch. I'd hate to be a femme in this city. You couldn't walk down the streets alone. Femmes in the city and femmes in the lesbian world are a big attraction. They are few and far between. I'm talking strictly visual appearance now. You see a femme and you would hear the sound of butches lusting after her body. I know, being one of them.

Now if you want to talk about the sexual role, that's where the fun comes in. Butches are supposed to make the initial moves, even though some of the femmes in this city are incredibly aggressive. And, talking stereotypes, the double standard applies, absolutely. A femme that sleeps around has the tag of a whore on her. But a butch that sleeps around is a good guy. It's absurd.

I know this stuff is out of fashion now. But I've been gay for twenty-five years. And this is the way it's been. But now it's getting into something I can't quite relate to—this sister movement. You're getting to more of a love-type relationship and less sexual identity. They claim they are getting further away from role playing. I haven't been impressed with what I've seen. But it used to be more he-she, male-oriented. Down to the point of wearing jockey shorts and whatever else would fit. I don't know why. When you would not think twice about dressing up in a tuxedo to go out to dinner. I couldn't afford one, but that was what people did.

Now you talk to these young couples, twenty-two, twenty-three years old, and you discuss your butch-femme relationship and they just look at you in horror and say, "You've got to be kidding." And we are a lot less than we used to be. I think, for example, that I am a much more sensitive person in some areas than Anita. And she really is more mechanically inclined. So maybe it's good to get rid of these labels. And it really goes out of the window in bed. You do what you enjoy, and who cares who gets the dominant position in bed?

Freddie and Anita do not bring these conventional roles into their bed—although Freddie told us that some of the butches and femmes she had known in earlier days certainly did.

FREDDIE: Oh, yeah, there are some women who really are extreme. Like a one-way butch. That's a woman who would not allow herself to be touched in bed. I knew one of them once. But I never personally experienced one, but I'm not for chasing butches to bed. I had a friend who absolutely would not allow a woman to make love to her. She was locked into the idea that she had to be one hundred percent dominant in bed. It was a classic. She wanted to have the only paycheck and she wanted the woman to keep an immaculate house and be sure there were three hot meals a day. And absolutely in bed: "Do not touch me."

But it's all changing for us now. Now, even though you might peg people one way, you'll go out to dinner and you'll see—my God, here's a butch putting dinner on the table. Even though the visual stereotype might be there, people don't carry through with it any-more. Now, no male in his right mind would take the role to the hilt, any more than any butch would take the role to the hilt. It's better that way.

While nearly twenty years of living together have softened these roles, and communication and sharing are strong, traditional male/female patterns characterize the relationship in other realms. Like many traditional couples, they pool their money and never think of who put in what. Anita is the bookkeeper and essentially gives Freddie an allowance. But no major purchases are made without Freddie's approval. The couple has different values about money. Anita likes to save it, and Freddie likes to spend it drinking and carousing after hours with the men she works with. Anita says this is still probably their greatest area of contention.

ANITA: Freddie works crazy hours. Normally her day is from six in the morning until six at night. But there are times when she'll go in midnight and work until six or eight the next day. And after work she would go out and have a couple of martinis or drinks for lunch. And sometimes not go back to work and just continue to drink and come home a little smashed. Or sometimes forget to come home and we had a problem. . . .

She has cut down now. And she keeps the drinking to one drink. And I asked her, if she was going to be late for dinner, to call me and she did. So she has done everything I have asked her to do to keep me from being worried.

I'm still not crazy about her drinking after work. They all are very close there and I certainly am not going to squelch it. But sometimes she'll have her beer and then she'll play liar's poker, which can be a deadly game. And I get concerned about that.

Freddie is very defensive:

FREDDIE: She had gotten angry. One night we had company coming and I didn't get home until ten. I did apologize that evening. But in other instances—like, I think that this may be difficult to justify, but—I think drinking is a vital part of my job. It's a guaranteed relaxing tool which you need when you're working under pressure. I'm under tremendous pressure down there. Every once in a while we get together and we just want to cut loose. She can say, "I don't want you to drink anymore."

And I say it's going to happen. It's sort of a nonnegotiable area. "You either learn to live with it or learn to live without me." To me, it's not a fair choice but it does work.

This is also related to the fact that I get along with straight people a lot better than Anita. Some of my best friends are straight and I'll keep them for a long time. I think she's a little jealous. I enjoy being close with them and going out after work. I enjoy drinking with them, playing liar's poker or whatever else we might do. And she's either very jealous or she doesn't quite understand what we've got going or she really resents it because she doesn't have it. It's something I refuse to give up. I flat-out won't give it up.

That problem was settled when Anita gave in and Freddie agreed to call more often—each woman trying to adapt to their differences. Though their decision-making involves considerable discussion, most of their problems get resolved because sooner or later Anita will give in to anything Freddie wants. Both agree that Anita has improved, however; that she has learned to be less dependent.

FREDDIE: I win all arguments. I don't feel good at all because I don't think it's really winning.

INTERVIEWER: She won't fight?

FREDDIE: Yeah. It gets back to who's competitive and who's not. Her role is extremely submissive, and she won't be aggressive enough to fight. It's the lousy femmes. It all goes back to the femmes. They won't fight.

We can talk real well but she does react poorly to criticism. I feel that she withdraws so damn much, it's almost easier to do something yourself rather than be angry.

However, it's better now. Early, I think I made all decisions. I don't particularly operate well on that level. One of the things that just drives me bananas is to go out to the store and she'll ask me: "Which pair of shoes do you like." Hell, if they feel good, buy 'em. I don't care what they look like. She does take offense at that. Maybe she *should* take offense at that. I don't know. It's the kind of decision

I hate making. That's the least of my worries—what her damn shoes look like. . . .

I'm afraid I have the most influence. Anita is used to being dominated, and it's like I say: Sometimes I think she says yes, when maybe she doesn't think yes, and I have to ask her several times to make sure that she still is going to maintain *Yes*, because I want her to be happy with the decision. You know, I don't want it to be my decision, but she waits for it to be my decision.

I think she might be beginning to be a little more independent as far as decisions. For example, she is paying our bills now.

Anita appears to be a very submissive person, and we did feel as if we were in the presence of a dominating husband with a wife who says yes all the time. For example, during our joint session even they were aware that Anita wasn't participating in the decision exercises we gave them. We asked who was more influential in reaching decisions.

ANITA: Oh, Freddie. She always is.

FREDDIE: I didn't tell her to say that.

ANITA: No, she just explained everything to me and I agreed.

FREDDIE: Yeah, but I didn't try to convince her. I just explained the story.

ANITA: We thoroughly agreed on all the answers.

FREDDIE: I'm talking too much. You do some talking.

ANITA: Now you know I'm not a talker.

FREDDIE: I know, but it looks bad.

INTERVIEWER: We don't care how it looks.

ANITA: But I don't have many opinions.

Although it does seem as if Anita is totally dominated, this is not entirely true. When Anita needs something, she puts her foot down.

ANITA: Freddie used to have the attitude: "That's the way it's going to be and that's tough. If you don't like it, go to hell." And it was exactly that way. I could do anything I wanted. I could rave and rant and pout and walk out of the house or anything. And that didn't change it. And I tried to explain that all I really would like is maybe "I'm sorry that I'm late," or something like that. But that's changed.

We don't argue much anymore. And when we do, it gets handled. There was a period where she could drink and call me up and really lay into me for everything that had happened in the prior three months that she didn't like. And I couldn't understand that. I mean, just, one night she dialed and just started in on all kinds of things . . . really upset me a great deal. And I said, "Well, I'm not going to talk to you if you talk like that anymore." And I hung up the phone. I was really upset. I couldn't understand what I did to deserve that.

I didn't sleep, I was so hurt. I went to sleep on the couch.

Freddie came in drunk, and went to bed and didn't even say anything to me on the couch. And I wasn't sleeping. I was just hurt. And I couldn't handle it, so I went into the bedroom and said, "What the hell is going on? Why do you blast me on occasion?" She just started all over again.

I almost didn't work the next day. But she didn't get up before me the next day, and I wasn't about to be in this house with her, so I went to work. Then about eight-thirty she called me at work and really apologized. She said that she didn't understand why it had happened and it wouldn't happen again. And I said, "Well, that's fine, but I want to talk about it when we get home because I don't want it to happen again."

So we talked about it, and she decided that maybe a day or two before her period begins, if she drinks, something bad happens. She cited several cases. And she's controlled that because she really cares a lot for me—I think more than either one of us realizes. And I think she'll do almost anything to keep this relationship.

We agree. Even though Freddie is generally dominant, she will never truly endanger the relationship. She has her tantrums, and afterward they talk it through as soon as they can.

FREDDIE: It's usually me that starts the argument, and our arguments last only so long as I can regain my composure. The last time I blew my cork. I tried to remain cool. I told myself I was not going to be upset: *I am going to be very nice and quiet.* But I walk in, with all these people here I didn't expect. And, by God—but that time she let up.

I couldn't. I banged my fist on the fireplace and it took me about ten minutes of yelling. And then everything was fine, and she settled down and I apologized and that's about it. And we don't talk about it, only for me to apologize and say, "Gosh, I'm sorry, I sort of blew my cool"—like that.

We have made up our minds that there will be no personal discussions at work that we cannot resolve in five minutes—so we don't have any day arguments.

The usual way it goes is: Anita cries, and I would say I usually started it and I always feel bad—in the first place because I didn't intend it to be that way and had no intention of hurting her feelings, and I was probably wrong to begin with. It was probably some petty thing of mine. She never picks an argument with me.

Their conflicts tend to follow a pattern: Freddie blows up, Anita feels hurt, Freddie then apologizes, and they talk everything out. Freddie almost always apologizes, and it is a rare argument that is not resolved to their mutual satisfaction.

But one issue has never been settled: They differ about sex. Freddie likes sex; Anita does not. And Anita's feelings have prevailed for nineteen years. This divergence was apparent from the beginning. The women did not have sex before they moved in together.

FREDDIE: We didn't have sex when we were getting acquainted with each other. And when we decided we wanted to be with each other permanently, even the first night we lived together, we didn't do anything sexually. That was about a week after she moved in. I found out immediately that was a problem, but we had so many other types of compatibility that I wasn't swayed in my desire to live with her.

This reflects the strength of Freddie's love for Anita. Freddie is aware of how much she likes sex. Nonetheless, she and Anita rarely make love and Freddie has *no* sex outside the relationship. When they do make love, genital sex of any kind is very infrequent. At the most, it happens once every three or four months; it has even occurred as rarely as twice a year. Anita refuses to touch Freddie *in any way* beyond kissing or rubbing her body against Freddie's. Freddie stimulates Anita to orgasm by touching her genitals, but Anita never touches Freddie. They never perform cunnilingus.

Freddie is very unhappy about this, but, like a number of other lesbians we have interviewed, she is willing to tolerate an almost sexless life because sex has never been the reason for, or the focus of, her commitment. Freddie is philosophical:

FREDDIE: It's not so important now. At first the excitement is there and you are younger and your desires are stronger. Used to be a lot more important and I would get more upset. It used to be traumatic. But nothing as far as breaking up. My desires aren't what they used to be.

Anita is defensive:

ANITA: I'm not much sexually oriented. Freddie is, and over the years she has changed a whole lot to please me and keep the relationship together. Because I haven't swung around in her direction. You can't do something you don't feel. That isn't fair.

We did have more when the relationship was new. But I have a different way of showing my attachment. I do it by giving in other ways. I realize this is probably not good. As sexually oriented as our society is—hetero or homo—I probably don't fit. I am almost asexual. It is a turn-off for me. I think we base too much on sex regardless of which side of the fence we are on. I see so many relationships that are totally based on a sexual relationship. You can't build a relationship on a twenty-minute session in bed. There has got to be something else. There's got to be more depth than that.

I base this relationship on a lot more than sex. I know Freddie feels that is the one true way she can express love. Me, I feel it in other ways. . . . I really don't have the urge, and since she does not force anything on me, she goes along with whatever I want. I fully realize how unfair that is and that I have a problem of some kind, and yet I refuse to look at it as a problem. I *don't* think—you will excuse the expression—that we should all be "hot to trot" all the time.

But I do wonder how fair I am. I can see how she might turn to someone else, because I've heard people say they got to have sexual satisfaction, sex becomes a drive, et cetera. I don't believe that. I should have been a nun or something.

But I'll tell you. I have friends that come to me and say that they have a problem and they are going to have sexual satisfaction somewhere else, and "I don't want to break up the relationship, but I'm just going to have an affair." And I look at this person in a little bit of disbelief and—say, this is a five- or six-year relationship—just say that all relationships have less sex over the years. And to hear someone say they are willing to throw the whole relationship in the air for twenty or thirty minutes in bed with someone else—it is hard for me to grasp. But I am not foolish enough not to think Freddie might come to that.

But in fact it has not come to that. They used to argue about being sexually mismatched, but their life together satisfies them and they remain very much in love to this day. For one thing, they share essential views about life. They believe it is important to be "closeted." They are conservative about politics in general and gay politics in particular. Both think gay people are "going to hell in a handbasket."

FREDDIE: We agree that we think gay society is going backwards, not forwards. We don't like the way gay men are handling the gay scene in society.

Well, for example, here in this city, the males are promiscuous. Men are more promiscuous, be they gay or straight. It's their nature. They seem to be flaunting it so much more and I don't think society is ready for that. I think it has hindered the gay movement rather than taking it forward. If they had left it as it was and just gradually passed bills and not rushed it, we would have come a lot further. We feel it has hurt the homosexual society.

ANITA: We act as normal as possible. We keep the drapes closed. We try not to call each other honey, and we don't do it in public unless it is an accident. We are private. We don't shove it down anyone's throats and I don't ask them what they do in bed.

I think gay people are getting out of line and I think they better slow down. We have always managed to survive, and just because we are this way doesn't mean it should ever be forced down anyone's throat. I don't agree with all the younger gay people, and all the older gay people are scared to death that these younger people are going to wreck it for us just when we have been able to maintain a peaceful living. These young kids just don't know.

Even though I would like to live legally and I would like to go out in public and hold Freddie's hand, I know I can't. I would like to live a normal life. I know why these gay kids push it. They want to feel normal, too. It would be nice to be normal—whatever *normal* is. To me, this is normal. But it just isn't going to happen. I would like to be ordinary Jane Doe 'cause I can't help what I am and who I am. But that isn't going to happen and it's best not to ruin things more.

Anita and Freddie believe in assuming a low profile, sufficient unto themselves, conservative and orderly and totally committed to each other, come what may. They were married in a gay church, they wear wedding rings, and they regard their marriage as having all the power of God and law.

This last point—the attitude of the church toward gay people—is a hard one for them. They go to an alternative church, but they are still bothered by some of the church's attitudes. In truth, neither of them would have chosen to be gay if she could be heterosexual. On the one hand, they understand the church's attitude; on the other, they cannot understand why they should be punished for something not in their power to change.

The relationship, whatever its problems and compromises, is for life. They talked about what gives them the most pleasure:

ANITA: Just being together. Having her at home or just going off somewhere and taking the animals. And we like nature and animals and plants, and we like to take walks, and just being together.

FREDDIE: Just knowing that when I leave work and know I'm coming home, that that's the best time of day because I know I'm going to see her. That's neat. And to know we're going to have a good dinner and be able to sit and talk and relax and be together. Being together is real important.

And sleeping with her. And waking up in the morning. Saturday breakfast and Sunday breakfast are my favorite meals of the week.

And what gives them the most worry?

FREDDIE: Well, that we can't have a public display of affection. You can't sit in a restaurant and hold hands. Or if you reach across and touch somebody in public you're always conscious that somebody is getting the wrong idea. We were at a party one night and singing in a group. As a natural response I put my arm around the guy next to me. It happened to be Anita. Talk about shrinking away in a hurry. And me: *God, what have I done in front of all these people I work with! I've touched Anita!* I quickly put my arm down.

ANITA: That bothers me to a degree. We're going to write *Fantasy Island* and see if we can't have our fantasy of having a public display of affection on *Fantasy Island*, with people around us and nobody noticing.

FREDDIE: We do get to kiss in the airport once in a while. "Anita, I haven't seen you in three months. How have you been!"

We asked them why they think their relationship has lasted.

FREDDIE: You have to treat each other as individuals and respect them for what they are. That's made all the difference in the world. Maybe I use her for a little slave labor every now and then, but that never hurt anybody. I do have a hell of a lot of respect for her.

ANITA: I go along with that. And be honest. And if you lose respect you fall out of love immediately. If I did that, it would be finished.

Also we have such rapport and peace of mind. I know people who have been married thirty years and they don't have any rapport, and I come home to Freddie and I am glad I am where I am.

Both Anita and Freddie also feel there are advantages to being women together.

FREDDIE: Two women are going to be more sensitive than a man and a woman. Now I don't think it's the men's fault—don't get me wrong. It is just that men are of a different nature. I used to think that men were no good, but as I have gotten older and matured I think society has laid a lot of trips on them, and I don't think many men know their own identity and so they can't be very sensitive.

ANITA: I agree. It's just harder to keep a hetero relationship together than a gay one.

And their advice to others:

FREDDIE: You are going to say what I'm going to say, so go ahead.

ANITA: How do you know?

FREDDIE: I know. But I'll say it: If you have a problem, sit down, talk it out, don't puff up like a big toad and throw a big fit and slam doors and go home to mother, so to speak. Life is a series of little things that you have to get through, so don't resolve things by holding stuff inside. Or by running to your friends with your problems instead of opening them up to the person who can help with them.

ANITA: I agree. Communication, that's the main thing. Whether it is straight or gay, no matter how bad it hurts. We have started doing it as we have gotten older; we are more free with it. You have to realize life is not like TV-utopia and a bowl of cherries. You gotta trust each other. Don't cheat on each other and don't play games. Just be women in love.

Freddie and Anita have many of the problems of married couples. Freddie is more independent than Anita would like. She likes to spend time with workmates and doesn't come home when she's expected. She likes to be free with money and forget about their budget. She dominates decision-making and she takes direction badly. Anita's complaints and her situation replicate those of wives, because essentially this is a relationship predicated on many of the conventions of heterosexual marriage. Both Freddie and Anita believe in order, authority, and tradition.

Yet there are differences. They both agree that communication and sharing are essential, and though Freddie may demonstrate a little less aptitude for the role than Anita, they both attempt to play the part of peacemaker when dissension arises. Freddie is much more tolerant of the almost asexual nature of their relationship than many husbands would be, and her monogamy in such circumstances is unusual. Among our couples, only lesbians accept such infrequency of sex and remain basically satisfied with and committed to their relationships. It may help that Freddie thinks of Anita as a "femme" and therefore less interested in sex than she is herself. She excuses Anita's lack of desire even though she fervently wishes it were otherwise. As with some long-term lesbian couples, the lack of sex is noted but not considered important enough to wreck the relationship.

It may be that since role playing like Anita's and Freddie's is out of fashion among lesbian couples—even as it is less common among heterosexuals—some of the accommodations based on behavior permissible to a "butch" or a "femme" will not be made in the future. Freddie and Anita have relied less on these roles over the years, but they continue to guide their daily lives.

# Natalie and Jill

We chose this couple because they live in a woman's world. Most of their friends, social life, and work revolve around lesbians. Their conflicts are common among lesbians who consider their sexuality political as well as personal. They argue about power, roles, personal and class privilege, independence, money, and monogamy.

Natalie and Jill have been a couple for more than five years. Their house, however, looks as if they have just begun to live together. It is a "Victorian brownshingle" in a university town, with a lot of dark wood paneling and wainscoting. What little furniture there is consists mostly of pillows and mattresses on the floor. The place seems to be in general disarray: stacks of paper everywhere, numerous plants occupying large areas, posters on the walls not quite staying up. Lists and notices of meetings are tacked up on a bulletin board, by the phone, and on the refrigerator door. The house is cluttered but not dirty. The couple rents the house for a modest sum and they consider themselves very lucky to have found it. Natalie is a mechanic in a "women's garage"; Jill has just started a dance exercise center. Neither makes much money right now.

Natalie, twenty-five, chunky and short, was wearing overalls and a plaid shirt when we met her. Jill is twenty-nine, a few inches taller, slim, and has delicate features nicely framed by her short curly hair. She was dressed in slacks and a peasant blouse. They are both lesbian feminists. Jill is very involved in lesbian separatist politics. When Natalie, seeking a place where she could live with her girl friend (she was living with her mother and father), heard about a lesbian feminist collective, she joined it, and met Jill there.

Their courtship would be stormy. In the beginning, when they first met, they were both with other partners. They were quite different and it took them a while just to be friends. Natalie, who describes herself as very "working-class," found Jill and the entire collective intimidating. All the members were middle-class and college-educated, while Natalie had gone only as far as high school. She resented their privileges, the assurance and poise their middle-class background bestowed. She thought Jill was nice, but part of the clique.

Jill was not as sensitive to the class difference (although she is now, because it is a central issue in their relationship). Her first impressions of Natalie were positive and physical.

> JILL: I thought she was attractive—beautiful blue eyes that seemed piercing.'. . . She seemed different from me and my friends . . . a sort of aggressive, part old-time lesbian appearance. She fit my stereotype of a lesbian. . . . I felt more comfortable with her partner.

Since they did not feel comfortable, they did not act on their attraction for more than a year. Then they started to talk about their primary relationships, and each became the other's confidante. Natalie's relationship began to come apart first. She then pursued Jill.

> JILL: She and her partner were obviously having a hard time and so were me and Fran, but it was under the surface. She started pursuing me . . . with a different kind of energy. She kept saying things like she would like to see me more often, and we went out one evening and then it became real obvious that I was attracted to her. I felt like: All right, I would like to have an affair with you but I don't want to lose my relationship with Fran. She was sort of not up for that. . . . She wanted me to be open to whatever would come about. She said that she was really hurt that I just wanted to have an affair with her. She wanted me to be open, so I said okay.

Jill and Natalie began to see each other. There were battles among all four members of the two couples, and within the collective as well.

> JILL: Our whole community was upset. Our partners were upset. Fran freaked out because she thought we were in a very good place. But it couldn't have been that good a place because Natalie and I were having a volcanic explosion. It was like I was ready to chuck everything in and ride off into the sunset. I didn't care if it was over in three weeks. I felt really alive and I wasn't going to give that up.

Everyone, however, urged Jill to go back to Fran.

> JILL: It was really hard. We felt very unsupported. . . . I felt there was no support for lesbian couples, even from the lesbian community. I can remember looking at Natalie and feeling really in

love with her and still thinking, *We can't do this.* . . . Sort of feeling like we were trying to go to the moon, or something that weird. There was no role. I have been married, so I know how easy you can just plod into that and it is like you have this whole niche set up for you.

Resistance to their relationship became so severe that one night the rest of the collective grabbed Jill and lectured her about why she should stay with Fran.

JILL: I came home one night after being out with Natalie and they were all sitting around the table drinking and smoking dope. They said, "Jill, we want to talk to you," and they called me into this courtroom atmosphere: "What are you doing? Natalie is not your kind of person. Fran is so wonderful. How can you make this decision?"

I felt really threatened and intimidated. One of the women was very powerful in her personal qualities and I freaked out. I called Natalie but she wasn't home, so I called a friend and said, "Get me out of here. I need someone to come and get me."

They wouldn't let me leave the apartment. I mean, I got held down physically. At one point Fran slapped me across the face. I felt like . . . it was the same kind of impact as if I had been grabbed by a group of men on the street and sort of raped or thrown around or something. It was psychologically very threatening, and for the next few weeks I was always afraid that someone was going to come up through my window or show up on my doorstep. I felt physically vulnerable. . . .

These were women I had known, depended on, and they attacked me. The first few months with Natalie, I was anxious and I leaned on her a lot for comfort.

The couple left the collective right after this incident. That was five years ago. Their dramatic departure from the collective made them very close, very needful of each other. But they had many issues to resolve and they had to work to remain a couple. They fight about differences in background, class, roles, about privacy, independence, money, sex, friends—just about everything. And when they fight, they fight hard.

Over time, they have made progress. Both women have changed.

NATALIE: At the beginning I was the more male. I was more aggressive. . . . I changed because, as I have grown within the women's community, I felt more uncomfortable. I didn't want to be in any type of role. I consciously changed.

Jill encouraged her to change. She hated Natalie's being "butch." Natalie knew how unhappy it made Jill.

NATALIE: It was a real fear of Jill's. I dressed more masculine. . . . She dresses very feminine. I am very conservative. I still wear my shirt and pants, but I feel like that is something I am trying to change and be more open, and not into a uniform.

That is important to Jill, who understands why Natalie prefers roles, but still doesn't approve:

JILL: She never grew out of the tomboy phase, and in her teens identified as a lesbian and was playing baseball. And really, at that point there were strong butch-femme roles. She sort of identified being tough with having power, whereas for myself, in about seventh grade I realized that nobody liked me as a tomboy. I decided it was more important to be liked, so I sort of redid myself and became ultrafeminine. By the end of college I was a dancer and a pom-pom girl and glamorous, and just all the stereotypes. Then I got married and so I have lots of practice with that whole kind of performance that Natalie never did.

The initial advantage to them of the butch-femme difference quickly dissipated.

JILL: I'd say when we first got together, part of the attraction was the difference between us. But then we got into the women's community and butch-femme roles were *out*, politically incorrect.

Nevertheless, they both feel that some inherent role differences remain which are at once pleasing and troublesome.

JILL: I felt her aggressive energy and that was really attractive. It is a quality I like. She was attracted because she thought of me as softer. But I like to dominate, and yet I also like people who can be strong and dominant. In my past relationship [with Fran] I felt dominant and I didn't want to be in that role. So that in the first days with Natalie I could have a revival of aspects of my femininity that I had felt were not okay to express the last couple of years. So at first we had a strong butch-femme thing. But I got uncomfortable with . . . my fluffy femme role. This is against my power and dignity, and I thought, *What am I doing in this place?* and I started wanting her not to look like a man. We started balancing things out.

Another thing that helped them change their roles was the reaction of Jill's family.

JILL: I got very uncomfortable when we would go and visit my family. I'd dress up and we'd arrive with me looking feminine and her looking masculine. I didn't like the fact that my family would be responding to us as, "Oh, this is the girl and this is the boy." I hated that, and so I wanted Natalie to express the feminine part of herself which is really there.

They consciously tried to modify their roles:

JILL: She would open doors for me and stuff, and she'd say, "Well, I just do that when I really like somebody and care about them." And

I said, "Yes, but it's such a male thing to do. You won't even let me walk in front of you." We stopped that.

Then there was the situation that she was more aggressive sexually. She would always initiate making love. We've drifted away from that too.

Both women agree that the shift in role behavior has been good. But they have not succeeded in overcoming a major problem between them: the difference in their backgrounds.

This is especially difficult for Natalie. She is from a working-class family and is clearly uneasy with people from more prosperous milieus. She resents "class privilege"; hence, issues of class intrude upon the couple's life every day.

NATALIE: It comes up constantly. There is a big difference in how we were brought up. . . . Even though I am adopting her middle-class values, I don't want to say that my working-classness is bad. . . . But there are issues. . . . She taught herself as a middle-class child to worry about her health. We never had the luxury of worrying about ourselves physically and I have never thought about it. You are more concerned about a roof over your head or money in your pocket or food to eat. I mean, I couldn't afford to go to a dentist! I think I went twice as a kid. . . . Now she says, "You're a bad person because you don't care about your health.". . . Because I smoke—though that's not necessarily working class. She lays all kinds of judgments on me like that.

It comes up when we deal with money. Money to me was to be spent. I had it, I spent it, and never saved it. If I saw something I wanted, I bought it and wasn't concerned about it. She is just the opposite. Saved her money right down to the quarter or the dime or nickel, which I thought was ridiculous. She's loosened up now and I have incorporated some of her—so that's better now.

Nonetheless, Natalie—who is the more devoted of the two and who is making every effort to ensure a lifetime relationship—thinks that if anything were to separate them, it would be the class difference.

NATALIE: I feel judged by her and she feels guilty, but she also feels she is right. It's all from *class*. Is it really possible for a middle-class person and a working-class person to maintain a relationship and work through all the hassles and feelings? It does come down to it that I would be much more comfortable with another working-class person than I would with Jill. And Jill—the same thing for her. We can't deal with it even though we're committed to deal with it. There is all this stuff pouring in each individual. You can't beat the class system.

Jill acknowledges that class is a major problem. But she discusses it from her own educated—and, indeed, more privileged—sensibility.

JILL: Our collective broke up over class issues. Rita, who had the highest-class background, felt the most guilty, defensive, and put down. Natalie also had angry confrontations. . . . This is our issue too. We have different values. What to eat, where to eat. I'd really like to read and I read all the time. Natalie will maybe read an Agatha Christie mystery, which I really get down on her for. She likes to watch a lot of TV. I feel like this is very working-class and not a good thing to spend your time doing. This was particularly true of her in the beginning and I would get down on her for doing nothing. She was sort of bored with herself and I was sort of bored with her.

I was worried about our future because it didn't seem that she was very comfortable with people who were middle-class and well educated. She felt intimidated and put down. She felt that way with me a lot. It was like the power balance in our relationship went from her being the more powerful to coming around to me being the more powerful. She looks more solid and secure, but as far as being out in the world and dealing with other people and the sort of status thing that the world puts out, I was on top.

Almost everything made Jill acutely aware of their differences and of Natalie's deficiencies.

JILL: The biggest thing that affected me was education, because in my family education was important. And in her family it was nothing. My family is very verbal, large vocabulary, reads nonstop, very articulate. She wouldn't know how to spell words. I just think, *My God, you don't know how to spell them,* and I would feel that reflected on me. . . . It didn't affect our relationship too much, but at those times I would feel, *Oh, my God, what am I doing? This is one of the most important things to me. And here she is not measuring up at all as far as that is concerned.* I am very concerned about what other people think and it was always like, well, what are other people going to think about this?

Jill is hopeful, however, that even this can be solved.

JILL: I think this is going to be a problem, but how we handle it will be a benchmark of how our relationship is doing. At this point, we are doing pretty well. But then something came up the other day. She didn't know something and I went through the same thing of: "Oh, my God, how could you not know that? My God, what am I doing?" If I ever fantasized about being with someone else, it would be with someone well educated.

This difference manifests itself in another area the couple talks about all the time: power. They constantly discuss who is more powerful, and how to keep things in balance. Both seem obsessed with the subject, and much of the conversation about class focuses on its consequences in their personal struggle for power.

Natalie, for example, feels that Jill has more influence because she has been taught to be verbal. Jill agrees, and admits it gives her the upper hand.

JILL: I have more influence in general. Again, that is our class background. I am more assertive and aggressive and think I am right and know more. Her way of being makes it seem like she is not so sure. . . . She is always asking me, to the point of where I just feel like: *"Do it yourself. Don't ask me."*

Natalie acknowledges that Jill's influence in the relationship is a consequence of her verbal ability, which she, too, attributes to class.

NATALIE: Jill wins more arguments because she's better at expressing things. Which is a class issue. Her education has given her a better sense of herself and she feels free to express what she is thinking.

Television is a big focus of their power struggle. Jill thinks TV is "dumb, boring, and useless." Natalie likes to watch it to relax. They get into heated arguments, which are about much more than television.

JILL: It seems like a silly thing, but it has been a big problem. I don't like coming home after work and seeing her watching TV when I walk in the door at six-thirty in the evening. I don't like it if she will spend all day Saturday and watch TV. I don't like it if I go out for a little while and I come back and she's watching TV. My parents said you should never watch TV before five in the evening, so someone watching TV during the day just bugs me. And the other part of my thinking is: "Don't you—aren't you interested in anything else besides watching TV?" TV is just a ridiculous, mind-bloating experience! Television is an expression of being exposed to things, and the differences between the way I was brought up and Natalie was brought up. It is a small thing but it brings up our class assumptions.

Jill is like a dog with a bone on all issues that relate to class. It is really important to her and she feels they are mismatched. Yet she is in love.

JILL: I feel like I love her, and it really has almost nothing to do with the way we interact, but it is serious. Just a couple months ago we were fighting about something, and I said, "Boy, I can really understand why you are talking about couples' prospects for being together—that the most important factor is socioeconomic background." It is really hard, and I know that if something ended up with us not being together, I would force myself, for the rest of my life, to get to know somebody first and find out how similar we were along our tastes, values, and educational level . . . and make sure we were as much the same in those ways as possible.

Jill and Natalie both agree that this problem affects not only what they fight about but *how* they fight. Jill doesn't like Natalie's style.

JILL: It is hard, because my personality is to put out what I think and if the other person is strong on their opinion, I'll go "Okay." But Natalie's personality is to put out what she thinks and, if I disagree with her, to just shut back in. She will get miffed and won't talk, and then I'll be upset and say, "Stick up for yourself. Don't agree with me. Just say something back."

But she takes my saying what I feel as saying that I automatically feel she is wrong. She won't come back with "No, I'm not." So that causes further argument because she is too timid. And then I feel like I can't disagree with her because it has too much impact.

This is a genuine problem: Natalie's preference for letting things drift away, against Jill's wish to have them discussed.

JILL: I can't feel comfortable unless it's all talked out. Her tolerance for having something slightly wrong is much greater than mine, so then I get mad at her for having something wrong and not bringing it up and talking about it and getting it out of the way. And I resent that I always have to bring things up.

Jill thinks there is improvement, but it is her responsibility to see that confrontation and communication occur.

JILL: It took her a long time to learn to get overtly angry with me. She is getting better at locating her feelings. . . . I would rather have it be really good, and then really angry, than sort of blah for a period of time while she is figuring out what is wrong. I am always afraid that she is just going to slip into this kind of apathy. And if I don't keep on top of things, we are just going to be this bored married couple.

Their fights do not appear to be boring. Natalie is able to keep the histrionics to a minimum but Jill really lets loose.

NATALIE: I am the logical one, less likely to lose my temper. I will keep the discussion on track. Jill will fly off the handle and be super-angry, say anything that comes to her mind. She would be the one to run out of the room. I would be the one to go to her and say, "Let's work this out."

JILL: We will start out irritated and then really fight. Things get louder. We get mad, start yelling. We do things like: One of us will hit the other one on the side of the arm or leg—though nothing that would hurt the other one. There is no fear that the other one is going to smack us in the face, but we will push, and do things that are physical. We don't tend to fight dirty and do attacks from the past. I have often gotten into the habit of saying, "I hate you, I just hate you," 'cause that is what I do when I really feel hurt and angry. She tends to say, "Fuck you," or something, but most of the time she tends to only say what she'd say when she wasn't angry, whereas I get more extreme.

At some point I usually will slam out of the room, come into my room, and get into bed. I will just feel like *That is it. I am going to stay here forever. She won't hold out as long as I will.*

And she will come in and say, "Do you want to talk about it?"

And I will sit up and we will talk, and we may get into a fight again and she'll go off. We do try not to let me go off, because it puts me into a power position 'cause I am in bed and she is having to stand there where she is more exposed and trying to work things out. It has been very hard for me to go to her and try and work things out.

But then what happens is usually one of us starts crying, and the other one will sit down with that person and hug them or hold them, and that person will say everything they are upset about, and the other one will listen and will understand. And then they will both listen. And there may be two or so places more where it gets tense, but you know, it gets dealt with. We finish in a good place.

If all of this weren't enough, the couple also has a troubled sex life to work out.

NATALIE: We have had a lot of problems around our sexual relationship because of the dynamics of our relationship in general. When I feel one-down to Jill or powerless in our relationship, I also, at those times, don't feel sexual towards her. So I'd say in the last year we have had a real struggle with our sex life just because of that. But I think that is changing.

Perhaps, but not fast enough for Jill. At present they have sex about once a month. Natalie is the less interested partner, and the one who initiates. That slows it down quite a bit. Jill understands the problem, but so far it hasn't been settled to her satisfaction.

JILL: The second year in our relationship I was very upset about sex. I felt we were not making love very much and I didn't even know why not. . . . The problem was coming from her. I wanted to make love more. I asked her, "What is going on with you?" and she really couldn't say.

Finally, after a year of going back and forth like this, she said, "It is just that I feel depowered by you and so it has made me want to pull away and not feel like making love."

Jill takes some of the responsibility.

JILL: To me everything had to be perfect. And that was another reason we started making love less. Natalie felt she had this major responsibility. She sort of opted out.

It was hard to make her opt in.

JILL: I didn't feel like I had as much power to initiate sex. I can maybe suggest it, and then if she took it from there it was okay. But I felt she didn't feel like a person that I could seduce, like I did in previous relationships. I felt she was remote. Either she decided to make love or we didn't make love. So I was in this condition of waiting, of: "Well, here I am waiting for you and wanting to make love. And I am getting really worried." We can't not make love for three weeks and have our relationship work out. And she just kept sort of resisting and said we would talk about it.

I do feel we are just starting to get it worked out. I realize I don't have to be powerless about it. If I feel like making love, I can just say I want to make love. I still get worried when a couple of weeks have gone by. I feel I have to be the watchdog. We have to make love X times; otherwise the relationship is doomed. Because that is how I interpreted things in my previous relationship.

Natalie uses sex to right the balance of power. It is a measure of how secure and accepted she feels. Both women say that when they do have sex, it feels good. And despite Natalie's withholding, both women believe that sex functions as a bond between them.

NATALIE: It is very important because it is one way of keeping in touch, feeling affectionate, keeping close, staying close. It is real important to stay physically close even though you may feel close on an emotional level. It's not so much the orgasm itself, although I feel this is a wonderful experience. It is the actual being close to each other and touching each other, feeling taken care of and taking care of someone else.

They are both monogamous, but there is some difference of opinion about it.

NATALIE: In the beginning, Jill mentioned that she wanted to be non-monogamous. But that was like all her feelings at that point. "I am never going to put all my energy into one person again," and blah, blah, blah.

Both of us now, though, agree on it. I want to be monogamous and feel comfortable with being monogamous. I don't feel I would have enough time or energy to put into more than one relationship, or I would have two lesser relationships instead of one great relationship.

The only argument we had was at some point Jill got the impression that if she ever stepped out on me I would immediately call a halt to our relationship. I relieved her by saying, "No. I would be very hurt and upset but it wouldn't be a case of *Get out of my life. I hate you.*" I could see someone having a fling and us still being able to maintain our relationship and get through it.

JILL: I thought I'd never again agree to that. But I did agree to it, though I always felt I was less committed to it. I felt at some point that I am going to want to have an affair and I am going to feel trapped, and I wish she were less conservative about this. I had never run into anybody else and I am still attracted to Natalie, but I always worried about it as a future issue. But when we talked about this questionnaire, I felt very relieved.

Actually, it is an accomplishment that their sex life is in as good order as it is. Their first sex together had been a disappointment.

JILL: I was feeling great about my sexuality, so I had this horrible sort of fantasy about what a torrid love affair Natalie and I were going to have. We didn't have ideal circumstances for the first time. We were in my room and I was worried that Fran was going to come home at any minute. We went to bed anyhow, and it was not fantastic or wonderful. . . . It was: "I don't know you very well," and there were differences in how we wanted to make love, and I was used to doing one thing and Natalie was used to doing something else. I was feeling like, *Oh, I'm not going to be made love to the way I need to be made love to*, and the whole thing was blown. The next day I felt, *Well, that takes care of that. It wasn't so great.* And I thought it was over.

But I said to myself, *Well, I can't just want to make love with her and then say goodbye.* So we tried again the next night. We were still having this conflict about how we were going to make love and I was thinking, *This just isn't going to work out.* We got up . . . and I made some coffee and we talked. And it was when we were talking that I fell in love with her, got this different sense of her. So it was not a wonderful fantasy, and it was a letdown. That bit the dust—but we still fell in love.

Fights and differences considered, both Natalie and Jill think their relationship is getting better, not worse. Jill feels it will last at least for the next couple of years, and Natalie is hoping for the long run. Both acknowledge that Jill is the more tentative. Jill thinks that her doubts arise from her marriage.

JILL: That really affected me. It's the reason I'm very careful that Natalie and I have no role division. Any time something reminds me of being married, I hate it. I don't tolerate routine very well. And it has added to my feelings of not getting enough space. It adds to my feelings about money. I don't want to be dependent again. Or giving up my own room. It doesn't mean you don't sleep together, but I felt an adult person needs to have their own room. So money has to be separate and you have to be independent. These things are pretty common in lesbian relationships anyway.

Indeed, these are common lesbian demands: privacy, independence, and absolute equality. Jill is reacting to what she considered a stifling experience that forced her to be dependent. So when we asked both partners what pleased them most, her remarks were predictable. So were Natalie's:

JILL: For me, it's feeling that I can do whatever I want to do and still fit into the context of the relationship. I don't feel trapped. And it's talking and sharing. It feels real good to communicate and have a good time together.

NATALIE: To me it is a sense of commitment. Feeling room to grow, to change, is real important. Feeling supported. Being supported to change and to grow within our relationship and to grow together also.

Both women felt that being in a lesbian relationship provides unique advantages.

JILL: There is much more emotional intensity between two women. The standard complaint from my heterosexual friends is that there is something missing. Another thing I hear is that their husbands are not interested in the same kind of sharing or talking about people. My best friend, I know, likes to talk to me more than she likes to talk to her husband about stuff that we see going on.

Jill also thinks lesbians have a sexual advantage.

JILL: I feel that two people of the same sex have more of an identity with what the other person is feeling and what the other person wants and what feels good to them. I feel there is less likely to be a conflict like between a heterosexual man saying, "I want this," and the woman saying, "I want this," and both wanting two different things and not knowing what to do about it. And men and women get stuck into roles, even if a particular man and woman work them out. To me, being a lesbian couple means that we are not stuck into something and therefore we are more free.

They also admitted to disadvantages: Jill misses the physical protection males provide. She feels that even though her family is supportive, they would be far more so if she would give them a son-in-law. Natalie wishes society approved more, but she is accustomed to doing without much support, and therefore does not miss it as keenly as Jill does.

Still, both feel the compensations of being women together are more than enough. Jill tends to downplay their competition (she says she likes to play tennis with Natalie because they both are on the same level; Natalie says Jill enjoys it because Jill always wins) and they both downplay many of their areas of incompatibility. They acknowledge each of their many differences, but they seem tied together by their attraction to each other—at least for the near future.

Their advice to others on how to conduct a relationship is probably the centerpost of their own involvement:

NATALIE: Couples have to be open to each other's differences and acknowledge them and accept them and talk about everything.

JILL: Yes, not let anything by. And no matter how uncomfortable it is, or how much you argue about things, if something is bothering you, bring it up. Find some way to talk about it. If you're not getting anywhere, get some help. But don't let things build up over a period of months or years.

Jill and Natalie don't let much build up. Their relationship seems exhausting, there is so much to handle. But that may be what keeps them interested.

Jill and Natalie are a young, feminist, counterculture couple. They are striving mightily to separate themselves from a world they consider "oppressive heterosexist." Often, lesbians who have been married regard the institution as a subversion of their identity. They want to live in a society where gender differences do not automatically bestow power on one person at the expense of another.

New values emerge: No one should be made dependent by a partner whose income is greater; no one should do more "dirty work" than the other; male values are to be rejected. Female values, defined as good communication, expression of feelings, time spent with friends, and equality, are to be exalted. Male values to be avoided: excessive ambition in work, being emotionally closed, trying to be more powerful than one's partner, and struggling for leadership rather than working things out through a group process.

Great sensitivity to these precepts guarantees that almost all the desired values will be present in lesbian relationships. It is not surprising that they encounter considerable difficulty in trying to avoid the pitfalls of traditional heterosexual marriages and to create egalitarian partnerships. Allocating duties and roles fairly and in a nonsexist way complicates even the most intimate experience.

For example, Jill and Natalie's sex life is troubled because it is not clear who has the right and responsibility to suggest or refuse sex. In heterosexual relationships the man is expected to initiate more and the woman to refuse more. But no one wants to be the "man" in a lesbian feminist couple. Further, refusal is regarded less as a "woman's right" than, in Jill's view, as a personal rejection. If Jill and Natalie were able to practice what they believe, each would initiate sex as often as the other. But Natalie takes the lead almost all the time. Jill doesn't feel comfortable suggesting sex because Natalie is likely to refuse her some of the time and Jill is demoralized by the rejection. Natalie doesn't especially like to make the first move either—and it is an awkward placement of responsibility because both women agree that Natalie is the one less interested in sex. Furthermore, because Natalie feels less powerful than Jill, she uses her role as initiator as a subtle means of securing more power. By not often proposing sex, she controls at least one area of their relationship. In fact, she employs infrequent initiation as a form of refusal. And since neither woman fancies this traditional male role, initiating sex is infrequent altogether—and then infrequency becomes another issue.

Trying to be a "new woman" is a demanding task. Jill and Natalie are rejecting traditional female dependencies and traditional male privileges at the same time. It requires enormous effort and negotiation. Fortunately for them, both women believe their struggle for true equality is worth the time and pain it entails.

# Marnie and Janet

This couple illustrates the issues and values of an upper-income feminist couple with children. They are mothers and successful career people at the same time, and they manage their multiple responsibilities very well. Like some other lesbians, they have played down the sexual component of their relationship, and it is not a major bond between them. Furthermore, the need to be closeted weighs heavily on them.

Janet and Marnie live in a luxurious suburb of an eastern city. Driving up to their house in the summer, a visitor to the neighborhood sees the artistry of hundreds of talented gardeners. Each house has a great expanse of perfectly manicured lawn, and all the shrubs look planned, pampered, and thriving. One sees an occasional homeowner out puttering in front, but mostly there are teams of professional gardeners working hard at the upkeep of perfection. This is a neighborhood expensive to live in and costly to maintain.

Marnie and Janet's home is a one-story house built in the late fifties or early sixties. It is not remarkable from the outside, except that it, too, is set back on a magnificent lawn and it is quite large. When you enter, you realize it is even bigger than it at first appears, and there is a huge pool with a cabana in the back. The rooms are elegantly appointed and look "decorated." The joint interview took place in the family kitchen, a spacious room with a carpeted floor, a table, chairs, and fireplace, adjacent to a yet larger room where the actual food preparation takes place. There is room for live-in help, but it is unoccupied because Marnie and Janet do much of the work themselves.

Marnie and Janet are feminists who have lived together about seven years. Now in their early forties, they have been active and dedicated almost all their adult lives. Marnie, red-haired, trim, and athletic-looking, is an investment broker respected nationwide. Janet is short, slim, blond, and quite beautiful. She is a hospital administrator. Between them they have three children, all under the age of twelve.

They met during their work in the women's movement, when both were married. That was about twelve years ago. They got together to plan campaign strategy on a women's issue. Neither was a lesbian at the time. Nonetheless, they vividly recall their first impressions:

MARNIE: I thought she was gorgeous. She was wearing some Indian jewelry and . . . I thought, *My goodness, what a striking woman.* And then, when I began working with her, I was struck by how competent and responsible and kind she was.

JANET: I thought she was very impressive. Sort of strong, dynamic. Capable, knowledgeable in her areas of expertise. Good natured, fun-loving—just in general a good friend. A person I was attracted to for her friendly and warm qualities. There was no immediate physical attraction because I don't usually do that first. It's more of a head-set. I'm attracted to people for . . . their mental qualities. And it grew that way because we began to work closely together on committees and I began to admire her very much.

Marnie and Janet worked with each other for years but nothing beyond friendship happened between them. They would come together in a big city for meetings and would cooperate on a project. It was years before either realized theirs was more than a platonic attraction.

While Marnie had been married for ten years, she had also had a brief relationship with another woman, and so she was more aware than Janet of the possibility that she could be sexually attracted to a woman. But it was not a primary interest of hers—particularly because she was pregnant and thinking of the future in terms of husband and family.

Neither was willing to recognize what they were feeling until they went on a trip for the organization they belonged to.

JANET: It was a dramatic incident [that made me understand I was attracted to her]. There was a casual gesture. She just touched my knee or something and I just realized what was going on in my head. But I tried to put it out of my mind. We were in different cities and I was married.

Janet tried not to think about it; not only was she married, she was happily married. But, in fact, she was so worried about the attraction that she rationalized it as mere curiosity about what it would be like to be with another woman. So she went out and had a sexual experience with a *different* woman. That did not work. Still, she thought she and Marnie could remain just friends, and when they went on the trip together, Janet told herself it was going to be just work.

It did not turn out that way. They started seeing each other as much as possible. It was serious. Both women faced the breakup of their marriages.

JANET: There was great sadness. Marnie was either going to move here or end our relationship, and that meant I had to face my relationship with my husband and improve that, or start something new. And I made the decision that I wanted something new.

And I determined two things: I didn't want to have a bad model in divorce and . . . I really wanted to remain friends if possible, because it was very important that he continue to be a father to the children. And I didn't want to create any situation where I would become public, or a custody problem or any difficulty with the children.

Janet had two children, both already in school, and Marnie's child was newly born by the time they decided they had to be together. Marnie was living in a different city, but since her child was not in school, there was no obstacle to her moving. Furthermore, since she was a well-established name in her profession, she could easily set up a new office. She moved in with Janet, and after renting for a few years they bought the house they now occupy.

They are not open about their relationship, although anyone who knows them well is aware that they are gay. But they do not like labels.

JANET: I have thought over the whole labeling issue. My view is that it is a pendulum swing. There are people who are very homosexual and there are people who are very heterosexual, and there are people who go back and forth at various points of their life. I have finally decided the only importance of labeling is political. You need the label for fights for civil liberties. I don't identify with the label. I don't draw strong lines about whether I would care for a man or a woman. But I do accept the political need.

Both Marnie and Janet are quiet about their relationship, but they invite friends to their home and expect to be accepted as they are. The ony place they try to be completely secret is in their professional lives. They do not deal solely with liberal clients and they do not expect their clients to approve of their personal lives.

The aspect of their relationship most noticeable to the outsider—and indeed to themselves—is how much of it revolves around home and family. Both of them have children, take care of each other's children, and spend a lot of time—in fact, most of their leisure time—doing things with their children.

MARNIE: Time without kids? But the kids are *always* there. Virtually. For a period we would keep every Thursday and we'd get a sitter and we'd go out and spend Thursday night alone together. But we both got so busy that it wasn't practical. From time to time we just go out with other adults. We're really only alone after nine when they go to bed.

Having three children and two very busy careers takes a lot of planning. They trade responsibilities a lot. They will each shop for the other's children or take them somewhere. The children treat both women as parents, and occasionally, just like children in other kinds of families, they try to see if they can gain some power by playing one against the other.

MARNIE: We have some issues over discipline, but we've learned to handle them. Like, if I disciplined one of the children and that child runs to her and says *"Waa!"* And then she'll come in and say, "What's going on?" in sort of an angry tone of voice. One child in particular tends to manipulate the situation, but we've talked about it and we've come up with ways to solve things. Never caused any big problem.

They are discreet about their relationship, even though the children know they are a couple.

JANET: We don't discuss it with the children, but then I don't think that parents discuss their sexuality with children. Children don't really want to acknowledge their parents' sexuality and I don't see any reason to discuss it unless they should ask. When they do ask, we answer whatever they ask, but they've never asked that particular question. They've asked what is homosexuality, what is a lesbian, and we've discussed those things in a factual manner. They certainly know that Marnie and I sleep together, that we hug each other and are affectionate. But we're affectionate with the children as well and half the other people that walk into the house, so where they draw the line or what they want to absorb is really going to be up to them. I haven't said, "Gee, kids, do you really realize what you got here?" And, "You got to face that right now, at the age of five and eleven." I'm sure they're aware of something but may not have a name for it.

Marnie and Janet are quite tied into other families as well. Janet still maintains a close relationship with her ex-husband. Marnie does not and is not pleased about Janet's doing so, but she does not interfere. They spend a good deal of time with Janet's parents.

JANET: I think they feel that I'm in a good environment and they like Marnie very much. . . . We all share a lot of interests and everybody has a good sense of humor and gets along well. That wasn't immediate, but over the years my parents treat Marnie's kid as a grandchild. They've grown a lot in the last ten years.

As committed as Marnie and Janet are—and as intertwined as they are—they still keep finances separate.

JANET: We don't keep an itemized list but we try to stay pretty straight as far as accounting. If one of us gets behind, we try to be sure to repay and not presume too long. But I think if something happened to either one of us, we'd support each other. There's no question about that. And neither one of us is fussy about money. But I think that's because we both have enough to get along with.

Housework used to be a big problem. Now they hire someone else. It was an issue until they did that.

MARNIE: We both have a tendency to get depressed if the house is terribly messy. But by the same token, with our feminist activities and our professions and raising the children, neither of us has a lot of time to spend on the house. So that's helped a great deal. Other than that, if one person cooks—that's usually me because she's tired of it—the other person cleans up. But nothing is set.

The emotional climate of their household is one of warm rationalism. They strike one as "married and settled." They talk about themselves in those terms as well. For example, though they may have disagreements, they do not have a lot of conflict.

MARNIE: When I get angry I traditionally have not talked about it. I just sort of bury it and walk away mad. And she won't let me do that. If I get angry at her for something, she makes me talk about it. It's not my style, but it's been very healthy for me and I can't even remember the things that have made me angry. More annoyances than anything else. One or the other will grab the other and say, "Hey, what's troubling you? You need to talk to me. Force it out and we'll talk about it." We don't have win-lose situations. We're both reasonable and busy people. You don't get into silly arguments.

JANET: I am not a confrontive person. I don't like to discuss things that are distasteful and we don't like encounters that are bad. We have emphatic discussions but we don't have arguments.

There are some things they don't discuss much. They have sex about once a month. Marnie would prefer it a bit more often. Janet is orgasmic a bit less often than she would like, but she doesn't mention it because she feels it would be "distressing" to Marnie. Marnie knows that their sex life needs work but is still more sexually satisfied than she used to be with men.

MARNIE: I was a very late comer to sexual activity. I didn't become sexually active until I was twenty-four or twenty-five. I never was that interested. I felt there were other ways to show love and affection, other than engaging in "The Act." Sometimes I found it downright uncomfortable to do that with men. I find men, even the most sensitive men—there comes a point in time where they don't care about your needs. They've got to fulfill themselves and they just don't care where you're at. Or even if they care, their body decides for them. Something shuts off down there and they just go forth. And then, having them fall asleep right after it happened. No—you know—touching and no affection or discussion or anything, and I found that a turn-off. With my current partner, I just always feel good about it even if it hasn't resulted in orgasm. It doesn't always.

Sex has decreased, but neither partner thinks this is significant of anything.

MARNIE: It's a natural tapering off. We've both been extremely busy and the fatigue level is crucial. You'll be working your way up to it and one or the other will just say, "Oh, I can't stay awake any longer," and just nod off. And, you know, the other one says, "Oh, well."
   We are comfortable and secure in one another's love and we don't have to do anything to prove that we love one another.

The two partners believe that the things keeping them together are humor, the women's movement, and family—although not necessarily in that order.

MARNIE: I think you should know about the sharing, the fun. You know we have the ability to have a great deal of fun together. . . . We have the ability to laugh, both in funny circumstances and at ourselves, if that's appropriate.

JANET: Yeah, I think generally we're both pretty happy people. It's nice to be around someone who's not morose or self-critical or beset with problems.

MARNIE: I think another component is the contribution we have both made to the women's movement and the ongoing contribution that we are making through our careers and through political involvement, whatever that may be. And we're both very supportive of one another, in career and extracurricular career—the women's movement.

The women's movement is largely what cements their relationship. They feel it brought them together and gives purpose to their lives.

JANET: I think many women have come to where we are, through the women's movement. . . . I think the women's movement has allowed women to get over competition, and value and not thwart each woman's career. . . . Our relationship allows and supports that. And it will be a long time before society allows that between a male and a female.

MARNIE: You run across so many exceptional women with such dedication and talent that it was natural—when you're working with such women, *for* women—to develop a strong, abiding love for women. And then, once you have developed a love for women and a respect for women, and a particular friend you love and respect, the next step is naturally: Why, if you love a woman, why limit the love for a woman to just intellectual and emotional? The last component is the perfectly natural thing to do.

JANET: I think our acculturation makes us better partners. We have been conditioned to be loving and open and gentle, whereas that is acculturated out of little boys. . . . Consequently, a relationship between two women tends to be much more open and loving, nurturing, supporting, than a heterosexual relationship.

We asked them if there were any disadvantages.

JANET: Not being open. When a heterosexual couple gets married, the joke stops at the wedding night. . . . Whereas a gay couple—no one thinks about: "My, how she suffered with him while he struggled through college," or "Wasn't she supportive when he was in that accident?"—the way they talk about married people. They only see sexuality. It's just incredibly prurient.

MARNIE: You have to be so careful. We have a little joke about [hugging in] airports. Everyone does it. Sometimes we feel just like going out to the airport.

JANET: You can't expect your partner to be invited to dinner like other partners. You can't talk about the pride and joy that you have in the accomplishment of the other.

Sometimes I have a strong desire to speak out against the

incredible bigotry I hear. Tell them: "How long have you known me and been my friend, and I'm gay," and deal with that. It happened in my own family. My own sister, who is liberal, politically and socially, made some real slur, and I felt like saying: "Don't put down a whole category of people. You don't know who might be in it, including your own sister." I wanted to say that. For the shock value, to make her grapple with her bigotry. But I didn't.

Janet and Marnie both see disadvantages to being gay in society, but advantages to being women together. They seem to be a very successful couple despite the cost of having to be private about their relationship. They give some advice to other couples:

JANET: Happiness is what individuals do. People decide if they're going to be unhappy or happy, and unless people make that individual decision it's unlikely they will be successful in a couple.

MARNIE: Don't force things. Don't force the other to be political. Things come back to haunt you at twenty-seven that you might have said at seventeen. Just give each other support and don't take anything for granted. Life is tough enough out there. Make life easier for each other.

*Epilogue:* This is a couple that did not last. We were saddened when we heard about their breakup, because they had appeared very happy and stable. But other events interceded in their lives and changed Janet's commitment to the relationship.

About a year after we interviewed them, Janet's mother became very ill and was hospitalized. There were other disrupting events as well: Her sister began to have marital problems, and the combined effect of these two traumas caused her to reexamine her life.

She realized that her sexual relationship with Marnie had been waning for some time. There was no longer any eroticism between them, and she had thrown herself into her work with a vengeance. Her affection or respect for her partner did not diminish in the least, but their relationship had become more that of best friends or roommates than a love affair. Things that might not have bothered her before took on importance: For example, she could not really love her partner's child as she loved her own and this troubled her. She resented the noise and disruption the child caused. Then, too, Marnie had lost a great deal of weight. While this was becoming, it affected the appeal she had once had for Janet. She seemed like another person. The more maternal, supportive, soft look of her partner had disappeared.

Janet was feeling more and more independent, more in need of privacy, autonomy, separateness. She came to the sad conclusion that her relationship with Marnie was over. Why was it over? Was it just "mid-life crisis"? Or was it something inherent in this relationship? Marnie was confused. She was still in love with Janet and could not understand why they had grown apart.

Janet was not sure herself. But she had some insights. For one thing, she had never truly resolved her questions about the end of her marriage. She had left her husband at the height of her immersion in the feminist movement. Whether her discontent within the marriage helped to precipitate her involvement with the movement or with Marnie, or whether it was the movement that inspired her relationship with Marnie and the end of her marriage, she will never know. But she does know that it was her growing dissatisfaction with the emotional inadequacies of men that attracted her to women, specifically to Marnie. Eroticism, love, and respect fused, and for many years it was beautiful as well as exciting.

But Janet's nostalgia for marriage and its rewards surfaced and grew stronger. When she saw husbands and wives and their children in the street, she became envious. She and Marnie, both so prominent in their careers, had kept their relationship secret from all but the closest of their friends. She missed the approval granted to marriage, and the social recognition married couples automatically acquire. She had come from a strong, close family herself, and she felt the need of those ties.

By comparison, she found her relationship with Marnie flawed. In her marriage, she and her husband had shared the same aspirations. But with Marnie, Janet said, "We were never working for something in common. Our estates were being built up separately to be separately inherited by our individual children." Finances were separate, never discussed; generously shared, but never combined. Ultimately, their relationship did not have the feel of a marriage to Janet, and she did not want to live with a roommate.

So they separated. They are still friends. They never say a bad word about each other. They both feel terrible that it is over. Marnie has been truly grief-stricken. What the future will bring for either of them is unclear. Janet is dating men; Marnie believes her future is in another female relationship. It was a good friendship that turned into a love affair, but never into a marriage, and now it has become a friendship once again.

# Five Gay Male Couples

## Henry and Gene

We chose Henry and Gene because their lifetime relationship has lasted since childhood. They have learned to cope with non-monogamy and still manage to keep an active sex life within the relationship. One works at home now, the other outside. They play different roles— although they are not similar to heterosexual couples.

We walked up to their duplex and rang the bell for apartment no. 1. The outside had elegant antique wrought-iron railings. The door opened into an extremely spacious entrance hall, and the apartment seemed to run the length of the block. Inside it was attractively and intensely decorated, with eye-catching photos of the couple and their friends, oils, and etchings taking up almost every available niche or wall space. The apartment looked like a retrospective of their life together.

Henry and Gene are casual, friendly men who welcomed us into their home. Gene gave us a tour, since much of the art was bought when Gene was a high-earning partner in an advertising firm. Now, however, Gene does free-lance illustration and earns far less money. He is of medium height, gray-haired, and distinguished. At fifty-five, and after thirty-eight years of living with Henry, he prefers to do things at home, working only when he feels like it. Henry, fifty-six, looks much like Gene, except that he is balding. He is an executive in a department store, where he earns a good, but not extraordinary, salary. Their combined earnings are enough to support their style of life, since most of the acquisitions (including the duplex) were made a while ago, and they now spend most of their time at home, living rather simply.

Henry and Gene were childhood sweethearts. They met in high school in a small town in Illinois and became best friends. They didn't think of their affection for each other as sexual until much later. None-theless, they were always very attached, so attached that after a death in Gene's family he moved in with Henry's family, who more or less adopted him throughout his high school years.

In high school the couple's intimacy was not completely fraternal, but they never labeled it homosexual.

> HENRY: We were thrown together and the sexual experimentation started and became more frequent, without being discussed or anything. It would just happen. But I think we loved each other without knowing it. Without putting it into words, either. It didn't dawn on me until after the war.

> GENE: Oh, in the beginning it was nonsexual. . . . I was fooling around more with this girl I was going with . . . because that's what we all did. We sat in cars and drove around—you know, necked—and we'd go to one of the person's houses and do like all teenagers did.

Life went on this way for a while, with nothing ever really defined between them. Then the Second World War came; both men enlisted and were sent off to different fronts.

> HENRY: We separated after induction and we never saw each other again throughout the war. We corresponded a couple of times weekly, if not daily. I did a lot of letter-writing and so did he. . . . We almost met once, just missed by an hour or so, and then he was sent overseas. I was sent over later and then I was wounded and sent back, but he didn't come back until December of 1945. In the meantime we had grown up, I guess, and realized about the love relationship, and our letters talked about missing each other and learning that there were gay people in the world. And so when he came back it was like a great realization, and bang—the whole thing, the whole world really opened up for us. It was really a sensation that only happens once. . . . We were on the seventh cloud. After being apart that long.

When Gene came home, it was to "his family"—which was Henry's family—and he moved back into his room with Henry. But that did not last long.

> GENE: I moved back with his family and immediately we decided that we wanted to go to Chicago. That was because his mother became suspicious of our behavior. . . . I mean, I'd been in the army and I knew what the world was about now, so I came back totally different from the person that I was when I left . . . and it became clear to his mother, and his brother was a priest and he said that Henry would have to talk to a psychiatrist. And it was a good psychiatrist. He just said, "Well, you're a homosexual. Go home and I'll talk to your family"—rather than trying to do something about it. So we knew we had to leave.

It was hard on Henry's family. They were very upset, but Henry was too much in love to let their feelings change his life.

HENRY: We were so much in love then that nothing, *nothing* would have stopped us. So strong. We would have faced any odds, including censorship of the family or whatever else faced us.

So Henry and Gene left the small town they had grown up in and started their adult relationship in Chicago. There were early conflicts, just getting to know each other and establishing the sexual relationship:

HENRY: The main problem, in the beginning, would be my greater commitment to Gene than his to me. He would go outside, just because he is more gregarious, and I had to learn that the outside thing doesn't mean a thing to him. We're rather opposite about that. I was more of a prude and I guess it was due to my Victorian mother. I had more of a sense of decorum than he did. Gene, being more open and friendly a personality, managed to get to bed with a lot of people at that time, which I did not and do not. But still, he's more in love with me now perhaps than me with him. It all turned out to have nothing to do with his love for me.

Sexual issues were a problem but they caused only one week's separation.

HENRY: Somehow or other our sexual relationship thinned out and it went haywire, and it upset me a lot and I decided to move out— and under protest and he didn't want me to. But I didn't see any other way, so I did—only to find out it was a big mistake.

They missed each other terribly during that week, resolved to put their sexual relationship in order, and did. After that, Henry became a little less insecure about Gene's non-monogamy, and Gene resolved to be more sexual with Henry. Now they have sex at least once a week. They talk it over if it starts to slacken off, and make an effort to mend the problem. Though Henry has had a couple of experiences outside the relationship, it really is not in his personality to be non-monogamous, and both men have come to accept that only Gene will take that freedom.

They lead a quiet, homey life. Their apartment is a social center:

HENRY: We like a lot of time alone, but this house is like an open house and a lot of close friends come by. . . . We were the first ones to move into this block in our group, and since then, perhaps six other good friends have moved around here, so they're very apt to ring the bell, and neighbors come by, too, and there's more often someone here. So we're in a sense not alone that much, but we're at home.

Gene works hard at maintaining the apartment. It is his special pleasure and he has time for it now that he is free-lancing.

HENRY: Gene runs the house. He does all the shopping. If I buy something, I get the wrong thing. He gets very exasperated. He doesn't even like to send me out for anything. And he is a great, absolutely superb cook. I wish he weren't sometimes. The food is so good I sometimes have a problem stopping eating. . . . Look at that table. I can't do a table the way Gene can. He puts all that stuff on it and it looks wonderful. It all comes out of his mind.

Gene sees it as a natural division of labor.

GENE: It just fell into place automatically this way. Because of my childhood and upbringing, I knew how to cook and to do household things, and he had never done that. He had been an only child in essence, and I grew up with seven brothers and sisters, and I was the oldest, so I knew how to do things for everyone. I know how to run the house. My mother was always pregnant and having babies, and since I was the oldest, I was the one to put the supper on the table. I also grew up being very handy. My father was a mechanical person. I learned how to repair cars and how to build bookshelves, how to do carpentry and painting and all that stuff. So I do everything.

They try to avoid assuming specialized roles and don't think of each other as mimicking husband and wife behavior, but they acknowledge that outsiders, seeing Gene's absolute dominion over all aspects of their domestic life, often classify Gene as the "wife."

HENRY: If Gene referred to me in conversation he would refer to me as his husband, and I would say the same thing. "Husband" doesn't fit very well either, but it's stupid, you know—there is no word that fits. So he made up one of his own and we call each other our "other." Gene says it's short for our "other half," and it rhymes with mother and brother so it means family.

They have a happy, peaceful sort of existence, with only a few bones of contention. The one that bothers Henry most is Gene's absolute aversion to travel. Gene is the quintessential homebody. He does not want to go anywhere, while Henry loves to go on trips. It has been an issue for many years.

HENRY: I can't get Gene to take a vacation with me. It irritates me enormously. I've begged and pleaded. . . . Last year I went to California and had such a good time. And all the while I'm there I just wish that Gene was with me. I mean I did so many fun things and had such a wonderful time without him. But I would have had a better time with him. I just can't get him out of here. He is firm about it . . . a homebody. . . . He doesn't like to leave his house. I love our apartment as a place to come home to. Gene likes to live here with the flowers. He feels vibrant here.

This issue becomes more complicated when it involves family responsibilities. Henry's family still has a strong affection for Gene, but he will not leave the house even to see them.

HENRY: When I visit home I do wish he would be with me, because when we all lived together Gene was like part of the family and I just wish that he would keep it up that way. Because when I go home they [say], "Why doesn't Gene come with you?" And I have to make up some reason for Gene not coming with me and coming to see his family. . . . Even when my mother died he wouldn't go home, and that hurt a lot. When that happened to *him* I went home with him, as I should have, and I thought he should have been with me, because it was a real hard experience.

Gene is not intransigent about much else, but he does not give on this issue.

GENE: I hate taking trips. I'm totally against traveling—I mean, I'm a person who likes to stay at home. We have been on a few major vacations, but I don't like to go and we have friction. But that is something we are just different about. It comes up every year and it's: "Why can't we go to Europe like everybody else?" and this kind of thing. . . . We went once. It's enough.

So Gene and Henry have a highly articulated homelife. They bring all the comforts of home in, rather than go out. Including people. They have created a sort of extended family comprised of men they have been friends with for many years or once had a passing sexual relationship with. Sometimes a few special people do become part of the actual family.

HENRY: We have in a sense adopted people. I mean we have one boy that we've known since he was eighteen who was like our son, I guess. He's now thirty-five and whenever he comes to town, he comes, like coming home to his parents. He comes here and stays for a couple of months, but with no questions asked. He just calls up and says, "I'm coming," and he comes and stays. There are a couple of others—a man who's forty now and we knew him since he was eighteen—and we've just about adopted these people.

There are always visitors, friends, sexual acquaintances. Both Henry and Gene seem able to enjoy a continuous stream of people and still feel they have time for each other. During the opera season things become strained, because Henry, an opera fanatic, goes every night. Gene does not get to see him as much as he would like. But Gene is delighted that Henry gets so much pleasure from this hobby, and understands that "he needs it and I feel that he deserves it."

A few remaining irritations surface between the two men over the subject of non-monogamy. Henry wishes that Gene's sexual behavior were different, but he accepts it.

HENRY: I know that when he doesn't make love to me it's not because he doesn't love me, but because his libido is lower than mine. . . . I know this is funny to say, but I'm not really his physical type. He's more gregarious. I'm more monogamous, and as long as he doesn't reject me too much, we're okay.

It turns out that Henry is interested in having sex only with Gene, and Gene is more interested in sex when he is with someone else.

HENRY: Gene is more interested in sex when he sees attractive people on the street. The neighborhood is full of them. He can't go to the grocery store without cruising somebody. I can spend the whole week and I don't see all that. But for him, the whole street is awash with beauty. To me Gene is the only one . . . a great turn-on.

This difference is reflected in Gene's sexual habits with other men and in Henry's role in the couple's sex life. Henry almost always initiates sexual contact. Gene is usually willing to have sex, but he is not always enthusiastic. This is one of the reasons the couple almost broke up many years ago. Henry tries not to pressure Gene ("I try and use a little self-control and not jump on him whenever I feel like it") and that means having sex only once a week rather than every day, as he would really like. For Gene it means trying to be accessible to Henry even though he doesn't always feel like it. Henry does most of the "work" (he is likely to be "active" in bed, performing oral and anal sex with his partner but not often receiving either from his partner) but this is a pattern they both accept and neither starts arguments about it.

Gene feels that their sex life is in order.

GENE: [Non-monogamy] is a minor issue for two reasons: Number one, I don't do it very much, and number two, he has come to understand me throughout the years, and he feels more secure now than he did in the beginning, naturally. I mean, he was afraid that I would disappear on one of these adventures of mine, and now that's impossible.

We have had only one serious disagreement lately. An old friend of ours was here about two years ago and I told Henry that I had had a relationship with him. I told him because I thought it was amusing. . . . Well, Henry became absolutely outraged. . . . I should have known better and not told him. . . . But I became angry because Henry became rude to the guy. The guy was still staying one more day and, you know, he says, "What's wrong with Henry? He's acting funny at breakfast." And so I became angry, saying, "What a way to treat a friend," and "This is absurd behavior." It was resolved by the passage of time and discussion.

Gene describes such situations as a "lark" and does not countenance histrionics from Henry. Henry apologizes, but it is not his emotional cup of tea. But as Gene says, it does not come up much anymore, and it all happens in the context of a lifetime relationship.

In our interview with both of them they were very protective of each other and worked as a "team" in presenting a story, retelling a specific incident, making sure the other's point of view was properly stated. When we asked them what they like most about their relationship, they were hard pressed for an answer. There was a moment of hesitation; then both said, "Everything." The secret of their success? Both agree that it is being able to talk things out.

GENE: I tell everybody, "You've got to sit and talk to each other." There is nothing more important.

Henry agreed and added his own insights:

HENRY: Tolerance. You've got to make allowances for the other person to go out and do his thing. If you really love him, you'll make allowances. And if you don't really love him, please forget about the whole deal. If the next year is what you really want, then you'll find a way to talk through any problem.

Henry and Gene have spent their lives together and nothing is going to break them up. As is true of many other gay couples in our study, their sex lives may not be entirely coordinated, but their emotional life is secure and well protected. Henry may have to make more allowances for Gene, but Gene is not any less committed. They pool their resources, own property together, and feel secure enough in their future for Gene to semi-retire. Except for Gene's non-monogamy, theirs resembles the long-term devoted relationships among our other three types of couples.

This is a childhood romance that flowered into adult commitment.

# Warren and Ted

This couple reflects some of the problems that can occur when one of the men is making the adjustment from a heterosexual marriage to a gay relationship. We chose them because they show how much men may need both "male" and "female" qualities in the same partner and how difficult that combination may be to achieve. In addition, Warren and Ted demonstrate what can happen when one partner is financially better off than the other, and how such an imbalance can affect the equality between the partners.

We had to drive way out of the city to reach their address, and when we arrived, we walked into a major construction project. Warren and Ted were in the process of building a very elaborate house, and since they were doing a lot of it themselves, there was a certain amount of chaos. It was snowing and we waded through slush, boards, and bricks. Thankful at last to get out of the slop, we discovered that the interior left something to be desired: The roof had several leaks, the heat was not quite working—and it was very cold. Clearly, this was going to be a wonderful home, but not until some time in the future. We were impressed by their ambition and wondered if this kind of joint enterprise helped or hurt a relationship.

They seemed much less affected by the discomfort than we. Warren met us at the door. He is a tall, handsome man of thirty-four with an angelic face and a confident manner of speaking. He is a broker in an old-line Wall Street firm and doing very well. Ted was also friendly but looked quite different. Where Warren seemed to have just emerged from his downtown office, Ted, thirty-six, looked as if he had come in from the backyard. He is a construction engineer and likes doing outdoor work, which was his contribution to the home they were building. He was a handsome man as well, dressed in jeans and a work shirt, and rather "woodsy" looking. At the time we talked to them, the two had known each other for four years and had lived together for two and a half.

They met at a gay steambath when Warren was still married. Warren's first impressions were based on Ted's physical attributes.

> WARREN: The first ones [impressions] are always physical because you make your original determination based on someone's physical appearance. I can still remember looking at his legs and thinking he had very nice legs. . . . My first emotional reaction was that he was an extremely gentle person who was always interesting. . . . I could tell he was a "good" person. He was the type I was used to from the Midwest and it just kind of showed.

> TED: It was two in the morning . . . and I was taken by his fire, the intensity of the individual. . . . Something snapped within me. . . . I was just there for sexual fantasy and certainly wasn't looking for someone anymore [he had just finished an unhappy relationship], but something just happened and I knew that I had to see more of this person.

Seeing more of him was not easy. At the time, Warren was confused about his sexual activities, deciding that he was mildly bisexual. He liked being married, loved his "beautiful home in a nice suburb," and was fighting the growing perception that he was gay. He gave Ted a phony name and even though he continued to contact him, he would not let Ted call him. Ted understood his dilemma and was sympathetic. But he was entranced and did not want Warren to vanish from his life. He did a little detective work.

> TED: Here was this married man who gave me a phony name, no last name, and the only thing I knew was approximately the year he had graduated from business school. And I knew he worked on Wall Street and I knew where he had worked in the past, and so we carried on for a good month before I did enough sleuthing on the side to put the story together. . . . He let slip such things as "How about meeting in Philadelphia, because I'll be there for this meeting?"
>     So I went to the meeting and said, "I'm trying to locate an investment broker from _____ at this meeting," and described him, and they said, "Oh, yes, but you have the wrong name. You mean Warren." I gave them a phony story and said I wanted to locate him

for some private work, and they told me the firm he worked for and everything. . . . About three weeks later we had planned a long weekend together, and I told him about what I had gone through to find out about him. And he revealed the torment that he had gone through in the last week trying to keep it secret, and knew that he was going to have to reveal himself to me because he knew there was more to our relationship, that it had developed that strongly.

They started to see a lot of each other, but it was still difficult because Warren had to lie to his wife and invent ways to see Ted. He began to have more and more difficulty keeping his two worlds separate.

WARREN: I had this awful experience of dreaming about him and waking up in the middle of the night in bed with my wife and calling my wife Ted.

Ted was having problems too.

TED: I had done this before and I wasn't about to get myself involved in another relationship where I was playing the second fiddle to a married man who had no intention of divorcing his wife. . . .
   We talked for hours and a lot of time with tears, because we were both scared. He could no longer just say goodbye to me and I knew it, and I was scared for him because I knew what he was going to have to do. And he didn't dislike his wife; he just wasn't attracted to her sexually. And so there were difficult times ahead. We would stay up all hours of the night talking and fall asleep in exhaustion.

Warren got up the courage to tell his wife, and they agreed to separate. It was very painful for him. He liked his wife. He even offered to stay if she would give him sexual freedom. She did not find this acceptable, however, and since they had no children, they handled the break in a reasonably short period of time.
   Ted helped Warren move out. Warren was basically in shock. He wanted Ted, but he was afraid of being gay, of entering the gay world, of leaving his life as a married man and embarking on a different kind of relationship. He moved from his rather elaborate house to a very modest place in the city. It was so depressing that the only thing Warren could do that night was cry.
   After the move, almost immediately things got better. But their early days had a lot of conflict. They were both feeling their way in the relationship. In addition, Warren was confronting his feelings about being gay. The transition was difficult.

WARREN: I was very emotionally unsteady at the time. . . . What I needed was someone who was very, very verbal, and tactile, and Ted is neither. He is very reserved. His feelings are quieter than most people's, but also a lot deeper. That was a source of conflict, that constantly milking him for verbal approval and reinforcement and stuff like that. That was a terrible drag on him, I now realize, because he had come out of something where there was always grasping going on and he was ready to carry on like a normal couple rather than having some schizo bug him all day long.

There were other problems:

WARREN: It was a very painful thing to him that he wasn't basically making any money in his job and so he was heavily into debt with me. We were sharing all household expenses, but he wasn't able to pay any, plus I was loaning him money. It never bothered me, but to him it was just painful. . . . He hated it because it was kind of a monthly event where we would have to go through the bills and he'd have to sign a promissory note and he'd have to sign an increase each month to the promissory note.

The money issue became less serious over time as Ted's business picked up, and their financial disparity lessened somewhat. But the conflict over communication and expressiveness endured.

TED: We've had long periods of talking through lots of anguish. We are both very intense personalities, but in our own way, and he needs a lot of reinforcement to know that I really care about him and need him. I'm a little more laid back maybe, because he can give me that feedback so much easier than I give it to him. . . . I had some conversation with friends about it, and I really worked at it and it took about a year and a half before we've started to feel it's been better.

Ted had some needs of his own:

TED: One of the demands I made before we ever got into this relationship was that there would be an extent of personal and sexual freedom and that it must be mutually agreed to by both of us. I would have the opportunity to go, at times that I determined, to the baths or bars. . . . Even though we agreed on it, it was very traumatic for him. I felt the need to get away once in a while, just to go to the baths with wild sexual fantasies, just to do my thing, and part of the agreement was that we would never follow up on someone there. . . . It is always done during weekdays, and the other person is let know so that you don't have the other person waiting at home with dinner or something like that. We don't exactly tell each other. We just say something that denotes that we will be home late. We are always home before dawn.

Warren was not ready for this in the beginning. He had been in a secure marriage and was used to having a monogamous partner. When Ted insisted on non-monogamy, the image of a gay community and the myth of the impossibility of a permanent relationship loomed before Warren. He was scared.

TED: I would come home totally exhausted about four or five in the morning, and he would be awake and the ashtray would be overfilled with burned-out cigarettes. He would be just heartbroken and so we would have to work it through. . . . There were lots of tears and talking, and most of all—even though it fell within the boundaries of our agreement—he needed reassurance that I didn't find someone I was more attracted to than him. So now when I come home, if he's awake we will talk for a little bit and I will assure him and tell him that I love him, and I am glad to be home and in bed with him, and it's fine.

Warren still becomes a little jealous, but he has grown accustomed to Ted's casual sex and it is no longer an issue. But problems of communication and decision-making abound.

WARREN: Ted is much more easygoing than I. He will just simply defer. He defers not only because he thought I was making better decisions, but because he didn't have more confidence in himself. Plus, at least on the surface, I am more aggressive.

I would like it to be more totally equal. I wish he would take more initiative in decision-making. For example, I will say, "Let's go to Bermuda," and I'm always the one to say it, and then once I say it, by and large I make the arrangements. I wish he would say, "Well, let's go to Los Angeles," or something like that. Or make decisions about shopping.

Ted feels his unwillingness to make decisions stems from nonemotional sources. He thinks it is solely a question of money.

TED: I have less ability to make decisions because I don't have the financial resources, so I let him pretty much determine things because he has to pay for it. . . . When my financial picture is bleak, it's hard for me to handle and puts additional stresses on our relationship. Because I wouldn't want to go anyplace, 'cause that would mean spending money and I didn't have money to spend. And I didn't want to entertain, because that would cost a hundred bucks to have eight guys over. . . . I would say no . . . and we would fight. . . . Also, as a result of my financial problems, I really get depressed and other problems creep into it, like sexual problems. When you are low mentally, you're not interested in a lot of lovemaking. . . . But I was reluctant to tell him some of these—about how sad and embarrassed and frustrated and angry I felt inside.

Warren doesn't entirely accept this. He feels Ted is abdicating responsibility.

WARREN: I think a lot of it is due to lack of initiative. Like I'll know at all times what we need from the store and he won't have the vaguest idea. If he goes, he will get a fetish about something and so for five weeks in a row he'll buy Bisquick.

It is very important for Warren that everything be on a parity, that everything is shared. This is difficult for Ted, because he is quieter and less skilled at confronting issues, and also because he doesn't like to suggest things that require an economic commitment. The couple solved the problem of housework by hiring help, but in general keeping the relationship in emotional equilibrium has been a struggle. Neither feels less masculine than the other and Ted doesn't feel that his passive exterior reflects "who's on top."

> TED: There are no masculine or feminine roles in our relationship. We are both masculine. Personality-wise, I tend to be more passive, quiet, and as people get to know me I become more outgoing. I think people would view Warren as being the more dominant personality and me the passive, although our sexual roles are completely reversed in that I am the dominant sexual partner. It's extremely important to him that I am, and that hasn't always been the easiest thing for me, since I have a lot of passive aspects of my sexual response that he's never been able to accommodate.

Warren wants Ted to be expressive and sharing and at the same time "all man" and, indeed, the sexually aggressive partner. He wants Ted to be equally involved in decision-making—but he is the one who keeps track of money scrupulously. As one might imagine, this leads to conflicts. One of the issues the couple faces is how to handle them.

Warren wants Ted to be more confrontational.

> WARREN: Well, what happens is we stonewall each other. Someone will break down but it gets so damned uncomfortable. Sooner or later we have to talk about it. And in the meantime I am likely to put on a big pout.

Ted, on the other hand, finds Warren's style a bit overwhelming.

> TED: Things get real emotional with outpouring of anger and tears. I don't get fiercely emotional. It takes a lot for me to boil, but Warren is a very hot, emotional person, very intense, and what appears to be a little firecracker can turn into a real bomb. At first I was so shocked by these reactions, I didn't know how to handle him and he didn't know how to handle me, and I took everything he said literally. And the first time it happened, I felt the relationship was over and I was just about ready to pack and leave. But that's just the way he is, and now I understand he just needs to vent it, and of course, he needs reassurance and talking about it later, as I do too. But I don't get fired up. I tend to get quiet and withdrawn.

*Quiet and withdrawn* drives Warren crazy. And he has to watch the way he fights or it will get worse.

> WARREN: If I come on too strong, I would just blow him away. If I don't come on too strong, sometimes he will get angry back. Then it can be one-upmanship. But if I get up a head of steam I can pretty much shut him up.

Ted recognizes Warren's frustration, and as a result they have developed a mutually satisfying style of dealing with problems.

TED: Initially I just wouldn't confront a situation. . . . I just would do anything to avoid any type of conflict. The longer I could put it off, great. And, boy, I could really do it. He would always confront me, and I told him that for a while earlier in our relationship I felt like it was either twenty questions or he was the judge and he was the prosecuting attorney and I was sitting on the chair and being on the witness stand and I was just getting drilled, and I resented it. He realized that he was using technique on me and I didn't feel comfortable anymore, and that I would feel less threatened and willing to bare my soul and discuss the topic, but I felt less skilled. Now I've become a lot more skilled at talking things out, and now I think I will confront a sensitive issue right away.

So they created new rules in order to minimize the impact of their conflict.

TED: We made an agreement that we would never go to bed without kissing each other good-night. We would never go to bed angry, or at least we wouldn't sleep in the same bed if we were, and there has been only one night when that happened and we couldn't resolve a particular issue.

But they have not yet worked out a way to avoid problems altogether. Both men told us that their arguments generally involve communication, and nearly always build to crisis point before they are settled.

TED: A typical argument. I don't smoke and I'm really offended when I go into a room and there are three ashtrays and they are full. So I will just dump some ashtrays in the garbage or the trays will just disappear, and he will ask for an ashtray and I will make some sort of sly comment, and then he will get on something else and we are like a badminton game. We are throwing it back and forth, and finally he stops it, 'cause I can keep it going for hours. . . .
Or he'll be in one of his moods and I'll ask him what the problem is and he generally breaks down and cries, and then we talk, or sometimes it culminates in real anger towards me for something I have or haven't done—maybe I haven't been as supportive of him or given him physical or verbal reinforcement. . . . He needs to know he's wanted and needed, and then it's hours and hours of conversation. Prior, I had always been where things blew up and everybody shut up and time just healed it. Now we have to talk it out if it takes all night.

Lately, some of the issues concern the house. Both men have been putting every spare minute they have into making it exactly what they want it to be. Although the house belongs to Warren, both see it as a symbol of their future together. Warren thinks they have settled their problems.

WARREN: We had one moment when I thought it was going to end. But what I think it was, was the death throes of my fantasies about how he should be and that I was going to remake him in an image that I wanted. And I think I realized that that simply wasn't going to happen, and that I couldn't kid myself anymore, so that I had a choice of either accepting him for who he was and what he was, because he wasn't going to change. And then once I did, things got better.

They do worry, however, about the pressures common to all gay couples and how they will affect their relationship.

WARREN: There are so many built-in conventions on gay couples that can destroy the relationship, even if it is very special. Everything from the Bible pumpers . . . and the crazies to parents who feel guilt and lay that trip on their children—that everything is wrong and that you can't have a relationship.

They are also concerned about the gay community:

TED: You got two choices. There's the frenetic gay life-style or there's one that more approaches the happy vine-covered cottage. We are headed towards the latter.

*Epilogue:* We interviewed Warren two and a half years later to find out what had happened to the relationship. The couple had lasted about a year longer, and then had broken up. The breakup was Warren's idea, and as an observer might have guessed, the major issue was expressiveness and communication. But there was more, and Warren's reasons give some insight on how the demands of masculinity affect a relationship.

We talked to Warren in his office. His secretary assumed we were there as clients. He greeted us in suit and tie and looked happy and successful. We asked him what had happened.

WARREN: I miscalculated who my partner was. I was in an emotional state when my marriage was over. I had had a loss of status and I needed security. So I picked someone and tried to impose a heterosexual model. But meanwhile I was changing and growing, and so I was getting all this home and family from him and I started to need a breath of fresh air. I needed new experiences.

Did new experiences mean other sexual partners?

WARREN: That wasn't the issue. He was static, stayed at home, that's all. He was a real decent man, a man of integrity. I wasn't wrong about that, but I got real bored. He didn't change and I did. I got tired of family, and his friends, his hobbies. I started to try new things, new people, the opera, the symphony, volunteer work. He resisted. First he didn't want to come along and then I didn't want him along.

Warren felt his lack of continuing commitment was typified by their economic arrangements:

WARREN: Our relationship had this balance-sheet logic. I assumed he had to contribute fifty percent. I kept records which became burdensome to him. He wasn't making it economically, and so there were more loans and gifts.

We asked Warren if this was not just his peculiar attitude about money. He said he had thought it was just an expression of himself at that moment. But now, in a new relationship, he does not behave the same way. Everything is shared. No accounts are kept, and the new partner has even fewer financial resources than Ted. What is the difference between the two relationships that made this change?

WARREN: Because now I *respect* someone. I don't mind writing a check. Now it's just a household expenditure.

So respect became the issue. Warren started to lose respect for Ted, and as that diminished, all that was emotionally satisfying started to deteriorate with it.

WARREN: He was so aggravating. He wouldn't fight. He wouldn't make decisions. He was passive-aggressive. *He had no guts.* He had no business guts; he had no social guts; he had no guts with me. He couldn't say *no*, he couldn't say *yes*. He had no input anywhere. Nothing came out of him.

How could he feel this way about a man he spent five years with? A man he said he had made his peace with and was planning a lifetime relationship with?

WARREN: When I met him, I perceived him as a "man of the earth." And he was honest and did have integrity. He was going to take care of me. But I should have known, that first evening when I moved into that awful apartment, that we were on different tracks.
    At the time you interviewed us I thought we were building a home together, but looking back, and trying to be honest, what I had was a workman who would help me build *my* home, and when it was done our relationship was over.

Warren feels that Ted needed a different kind of person—someone nonthreatening who would "bring him out." And that wasn't Warren. It was a sad ending for them both, although Warren never faltered in his decision once he realized he no longer respected Ted. We asked Warren if perhaps he had not constructed a "catch-22" for Ted: That is, had he not demanded that Ted assert himself, and then turned punishing and dominating when Ted did? Had he not held money over Ted's head—which Ted felt inadequate about and which made him feel that he didn't have the right to make decisions?
    Warren agreed that this might be true.

WARREN: Ted was overwhelmed by me. If he came up with
anything, it was discounted. It must have made him crazy. He would
say I didn't take his opinion into account. He was right. But by then
I had lost respect and there was nothing to be done.

Warren, in fact, made some demands on Ted which are not unusual in heterosexual relationships. Warren wanted Ted to be "all
man," to be as strong-minded and directive of the relationship as he
was. He wanted a will to match his own. On the other hand, he wanted
expressiveness; he wanted a nurturing, communicative, physically affectionate partner who could fulfill all his current needs. It is a combination hard to find. Nonetheless, now Warren thinks he has found the
right man.

WARREN: I didn't realize how far away I was from a real relationship
until this one. When you get into a relationship and you go further
and further and go places you've never been, you see how protected
you really were. This is the man I am going to spend my life with.
He has the qualities of goodness I need. I respect him and I can't
imagine anything he could do to lose that respect. He's high-energy
and curious and I don't feel trapped. He has his own business and
his own friends and we're independent, and yet the most important
time we spend is the time we spend in our home together and with a
group of wonderful friends. We're both powerful people. We're both
tough. Life has never been better.

And Ted?
He too is in another relationship and, by all reports, happy.

# Lawrence and Bernard

We picked this couple because their homelife follows the model of a
traditional marriage. This is not true for all aspects of their relationship
but it does guide much of their daily life. The occasional identity crisis
that results is ameliorated by the fact that both men intend to pursue
careers. They feel a mutual bond in their joint financial responsibility
for their apartment and also in their desire to make their relationship
last, even though they live in a gay community where they perceive
long-term couples as rare.

Lawrence and Bernard live in a small two-bedroom apartment in a
city known for high rents and limited spaces. They live in Tribeca, a
commercial neighborhood in New York recently rehabilitated by art-
ists, students, and other people with not much money but a need for
roomy living and working quarters. Although this couple did not ac-

quire a lot of space, their rent is moderate—which is important, since neither one has much money now.

Lawrence, twenty-five, is just finishing college and plans, with friends, to open a small store of specialty items. He has been gathering inventory for a while, and the overflow makes the small apartment seem even smaller. Bernard, twenty-nine, came here from Cuba when he was six years old. His father was a professor and Bernard is following in his footsteps, studying for a graduate degree in comparative literature. Lawrence and Bernard have been a couple for about two years, but have been living together for only one year.

Lawrence is tall and very thin. He greeted us at the door wearing a skintight T-shirt and soft black leather pants. Bernard is more muscular, shorter and was more conventionally dressed, but he, too, owns black leather clothes. Both men consider these more costume than regular apparel and usually restrict their wear to those times when they go to gay bars—which is where they met.

> LAWRENCE: It was sort of strange. We were in a back-room bar. We were in the world-famous Pen and I was standing in the bar and Bernard was looking at me and cruising me, and I was sort of checking him out. But I was in my usual very stoned state and a friend of mine came out of the back room and collapsed in my arms, and Bernard shot across the room and disappeared. And I carried him over to another group of friends and then I went into the back room, and standing under this light and looking at what was going on was Bernard. . . . I inched my way over and he recognized me and we started talking. And he said, "Do you want to go somewhere more comfortable?"
>
> And I said, "Yes, I only live three blocks from here."
>
> And he said, "I only live six blocks from here."
>
> So I went to his house because it's interesting to see other people's houses. And that's how we met. . . . My first impressions were that he was oversexed and one of the few people I could talk to.

Bernard was in a less open frame of mind.

> BERNARD: I wasn't interested in having a relationship with anyone. I wasn't having a good time that evening, and I didn't want to be where I was, and I felt I had been dragged there by friends against my will. I was on my way out the door when I met him. He seemed like a really nice person, and he was the first person that I had met that I felt I could talk to and have an intelligent conversation with for more than thirty seconds in about two months.

They started seeing each other immediately, spending a lot of time at Lawrence's apartment. Even though they had sex that first night, the rest of the relationship progressed more slowly.

> BERNARD: We went to a lot of movies. There's a sort of process you go through of meeting someone's friends socially and getting either

approval or disapproval. And we spent a lot of time together alone, just talking and doing things like watching television or other equally exciting intellectual activities. . . . I really got along with him well because he was the first person that I had ever seen for any extended period of time where I didn't feel obligated to be doing something. I could just be comfortable sitting there reading and he would be sitting there reading, and we would be pleased just to be there together.

Staying at home and entertaining Bernard at his place wasn't at all difficult for Lawrence. It was his way to catch a man, and how he likes to live.

LAWRENCE: I'm almost impossible to get out of the house. I am a real extreme homebody. . . . I brought out this huge, elaborate dinner for him that I had been preparing for two days. I brought it out and he ate it and as usual, he fell in love. You know what they say, "You get a man through his stomach." Well, it really is that way. He came over, he ate my dinner, he fell in love with me, and he's been eating my dinners ever since.

Lawrence was ready to settle down. He had been going to gay bars, especially disco bars, three or four nights a week, "dancing until dawn." He would come home in the early morning, grab his books, and go to school. He watched his other gay friends undergo the ravages of such a pace, and had resolved before he met Bernard that he was going to change his way of life.

The two men saw a lot of each other. Bernard was essentially living at Lawrence's, but that apartment was tiny. So Lawrence looked for a place big enough for both of them.

LAWRENCE: I knew it was permanent when I said, "Yes, I'll move in with you." Because both of our leases were up at the same time, but he had to move. And when we decided to live together and get this place, we knew we had to make it last, because even if we were to break up, neither one of us could move. . . . Apartments are so hard to find and so expensive. And we've put so much money in this apartment. We just know we won't ever leave here unless we move out of the city.

Moving was full of decision-making. It provoked a number of incidents that drew the couple closer together. One involved a terrible incident with the superintendent of Lawrence's building:

LAWRENCE: I was hesitant to make this commitment to the new apartment, but I really had to leave. The neighbors did not like me and the super hated me with an absolute passion. The neighbors did not harass me because I was gay. [But] he used to call me faggot in the hallway and drive by in the car and scream obscenities at me while walking down the street, and I tried to get him off my back but the management wouldn't help me. He threatened to kill me, and I went to the police and they couldn't do anything unless he did something, and one day—luckily I was with Bernard—because on the street he did try to attack me, and Bernard just sort of said, "If you want to bother him, you're going to have to bother me," and he just backed off. I think you'd call him homophobic.

Bernard and Lawrence do not suffer lightly comments about their sexual preference. Witness this incident:

LAWRENCE: Well, I'm a fighter, and so is he, and that's what I like about him. If someone bothers me, I may get killed but you're going down with me. . . . At Christmas we were coming back from Washington on the train, and there was this drunk man on the train who was causing everyone in the car an awful amount of grief and displeasure, and the man said something to me and I got up and smashed him across the car and there was this big brouhaha. Bernard was in the bathroom. And this guy got even madder and was calling me names and things, which of course were all true, but I didn't really care. The guy said, you know, "You goddamned faggot," or something like that, and Bernard just walked out of the bathroom and he walks up to me and says to him, "Who are you calling a faggot?" and punched him again. Poor man! It was so funny. He was so flattened, and then I went after the guy with a . . . cane, and of course the man screamed about how the horrible faggots are doing this, and they threw him off the train.

Even though Lawrence was used to living alone, he was afraid *not* to move in with Bernard, for reasons other than the cost:

LAWRENCE: So ultimately, even though I liked living alone and was never really wanting to live with him, the deciding factor was that I couldn't stand living where I was and he couldn't stand living where he was and he couldn't move without me, and I couldn't move without him. I know this sounds weird, but in a way I felt like I might lose him. Because I felt that if he couldn't find an apartment near here, he might move out of this area [of the city]. So I felt for our future it was important for me to get the right place for us.

This triggered the great apartment hunt—and Lawrence was a bear about it.

LAWRENCE: I was very lucky. I hit this one very quickly. And there was a person here renting it and I had to talk her out of renting it. It was real blood and guts. I couldn't believe it. . . . It was like a first-come, dog-eat-dog business, and I went to the apartment and she was there and I said, "Oh, you don't want to live here" [he laughs], and I went through this whole thing about how horrible the neighborhood was and, "Oh my God, they're going to come crawling through these windows," and you know. "There's a disco down the street and the faggots are all over at night making noise."
And she said, "Oh, that sounds horrible."
And I said, "Oh, it is, it is, especially for this kind of rent," and then I rushed up to the agency and called him and we made it

before she did. We had signed the lease when she called and said, "I'll take it." Dog eat dog. So the apartment makes it permanent.

In the first months of the relationship, the couple had lots of differences over small things. One was Lawrence's smoking. Lawrence, however, was ready to fight to the death to preserve his habits.

LAWRENCE: We have conflicts but they're minimal. Drives him absolutely insane. In the beginning, he was not confident enough to put his foot down, because I would have thrown him out. But I still say things that are nasty, like "If you don't like it, get the hell out of here," because I feel that's my right.

Another thing was the apartment. I signed the lease, and my stance is that it is my apartment and not his. Which sounds cold, but let me explain. I am very into decorating. One of the things I liked about living alone is that nobody told me what I could do with my apartment—you know, where I had to put anything. . . . So one of the things I agreed is that I would have complete control of decorating the apartment—and that did and does cause problems occasionally. Like that paint in the living room. He hated it at first. When I bought the paint he said, "Oh my God, it's going to look horrible. You can't do that."

And I said, "Remember our agreement?"

And then I go and do it and he comes out and he says, "Oh that's just lovely." His taste is completely different from mine, so I just made it clear—I know it sounds cruel and rude, but it has to be clear—how it was going to work. I'm very nice, very diplomatic, I ask his opinion, but we do it my way. We don't argue about it much anymore.

Bernard seems to have accepted the arrangement well.

BERNARD: We don't do anything big without one another. Well [he laughs], he would decide to do it and then he would ask me and then he would do it whether I said yes or no. [He laughs again.] I may sound like I resent that, but I *don't*. I think he has much better taste than I do, so I don't really care.

The couple has also come to an agreement about which areas of the household each finds interesting, and they have amicably divided the shopping.

LAWRENCE: He doesn't care what I do. It's all my stuff. He owns very few things in the house. We're a great combination. I love the *tchotchkies* and he loves the mechanical things. So he runs out and buys microwaves and air-conditioners, and I run out and buy my crystal, and there's no problem at all. He rarely buys anything that I don't see first and give an okay, and I don't buy anything important unless he sees it first.

Another area of conflict has continued from the beginning. Lawrence still likes to go out to dance occasionally. Bernard hated it then and hates it now.

LAWRENCE: It's like the Saturday Night Rag that we have. Every Saturday night I get twisted out of shape, because he doesn't like rock and he doesn't like disco either. He won't go out dancing. It's one of our problems. He likes to go to the Pen [a gay bar] and screw around all night, and I like to do disco dancing. It just never quite works because I don't think it's fair for me to go out discoing while he goes to the Pen and gets into these things. . . . Well, if he goes to the Pen then I have the right to go to the Pen and he doesn't like going dancing and it's hard for me to force him. So we go back and forth and what it usually ends up doing is that we don't do either. We stay home and get tanked. . . .

I've threatened to end the marriage over that. I've made quite a few comments that if it's a choice between him and my music, I would probably pick my music. That's very cruel to say, but then, in reality, I've actually given up my music to be with him. Little by little I'm getting over my Saturday Night Rags. I guess over the years and years of spending Saturday nights out, it's very difficult to spend them at home. It's like my body wants to go out and have a Saturday nght and it just doesn't work anymore. I used to get depressive about it, but now I've changed for him.

Bernard sees the problem in a different light:

BERNARD: I am perfectly willing to go out with him, but I tell him, "You have to decide where you want to go and tell me at a reasonably early time in the evening and then I will go along with you and gear myself up for it." His normal procedure is to sit around and get stoned or something until about one o'clock, and then about one o'clock in the morning he decides, "Oh, well, we're going to this disco," or we're going to do this or that. By which time I am ready to go to bed because I have been sitting there all night watching *Saturday Night Live* or reading the Sunday *Times*, or whatever, and I'm really tired.

"Why didn't you say this two hours ago when I would be more up for it?" And then I say, "Well, if you really want to go, I'll go."

And he says, "Well, you really don't want to go. We'll stay home."

And I'll say, "No, if you don't go out tonight, you'll be in a foul mood tomorrow." And we'll go back and forth and usually wind up staying home and he'll be in a foul mood the next day.

I suspect he will have to end up making more plans to go out with other people who like to dance. . . . It's not that I'm unwilling to dance. It's just that he doesn't perceive me as having a good time when I go out, and he dislikes the feeling that he's dragging me against my will. I try and tell him that if it was really against my will I wouldn't go. It's just that I don't really have a wonderful time, you know. Stay there till six in the morning and say, "Wow, it's really great." I go. I dance. I want to leave. I don't want to dance for six hours straight. My idea of a good time is not going places that have just opened up, standing out in the street and having someone look at you and decide if you're good enough to come in or not. That I resent like you wouldn't believe.

This is the couple's biggest area of disagreement. Everything else is small by comparison. In any event, they don't fight about it very much. When they do, it ends very quickly.

LAWRENCE: Oh, I'll get bent out of shape and I sit in the living room, and then because I'm bent out of shape he comes marching into the bedroom and slams the door. This is the way it always works, like a script. He comes in here and he'll read and then one of us about a half hour later will feel bad or guilty and just cannot argue anymore and live like that, and we usually go in and say, "I'm sorry," and then everything's all right. . . . It's all laughable. It always ends nicely. I always call him a pointy-head intellectual and he always calls me a fascist, and that's the end of it.

BERNARD: I tend to withdraw from an issue. . . . He wants to face it. . . . I have a tendency to get up and walk in the other room and shut the door, which is a really obnoxious habit. I realize that. I'm sure he's told you that. [He laughs.] And what he does now is very good, because he knows that if he just ignores me, in about five minutes, like a spoiled child, I will come out and say I'm sorry because no one has come in to get me. [He laughs.] . . .
   Sometimes if it's a real issue, I'll talk to a third party. Some third party will say, "Yes, you're really being an idiot, and you should apologize, because that's really stupid." And I do that. Because if a third party says, "You're being an idiot," that's different from having your lover say, "You're being an idiot."

Lawrence and Bernard spend almost all of their free time together. Lawrence, the ex-swinger, chafes a little at the restriction.

LAWRENCE: One of our problems is that we never do anything alone. I mean, God forbid one of us should go out by ourselves—God forbid! [He laughs.] I don't want it that way. . . . Lately it's gotten a little better. I've actually gone out once or twice by myself. . . . It was strange to be out, actually just out by myself, not on a specific errand.

This seems to be a common early adjustment among couples who want to be together a lot in the beginning and then, as they become more secure in the relationship, feel they need more "space." Both men agree that their transition has been generally smooth. Both men also feel they have an equal say in everyday decisions and in the resulting changes. If the truth were known, however, Lawrence considers himself the power behind the throne:

LAWRENCE: He thinks he makes all the decisions, but I just let him think that. . . . Actually I think it's at a happy medium. I have to avoid giving in to him. I could do that easily and I don't want to. I mean I could easily sit back and let him run my life, and be the nice submissive housewife sitting at home, cleaning and decorating, but that's not what I really want. And I'm going to fight not to let myself ever get into that, because if that happened, it would have to end the relationship.

Assigning who does what in the house is an uncomplicated task, but a task nonetheless. Even though Lawrence wants to avoid assuming any roles, he falls into them easily, given his talents and interests. Bernard is an ardent feminist and doesn't want to encourage a division of labor that has historically oppressed "wives." So he, too, strives to avoid roles. But this is easier said than done.

LAWRENCE: It's just that I'm home during the day, so I do all the chores . . . like groceries, cleaning the house, doing the laundry, all the domestic chores I do during the day, plus I study during the day or late at night. So, generally when he gets home, dinner's ready. . . . It's just like a marriage. It drives me crazy. I'm in the kitchen; he sits down; dinner comes out. After dinner he does the dishes. It's very, very routine.

Bernard makes an effort:

BERNARD: I'm a feminist. You can't believe how strongly I feel on that point. I'm one of those people who don't think you should have meetings in non-E.R.A. states. . . . But if you forced me into stating who does what, I would guess that I do more of the repair type of work and he does more of the cooking and shopping. And I will say I always do the dishes and probably forty percent of the cleaning. He probably thinks he does most of it, but I think I do a substantial amount. . . . He insists that I clean out my own closet and things like that . . . but that's the type of material he decides that I should do.

Bernard doesn't want this to deteriorate into "roled behavior."

BERNARD: Well, jokingly we will refer to him as my wife because he cleans up after me. But sexually there's not any kind of traditional role. And I don't really think there is in other aspects of our life except for the fact he's not working that much.

Lawrence feels the same way, though he is a little more comfortable with their division of labor—but constantly aware of its pitfalls:

LAWRENCE: He will deny it vigorously, but I do all the housework. I am the only one who cleans this house. His attitude is that he does half the housework because he washes the dishes after dinner. Okay. But he's never had to polish the furniture. . . . Like I was off the last week and I spent the whole day cleaning, and literally everything was cleaned. But then I am fanatically clean, much more than he is. . . . I, in a great way, enjoy housework. I can really get off on it if I really let myself. Like I can put on disco music and just go around the house all day while I do my housework. . . .
    In a way, if I allowed myself to, I would probably take on all the female roles in the relationship, in terms of cleaning and that type of nonsense. But I don't want it that way. It's a conflict. I do, but then I don't, for my mental happiness. . . . Because I would be living for him. I can see why women's lib . . . how women really do get beat down living with straight men . . . how they just become an offshoot

of the male, not really their own selves, and that's what I'm trying to prevent because I could easily get into that. Like, I could get into the role of not working, and him supporting me. That's been discussed at length and he would support me—but I'm making it very clear that will never happen. I don't want to be *Miss Housewife*. . . . I've known three or four people in that type of relationship and they were all just terribly miserable, trapped in it. My friends all unanimously consider me the best housewife they have ever met. [He laughs.]. . . Even many straight friends have told me that I would make someone a wonderful wife and it's a standard joke throughout my friends that I am the one who will compulsively clean out ashtrays. But I don't really want that to be. It's a conflict in me that I want to be, you know, the *housewife*, and then I don't want to be. Because I know what it will do to me.

Both partners' families are part of the couple's life and, in fact, members of both families have spent the night in the apartment. But the nature of the couple's relationship has never been discussed. When their parents come, they sleep on the couch in the living room and the men share their bedroom as always, but there has never been an open acknowledgment of the kind of relationship Lawrence and Bernard have. They are a new couple, but we have heard stories in which the same unspoken familial response to the relationship lasted ten to twenty years or more. While there is no criticism from the families, there is no support either.

The couple generally receives support from their numerous and varied friends, both heterosexual and homosexual. Both partners like almost all of each other's friends and see them as a great strength in their relationship. Both consider it an obligation to be nice to the few of their partner's friends whom they do not like. Arguments over social issues are minimal, although they have had one or two over what is considered proper decorum.

> LAWRENCE: Well, for example, at our Christmas party I wanted to wear a pair of gym shorts and that's it, and he just thought that was exceedingly rude, to wear nothing but gym shorts to your own Christmas party, so I dressed.

Jealousy is a problem, but not a major one. They experiment with some non-monogamy, but it has not been very successful and the latest thought is to try to be monogamous—with a few exceptions to the rule.

> LAWRENCE: He's much more jealous than I am. I'm really surprised. If I just make even funny comments about having sex that day with someone else, even though it's in jest and he knows it, he just gets all bent out of shape. I think it's really funny, because you see, in the beginning I was very jealous. I'm very possessive when I meet people, but then after a few months, when I feel secure in the relationship, it goes away. Like I really don't care if he has sex with other people. It wouldn't faze me a bit. I mean, he's never had it.

Well, I shouldn't say "never." I may not know, but if gets down to where we're allowed sex outside, it would be okay with me. I just don't want to hear about it. . . .

Sometimes we'll go to the Pen, which is this orgy bar for gay leather men where you sort of walk around and have sex with one or as many as you want of the thousands of men that go there on a Saturday night. We sort of compete a little for looks from people, but it's no big deal because we can't have sex on the outside. It's just on a subconscious level.

Having sex on the outside takes on a particular definition for them, since occasionally at the Pen they do more than look.

LAWRENCE: I know most of the people who work there, and I can easily go and chitchat all night. Generally, when we go I do avoid him. I don't like to see him having sex with someone else. That bothers me for some reason—I don't know why. I mean, we have brought third parties home, and then it doesn't bother me at all, but for some reason there, I just don't want to see what he's doing. . . . We don't go much. Maybe four times a year. We don't want to jeopardize the relationship by screwing around. The last time, for example, I refused to go in. I said, "I'm not ready for this place tonight."

And he said, "Oh, fine, let's go to another place," and we went off. . . .

I find going there very difficult and you have to be in a good psychological mood to be able to go there and do that stuff. . . .

I should add that I'm allowed to go to the Pen and play around if he's not in the city. That's an understanding. . . . I don't tell him the details. But I know he does the same when he's away. But this is very seldom, let me tell you.

Bernard talks about the same problems. Their solutions include rules of sexual conduct and trying not to compete with each other.

BERNARD: We're not competitive. Although if you're having a bad evening and you're in a lousy mood and you think everyone is looking at the person you're with, you obviously have something horribly wrong with you because nobody is chasing your ass. But that's really minor. . . . We came to a kind of agreement when we first started, that for the time being it would be better if neither of us did things with other people. Certainly not with the other person's knowledge . . . And I think it's gotten to the point now, well, it doesn't matter so much. We both feel secure enough not to be threatened by other people. . . . We have not gone home with somebody else, and I don't think that you can do that without the other person's knowledge. I don't think either of us would feel right about going home with someone and staying all night and having sex and coming back the next morning and saying, "I had a real good time last night and met person X and did this and this and this." That, I think we would both agree, would be really destructive. I don't know what I would do if he did it. I know he would probably murder me—uh, figuratively—if I did it. We just don't do that.

So Bernard and Lawrence have—from a lesbian's or heterosexual's vantage point—a strange kind of monogamy but one that is not uncommon among our male couples. Greater importance is attached to not seeing or hearing about a non-monogamous incident than is attributed to its actual occurrence.

They are able, occasionally, to go out together and have other partners—as long as they come home together. From time to time they can share someone and not feel the same jealousy they might if each person were going off by himself. They can feel twinges of envy if they are not equally admired—but they try to keep all this under control so that they are not, to quote Lawrence, "screwing around," and thus hurting their relationship.

Their sex life with each other has tapered off somewhat.

LAWRENCE: It's gone steadily down since we met. At first, it was about eight times a day and then it's gone down to about two times a week, which is more about my speed. He's very good about it. He gets uptight because he suffers when he doesn't have sex, and I can just go, you know, a long time without sex.

Sexual frequency is an issue, but a controllable one. Lawrence is simply not as interested as Bernard.

LAWRENCE: About a fourth of the time he initiates, I have sex with him even though I'm not that interested. Or I say I'm not in the mood, I got a headache—you know. But most of the time I say yes. I'm very honest. I tell him it's my wifely duty. I really do.

Lawrence feels that it's not his partner's attractiveness that is the issue—it is his own psychological makeup.

LAWRENCE: When I'm alone, without a lover . . . I like sex all the time. When I have a lover, for some reason the need of sex disappears. I guess I think it's because I think I'm looking for sex, and what I'm really looking for is an emotional relationship. And when I have the emotional relationship, then the sex doesn't mean anything. And, of course, after two years you get a little bored. [He laughs.]

Bernard wishes it were otherwise, but he has come to recognize that he has to make some compromises.

BERNARD: I think that differences in sexual desire between two people is something that probably destroys more relationships than anything else, and I think it's the person who has the stronger desire who has to adjust to it. I'm sure he's compromised too. I don't think it's anything negative to do with me. I just know that if he went blissfully along his own way, he would have sex about once every two weeks or something like that. . . . He's a very physically affectionate person, though. It's just that he doesn't have sex to the point of orgasm very often.

It was an issue in the beginning because I—you know—you feel that you're not doing what you're supposed to do if the other person doesn't have an orgasm, and he was repeatedly insistent to say that it didn't make any difference to him, that he was more interested in *my* having an orgasm. And after six or seven months, I finally decided that if he said that all the time, it must be true or he wouldn't keep saying it. So I kind of gave up. He does make his wishes known if he wants me to do something in particular, or if he wants to reach orgasm himself. God, this sounds so horribly scientific! Anyhow, he's usually blunt about it then, so we're probably making love according to his desires.

The couple is very happy, very secure. They have already made many compromises with an ease that would be the envy of many couples. But they do not talk about the future very much.

LAWRENCE: I think we are both world-wise enough to know that relationships can't be planned, and I think that is why this has lasted this long and why I think it's going to last a long time, because we're not shooting for any particular goal. We're just letting it happen as it happens. And I think that's probably why we're doing really well, you know.

Bernard agrees:

BERNARD: I know what my attitude is and I think his attitude is pretty much the same. That we both enjoy it right now and we've both been around long enough and seen enough other relationships to know that objectively the chances of our being together ten or fifteen years from now are fairly small. Yet both of us feel a strong sense of commitment and we're more interested in now, and building our relationship now, than in projecting ten years from now, because we don't know what will happen. We have to just sort of live day by day.

I think my favorite expression is just that if each person is willing to go ninety percent of the way towards meeting the other person's desires, you will probably meet in the middle and that gives you as good a chance as any.

Bernard and Lawrence fulfill important needs for each other, and while the bar scene beckons, it offers few rewards to compete with the homelife they have created. They try to protect each other's feelings, and they seem to be successful—at least thus far—in keeping their outside sex emotionally uninvolved. They are a "companionate" couple. Each gives to, and demands, a lot of time from the other, and they have acquired a circle of friends who sustain their feelings about being a couple with a valuable relationship to protect.

While they maintain separate ownership of objects, they pool everyday expenses. The apartment, which was difficult to find and would be even more difficult to replace, has become a part of the complex of needs that keeps them together. Their most demanding task at the moment is believing in their future, when the prevailing attitude among their friends and other gay men they know is that relationships are fragile and unlikely to last a lifetime.

# Steve and Ben

Steve and Ben are two men who embrace the traditional male values. Both try to be independent, self-sufficient, and in control—which provokes competition and inhibits exchange of affection between them. Their competitiveness becomes a problem when it extends into the world of gay bars and cruising places they frequent together. They are working to make their non-monogamy less destructive to the relationship, more recreational, and more equally practiced.

When we went to interview the couple, we found ourselves on an industrial pier where there was a mixture of modest houseboats, commercial fishing boats, and a few private sailboats. We walked down to the water's edge, not quite knowing where to go next, and might have spent the day on the wrong pier if Ben had not come and found us. He took us to another part of the dock. Wedged between two commercial fishing boats was the small sailboat he lives on with Steve.

Ben is a twenty-six-year-old fisherman who works most of the time in nearby waters, while Steve, thirty-one, also a seaman, works on a fishing boat that is often gone for weeks at a time. At the time we interviewed them, they had been together for a little over five years.

They looked like "Marlboro men." Both are well-developed, handsome, with dark hair, moustaches, and blue eyes. They both wore jeans, Ben's topped with a dark turtleneck, and Steve's with a plaid flannel shirt. The small boat they call home is sparely outfitted. All in all, it was a rather romantic picture.

The couple met on a boat. Steve was working on a ferry at the time and their meeting was serendipitous:

> BEN: I hopped on the ferryboat. I was the last one on, which meant thirty seconds later the gate went down. If I had missed that boat I would never have met him. I looked at the boat and thought it was great and I wanted to see the engine room. I was taken down there by one of the deckhands and the chief engineer looked over at Steve and told him to give me a tour. So he gave me the grand tour.
>
> I didn't know anyone in town, so he gave me his phone number. . . . When I got to town, I came up to his house to visit him and we

proceeded to get slightly plastered. By about two o'clock we still hadn't determined if either of us was gay or not. And he finally said, "Look, I've got to go to bed. Where would you like to sleep? Here on the sofa or in the double bed with me?" And I was thinking, *Oh, my God!* And so we finally ended up hopping into bed together and I decided that he was gay.

Steve was also unsure.

STEVE: I was nervous. I thought he might be straight. I didn't know. . . . But I told him, "Okay, you can sleep with me. I don't bite." I went to the bathroom, came out, and he was in bed. And I could see he didn't have his shirt on, but I didn't know if he left his shorts on or not. And I thought, *I used to sleep with my straight boyfriends when I was growing up and I left my shorts on.* I didn't know, and I was nervous, and about ten minutes later I kind of brushed my hand along his side and I noticed he was naked. So then we both figured it all out.

Things, however, did not proceed smoothly.

STEVE: Unfortunately, we had been drinking. I got excited and I was all over him and he got sick and he ended up going to the bathroom and throwing up for a whole hour. So I couldn't touch him again, and I thought, *Oh, no, I've brought home some drunk or something.* But the next morning everything was fine, and we've been together ever since.

The relationship was rocky in the beginning. Both Ben and Steve place great importance on independence, self-reliance, and a strong separate identity. In the beginning there was a tug of war for control and dominance. Ben fell heavily in love right away; Steve was more cautious.

BEN: I knew at the time that Steve was not ready for another relationship, although he wanted a friend. And I really didn't want to come on too heavy, and it would have been too heavy to say, "I love you." It was probably a month and a half later, afterwards, I told him [what] I thought: "I kind of like you a lot. I think I love you, in fact" type of thing.

But Ben could not step lightly enough.

BEN: There were quite a few conflicts in the beginning. In a way, it was almost as if I had invaded his territory. And taken over. That bothered him. It's still not resolved. It was almost as if he resented me and wanted me at the same time, and he had a tough time resolving that. . . . I was and I still am a relatively, I guess, a very forceful person—pushy, I've been told. And when I first got together with Steve, I really wanted to impress him, so I was doing all these things for him and in a way it was almost as if I was . . . invading his space and his house. . . .

One incident is this fence which he was building at the time, and I wanted to impress him, so I took over and finished the fence for him. And he resented that in a way because it was like saying it was something that he didn't know how to do—which I can understand why he would resent that. But I wasn't thinking that. I was just thinking, you know, if I impress him, he'll see how good a person I am and how necessary I am for his life and he'll want to keep me.

At first, that was not Steve's response.

STEVE: Ben has a very domineering personality, and where I had been doing things like building a fence, I allowed him to just step in and do it for me. And I started losing all my power and letting him take over a lot of things. Which really upset me, so finally I kicked him out. I said, "I can't do it." And he was gone.

But not for long. Ben came back and Steve tried twice more.

STEVE: I told him I couldn't live with him. . . . I told him I was losing my sense of individuality. I was going to move to Seattle or Tacoma. I said I was going to, and he curled up on the sofa in a little ball and didn't talk for the whole day. And I felt, *I just can't move away. He'd die.* So I stayed. And I guess I felt a little better then, knowing that he cared that much. So we tried to better the situation and get a bigger place . . . but I started feeling the same way, so I did go north. And I went looking for a job and I was up there for a week or so, and I called home and he said he had met somebody. I got so jealous I didn't go all the way to Seattle. I stopped and came back.

But by now he was having this affair. So I said, "Okay, I'll stay in this apartment and you can get your apartment, and we can still be friends." I figured I can be there when he goes through this lover.

But then he said, "What if we have a two-bedroom apartment?"

I said, "Well, that might work." . . . So we did, and I was on my own and he saw his friend, and it was fun because I had my space. But then I started getting lonely and crawling into his bedroom, asking him if I could crawl into bed with him. So I started to crawl in bed with him. And so doing that for about a month, and then we started to get close again, and sleeping together. . . . I learned that I want to be with Ben, but I have to be able to remain myself.

They still jockey with each other over issues of competition and dominance.

BEN: We have a conflict any time I tell him how to do something. And that's a lot of time, because as I said, I'm a very pushy person. Everything from, you know—"Pick that parking space" to "Don't hold the paintbrush that way." But I'm learning more and more to keep my mouth shut. For instance, take driving. I'm a backseat driver. Today I said, "Turn down Market." And I said, "You're supposed to turn here."

He said, "No."

Then it was, "Yes you are." Then, "Oops, my God, I'm wrong, I'm sorry."

Things like that happen at least once a day. . . . I do feel that I apologize a lot when I'm wrong, and I've been wrong a lot. I don't try to bury it. I admit it. And I am working on not trying to do what I want to do and not letting Steve have his say. And it's getting more successful. Steve is telling me more often to shut up, or he has a right to say what he wants to. He is going through counseling to learn how to be stronger with me and I had some counseling on not being so pushy. I try hard, but I make mistakes and I need Steve to tell me when I'm making mistakes. . . . We've made a lot of concessions and a lot of good communication goes on now.

Steve agrees that things have changed and are controllable, but little things can bring up the dominance issue in an instant.

STEVE: I get annoyed when we're going somewhere and he'll walk so fast. It makes me feel like walking slower. And I tell him, "Would you slow down." And he gets exercised about it and I get upset.

Steve's strong feelings about keeping the relationship in balance complicate their expressions of affection. This is a cause of stress to both men.

STEVE: I feel a little guilty 'cause I don't like him to be so close and hugging me and holding me and stuff—even around gay people. I can take only so much. . . . Then I start feeling a little helpless, like if he keeps hugging me I feel obligated to give him his way. I start feeling a little . . . weak.

Steve feels that Ben's open display of affection has other, underlying motives.

STEVE: There's times that I like it and times that I feel that he's just being insecure, and that's why he's being so affectionate. But there are other times when he'll be real affectionate, and then he'll see somebody and he'll immediately become less affectionate to me and just want to go and talk to his other friend. And so I get the feeling sometimes that he's just kind of using me because he needs to hold on to somebody.

Ben agrees that his affectionate behavior is an issue, but claims his motives are genuine.

BEN: I thrive on physical contact. I have been afraid in the past that I have been too clutching, but this is simply the way that I think rather than a psychological smothering of somebody. It is simply the way I like to be with him. I like to be close to him and touch him. I don't really feel I get enough of it from Steve. It was a big bone of contention between me and my ex. It was always me constantly coming up to him and touching him and rubbing his back or holding his arms, something like that. He almost never did it to me. I am constantly telling Steve that I love him. Because it's true. . . . I do, and I like expressing that emotion. It makes me feel good and I don't begrudge Steve that he doesn't give me enough of it. I realize that I would like more, but I understand the space he's in.

The pair turn the tables a bit when it comes to expressing affection outside the relationship. Ben is much more likely to be non-monogamous—and more insistent about his needs. Steve agrees on non-monogamy, but is more jealous about how it is practiced.

BEN: I enjoy sex with other people. I need sex with other people. It's one of the things I have to do. It's a drive. . . . We have our little rules to live by, though. Generally I try and restrict any tricking when Steve is out on the boat for a long time. And he tries to do the same for me. . . . Steve is more jealous. But I have felt that any relationship I have, that if I can't trust them, the relationship isn't going to work. For me that means they can do what they want to, when they want to, with whom they want to do it. So I feel no jealousy toward Steve, and for that matter—like tricking—I feel strong enough, that he loves me and I love him, there ain't nobody in this town that can separate us. And I don't care what he does as long as he comes home. . . .

Steve feels a bit differently at times. I can take advantage of that 'cause there have been times when I have run off and tricked or whatever at the tubs, and he would much rather have me be home by six-thirty. And I've stayed out till noon, and that type of thing has bothered him quite a bit—which I guess he feels it's not a good thing for the relationship. Not that it's bad to go to the tubs to trick, just that you should at least come home early.

It usually gets resolved well. I kind of come home like a little puppy with his tail between the legs and I realize that I've done something wrong, but I've gone out and done it anyway. And usually I'll say, "Well, I'll try not to do it again," but that's really as far as it ever goes. It's not something that's brought up again and again and again. It's not a grudge-type thing.

Steve basically agrees, but he thinks Ben can be thoughtless about the way he acts toward other men when Steve is around.

STEVE: He's got to watch it. Like one day we went over to a friend of his for dinner and I walked into the kitchen and they were kissing . . . and I got extremely jealous. And I told him. I got real upset. I was real mad because I didn't want this done in front of me when I was around. I wanted to leave right then, and after we got in the car I was ready . . . to call it quits. I was really mad. But he tries not to touch any people when I'm around now.

I'm getting better. For instance, I wanted to have a fling and he had a friend he wanted to have lunch with one day, so I told him, "Well, why don't you spend the night with him and I'll go off and do something." That was the first time we just both went our separate ways. And in the morning we loved each other that much more. I just needed some independence. . . . I realize now that I don't have to be bothered. I realize that his nonsexual friends last longer than his sexual friends. So jealousy is not much of an issue now.

This is not entirely true. These men cannot help but vie with each other, and while they have reached a secure and loving point in their relationship, and are able to give each other sexual freedom without much conflict, they still are *competitive* about which of them is doing better in the sexual marketplace.

STEVE: Well, we get jealous if the other person is getting more of someone's attention. I think it's better now, but, like, if I would go out and have sex with somebody and I would tell him, he would be real cool and kind of irritable. And then he'd go out and do something and he'd be better. It's kind of a jealousy that I've done something and he hasn't. And I would get the same way with him. It was competitive. . . .

It just happened three days ago. He had sex a couple times while I was away and I was feeling angry with him when I came back, but I didn't understand myself. And finally after being back a couple days, I realized what it was. I just needed to go out and be with someone else. . . . I went out and had my sex and I felt better. I quit being angry. I quit being irritable and I quit snapping. And we both realized this was very important, that we've reached another stepping-stone in how to grow.

They are still making efforts to control competition and jealousy.

BEN: If somebody hits on me in a bar, Steve doesn't particularly like it. Those times are our strongest competition. Example: Once in this bar we go to, two guys hit on me in one day. Which made me feel pretty damn good when two guys hit on me. And Steve didn't like it. We kind of feel when we're out together, we're out together. But still, when two people hit on you, that's something special. It's really an ego trip there, so I kind of flirted with them a little bit and in a way I flaunted it in front of Steve, and he was really, really pissed off—to the point where he was ready to throw one of the candles across the room. I managed to get him to sit down. I put the candle down and we talked a bit. I kind of brought him out. I wanted him to be angry. And so he ended up getting angrier and angrier.

I said, "Look, Steve, you know you want to hit me, so go ahead and do it."

He said, "Okay," and he hit me on my shoulder twice.

And I said, "Look, you're still mad, do it again." And he did it again, and a lot of people in the bar were turning around and looking. . . . He calmed right down. . . .

Now we don't usually hit each other, but the competition is there in the bars, and it had to be handled. And we've had people tell us that whenever we're in the bar together, we're usually uptight because of the competition. It threw me. I didn't know it was that obvious. One person said that every time he sees us in a bar, we're at each other's throat.

The competition is about who is more attractive to others, even over who can perform better. There is a lot of "who's more masculine than whom" in this couple, and they use other men as a testing ground.

BEN: I could never be monogamous. Steve's in the same space as I am, but he's too insecure to do it. He's told me lots of times, "I wish I could do what you do." And that's part of the competition right there—I do it more often than he does. . . . He has problems tricking, problems being relaxed, doing it, that sort of thing. He's going to counseling to work it out, because he wants to be able to trick well. And I'm trying to support him that way. I don't want to live in a double standard. I don't tell someone I can trick and they can't. I know relationships, like, where one does and the other doesn't. They say, "I can and you can't." It turns my stomach.

They compete in all masculine activities, from fixing the sailboat to cruising, and even having sex together. Their sex life is sporadic, since both of them are on boats away from each other for long stretches at a time. But when they are in town they have frequent, almost daily, sex together. Each insists that he is the person who initiates sex and that he has the greater sexual appetite. It is male to initiate, male to be "horny," and each claims that as an important part of his own persona.

Surprisingly, there is little competition over household issues. They split the household chores right down the middle, keep separate bank accounts, and never have fights about money. Generally, they share similar values on most things. They are open about their relationship and Ben is not afraid or shy about showing physical affection to Steve, in public or in front of his family. Steve feels a bit squeamish about both, but it is no longer an important issue between them.

They have heated arguments, but they always know how to handle them. As Ben says, they usually resolve them and resume being affectionate.

BEN: I'll blow up or something. Or I tell Steve how to do something and he says, "Look, I know what I'm doing."
And I'll say, "I know, but I think my way is better."
And we'll kind of snap and growl and he usually goes off and does it his own way anyway. And I usually back right down again. I can even confuse Steve. Because I just get pissed off at him real fast, and then turn around and be all lovey-dovey, hugging and kissing kind of thing, minutes later. He's had difficulty coping with that. But I don't carry a grudge. It's not worth it. And I don't like to be angry at Steve. Regardless of whether I feel I'm right or wrong, I would rather forgive everything, forgive and forget.

STEVE: I usually feel it's all his fault, right? I reach a saturation point and if I yell at him, it's a fight. It gets loud and then I can see that neither one of us is going to agree with the other. The more we talk, the angrier we get. So I say I just don't want to talk about it anymore. . . . He sometimes will run up and just lay on the bed, in which case I'll feel real guilty. . . . Usually we make up within a half hour. . . .

It's rarely physical. I slapped him once. We were having a problem with the boat and he started yelling and screaming at me to do this, and I couldn't take it anymore. I just slapped him across the face. Which shook the boat and crashed it into the dock. So it's rarely physical.

Ben and Steve take themselves and their behavior with a grain of salt. They know they are overcompetitive and are likely to smile at their own conduct. Occasionally each will admit to being the person who is guilty of misbehaving. They are proud of being able to temper their jealousy and competition, and they feel stronger now as a couple than they have ever been. When we asked them what makes them happiest about their relationship, they both replied that it was the quality of their companionship and the reciprocity of real affection. They also feel being a gay couple has distinct benefits:

BEN: I think gay couples have a lot less game-playing. The whole business of "You do this and I do that" kind of thing. I think that exists less in gay couples—they just don't let the world influence them like heterosexual couples.

On the other hand, they both recognize that they are often in a tug of war for the *same* role, and so they both advise giving the other person "space," "independence," "separation," and "respect."

BEN: Trust the other person. That means let him be himself, and that means he'll come home to you.

Ben and Steve are working hard at being macho enough for their own self-respect but not so macho that the other person cannot feel good about his need to be his "own man." They have tested the relationship and concluded that it was important to them. They resisted needing each other and found that they wanted to be together. They are going to counseling so that Steve can "trick" and thus regard sex outside the relationship as lightly as Ben does. Together, they are trying to learn how to be interdependent, to express their emotions to each other so that the relationship can be less defensive and more collaborative.

# Gary and Joel

We picked Gary and Joel because we wanted to document an affluent non-monogamous couple living in a sophisticated gay world. We wanted a long-term committed couple who had weathered the storms of non-monogamy—including affairs—and remained happy, basically without conflict, and together. In addition, like other long-term couples Gary and Joel have gone through many changes in their careers and mode of living, and we wanted to see how they had accommodated these changes as a couple.

Gary and Joel live in an elegant town house. Perhaps *elegant* is not a precise enough description. It is truly fabulous. It looks as if it ought to house an embassy or a national institution. But it is home for Gary, Joel, their friends, and an assortment of cats.

The house used to belong to a famous art collector. The entryway is flanked by marble statues, the entrance hall is marble, and the large public rooms have eighteen-foot ceilings. There are three winding staircases that divide the house into three parts. On each landing is a large canvas by Robert Motherwell, Mark Rothko, or another established artist. The setting is quite intimidating, but Gary and Joel's friendliness puts visitors at ease.

Gary, thirty-seven, is responsible for the decor. He used to be a successful clothing designer, and has become a sculptor in the past year. Joel, forty-seven, actually owns the town house, and while Gary is financially secure, it is Joel's family money that has allowed them to live so palatially. He is from a wealthy Italian-American family and, after having seriously considered the priesthood, is now a research physician. He does not need his salary.

Gary and Joel come from quite different backgrounds. Gary is Jewish, from a middle-class family, and has cut himself off from his past. Joel is close to his family, close to many of his religious traditions, and more driven professionally than Gary. Friends told them their relationship wouldn't last—but they have been together for fifteen years and expect to be for the rest of their lives. They had a memorable first meeting.

GARY: Joel was in Gump's on April second. He was there waiting for an elevator to go upstairs, not noticing anybody looking at him, and I was there absolutely fainting dead away looking at him and not being noticed. The elevator finally came. He walks into the back. I stood right next to him and the elevator fills up, and I was there with my huge portfolio at the time. The elevator closed, and everybody looking forward, I just put out my pinky and grabbed his hand. It was the first time he noticed me.

We got out on the third floor, and there is a furniture

department which was like a maze, and he started wandering around there and he started feeling for my cock—which was so excited at the time I couldn't believe it. And my first words to him were, "Don't worry, it's big," thinking that's the reason he started feeling me. And I got so scared that I gave him my card . . . not knowing what would happen. He called me the next day and I went over to his place and we made love; and that's our anniversary.

Joel also remembers that encounter vividly:

JOEL: I was in the elevator, totally oblivious that I was being noticed. Gary had recently returned from Palm Springs and was very tanned and attractive and had a sunny face . . . and when I looked up I realized there was a tremendous innocence about him, and that was very appealing to me. I put my hand on the rail in the back of the elevator to steady myself as the elevator went up, and he interlinked his pinky with my pinky. I got off the elevator, thinking this would be a good place to have some conversation with him. I made it quite obvious that I wanted to leave the store and go to my apartment with him at that moment. But he gave me his card. I was disturbed at the moment because I thought I might never see him again.

I shopped longer, hoping I would see him again, but I didn't, and later on that afternoon I was meeting friends, and I mentioned to them that I had met someone . . . and I thought I was in love. And they said, "Oh, how ridiculous. How could that possibly be?" You see, at this point I had quite a reputation about town. . . . I was rather promiscuous and they thought this was just a passing fancy. But I felt different about it. The next morning at eight A.M. I called him . . . and we've been together ever since.

There was an enormous physical attraction, but both men say it was something else that drew them to each other.

JOEL: I am not concerned about physical beauty *per se*. There is a whole aura about a person and Gary has that aura. . . . It was the innocence, the naïveté, the youth, the honesty, the expectation, the friendliness, the warmth.

Gary, in fact, lived very differently from Joel. He had never participated in the bar scene, never was promiscuous, and had always wanted to be in a relationship. Nonetheless, he was the slower one to say "I love you." Joel was sure immediately, but Gary needed a little more time. Still, they made a commitment to each other fairly quickly.

In the beginning their relationship was complicated by Joel's family obligations. His brother moved in with them early on, and that caused a serious rift.

JOEL: I tried to convince Gary that this was a temporary thing, but it didn't seem temporary to him and he wanted our privacy very much. I wasn't very objective about it. My brother suspected the relationship and might have been uncomfortable, which manifested in some hostility that Gary was able to sense.

Joel had his own complaints about Gary's family:

JOEL: It disturbed me that they decided I was the one who had made Gary gay. They felt I was the one who took him off the straight and narrow path. They confronted him with "We thought you were cured," and "You were going to be married and give us a grandchild," and "It's Joel has taken you away from all this." Which, of course, was not true. It was mutual, and really Gary who picked me up.

Joel's brother lived with them for a year. Gary couldn't take it.

GARY: We were starting out in a Victorian flat where there were no doors to the two bedroom alcoves. We learned to have silent sex. Joel couldn't see what was happening to us. And having Vic there, not understanding who I was, why I was there, why would he choose someone ten years younger from a middle-class Jewish family when he was from a Catholic upper-class background. And I did not treat Vic [respectfully] like everyone else had. . . . And Joel got torn between us.

Finally Gary moved out. He went to Denver.

GARY: I left Joel. Not as much to leave him as . . . because I couldn't be married to somebody who was also married to his family. Catholic families are incredibly worse than Jewish families. . . . Joel would come visit me on weekends, or I would go visit him. . . . And he made the commitment of leaving his family and coming to live with me. That's when I started totally feeling that we were married.

Once the commitment was established they both moved back to California. Gary's family became more accepting. ("My mother kept saying she was so proud that I married a doctor—couldn't he be Jewish?") Friends, however, did not like the match and Joel's friends snubbed Gary.

GARY: Joel was the one who entertained everybody. . . . He'd fix them up with dates and then go get his own. He was the only one lively enough to take care of them, to see to their needs. When he met me he stopped going to the bars and they resented the fact that he wasn't around. They really did not like me.

These friends were so disruptive that Joel eventually stopped seeing them. But the early years brought other complications. For Gary, the biggest were family problems. For Joel, there were sexual adjustments he had to make.

JOEL: I have always impressed people as being the masculine type and therefore it was always assumed that I would do the fucking. So I kind of got used to the idea and assumed that apparently this was the role that I was supposed to play. Not that I was antagonistic to the idea of being buggered, but the physical aspects of it terrified me, so that I never even allowed it to happen except once, and it was horrendous because it was the wrong person who did it. And so therefore I was predisposed away from being passive. . . . I just assumed that I would be the active one and that is the way it would be between Gary and I.

It was not. They had arguments about how to have sex, and Gary resisted receptivity to Joel's preference.

JOEL: I would joke about some other young men whom we would have as acquaintances—saying, "I wonder which one is quick to lift his legs to heaven"—not knowing it was upsetting Gary tremendously because it made him feel in some way inferior. It made him feel that I was forcing him into a passive role situation. Without articulating it, an air of contention began to develop. And when I would make attempts to fuck Gary, he, having not much experience, would resist, and that would be that.

And so for a long time I felt as though I was being deprived of something I had grown used to. He was willing to have sex in other ways—fellatio, mutual masturbation, body-rubbing, et cetera, any way except anal intercourse. And that was okay with me and it became not that important. And we also had some other ways of physical satisfaction.

Another way of compensating was to become involved with other people. Joel felt it was important for Gary to have sex outside the relationship. He didn't want Gary to feel confined and therefore resentful. Joel had been "out" in the gay world much longer than Gary; he thought it natural for his partner to "sow a few wild oats."

Unfortunately, he was projecting his own sexual philosophy on Gary and was unable to imagine how Gary would behave. Joel wanted Gary to have only impersonal sex—as impersonal as possible, because that had always satisfied him. But Gary, unlike Joel and his friends, was a true romantic. He couldn't go to the baths or bars. He had affairs with friends and built those affairs into relationships.

This difference exposed the relationship of Gary and Joel to some risk.

GARY: We have always had an open marriage. However, Joel prefers total anonymity. . . . He doesn't want to know, speak to, have anything further to do with whomever he has sex with, and that's dropped and that's it. And he gets his jollies that way. I am totally the opposite. I cannot make love to anybody I don't know. I do not like being anonymous. . . . I can't stand the thought of having a one-night stand, and so it's usually with people I know. And I overdo it. Joel thinks I'm nuts and he thinks I think he is nuts. 'Cause I overdo it sometimes to the detriment of our relationship.

What happened is what happens in many long-term gay male relationships. About five years ago, one of Gary's one-night stands turned into a love affair. For nine months Gary and Joel's relationship looked as if it might not survive. Gary went to the East Coast with a man he had first thought of as "just a trick," and set up housekeeping. He and Joel continued to write, meet, and talk, to have long tearful sessions. Finally, Gary came back to Joel. Now they are somewhat less eager to get involved with other people. They have learned that a lot of outside sex allows an opening for another emotional attachment, and both men want to preserve what they have.

They talked to friends about their relationship and their sex life—and it helped both. They solved the problem of "who was going to be on top" and learned to be more egalitarian about initiating sex. Their sex life has become much more satisfying and they have sex almost every day.

The larger issue is time together. Gary believes in a "companionate relationship." Joel agrees, but cannot seem to find the time. He is a "workaholic." Yet Joel says his happiest times are spent alone together with Gary.

> JOEL: We get away for a full month in the summer and we love it. It's marvelous. We never get tired of being with each other. We're never bored. We both love the same things. We can be together for interminable amounts of time.

But work has gotten in the way more often than not. Joel spends every night at the lab and also part of the weekend. When he takes time off, his family responsibilities often necessitate more time away from Gary. Gary, on the other hand, is absolutely flexible about time. He receives money from a former business and sculpts all day at home. Joel knows their schedules and needs are out of sync and he worries.

> JOEL: Gary works at home and I get a great deal of pleasure watching him. I'm more profligate with time. I spend more time away from him than I would like, and I feel very guilty about it. He is much more firm and much more adamant about the time that he will spend with others . . . so he is much more jealous of the time we have together than I am.

Having enough time together is an issue in their relationship, but because Gary is sympathetic to Joel's ambition they rarely have a real fight about it. Gary used to be in a time-consuming occupation himself, so he is able to empathize with Joel. Because Gary wants as much time together as possible, and because he wants to help Joel protect himself from getting "used up" by family, friends, co-workers, and others, Gary takes on the organization of the household and the everyday decisions. Working at home makes it easier. Both partners bristle at the thought that Gary has a "female role."

> GARY: I am very anti gay people who refer to each other as *she,* or this is *butch* or this is *femme.* As a matter of fact, some people ask me

who Joel is and I say he's my husband, and Joel will answer me the same thing.

Even though Gary does all the housework now, it was not always that way. It depends on who is doing what at the time.

JOEL: I used to do it all while I was going to school and Gary was working. I used to be what is commonly known in gay parlance as a "clean queen." Nothing was ever clean enough for me, so I would have to shine and polish. Now I've gotten quite tired of it and it doesn't matter so much to me if there is dust. But you see there isn't any. Gary is doing about ninety percent of it now. He does all the housecleaning and the cooking and marketing and all of that. He loves to cook and we like to cook together, but Gary and I, if we ever have arguments, we have them in the kitchen. For example, if the recipe calls for half a stick of butter, I think, "Well, a whole stick would be better." It's the only place we argue.

But—this is not an excuse—but part of it is most people don't have nearly as large a place as this or as complicated to take care of. And it's not because we can't afford it, but I simply don't like the idea of having a stranger come into the house and do it. First of all, they are not going to do it as well as we would, and I just don't want to work my life around somebody else being here. Gary really does have the time. I don't get home until after seven o'clock at night. . . .

However, if because Gary works at home anyone thought of him as the feminine partner, that's mistaken, ludicrous. I think people are too sophisticated for that.

Very little really disturbs the harmony of Gary and Joel's relationship. The conflicts they do have, except for the one over Gary's single serious affair, are usually brief, situational, and over "in three seconds." They had to *learn* how to communicate, however; it was not something they knew how to do at the start.

GARY: It was much different in the beginning of the relationship, because we didn't realize how much we didn't communicate. You tend to overlook familiar things and they don't come out. We were ignorant—or afraid—about how to discuss things. Part of it was background. Part of it was style. Joel would just give in to me without feedback. I was frustrated because I am not guilty that way. This is when I notice he is not Jewish.

Over the years they have come to understand and know each other much better.

JOEL: We try not to make arguments a matter of who wins. I don't have any notches in my belt, and he doesn't have any notches in his belt that I'm aware of. I don't think we keep track and I don't think it's important.

We talk things out better than we used to. We confront things better. In years past we might have harbored resentments; we don't any longer. We have a lot of "I" dialogues. For example, "I feel down" or "I feel wonderful," and then, of course, the other person is supposed to say, "Why?" and that helps things get talked about on the right basis. . . . Perhaps sometimes we don't share enough, but that is because of the closeness, of the number of years we've been together, of that whole osmosis thing; we assume that our partner sometimes knows more than he does.

For some years, I would just clam up and I can remember Gary saying, "Where is your head?" And I would say, "I'm here," when I was really somewhere else. Eventually, of course, I would let Gary in, but it took a while, and now I'm much more willing to open up. . . . I spent a lot of time in boys' boarding school and then seminary, and learned to be solitary and introspective, and it's taken time to . . . unroot that from my psyche.

The essence of this relationship, which they reiterate time and again, is that they enjoy each other's company. Each respects the other's mind; they like discussing things with one another. They pride themselves on not having what Gary calls "trivial chitchat," and they both would rather be with each other more than with anyone else. They tend to protect each other too. They recognize some areas that could cause competition, and they manage those areas consciously.

GARY: If he wants to make some suggestions about my clothing designs, I don't let him. But sculpture is another thing. I look forward to his comments, but I feel I am professional enough so that I don't need outside help and resent it. And even though he continues doing it, he has toned down about ninety percent. It is the other ten percent when I can smack him. [He laughs.]

JOEL: I used to take art lessons before I met Gary. The guy I studied with thought I had a fabulous talent. But this was while I was single. When I met Gary, I thought, *No, I don't want that to be a bone of contention.* So when we started living together, I gave it up. I think each of us is very good at what he does. And we're happy that we do different things.

Gary and Joel have had to work at keeping a balance of power in the relationship. They have also had to work to reach a point where each of them can feel at ease about giving the other room to be different. They think a lot about the areas in which they want to be "bonded" and those in which they need to be independent. It is very important for them to be economically intertwined (everything is fifty-fifty and they have both joint and separate checking and savings accounts), and they think it is just as important to have a mutually satisfactory group of friends. This last requirement is one that they have had trouble meeting—not because they like different kinds of people but because both would like to be friends with other couples, and they say those are hard to find.

GARY: We would like to develop friends with couples. It's difficult to be friends with singles. They're always looking to see what time they can go to a bar. Or they don't reciprocate like couples do because they're not set up for it or because they are selfish.

They also wish, from time to time, they could have a family.

GARY: I would love children. I would absolutely love it. I relate to them very well. We are surrogate parents to children of two different families. . . . Some of our closest friends' kids have grown up knowing us and now they're late teenagers and they call *us* when there are problems, not their parents.

Both of them agree on the necessity of a homelife and the importance of their partnership. They have more independent views about some of their sex life, but they are closer to agreement than they used to be. Gary would like to be less involved with Joel's family. Joel feels tremendously responsible to his family, and that is not going to change. Gary would also like to be more public and political about their gayness, but Joel feels very strongly about keeping it private.

JOEL: I think that those who have come out have hurt themselves. As a scientist, I think I make a tremendous contribution—and people who listen to me just might turn me off if they thought I was a homosexual. I do not impose or propose, but expose; they go away enlightened because I present things in a very objective way. I think I would lose my credibility with too many people if I came out.

Gary disagrees, but he allows Joel to go his own way on this.

Together they are a very comfortable couple to be with. Joel says the best way to make a relationship last is to "give your lover a loose leash." Gary says to "start out monogamous, develop interests and friends together, and ignore outside influences." The secret of their own success is not their similarity. They are different people with very different impulses. The key to their ability to stay in love and to stay together is their skill at compromising, their willingness to talk, and, as Joel says, "not to make black-and-white rules."

They have also conquered two problems our gay male couples often have: competition, and exposure to risk from outside affairs. Gary and Joel consciously skirt areas that might draw them into sexual or any other kind of competition. And, while they are secure about their commitment and generally unpossessive, they have learned that, because of the nature of Gary's personality, a little less sexual opportunity is a good idea for both of them.

They really have no other risks. They are both wealthy enough that neither wields economic dominance over the other, and both are happy in their work. There are some job-related stresses: Gary is more companionate than Joel, but Joel doesn't feel pressured, because Gary agrees with his values even if Joel's attachment to his work sometimes makes it hard for him to be around as much as Gary would like. The key here is that they share the same values and have the same goals for the relationship. They have divided up responsibilities in a way they find natural and equitable and they are not troubled by Gary's staying home more these days.

They are not without some tensions. Joel's family is still seen as a burden and intrusion by Gary and they both are trying to figure out a way to have more time together. But all of this is backed by the assumption that they will be together forever. Gary and Joel come as close to an institutional model of marriage as a gay couple can.

# Notes

[  ] Notes in brackets give additional details for readers interested in the statistical analyses that led to our conclusions.

$N$ refers to the number of people or number of couples on which a percentage is based.

# Introduction

1. The way in which participants were sought did not guarantee a sample representative of the population of the United States. We did succeed, however, in getting a very large group of participants. The issue of representativeness becomes less troublesome as the number of participants increases. (See also Note 4.)

2. We sent questionnaires to 7,397 heterosexual couples (both married and cohabiting), 1,875 gay male couples, and 1,723 lesbian couples. Usable questionnaires were returned by 4,314 heterosexual couples, 969 gay male couples, and 788 lesbian couples. This reflects a return rate of 58 percent for heterosexuals, 52 percent for gay men, and 46 percent for lesbians. For a number of reasons, these rates are not higher: First, for ethical considerations we destroyed names and addresses of volunteers as soon as the questionnaires were mailed, which meant we could not follow up with reminders or a second wave of questionnaires. Second, with the first very large mailing we encountered some difficulties: The names and addresses of the gay men and lesbians in this mailing were collected more than six months before the questionnaires were ready to go out, and some of these couples had either broken up or moved in the interim. Then, too, we were initially unaware that undeliverable questionnaires would not be returned by the postal service, but rather were destroyed without any record. Therefore, when calculating our return rate we must count the undeliverable as unreturned. In subsequent mailings we made sure that the undelivered questionnaires were returned by the postal service. Additionally, we left some of the gay and lesbian questionnaires at drop-off points or gave them to cooperating groups or organizations to distribute to people who might want to participate; we did not always succeed in getting unused questionnaires returned.

Another factor that we feel accounts for the response rate is that we would not include a couple unless both partners filled out questionnaires; we know that some were requested by one partner without the other's acquiescence, and where one partner was unwilling, we told the couples not to return the other's questionnaire. We also know that volunteers were often unaware of the length of the questionnaires. In light of these factors, we feel that our response rate is very good.

[If we make the somewhat questionable assumption that each partner in a couple has a propensity to complete and return his or her questionnaire, and that it is independent of his or her partner's propensity to do the same, then we can infer this propensity from the actual return rate, which is based on *couples'* returns. The individual propensity to return would be the square root of the couple return rate. That would be .76 for heterosexuals, .72 for gay men, and .68 for lesbians. Of course, partners' propensity to complete and return their questionnaires are not independent of each other, and indeed each may act as a goad to the other. So we feel that the true propensity to return a questionnaire is somewhere between the couple return rate and its square root.]

3. We chose not to include in our study couples who live apart. This decision was not meant as a reflection on these couples, who are very interesting in their own right, but simply to limit the scope of an already enormous undertaking. Also, because many of the questions we wanted to ask presuppose a couple's living together, we would have required a separate set of questionnaires and interviews to capture the nature of these relationships.

4. A caution to the reader about the limitations of our sample of participants: It does not represent all of the couples in the United States, and it would be misleading if our findings were applied to all groups within the country. For instance, a large number of our couples come from the New York, San Francisco, and Seattle areas. More important, our couples are primarily white and disproportionately well educated. We have more high salaries and prestigious occupations among our couples than would be found in the general population. Thus we need to be tentative about applying our findings to working-class or poor people, or to people with only a grade-school education. While we attempted to attract racial minorities and working-class people to the study, we were more successful in getting middle-class and affluent participants. We chose a greater number of people without a college education for the interviews, and therefore the quoted material does give a better flavor of this part of the American population.

These limitations apply to all four kinds of couples. In addition, among the gay men and lesbians there are few of the *truly* closeted. We do have many people who keep their sexuality private from co-workers and family, but not many who are so closeted that *no one* knows they are gay.

We must also caution the reader about areas in which the different kinds of couples are not fully comparable. The gay male and lesbian couples were more likely to have learned about the study by word of mouth and by knowing other people who had taken part. As a group their relationships are of shorter duration than the married couples', but the gay men's are actually of longer duration than the cohabitors'. The lesbian relationships on average are of shorter duration than those of the gay men. Finally, our married couples are more religious than the other couples and have more conservative political beliefs.

5. We should note that everyone in the study is a volunteer. This means that when we compare heterosexuals to homosexuals, we are comparing volunteer to volunteer. Whatever biases may be introduced into the data because of a volunteer sample should not account for the differences we find between the various types of couples.

6. It was our plan to interview 300 couples, but because of the vagaries of selection and scheduling, we eventually interviewed more than 300. The actual numbers are:129 heterosexual couples, 98 gay male couples, and 93 lesbian couples.

7. For cohabitors we had only two duration categories: short and medium. This is because we found an exceedingly small number of such couples who had been together for more than ten years. The rarity of such couples, we feel, is largely due to the relative novelty of unmarried cohabitation as a social phenomenon.

8. Social class is a very difficult concept to measure, particularly in the United States in the 1980's. We chose education as the single best yardstick because it has been commonly used for this purpose in sociological research.

[The educational category into which a couple was placed does not necessarily reflect that of both partners. To arrive at the education level of a *couple*, we made the assumption that the partner with the higher education would be more likely to affect the couple's values and living conditions. Therefore, some people are included in a higher education category than they have themselves attained.]

9. Within each of the categories based on education and duration, we chose ten gay male couples, ten lesbian couples, eight married couples, and eight cohabiting couples. This

was the basic design, but in actuality there were a few extra couples in some of the categories (see note 6).

10. Two different kinds of follow-up questionnaires were sent. We randomly chose a large group of people we had not interviewed to receive a brief follow-up questionnaire, asking only about the current state of their relationship. These were sent to the following percentages of the original questionnaire sample: 34 percent of married couples; 53 percent of cohabitors; 68 percent of gay male couples; and 59 percent of lesbian couples. Only one reminder was sent to these people if they failed to return their questionnaires. The return rate was: 82 percent of married couples, 67 percent of cohabitors, 75 percent of gay male couples, and 73 percent of lesbian couples.

The people whom we had interviewed received a longer form which asked if they were still together or, if not, how the relationship had ended. In addition they were asked a number of other questions reflecting new ideas that had occurred to us as we looked at the data from the original questionnaires and interviews. We kept sending question-naires to these people until we achieved a return rate of 88 percent of the heterosexuals, 99 percent of the gay men, and 98 percent of the lesbians.

11. This meant that in the heterosexual couples, roughly half the women were inter-viewed by women and half by men, and the same held true for male partners. In the same-sex couples, it meant that not all lesbians were interviewed by women (or men) and not all gay men by men (or women). In this way we could reduce the bias that might result from the effect of the interviewer's gender on the information gathered in the interview.

12. The first questionnaires were mailed out in the spring of 1978 and interviewing began in the Seattle area and the San Francisco Bay area in early summer. Question-naires continued to be sent out all over the country until late 1979. Interviews were conducted in the New York metropolitan area beginning in the spring of 1979. Follow-up questionnaires were first sent out in late 1979 and were continued into early 1981.

13. The data from questionnaires are presented in figures in the text and in notes at the end of the book, usually in the form of percentages. Data are presented in this manner for clear communication to a nonacademic audience. However, the presentation does not generally reflect the manner in which the data have been analyzed. If data are discussed as having noteworthy differences, this means that an underlying statistical analysis sup-ports that noteworthiness. Details of these analyses are presented in brackets in the endnotes.

[Two major kinds of analyses were done, each with different causal assumptions. Multiple regression analyses were performed when it was reasonable to assume that the independent variables were clearly antecedent to the dependent variable. For example, a measure of the couple's sexual frequency was regressed on such measures as the couple's mean age, its duration, its mean income, etc. When the causal priority of two variables was not clear, partial correlations were used instead, with such variables as age, duration, income, etc., used as controls. For example, the relationship between the couple's re-ported sexual frequency and a partner's reported satisfaction with his or her sex life was analyzed in this manner because of the reciprocal causality probably involved.

Sometimes the variables in these analyses are based on the individual as the unit of analysis, such as his or her age, and at other times they are based on the couple, such as the mean age or the age difference, or the absolute age difference. The nature of the causal argument and the nature of the dependent variable dictated which type of analysis was done. In the percentage tables and notes presented, variables were collapsed, usually into dichotomies or trichotomies. In the multivariate analyses, however, the full variation was used. The exact wording of items and the scale points are presented in the composite questionnaire beginning on page 603, and the reliability coefficients of created scales are listed in the relevant endnotes. The control variables used for the regression analyses and partial correlations are presented in the endnotes where the findings are discussed.

There are no statistical tests presented in this book for two reasons: First, the sample is not random; and second, the number of cases is so large that the usual standards of statistical significance would cause us to be swamped by a proliferation of substantively unimportant findings. After a good deal of thought we settled upon a very simple rule to use in judging a finding worthy of discussion. We decided, on the basis of our experience with the data and our more general experience with data on related topics, that correla-tion coefficients and standardized regression coefficients that exceeded an absolute value of .15 would be our approximate cutoff point. We recognize the arbitrariness of this rule, but it is one we found we could apply easily and consistently across all of our analyses. Occasionally we discuss findings based on a slightly smaller coefficient, but only when it is part of a group of closely related findings, all of which achieve the proper coefficient. We also chose to apply the same standard to dummy variables even though they have statistical properties different from those of our interval scales.

Almost all of the regression and partial correlation analyses were done in one of two ways: either within each type of couple separately, or within each type of person separately. So, for example, there were four regression analyses for the dependent variable of sexual frequency: one for married couples, one for cohabitors, one for gay men, and one for lesbians, each with the couple as the unit of analysis. There were, however, six regression analyses using satisfaction with the quality of the couple's sex life as the dependent variable: one for husbands, one for wives, one for male cohabitors, one for female cohabitors, one for gay men, and one for lesbians, each with the person as the unit of analysis. We recognize that in doing the latter analyses we do not have independent observations in the gay male and lesbian analyses, but we have no reason to believe we would bias our results.

We had to have slightly different conceptualizations for heterosexual and same-sex couples because the latter do not have gender as a marker for creating separate variables. For example, it is possible to regress a measure of the husband's satisfaction with the relationship against a measure of his income and a measure of his wife's income. For a gay man, we would instead regress each man's satisfaction against his own income and against his partner's. These two examples reflect essentially the same independent variables, but they must be discussed in substantively different ways. Other kinds of analyses pose other problems, however. For example, it is possible to regress a measure of a married couple's conflict against both the husband's income and the wife's income. For the same-sex couples, a similar procedure is impossible, and it was necessary to compromise by regressing the dependent measure against the absolute difference in the couple's incomes as well as their total income. This way we would know about income differences as well as overall couple income. In order then to bring the heterosexual couples into line, we would perform additional analyses for them, in one case using total income and the absolute difference of the incomes as independent variables, and in another analysis, using total income and the signed difference as independent variables. With this approach we brought the substance of the analyses into as close alignment as possible.

Sometimes in the text we discuss comparisons between entire distributions—for example, the gay men compared to the lesbians. When we do this, it reflects that the means of the distributions are different in what seems like a substantively important way.

When we compare different types of couples, the danger arises that we may mistakenly conclude that they are, on average, different, but this difference may reflect other differences between couple types, such as the fact that our married couples have been together longer than any of the other kinds of couples. For example, we may find that, on average, gay men are less possessive than married couples. Is this a real difference or is it spurious, owing to the difference in the distribution of the couple's duration together? There is no ultimate solution to this problem. But the statistical analyses allow us to come close. If, for example, among gay men, those who have been together a short time are no more or less possessive than those who have been together a longer time, and if the same holds true for married couples, then it is probably safe to compare the gay men as a whole to the married couples as a whole, without fear that differences in duration together are really accounting for the apparent difference in possessiveness between the two types of couples. This is the procedure we have followed, so when in the text we present and discuss differences between types of couples, this means we have already considered and discarded as many alternative reasons for them as possible. However, it is conceivable that we could have found that couples of short duration *are* more possessive than those who have been together a long time. In that case we would not present a comparison between all of our gay male couples and all of our marrried couples. Rather, we would only compare gay men in short-term relationships with married couples in short-term relationships, and gay men in long-term relationships with married couples in long-term relationships.]

# The American couple in historical perspective

1. Rudy Ray Steward, *The American Family: A Demographic History* (Beverly Hills, Cal.: Sage Publications, 1978).

2. Hugh Carter and Paul C. Glick, *Marriage and Divorce: A Social and Economic Study*, rev. ed. (Cambridge, Mass.: Harvard University Press, 1976).

3. Ibid.

4. U.S. National Center for Health Statistics, *Monthly Vital Statistics Report*, Vol. 31, No. 12 (March 14, 1983).

5. Andrew Cherlin, *Marriage, Divorce and Remarriage* (Cambridge, Mass.: Harvard University Press, 1981).

6. Carter and Glick, *Marriage and Divorce*.

7. Cherlin, *Marriage, Divorce and Remarriage*.

8. U.S. Bureau of the Census, *Current Population Reports*, series P-20 (1981, 1982) and series P-23 (1981, 1982), (Washington, D.C.: U.S. Government Printing Office).

9. Carter and Glick, *Marriage and Divorce*.

10. *Family Planning Perspectives*, Vol. 15, No. 1 (January/February 1983), pp. 38–39.

11. Ibid.

12. Paul C. Glick, "A Demographer Looks at American Families," *Journal of Marriage and the Family*, Vol. 37, No. 1 (February 1975), pp. 15–26. Also, Carter and Glick, *Marriage and Divorce*.

13. Ernest Porterfield, "Black-American Intermarriage in the United States," *Marriage and Family Review*, Vol. 5, No. 1 (Spring 1982), pp. 17–34. See Also Graham Spanier and Paul Glick, "Mate Selection Differentials Between Whites and Blacks in the United States," *Social Forces*, Vol. 58, No. 3 (March 1980), pp. 707–725. They state that in 1975 about 4.4 percent of married black men and about 2.4 percent of married black women had partners of a different race (usually white).

14. Andrew Hacker, "Divorce à la Mode," *The New York Review of Books* (May 3, 1979). See also U.S. Bureau of the Census, *Statistical Abstract of the United States* (Washington, D.C.: U.S. Government Printing Office, 1978), tables 114, 118, 119.

15. Carter and Glick, *Marriage and Divorce*. Also, Spanier and Glick, "Mate Selection Differentials between Whites and Blacks in the United States." These authors have shown that black women are more likely to marry men of a lower educational level than themselves. This is one of the outcomes of a "marriage squeeze" for black men and women which the authors feel may make marital instability more likely.

16. U.S. Bureau of the Census, *Statistical Abstract of the United States* (1978), tables 114, 118, 119. See also Hacker, "Divorce à la Mode."

17. U.S. Bureau of the Census, *Current Population Reports*, series P-20 (1981, 1982) and series P-23 (1981, 1982).

18. Joseph Goldstein, Anna Freud, and Albert J. Solnit, *Beyond the Best Interests of the Child* (New York: The Free Press, 1973). See also Lenore Weitzman, *The Marriage Contract: Spouses, Lovers and the Law* (New York: The Free Press, 1981), pp. 98–120. Also, Cherlin, *Marriage, Divorce and Remarriage*, pp. 26–27.

19. U.S. Bureau of the Census, *Current Population Reports*, series P-20, No. 312 (June 1975) and No. 323 (March 1977), (Washington, D.C.: U.S. Government Printing Office).

20. U.S. National Center for Health Statistics, *Monthly Vital Statistics Report*, Vol. 31, No. 12 (March 14, 1983).

21. Paul C. Glick and Arthur J. Norton, "Marrying, Divorcing and Living Together in the U.S. Today," *Population Bulletin*, Vol. 32, No. 5 (Washington, D.C.: Population Reference Bureau, Inc., October 1977), pp. 36–37. Another measure of divorce trends is the

divorce ratio (the number of persons currently divorced per 1,000 persons currently married). The divorce ratio increased, from 47 in 1970, to 100 in 1980, and 109 in 1981. Note that the divorce ratio is not a measure of the incidence or frequency of divorce but rather of the prevalence of divorce (i.e., a measure of the previously married persons whose marriages have ended in divorce). See U.S. Bureau of the Census, *Current Population Reports*, series P-20 and series P-23, especially "Population Profile of the United States: 1981."

22. U.S. Bureau of the Census, *Statistical Abstract of the United States*, No. 122 (1977), (Washington, D.C.: U.S Government Printing Office), p. 84.

23. U.S. Bureau of the Census, *Statistical Abstract of the United States* (1978), tables 114, 118, 119.

24. Carter and Glick, *Marriage and Divorce*. Also Arthur J. Norton, "Family Life Cycle: 1980," *Journal of Marriage and the Family*, Vol. 45, No. 2 (May 1983), pp. 267–275. Also, Arthur J. Norton and Paul C. Glick, "Marital Instability in America: Past, Present and Future," *Journal of Social Issues*, Vol. 32, No 1 (1976), pp. 5–20.

25. Cherlin, *Marriage, Divorce and Remarriage*. Also, Norton, "Family Life Cycle: 1980."

26. U.S. National Center for Health Statistics, *Monthly Vital Statistics Report*, Vol. 31, No. 12 (March 14, 1983).

27. Cherlin, *Marriage, Divorce and Remarriage*, p. 26.

28. U.S. Bureau of the Census, *Current Population Reports*, series P-20 (1981, 1982) and series P-23 (1981, 1982).

29. A. Regula Herzog, Jerald G. Bachman, and Lloyd D. Johnston, "Paid Work, Child Care, and Housework: A National Survey of High School Seniors' Preferences for Sharing Responsibilities Between Husband and Wife," *Sex Roles*, Vol. 9, No. 1 (January 1983), pp. 109–135.

30. Alex Comfort, *The Joy of Sex* (New York: Simon & Schuster, 1972). Also, Charles Silverstein and Edmund White, *The Joy of Gay Sex* (New York: Simon & Schuster, 1977). Also, Emily Sisley and Bertha Harris, *The Joy of Lesbian Sex* (New York: Simon & Schuster, 1977).

31. William H. Masters and Virginia E. Johnson, *Human Sexual Response* (Boston: Little, Brown, 1966). Also, *Human Sexual Inadequacy* (Boston: Little, Brown, 1970). Also, *Homosexuality in Perspective* (Boston: Little, Brown, 1979). Also, Helen Singer Kaplan, *The New Sex Therapy: Active Treatment of Sexual Dysfunctions* (New York: Brunner/Mazel, 1974).

32. Graham B. Spanier, "Married and Unmarried Cohabitation in the United States: 1980," *Journal of Marriage and the Family*, Vol. 45, No. 2 (May 1983), pp. 277–288.

33. U.S. Bureau of the Census, *Current Population Reports*, series P-20, No. 349, "Marital Status and Living Arrangements: March 1979" (Washington, D.C.: U.S. Government Printing Office, 1980).

34. Spanier, "Married and Unmarried Cohabitation in the United States: 1980."

35. Richard R. Clayton and Harwin L. Voss, "Shacking Up: Cohabitation in the 1970s," *Journal of Marriage and the Family*, Vol. 39, No. 2 (May 1977), pp. 273–283.

36. Jessie Bernard, *The Future of Marriage* (New York: World Press, 1972).

37. Clayton and Voss, "Shacking Up: Cohabitation in the 1970s."

38. This is why all of our tabulations of cohabitors stop at medium-duration couples (two to ten years) and do not measure couples of more than ten years duration. For statistical analysis, there are simply too few couples in our study who have been together more than ten years.

39. Paul C. Glick and Graham B. Spanier, "Married and Unmarried Cohabitation in the United States," *Journal of Marriage and the Family*, Vol. 42, No. 1 (February 1980), pp. 19–30. Also, Spanier, "Married and Unmarried Cohabitation in the United States: 1980."

40. Cherlin, *Marriage, Divorce and Remarriage*, pp. 14–17.

41. Judith Blake, "Structural Differentiation of the Family: A Quiet Revolution in America," *Societal Growth: Processes and Implications*, ed. Amos H. Hawley (New York: The Free Press, 1979), pp. 179–201.

42. Weitzman, *The Marriage Contract*.

43. Letitia Anne Peplau, "Research on Homosexual Couples: An Overview," *Journal of Homosexuality*, Vol. 8, No. 2 (Winter 1982), pp. 3–8. This *Journal* special edition, on couples, was edited by Letitia Anne Peplau and Randall W. Jones.

44. Clellan S. Ford and Frank A. Beach, *Patterns of Sexual Behavior* (New York: Harper & Row, 1951), especially chapter XIII, "Human Sexual Behavior in Perspective," pp. 250–267.

45. See Jonathan Katz, *Gay American History: Lesbians and Gay Men in the U.S.A.* (New York: Avon, 1976); Arno Karlen, *Sexuality and Homosexuality: A New View* (New York: W. W. Norton, 1971); and Jeffrey Weeks, "Discourse, Desire and Sexual Deviance: Some Problems in the History of Homosexuality," *The Making of the Modern Homosexual*, ed. Kenneth Plummer (Totowa, N.J.: Barnes & Noble, 1981).

46. Carroll Smith-Rosenberg, "The Female World of Love and Ritual: Relations Between Women in Nineteenth-Century America," *Signs*, Vol. 1, No. 1 (Autumn 1975), pp. 1–29.

47. Lillian Faderman, *Surpassing the Love of Men: Romantic Friendship and Love Between Women from the Renaissance to the Present* (New York: William Morrow, 1981).

48. Faderman, *Surpassing the Love of Men*. Also, Smith-Rosenberg, "The Female World of Love and Ritual."

49. Faderman, *Surpassing the Love of Men*.

50. Richard von Krafft-Ebing, *Psychopathia Sexualis*, 12th edition (1902), trans. Franklin S. Klaf, reprinted (New York: Stein and Day, 1965).

51. *The Standard Edition of the Complete Psychological Works of Sigmund Freud*, trans. James Strachey (London: Hogarth Press, 1953).

52. Alan P. Bell and Martin S. Weinberg, *Homosexualities: A Study of Diversity Among Men and Women* (New York: Simon & Schuster, 1978).

53. Kinsey et al. found that 37 percent of their male sample had "at least some overt homosexual experience to the point of orgasm between adolescence and old age" and that 4 percent of males were exclusively homosexual throughout their lives. Approximately 13 percent of all women had an adult same-sex experience, and somewhat less than 3 percent were homosexual throughout their lives. See Alfred C. Kinsey, Wardell B. Pomeroy, and Clyde E. Martin, *Sexual Behavior in the Human Male* (Philadelphia: W. B. Saunders, 1948); and Alfred C. Kinsey, Wardell B. Pomeroy, Clyde E. Martin, and Paul H. Gebhard, *Sexual Behavior in the Human Female* (Philadelphia: W. B. Saunders, 1953).

54. Sir John Wolfenden, *Report of the Committee on Homosexual Offenses and Prostitution* (London: Her Majesty's Stationery Office, 1957).

55. Evelyn Hooker, "Male Homosexuality in the Rorschach," *Journal of Projective Techniques*, Vol. 22 (March 1958), pp. 33–54. Also, "The Adjustment of the Male Overt Homosexual," *Journal of Projective Techniques*, Vol. 21 (March 1957), pp. 18–31.

56. Mark Freedman, *Homosexuality and Psychological Functioning* (Belmont, Cal.: Brooks/Cole, 1971).

57. See the Symposium on Homosexual Couples in the *Journal of Homosexuality*, Vol. 8, No. 2 (Winter 1982), and the bibliography of articles in Peplau, "Research on Homosexual Couples: An Overview."

58. Martin S. Weinberg and Colin J. Williams, *Male Homosexuals: Their Problems and Adaptations* (New York: Oxford University Press, 1974).

59. Bell and Weinberg, *Homosexualities*.

60. Letitia Anne Peplau, Christine Padesky, and Mykol Hamilton, "Satisfaction in Lesbian Relationships," *Journal of Homosexuality*, Vol. 8, No. 2 (Winter 1982), pp. 23–36.

# Money

## Introduction

1. F. Ivan Nye, et al., *Role Structure and Analysis of the Family* (Beverly Hills, Cal.: Sage Publications, 1976), pp. 82–83.

2. Eighteen percent of wives felt it was not important for their husbands to provide them with financial security, while 49 percent felt it was important, and 33 per cent responded neutrally to the question ($N = 3,639$). [The question asked was 1j in the Ideal Relationship part of the composite questionnaire.]

3. For example, see Robert O. Blood, Jr., and Donald M. Wolfe, *Husbands and Wives* (New York: Free Press, 1960), p. 241; and John Scanzoni, *Opportunity and the Family* (New York: Free Press, 1970).

## Income and power

1. [A measure of the couple's power balance was constructed using the difference between the two partners' ratings on item 5 of the Relationship questions in the composite questionnaire. The intra-couple correlations are: married: $r = -.313$; cohabitors: $r = -.469$; gay men: $r = -.413$; lesbians: $r = -.205$. Because of the wording of the items, a negative correlation reflects consensus. This measure was regressed against the following measures: the number of years the couple has lived together, the couple's average age, the couple's age difference, the total couple income, and the couple's income difference. The standardized regression coefficients for the last variable are: married couples: $-.174$; cohabitors: $-.182$; gay men: $-.233$; lesbians: $-.080$. A similar analysis using as the dependent measure the couples' answers to question 4f of the Relationship questions produced substantially the same results. Because of the rather low intra-couple correlations, the analyses were done separately for each partner's rating of the couple's power balance, but the findings were very similar to those presented.]

2. Fifty-six percent of wives who earn less than $10,000 ($N = 2,241$) do not discuss with their husbands how much they should have for personal spending money, as compared to 61 percent of those earning between $10,000 and $30,000 ($N = 1,209$), and 78 percent of those with an income above $30,000 ($N = 96$). [The question analyzed is Family Relations question 28a.]

3. Thirty-three percent of wives earning less than $10,000 ($N = 2,251$) have a personal savings account, as compared to 40 percent of those earning between $10,000 and $30,000 ($N = 1,206$), and 57 percent of those earning more than $30,000 ($N = 96$). [The question analyzed is Family Relations question 26.]

4. Thirty-four percent of husbands ($N = 3,638$) and 26 percent of wives ($N = 3,624$) do not feel that both spouses should share the responsibility for earning a living for the household. Thirty-three percent of husbands say it is better for the man to work in the outside world and the wife to stay at home ($N = 3,637$); 24 percent of wives share this view ($N = 3,631$). And 31 percent of husbands feel that the man should have major responsibility for the couple's financial plans, even if the wife is employed ($N = 3,642$). Twenty-six percent of the wives take this position ($N = 3,639$). [The relevant items are Opinion statements 4, 8, and 10.]

5. [The two items correlate $r = -.473$ for husbands and $r = -.487$ for wives. The second item was reversed before the two were added.]

6 [The regression analysis described in Note 1 of this section was repeated with an additional variable: the husband's belief in the provider role. The standardized regression coefficient for this measure is $-.139$. The same analysis was repeated again, this time substituting the wife's belief in the provider role, and the regression coefficient is $-.198$.]

7. [The same regression analyses as in the previous note were performed, except that the dependent variable was the partners' relative influence over whether or not to move to another city, state, or country (Relationship question 17e). The standardized regression coefficient for income difference is − .150, and for the man's belief in the provider ideology is − .158. The coefficient when the wife's belief in the provider role was substituted is − .136.]

8. Fewer than 1 percent of the gay men stay home to be full-time homemakers ($N =$ 1,921). Additionally, only 10 percent feel it is important that their partners provide them with financial security ($N = 1,922$). [The first of these statements is based on item 2a of the Statistical Information section of the questionnaire. The second is from 1j in the Ideal Relationship section.]

9. Lesbians place the highest value on self-sufficiency of any group in the study. Sixty-seven percent feel it is extremely important to be self-sufficient and only 10 percent feel it is not important. ($N = 1,547$). They place much more importance on self-sufficiency than do husbands, wives, and gay men in particular. [The data are based on item 4k on the Ideal Relationship part of the questionnaire.]

10. An important complicating factor in much of this discussion is whether the couple pools its money or keeps resources separate. We deal in detail with the whole issue of pooling in the chapter with that title.

11. Cohabiting women are very close to the lesbians in wanting to be self-sufficient, and surpass the married couples and the gay men by a sizable degree. They are nearly the same as the male cohabitors. Sixty-five percent of the women think it is extremely important for them to be self-sufficient ($N = 650$).

12. That their partners should be self-sufficient is felt more strongly by male cohabitors than by husbands, and even a bit more than by gay men. Sixty percent of the male cohabitors feel it is very important for their partners to be self-sufficient ($N = 651$), as compared to only 46 percent of husbands ($N = 3,641$) and 57 percent of gay men ($N = 1,926$). [The item used was 2p of the Ideal Relationship questions.]

13. Sixty-seven percent of female cohabitors who earn less than $10,000 ($N = 311$) do not discuss with their partners how much they should have for personal spending money, as compared to 75 percent of women with income between $10,000 and $30,000 ($N = 314$) and 94 percent of those earning more than $30,000 ($N = 16$). Sixty-nine percent of the women with the lowest income ($N = 309$) have their own private savings accounts, as compared to 86 percent of those in the middle income group ($N = 316$) and 100 percent of those in the high income group ($N = 16$).

14. [The same regression analyses as those described in Note 1 of this section were performed, using as the dependent measure, instead of relative power, the partners' relative influence over how much to spend on furniture items. This is Relationship question 17l. The intra-couple correlations are: married: $r = − .228$; cohabitors: $r = − .526$; gay men: $r = − .482$; lesbians: $r = − .287$. The standardized regression coefficients for the couple's income difference are: married couples: − .051; cohabitors: − .308; gay men: − .325; lesbians: − .178.]

15. In 63 percent of married couples, both partners have equal influence over spending on furniture. Among those couples where influence is unequal, in 26 percent the wife has more influence, while in only 11 percent is it the husband ($N = 3,496$).

16. In 63 percent of marriages the wife has greater influence over money spent on groceries, as compared with 28 percent of those where the influence is equal, and only 9 percent where the husband has greater influence ($N = 3,312$). [This is based on item 17i of the Relationship questions.]

17. [The same regression analyses as those described in Note 14 of this section were performed, using as the dependent measure the partners' relative influence over how much to spend on entertainment. This was Relationship question 17j. The intra-couple correlations are: married couples: $r = − .273$; cohabitors: $r = − .336$; gay men: $r = − .300$; lesbians: $r = − .230$. The standardized regression coefficients for the couple's income difference are: married couples: − .080; cohabitors: − .227; gay men: − .394; lesbians: − .164.]

18. [Partial correlations were computed between an individual's satisfaction with the amount of money coming in (Relationship question 1i) and his or her overall satisfaction

with the relationship (Relationship question 2), controlling for the length of time the couple has been together and the individual's age. The partial correlations are: husbands: .224; wives: .227; male cohabitors: .252; female cohabitors: .277; gay men: .200; lesbians: .104.]

19. [Regression analyses were performed where the dependent measure was the individual's happiness with the couple's income, and the independent variables included the number of years the couple have been together, the individual's age, the individual's income, and his or her partner's income. In the analysis for the husbands, the standardized regression coefficient for the man's income is $-.272$, and for the woman's, it is $-.124$. The parallel coefficients for the analysis for the wife are $-.342$ and $-.042$. It may be that in very untraditional couples or in couples where the wife earns a very high income, there is a different pattern. The regression analyses were repeated among couples where the wife works full time and again among couples where the wife's earnings are over $20,000. In both cases, the man's income continues to have a stronger regression coefficient than the woman's.]

20. [The same regression analyses as described in the previous note were conducted for cohabitors. For male cohabitors, the standardized regression coefficient for his own income is $-.212$, and for his partner's income it is $-.049$. For the women, her own income is $-.243$, while that of her partner is $-.089$.]

21. We find, for example, that the higher the incomes of husbands and male cohabitors, the more they describe themselves as outgoing, aggressive, and forceful. We combined these three self-descriptions to form a measure of the person's self-perception as masculine, since these three items have been used on "masculinity" scales by psychologists. Among husbands, 26 percent of those who earn less than $10,000 feel they are very masculine ($N = 337$), as compared to 32 percent of those earning between $10,000 and $30,000 ($N = 2,247$), and 46 percent of those with incomes over $30,000 ($N = 1,000$). The comparable figures for male cohabitors are 34 percent ($N = 177$), 42 percent ($N = 369$) and 56 percent ($N = 89$). We also note that husbands who feel more masculine are more satisfied with their relationships and that male cohabitors who feel more masculine are more strongly committed to the future of their relationships. Among husbands 79 percent of those who say they are very masculine are very happy with their relationship ($N = 1,274$), as compared to 71 percent of those who feel somewhat less masculine ($N = 1,338$), and 65 percent of those who do not feel masculine ($N = 1,002$). As for male cohabitors, among those who say they are very masculine, 63 percent expect their relationship to last ($N = 259$), and 63 percent of those who say they are moderately masculine agree ($N = 191$), as compared to 45 percent of those who say they are not masculine ($N = 166$).

[The items used for the masculinity scale are Relationship questions 20d, 20e, and 20g. The alpha reliabilities for the three items are: husbands: .763; male cohabitors: .803. For the most recent work on developing measures of masculinity, see Janet T. Spence and Robert L. Helmreich, *Masculinity and Femininity: Their Psychological Dimensions, Correlates, and Antecedents* (Austin: University of Texas Press, 1978); and Sandra L. Bem, "The Measurement of Psychological Androgyny," *Journal of Consulting and Clinical Psychology*, Vol. 42, No. 2 (April 1974), pp. 155–162. Zero-order correlations between the masculinity scale and the man's income are $r = -.149$ for husbands ($N = 3,588$) and $r = -.210$ for male cohabitors ($N = 640$). The correlations between masculinity and happiness with the relationship is $r = .144$ for husbands ($N = 3,617$) and between masculinity and commitment is $r = .189$ for male cohabitors ($N = 622$). Commitment to the future of the relationship is measured by Relationship question 27c. It is important to note that a more common interpretation would be that men who are more masculine earn more money and we do not deny the validity of this argument. We also believe however, and we get a sense of this in the interviews, that men derive their sense of masculinity from their success in the world of employment and that they use their earnings as a mark of that success.]

22. [The same regression analysis performed for married couples (see Note 19) was done for gay men. The regression coefficient for a man's own income is $-.220$ and for his partner's income is $-.251$.]

23. We feel, of course, that such a change would be anathema to the captains of industry who want as much productivity as possible from their employees. Perhaps this is one reason industry has been slow to warm to two-paycheck couples. It may be that corporate decision-makers feel that once a man loses his sense that he exists solely for his family's

welfare, he becomes less completely oriented to his work and therefore a less valuable employee.

24. However, among our couples, 9 percent of the gay couples report currently paying alimony or child-support payments incurred by one partner or the other.

25. It might startle captains of industry if we were to suggest, with tongue in cheek, that they might hire gay male couples and promote one at a time in order to have extremely ambitious and productive employees.

26. Sixty-seven percent of the lesbians between twenty-six and forty in our study have incomes below \$15,000 ($N = 1,027$). This is in contrast to 27 percent of comparably aged husbands ($N = 1,872$), 46 percent of male cohabitors ($N = 412$), and 55 percent of gay men ($N = 1,237$). Their average income is the same as female cohabitors (67 percent, $N = 384$).

## Money management

1. [The relevant questionnaire items are Relationship questions 21j and 21k. For the analyses using these items, the two partners' scores were summed. The intra-couple correlations are: married couples: $r = .500$ and $r = .496$; cohabitors: $r = .525$ and $r = .474$; gay men: $r = .485$ and $r = .491$; lesbians: $r = .487$ and $r = .549$. For all four types of couples, the amount of conflict over money is less in couples of longer duration. In order to avoid confounding between duration and type of couple, Figure 6 presents only the data for couples together between two and ten years. Similar profiles are found in the short-duration couples and in the long-duration couples.]

2. Married couples are much more likely to favor pooling their money than are the other kinds of couples, particularly in the first few years together. See Figure 8.

3. In marriages where the wife is a full-time homemaker, she has greater involvement in grocery shopping in 82 percent of the couples, her husband has greater involvement in 4 percent, and it is equal in 14 percent ($N = 894$). When she is employed full time she has greater involvement in grocery shopping in 59 percent of the couples, the man has greater involvement in 12 percent, and they share equally in 29 percent ($N = 1,369$). See also the discussion in Note 2 of the chapter on Pooling. [The grocery shopping item is Relationship question 9l.]

4. For the percentages of cohabitors, gay men, and lesbians who favor pooling their money, see Figure 8.

5. When cohabitors have a greater commitment to their future together, they are more likely to favor pooling of their money and property. This is discussed in detail in the chapter on Pooling.

6. Fifty-seven percent of the male "ideological" cohabitors have been previously married ($N = 129$) as compared to 49 percent of the "trial married" men ($N = 388$). For females, the percentages are 50 percent ($N = 120$) and 42 percent ($N = 424$).

7. In 62 percent of our cohabiting couples, the man has a higher income than the woman. In 14 percent the incomes are approximately equal, and in the remaining 23 percent the woman has the higher income.

8. Cohabiting couples are more likely to report fighting about money management at least once every few months if the woman has more influence over money spent on leisure (57 percent, $N = 49$) than if the influence is equal (42 percent, $N = 380$) or the man has greater influence (52 percent, $N = 144$). The same pattern holds true for spending on furniture: 52 percent if the woman has more influence ($N = 126$), 45 percent if influence is equal ($N = 372$), and 49 percent if the man has more influence ($N = 87$).

9. We divided couples into those who fight about money management more than approximately once every few months and those who fight less than that often. When they say influence is equal over spending on entertainment, they report less fighting than if they feel influence is not equal. For married couples it is 41 percent ($N = 2,120$) versus 47 percent ($N = 1,202$); for cohabitors, 42 percent ($N = 380$) versus 53 percent ($N = 193$); for gay men 42 percent ($N = 609$) versus 56 percent ($N = 254$); and for lesbians 35

percent ($N$ = 538) versus 42 percent ($N$ = 156). Similar differences are found when the couples rated the equality or inequality of influence over spending on furniture.

10. Recall that there is some evidence that among cohabiting couples, where influence over spending is not equal, conflict is greater when the woman has more influence than when the man does.

11. There is, of course, a minority of professionally employed wives who earn large salaries and choose not to commingle money or property with their husbands'. They are unaccountable to their husbands for purchases they may make, and they do not review his spending decisions. Such women tell us that this makes money conflict almost nil. Even these wives, however, can be faced with a purchase of such magnitude—for example, buying a house—that discussion and joint action become necessary. Nonetheless, it appears true that by avoiding day-to-day decision-making they can often cut down on the amount of conflict.

## Pooling

1. We assess people's attitudes toward pooling with item 5 of the Opinion statement part of the questionnaire. [We prefer to use an item about people's attitudes, rather than whether they do indeed pool, for two reasons: It is very difficult to measure the actualities of pooling, since its mechanics can be very complex. But more important, we feel that couples' actual pooling may be caused by many factors, some of which are not within the partners' control. Some may pool because one partner wants to, even though the other may not.]

2. Seventy-two percent of full-time homemakers want to pool ($N$ = 892). The percentage for wives employed part time is 69 percent ($N$ = 802) and for wives employed full time 68 percent ($N$ = 1,375). Among high-earning wives (over $30,000) the percentage is 61 percent ($N$ = 97), as compared to low-earning wives (under $10,000) 71 percent ($N$ = 2,252). Among wives whose husbands earn over $30,000, 71 percent favor pooling ($N$ = 999), and among those with husbands earning below $10,000, it is 69 percent ($N$ = 339). [Zero-order correlation between the wife's income and her attitude toward pooling is $r$ = .061. The correlation with her husband's income is $r$ = .044.]

3. Sociologist Lenore Weitzman has written extensively on the legal complexities of living together without being married (see her book *The Marriage Contract* [New York: Free Press, 1981]). As Weitzman points out, fifteen American states and the District of Columbia make cohabitation a crime. While such laws are rarely enforced, they show that legal vulnerability, rather than legal protection, exists. Furthermore, as Weitzman points out, cohabitors are not eligible for social security benefits that go to spouses, they get no tax benefits, they have problems insuring each other, and the legal rights of their children are unclear. There is a great deal of litigation over cohabitors' property rights, but the outcomes hinge on whether or not there is an explicitly written agreement. If no agreement exists, legal title to property determines ownership. To cohabitors, the courts have generally denied the rights to each other's income and/or property that they grant to husbands and wives. The same holds true for same-sex couples.

4. [Alpha reliability coefficients for this three-item scale are: for husbands .653, and for wives .667. The items are Opinion statements 9, 7, and 6.]

5. [Zero-order correlations between the institutional-voluntary dimension and people's attitudes toward pooling are: for husbands: $r$ = .270; for wives: $r$ = .301.]

6. [Zero-order correlation between the husband's attitude toward pooling and the number of years the couple has been together is $r$ = −.069. The wife's correlation is $r$ = −.108. In interpreting these correlations it is very important to recognize that these are cross-sectional data and not longitudinal. None of the possible alternative explanations for the lack of an association (for example, that couples actually want to pool more as time goes on, but the larger attrition among those who favor pooling causes an apparent lack of difference) seem to be plausible.]

7. See Figure 8. [Correlations between attitude toward pooling and the number of years

the couple has been together are $r = -.211$ for gay men and $r = -.189$ for lesbians. In this case it is extremely important to recognize the cross-sectional quality of the data. It is very possible that pooling is associated with couples staying together, and this may account in part for the fact that long-term couples are more inclined to favor pooling. On the basis of the interviews, however, we also feel that it takes time for many gay and lesbian couples to decide to pool.]

8. Among male cohabitors who would like to marry their partners, 42 percent favor pooling ($N = 365$), as compared to 14 percent of those who do not want to marry ($N = 118$). The comparable figures for women are 31 percent ($N = 415$) and 15 percent ($N = 108$).

[The marriage item is 23b of the Lifestyle questions. Partial correlations were computed between commitment and pooling, and between the desire to marry and pooling. The control variables were the number of years the couple has lived together and the partners' ages. The partials between commitment and pooling are: male cohabitors: .321; female cohabitors: .296. The partials between wanting to marry and pooling are: .328 and .265. We use partial correlations because we think a causal argument can be made in both directions: When people are more committed, they wish to pool; and when people pool they become more committed. Our commentary on these two patterns is in the text.]

9. Where the male cohabitor believes in pooling, 41 percent of couples fight about income at least once every few months ($N = 203$), as compared to only 26 percent of couples where the male does not favor pooling ($N = 233$). When it is the woman who believes in pooling, the percentage of couples fighting is 40 percent ($N = 174$), as opposed to 29 percent where she does not believe in it ($N = 277$). The parallel percentages for male cohabitors, when we consider fighting about money management, are 51 percent ($N = 200$) versus 43 percent ($N = 232$). For females: 49 percent ($N = 171$) versus 43 percent ($N = 275$).

[The causal interpretation is not without ambiguity. On the basis of the interviews, we believe that pooling increases the chance of conflict. It is also possible that some couples sense they are mismatched in their feelings about how to manage money and so they choose not to pool, because otherwise they anticipate conflict. Both arguments are compatible.]

10. [Correlations between people's attitudes toward pooling and their satisfaction with how they manage money are: husbands: $r = .059$; wives: $r = .123$; male cohabitors: $r = .037$; female cohabitors: $r = -.014$; gay men: $r = .070$; lesbians: $r = .014$. Satisfaction with how the couple manages money is measured by Relationship question 1k.]

# Work

## Introduction

1. This is the image of middle-class white post-industrial society. In reality, of course, poor women worked. Throughout this chapter we try to use the word *employed* or the expression *worked outside the home* when contrasting these women to those who are not wage-earners but work as full-time homemakers. Sometimes, however, for clarity and/or brevity we use the expression *working wives* to identify women who are employed. This shorthand is not meant to indicate that homemaking is not work.

## Having a job

1. We are speaking here primarily of first marriages. Women who are divorced or divorcing find it necessary to contemplate entry into the labor force unless they have independent means or large settlements from their husbands. There are also, of course, heterosexual women who do not wish to marry, and they, too, find it necessary to plan how they will support themselves. Whether single by desire or by happenstance, an unmarried woman, particularly one with children, is usually at an economic disadvantage because of women's lesser access to high-paying jobs. Thus, women who are heads of their families have been called the new poor. Like women in the working class, they take jobs out of necessity and tend to earn less than men with comparable education and job experience. See National Research Council, *Women, Work, and Wages: Equal Pay for Jobs of Equal Value* (Washington, D.C.: National Academy Press, 1981).

2. In contrast to the 34 percent of husbands and 25 percent of wives who feel couples should not share the responsibility for earning a living (Figure 12), fully 64 percent of husbands ($N$ = 3,640) and 60 percent of wives ($N$ = 3,600) feel a wife should not be employed if there are small children in the home. [The first item is Opinion statement 4 and the second, Opinion statement 11.]

3. [A regression analysis was performed using as the dependent variable the couple's mean score on the amount of conflict they have over whether both partners should work (Relationship question 21m). The independent variables included duration, the couple's mean education level, their mean age, their mean income level, the difference in their incomes, whether each partner is employed full time, and whether they were previously married. The standardized regression coefficient for duration is .156, which means that there is more conflict in couples of shorter duration. The intra-couple correlation for the amount of conflict is $r$ = .399. One should exercise care in interpreting this finding. It is possible that people who have married in recent years are more argumentative on this issue, but this is unlikely, since age was a control variable in the analysis. There are other more plausible explanations. First, couples may resolve their differences over time, or at least realize that there is no longer any use in arguing. Second, it may be that couples who do not see eye to eye on this issue are more likely to break up and not survive to become long-duration couples.]

4. While cohabitors feel strongly about both partners' working, when they were asked about whether mothers of small children should work outside the home, only 33 percent of the men ($N$ = 571) and 43 percent of the women ($N$ = 593) said yes.

5. Among male cohabitors who want to marry their partners, 63 percent reject the provider role ($N$ = 367), as compared to 69 percent of those who do not want to marry ($N$ = 118).

6. [The zero-order correlations between a male cohabitor's belief that it is preferable for a husband to work and the wife to take care of the home (Opinion statement 8) and the amount of conflict the couple has over both working is $r$ = .176. The correlation between the latter measure and the man's belief that husbands should have major responsibility for the couple's financial plans even if the wife works is $r$ = .165. The intra-couple correlation on whether both should work is $r$ = .338.]

7. [The partial correlation between the couple's mean rating of how much they fight over whether both should work and the male cohabitor's satisfaction with the overall relationship (controlling for duration, both ages, both incomes, both educational levels, and whether each has been married) is $-.142$. The partial correlation for the woman's overall satisfaction is $-.165$.]

8. Nine out of 1,921 gay men and 10 out of 1,554 lesbians say that taking care of the house is their full-time job.

9. When asked if one of the things they want in a relationship is for their partner to provide them with financial security, fewer than 10 percent of the gay men answered in the affirmative ($N$ = 1,922). [Ideal Relationship question 1j.]

10. Twenty-four percent of the gay men feel it is very important for them to have the masculine qualities of being aggressive, forceful, and outgoing ($N$ = 1,904). The husbands are close, 23 percent feeling the same way ($N$ = 3,614), followed by the male cohabitors at 21 percent ($N$ = 643). Fewer women feel the same way: of lesbians 18

percent ($N$ = 1,546); female cohabitors 15 percent ($N$ = 643); and wives 10 percent ($N$ = 3,588).

[The items are Ideal Relationship questions 2a, 2d, and 2o. Alpha reliability coefficients for the three items are: husbands: .623; wives: .522; male cohabitors: .586; female cohabitors: .540; gay men: .616; lesbians: .525. Even though these reliabilities are only moderate, these three items are used because they are the same as on the measure of an individual's self-perception as actually being masculine; for that measure the reliabilities are substantially higher.]

11. As for the wives taking on the breadwinner role, we find that only 4 out of 3,632 husbands describe their work as taking care of the house full time. Among the lesbians, only 8 percent say they want their partners to provide financial security ($N$ = 1,573).

12. [Partial correlations were performed between the couple's rating of how much they fight about whether both should work and the two spouses' satisfaction with their relationship and their commitment to its future. The control variables were duration, both ages, both incomes, both education levels, and whether each had been previously married. The partial for the husband's satisfaction is −.241, and for the wife's −.265. For the husband's commitment to the future of the relationship it is −.157, and for the wife's it is −.179. The assumption we make throughout this discussion, based on other questionnaire data and on the interviews, is that when married couples fight about whether both should work they are almost invariably fighting about whether the *wife* will work. It might be argued that what is really happening here is that a person in an unsatisfying relationship casts around for causes of his or her dissatisfaction, and on the basis of cultural stereotypes, chooses the wife's work as part of the problem.]

13. [Partial correlations were calculated between whether or not a wife is a full-time homemaker and her satisfaction with the relationship, her commitment to its future, her husband's satisfaction, and his commitment. The control variables were duration, both partners' ages, and whether they were married previously. None of the coefficients exceeds a magnitude of .060. Similar analyses were done using whether the wife worked full time outside the home or not. Again, the correlations are very small.]

14. Only 42 percent of couples where the wife is employed full time fight about her working. This is in contrast to 60 percent of couples where she works part time, and 56 percent of those where she is a full-time homemaker.

15. Among couples with small children, 50 percent of those where the wife is employed full time fight more than once every few months about how the children are raised ($N$ = 264), as compared to 47 percent of those where she works part time ($N$ = 359) and 45 percent of those where she is a full-time homemaker ($N$ = 508). [Relationship question 21n.]

16. For example, see Lois Wladis Hoffman, "Effects of Maternal Employment on the Child: A Review of the Research," *Developmental Psychology*, Vol. 10, No. 2 (March 1974), pp. 204–228.

17. See Viktor Gecas, "The Socialization and Child Care Roles," in F. Ivan Nye, *Role Structure and Analysis of the Family* (Beverly Hills, Cal.: Sage Publications, 1976), pp. 33–59.

18. Economist Gary Becker (*A Treatise on the Family* [Cambridge, Mass.: Harvard University Press, 1981]) has argued that it would be irrational for men to stay at home and women to be employed because men's wages are higher than women's and therefore a man's employment would profit the family more than if the wife was employed. We feel that tradition plays as great a part as rationality in the patterns we observe.

19. See Note 2.

20. Twenty-one percent of wives ($N$ = 3,631) and 16 percent of husbands ($N$ = 3,640) actively disagree with the statement that mothers of small children should not work outside the home. [Opinion statement 11.]

21. The percentage of cohabitors who actively approve of mothers of small children being employed is over twice that of our married couples. For male cohabitors it is 33 percent ($N$ = 571), as compared to husbands, 16 percent. For female cohabitors it is 43 percent ($N$ = 593), in contrast to wives, 21 percent.

22. [Multiple regression analyses were performed, with attitude toward mothers of small children working as the dependent variable and these independent variables: age, education, and whether or not the person has been married previously. The standardized

regression coefficients for age are: husbands: $-.149$; wives: $-.156$; male cohabitors: $-.188$; female cohabitors: $-.215$. A negative coefficient means that younger people are more permissive.]

23. On the way we measure power and how it is related to partners' relative income, see the chapter "Income and power." In looking at Figure 16 it is important to note that the power-balance difference in married couples depends on whether the wife is employed or not. This should not obscure, however, the general pattern: The majority of couples feel that power is shared equally. Among couples who say it is not, the husband tends to be more powerful.

24. It is not easy to measure respect in the context of intimate relationships. When asked directly if they respect their partners, people almost invariably say yes. On the follow-up questionnaire sent to people whom we interviewed, there were two items that we feel indirectly measure respect. We asked heterosexual men if their partners are the sort of persons they themselves would like to be. When the woman is employed full time, 35 percent of their partners say no ($N = 46$). When she is a full-time homemaker, fully 47 percent say no ($N = 17$). We also asked the men to judge how often they and their partners have a stimulating exchange of ideas. Sixty-nine percent of the men living with fully employed partners said at least three or four times a week ($N = 48$), in contrast to only 47 percent of those whose partners are full-time homemakers ($N = 18$). [The two measures correlate $r = .467$.]

25. On the follow-up questionnaires sent to people whom we interviewed, two questions were asked to measure self-respect. People could agree or disagree with the statement "I certainly feel useless at times." Among heterosexual women who are employed full time, 62 percent disagreed with this statement ($N = 53$), as compared to 48 percent of women employed part time ($N = 23$) and 47 percent of full-time homemakers ($N = 17$). They could also agree or disagree with "I take a positive attitude toward myself." Seventy-four percent of women employed full time agreed, as compared to 70 percent of those employed part time, and 53 percent of full-time homemakers. These women may derive some of their self-respect from their experience in the world of work. We often heard women say this in interviews. It may also be true that those with a positive sense of their worth are more inclined to enter the world of work.

26. For a discussion of the nature of part-time work, see Sheila B. Kamerman and Paul W. Kingston, "Employer Responses to the Family Responsibilities of Employees," in S. B. Kamerman and Cheryl D. Hayes, eds., *Families That Work: Children in a Changing World* (Washington, D.C.: National Academy Press, 1982), pp. 144–208.

27. [Relationship question 13.]

28. Among husbands who say they are unemployed ($N = 95$) or "househusbands" ($N = 4$), 69 percent do less than ten hours of housework, while 27 percent do between ten and twenty hours, and 4 percent do more than twenty hours. These percentages stand in sharp contrast to the housework done by wives employed full time (see Figure 17).

29. [Figure 18 represents couples where both husband and wife are employed full time and strongly endorse the equal sharing of housework. Opinion statement 1.]

30. Eighteen percent of marriages where the wife works full time have hired help for indoor housework ($N = 1,374$). The percentage is the same for couples where the wife works part time ($N = 804$), and it is 13 percent for couples where the wife is a full-time homemaker ($N = 895$). We would not interpret these data to reflect a wholesale replacement of wives by paid help. Housework remains very much the wife's work, even if she is fully employed outside of the home. [The paid help item is Relationship question 14.]

31. See Note 11.

32. In marriages where the husband does no housework, 39 percent fight more than once every few months about how the house is kept ($N = 158$). This is in contrast to 45 percent of couples where the husband does five or fewer hours of housework ($N = 1,659$), 54 percent of those where he does between six and ten hours ($N = 1,164$), and 56 percent of those where he does more than ten hours ($N = 636$). [The conflict measure is Relationship question 21a.]

33. Among female cohabitors, 78 percent endorse equal sharing of housework, while 15 percent have neutral feelings, and 7 percent reject the idea ($N = 647$). The comparable figures for male cohabitors are 67 percent, 23 percent, and 10 percent ($N =$

649). It should be noted that even though the majority endorse equal sharing, more women feel this way than men.

34. Only 7 percent of male cohabitors would like their partners to provide financial security ($N$ = 649). This is the same percentage as for husbands. The percentage for female cohabitors is 23 percent ($N$ = 651), less than half the percentage for wives. Figure 13 shows cohabitors' feelings about both partners' working to support the household.

35. In addition to the data in Figure 19, we also find that among couples where both partners are employed full time, 18 percent of wives do more than twenty hours of housework per week, as contrasted with 4 percent of husbands, 8 percent of female cohabitors, and 3 percent of male cohabitors. Sociologist Barbara Risman (in a personal communication) has suggested that part of the difference between male and female time spent in housework has to do with different standards, that is, females like the house cleaner than men. She points out that all standards of cleanliness are culturally relative and socially constructed. Females may be obsessive about housework because traditionally a woman's self-image has been tied up in her house's appearance. Risman believes that if a person's sense of self is attached to how "shiny a refrigerator is," that person is going to tend to such details more than if the house has no relationship to personal competence. Therefore, many men may do what they think is necessary, but it is not as much as their female partners would like or would do themselves. The problem is that by the time a man thinks cleaning is necessary, his female partner cannot stand the mess and does all the cleaning herself.

36. Sixty-eight percent of these women ($N$ = 22) do more than twenty hours of housework per week, as compared to 79 percent of all married homemakers ($N$ = 886). This difference is small when compared to the cohabiting women who are employed full time or to husbands and male cohabitors (see Figure 19).

37. Fifty-eight percent of cohabiting women who work full time do fewer than ten hours of housework, while 34 percent do between ten and twenty, and 8 percent do more than twenty ($N$ = 413). The comparable percentages for women working part time are: 54 percent, 33 percent, and 13 percent ($N$ = 141).

38. Thirty-nine percent of these women do more than ten hours of housework, as compared to 20 percent of the men ($N$ = 218).

39. Forty-eight percent of these women do more than ten hours of housework each week, as compared to 24 percent of the men ($N$ = 115). Indeed, under these circumstances she does more housework than the woman who earns less than her partner (see preceding note).

40. [The partial correlation between the woman's rating of whether her partner does his "fair share" of the housework (Relationship question 16) and how much they fight over the housework (controlling for duration, both ages, and whether each partner has ever been married) is −.158. The partial between the fair-share item and the woman's satisfaction with her relationship is .217.]

41. Among husbands who are employed full time, 84 percent do ten or fewer hours of housework ($N$ = 3,102), as compared to 76 percent of those employed part time ($N$ = 182), and 72 percent of those who are unemployed ($N$ = 95). The comparable figures for male cohabitors are 79 percent ($N$ = 493), 69 percent ($N$ = 83) and 69 percent ($N$ = 59). The data for wives are in Figure 17 and for gay men and lesbians in Figure 20. For female cohabitors, see Note 37.

42. [The measurement of masculinity is discussed in Note 21 of Money: Income and Power. Alpha reliability coefficients for gay men and lesbians are .794 and .741. Femininity is measured by the same kinds of self-descriptions, using the adjectives *compassionate, tender,* and *understanding* (Relationship questions 20c, 20f, and 20p). The alpha reliability coefficients for gay men and lesbians are .673 and .702. Zero-order correlations between these measures and the amount of housework done by gay men and lesbians are all below .050.]

43. See Note 8.

44. Among people who work full time, 37 percent of gay men do more than ten hours of housework per week ($N$ = 1,487), as compared to 31 percent of lesbians ($N$ = 1,069).

## Job satisfaction, ambition, and success

1. Christopher Lasch, *Haven in a Heartless World: The Family Besieged* (New York: Basic Books, 1977).

2. Among wives who are employed part time, 77 percent of those who are satisfied with their work are very satisfied with their marriage ($N = 401$), as compared to 73 percent of those who feel neutral about their work ($N = 308$), and 66 percent of those who dislike their work ($N = 87$). The comparable figures for wives who are employed full time are 75 percent ($N = 696$), 66 percent ($N = 519$), and 66 percent ($N = 152$).

[The partial correlation between satisfaction with work and satisfaction with the relationship is .153 (controlling duration, age, and whether she has been previously married). For the other groups in the study the comparable partials are less than .100. Satisfaction with work is measured by item 3 of the Statistical Information part of the questionnaire.]

3. [Partial correlations were computed between the amount of conflict the couple has over the effect of the wife's job on their relationship, and her satisfaction both with her work and with her marriage (controlling the same variables as in the preceding note). The correlations are −.141 and −.212.]

4. Among husbands under twenty-six years of age, 44 percent are very satisfied with their work ($N = 258$) as compared to 39 percent of male cohabitors of the same age ($N = 116$). For men between the ages of twenty-six and forty, the percentages are 52 percent ($N = 1,832$) versus 46 percent ($N = 397$); and for men over forty they are 64 percent ($N = 1,298$) versus 52 percent ($N = 90$). It may also be true that a man who feels good about his work is more confident of his future and more willing to make a commitment to marry. Such a man may also be more attractive to a woman seeking a husband. We believe, however, that it gives people pleasure to be responsible for the welfare of others, and for husbands this is expressed in satisfaction with their jobs. In the interviews with husbands, we often sensed this.

5. Twenty-seven percent of our gay men ($N = 1,887$) feel they have had problems on the job because they were known to be, or suspected of being, gay. A somewhat larger number of lesbians (32 percent) report the same experience ($N = 1,514$). [See Lifestyle question 16a.]

6. The lesbians in our study are somewhat more closeted than the gay men. Twenty-eight percent of the women under twenty-six want few or no heterosexuals to know they are lesbians ($N = 319$), and this is also true for 36 percent of those between twenty-six and forty ($N = 1,025$), and 44 percent of those over forty ($N = 208$). The comparable figures for gay men are: 16 percent ($N = 245$), 20 percent ($N = 1,244$), and 35 percent ($N = 430$). It is impossible to infer from these data that lesbians are more closeted than gay men in general. The very closeted are likely to have avoided participating in our study. Indeed, the very closeted may even avoid being part of a couple. [See Lifestyle question 18.]

7. [The partial correlation between a wife's assessment of her husband as accomplished in his work and her happiness with her relationship in general is .216. The control variables are duration, both spouses' ages, both incomes, and both educational levels. The measure of the wife's perception of the husband as a success is Relationship question 19f.]

8. It is commonly held among sociologists that wives derive their position in society from their husbands' social standing or occupational status. For example, Robert F. Winch wrote in 1971: "It is generally the case in Western societies that a woman . . . assumes the socioeconomic status . . . of her husband. The recognition that the woman takes her socioeconomic status from her husband is of course the crux of the interest of single girls, and their parents, in the 'prospects' of their young men. Popenoe [another family sociologist] has telescoped much discussion into the remark that a man marries a wife but a woman marries a standard of living." (*The Modern Family,* 3rd ed. [New York: Holt, Rinehart & Winston, 1971], pp. 230–231.) There is never any mention in these discussions of the husband deriving his position in society from his wife's accomplishments.

9. [The partial correlation between the husband's rating of his wife as accomplished at

her job (only for employed wives) and his overall satisfaction with the relationship is .191 (same controls as in Note 7).]

10. Among husbands who endorse the notion that both spouses should share the responsibility for earning a living to support the household, 91 percent have employed wives ($N = 1,118$), as compared to 78 percent of husbands who have neutral or mixed feelings on this issue ($N = 1,255$), and 57 percent of husbands who reject the idea ($N = 1,209$). Another factor in the finding of a correlation between happiness with the relationship and having a partner who is a success at work is that a successful partner is probably a happier person, and this may make him or her easier to live with. A person whose business is failing or who is not meeting his or her own goals at work is probably difficult to live with.

11. [The partial correlation between the female cohabitor's rating of her partner as accomplished at his job and her overall satisfaction with the relationship is .182 (same control variables as in Note 7).]

12. [The partial correlation between the male cohabitor's rating of his partner as a success on her job and his satisfaction with their relationship is .102 (same control variables as in Note 7).]

13. Cohabitors are more competitive with each other than any of the other kinds of couples. Twenty-six percent of the men describe themselves as competitive ($N = 651$), and 23 percent of the women feel the same ($N = 648$). This is in contrast to 16 percent of husbands ($N = 3,627$), 18 percent of wives ($N = 3,627$), 20 percent of gay men ($N = 1,928$), and 20 percent of lesbians ($N = 1,557$). [See Relationship question 20j.]

14. Among couples where the wife works full time, 45 percent of the husbands say they are very ambitious ($N = 1,367$), as compared to 42 percent of those where the wife works part time ($N = 800$), and 39 percent where she is a full-time homemaker ($N = 894$). It is possible that ambitious men are more likely to marry women who wish to work in the labor force or that these men are more likely to encourage their wives to work. However, we find no correlation between a man's ambition and his attitudes toward his wife's working. [The ambition item is Relationship question 20m.]

15. When their wives are employed full time, 19 percent of husbands describe themselves as competitive with her ($N = 1,368$), as compared to 16 percent of the husbands of part-time employed women ($N = 798$), and 13 percent of the husbands of women who are full-time homemakers ($N = 893$). Part of the husbands' competitiveness may be in reaction to competitiveness on the part of their wives. We find that when wives are employed, both they and their husbands tell us the women are more competitive. Twenty-one percent of wives employed full time say they are competitive with their husbands ($N = 1,368$), as compared to 17 percent of those employed part time ($N = 797$), and 15 percent of those who are full-time homemakers ($N = 892$). [Perception of one's partner's competitiveness is measured by Relationship question 19e.]

16. Among husbands who describe their wives as competitive, 65 percent are very satisfied with their relationship ($N = 670$), as compared to 77 percent of those who say she is not competitive ($N = 1,679$). The comparable figures for wives are 60 percent ($N = 599$), versus 80 percent ($N = 2,033$).

[Partial correlations were computed between ratings of one's partner's competitiveness and satisfaction with the relationship, controlling for duration, both partners' ages, education levels, and incomes. The association is stronger for wives ($-.242$) than for husbands ($-.146$). The same partials were computed for commitment to the future of the relationship, and again we find that the wife is more strongly affected by her partner's competitiveness. The partial for wives is $-.161$, while for husbands it is only $-.082$.]

17. [Zero-order correlations between income level and an individual's rating of himself or herself as accomplished are: husbands: $r = -.278$; wives: $r = -.171$; male cohabitors: $r = -.391$; female cohabitors: $r = -.316$; gay men: $r = -.382$; lesbians: $r = -.261$. A negative correlation means that people with higher incomes feel more accomplished.]

18. [The partial correlation between gay men's self-rating as accomplished and their partner's income, controlling for their own income, is .149. A positive correlation means that the higher the partner's income, the less accomplished a gay man feels.]

19. Twenty percent of lesbians feel it is extremely important to have an accomplished partner ($N = 1,558$). The comparable figure for female cohabitors is 23 percent ($N = 648$).

20. Eighteen percent of gay man say they are competitive with their partners ($N = 1,926$), compared with 19 percent of husbands and 21 percent of wives in couples where the wife is employed full time ($N = 1,368$).

## Work versus the relationship

1. *Don Juan.*

2. Erik H. Erikson, *Childhood and Society* (New York: W. W. Norton, 1950).

3. We recognize that when we speak of people as relationship-centered or work-centered we are dealing with some subtle themes. A person may feel that the relative emphasis in his or her life may shift with different events and at different stages of a relationship or a career. There may be other interests outside the relationship and outside of work which are more nearly the main focus of one's life. We mean by these concepts very much what the questionnaire item reflects. We purposely used the term *emotional energy* because we want to focus on the priority that a relationship or work has in an individual's everyday emotions. We are not necessarily interested here in the question of which of the two one would sacrifice for the other. [The item is Relationship question 22a.]

4. The wives' data can be broken down further: 53 percent of wives who are employed full time are relationship-centered ($N = 1,367$), as compared to 58 percent of wives who work part time ($N = 798$), and 67 percent of wives who are full-time homemakers ($N = 877$).

5. [Partial correlations between the femininity measure and the measure of being relationship-centered versus work-centered. (controlling for duration, age, education, and whether previously married) are: husbands: .263; wives: .213; male cohabitors: .242; female cohabitors: .216; gay men: .197; lesbians: .215. Alpha reliability coefficients for the femininity measure are: husbands: .722; wives: .697; male cohabitors: .738; female cohabitors: .640.]

6. See Joseph E. Garai and Amram Scheinfeld, "Sex Differences in Mental and Behavioral Traits," *Genetic Psychology Monographs,* Vol. 77, Second Half (May 1968). Also, Judith M. Bardwick, *Psychology of Women* (New York: Harper College Books, 1971). Also, Patricia W. Lunneborg and Linda M. Rosenwood, "Need Affiliation and Achievement: Declining Sex Differences," *Psychological Reports,* Vol. 31, No. 3 (December 1972), pp. 795–798. Also Phillip Shaver and Jonathan Freedman, "Your Pursuit of Happiness," *Psychology Today,* Vol. 10, No. 3 (August 1976), pp. 26–29ff.

7. By our measure, 48 percent of wives ($N = 3,629$), 51 percent of female cohabitors ($N = 649$), and 48 percent of lesbians ($N = 1,558$) describe themselves as very feminine. While there are fewer men who give this description of themselves, there is still a substantial number, particularly among the gay men: 22 percent of husbands ($N = 3,626$), 26 percent of male cohabitors ($N = 650$), and 36 percent of gay men ($N = 1,928$). There are a large number of men who do not describe themselves as feminine: of husbands, 50 percent; male cohabitors 44 percent; and gay men 35 percent. But there are also some women in the same category: of wives, 25 percent; female cohabitors 22 percent; and lesbians 23 percent.

8. It may be that as a consequence of being highly invested in one's relationship or being less invested in work, a person comes to take on a more feminine sense of himself or herself, or a greater willingness to describe himself or herself in feminine terms. It may also be that the care of a relationship requires that one develop the "feminine" qualities of compassion, tenderness, and understanding.

9. Even though we find that on average, heterosexual women describe themselves as more compassionate, tender, and understanding than their partners, when we ask people how important it is for a partner to have these characteristics, the women put more

stress on them than do the men. Sixty percent of wives ($N$ = 3,641), and 57 percent of female cohabitors ($N$ = 651) say it is extremely important to have a partner who is understanding of others, as compared to only 39 percent of husbands ($N$ = 3,634) and 43 percent of male cohabitors ($N$ = 648). The comparable percentages for the desirability of a partner's being compassionate are: for wives: 60 percent ($N$ = 3,635); female cohabitors: 60 percent ($N$ = 651); husbands: 39 percent ($N$ = 3,632); and male cohabitors: 39 percent ($N$ = 649). For tenderness the figures are: wives: 50 percent ($N$ = 3,640); female cohabitors: 52 percent ($N$ = 651); husbands: 28 percent ($N$ = 3,636); and male cohabitors: 31 percent ($N$ = 651). [See Ideal Relationship questions 2g, 2i and 2l.]

10. See Note 7. We should also note that even when we consider whether the wife is employed or not, husbands are still less relationship-centered than male cohabitors are. Thirty-seven percent of the husbands of full-time homemakers are primarily relationship-centered ($N$ = 885), as compared to 40 percent of the husbands of women who are employed part time ($N$ = 795), and 42 percent of the husbands of women who are employed full time ($N$ = 1,362). Forty-six percent of male cohabitors are relationship-centered.

11. [The partial correlations between masculinity and whether a person is relationship-centered (controlling the same variables as in Note 5) are: male cohabitors: .023; husbands: .013.]

12. See Figure 22.

13. See Note 7.

14. [The partial correlation between masculinity and whether a gay man is work-centered or relationship-centered is .036.]

15. For example, Talcott Parsons and Robert F. Bales, *Family, Socialization, and Interaction Process* (New York: Free Press, 1955); and Gary S. Becker, *A Treatise on the Family* (Cambridge, Mass.: Harvard University Press, 1981).

16. See, for example, Alan C. Kerckhoff and Keith E. Davis, "Value Consensus and Need Complementarity in Mate Selection," *American Sociological Review*, Vol. 27, No. 3 (June 1962), pp. 295–303.

17. The 47 percent of married couples with only one relationship-centered partner breaks down into 34 percent where it is the wife who is relationship-centered and 13 percent where it is the husband. This is a ratio of 72 to 28.

18. Among the 41 percent of cohabitors with only one partner relationship-centered, in 15 percent it is the man, and in the remaining 26 percent it is the woman. The woman-to-man ratio is 63 to 37, which is less skewed than among married couples.

19. See Robert F. Winch, "The Theory of Complementary Needs in Mate Selection: Final Results on the Test of the General Hypothesis," *American Sociological Review*, Vol. 20, No. 5 (October 1955), pp. 552–555.

20. [Partial correlations were computed between people's rating of their partners as either relationship-centered or work-centered, on the one hand, and on the other, first, their satisfaction with their relationships, and second, their commitment to their future (Relationship question 22b). The control variables were duration, both partners' ages, both incomes, both education levels, and whether each partner had previously been married. The correlations for satisfaction are: husbands: .195; wives: .375; male cohabitors: .128; female cohabitors: .250; gay men: .255; lesbians: .181. The correlations for commitment to the future are: husbands: .093; wives: .193; male cohabitors: .164; female cohabitors: .238; gay men: .164; lesbians: .147. Analyses were performed to test for any interaction effects between the two partners' ratings on relationship-centeredness versus work-centeredness. We were interested to know if a couple's consisting of two work-centered partners would cause even more dissatisfaction, or actually less. We found no evidence for an interaction effect in any of the four kinds of couples.]

21. Let us consider how often couples fight about the intrusion of work on their relationship, where they have been together between two and ten years and both partners are employed full time. Fifty percent of these married couples fight about the husband's work at least once every few months ($N$ = 585), and 50 percent of cohabitors fight about the man's work ($N$ = 132). This is in contrast to 39 percent of married couples fighting about the wife's work ($N$ = 580), and 45 percent of cohabitors fighting about the woman's work ($N$ = 131). The comparable figures for gay men and lesbians are 40 percent ($N$ = 592) and 41 percent ($N$ = 381). Similar patterns are found for couples of shorter and longer durations. [The conflict items are Relationship questions

21b and 21d. The intra-couple correlations are: husband's job: $r = .498$; wife's job: $r = .472$; male cohabitor's job: $r = .497$; female cohabitor's job: $r = .465$; gay man's job: $r = .324$; lesbian's job: $r = .474$.]

22. On the basis of these questions we measured how much people are committed to an ideology of separateness. When husbands have such an ideology, couples fight more about the impact of his work on the marriage. Fifty-five percent of husbands who believe in a lot of autonomy for themselves say they fight at least once every few months about their work ($N = 1,297$), as compared to 42 percent of men whose feelings are more moderate on the subject of personal autonomy ($N = 1,709$), and 28 percent of men who do not feel a need for personal autonomy ($N = 266$).

[The personal autonomy items and scale properties are discussed in Note 36. The partial correlation between an ideology of autonomy and the amount of fighting about the husband's work is .166. The control variables were duration, both partners' ages, both incomes, both education levels, and whether each has been previously married. When the actual amount of time the couple spends together is added as a control variable, the partial correlation is not substantially reduced.]

23. [The partial correlation between the wife's assessment of how much they fight over the impact of her husband's job and her happiness with her relationship is $-.234$. The partial between fighting and her commitment to the future of her marriage is $-.167$. The control variables were duration, age, education, and whether or not she was previously married.]

24. [The partial correlation between the husband's estimate of how much they fight about the effect of his wife's job on their relationship and his satisfaction with his marriage (comparable controls as in preceding note) is $-.222$. The partial with the husband's commitment to the future of the relationship is $-.144$.]

25. [The partial correlations between fighting over the impact of one's partner's job and one's satisfaction with one's relationship are: male cohabitors: $-.226$, female cohabitors: $-.266$, and gay men: $-.178$.]

26. [The partial correlation for lesbians is $-.193$.]

27. Sixty-six percent of wives under twenty-six feel they would like to spend more time with their husbands ($N = 499$), as compared to 59 percent of wives between twenty-six and forty ($N = 1,936$), and only 41 percent of those over forty ($N = 1,203$). For female cohabitors, the percentages are 45 percent ($N = 209$), 49 percent ($N = 384$), and 30 percent ($N = 57$).

[We should be cautious about inferring change from cross-sectional data. It may be that younger women were part of a generation with greater need for companionship. Or it may be that women with strong needs leave their relationships, and only the less needful remain in a relationship when they are older. Our interview data suggest, however, that it is reasonable to make an argument based on personal change over the years. The item about spending time with one's partner is Lifestyle question 3.]

28. Fifty-eight percent of younger husbands told us that there are times when they want to do things without their partners ($N = 280$), as compared to 57 percent of husbands between twenty-six and forty ($N = 1,880$) and 40 percent of husbands over forty ($N = 1,484$). The comparable percentages for male cohabitors are 71 percent ($N = 137$), 67 percent ($N = 416$), and 48 percent ($N = 98$).

[The question asked is Opinion statement 14. We find similar patterns when we ask men if their partners should have time away from them (Opinion statement 15). It is important to recognize that these data are cross-sectional, and care must be taken in inferring longitudinal change. It may be that younger men have grown up in a period that emphasizes personal autonomy. From the interviews, however, with both men and women, we get the impression that both sexes have noticed changes in the men as they have aged. It is interesting that younger and older men are equally pleased with the amount of time they and their partners actually spend together.]

29. [We developed a measure of how much time and how many activities couples share. The items on this companionship scale include dinners together (Lifestyle question 2), evenings at home together (question 1), movies, theater, and concerts together (question 5a), and socializing with friends together (question 27). The last two items are reverse-scored before the items are summed. Alpha reliability coefficients are: husbands: .513; wives: .505; male cohabitors: .620; female cohabitors: .606; gay men: .639; lesbians: .642. For husbands, the zero-order correlation between age and companion-

ship is $r = .155$, and for male cohabitors it is $r = .162$. For wives it is $r = .077$, and for female cohabitors, $r = .077$. This suggests that a larger proportion of older men's time is spent with their partners, while women have a constant proportion of time for themselves.]

30. See Note 27.

31. Not only do the lesbians put the greatest stress on self-sufficiency (see Note 9 of Money: Income and Power) but they also prize success at work as much as or more than any of the kinds of couples. Sixty-three percent feel it would be extremely important that they themselves be accomplished ($N = 1,566$), as compared to 57 percent of husbands ($N = 3,643$), 54 percent of wives ($N = 3,634$), 60 percent of male and female cohabitors ($N = 650$ each), and 59 percent of gay men ($N = 1,926$). Lesbian periodicals sometimes stress the importance of shedding the image of the dependent female, and this is sometimes a topic of conversation in lesbian political and social groups, which are more commonly attended by younger women. When a woman immerses herself in the gay world, she is more likely to embrace the need for private time away from her partner as an indication that she has created a life of her own, outside her relationship. We find that the more involved a woman is in the gay world, the more she endorses the importance of separateness and autonomy. [The correlation between involvement in the gay world and ideological separateness is $r = .266$). The measure placing importance on success is Ideal Relationship question 4p.]

32. Fifty-one percent of lesbians under twenty-six would like to spend more time with their partners ($N = 317$). This is also true of 52 percent of those between twenty-six and forty ($N = 1,033$), and 49 percent of those over forty ($N = 209$). Only 38 percent of lesbians feel that the amount of time they have together corresponds to what they would like ($N = 1,559$), as compared to fully 50 percent of the gay men ($N = 1,931$).

33. Fifty-nine percent of gay men under twenty-six want time away from their partners ($N = 246$), as compared to 51 percent of men between twenty-six and forty ($N = 1,242$), and 31 percent of men over forty ($N = 435$). The findings are similar when we ask them if they want their partners to have separate time too.

[We infer that they tend to be well matched in their need for autonomy, because we find no correlation between age and whether they feel they have too much or too little time together ($r = .065$). The intra-couple correlation of age is $r = .642$. See the warning on interpretation in Note 28.]

34. [The data in Figure 25 are based on Lifestyle questions 5d and 5e.]

35. [Partial correlations were computed between the amount of time spent in shared activities and the partners' satisfaction with the relationship and their commitment to its future. The control variables were duration, the two ages, two incomes, two education levels, and whether or not each partner had been married previously. The partials for satisfaction are: husbands: $-.221$; wives: $-.256$; male cohabitors: $-.147$; female cohabitors: $-.151$; gay men: $-.217$; lesbians: $-.247$. For commitment, the partials are: husbands: $-.216$; wives: $-.235$; male cohabitors: $-.253$; female cohabitors: $-.225$; gay men: $-.246$; lesbians: $-.309$.]

36. [The three items are Ideal Relationship question 1f and Opinion statements 14 and 15. Alpha reliability coefficients are: husbands: .555; wives: .613; male cohabitors: .583; female cohabitors: .665; gay men: .577; lesbians: .678.]

37. Among heterosexual couples, women are more likely to spend time alone with friends than are men. Thirty percent of wives are alone at least half the time they see friends ($N = 3,604$), as compared to only 15 percent of husbands ($N = 3,572$). The figures for cohabitors are: for women: 45 percent ($N = 645$); men: 26 percent ($N = 649$). The large difference between male and female cohabitors (almost all of whom are employed) suggests that the overall gender differences among heterosexual couples are not due to many wives being out of the labor force. A similar pattern is found when we ask about whether they attend clubs and political groups alone or together.

38. Twenty-three percent of male cohabitors ($N = 647$) and 28 percent of females ($N = 643$) go to movies and concerts without their partners half the time or more. The comparable figures for husbands and wives are 17 percent ($N = 3,519$) and 21 percent ($N = 3,483$); and for gay men and lesbians, 26 percent ($N = 1,921$) and 18 percent ($N = 1,549$). Twenty-four percent of cohabitors dine together four or fewer nights per week ($N = 650$), as compared to 13 percent of married couples ($N = 3,615$), 21 percent of gay male couples ($N = 961$), and 21 percent of lesbian couples ($N = 779$).

39. See Note 27 for a comparison between wives and female cohabitors. Among heterosexual men, 52 percent of husbands would like to spend more time with their partners ($N$ = 3,634), as compared to 48 percent of male cohabitors ($N$ = 648).

40. Any causal argument here is complex. The social forces that contribute to women being more relationship-centered are likely to be involved in shaping the employment opportunities of women and women's attitudes toward the world of work.

# Sex

*Physical contact*

1. [The measure is the mean of the partners' scores on Relationship question 29. Intracouple correlations are: married couples: $r$ = .833; cohabitors: $r$ = .782; gay men: $r$ = .855; lesbians: $r$ = .852.]

2. It is also true that cohabitors, especially early in their relationships, attach greater importance to sex than other kinds of couples do. When we asked couples who had been together less than two years how important they felt sexual compatibility was in a relationship, 52 percent of male cohabitors ($N$ = 352) and 60 percent of females ($N$ = 354) said it was extremely important. This is in contrast to 43 percent of husbands ($N$ = 343), 48 percent of wives ($N$ = 383), 39 percent of gay men ($N$ = 630), and 42 percent of lesbians ($N$ = 726). [These percentages are based on Ideal Relationship question 1k.]

3. Fully 82 percent of our gay men have been non-monogamous during their relationships.

4. Among gay men together less than two years, 67 percent feel sexual compatibility is very important in a relationship ($N$ = 630), as compared to 64 percent of those together between two and ten years ($N$ = 952) and 59 percent of those together ten years or more ($N$ = 348).

[Care should be exercised in interpreting these data because they are cross-sectional and not longitudinal. It is very possible that the men who do not place a great emphasis on sexual compatibility have a greater chance of surviving as couples and are therefore more numerous in the longer-duration group. From the interviews we get the impression, however, that sexual compatibility becomes less critical as couples stay together longer. A regression analysis where the importance of sexual compatibility was the dependent variable was performed. The independent variables were: duration, age, income, partner's income, education, involvement in the gay world, covertness, church or synagogue attendance, attitudes toward sex without love, employed or not, partner employed or not, an ideological commitment to separateness or companionship, and both partners' self-perception of masculinity and femininity. The standardized regression coefficient for duration is .153.]

5. Only 28 percent of our lesbians have been non-monogamous since the beginning of their relationships.

6. The fact that lesbians in couples of long duration have significantly less frequent sex than other couples is clear from Figure 27. We can consider age separately. If we look at people between forty-one and fifty-five who have been with their partners between two and ten years, lesbians still have a much lower sexual frequency. The percentages of people reporting a sexual frequency of at least once a week are: lesbians: 31 percent ($N$ = 74); wives: 75 percent ($N$ = 105); female cohabitors: 72 percent ($N$ = 29); husbands: 72 percent ($N$ = 166); male cohabitors: 74 percent ($N$ = 43); gay men: 65 percent ($N$ = 131).

7. Exactly this point has been argued by anthropologist Donald Symons in his book *The Evolution of Human Sexuality* (New York: Oxford University Press, 1979), pp. 286–305. It is interesting to note that in our study, lesbians are more likely than any of the other kinds of couples to wish they had a higher sexual frequency. On the follow-up questionnaire sent to people we had interviewed, we asked, "Would you prefer to have sexual relations more or less frequently with [your partner]?" Eighty-three percent of the les-

bians answered more ($N = 121$) as compared to only 56 percent of the gay men ($N = 147$), 80 percent of heterosexual men ($N = 96$) and 70 percent of heterosexual women ($N = 94$).

8. Because of the large number of couples in the study, we are able to use statistical techniques to tell us which factor is more important in the decline of sexual frequency: the length of time the couple has been together, or the age of the participants. For married couples the impact of age and duration are approximately equal, although there is a slight suggestion in the data that the husband's age is more important than the wife's. For cohabiting couples it is simply duration that matters; neither partner's age is at all important. For gay men and lesbians the length of time together is more important than age, but age has a separate effect worthy of note.

[The multiple regression analyses used the mean of the partner's frequency ratings as the dependent variable and the following independent variables: duration, couple mean age, couple age difference, couple mean education level, couple total income, couple education difference (absolute value for same-sex couples), whether there are children living at home, couple income difference (absolute difference for same-sex couples), couple mean church or synagogue attendance, couple mean physical attractiveness, difference in partners' attractiveness (absolute difference for same-sex couples), couple mean attitude about sex without love, same-sex couples' mean homosexual covertness, their mean involvement in gay life, whether both partners work full time, couple's mean attitude toward companionship versus separateness, couple's mean masculinity score, femininity score, difference in partners' masculinity and in partners' femininity (absolute differences for same-sex couples). For married couples, when the analysis is done with the couple's mean age as an independent variable, the age effect is .168 and the duration effect .142. When only the husband's age is used, the age effect is .172 and the duration effect .142. When the wife's age is used, its effect is .138 and the duration effect is .157. Among cohabitors the duration effects are between .154 and .157, while the age effects are between .015 and .027. For gay men the duration effect is .371 and the age effect .143. For lesbians the effects are .285 and .170.]

9. We cannot determine whether it is the frequency of sex that increases satisfaction with the couple's sex life, or whether couples who have an enjoyable sex life will strive to increase its frequency. We assume that, in fact, both factors affect each other. We do think, however, on the basis of the interviews, that sexual frequency, whatever all of its causes are, does have an impact on couples' happiness. Many people with whom we spoke had only one complaint about their sex life and that was its infrequency. They said that they could not fault the quality of the experience. In some couples it may be that one partner's unhappiness with the quality leads to a lower frequency, which then in turn reduces the other partner's satisfaction.

[Partial correlations were computed between sexual frequency and people's rating of the quality of their sex life (Relationship question 1m). The control variables were duration, age, partner's age, education level, partner's education level, homosexual covertness, involvement in the gay world, and whether one had been previously married. The partial correlations are: husbands: .462; wives: .464; male cohabitors: .550; female cohabitors: .501; gay men: .502; lesbians: .477.]

10. Only 30 percent of married couples who have sex at least once or twice a week report fighting about sex once every few months or more ($N = 2,372$), as compared to 41 percent of married couples who have less frequent sex ($N = 1,062$). The comparable figures for cohabitors are 41 percent ($N = 524$) versus 56 percent ($N = 95$) and for lesbians, 39 percent ($N = 399$) versus 53 percent ($N = 336$).

[Partial correlations between sexual frequency and the amount of conflict over sex (using the same controls as in Note 9) are: for married couples: $-.205$; for cohabitors: $-.224$; for gay men: $-.071$; and for lesbians: $-.162$. The couple's mean rating on conflict over sex was used. Intra-couple correlations on this measure are: married couples: $r = .558$; cohabitors: $r = .564$; gay male couples: $r = .519$; lesbian couples: $r = .601$.]

11. The way the frequency of sex affects people's general happiness with their relationship, and the impact their happiness has on how often they have sex, constitute a complex issue. We feel that satisfaction with the relationship is bound to influence how often the partners want to have sex. On the other hand, we are quite sure that for many people, having a lot of sex has an independent effect on their feelings about how well they are doing as a couple. Not only does it increase feelings of intimacy and provide

physical pleasure, but people often use it as a measure of the relationship's viability. [Partial correlations between sexual frequency and happiness with the overall relationship (same controls as in Note 9) are: husbands: .243; wives: .250.]

12. [Partial correlations between sexual frequency and happiness with the relationship are: gay men: .188; male cohabitors: .253; lesbians: .124; female cohabitors: .139.]

13. [Regression analyses were performed using the person's satisfaction with the quality of the couple's sex life as the dependent variable and the following independent variables: duration, age, income, partner's income, sex-role traditionalism, education, whether married before, gay involvement, gay covertness, whether trial married or ideological cohabitors, church or synagogue attendance, attitudes toward sex without love, whether the partners work full time, presence or absence of children, whether ideologically companionate or separate, each partner's masculinity, each partner's femininity, one's own physical attractiveness and one's rating of one's partner's attractiveness, and the amount of nonsexual conflict. The unstandardized regression coefficients for the last variable are: husbands: $-.174$; wives: $-.198$; male cohabitors: $-.252$; female cohabitors: $-.169$; gay men: $-.116$; lesbians: $-.107$. The conflict measure is made up of four items which we feel have little to do with sex, affection, intimacy, or communication. These are Relationship questions 21a, 21j, 21k, and 21m. Alpha reliability coefficients are: husbands: .778; wives: .738; male cohabitors: .756; female cohabitors: .729; gay men: .738; lesbians: .719.]

14. [In the regression analysis for married couples detailed in Note 8, the standardized regression coefficient for the presence or absence of children living at home (a positive coefficient meaning less sex if there are children) is $-.034$.]

15. We asked people if they felt it was difficult for a relationship such as theirs to last a long time. Gay men and lesbians are much more likely than married couples to answer in the affirmative. It is very interesting that they offer the same response in relationships of short duration as well as long duration. Among lesbians together less than two years, 30 percent feel it is hard for relationships to last ($N = 721$). For lesbians together between two and ten years the percentage is 28 percent ($N = 708$), and for those together over ten years, it is 26 percent ($N = 126$). For gay men, the comparable percentages are: 31 percent ($N = 629$), 27 percent ($N = 947$), and 29 percent ($N = 345$). For husbands, the figures are 13 percent ($N = 345$), 16 percent ($N = 1,520$), and 14 percent ($N = 1,777$), and for wives, 15 percent ($N = 382$), 13 percent ($N = 1,507$), and 12 percent ($N = 1,748$). [The item is Opinion statement 2.]

## Initiating and refusing

1. [Sexual initiation is measured by Relationship question 4n, and refusal by question 4o.]

2. Among male cohabitors below the age of twenty-six, 22 percent would be bothered by their partner initiating sex ($N = 135$), as compared to 28 percent of men between the ages of twenty-six and forty ($N = 416$) and 42 percent of men above that age ($N = 97$). [The questionnaire item is Relationship question 23b. The zero-order correlation between the cohabiting woman's age and whether it is she or her partner who initiates sex (a positive correlation meaning younger women initiate more) is $r = -.011$.]

3. Gay men are less bothered by the prospect of their partners' waiting for them to initiate than anyone else in the study, even less than the husbands. Thirty-three percent of the gay men would not be bothered if their partners left the initiation to them ($N = 1,911$) as compared to 36 percent of the husbands ($N = 3,629$), 40 percent of male cohabitors ($N = 649$), 41 percent of lesbians ($N = 1,556$), 47 percent of female cohabitors ($N = 651$), and 49 percent of wives ($N = 3,618$). [The item used is Relationship question 23d.]

4. [The partial correlations between the couple's score on who initiates sex (the difference between the two partners' scores) and their score on who raises in conversation the subject of trouble in the relationship (Relationship question 4d) among lesbians is .241. The partial correlation with their score on who gives a spontaneous hug or kiss

(Relationship question 4e) is .306. The control variables were the same as those listed in Note 9 of the preceding chapter. The intra-couple correlation for sexual initiation is −.511. For the first expressiveness measure it is −.501, and for the second, −.382.]

5. In 53 percent of married couples the wife is the partner more likely to begin to talk about what is troubling the relationship when there is tension, while in only 18 percent is it the husband, and in the remaining 29 percent both partners do it approximately equally ($N$ = 3,605). The comparable figures for cohabitors are: female: 48 percent; male: 24 percent; and equal: 28 percent ($N$ = 652). In 33 percent of married couples the wife is more likely to give a spontaneous hug or kiss when something good has happened, as compared to 19 percent in which the husband does so, and 48 percent where it is equal ($N$ = 3,592). The parallel percentages for cohabitors are: female: 34 percent; male: 15 percent; and both equal: 51 percent ($N$ = 649).

[Intra-couple correlations for the first expressiveness measure are: married couples: $r$ = −.459; cohabitors: $r$ = −.536. For the second measure: married couples: $r$ = −.470; cohabitors: $r$ = −.492.]

6. [The partial correlation between the couple's score on who initiates sex and their score on who starts to talk about trouble when there is tension between them is .229. The partial correlation between initiation and spontaneous hugs and kisses is .291. The intra-couple correlation for initiation is −.580. For the first expressiveness measure it is −.475, and for the second, −.505.]

7. [Partial correlations between which partner is more expressive and which intitiates sex more were computed. When we use the item of raising the question of trouble, the correlation for married couples is .198 and for cohabitors .219. When we use the spontaneous hug item, the correlations are .303 and .249. It is these latter correlations that are reflected in the data in Figure 30. The control variables were: duration, age of both partners, education level of both partners, whether each spouse had been previously married, and whether each of the cohabitors had ever been married. Intra-couple correlations for initiation are: married couples: $r$ = −.538; cohabitors: $r$ = −.577.]

8. [The preceding note describes the underlying analysis, since the measures used reflect the *relative* expressiveness and the *relative* likelihood of initiating within the couple. Separate analyses using the male partner's ratings alone or the female partner's ratings alone give very similar results.]

9. [Partial correlations (using the same controls as in Notes 4 and 7) between which partner is more likely to give a spontaneous hug and which is more likely to refuse sex are: married couples: −.288; cohabitors: −.258; gay men: −.302; lesbians: −.310. Intra-couple correlations for refusal are: married couples: $r$ = −.576; cohabitors: $r$ = −.620; gay male couples: $r$ = −.649; lesbian couples: $r$ = −.650.]

10. In 48 percent of cohabiting couples where the woman is the more powerful, she is also the more likely to refuse sex ($N$ = 44), as compared to 34 percent of couples where power is approximately equal ($N$ = 453), and only 25 percent of those where the man is more powerful ($N$ = 156). [The partial correlation between the couple's power balance and their relative refusal is .200. The controls were the same as in Note 7.]

11. When power is unequal in lesbian couples, the more powerful partner is the one more likely to refuse in 46 percent of the couples, while the less powerful partner refuses in only 19 percent ($N$ = 162). [The partial correlation between the couple's power balance and their relative refusal is .232. The controls are the same as in Note 4.]

12. When commitment is unequal in gay male couples (one partner more in love than the other), the less committed partner is the one more likely to refuse sex in 49 percent of the couples, while it is the more committed who refuses in only 22 percent ($N$ = 237). [The partial correlation between the couple's relative commitment and their relative refusal is −.225. The controls are the same as in Note 4. The relative commitment item is Relationship question 7. The intra-couple correlation for this item is $r$ = −.375. Because of the wording of the item, a negative correlation reflects consensus.]

13. In married couples where the husband is more in love than the wife, she refuses more in fully 58 percent of the cases ($N$ = 312), as compared to only 40 percent of the cases where they are approximately equally in love ($N$ = 2,882) and to 35 percent of the cases where she is more in love ($N$ = 462). [The intra-couple correlation on the relative commitment item is $r$ = −.259.]

14. The causal relationship between equality on the one hand, and the quality of a

couple's sex life and their happiness with their relationship on the other, is probably complex. It may be that people are happier when initiation of refusal are equal because neither partner assumes the role of the supplicant and neither assumes the role of the rejector, and thus neither person feels undesired and neither feels guilty of having less desire than his or her partner. Or it may be that this reflects a genuinely balanced sexual desire and compatibility between the two partners. Or it may be that partners who have good communication and are sensitive to each other's moods do not set up situations that force one of them into refusing too much or one into always asking. Our data do not tell us how much weight to give to these various explanations. It is also possible that the equality of sexual initiation and acceptance is so confirming to both partners' sense of being desired that it gives them a greater attachment to their relationship.

[Partial correlations (using the same control variables as in Notes 4 and 7) were performed between the equality of sexual initiation and happiness with the quality of their sex lives. The correlations are: for husbands: .288; wives: .275; male cohabitors: .306; female cohabitors: .297; gay men: .249; lesbians: .261. Similar partial correlations for equality of refusal are: husbands: .364; wives: .348; male cohabitors: .309; female cohabitors: .287; gay men: .312; lesbians: .370. Similar partial correlations between equality of refusal and happiness with the overall relationship were performed. The results are: husbands: .213; wives: .206; male cohabitors: .136; female cohabitors: .168; gay men: .179; lesbians: .203. The weak relationship for the male cohabitors should be noted.]

15. [Partial correlations (with the same controls as in Notes 4 and 7) between equality of refusal and sexual frequency are: married couples: .205; cohabitors: .205; gay men: .215; lesbians: .235.]

16. When husbands initiate more than wives, 72 percent of the men are very satisfied with their relationship ($N$ = 1,858), as compared to only 66 percent when the wife initiates more ($N$ = 483). The comparable percentages for the wife's satisfaction are 72 percent ($N$ = 1,861) versus 68 percent ($N$ = 485). For the male cohabitors there is no difference, but for the females, 67 percent are very happy with their relationship when the man initiates more ($N$ = 251) as compared to 57 percent of those in couples where the woman intiates more ($N$ = 112). When wives refuse more than husbands, 70 percent of the women are very satisfied with their relationship ($N$ = 1,507) as compared with only 56 percent where the man refuses more ($N$ = 321). The comparable figures for the man's satisfaction with the relationship are 67 percent ($N$ = 1,500) versus 59 percent ($N$ = 321). The comparable numbers for female cohabitors are 68 percent ($N$ = 216) versus 55 percent ($N$ = 97), and for males, 65 percent ($N$ = 214) versus 60 percent ($N$ = 97).

17. Questions about sex acts were asked only of people who were interviewed in person. In the individual part of the interview, the person was shown a list of sex acts and asked to answer, for each item on the list, *how often it was part of the couple's lovemaking.* They were to choose one of these answers: *always, usually, sometimes, rarely,* or *never.* The acts listed for heterosexuals were: kissing or necking; one partner touching the other's genitals to orgasm; cunnilingus; fellatio; intercourse; intercourse with either partner on top; one partner stimulating the other's genitals with an object. The acts for gay men were: kissing or necking; one partner touching the other's genitals to orgasm; performing or receiving oral sex; performing or receiving anal sex; one partner rubbing his body against the other's to achieve orgasm; one partner stimulating the other's genitals with an object. The acts for lesbians were: kissing or necking; one partner touching the other's genitals; one touching the other's genitals to orgasm; performing and receiving oral sex; one partner rubbing her body against the other's to achieve orgasm; one partner stimulating the other's genitals with an object. All items were worded to be clear and unambiguous to an unsophisticated respondent.

[The total number of heterosexual couples with completed interview data is 129, of whom 52 are cohabitors and 77 are married couples. Because of the sample size, these two subgroups are combined for statistical analyses. The total number of gay male couples with completed interview data is 98 and the number of lesbian couples is 93. Couples who no longer had a sexual relationship were not asked the sex act questions. For statistical analyses, the verbal responses were coded as followed: *always* = 1; *usually* = 2; *sometimes* = 3; *rarely* = 4; *never* = 5.]

18. Among heterosexual couples who report a lot of conflict over matters not related to sex, communication, or affection, 48 percent report not kissing every time they have sex

($N$ = 29), while the percentage for those reporting less conflict is 29 percent ($N$ = 76). The comparable figures for gay men are 53 percent ($N$ = 15) versus 39 percent ($N$ = 56).

[The couple's score for the amount of conflict they experience in areas outside the realm of sex, affection, and communication was correlated with the mean of the two partners' rating on kissing or necking. The correlation for heterosexuals was $r$ = $-$.261 and for gay men it was $r$ = $-$.202. This indicates that couples who have a high level of conflict are less likely to kiss every time they have sex. Regression analyses where kissing was the dependent variable, and conflict one of a large number of possible causal variables, showed that the pattern holds even with other variables controlled. What should be noted is that there is no relationship between conflict and kissing for lesbians ($r$ = .044). We feel this reflects the fact that kissing is such an essential part of sex for lesbians that they have sex only under circumstances where they would be willing to kiss. It may also be that only in couples that include a man does the couple have sex even when circumstances are not conducive to kissing. Intra-couple correlations for the kissing measure are: heterosexuals: $r$ = .280; gay men: $r$ = .627; lesbians: $r$ = .133.]

19. Among heterosexual couples, 94 percent report that intercourse is usually or always part of their sexual relations ($N$ = 113).

20. We have already shown that heterosexual men are more commonly the sexual initiators than their partners. We also find that they want sex more often than their partners. Sixty-two percent of the men want sex a good deal more than they currently have it ($N$ = 96), as compared to only 48 percent of the women ($N$ = 94). [These percentages are based on data from the version of the follow-up questionnaire sent to the couples who had been interviewed. They were asked: "Would you prefer to have sexual relations more or less frequently with your partner?" This variable was tabulated only for couples who were still together at the time of the follow-up.]

21. Heterosexual men in couples who have intercourse every time they have sex are no more satisfied with their sex life than those who report less frequent intercourse. The same holds true when we look at how content they are with their relationships overall, and when we ask them if they expect their relationships to last. When we look at the heterosexual women, however, we see a different picture. If both partners say they have intercourse every time they have sex, they are more satisfied with their sex life (80 percent saying they are satisfied [$N$ = 40]) than if they say they have intercourse less regularly (73 percent [$N$ = 70]). Moreover, the women in couples where both say they always have intercourse are more likely to say they are very happy with their relationship ( 93 percent [$N$ = 40]) than those who have intercourse less regularly (69 percent [$N$ = 70]). Finally, they are more apt to feel that the relationship will last beyond five years (72 percent [$N$ = 39], versus 63 percent [$N$ = 67]).

[Partial correlations were computed between the frequency of intercourse and happiness with the quality of sex life, each person's overall happiness with the relationship, and his or her commitment to the future of the relationship. The control variables were: duration, education, age, church or synagogue attendance, amount of nonsexual conflict, partner's age, partner's education, and marital status. For heterosexual men, the three partial correlations are: .041, .073, and .095. For the women they are: .313, .324, and .163. Intra-couple correlation for the frequency of intercourse is $r$ = .386.]

22. For a discussion of the physiology of women's sexual response, see William H. Masters and Virginia E. Johnson, *Human Sexual Response* (Boston: Little, Brown, 1966).

23. Among heterosexual men who feel that sex without love is acceptable, 53 percent usually engage in cunnilingus when they have sex ($N$ = 72) as compared to 27 percent of those who do not approve of sex without love ($N$ = 37). The percentages for heterosexual women are 58 percent ($N$ = 64) and 24 percent ($N$ = 46). The percentages for men when we consider fellatio are 44 percent ($N$ = 72) versus 27 percent ($N$ = 37) and for women, 44 percent ($N$ = 64) versus 30 percent ($N$ = 46). When we consider couples who sometimes have intercourse with the woman on top, the figures for the men are 20 percent ($N$ = 71) versus 16 percent ($N$ = 46), and for women 25 percent ($N$ = 63) versus 13 percent ($N$ = 46).

[The measure of attitudes toward sex without love is Opinion statement 19. A regression analysis where the frequency of cunnilingus was the dependent measure yielded a standardized regression coefficient of $-$.559 for the measure of attitudes toward sex without love (couple mean). A similar regression analysis with the frequency of fellatio as the dependent variable yielded a coefficient of $-.377$, and an analysis of frequency of intercourse with the woman on top a coefficient of $-.190$. Similar results were found when the man's attitudes toward sex without love and the woman's attitudes were used in separate regression analyses. The other independent variables include: duration, couple mean age, couple mean education, couple mean income, the presence or absence of children, the couple's previous marital status, the couple's mean church or synagogue attendance. Intra-couple correlations are: cunnilingus: $r = .655$; fellatio: $r = .707$; intercourse with the woman on top: $r = .446$. Intra-couple correlations for the sex without love measure in the entire group of married couples is $r = .413$, and in the entire group of cohabitors, $r = .323$.]

24. Among couples where it is usual for the man to perform oral sex, only 40 percent agree they have intercourse every time they have sex ($N = 37$). This is in contrast to 54 percent of the couples in which the man performs oral sex only sometimes ($N = 46$), and 63 percent of those where he performs oral sex rarely or never ($N = 28$). When we look at the comparable figures for the woman performing oral sex, they are 41 percent ($N = 32$), 54 percent ($N = 47$), and 59 percent ($N = 32$). [The correlations between the frequency of intercourse and the frequency of fellatio is $r = -.184$, and the frequency of cunnilingus $r = -.194$.]

25. Fifty-seven percent of the couples where the man is the more powerful partner have sex with the woman on top with some regularity ($N = 21$), as compared to 76 percent of the couples where power is shared equally or the woman is more powerful ($N = 88$). [The partial correlation (same controls as in Note 21) between the equality of power and the frequency of intercourse with the woman on top is $.164$.]

26. [The partial correlation (same controls as in Note 21) between the frequency of the man touching the woman to orgasm and the balance between the partners regarding who "runs the show in the relationship" (Relationship question 4f) is $-.157$. This means that the more the man runs the show, the *less* he touches his partner to orgasm. Intra-couple correlation for the frequency of the man touching the woman to orgasm is $r = .327$ and the intra-couple correlations for all married couples for "running the show" is $r = -.355$ and for all cohabitors, $r = -.404$.]

27. Among couples together less than two years, in 71 percent the man touches the woman to orgasm with some regularity ($N = 42$) as compared to 87 percent of couples together between two and ten years ($N = 47$), and 90 percent of couples together longer than ten years ($N = 21$).

[The correlation between duration and the frequency of the man touching the woman to orgasm is $r = -.193$, indicating a higher frequency in couples of longer duration. It is interesting that the correlation is so large in spite of the fact that the correlation with the woman's age is $r = +.104$. Multiple regression analyses (using the same independent variables as in Note 23) show a large standardized coefficient for duration when age is not in the equation, and a very large coefficient when age *is* in the equation. Care should be taken in interpreting these findings because the data are cross-sectional and not longitudinal. It may be that couples who married longer ago especially favor the man touching the woman to orgasm. This interpretation, though, has little plausibility. It may also be that couples in which the man touches the woman to orgasm are more likely to survive. This may be true, but we doubt that it accounts entirely for the findings. We favor the argument that a socialization effect occurs with time.]

28. [Multiple regression analyses were performed where the frequency of various sexual acts were the dependent variables, and included among the independent variables was a measure of the woman's attractiveness. The other independent variables include: the male partner's attractiveness, duration, the partners' ages, incomes, educations, church or synagogue attendance, previous marital status, work status, attitudes toward sex without love, masculinity, femininity. The standardized regression coefficient for the woman's attractiveness for the frequency of fellatio is $.205$; for the frequency of cunnilingus, $.199$; and for the frequency of intercourse with the woman on top, $.193$. The items that went into the woman's attractiveness scale are Relationship questions 20h and 20q from her questionnaire, and questions 19k and 19n from her partner's. The alpha reliability coefficient for the four items for all of the married couples is $.744$ and for all of the cohabitors it is $.725$.]

29. Ninety percent of heterosexual men for whom receiving oral sex is usual are satisfied with their sex life ($N = 42$), as compared to only 66 percent of those who receive oral sex

less often ($N$ = 68). The former are also more likely to be very satisfied with their overall relationship (83 percent [$N$ = 42], versus 75 percent [$N$ = 68]). [Partial correlations (with the same control variables as in Note 21) between frequency of fellatio and quality of sex life yield a coefficient of .402 and for overall satisfaction with the relationship, .230.]

30. Among heterosexual men for whom performing oral sex is a usual part of sex, 90 percent are satisfied with their sex life ($N$ = 48), as compared to only 65 percent of those who perform oral sex less often ($N$ = 62). The former are also more likely to be very satisfied in general with their relationship (79 percent [$N$ = 48], versus 77 percent [$N$ = 62]). [The partial correlation between the frequency of cunnilingus and the quality of sex life is .370 and happiness with the entire relationship, .196.]

31. Heterosexual couples who engage in fellatio frequently are more likely to report being very sexually compatible (81 percent of men [$N$ = 31] and 63 percent of women [$N$ = 32]) than couples who engage in fellatio less often (52 percent of men [$N$ = 54] and 40 percent of women [$N$ = 50]). Those who engage frequently in cunnilingus are also more compatible (79 percent of men [$N$ = 38] and 58 percent of women [$N$ = 38]) than couples who engage in cunnilingus less often (49 percent of men [$N$ = 47] and 41 percent of women [$N$ = 44]). But compatibility has different meanings for men and women. If the man feels they are sexually incompatible, they are more likely to fight about sex (40 percent of these couples fight about it at least once every few months [$N$ = 40], as compared to only 25 percent of those who feel they are compatible [$N$ = 55]). However, if the woman feels they are incompatible, this does not have any impact on their fighting (29 percent whether she says they are compatible or not).

[Sexual compatibility is measured on the follow-up questionnaire sent to couples who were interviewed. The question: "How compatible are you and your partner with respect to the ways you would prefer to make love?" The response format is a nine-point scale ranging from 1 = *Extremely compatible*, to 9 = *Not at all compatible*. Partial correlations (controlling for the same variables as in Note 21) between the wife's compatibility rating and the frequency of fellatio is .272 and cunnilingus .231. For husbands they are .379 and .363. The partial correlation between the man's rating of compatibility and fighting over the couple's sex life is −.212, while the partial correlation for the woman is .034. These last findings suggest that women are much more likely than men to keep to themselves their feelings that their sexual desires are not compatible, while men make their feelings known in a manner that can cause open conflict.]

32. Among men who say that cunnilingus is usually part of their sexual relations, 29 percent also say intercourse with the woman on top is usually part ($N$ = 38); only 11 percent of men with less frequent cunnilingus say that intercourse with the woman on top is usual ($N$ = 75). Among men for whom fellatio is usual, 31 percent say the woman is frequently on top in intercourse ($N$ = 32), as compared with 11 percent of men for whom fellatio is not usual ($N$ = 81). Forty-eight percent of men for whom their partners' physical attractiveness is extremely important perform oral sex as a usual part of having sex ($N$ = 25), and 44 percent receive oral sex as a usual part of having sex ($N$ = 25). These figures are in contrast to 41 percent ($N$ = 34) and 26 percent ($N$ = 34) of men who do not feel physical attractiveness is important.

[Partial correlations (controlling for the same variables as in Note 21) between frequency of cunnilingus and frequency of intercourse with the woman on top is .205. The partial correlation of the latter with the frequency of fellatio is .341. The measure of ideal partner attractiveness is the sum of Ideal Relationship items 2b and 2f. Among all of the husbands, the two items correlate $r$ = .463 and among all male cohabitors, $r$ = .472.]

33. This is consistent with the finding that these men are more able to separate sex and love (see Note 23), and we also find that they are more likely to have sex outside their relationships. [The partial correlation (using the same controls as in Note 21) between the frequency of cunnilingus and the number of non-monogamous sex partners the man has had (Relationship question 36b) is −.150.]

34. [The same partial correlations as in Note 29 were done for heterosexual women. The partial correlation between frequency of cunnilingus and quality of sex life is .062, and between cunnilingus and happiness with the relationship is .033. The partials for fellatio are .082 and .042.]

35. For 72 percent of the heterosexual couples, the frequency of cunnilingus and fel-

latio are the same. For 16 percent there is more cunnilingus, and for 12 percent more fellatio ($N = 113$.)

36. Seventy-nine percent of lesbians who perform oral sex regularly are happy with the quality of their sex life ($N = 72$) as compared to 49 percent of those who perform oral sex less often ($N = 81$). The figures for receiving oral sex are 75 percent versus 53 percent. Eighty-eight percent of those who perform oral sex often are very satisfied with their overall relationship ($N = 74$) as compared to 81 percent of those who perform oral sex less frequently ($N = 81$). The comparable percentages for those receiving oral sex are 86 percent and 83 percent. Forty-one percent of lesbian couples with frequent oral sex fight about their sex life more than once every few months ($N = 74$), as compared to 52 percent of those with less frequent oral sex ($N = 81$).

[Partial correlations between the frequency of receiving oral sex and satisfaction with the quality of sex life is .214, and with satisfaction with the overall relationship it is .206. The parallel partial correlations for performing oral sex are .219 and .218. The partial correlation between the frequency of oral sex and the amount of fighting over sex is $-.175$. The control variables were essentially the same as in the analyses described in Note 21, but with the substitution of variables relevant to lesbians, such as covertness and involvement in the gay world. The intra-couple correlation for the frequency of oral sex is $r = .695$.]

37. In 72 percent of the lesbian couples, oral sex is performed and received equally by each partner, and in only 9 percent is there a sizable disparity ($N = 70$). [The zero-order correlation between receiving oral sex and performing oral sex is $r = .587$.]

38. [The absolute difference between how much a woman performs oral sex and how much she receives it was correlated with the couple's mean educational level. The correlation is $-.366$, which suggests that women with lower educational levels have a greater likelihood of specialized roles in oral sex.]

39. [The signed difference between the amount a woman performs oral sex and the amount she receives it is not correlated with the signed difference in the two partners' self-ratings of masculinity ($r = -.115$) and with the signed difference in their self-ratings of femininity ($r = .007$). The measurement of masculinity has been described in Note 21 of Money: Income and Power, and of femininity in Note 42 of Work: Having a Job.]

40. Lesbians who describe themselves as very feminine (compassionate, tender, and understanding) are more likely to perform oral sex (53 percent) and receive oral sex (54 percent [$N = 79$]) than are lesbians who describe themselves as less feminine (42 percent performing and 41 percent receiving [$N = 76$]). [The correlation between the frequency of oral sex and the couple's mean femininity score is $r = .190$.]

41. See, for example, Emily Sisley and Bertha Harris, The Joy of Lesbian Sex (New York: Simon & Schuster, 1977); Betty Dodson, Liberating Masturbation: A Meditation on Self-Love (New York: Betty Dodson, 1974).

42. In interviews with lesbians we were occasionally told of other women they had known or heard of who insisted on a sexual pattern where only one partner performed oral sex and would not allow reciprocation. A few lesbians used the term "one-way butch" to describe such women.

43. Sixty-nine percent of the women under twenty-six perform oral sex often ($N = 16$), in contrast to 48 percent of those between twenty-six and forty ($N = 112$) and 33 percent of those over forty ($N = 33$). The comparable percentages for those who say they receive oral sex often are 56 percent, 49 percent, and 37 percent.

[The correlation between the frequency of oral sex and the couple's mean age is $r = .190$. Because of the coding of the oral sex questions, the positive correlation means that older women have less oral sex. The intra-couple correlation of age is $r = .637$.]

44. [The partial correlation between the frequency of performing oral sex and whether a lesbian had had sex with other women before meeting her current partner is $-.151$, indicating that the sexually experienced are more likely to perform oral sex. Sexual experience is measured by an item on the follow-up questionnaire sent to people whom we had interviewed: "Was your partner the first woman with whom you had sexual relations?" The responses were coded 1 = Yes, and 2 = No.]

45. Fifty-five percent of our gay men engage in oral sex usually or always when they have sex ($N = 140$), as compared to 19 percent who engage in anal sex that regularly

($N$ = 140), and 5 percent who engage in body rubbing to the point of orgasm ($N$ = 139). Sixty-three percent masturbate their partners to orgasm usually or always when they have sex ($N$ = 141).

46. Sixty-eight percent of gay men who perform oral sex often are happy with their sex life ($N$ = 105) as compared to 58 percent of those who perform it less often ($N$ = 43). The percentages for receiving oral sex are 71 percent and 49 percent.

[Partial correlations between the frequency of receiving oral sex and happiness with the quality of their sex life is .289. For performing oral sex it is .168. The control variables were essentially the same as in Note 36. The intra-couple correlation for the frequency of oral sex is $r$ = .382.]

47. [The partial correlations (same control variables as in Note 21) between gay men's sex acts and their happiness with the couple's sex life are as follows: performing anal sex: .187; receiving anal sex: .247; rubbing against one's partner to achieve orgasm: .233; being rubbed against by partner: .282; touching one's partner to orgasm: .151; being touched by one's partner to orgasm: .217. The intra-couple correlation on the frequency of anal sex is $r$ = .647.]

48. [The partial correlation between performing oral sex and the equality of commitment within the couple is .176. Equality of commitment is measured by Relationship question 7, scored such that a departure from equality is the absolute difference between an individual's response and the equality point of "5." Because of this scoring, the positive partial correlation reflects that there is more oral sex performed when the commitment is equal.]

49. In 68 percent of the gay male couples, oral sex is performed and received the same amount by each partner, and in only 13 percent is there a large disparity ($N$ = 70). [The zero-order correlation between receiving oral sex and performing oral sex is $r$ = .336.]

50. [The partial correlation between the absolute difference of a man's frequency of performing versus receiving oral sex and his happiness with the quality of the couple's sex life is .153.]

51. Only 4 percent of our gay men say they have oral sex rarely or never ($N$ = 139), as compared to fully 30 percent who say they rarely or never have anal sex ($N$ = 140).

52. See John H. Gagnon and William Simon, *Sexual Conduct: The Social Sources of Human Sexuality* (Chicago: Aldine, 1973), pp. 244–251.

53. [The zero-order correlation between the frequency of receiving anal sex and the number of lifetime male sex-partners (Relationship question 34a) is $r$ = −.165. Note that because of the wording of the item, a negative correlation means that the more sex partners, the greater the frequency of anal sex. The comparable correlation between number of partners and the frequency of performing anal sex is $r$ = −.125]

54. [Partial correlations (with the same control variables as in Note 21) were computed between the following differences: how much a man performs anal sex versus how much he receives anal sex, on the one hand, and on the other, first the couple's balance of power, and second, the difference between his rating of masculinity and his partner's rating of his own masculinity. The first partial is −.030 and the second .049.]

55. [Partial correlations were calculated between which partner is more likely to penetrate the other, and two other variables: first, which partner is more likely to take on a rational versus emotional approach to problems (Relationship question 4j), and second, which partner is more likely to keep his feelings to himself (Relationship question 4m). The partials are .212 and .202. The intra-couple correlation for the first of these items among the entire group of gay men is $r$ = −.379, and for the second it is $r$ = −.495.]

56. [The partial correlation between which partner is more likely to penetrate the other and which is more likely to give in during an argument (Relationship question 4b) is .155. The intra-couple correlation among all gay men for the latter item is $r$ = −.147.]

57. [The correlation between the frequency of anal sex and the couple's mean masculinity score is $r$ = .171.]

58. Fifty-seven percent of heterosexual men rated their sexual relationship as very compatible ($N$ = 96) as opposed to only 46 percent of their partners ($N$ = 94). The percentage for lesbians is 55 percent ($N$ = 121), and for gay men it is 45 percent ($N$ = 149).

59. See Note 4 in the preceding chapter, Sex: Physical Contact.

## Beauty, competitiveness, and possessiveness

1. The major research on the effects of physical appearance has been the work inspired by social psychologists Elaine (Walster) Hatfield and Ellen Berscheid. For a review of their research and that of other social psychologists, see Berscheid and Walster, "Physical Attractiveness," *Advances in Experimental Social Psychology*, Vol. 7, ed. L. Berkowitz (New York: Academic Press, 1974), pp. 157–215.

2. See the following pieces of research: Elaine Walster, Vera Aronson, Darcy Abrahams, and Leon Rottmann, "Importance of Physical Attractiveness in Dating Behavior," *Journal of Personality and Social Psychology*, Vol. 4, No. 5 (November 1966), pp. 508–516. Also, Karen K. Dion and Ellen Berscheid, "Physical Attractiveness and Peer Perception Among Children," *Sociometry*, Vol. 37, No. 1 (March 1974), pp. 1–12. Also, David Landy and Harold Sigall, "Beauty Is Talent: Task Evaluation as a Function of the Performer's Physical Attractiveness," *Journal of Personality and Social Psychology*, Vol. 29, No. 3 (March 1974), pp. 299–304. Also, Margaret M. Clifford and Elaine Walster, "The Effect of Physical Attractiveness on Teacher Expectations," *Sociology of Education*, Vol. 46, No. 2 (Spring 1973), pp. 248–258. Also, Thomas F. Cash, Barry Gillen, and D. Steven Burns, "Sexism and 'Beautyism' in Personnel Consultant Decision Making," *Journal of Applied Psychology*, Vol. 62, No. 3 (June 1977), pp. 301–310.

3. [Regression analyses were performed, with the individual's satisfaction with the quality of his or her sex life as the dependent variable, and the following independent variables: duration, age, income, partner's income, sex-role traditionalism, education, whether previously married, involvement in the gay world, homosexual covertness, voluntary versus institutional marriage, trial marriage versus ideological cohabitation, church or synogogue attendance, whether the person works full time or not, whether his or her partner works full time or not, the presence or absence of children, the amount of conflict over nonsexual matters, each partner's masculinity, each partner's femininity, the person's own attractiveness, and the person's assessment of his or her partner's attractiveness. The standardized regression coefficients for partner's attractiveness are: husbands: .176; wives: .170; male cohabitors: .179; female cohabitors: .154; gay men: .178; lesbians: .099. The measure of one's partner's attractiveness is the sum of Relationship questions 19k and 19n. The inter-item correlations are: husbands: $r = .595$; wives: $r = .623$; male cohabitors: $r = .526$; female cohabitors: $r = .495$; gay men: $r = .562$; lesbians: $r = .494$.]

4. Seventy-nine percent of husbands who feel their partners are very attractive are very happy with their relationship, as compared to 69 percent of those who feel they are moderately attractive, and 51 percent of those who do not rate them as attractive. The comparable figures for wives are 79 percent, 71 percent, and 56 percent; for male cohabitors 71 percent, 61 percent, and 57 percent; for female cohabitors 72 percent, 66 percent, and 47 percent; and for gay men, 77 percent, 68 percent, and 56 percent.

[The same regression analyses as in the preceding note were performed, but with satisfaction with the overall relationship as the dependent variable. The standardized regression coefficients are: husbands: .172; wives: .132; male cohabitors: .192; female cohabitors: .143; gay men: .158; lesbians: .064. It should be noted that the heterosexual women have fairly marginal coefficients. However, if instead of using the two-item measure of partner's attractiveness as the independent variable, we use the rating of his being sexy-looking, then the coefficients are larger. For lesbians, the coefficients are small under any circumstances.]

5. Sixty-three percent of male cohabitors who find their partners very attractive are very committed to the future of their relationship, as compared to 54 percent of those who find them moderately attractive, and 46 percent of those who do not feel they are attractive. [The standardized regression coefficient for the man's assessment of his partner's physical attractiveness (the dependent variable being his commitment to the future of the relationship) is .173. The coefficients for the other groups are all below .115.]

6. [The regression coefficient for the cohabiting woman's physical attractiveness (where

sexual frequency is the dependent variable) is .228. The regression analysis is almost the same as described in Note 8 of the chapter on Sex: Physical Contact, except that there were two independent variables dealing with attractiveness, one for the man's looks and one for the woman's. The attractiveness measure is described in Note 28 of the chapter on Sex: Initiating and Refusing.]

7. For example, 34 percent of male cohabitors ($N$ = 290) and 20 percent of females ($N$ = 288) together between two and ten years feel it is very important to have a sexy-looking partner. The comparable percentages for husbands and wives are 31 percent ($N$ = 1,521) and 16 percent ($N$ = 1,508), and for gay men, 34 percent ($N$ = 951) and lesbians, 18 percent ($N$ = 710). The comparisons are even stronger in the couples together less than two years. [The measure is Ideal Relationship question 2b.]

8. [The lesbian regression coefficients for rating of one's partner's physical attractiveness are: quality of sex life: .099; overall happiness with the relationship: .064; and commitment to the future of the relationship: .023.]

9. Seventeen percent of husbands who feel they are very attractive would resent it if their partners were sexually more attractive to others ($N$ = 507), as compared to 12 percent of husbands who feel they are moderately attractive ($N$ = 2,540) and 10 percent of those who say they are not attractive ($N$ = 524). The comparable percentages for wives are: 32 percent ($N$ = 465), 25 percent ($N$ = 2,270), and 21 percent ($N$ = 825); for male cohabitors: 18 percent ($N$ = 141), 12 percent ($N$ = 449), and 13 percent ($N$ = 48); and for female cohabitors: 34 percent ($N$ = 137), 27 percent ($N$ = 441), and 17 percent ($N$ = 65).

[People's self-ratings of their physical attractiveness is the sum of Relationship questions 20h and 20q. Inter-item correlations are: husbands: $r$ = .717; wives: $r$ = .665; male cohabitors: $r$ = .682; female cohabitors: $r$ = .591; gay men: $r$ = .667; lesbians: $r$ = .613. People's resentment at the prospect of their partners' receiving more attention from others is measured by Relationship question 23g. The standardized coefficients when this measure was regressed against ratings of one's physical attractiveness (controlling the same variables as in Note 3) are: husbands: .219; wives: .166; male cohabitors: .150; female cohabitors: .185; gay men: .090; and lesbians: .111.]

10. It is clear from Figure 40 that among heterosexuals, more women resent their partners being more attractive to others than vice versa. This reflects, we believe, the cultural stereotype that allows and encourages women to have greater vanity than men, as well as the fact that women's looks are a more central aspect of their evaluation in this society than is the case for men. (See Stanley J. Morse, Joan Gruzen, and Harry Reis, "The 'Eye of the Beholder': A Neglected Variable in the Study of Physical Attractiveness," *Journal of Personality*, Vol. 44, No. 2 [June 1976], pp. 209–225.) We also believe that because women's looks are so important to men, women are more troubled at the prospect of not being judged attractive. Among gay men, 19 percent would be bothered if their partners were found more sexually attractive, as compared to 31 percent who feel neutral on the matter, and 50 percent who would not be bothered ($N$ = 1,916). The percentages for lesbians are 15 percent, 29 percent, and 56 percent ($N$ = 1,550).

11. Among gay men who would be very bothered by their partners' being found more attractive, 52 percent report fighting over their sex life at least once every few months ($N$ = 348), as compared to 46 percent of those who feel neutral about their partners' being more attractive to others ($N$ = 580) and 31 percent of those who would not be at all bothered ($N$ = 936). The comparable figures for lesbians are: 64 percent ($N$ = 235), 51 percent ($N$ = 436), and 39 percent ($N$ = 837). [Partial correlations between how bothered a person would feel if his or her partner were found more attractive and the amount of fighting about sex are: gay men: .200; lesbians: .191; husbands: .139; wives: .102; male cohabitors: .133; female cohabitors: .059.]

12. We have purposely avoided the term *jealousy* because of the ambiguities in its meaning. When we discuss *possessiveness*, we mean how troubled a person is at the prospect of his or her partner's having sex with another person. When we discuss *suspicion*, we are concerned with the person's belief that his or her partner has had sex with someone else. In common usage, the word *jealousy*, we feel, has a mixture of these two meanings. [Possessiveness is measured by Relationship question 23i.]

13. [The partial correlation between a wife's possessiveness and the loneliness she feels she would experience if her relationship were to end (Relationship question 26g) is .216. The partial for female cohabitors is .193.]

14. [Partial correlations comparable to those in Note 13 are: for gay men: .152; for lesbians: .174.]

15. [This variable is measured by Opinion statement 19. The wording of the item asks about sex between a man and a woman, and so may not be a good measure for gay men and lesbians. However, there is some evidence of its adequacy. A question on the follow-up questionnaire that was sent to people who were interviewed asked if the individual (were he or she not attached) would be capable of having sex with a stranger when there was no anticipation of a further relationship (see Note 30 of the next chapter, Sex: Non-monogamy). This measure correlates with Opinion statement 19: .387 for lesbians, .227 for gay men, .346 for heterosexual men, and .596 for heterosexual women. Zero-order correlations between attitudes toward sex without love and possessiveness are: husbands: $r = .319$; wives: $r = .332$; male cohabitors: $r = .256$; female cohabitors: $r = .239$; gay men: $r = .283$; lesbians: $r = .219$.]

16. [The item is Relationship question 23j.]

17. Forty-eight percent of gay men who have been together less than two years are possessive ($N = 630$), as opposed to 30 percent of those together between two and ten years ($N = 949$) and 26 percent of those together more than ten years ($N = 347$). [A regression analysis (using the same independent variables as in Note 3) produced a standardized coefficient for duration of .194. It is important to realize that this is a cross-sectional analysis and we should not be too eager to infer that possessiveness declines over time. It may be that possessiveness is a destructive emotion and that the relationships of gay men who are more possessive do not survive. It is more plausible that those who are not possessive are better able to deal with non-monogamy when it occurs, while the possessive ones are more likely to break up if one of the partners does have sex outside the relationship. In spite of these other very plausible interpretations, the strong sense we get from the interviews is that, over time, gay men come to realize that their partners can be non-monogamous without jeopardizing the relationship and so they are less bothered by the prospect of outside sex.]

18. Seventy-nine percent of lesbians together less than two years are possessive ($N = 724$), as compared to 69 percent of those together between two and ten years ($N = 707$) and 64 percent of those together longer than ten years ($N = 64$). [The regression coefficient for duration among lesbians is .155. See the preceding note for a description of the regression analysis and for a warning on the interpretation of the duration effect.]

19. Among wives who are possessive, 87 percent say it is very likely that their marriages will last ($N = 2,971$), as opposed to only 73 percent of those who are less possessive ($N = 577$). [The partial correlation coefficients between possessiveness and commitment to the future of the relationship are: wives: .172; husbands: .114; male cohabitors: .069; female cohabitors: .063; gay men: .035; lesbians: .131.]

20. [Zero-order correlations between husbands' score on the voluntary-institutional dimension and their commitment to the future of the relationship is $r = .222$. The wives' correlation is $r = .217$.]

21. Eighty-nine percent of "institutional" husbands are possessive ($N = 1,827$), as opposed to 74 percent of husbands who are intermediate between "institutional" and "voluntary" ($N = 1,321$), and 50 percent of "voluntary" husbands ($N = 428$). The comparable percentages for wives are 93 percent ($N = 1,477$), 83 percent ($N = 1,419$), and 63 percent ($N = 655$). [Regression analyses were performed with possessiveness as the dependent variable and the same independent variables as in Note 3. The standardized regression coefficient for husbands for the voluntary-institutional dimension is .359, and for wives it is .364.]

---

## Non-monogamy

1. [Whether people have ever been non-monogamous within their current relationship is measured by Relationship question 35. Their awareness of their partners' non-monogamy is measured by question 42.]

2. Figure 46 shows that married couples are the most likely of our couples to prize monogamy.

3. [The question is Ideal Relationship item 1i. The gay men are a notable exception to the pattern in Figure 46. A full discussion of the meaning of non-monogamy in the gay male world is found later in this chapter.]

4. [The data in Figure 47 are based on Relationship questions 36a and 36b.]

5. Part of the reason that husbands have had more non-monogamous partners than male cohabitors have is that, on average, they have been with their partners longer, and therefore longer "at risk." However, even if we consider the length of the relationships, the husbands have a small edge. For example, 22 percent of non-monogamous husbands who have been with their wives less than two years have had more than five outside partners ($N = 49$), as compared to only 10 percent of comparable male cohabitors ($N = 73$). By a similar analysis, we find that female cohabitors actually have a slight edge on wives when it comes to the number of outside sex partners.

6. We simply mean that over the entire course of a relationship there is always the possibility that a first act of non-monogamy will occur. It is, however, probably quite safe to assume that the longer a relationship continues to be monogamous, the greater the chance it will be monogamous in the future. In interpreting the data in Figure 49 (as well as Figures 50 and 51) it is critical to realize that we cannot assume that couples in the tenth year of their relationship give a perfect picture of what couples in a two-year relationship will be like in eight years. There are two main reasons that this may not be true: First, the two kinds of couples began their relationships at different points in history and therefore under different conditions. Second, some two-year couples do not survive to their tenth anniversary; the ten-year couples represent only survivors and are therefore less likely to possess the qualities that might have broken up couples prior to their tenth year. We try to be very tentative when we make interpretations about changes in couples' lives based on comparisons of different couples at different stages in their lives. When we do this, the comparison is usually based on strong impressions we have gotten from the interviews.

7. Based on an analysis of the follow-up data. See the chapter on Who Broke Up. [One should exercise caution about inferring longitudinal patterns on the basis of the cross-sectional data presented in this entire discussion of monogamy.]

8. [Again it is important to warn against making longitudinal inferences from cross-sectional data. It may be that the gay men who favor monogamy do not last as couples, and so we find a greater concentration of the non-monogamous among the couples of long duration. For instance, if in a short-duration relationship one partner favored monogamy more strongly than the other, he might choose to leave the relationship when his partner departed from monogamy. Our follow-up data do not suggest that this pattern occurs. It may also be that the relationships that survive to long duration are fundamentally more durable in many ways and can therefore tolerate non-monogamy better. We believe there may be some truth to this interpretation. However, time and again, our experience with couples whom we have interviewed strongly supports the interpretation in the text.]

9. Fifty-three percent of non-monogamous lesbians have had only one outside partner, and 78 percent have had only one or two partners ($N = 368$).

10. It is not important to our argument whether heterosexual women have numerically more affairs than their partners. What is significant is that *when* a woman has sex outside her relationship, it is more likely to be a "meaningful love affair" (Relationship question 40a). Let us consider an example from Figure 51. Among husbands married more then ten years, 30 percent have at some time had extramarital sex, but only 11 percent have ever had an affair. Translated differently, approximately 37 percent of non-monogamous husbands have ever had a serious affair. The picture of wives married more than ten years is quite different. Only 22 percent have ever been non-monogamous, but of these, fully half have had a meaningful affair. Another good example is the cohabitors who have been together between two and ten years. Of the 47 percent of men who have been non-monogamous, only about 15 percent have had an affair. Among the women, of the 42 percent who have been non-monogamous, about 31 percent have had an affair.

11. Among highly companionate husbands, 7 percent ($N = 1,676$) were non-monogamous in the preceding year, as compared to 14 percent of less companionate husbands ($N = 1,853$) and fully 44 percent of very "separate" husbands ($N = 62$). The comparable percentages for wives are: 5 percent ($N = 1,274$), 9 percent ($N = 2,222$), and 22 percent ($N = 110$). For male cohabitors: 14 percent ($N = 181$), 23 percent ($N = 431$), and 45

percent ($N$ = 31). For female cohabitors: 13 percent ($N$ = 134), 17 percent ($N$ = 457), and 37 percent ($N$ = 57). For gay men: 64 percent ($N$ = 704), 76 percent ($N$ = 1,110), and 88 percent ($N$ = 100). For lesbians: 7 percent ($N$ = 616), 20 percent ($N$ = 881), and 39 percent ($N$ = 57).

[The items measuring non-monogamy in the preceding year are Relationship questions 38a and 38b. Partial correlations between a dichotomous variable (whether or not a person had been non-monogamous during the preceding year) and the person's score on companionate versus separate living (see Note 29 of Work: Work Versus the Relationship) provide these correlations: husbands: .203; wives: .139; male cohabitors: .203; female cohabitors: .144; gay men: .166; and lesbians: .235. It should be noted that the statistical relationship is stronger for heterosexual men than for heterosexual women. A word of warning is in order about inferring causality. While we do believe that living separate lives makes non-monogamy more likely, it is also probably the case that couples sometimes lead more separate lives because of their outside involvements, such as other sex partners. They may also be somewhat alienated from their partners and seeking an alternative.]

12. [Partial correlations between having an ideology that stresses independence from one's partner and endorsing monogamy as a personal ideal are: husbands: −.187; wives: −.196; male cohabitors: −.206; female cohabitors: −.156; gay men: −.285; and lesbians: −.307.]

13. [Multiple regression analyses were performed with the dependent variable being whether or not a person had been non-monogamous in the preceding year, and the following independent variables: duration, age, income, partner's income, sex-role traditionalism, education, having been married before, involvement in the gay world, homosexual covertness, voluntary versus institutionally married, trial married or ideological cohabitation, church or synagogue attendance, belief in sex without love, presence of children, the amount of nonsexual conflict, and ideological commitment to a separate life from one's partner. The standardized coefficients for the latter variable are: gay men: .153; lesbians: .173. While the coefficients of others groups are lower, it should be noted that they are higher for heterosexual men than women: husbands: .119 and male cohabitors: .135, as compared to wives: .069 and female cohabitors: .017.]

14. [Regression analyses for gay men and lesbians, with the same independent variables as listed in Note 13, were performed with two different non-monogamy dependent variables: one, the dichotomy of whether or not a person had been non-monogamous in the past year, and the other, the number of non-monogamous partners a person has had during the course of the relationship. The independent variable of interest is the person's involvement in the gay world, which is the sum of four items: whether the person lives in a "gay ghetto" (Lifestyle question 14), whether he or she goes to gay (or lesbian) bars (question 9a) or other gay places (question 11), and involvement in the gay rights movement (question 8). Alpha reliability for the scale for gay men is .518 and for lesbians it is .572. The regression coefficient for this variable for gay men when non-monogamy in the past year is the dependent variable is .153, and when number of partners is the dependent variable it is −.167. When the gay ghetto variable is used instead of the gay involvement scale, the results are not substantially altered. We should note that gay men may choose to live in a largely gay social environment because they wish to have non-monogamous opportunities; this would complicate the causal argument.]

15. [Comparable analyses to those described in the preceding note were performed for lesbians. The standardized regression coefficient for gay involvement is −.011 for non-monogamy in the past year and −.046 for number of non-monogamous partners.]

16. [Regression analyses like those described in Note 13 were performed, with the dependent variable being whether a person had ever been non-monogamous in the course of his or her relationship. There is a large effect for duration: The longer the couple has been together, the more likely the partners have been non-monogamous; but with duration controlled, there is a significant age effect for the women. The younger have a greater likelihood of having been non-monogamous. The standardized regression coefficients are: for wives: .210; for female cohabitors: .151; and for lesbians: .155. Note that a low score on the dependent variable indicates non-monogamy.]

17. [Our measure of "loving less" is Relationship question 7. We use the term as a shorthand for the more cumbersome expression *asymmetric commitment*. The correlation between relative commitment and relative power in our couples is only moderate: for

married couples, $r = -.091$; for cohabitors: $r = -.322$; for gay men: $r = -.086$; and for lesbians: $r = -.161$.]

18. Willard Waller, *The Family: A Dynamic Interpretation* (New York: Dryden, 1938). Waller was actually borrowing on an idea of E. A. Ross (*Principles of Sociology* [New York: Century, 1921]).

19. The less committed partner can take greater liberties because he or she feels less vulnerable to the prospect of the relationship's ending. This is particularly true among cohabiting couples. We find, for example, that a person who fears he or she would be unable to avoid loneliness if the relationship were to end also tends to be the more highly committed partner. [The zero-order correlations between relative commitment and difficulty avoiding loneliness (Relationship queston 26g) are: male cohabitors: $r = .143$; female cohabitors: $r = .177$.]

20. See Peter M. Blau, *Exchange and Power in Social Life* (New York: Wiley, 1964), p. 133. Also, Richard M. Emerson, "Power-Dependence Relations," *American Sociological Review*, Vol. 25, No. 1 (February 1962), pp. 31–41.

21. [The religiosity question is Statistical Information item 8b. The zero-order correlations between this question and attitudes toward sex without love are: husbands: $r = .439$; wives: $r = .391$; male cohabitors: $r = .202$; female cohabitors: $r = .200$; gay men: $r = .304$; lesbians: $r = .275$. The correlations between church or synagogue attendence and anti-pornography sentiments (Opinion statement 17) are: husbands: $r = .361$; wives: $r = .328$; male cohabitors: $r = .197$; female cohabitors: $r = .138$; gay men: $r = .159$; lesbians: $r = .117$. The correlations between church or synagogue attendance and acceptance of positive portrayals of homosexuals and lesbians in public schools (Opinion statement 21) are: husbands $r = -.237$; wives: $r = -.270$; male cohabitors: $r = -.142$; female cohabitors: $r = -.207$.]

22. [Zero-order correlations were computed for husbands, wives, male cohabitors, female cohabitors, gay men, and lesbians, between church or synagogue attendance, on the one hand, and on the other: sexual frequency, satisfaction with the quality of the couple's sex life, conflict over sex, which partner initiates sex, displeasure at the prospect of one's partner initiating sex (Relationship question 23b), and displeasure at the prospect of one's partner waiting for sex to be initiated (Relationship question 23d). None of the correlations attained a magnitude of .100.]

23. [Multiple regressions were performed with the same independent variables as in Note 13. When the dependent variable was whether the person had ever been non-monogamous during his or her current relationship, the standardized regression coefficients for church or synagogue attendance are: husbands: $-.079$; wives: $-.057$; male cohabitors: $-.042$; female cohabitors: $-.045$; gay men: $-.061$; lesbians: $.034$. With non-monogamy within the past year as the dependent variable, the coefficients become: husbands: $-.063$; wives: $-.011$; male cohabitors: $-.042$; female cohabitors: $-.021$; gay men: $-.042$; lesbians: $.039$.]

24. "Manners of Deceit and the Case for Lying," *Esquire*, Vol. 88, No. 6 (December 1977), pp. 134, 194.

25. For example, Nena O'Neill and George O'Neill, *Open Marriage: A New Life Style for Couples* (New York: M. Evans, 1972). Also, Roger W. Libby and Robert N. Whitehurst, eds., *Marriage and Alternatives: Exploring Intimate Relationships* (Glenview, Ill.: Scott, Foresman, 1977), pp. 112–185, 302–356.

26. [Relationship question 41.]

27. Married couples are less likely than any other kind of couple to have an understanding that allows non-monogamy under some circumstances. The percentages are: married couples: 15 percent; cohabitors: 28 percent; gay men: 65 percent; lesbians: 29 percent. [In these percentages a couple is considered to have a non-monogamous understanding only if both partners say they do. When we tabulate peoples' responses individually, the percentages are a bit higher. Twenty-six percent of husbands ($N = 3,533$) and 23 percent of wives ($N = 3,558$) say they have an understanding that will allow non-monogamy under some circumstances. The figures for male and female cohabitors are 38 percent ($N = 628$) and 36 percent ($N = 633$). For gay men it is 72 percent ($N = 1,902$), and for lesbians 37 percent ($N = 1,519$).]

28. Seventeen percent of lesbians who have been non-monogamous in the past year report having had sex with someone they had met that same day or with a stranger ($N$

= 236), as compared to fully 90 percent of comparable gay men ($N$ = 1,373). This does not mean that 90 percent of the men's sex partners were strangers, but simply that 90 percent of them have shown the capability to have sex with a stranger. [The item on which these data are based is Relationship question 38c. This question was not asked of heterosexuals.]

29. The word *trick* is defined as a "short-term sex partner" and to *trick out* means "to be unfaithful to a regular lover." See Bruce Rodgers, *The Queens' Vernacular: A Gay Lexicon* (San Francisco: Straight Arrow Books, 1972), p. 200. While the etymology of the term is not clear, it has been suggested that it was borrowed by the gay male culture from street prostitutes, who use the word to refer to a client.

30. On the follow-up questionnaire sent to people who were interviewed, one question was: "If you were not involved in a relationship with someone, what would be your attitude toward having sex with someone you had just met and whom you could expect never to see again?" Seventy-three percent of gay men said it was something they could do with no trouble at all ($N$ = 166). Only 14 percent of the lesbians ($N$ = 150) and 20 percent of the heterosexual women ($N$ = 106) gave the same answer. Thirty-four percent of heterosexual men said that they could, and an additional 40 percent said they could do it but with some reservations ($N$ = 106).

31. [Partial correlations between sexual frequency and having been non-monogamous in the past year are: husbands: $-.016$; wives: $-.031$; male cohabitors: $-.040$; female cohabitors: $-.019$.]

32. [Partial correlations between an individual's satisfaction with the quality of his or her sex life at home and whether he or she has been non-monogamous in the past year are: husbands: $-.086$; wives: $-.047$; male cohabitors: $-.007$; female cohabitors: $-.102$.]

33. [Partial correlations between whether a person has been non-monogamous in the past year and his or her satisfaction with the overall relationship are: husbands: $-.122$; wives: $-.093$; male cohabitors: $-.113$; female cohabitors: $-.105$.]

34. Ninety percent of husbands who have been monogamous in the past year are highly committed to the future of their relationship ($N$ = 3,099) as compared to 72 percent of those who have been non-monogamous ($N$ = 388). The comparable figures for wives are 91 percent ($N$ = 3,235) versus 71 percent ($N$ = 285). For male cohabitors it is 61 percent ($N$ = 485) versus 47 percent ($N$ = 132), and for female cohabitors 64 percent ($N$ = 502) versus 45 percent ($N$ = 114). These data can be looked at in another way: Only 9 percent of highly committed husbands have had sex outside their relationship in the past year ($N$ = 3,067) as compared to fully 26 percent of the less committed ($N$ = 388). The parallel data for wives is 6 percent ($N$ = 3,136) versus 21 percent ($N$ = 384); for male cohabitors 17 percent ($N$ = 360) versus 27 percent ($N$ = 257), and for female cohabitors 14 percent ($N$ = 370) versus 26 percent ($N$ = 246).

[Partial correlations between whether a man has been non-monogamous in the past year and his expectation that the relationship will last are $-.149$ for husbands, and $-.146$ for male cohabitors. For wives it is $-.147$, and for female cohabitors $-.146$. Because of the direction of the scales, a negative correlation means less commitment to the future among people who have been non-monogamous.]

35. Seventy-two percent of lesbians who have been monogamous in the past year are satisfied with the quality of their sex life together ($N$ = 1,304), as compared to 57 percent of those who have not been monogamous ($N$ = 239). Eighty percent of the former are very satisfied with the overall relationship ($N$ = 1,314) as compared to 59 percent of the latter ($N$ = 239); and 73 percent of the former are very committed to its future ($N$ = 1,273), as compared to 47 percent of the latter ($N$ = 230). Let us look at these data in another way: Thirteen percent of lesbians who are satisfied with the quality of their sex life together have been non-monogamous in the past year ($N$ = 1,076), as compared to 19 percent of those who have mixed feelings about the quality of their sex life ($N$ = 313), and 27 percent of those who are dissatisfied with its quality ($N$ = 154). Twelve percent of those who are generally happy with the relationship have been non-monogamous ($N$ = 1,192), as compared to 27 percent of those who are less happy ($N$ = 361). Finally, 10 percent of lesbians who are highly committed to the future of the relationship have been non-monogamous ($N$ = 1,038) as opposed to 26 percent of those who are less committed ($N$ = 465).

[Partial correlations between whether a lesbian has had non-monogamous sex in the past year and her evaluation of the quality of her sex life with her partner is − .153. The partial with her overall satisfaction with her relationship is − .161, and with her commitment to its future is − .195.]

36. [Partial correlation between a gay man's having been non-monogamous in the past year and his overall happiness with his relationship is − .083; and with his commitment to the future of his relationship it is − .047. The partial correlations, when we consider the frequency of non-monogamy in the past year (Relationship question 38a) or the number of non-monogamous partners over the course of the relationship, are all equally small.]

37. [The partial correlation between the frequency of non-monogamous sex in the past year and the couple's sexual frequency together is − .165, and between the number of non-monogamous partners and sexual frequency is .181 (note that here a positive correlation means a negative relationship). The partial correlations for the two non-monogamy measures and the gay man's satisfaction with the quality of the couple's sex life are − .160 and .166.]

38. There is already evidence that the advent of this serious disease has changed the attitudes of some gay men about non-monogamy. In an unpublished study, San Francisco psychotherapists Leon McKusick, William Horstman, and Arthur Carfagni ("Report on Community Reactions to AIDS Survey"), found that since learning about AIDS, men in their study say they are more in favor of monogamy and more committed to their current partners.

# Who broke up—and why

1. We have taken into account the length of time the couple has been together because we feel it is likely that some factors might break up relationships in their early years, while others might take their toll at a later point. [When we talk about factors associated with couples' breaking up in the early years, in contrast to breaking up at a later point, we are making cross-sectional comparisons, and care should be exercised in inferring that our long-term couples are the same as the short-term couples who have not broken up.]

2. Thirty-seven percent of male cohabitors together less than two years had told us it was extremely likely that they and their partners would stay together ($N = 341$). The figure is 39 percent for female cohabitors ($N = 338$), 37 percent of gay men ($N = 607$), and 43 percent for lesbians ($N = 703$). The lesbian prophecy proved to be the most optimistic.

3. [Among married couples together less than two years, the zero-order correlation between whether they broke up (low score) and the couple's mean rating of how much they fought over money management is $r = .289.$]

4. [The zero-order correlation between breaking up and conflict over money management among couples together more than two years is $r = .043.$]

5. [For gay men, zero-order correlations between breaking up and conflict over money management are $r = .179$ for those together less than two years, and $r = .225$ for those together more than two years. The correlation for all of the gay men is $r = .187$. For lesbians together less than two years, the correlation is $r = .199$. For those together longer there is a substantial negative correlation between breaking up and having been satisfied with the way money was managed ($r = −.154$).]

6. [The correlation between cohabitors' (mean) score on pooling and whether they broke up is $r = −.208$. There is no difference between the correlation for couples together under two years and couples together longer. The intra-couple correlation on pooling is $r = .357.$]

7. [The correlation between pooling and breaking up for gay men together less than two years is $r = −.167$. The correlation for men together longer is $r = −.123.$]

8. [The correlation between breaking up and how the couple feels about pooling is $r = −.149$. The correlations for short-term and long-term couples are almost the same.]

9. [The correlations between breaking up and either partner's feelings about pooling, either in short-term or long-term married couples, do not exceed a magnitude of $-.090$.]

10. [The correlation between breaking up and the wife's feeling that she would have difficulty maintaining her standard of living if the relationship were to end (Relationship question 26d) is $r = -.158$ in couples together less than two years. A negative correlation means that wives who would find it difficult are less likely to be in relationships that break up.]

11. [For wives in short-term relationships, the correlation between breaking up and feeling it important to be self-sufficient (Ideal Relationship question 4k) is $r = .153$.]

12. [Among cohabitors together less than two years, the correlation between breaking up and the equality of influence over spending on furniture is $r = -.195$. For couples of longer duration it is $r = -.186$. Inequality of influence is measured as the absolute departure from the equality midpoint of "5." A negative correlation means that where influence is unequal, couples are more likely to break up.]

13. [For lesbians together less than two years, the correlation between breaking up and finding their partners self-sufficient is $r = -.152$, while for couples of long duration the correlation is $r = -.228$. For couples of long duration the correlation with finding a partner forceful is $r = -.150$. When these couples perceive themselves to be forceful, the correlation is $r = -.252$. A negative correlation means that couples are more likely to break up when partners are not self-sufficient and forceful.]

14. [In lesbian couples of long duration, the correlation between breaking up and the absolute value of their income difference is $r = -.222$. The correlation with the inequality of influence over entertainment spending is $r = -.177$, and with inequality of influence over furniture spending, $r = -.224$.]

15. [On the follow-up questionnaire we asked, "When your relationship as a couple began breaking up, who wanted it to end?" The response possibilities are: "I wanted it to end but [my partner] did not"; "We both wanted it to end, but I wanted it more"; "We equally wanted it to end"; "We both wanted it to end, but [my partner] wanted it more"; and "[My partner] wanted it to end, but I did not." Among lesbians the correlation between which partner wanted it to end and which had more power when they filled out their original questionnaires is $r = .222$.]

16. [Among gay men together less than two years, the correlation between breaking up and satisfaction with the couple's income is $r = -.149$, and the correlation with the amount of fighting about income is $r = .148$. For couples of longer duration, the correlation with fighting is $r = .156$. For lesbians together less than two years, the correlation with satisfaction with the couple's income is $r = -.206$, and for couples together longer, the correlation with conflict over income is $r = .178$.]

17. [The correlation among married couples between breaking up and conflict over income is $r = .066$. The correlations for husband's satisfaction and wife's satisfaction with income are $r = -.021$, and $r = -.045$. For cohabitors the comparable correlations are $r = .094$, $r = -.042$, and $r = -.111$. When we consider heterosexual couples of short or long duration, we get very similar correlations.]

18. [The correlation between breaking up and fighting about the wife's job is $r = .288$ in couples together less than two years, and $r = .158$ in couples of longer duration. The correlations for fighting over the man's job are $r = .186$, and $r = .026$.]

19. [Among married couples of short duration, the correlation between breaking up and conflict over the wife's working is $r = .177$.]

20. [Among cohabitors together less than two years, the correlation between conflict over the intrusion of the woman's work and the couple breaking up is $r = .273$. The correlation for couples together a longer time is $r = .195$. The correlations for the intrusion of the man's work are $r = .137$, and $r = .089$.]

21. [This form of conflict is destructive for gay men in short-term relationships ($r = .163$), and for lesbians in longer relationships ($r = .152$).]

22. [Among gay men who broke up, the correlation between which partner wanted the relationship to end and the difference between the partners' level of ambition is $r = .225$. For lesbians the correlation is $r = .214$. Among lesbians who broke up, the correlation between which woman wanted it to end and which was more work-centered is $r = .226$. The comparable correlation for gay men is $r = .204$.]

23. [Among couples together less than two years, the correlation between breaking up and a husband's feeling of how important it is that he be a success at work (Ideal Relationship question 4p) is $r = -.151$. The comparable correlation for male cohabitors is $r = -.181$.]

24. [Among couples together a short time, the correlation between breaking up and the importance the wife places on being a success is $r = .152$. A positive correlation means that couples are *more* likely to break up when the wife is ambitious. The opposite is true when husbands are ambitious.]

25. While many a husband can take pride in his wife's entry into and achievement in the world of work, the stress of having a wife heavily invested in her job is more than some men can handle. It may also be that her desire to succeed is something he finds unseemly in his partner. In either event, he feels that she is putting her work before her relationship, which is not how he envisions a wife's role. This is bad news for the professional woman who would like to be as aggressive at her job as her husband is at his and have this enhance rather than hurt her relationship.

[Among married couples who had broken up, the correlation between the wife's rating of her own ambition and her saying that it was her husband who wanted the relationship to end is $r = .400$. The correlation between her ambitiousness and her husband saying it was he who wanted it to end is $r = .413$]

26. [The correlation in new marriages between breaking up and the husband's assessment of whether his wife does her "fair share" of the housework is $r = -.157$. The comparable correlation for male cohabitors is $r = -.163$. A negative correlation means that when she does less than he considers fair, they are more likely to break up.]

27. [Among married couples together less than two years, the correlation between breaking up and the number of evenings they dine together is $r = .248$. For cohabitors the comparable correlation is $r = .204$. (A positive correlation means couples who dine together infrequently are more likely to break up.) For all cohabitors the correlation between taking separate vacations and breaking up is $r = .249$ (Lifestyle question 4). Among gay men the correlation between breaking up and spending time alone with friends is $r = .203$, while for lesbians the comparable correlation is $r = .182$. For gay men together more than two years, the correlation with dining together is $r = .162$. For lesbians the correlation among couples together more than ten years between breaking up and taking separate vacations is $r = .182$, and for going to movies and concerts alone it is $r = .207$.]

28. [Among married couples together less than two years, the correlation between breaking up and fighting over their sexual relationship is $r = .162$. It is interesting that when we consider satisfaction with the quality of their sex life, it is only the husband's feelings that are correlated with breaking up ($r = -.152$ among those in new marriages). Among cohabitors we find the same pattern: Only among men in short-term relationships is there a correlation between satisfaction with the quality of the couple's sex life and breaking up ($r = -.155$). But we find that for relationships of all durations, the more cohabitors fight about sex, the more likely they are to break up ($r = .161$). For gay men we find a correlation, among those together less than two years, between breaking up and satisfaction with the quality of their sex life ($r = -.211$) as well as a correlation among those together more than ten years ($r = -.160$). With lesbians, sex seems to be related to breaking up only among those together more than two years. The correlation with sexual satisfaction is $r = -.181$, and with conflict over sex, $r = .206$. There is evidence that this pattern is magnified among the women together a long time. It we look at those together more than ten years, the correlations are $r = -.455$, and $r = .321$.]

29. [The correlations between breaking up and sexual frequency for short- and long-duration married couples are $r = -.029$ and $r = -.084$. For cohabitors they are $r = -.094$ and $r = .010$. For gay men: $r = -.020$ and $r = -.065$. For lesbians: $r = .058$ and $r = -.049$.]

30. [In marriages of less than two years' duration, the correlation between the husband's rating of himself as feminine and the couple breaking up is $r = -.298$. The comparable correlation for male cohabitors is $r = -.201$. A negative correlation means that when the man is not tender, compassionate, and understanding, the couple is more likely to break up.]

31. [In marriages of less than two years' duration, the correlation between breaking up

and whether the husband considers it important that his wife be good-looking (Ideal Relationship question 2f) is $r = .175$. For cohabitors in short-term relationships, the correlation between breaking up and the man feeling it important that his partner be sexy-looking (Ideal Relationship question 2b) is $r = .145$.]

32. [We calculated a measure of the difference between the two partners' physical attractiveness (a high score means the woman is more attractive). The correlation between this measure and the man's saying that he wanted the relationship to end more than his partner did is $r = -.311$. The correlation with the woman saying that she wanted it to end more is $r = .327$. Married and cohabiting couples are combined to enlarge the number of cases ($N = 38$).]

33. [The correlation between breaking up and the wife's having been non-monogamous in the preceding year is $r = .261$ for short-term couples, and $r = .173$ for couples of longer duration. For husbands, there is no correlation in the first few years of marriage ($r = -.068$), while in long-term relationships it is $r = .184$. A positive correlation means that non-monogamous couples are more likely to break up.]

34. [The correlation for lesbians between breaking up and having been non-monogamous in the past year are: short-duration couples: $r = .158$; longer-duration couples: $r = .238$.]

35. [The correlation between a lesbian's having been non-monogamous in the past year and being the partner who wanted the relationship to end is $r = .174$.]

36. [Among heterosexual couples there is no correlation between whether the man has been non-monogamous in the past year and which partner wanted the relationship to end ($r = .013$). We take this finding as suggesting that the man's non-monogamy is no more likely to cause him to want to leave the relationship than it is likely to cause his partner to want it to end. However, the correlation between the woman's having been non-monogamous in the past year and her wanting the relationship to end is $r = .206$.]

37. [Among gay men together less than two years, the correlation between breaking up and having been non-monogamous in the past year is $r = .019$. However, the correlation between breaking up and the frequency of non-monogamy in the past year is $r = .149$. This suggests that gay male couples are less likely to survive if they are frequently non-monogamous early in their relationship. It does not seem to matter at later stages of the relationship.]

38. [The correlation in gay male relationships of less than two years between breaking up and having a meaningful affair is $r = .147$. For relationships of more than two years the correlation is $r = .064$.]

39. [For male cohabitors in relationships of less than two years' standing, the correlation between breaking up and having been non-monogamous in the past year is $r = .188$. The correlation for couples together more than two years is $r = .064$. For female cohabitors' non-monogamy, the correlations are $r = .072$ and $r = .042$.]

40. [For the gay men the correlation between having a non-monogamy understanding and breaking up is $r = -.001$ among those together less than two years and $r = .022$ for those together two years or more. For married couples this factor is associated with breaking up only among couples together less than two years ($r = -.176$), and for cohabitors and lesbians only for couples together more than two years ($r = -.153$ and $r = -.189$). A negative correlation means that couples with an understanding are more likely to break up.]

41. On the follow-up questionnaire sent to gay men and lesbians whom we had interviewed there was a question about how they had met: "When you and your partner first met, was it in a place where gay people [lesbians] go to be with other gay people [lesbians]? (Such as a gay bar, gay [lesbian] community center, [steam bath], gay coffee house, etc.)" Sixty-two percent of the male couples had met in such a way ($N = 82$), as compared to only 25 percent of the lesbian couples ($N = 78$).

42. [On the original questionnaire, the gay men's responses indicate they are substantially less well matched in education level (intra-couple $r = .200$) than are the cohabitors ($r = .383$), the married couples ($r = .413$), and the lesbians ($r = .837$).]

43. [Among gay men together less than two years, the correlation between breaking up and the absolute difference in their education levels is $r = .161$. This means that the more dissimilar their educational backgrounds, the greater the chance of their breaking up.]

44. [Among lesbian couples together more than two years, the correlation between breaking up and their involvement in the gay world (going to gay places, living among many gay people, participation in the gay movement) is $r = .229$.]

45. This means that cohabitors who stay together a long time without marrying afford the best view of what cohabitation as a *way of life* means.

46. [Among cohabitors together less than two years, who then marry (low score), we find these traditional patterns: The man is bothered by the prospect of earning less than the woman (Relationship question 23h, $r = .205$); the woman feels that men should have more say in a couple's financial plans (Opinion statement 10, $r = .206$); and the woman believes in the male provider role ($r = .147$). Among couples together more than two years, who then marry, we find these patterns: The man feels that men should have more financial say ($r = .165$), and believes in the male provider role ($r = .169$); the woman rejects the idea of sex without love ($r = .167$), and she would be bothered if the man waited for her to initiate sex ($r = .150$). In all of these analyses the dependent variable is whether the couple married or continued to live together. Couples who broke up are not included in the analyses.]

47. [The correlations between marrying and wanting to spend more time with one's partner are: males: $r = .148$, and females: $r = .219$.]

48. [In couples together less than two years, marrying is correlated with possessiveness: men: $r = .175$; women: $r = .221$. These couples are also less likely to have an understanding that permits non-monogamous sex ($r = -.286$).]

49. [The correlations between marrying and endorsing pooling are: men in short relationships: $r = .164$; women in short relationships: $r = .231$; men in longer relationships: $r = .169$; women: $r = .260$. A positive correlation means that couples who favor pooling are more likely to marry.]

50. [Among cohabitors together more than two years, the correlation between marrying and the man's feeling his partner is sexy-looking is $r = .195$, and the correlation with his satisfaction with the quality of their sex life is $r = .172$. For all cohabiting couples, the correlation between marrying and the frequency of sex is $r = .155$.]

51. [In couples together less than two years, the correlation between marrying and the man finding the woman ambitious is $r = .167$, and with his considering her accomplished: $r = .209$. The correlation with the woman finding the man ambitious is $r = .208$. Among couples together more than two years, the correlation between marrying and the man finding the woman ambitious is $r = .152$.]

52. [Among lesbian couples who have broken up, the correlation between which woman wanted it to end and which is more forceful, aggressive, and outgoing (the signed differences between their self-ratings on the masculinity scale) is $r = .153$. The correlation with which woman did less housework (the difference between the two scores on the housework question) is $r = .240$.]

53. [Among gay men who broke up, the correlation between which man wanted the relationship to end and which was more powerful is $r = -.154$. The correlation with which is better educated (the signed difference between their education levels) is $r = -.312$. For which is more masculine, $r = -.365$; and for which has the higher income, $r = -.143$.]

54. [Among gay male couples who broke up, the correlation between which one wanted it to end and which is younger (the signed difference in ages) is $r = .324$. The correlation with which is more self-sufficient is $r = .225$; with which is more ambitious, $r = .184$; and with which is physically more attractive, $r = .190$.]

55. [Among cohabitors together less than two years, the correlation between breaking up and the equality of power is $r = -.174$; and with the equality of commitment it is $r = -.159$. Among couples together more than two years, the correlation between breaking up and the equality of commitment is $r = -.212$.]

56. [Among married couples the correlations between breaking up and the equality of power in short-term and long-term couples are $r = .064$, and $r = -.018$. The comparable correlations with equality of commitment are $r = -.022$ and $r = -.111$.]

# Appendix: Participants in the study

## Table 1: How couples learned of the study

|  | Married couples | Cohabiting couples | Gay male couples | Lesbian couples |
|---|---|---|---|---|
| Read about it in a publication or newspaper |  |  |  |  |
| Gay publication | — | — | 30% | 26% |
| Other | 58% | 72% | 18 | 19 |
| Heard the researchers talk on TV, radio, or public address | 34 | 23 | 10 | 9 |
| Heard the study described on TV or radio news | 18 | 14 | 4 | 3 |
| Learned about it in a personal conversation with the researchers | 1 | 3 | 3 | 2 |
| Learned about it from someone who had already participated or intended to participate | 4 | 5 | 23 | 27 |
| Heard about it from someone who knew about it but did not intend to participate | 1 | 2 | 4 | 5 |
| Saw a notice posted in a bar, supermarket, laundromat, etc. | 1 | 1 | 1 | 1 |
| Saw a notice posted in a gay bar, coffee house, community center, etc. | — | — | 9 | 13 |
| Other | 6 | 3 | 8 | 8 |
| Ever taken part in a study of gay people before | — | — | 16% | 18% |

Note: Based on Statistical Information questions 30 and 31. The percentages add up to more than 100 percent because of multiple responses.

## Table 2: Region

|  | Married couples | Cohabiting couples | Gay male couples | Lesbian couples |
|---|---|---|---|---|
| New England | 5% | 4% | 3% | 6% |
| Middle Atlantic | 18 | 22 | 22 | 15 |
| North Central | 23 | 14 | 8 | 10 |
| South Atlantic | 12 | 8 | 8 | 7 |
| South Central | 8 | 4 | 4 | 3 |
| Mountain | 5 | 5 | 2 | 4 |
| Pacific Northwest | 10 | 18 | 17 | 23 |
| California and Hawaii | 18 | 24 | 35 | 31 |
| U.S. territories, Canada, and other foreign | 1 | 1 | 1 | 1 |
| Number of couples | 3,574 | 642 | 957 | 772 |

*Note:* Based on Statistical Information question 9

*New England*: Maine, New Hampshire, Vermont, Massachusetts, Rhode Island, Connecticut. *Middle Atlantic*: New York, New Jersey, Pennsylvania.

*North Central*: Ohio, Indiana, Illinois, Michigan, Wisconsin, Minnesota, Iowa, Missouri, North Dakota, South Dakota, Nebraska, Kansas.

*South Atlantic*: Delaware, Maryland, District of Columbia, Virginia, West Virginia, North Carolina, South Carolina, Georgia, Florida.

*South Central*: Kentucky, Tennessee, Alabama, Mississippi, Arkansas, Louisiana, Oklahoma, Texas.

*Mountain*: Montana, Idaho, Wyoming, Colorado, New Mexico, Arizona, Utah, Nevada.

*Pacific Northwest*: Alaska, Oregon, Washington.

## Table 3: Number of years couple has lived together

|  | Married | Cohabiting | Gay male | Lesbian |
|---|---|---|---|---|
| Less than 2 years | 8% | 55% | 32% | 46% |
| Between 2 and 5 years | 19 | 34 | 29 | 32 |
| Between 5 and 10 years | 24 | 10 | 21 | 14 |
| Between 10 and 15 years | 13 | 1 | 8 | 5 |
| Between 15 and 20 years | 8 | 0 | 4 | 2 |
| Between 20 and 30 years | 14 | 0 | 4 | 1 |
| More than 30 years | 14 | 0 | 2 | * |
| Average years | 13.9 | 2.5 | 6.0 | 3.7 |
| Median years | 9.8 | 1.7 | 3.5 | 2.2 |
| Number of couples | 3,656 | 653 | 1,938 | 1,576 |

*Less than ½%          *Note*: Based on item 2c of the questionnaire

# Table 4: Age

| | Husbands | Wives | Cohabiting men | Cohabiting women | Gay men | Lesbians |
|---|---|---|---|---|---|---|
| Under 21 | 1% | 1% | 2% | 6% | 1% | 2% |
| Between 21 and 30 | 27 | 35 | 48 | 59 | 35 | 47 |
| Between 31 and 40 | 31 | 31 | 35 | 26 | 42 | 37 |
| Between 41 and 50 | 19 | 17 | 10 | 6 | 14 | 10 |
| Between 51 and 60 | 15 | 11 | 4 | 2 | 7 | 3 |
| Over 60 | 7 | 5 | 1 | 1 | 1 | 1 |
| Average age | 39.9 | 37.3 | 32.3 | 29.7 | 35.2 | 32.2 |
| Median age | 36.4 | 33.9 | 30.5 | 28.2 | 33.3 | 30.6 |
| Number of people | 3,638 | 3,634 | 649 | 650 | 1,927 | 1,568 |

*Note*: Based on item 1 of the questionnaire

# Table 5: Race

| | Husbands | Wives | Cohabiting men | Cohabiting women | Gay men | Lesbians |
|---|---|---|---|---|---|---|
| White | 96% | 97% | 94% | 96% | 94% | 95% |
| Black | 1 | 1 | 2 | 2 | 2 | 1 |
| Asian or Asian-American | 1 | 1 | * | 1 | 1 | 1 |
| Chicano or Mexican-American | 1 | 1 | 2 | * | 1 | 1 |
| Native American or Indian | * | * | * | * | * | 1 |
| Puerto Rican | * | * | * | * | * | 1 |
| Other | 1 | * | 1 | 1 | 1 | * |
| Number of people | 3,629 | 3,612 | 645 | 652 | 1,930 | 1,549 |

*Less than ½%

*Note*: Based on Statistical Information question 4

# Table 6: Education

|  | Husbands | Wives | Cohabiting men | Cohabiting women | Gay men | Lesbians |
|---|---|---|---|---|---|---|
| Twelve years or fewer | 13% | 19% | 14% | 15% | 12% | 12% |
| Some college | 20 | 29 | 28 | 30 | 22 | 29 |
| Bachelor's degree | 34 | 33 | 31 | 36 | 38 | 32 |
| Higher degree | 33 | 19 | 27 | 19 | 28 | 27 |
| Average years of education | 15.5 | 14.9 | 15.3 | 15.1 | 15.4 | 15.7 |
| Number of people | 3,644 | 3,629 | 651 | 651 | 1,930 | 1,559 |

*Note*: Based on Statistical Information questions 1a and 1c

# Table 7: Employment

|  | Husbands | Wives | Cohabiting men | Cohabiting women | Gay men | Lesbians |
|---|---|---|---|---|---|---|
| Employed full time | 86% | 38% | 76% | 63% | 78% | 69% |
| Employed part time | 5 | 23 | 13 | 22 | 11 | 16 |
| Employed but not at work (illness, strike, etc.) | 1 | 1 | 1 | * | 1 | 2 |
| Unemployed | 2 | 10 | 9 | 11 | 7 | 11 |
| Retired | 6 | 3 | 1 | * | 2 | 1 |
| Full-time care of household | * | 25 | 0 | 3 | * | 1 |
| Number of people | 3,632 | 3,600 | 650 | 651 | 1,921 | 1,554 |

*Less than ½%

*Note*: Based on Statistical Information question 2a

# Table 8: Occupation

| | Husbands | Wives | Male cohabitors | Female cohabitors | Gay men | Lesbians |
|---|---|---|---|---|---|---|
| Professional, technical, and related | 44% | 35% | 41% | 39% | 42% | 44% |
| Managers and administrators | 29 | 11 | 20 | 12 | 25 | 15 |
| Sales | 7 | 4 | 7 | 5 | 7 | 4 |
| Clerical and related | 3 | 17 | 5 | 24 | 11 | 16 |
| Crafts and related | 7 | 1 | 12 | 2 | 4 | 5 |
| Operatives | 3 | 1 | 6 | 3 | 2 | 4 |
| Laborers | 2 | * | 2 | 1 | 1 | 2 |
| Farm workers | 1 | * | 1 | 0 | * | * |
| Service workers | 3 | 5 | 4 | 8 | 7 | 8 |
| Students | 1 | 1 | 2 | 3 | 1 | 1 |
| Homemakers (full time) | * | 25 | 0 | 3 | * | 1 |
| Other | * | 0 | * | 0 | * | 0 |
| Number of people | 3,540 | 3,434 | 634 | 631 | 1,820 | 1,499 |

*Less than ½%

*Note*: Based on Statistical Information questions 2a, 2d, and 2e. If an individual answered, "Taking care of the household is my full-time job," on question 2a, his or her answers about a former occupation were disregarded.

# Table 9: Annual personal income

| | Husbands | Wives | Cohabiting men | Cohabiting women | Gay men | Lesbians |
|---|---|---|---|---|---|---|
| Under $5,000 | 4% | 47% | 13% | 22% | 10% | 17% |
| Between $5,000 and $9,999 | 6 | 17 | 15 | 26 | 18 | 25 |
| Between $10,000 and $14,999 | 15 | 18 | 21 | 26 | 27 | 27 |
| Between $15,000 and $24,999 | 35 | 13 | 28 | 21 | 28 | 23 |
| Between $25,000 and $49,999 | 31 | 4 | 18 | 4 | 14 | 7 |
| $50,000 and above | 9 | 1 | 5 | 1 | 3 | 1 |
| Number of people | 3,608 | 3,577 | 644 | 651 | 1,909 | 1,550 |

*Note*: Based on Statistical Information question 13a

# Table 10: Marital status

|  | Cohabiting men | Cohabiting women | Gay men | Lesbians |
|---|---|---|---|---|
| Single, never married | 50% | 55% | 83% | 74% |
| Single, previously married | 44 | 42 | 15 | 22 |
| Currently married, but separated from spouse | 6 | 3 | 2 | 4 |
| Number of people | 649 | 650 | 1,916 | 1,542 |

*Note*: Based on Statistical Information question 14a

# Table 11: Number of marriages

|  | Husbands | Wives | Cohabiting men | Cohabiting women | Gay men | Lesbians |
|---|---|---|---|---|---|---|
| None | — | — | 50% | 55% | 83% | 74% |
| One | 80% | 83% | 41 | 36 | 15 | 22 |
| Two | 17 | 15 | 8 | 7 | 1 | 3 |
| Three | 2 | 2 | 1 | 1 | * | 1 |
| Four or more | 1 | * | * | * | 0 | * |
| Number of people | 3,637 | 3,632 | 649 | 650 | 1,916 | 1,542 |

*Less than ½%

*Note*: Based on Statistical Information question 14d

## Table 12: Children

| | Husbands | Wives | Male cohabitors | Female cohabitors | Lesbians |
|---|---|---|---|---|---|
| *Children from past or current relationship* | | | | | |
| One | 16% | 17% | 11% | 9% | 5% |
| Two | 28 | 27 | 13 | 11 | 5 |
| Three | 14 | 13 | 7 | 4 | 2 |
| Four | 7 | 7 | 1 | 2 | 1 |
| Five | 2 | 2 | 1 | * | * |
| Six or more | 2 | 2 | 1 | * | * |
| None | 31 | 32 | 66 | 74 | 86 |
| *Children living at home more than six months per year* | | | | | |
| One | 21% | 22% | 4% | 8% | 4% |
| Two | 18 | 19 | 1 | 7 | 2 |
| Three | 6 | 7 | 1 | 1 | 1 |
| Four | 2 | 2 | 0 | * | * |
| Five | * | * | * | * | * |
| Six or more | * | * | 0 | 0 | * |
| None | 53 | 50 | 94 | 84 | 92 |

*Less than ½%

*Note*: Based on Family Relations question 2. Gay men were not asked about children.

## Table 13: Current religious preference

| | Husbands | Wives | Cohabiting men | Cohabiting women | Gay men | Lesbians |
|---|---|---|---|---|---|---|
| Protestant | 38% | 43% | 16% | 20% | 23% | 19% |
| Roman Catholic | 14 | 16 | 8 | 11 | 14 | 12 |
| Jewish | 13 | 13 | 14 | 12 | 6 | 8 |
| Other | 6 | 6 | 9 | 9 | 8 | 10 |
| No religious preference | 29 | 22 | 53 | 48 | 49 | 51 |
| Number of people | 3,620 | 3,610 | 640 | 646 | 1,920 | 1,548 |

*Note*: Based on Statistical Information question 8a

# Table 14: Church or synagogue attendance

| | Husbands | Wives | Cohabiting men | Cohabiting women | Gay men | Lesbians |
|---|---|---|---|---|---|---|
| Once a week or more | 21% | 24% | 3% | 4% | 9% | 6% |
| Once a month or more, but less than weekly | 13 | 15 | 4 | 5 | 7 | 7 |
| Once a year or more, but less than monthly | 26 | 25 | 26 | 27 | 24 | 23 |
| Less than once a year | 40 | 36 | 67 | 64 | 60 | 64 |
| Number of people | 3,631 | 3,632 | 645 | 647 | 1,910 | 1,559 |

*Note*: Based on Statistical Information question 8b

# Table 15: Political outlook

| | Husbands | Wives | Cohabiting men | Cohabiting women | Gay men | Lesbians |
|---|---|---|---|---|---|---|
| Extremely conservative | 4% | 3% | 3% | 1% | 2% | 1% |
| Conservative | 22 | 15 | 10 | 4 | 6 | 4 |
| Moderate | 41 | 44 | 33 | 34 | 28 | 23 |
| Liberal | 26 | 31 | 36 | 44 | 43 | 42 |
| Extremely liberal | 7 | 7 | 18 | 17 | 21 | 30 |
| Number of people | 3,608 | 3,601 | 635 | 643 | 1,916 | 1,535 |

*Note*: Based on Lifestyle question 6

## Table 16: Involvement in organized gay and lesbian activities

| | Gay and lesbian activities | | Lesbian activities |
| --- | --- | --- | --- |
| | Gay men | Lesbians | Lesbians |
| Very involved | 15% | 9% | 10% |
| Somewhat involved | 21 | 23 | 26 |
| Slightly involved | 26 | 25 | 23 |
| Not at all involved | 38 | 43 | 41 |
| Number of people | 1,927 | 1,545 | 1,520 |

Note: Based on Lifestyle questions 12a and 12b

## Table 17: Openness about homosexuality

| | Gay men | Lesbians |
| --- | --- | --- |
| "I do not care who knows I am gay." | 36% | 23% |
| "There are a few heterosexuals I do not want to know I am gay." | 41 | 42 |
| "There are a large number of heterosexuals I do not want to know I am gay." | 21 | 33 |
| "I do not want any heterosexuals to know I am gay." | 2 | 2 |
| Number of people | 1,919 | 1,552 |

Note: Based on Lifestyle question 18

## Table 18: Gay neighbors and co-workers

| | Neighbors | | Co-workers | |
| --- | --- | --- | --- | --- |
| | Gay men | Lesbians | Gay men | Lesbians |
| All | 1% | 2% | 4% | 3% |
| Most | 10 | 2 | 5 | 5 |
| Half | 10 | 3 | 6 | 5 |
| Few | 51 | 46 | 60 | 56 |
| None | 28 | 47 | 25 | 31 |
| Number of people | 1,905 | 1,528 | 1,751 | 1,373 |

Note: Based on Lifestyle questions 14 and 15a

# COUPLES SURVEY

Dr. Philip W. Blumstein/Dr. Pepper Schwartz

## The Questionnaire

All couples began their participation with questionnaires of approximately thirty-eight pages, including questions on a variety of subjects. The four different versions of the basic questionnaire differed little. Married and cohabiting couples received one Male Questionnaire and one Female Questionnaire. The only basic differences between these two were the gender of the pronouns used throughout and a few questions about giving and receiving alimony or child-support payments. Several special sections within each questionnaire specifically queried married people only or cohabitors only. The lesbian version used only female pronouns and asked some extra questions about lesbian life-styles, and the gay-male version had male pronouns and special gay-male questions. An important consideration in creating the questionnaires had been to ensure that all types of couples were asked exactly the same questions in exactly the same way. What follows is a composite of the four kinds of questionnaires, specifically designed to enable anyone to answer the questions, whatever his or her type of couple relationship.

The symbols appearing in front of some of the questions indicate to whom they were addressed:

* gay male
# lesbian
** heterosexual
† heterosexual female
@ heterosexual male
$ cohabitor

Questions with no symbols were asked of everyone.

The composite questionnaire is included here for two reasons: first, so that interested readers can see the specific kinds of information we had access to in the survey. Second, readers may want to fill it out themselves for their own purposes. However, please do not send it in to the authors; it will not be used as part of any new survey.

Copyright © 1978 Philip W. Blumstein and Pepper Schwartz

1.  In what year were you born?

    _____

** 2a. Are you and your partner married?
    **1** Yes
    **2** No (IF "NO," SKIP TO QUESTION 3a.)

** b.  How long ago did you and [he] [she] get married?

    _____years    _____months

3a. How long ago did you and your partner first meet?

    _____ years    _____ months

b.  How long ago did you and [he] [she] begin "going out together"?

    _____ years    _____ months

c.  How long ago did you and [he] [she] begin living together?

    _____ years    _____ months

4.  When you and your partner *began* living together, who moved? (PLEASE CIRCLE THE NUMBER IN FRONT OF YO
    ANSWER.)
    **1** I moved in with [him] [her]
    **2** [He] [she] moved in with me
    **3** We moved together into a new residence

5a. Do you and your partner currently live together full-time?
    **1** Yes (IF "YES," SKIP TO QUESTION 6a)
    **2** No

b.  If "no," about how many days each week do you live apart?
    _____ days

6a. Does your job involve travel that keeps you away from home more than two days at a time?
    **1** Yes
    **2** No (IF "NO," SKIP TO QUESTION 7a.)
    **X** I do not have a job (SKIP TO QUESTION 7a.)

b.  How many days were you away from your partner in the last year because of work-related travel?
    **1** Less than one week
    **2** One to three weeks
    **3** Three to six weeks
    **4** More than six weeks

7a. Has there been any extended period(s) of time when you and your partner lived apart after you began living together?
    **1** Yes
    **2** No (IF "NO," SKIP TO THE NEXT SECTION "IDEAL RELATIONSHIP.")

b.  If "yes," how many such periods have there been?

    _____

c.  What, approximately, is the *total* length of time you were apart?

    _____ years    _____ months

d. What was the reason(s) for your living apart? *(CIRCLE ALL THAT APPLY.)*

  **1** Job-related reasons

  **2** Military service

  **3** Personal differences (for example, trial separation, "broke up" for a period of time, etc.)

  **4** One or both of us "away" at school

  **5** Other (specify) _____

  _____

  _____

---

# IDEAL RELATIONSHIP

1. In an *ideal* relationship, how important to you would each of the following be? Tell us about the kind of relationship you would like to have, whether this describes your current relationship or not. (On each line, circle *the one* number—**1** to **9**—that most closely fits your true feelings. Circle **1** if you think that the statement is *extremely important,* circle **9** if you think it is *not at all important,* or circle one of the numbers between **1** and **9** if your feelings are in between.)

| | Extremely important | | | | | | | | Not at all important |
|---|---|---|---|---|---|---|---|---|---|
| a. That we can confide all of our personal feelings to each other .................. | 1 | 2 | 3 | 4 | 5 | 6 | 7 | 8 | 9 |
| b. That our relationship is permanent .............. | 1 | 2 | 3 | 4 | 5 | 6 | 7 | 8 | 9 |
| c. That my partner is well liked by my friends ............ | 1 | 2 | 3 | 4 | 5 | 6 | 7 | 8 | 9 |
| d. That we both have the same hobbies and interests ...... | 1 | 2 | 3 | 4 | 5 | 6 | 7 | 8 | 9 |
| e. That we both have the same feelings about women's issues .................. | 1 | 2 | 3 | 4 | 5 | 6 | 7 | 8 | 9 |
| f. That our relationship does not interfere with other important parts of my life ........... | 1 | 2 | 3 | 4 | 5 | 6 | 7 | 8 | 9 |
| g. That I have someone to grow old with ............... | 1 | 2 | 3 | 4 | 5 | 6 | 7 | 8 | 9 |
| h. That my partner is sexually faithful to me ............ | 1 | 2 | 3 | 4 | 5 | 6 | 7 | 8 | 9 |
| i. That I am sexually faithful to my partner .............. | 1 | 2 | 3 | 4 | 5 | 6 | 7 | 8 | 9 |
| j. That my partner provides me with financial security ...... | 1 | 2 | 3 | 4 | 5 | 6 | 7 | 8 | 9 |
| k. That I find my partner sexually compatible .............. | 1 | 2 | 3 | 4 | 5 | 6 | 7 | 8 | 9 |

| | | Extremely Important | | | | | | | | Not at all |
|---|---|---|---|---|---|---|---|---|---|---|
| l. | That we both have the same social class background .... | 1 | 2 | 3 | 4 | 5 | 6 | 7 | 8 | 9 |
| m. | That I am well liked by my partner's friends .......... | 1 | 2 | 3 | 4 | 5 | 6 | 7 | 8 | 9 |
| *#n. | That we both have the same feelings about gay rights .... | 1 | 2 | 3 | 4 | 5 | 6 | 7 | 8 | 9 |
| *#o. | That my partner can pass as straight when we are among straight people ........... | 1 | 2 | 3 | 4 | 5 | 6 | 7 | 8 | 9 |

2.  How much of each quality would you want in an *ideal* partner? Tell us about the kind of partner you would like to have, whether this describes your current partner or not.

| | | Extremely | | | | | | | | Not at all |
|---|---|---|---|---|---|---|---|---|---|---|
| a. | Forceful ................. | 1 | 2 | 3 | 4 | 5 | 6 | 7 | 8 | 9 |
| b. | Sexy-looking ............ | 1 | 2 | 3 | 4 | 5 | 6 | 7 | 8 | 9 |
| c. | Affectionate ............. | 1 | 2 | 3 | 4 | 5 | 6 | 7 | 8 | 9 |
| d. | Aggressive .............. | 1 | 2 | 3 | 4 | 5 | 6 | 7 | 8 | 9 |
| e. | Romantic ............... | 1 | 2 | 3 | 4 | 5 | 6 | 7 | 8 | 9 |
| f. | "Movie star" good-looking . | 1 | 2 | 3 | 4 | 5 | 6 | 7 | 8 | 9 |
| g. | Understanding of others .... | 1 | 2 | 3 | 4 | 5 | 6 | 7 | 8 | 9 |
| h. | Ambitious ............... | 1 | 2 | 3 | 4 | 5 | 6 | 7 | 8 | 9 |
| i. | Compassionate ........... | 1 | 2 | 3 | 4 | 5 | 6 | 7 | 8 | 9 |
| j. | Muscular build .......... | 1 | 2 | 3 | 4 | 5 | 6 | 7 | 8 | 9 |
| k. | Accomplished in [his] [her] chosen field ............. | 1 | 2 | 3 | 4 | 5 | 6 | 7 | 8 | 9 |
| l. | Expresses tender feelings easily .................. | 1 | 2 | 3 | 4 | 5 | 6 | 7 | 8 | 9 |
| m. | Shy .................... | 1 | 2 | 3 | 4 | 5 | 6 | 7 | 8 | 9 |
| n. | Athletic ................. | 1 | 2 | 3 | 4 | 5 | 6 | 7 | 8 | 9 |
| o. | Outgoing ............... | 1 | 2 | 3 | 4 | 5 | 6 | 7 | 8 | 9 |
| p. | Self-sufficient ............ | 1 | 2 | 3 | 4 | 5 | 6 | 7 | 8 | 9 |

3.  What would your *ideal* partner be like in relation to you?

| | | | | | | | | | | | |
|---|---|---|---|---|---|---|---|---|---|---|---|
| a. | Much *taller* than I am | 1 | 2 | 3 | 4 | 5 | 6 | 7 | 8 | 9 | Much *shorter* than I am |
| b. | Much *more* intelligent than I am | 1 | 2 | 3 | 4 | 5 | 6 | 7 | 8 | 9 | Much *less* intelligent than I am |

| | | Extremely | | | | | | | | | Not at all |
|---|---|---|---|---|---|---|---|---|---|---|---|

*# c. Much *more* masculine than I am    1   2   3   4   5   6   7   8   **9**   Much *less* masculine than I am

d. Much *younger* than I am   1   2   3   4   5   6   7   8   **9**   Much *older* than I am

*# e. Much *more* feminine than I am    1   2   3   4   5   6   7   8   **9**   Much *less* feminine than I am

f. Physically much *stronger* than I am    1   2   3   4   5   6   7   8   **9**   Physically much *weaker* than I am

4. What kind of person would you *ideally* like to be yourself?

| | | Extremely | | | | | | | | Not at all |
|---|---|---|---|---|---|---|---|---|---|---|
| a. | Outgoing | 1 | 2 | 3 | 4 | 5 | 6 | 7 | 8 | 9 |
| b. | "Movie star" good-looking | 1 | 2 | 3 | 4 | 5 | 6 | 7 | 8 | 9 |
| c. | Compassionate | 1 | 2 | 3 | 4 | 5 | 6 | 7 | 8 | 9 |
| d. | Ambitious | 1 | 2 | 3 | 4 | 5 | 6 | 7 | 8 | 9 |
| e. | Romantic | 1 | 2 | 3 | 4 | 5 | 6 | 7 | 8 | 9 |
| f. | Sexy-looking | 1 | 2 | 3 | 4 | 5 | 6 | 7 | 8 | 9 |
| g. | Express tender feelings easily | 1 | 2 | 3 | 4 | 5 | 6 | 7 | 8 | 9 |
| h. | Aggressive | 1 | 2 | 3 | 4 | 5 | 6 | 7 | 8 | 9 |
| i. | Affectionate | 1 | 2 | 3 | 4 | 5 | 6 | 7 | 8 | 9 |
| j. | Athletic | 1 | 2 | 3 | 4 | 5 | 6 | 7 | 8 | 9 |
| k. | Self-sufficient | 1 | 2 | 3 | 4 | 5 | 6 | 7 | 8 | 9 |
| l. | Understanding of others | 1 | 2 | 3 | 4 | 5 | 6 | 7 | 8 | 9 |
| m. | Shy | 1 | 2 | 3 | 4 | 5 | 6 | 7 | 8 | 9 |
| n. | Muscular build | 1 | 2 | 3 | 4 | 5 | 6 | 7 | 8 | 9 |
| o. | Forceful | 1 | 2 | 3 | 4 | 5 | 6 | 7 | 8 | 9 |
| p. | Accomplished in my chosen field | 1 | 2 | 3 | 4 | 5 | 6 | 7 | 8 | 9 |

## OPINION STATEMENTS

The following are general statements about [couples]** [gay male couples who live together]* [lesbian couples who live together]# but not necessarily about *your* relationship. [*If you and your partner are married*, think of the statements as referring to married couples. *If you and your partner are not married*, think of the statements as referring to unmarried couples who live together.]** How much do you agree or disagree with each statement?

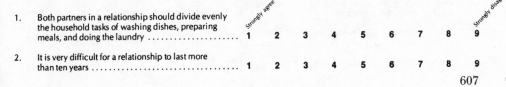

1. Both partners in a relationship should divide evenly the household tasks of washing dishes, preparing meals, and doing the laundry   *Strongly agree*   1   2   3   4   5   6   7   8   9   *Strongly disagree*

2. It is very difficult for a relationship to last more than ten years   1   2   3   4   5   6   7   8   9

3. If both partners work full-time, both of their career plans should be considered equally in determining where they will live ............................ 1 2 3 4 5 6 7 8 9

4. The two partners should share the responsibility for earning a living for the household ................. 1 2 3 4 5 6 7 8 9

5. The two partners should pool all their property and financial assets ....................:........... 1 2 3 4 5 6 7 8 9

6. A member of a couple that has been together a long time should not accept a job he or she wants in a distant city, if it means ending the relationship...... 1 2 3 4 5 6 7 8 9

7. Couples should try to make their relationship last a lifetime ........................................ 1 2 3 4 5 6 7 8 9

The following statements refer to [heterosexual]*# married couples. How much do you agree or disagree with each?

8. It is better if the man works to support the household and the woman takes care of the home ............. 1 2 3 4 5 6 7 8 9

9. Marriage is a lifetime relationship and should never be terminated except under extreme circumstances ..... 1 2 3 4 5 6 7 8 9

10. Even if the wife works the man should have major responsibility for the couple's financial plans ........ 1 2 3 4 5 6 7 8 9

11. When there are small children in the home, it is better for the mother not to work........................ 1 2 3 4 5 6 7 8 9

12. It is better for parents to break up than expose children to an unhappy marriage ................. 1 2 3 4 5 6 7 8 9

13. Extramarital sexual relations are always wrong...... 1 2 3 4 5 6 7 8 9

How much do you agree or disagree with the following statements?

14. There are times when I am with my friends and I do not want my partner along ....................... 1 2 3 4 5 6 7 8 9

15. It is important to me that my partner spend some time without me .................................... 1 2 3 4 5 6 7 8 9

16. There is nothing wrong with a man and woman living together without getting married ................. 1 2 3 4 5 6 7 8 9

17. There should be stronger laws against the selling of erotic books and magazines ...................... 1 2 3 4 5 6 7 8 9

18. Sex education should be taught in public schools .... 1 2 3 4 5 6 7 8 9

608

| | | Strongly agree | | | | | | | | Strongly disagree |
|---|---|:---:|:---:|:---:|:---:|:---:|:---:|:---:|:---:|:---:|
| 19. | A man and woman should not have sexual relations unless they are in love .......................... | 1 | 2 | 3 | 4 | 5 | 6 | 7 | 8 | 9 |
| 20. | There should be laws prohibiting discrimination against lesbians and homosexuals in employment and housing .................................. | 1 | 2 | 3 | 4 | 5 | 6 | 7 | 8 | 9 |
| 21. | Public schools should present positive portrayals of homosexuals and lesbians ...................... | 1 | 2 | 3 | 4 | 5 | 6 | 7 | 8 | 9 |
| 22. | Being a homosexual or lesbian should disqualify a person from being a schoolteacher................ | 1 | 2 | 3 | 4 | 5 | 6 | 7 | 8 | 9 |

---

## RELATIONSHIP QUESTIONS

1. How satisfied are you with these parts of your relationship?

| | | Extremely satisfied | | | | | | | | Not at all satisfied | Does not apply to our situation |
|---|---|:---:|:---:|:---:|:---:|:---:|:---:|:---:|:---:|:---:|:---:|
| a. | Our moral and religious beliefs and practices ....... | 1 | 2 | 3 | 4 | 5 | 6 | 7 | 8 | 9 | |
| b. | How my partner's job affects our relationship .......... | 1 | 2 | 3 | 4 | 5 | 6 | 7 | 8 | 9 | X |
| c. | How we communicate ..... | 1 | 2 | 3 | 4 | 5 | 6 | 7 | 8 | 9 | |
| d. | How my job affects our relationship .............. | 1 | 2 | 3 | 4 | 5 | 6 | 7 | 8 | 9 | X |
| **e. | My partner's attitudes about having children.......... | 1 | 2 | 3 | 4 | 5 | 6 | 7 | 8 | 9 | |
| f. | How the house is kept...... | 1 | 2 | 3 | 4 | 5 | 6 | 7 | 8 | 9 | |
| g. | The amount of influence I have over the decisions we make ................. | 1 | 2 | 3 | 4 | 5 | 6 | 7 | 8 | 9 | |
| h. | Our social life ............ | 1 | 2 | 3 | 4 | 5 | 6 | 7 | 8 | 9 | |
| i. | The amount of money coming in ............... | 1 | 2 | 3 | 4 | 5 | 6 | 7 | 8 | 9 | |
| j. | How we express affection for each other ............ | 1 | 2 | 3 | 4 | 5 | 6 | 7 | 8 | 9 | |
| k. | How we manage our finances ................ | 1 | 2 | 3 | 4 | 5 | 6 | 7 | 8 | 9 | |
| **#l. | How we raise the children .. | 1 | 2 | 3 | 4 | 5 | 6 | 7 | 8 | 9 | X |
| m. | Our sex-life .............. | 1 | 2 | 3 | 4 | 5 | 6 | 7 | 8 | 9 | |
| 2. | How satisfied are you with your relationship in general? ................ | 1 | 2 | 3 | 4 | 5 | 6 | 7 | 8 | 9 | |
| 3. | How would *your partner* rate [his] [her] satisfaction with your relationship in general? | 1 | 2 | 3 | 4 | 5 | 6 | 7 | 8 | 9 | |

4. Who is more likely to do each of the following things in your relationship, you or your partner?

*I do this much more* ... *We do this equally* ... *[He] [She] does this much more*

| | | I do this much more | | | | We do this equally | | | | [He][She] does this much more |
|---|---|---|---|---|---|---|---|---|---|---|
| a. | Pay the other compliments ..................... | 1 | 2 | 3 | 4 | 5 | 6 | 7 | 8 | 9 |
| b. | Say that one sees the other's point of view when we are having an argument ........................ | 1 | 2 | 3 | 4 | 5 | 6 | 7 | 8 | 9 |
| c. | Do favors for the other, even when they are not asked for ................................... | 1 | 2 | 3 | 4 | 5 | 6 | 7 | 8 | 9 |
| d. | Begin to talk about what is troubling our relationship when there is tension between us ................ | 1 | 2 | 3 | 4 | 5 | 6 | 7 | 8 | 9 |
| e. | Give the other a spontaneous hug or kiss when something good or exciting has occurred ............... | 1 | 2 | 3 | 4 | 5 | 6 | 7 | 8 | 9 |
| f. | See oneself as running the show in our relationship ... | 1 | 2 | 3 | 4 | 5 | 6 | 7 | 8 | 9 |
| g. | Offer advice when the other is faced with a problem .. | 1 | 2 | 3 | 4 | 5 | 6 | 7 | 8 | 9 |
| h. | Sense that the other is disturbed about something .... | 1 | 2 | 3 | 4 | 5 | 6 | 7 | 8 | 9 |
| i. | Give in to the other's wishes when one of us wants to do something the other does not want to do ........ | 1 | 2 | 3 | 4 | 5 | 6 | 7 | 8 | 9 |
| j. | Take on a problem in a rational rather than emotional way ............................... | 1 | 2 | 3 | 4 | 5 | 6 | 7 | 8 | 9 |
| k. | Contribute the most in reaching a solution when we face a dilemma............................... | 1 | 2 | 3 | 4 | 5 | 6 | 7 | 8 | 9 |
| l. | Criticize the other's judgment .................... | 1 | 2 | 3 | 4 | 5 | 6 | 7 | 8 | 9 |
| m. | Keep one's feelings to oneself .................... | 1 | 2 | 3 | 4 | 5 | 6 | 7 | 8 | 9 |
| n. | Let the other know one would like to have sex ....... | 1 | 2 | 3 | 4 | 5 | 6 | 7 | 8 | 9 |
| o. | Refuse to have sex ............................. | 1 | 2 | 3 | 4 | 5 | 6 | 7 | 8 | 9 |

*I much more* ... *Both equally* ... *[He][She]*

| | | I much more | | | | Both equally | | | | [He][She] |
|---|---|---|---|---|---|---|---|---|---|---|
| 5. | In general, who has more say about important decisions affecting your relationship, you or your partner? ................................ | 1 | 2 | 3 | 4 | 5 | 6 | 7 | 8 | 9 |
| 6. | Who do you think *should* have the final say about important decisions affecting your relationship, you or your partner? ............................... | 1 | 2 | 3 | 4 | 5 | 6 | 7 | 8 | 9 |
| 7. | Who is more committed to the relationship, you or your partner? ............................... | 1 | 2 | 3 | 4 | 5 | 6 | 7 | 8 | 9 |
| 8. | Who has altered his or her habits and ways of doing things more to please the other, you or your partner?................................. | 1 | 2 | 3 | 4 | 5 | 6 | 7 | 8 | 9 |

9. Certain household tasks are necessary to keep things running smoothly. Who does each of these tasks more often, you or your partner?

| | | I do this all of the time | | | | We do this equally | | | | [He] [She] does this all of the time | Neither of us does this |
|---|---|---|---|---|---|---|---|---|---|---|---|
| a. | Repairing things around the house ............... | 1 | 2 | 3 | 4 | 5 | 6 | 7 | 8 | 9 | X |
| b. | Doing the dishes ......... | 1 | 2 | 3 | 4 | 5 | 6 | 7 | 8 | 9 | X |
| c. | Cooking breakfast ........ | 1 | 2 | 3 | 4 | 5 | 6 | 7 | 8 | 9 | X |
| d. | Cooking the evening meal .. | 1 | 2 | 3 | 4 | 5 | 6 | 7 | 8 | 9 | X |
| e. | Vacuuming the carpets ..... | 1 | 2 | 3 | 4 | 5 | 6 | 7 | 8 | 9 | X |
| f. | Doing the laundry ......... | 1 | 2 | 3 | 4 | 5 | 6 | 7 | 8 | 9 | X |
| g. | Making arrangements to have repairs done around the house ................. | 1 | 2 | 3 | 4 | 5 | 6 | 7 | 8 | 9 | X |
| h. | Making complaints to the landlord/lady ............. | 1 | 2 | 3 | 4 | 5 | 6 | 7 | 8 | 9 | X |
| i. | Cleaning the bathroom ..... | 1 | 2 | 3 | 4 | 5 | 6 | 7 | 8 | 9 | X |
| j. | Caring for pets ........... | 1 | 2 | 3 | 4 | 5 | 6 | 7 | 8 | 9 | X |
| k. | Taking out the trash ........ | 1 | 2 | 3 | 4 | 5 | 6 | 7 | 8 | 9 | X |
| l. | Doing the grocery shopping | 1 | 2 | 3 | 4 | 5 | 6 | 7 | 8 | 9 | X |
| m. | Taking care of the lawn ..... | 1 | 2 | 3 | 4 | 5 | 6 | 7 | 8 | 9 | X |
| n. | Ironing my clothes ......... | 1 | 2 | 3 | 4 | 5 | 6 | 7 | 8 | 9 | X |
| o. | Mixing drinks for company . | 1 | 2 | 3 | 4 | 5 | 6 | 7 | 8 | 9 | X |
| p. | Driving the car when we are going somewhere in town together ................. | 1 | 2 | 3 | 4 | 5 | 6 | 7 | 8 | 9 | X |
| #** q. | Punishing the children ..... | 1 | 2 | 3 | 4 | 5 | 6 | 7 | 8 | 9 | X |
| #** r. | Taking the children to their activities and appointments . | 1 | 2 | 3 | 4 | 5 | 6 | 7 | 8 | 9 | X |
| #** s. | Playing with the children ... | 1 | 2 | 3 | 4 | 5 | 6 | 7 | 8 | 9 | X |

10. Why do you and your partner divide household tasks in the way that you have indicated above?

_____
_____
_____
_____
_____

| | | Extremely satisfied | | | | | | | | Not at all satisfied | I don't do household chores |
|---|---|---|---|---|---|---|---|---|---|---|---|
| 11. | In general, how much satisfaction do you get from doing household chores? ........ | 1 | 2 | 3 | 4 | 5 | 6 | 7 | 8 | 9 | X |

611

12. How often do you and your partner perform these tasks *together* (at the same time)?

| | Always | | | | Half the time | | | | Never | Neither ever |
|---|---|---|---|---|---|---|---|---|---|---|
| a. Cooking meals . . . . . . . . . . . | 1 | 2 | 3 | 4 | 5 | 6 | 7 | 8 | 9 | X |
| b. Taking care of the yard . . . . . | 1 | 2 | 3 | 4 | 5 | 6 | 7 | 8 | 9 | X |
| c. Doing household cleaning . . | 1 | 2 | 3 | 4 | 5 | 6 | 7 | 8 | 9 | X |
| d. Doing the grocery shopping | 1 | 2 | 3 | 4 | 5 | 6 | 7 | 8 | 9 | X |

13. On the average, how many hours a week do you personally spend on household chores (including cooking, grocery shopping, laundry, etc.)?

   1 None
   2 Five hours or less
   3 6 to 10 hours
   4 11 to 20 hours
   5 21 to 30 hours
   6 31 to 40 hours
   7 41 to 50 hours
   8 51 to 60 hours
   9 61 or more

14. On the average, how many hours a week do you have *hired help* doing indoor household work?

   1 None
   2 One or two hours
   3 3 to 5 hours
   4 6 to 10 hours
   5 11 to 15 hours
   6 More than 15 hours

#**15. On the average, how many hours a week are indoor household chores done by children living with you?

   1 None
   2 One or two hours
   3 3 to 5 hours
   4 6 to 10 hours
   5 11 to 15 hours
   6 More than 15 hours
   X No children living with us

16. Considering the chores in your household, do you feel your partner does [his] [her] "fair share"? . . . . . .

| Much more than [his] [her] fair share | | | | Exactly [his] [her] fair share | | | | Much le [her] s |
|---|---|---|---|---|---|---|---|---|
| 1 | 2 | 3 | 4 | 5 | 6 | 7 | 8 | 9 |

17. For each of the different decisions listed below, first tell us *(ON THE LEFT SIDE OF THE LINE)* who usually has the *most influence*. Then tell us *(ON THE RIGHT SIDE OF THE LINE)* whether you feel each decision is a *major one* or a *minor one.*

| | Who Usually Has Most Influence? | | | | | | | | | | Major or Minor Decision? | | | | | | | | |
|---|---|---|---|---|---|---|---|---|---|---|---|---|---|---|---|---|---|---|---|
| | I have all | | We have equal influence | | | [He] [She] has all | | We never make this decision | | Very major | | | | | | | | Very mino |
| a. What groceries to buy . . . . . . . . . . . . . . . | 1 | 2 | 3 | 4 | 5 | 6 | 7 | 8 | 9 | X | 1 | 2 | 3 | 4 | 5 | 6 | 7 | 8 | 9 |
| b. How to decorate our home . . . . . . . . . . . . | 1 | 2 | 3 | 4 | 5 | 6 | 7 | 8 | 9 | X | 1 | 2 | 3 | 4 | 5 | 6 | 7 | 8 | 9 |

|  | | I have all | | We have equal influence | | | | [He] [She] has all | We never make this decision | | Very major | | | | | | | Very minor |
|---|---|---|---|---|---|---|---|---|---|---|---|---|---|---|---|---|---|---|---|

c. Where to go on a
vacation . . . . . . . . . . . 1  2  3  4  5  6  7  8  9  X | 1  2  3  4  5  6  7  8  9

d. When to go out
to eat . . . . . . . . . . . . . 1  2  3  4  5  6  7  8  9  X | 1  2  3  4  5  6  7  8  9

e. Whether to move to
another city, state
or country . . . . . . . . . 1  2  3  4  5  6  7  8  9  X | 1  2  3  4  5  6  7  8  9

f. Where to go out for
an evening . . . . . . . . . 1  2  3  4  5  6  7  8  9  X | 1  2  3  4  5  6  7  8  9

g. Whom to invite to
our home . . . . . . . . . . . 1  2  3  4  5  6  7  8  9  X | 1  2  3  4  5  6  7  8  9

h. How to discipline the
children . . . . . . . . . . . . 1  2  3  4  5  6  7  8  9  X | 1  2  3  4  5  6  7  8  9

i. How much money to
spend on groceries . . . 1  2  3  4  5  6  7  8  9  X | 1  2  3  4  5  6  7  8  9

j. How much money to
spend on entertainment 1  2  3  4  5  6  7  8  9  X | 1  2  3  4  5  6  7  8  9

k. How much money to
spend on my own
clothes . . . . . . . . . . . . 1  2  3  4  5  6  7  8  9  X | 1  2  3  4  5  6  7  8  9

l. How much money to
spend on furniture and
home furnishings . . . . 1  2  3  4  5  6  7  8  9  X | 1  2  3  4  5  6  7  8  9

18.  How often does your partner do each of the following?

|  | | Always | | | | | | | | Never |
|---|---|---|---|---|---|---|---|---|---|---|

a. Makes sure our household
runs smoothly . . . . . . . . . . . 1     2     3     4     5     6     7     8     9

b. Confides [his] [her] inner-
most thoughts and feelings to
me . . . . . . . . . . . . . . . . . . . . 1     2     3     4     5     6     7     8     9

c. Tries to bring me out of it
when I am restless, bored, or
depressed . . . . . . . . . . . . . . . 1     2     3     4     5     6     7     8     9

d. Sees [himself] [herself] as the
decision-maker in our
relationship . . . . . . . . . . . . . . 1     2     3     4     5     6     7     8     9

e. Knows what I am feeling even
when I do not say anything . . 1     2     3     4     5     6     7     8     9

f. Tells me what [he] [she]
likes most about me . . . . . . . 1     2     3     4     5     6     7     8     9

g. Suggests a workable solution
when we face a dilemma . . . 1     2     3     4     5     6     7     8     9

h. Acts very affectionately
toward me . . . . . . . . . . . . . . 1     2     3     4     5     6     7     8     9

i. Tells me [his] [her] feelings
about the future of our
relationship . . . . . . . . . . . . . . 1     2     3     4     5     6     7     8     9

j. When we argue, apologizes
for [his] [her] behavior even
when [he] [she] thinks [he]
[she] is right . . . . . . . . . . . . . 1     2     3     4     5     6     7     8     9

613

19. How would you *realistically* describe your partner?

|   |   | Extremely |   |   |   |   |   |   |   | Not at all |
|---|---|---|---|---|---|---|---|---|---|---|
| a. | Ambitious | 1 | 2 | 3 | 4 | 5 | 6 | 7 | 8 | 9 |
| b. | Athletic | 1 | 2 | 3 | 4 | 5 | 6 | 7 | 8 | 9 |
| c. | Expresses tender feelings easily | 1 | 2 | 3 | 4 | 5 | 6 | 7 | 8 | 9 |
| d. | Forceful | 1 | 2 | 3 | 4 | 5 | 6 | 7 | 8 | 9 |
| e. | Competitive with me | 1 | 2 | 3 | 4 | 5 | 6 | 7 | 8 | 9 |
| f. | Accomplished in [his] [her] chosen field | 1 | 2 | 3 | 4 | 5 | 6 | 7 | 8 | 9 |
| g. | Compassionate | 1 | 2 | 3 | 4 | 5 | 6 | 7 | 8 | 9 |
| h. | Muscular build | 1 | 2 | 3 | 4 | 5 | 6 | 7 | 8 | 9 |
| i. | Outgoing | 1 | 2 | 3 | 4 | 5 | 6 | 7 | 8 | 9 |
| j. | Affectionate | 1 | 2 | 3 | 4 | 5 | 6 | 7 | 8 | 9 |
| k. | Sexy-looking | 1 | 2 | 3 | 4 | 5 | 6 | 7 | 8 | 9 |
| l. | Aggressive | 1 | 2 | 3 | 4 | 5 | 6 | 7 | 8 | 9 |
| m. | Self-sufficient | 1 | 2 | 3 | 4 | 5 | 6 | 7 | 8 | 9 |
| n. | "Movie star" good-looking | 1 | 2 | 3 | 4 | 5 | 6 | 7 | 8 | 9 |
| o. | Romantic | 1 | 2 | 3 | 4 | 5 | 6 | 7 | 8 | 9 |
| p. | Shy | 1 | 2 | 3 | 4 | 5 | 6 | 7 | 8 | 9 |
| q. | Understanding of others | 1 | 2 | 3 | 4 | 5 | 6 | 7 | 8 | 9 |

20. How would you *realistically* describe yourself?

|   |   | Extremely |   |   |   |   |   |   |   | Not at all |
|---|---|---|---|---|---|---|---|---|---|---|
| a. | Accomplished in my chosen field | 1 | 2 | 3 | 4 | 5 | 6 | 7 | 8 | 9 |
| b. | Muscular build | 1 | 2 | 3 | 4 | 5 | 6 | 7 | 8 | 9 |
| c. | Compassionate | 1 | 2 | 3 | 4 | 5 | 6 | 7 | 8 | 9 |
| d. | Outgoing | 1 | 2 | 3 | 4 | 5 | 6 | 7 | 8 | 9 |
| e. | Aggressive | 1 | 2 | 3 | 4 | 5 | 6 | 7 | 8 | 9 |
| f. | Express tender feelings easily | 1 | 2 | 3 | 4 | 5 | 6 | 7 | 8 | 9 |
| g. | Forceful | 1 | 2 | 3 | 4 | 5 | 6 | 7 | 8 | 9 |
| h. | Sexy-looking | 1 | 2 | 3 | 4 | 5 | 6 | 7 | 8 | 9 |
| i. | Affectionate | 1 | 2 | 3 | 4 | 5 | 6 | 7 | 8 | 9 |
| j. | Competitive with my partner | 1 | 2 | 3 | 4 | 5 | 6 | 7 | 8 | 9 |
| k. | Shy | 1 | 2 | 3 | 4 | 5 | 6 | 7 | 8 | 9 |

| | Extremely | | | | | | | | Not at all |
|---|---|---|---|---|---|---|---|---|---|
| l. Self-sufficient | 1 | 2 | 3 | 4 | 5 | 6 | 7 | 8 | 9 |
| m. Ambitious | 1 | 2 | 3 | 4 | 5 | 6 | 7 | 8 | 9 |
| n. Romantic | 1 | 2 | 3 | 4 | 5 | 6 | 7 | 8 | 9 |
| o. Athletic | 1 | 2 | 3 | 4 | 5 | 6 | 7 | 8 | 9 |
| p. Understanding of others | 1 | 2 | 3 | 4 | 5 | 6 | 7 | 8 | 9 |
| q. "Movie star" good-looking | 1 | 2 | 3 | 4 | 5 | 6 | 7 | 8 | 9 |

21. Even though you may be quite satisfied with your relationship, you and your partner may sometimes have serious differences of opinion on some issues. How often do you and [he] [she] have *open disagreements or fights* in the following areas?

| | Daily or almost every day | Three or four times a week | Once or twice a week | Two or three times a month | Once a month | Once every few months | About once a year | Less than once a year | Never | Does not apply to our situation |
|---|---|---|---|---|---|---|---|---|---|---|
| a. How the house is kept | 1 | 2 | 3 | 4 | 5 | 6 | 7 | 8 | 9 | |
| b. How my partner's job affects our relationship | 1 | 2 | 3 | 4 | 5 | 6 | 7 | 8 | 9 | X |
| c. Our social life | 1 | 2 | 3 | 4 | 5 | 6 | 7 | 8 | 9 | |
| d. How my job affects our relationship | 1 | 2 | 3 | 4 | 5 | 6 | 7 | 8 | 9 | X |
| **e. My partner's attitudes about having children | 1 | 2 | 3 | 4 | 5 | 6 | 7 | 8 | 9 | |
| f. Relations with my relatives | 1 | 2 | 3 | 4 | 5 | 6 | 7 | 8 | 9 | |
| g. Relations with [his] [her] relatives | 1 | 2 | 3 | 4 | 5 | 6 | 7 | 8 | 9 | |
| h. Our moral and religious beliefs and practices | 1 | 2 | 3 | 4 | 5 | 6 | 7 | 8 | 9 | |
| i. How we communicate | 1 | 2 | 3 | 4 | 5 | 6 | 7 | 8 | 9 | |
| j. The amount of money coming in | 1 | 2 | 3 | 4 | 5 | 6 | 7 | 8 | 9 | |
| k. How we manage our finances | 1 | 2 | 3 | 4 | 5 | 6 | 7 | 8 | 9 | |
| l. How we express affection for each other | 1 | 2 | 3 | 4 | 5 | 6 | 7 | 8 | 9 | |
| m. Whether we both should work | 1 | 2 | 3 | 4 | 5 | 6 | 7 | 8 | 9 | |
| #**n. How we raise the children | 1 | 2 | 3 | 4 | 5 | 6 | 7 | 8 | 9 | X |
| o. Our sex life | 1 | 2 | 3 | 4 | 5 | 6 | 7 | 8 | 9 | |
| p. Sex outside our relationship | 1 | 2 | 3 | 4 | 5 | 6 | 7 | 8 | 9 | |
| *#q. Our openness about being [gay] [lesbians] | 1 | 2 | 3 | 4 | 5 | 6 | 7 | 8 | 9 | |
| r. Our relationship in general | 1 | 2 | 3 | 4 | 5 | 6 | 7 | 8 | 9 | |

22. How much emotional energy would you say you and your partner give to your relationship, as compared to work and other outside activities?

|  | All to our relationship | | | | Equal amounts to each | | | | All to work and other activities |
|---|---|---|---|---|---|---|---|---|---|
| a. Me | 1 | 2 | 3 | 4 | 5 | 6 | 7 | 8 | 9 |
| b. My partner | 1 | 2 | 3 | 4 | 5 | 6 | 7 | 8 | 9 |

23. How bothered would you be if your partner behaved in each of the following ways?

|  | Extremely bothered | | | | | | | | Not at all bothered |
|---|---|---|---|---|---|---|---|---|---|
| a. Cried when emotionally upset | 1 | 2 | 3 | 4 | 5 | 6 | 7 | 8 | 9 |
| b. Initiated sex | 1 | 2 | 3 | 4 | 5 | 6 | 7 | 8 | 9 |
| c. Avoided making decisions | 1 | 2 | 3 | 4 | 5 | 6 | 7 | 8 | 9 |
| d. Waited for me to initiate sex | 1 | 2 | 3 | 4 | 5 | 6 | 7 | 8 | 9 |
| e. Had a very close (nonsexual) friendship with a man | 1 | 2 | 3 | 4 | 5 | 6 | 7 | 8 | 9 |
| f. Had a very close (nonsexual) friendship with a woman | 1 | 2 | 3 | 4 | 5 | 6 | 7 | 8 | 9 |
| g. Was more sexually attractive to other people than I am | 1 | 2 | 3 | 4 | 5 | 6 | 7 | 8 | 9 |
| h. Earned much more money than I did | 1 | 2 | 3 | 4 | 5 | 6 | 7 | 8 | 9 |
| i. Had sex with someone else | 1 | 2 | 3 | 4 | 5 | 6 | 7 | 8 | 9 |
| j. Had a meaningful affair with someone else | 1 | 2 | 3 | 4 | 5 | 6 | 7 | 8 | 9 |

24. Compared to *three months ago*, how would you rate your relationship with your partner?

|  | Much better | | | | The same | | | | Much worse |
|---|---|---|---|---|---|---|---|---|---|
| | 1 | 2 | 3 | 4 | 5 | 6 | 7 | 8 | 9 |

25a. How often have you seriously considered ending your relationship with your partner?

1 Never

2 Once

3 Two or three times

4 More than three times

b. How often have you and [he] [she] seriously discussed ending your relationship?

1 Never

2 Once

3 Two or three times

4 More than three times

c. If you and [he] [she] did decide to end your relationship, whose life would this disrupt more, yours or [his] [hers]? . .

_Mine much more_         _Both equally_         _[His] [Hers] much more_

| 1 | 2 | 3 | 4 | 5 | 6 | 7 | 8 | 9 |

26. If something were to happen to your partner and you were forced to live without [him] [her], how difficult would it be for you to do each of the following?

_Extremely difficult_         _Not at all difficult_

a. Do household tasks (such as cleaning, laundry, and managing the household) . . . . . . .

| 1 | 2 | 3 | 4 | 5 | 6 | 7 | 8 | 9 |

b. Find another partner . . . . . . .

| 1 | 2 | 3 | 4 | 5 | 6 | 7 | 8 | 9 |

c. Cook appetizing meals . . . . .

| 1 | 2 | 3 | 4 | 5 | 6 | 7 | 8 | 9 |

d. Maintain my present standard of living . . . . . . . . . . . . . . . .

| 1 | 2 | 3 | 4 | 5 | 6 | 7 | 8 | 9 |

e. Make household repairs (such as plumbing or electrical repairs) . . . . . . . . . . . . . .

| 1 | 2 | 3 | 4 | 5 | 6 | 7 | 8 | 9 |

f. Find or continue employment . . . . . . . . . . . . .

| 1 | 2 | 3 | 4 | 5 | 6 | 7 | 8 | 9 |

g. Avoid loneliness . . . . . . . . . .

| 1 | 2 | 3 | 4 | 5 | 6 | 7 | 8 | 9 |

27. How likely is it that you and your partner will still be together . . . _(CIRCLE ONE ANSWER ON EACH LINE.)_

_Extremely likely_         _Extremely unlikely_

a. Six months from now? . . . . . .

| 1 | 2 | 3 | 4 | 5 | 6 | 7 | 8 | 9 |

b. One year from now? . . . . . . .

| 1 | 2 | 3 | 4 | 5 | 6 | 7 | 8 | 9 |

c. Five years from now? . . . . . .

| 1 | 2 | 3 | 4 | 5 | 6 | 7 | 8 | 9 |

d. Twenty years from now? . . . .

| 1 | 2 | 3 | 4 | 5 | 6 | 7 | 8 | 9 |

28a. Have you and your partner had sexual relations _during the last year?_

     **1** Yes _(IF "YES," SKIP TO QUESTION 29.)_

     **2** No

*# b. If not, have you and [he] [she] ever had sexual relations?

     **1** Yes

     **2** No _(IF "NO," SKIP TO QUESTION 30.)_

*# c. If you and [he] [she] have had sexual relations in the past, but not in the last year, when did you stop?

     **1** Before we started living together _(SKIP TO QUESTION 30.)_

     **2** After we started living together _(SKIP TO QUESTION 30.)_

29. About how often _during the last year_ have you and your partner had sexual relations?

     **1** Daily or almost every day

     **2** Three or four times a week

     **3** Once or twice a week

     **4** Two or three times a month

     **5** Once a month

     **6** Once every few months

     **7** A few times

30. How long ago did you and your partner first consider yourselves a couple (regardless of when you started living together)?

_____ years      _____ months

*#31. Do you and your partner consider yourselves lovers?

1   Yes

2   No

*# 32. Do you and your partner consider yourselves married? (This is not restricted to a legal marriage or one involving a religious ceremony.)

1   Yes

2   No

*# 33a. Do you currently think of yourself as: (SELECT ONLY ONE.)

1   Exclusively heterosexual (SKIP TO QUESTION 34.)

2   Predominantly heterosexual, only slightly homosexual (SKIP TO QUESTION 34.)

3   Predominantly heterosexual, but significantly homosexual (SKIP TO QUESTION 34.)

4   Equally homosexual and heterosexual (SKIP TO QUESTION 34.)

5   Predominantly homosexual, but significantly heterosexual

6   Predominantly homosexual, only slightly heterosexual

7   Exclusively homosexual

*# b. If you consider yourself exclusively or predominantly homosexual, at what age did you first decide you were definitely homosexual?

_____ years old

*#† 34. With how many people have you ever had sexual relations (including your current partner)?

a. With men

1   None

2   One

3   Two

4   3 to 5

5   6 to 10

6   11 to 20

7   21 to 50

8   51 to 100

9   101 or more

*#@ b. With women

1   None

2   One

3   Two

4   3 to 5

5   6 to 10

6   11 to 20

7   21 to 50

8   51 to 100

9   101 or more

35. Have you had sexual relations with anyone other than your current partner since you have been living together?

1   Yes

2   No (IF "NO," SKIP TO QUESTION 41.)

618

\*#†36.  How many people have you had sexual relations with, other than your current partner, *since you have been living together?*

   a.  With men

   1  One
   2  Two
   3  3 to 5
   4  6 to 10
   5  11 to 20
   6  21 to 50
   7  51 to 100
   8  101 or more

\*#@ b.  With women

   1  One
   2  Two
   3  3 to 5
   4  6 to 10
   5  11 to 20
   6  21 to 50
   7  51 to 100
   8  101 or more

   37a.  How long was it after you and your current partner started living together that you first had sexual relations with someone else?

   1  A few days
   2  A week or two
   3  A month or two
   4  Three to 6 months
   5  More than 6 months, but less than a year
   6  1 to 2 years
   7  3 to 5 years
   8  6 to 10 years
   9  11 years or more

   b.  Does your partner know that you have had sexual relations with others during your relationship?

   1  Yes, I am certain [he] [she] knows
   2  Yes, I feel fairly sure [he] [she] knows
   3  I am not sure whether [he] [she] knows or not
   4  No, I feel fairly sure [he] [she] does not know
   5  No, I am certain [he] [she] does not know

   38.  How often in *the last year* (or since you have been living with your partner, if that is less than one year) . . .

\*#† a.  . . . have you had sexual relations with a man [*other than* your current partner]?

   1  Daily or almost every day
   2  Three or four times a week
   3  Once or twice a week
   4  Two or three times a month
   5  Once a month
   6  Once every few months
   7  A few times
   8  Never

*#@ b.  . . . have you had sexual relations with a woman [*other than* your current partner]?

    **1**   Daily or almost every day

    **2**   Three or four times a week

    **3**   Once or twice a week

    **4**   Two or three times a month

    **5**   Once a month

    **6**   Once every few months

    **7**   A few times

    **8**   Never

*#c.  . . . have you had sexual relations with someone you met that same day or with a stranger?

    **1**   Daily or almost every day

    **2**   Three or four times a week

    **3**   Once or twice a week

    **4**   Two or three times a month

    **5**   Once a month

    **6**   Once every few months

    **7**   A few times

    **8**   Never

39.   Please indicate your satisfaction or dissatisfaction with the following aspects of the sexual experiences you have had with persons other than your partner since you have been living together.

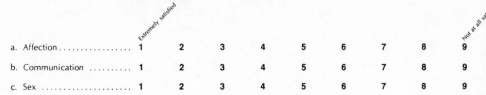

| | Extremely satisfied | | | | | | | | Not at all satisfied |
|---|---|---|---|---|---|---|---|---|---|
| a. Affection . . . . . . . . . . . . . . . . | 1 | 2 | 3 | 4 | 5 | 6 | 7 | 8 | 9 |
| b. Communication . . . . . . . . . | 1 | 2 | 3 | 4 | 5 | 6 | 7 | 8 | 9 |
| c. Sex . . . . . . . . . . . . . . . . . . . . | 1 | 2 | 3 | 4 | 5 | 6 | 7 | 8 | 9 |

40a.  Have you had a meaningful love affair since you and your partner have been living together?

    **1**   Yes

    **2**   No *(IF "NO," SKIP TO QUESTION 41.)*

  b.  If "yes," how many love affairs have you had?

    ———————

  c.  How many lasted more than a year?

    ———————

  d.  Are you currently having a meaningful love affair with someone other than your partner?

    **1**   Yes

    **2**   No *(IF "NO," SKIP TO QUESTION 41.)*

  e.  Does your partner know about this love affair?

    **1**   Yes, I am certain [he] [she] knows

    **2**   Yes, I feel fairly sure [he] [she] knows

    **3**   I am not sure whether [he] [she] knows or not

    **4**   No, I feel fairly sure [he] [she] does not know

    **5**   No, I am certain [he] [she] does not know

41. Which *one* of the following statements best describes your and your partner's current understanding concerning sex outside of your relationship?

    **1**  We have discussed it and decided that under *some* circumstances it is all right

    **2**  We have discussed it and decided that under *no* circumstances is it all right

    **3**  We have discussed it and do not agree *(PLEASE EXPLAIN HOW EACH OF YOU FEELS.)*

    _____

    _____

    _____

    **4**  We have *not* discussed it but I feel we would agree that under some circumstances it is all right

    **5**  We have *not* discussed it but I feel we would agree that under *no* circumstances is it all right

    **6**  We have *not* discussed it but I feel that we would not agree *(PLEASE EXPLAIN HOW EACH OF YOU FEELS.)*

    _____

    _____

    _____

42. Has your partner had sexual relations with others during your relationship?

    **1**  Yes, I am certain [he] [she] has

    **2**  Yes, I feel fairly sure [he] [she] has

    **3**  I am not sure whether [he] [she] has or not

    **4**  No, I feel fairly sure [he] [she] has not

    **5**  No, I am certain [he] [she] has not

---

## FAMILY RELATIONS

#**1. Do you *personally* have any children from [your current relationship] or from a prior relationship?

    **1**  Yes

    **2**  No *(IF "NO," SKIP TO QUESTION 3.)*

#**2. If "yes," what is the age and sex of each child, and how much of the year does each child live with you and your partner?

| | Age | Sex | From current (C) or prior (P) relationship** | Full-time | 7-11 months | 2-6 months | Less than 2 months | On weekends only | Visits occasionally | Never visits |
|---|---|---|---|---|---|---|---|---|---|---|
| a. First child | _____ | M  F | C  P | 1 | 2 | 3 | 4 | 5 | 6 | 7 |
| b. Second child | _____ | M  F | C  P | 1 | 2 | 3 | 4 | 5 | 6 | 7 |
| c. Third child | _____ | M  F | C  P | 1 | 2 | 3 | 4 | 5 | 6 | 7 |
| d. Fourth child | _____ | M  F | C  P | 1 | 2 | 3 | 4 | 5 | 6 | 7 |
| e. Fifth child | _____ | M  F | C  P | 1 | 2 | 3 | 4 | 5 | 6 | 7 |
| f. Sixth child | _____ | M  F | C  P | 1 | 2 | 3 | 4 | 5 | 6 | 7 |

(header note: *Amount of time child lives with us each year*)

**3. Ideally, how many children would you and your partner like to have altogether?

_____

**4. How many children do you and your partner expect to have altogether?

_____

5a.  Do your parents presently live together?

    1  Yes *(IF "YES," SKIP TO QUESTION 6.)*

    2  No

b.  Is either of your parents deceased?

    1  Neither deceased

    2  Father only deceased

    3  Mother only deceased

    4  Both deceased *(IF "BOTH," SKIP TO QUESTION 11.)*

c.  Are your parents divorced or separated?

    1  Yes

    2  No

6.  How old are your parents?

a.  Your mother

    _____

    X  No mother

b.  Your father

    _____

    X  No father

7.  About how far from you do your mother and father live?

a.  Your mother

    1  Less than one mile

    2  One to 10 miles

    3  11 to 100 miles

    4  101 to 500 miles

    5  501 to 1,000 miles

    6  More than 1,000 miles

    X  No mother

b.  Your father

    1  Less than one mile

    2  One to 10 miles

    3  11 to 100 miles

    4  101 to 500 miles

    5  501 to 1,000 miles

    6  More than 1,000 miles

    X  No father

8.  How often do you and your parents visit one another (including when you go to see them and they come to see you)?

a.  Your mother

    1  Daily or almost every day

    2  Three or four times a week

    3  Once or twice a week

    4  Two or three times a month

    5  Once a month

    6  Once every few months

    7  About once a year

    8  Less often than once a year

    9  Never

    X  No mother

b. Your father

    **1** Daily or almost every day

    **2** Three or four times a week

    **3** Once or twice a week

    **4** Two or three times a month

    **5** Once a month

    **6** Once every few months

    **7** About once a year

    **8** Less often than once a year

    **9** Never

    **X** No father

9. About what proportion of the time is your partner with you when you visit your parents or meet them *outside* your own home?

|  |  | Always | | | | Half the time | | | | Never | Does not apply to our situation |
|---|---|---|---|---|---|---|---|---|---|---|---|
| a. | Your mother .............. | 1 | 2 | 3 | 4 | 5 | 6 | 7 | 8 | 9 | X |
| b. | Your father .............. | 1 | 2 | 3 | 4 | 5 | 6 | 7 | 8 | 9 | X |

10. Overall, how often do you have any kind of contact (by phone, mail, visits, etc.) with your parents?

a. Your mother

    **1** Daily or almost every day

    **2** Three or four times a week

    **3** Once or twice a week

    **4** Two or three times a month

    **5** Once a month

    **6** Once every few months

    **7** About once a year

    **8** Less often than once a year

    **9** Never

    **X** Does not apply in my situation

b. Your father

    **1** Daily or almost every day

    **2** Three or four times a week

    **3** Once or twice a week

    **4** Two or three times a month

    **5** Once a month

    **6** Once every few months

    **7** About once a year

    **8** Less often than once a year

    **9** Never

    **X** Does not apply in my situation

11. How often do *you personally* initiate any kind of contact (by phone, mail, in person, etc.) with *your partner's* parents?

   a. Your partner's mother

      1 Daily or almost every day

      2 Three or four times a week

      3 Once or twice a week

      4 Two or three times a month

      5 Once a month

      6 Once every few months

      7 About once a year

      8 Less often than once a year

      9 Never

      X Does not apply to our situation

   b. Your partner's father

      1 Daily or almost every day

      2 Three or four times a week

      3 Once or twice a week

      4 Two or three times a month

      5 Once a month

      6 Once every few months

      7 About once a year

      8 Less often than once a year

      9 Never

      X Does not apply to our situation

12. Considering *all of your relatives* and *all of your partner's relatives*, list the four relatives with whom you have the most contact of any kind. Only include people you have contact with at least once a year. Be sure to specify whether they are your relatives or your partner's.

   a. I have the most contact with _____

   b. I have the second most contact with_____

   c. I have the third most contact with_____

   d. I have the fourth most contact with_____

13. Overall, do you have more contact of any kind with your relatives or with your partner's relatives? . . . . . . . . .

    More with my relatives — 1    2    3    4    Equal with both relatives — 5    6    7    8    More with (his) (her) relatives — 9

14. Overall, do you have more contact with relatives (including both yours and your partner's) or with friends? . . .

    More with relatives — 1    2    3    4    Equal with relatives and friends — 5    6    7    8    More with friends — 9

15. Did either of your parents send you a Christmas or Channukah card last year?

   a. From both parents together

      1 No

      2 Yes, addressed to me alone

      3 Yes, addressed to both my partner and to me

      X Does not apply to my situation

b. From mother alone

   **1**  No

   **2**  Yes, addressed to me alone

   **3**  Yes, addressed to both my partner and to me

   **X**  Does not apply to my situation

c. From father alone

   **1**  No

   **2**  Yes, addressed to me alone

   **3**  Yes, addressed to both my partner and to me

   **X**  Does not apply to my situation

16. Did you send your parents a Christmas or Channukah card last year?

   **1**  No

   **2**  Yes, signed from me alone

   **3**  Yes, signed from me and my partner

   **X**  Does not apply in my situation

17. To what extent do your partner's parents make you feel like you are "one of the family"?

| | Very much | | | | | | | | Not at all | Does not apply to my situation |
|---|---|---|---|---|---|---|---|---|---|---|
| a. [His] [her] mother | 1 | 2 | 3 | 4 | 5 | 6 | 7 | 8 | 9 | X |
| b. [His] [her] father | 1 | 2 | 3 | 4 | 5 | 6 | 7 | 8 | 9 | X |

18. How satisfied are you with your relationship with your parents?

| | Extremely satisfied | | | | | | | | Not at all satisfied | Does not apply to my situation |
|---|---|---|---|---|---|---|---|---|---|---|
| a. Your mother | 1 | 2 | 3 | 4 | 5 | 6 | 7 | 8 | 9 | X |
| b. Your father | 1 | 2 | 3 | 4 | 5 | 6 | 7 | 8 | 9 | X |

19. Would you prefer to see your parents and your partner's parents more or less than you do now?

| | Much more | | | | Neither more nor less | | | | Much less | Does not apply to my situation |
|---|---|---|---|---|---|---|---|---|---|---|
| a. Your mother | 1 | 2 | 3 | 4 | 5 | 6 | 7 | 8 | 9 | X |
| b. Your father | 1 | 2 | 3 | 4 | 5 | 6 | 7 | 8 | 9 | X |
| c. [His] [her] mother | 1 | 2 | 3 | 4 | 5 | 6 | 7 | 8 | 9 | X |
| d. [His] [her] father | 1 | 2 | 3 | 4 | 5 | 6 | 7 | 8 | 9 | X |

20. How much do you agree or disagree with the following statements?

|  |  | Strongly agree | | | | | | | | Strongly disagree |
|---|---|---|---|---|---|---|---|---|---|---|
| a. | Adult children have an obligation to keep in contact with their parents .............................. | 1 | 2 | 3 | 4 | 5 | 6 | 7 | 8 | 9 |
| b. | [Partners in a heterosexual marriage]*# [People who are married]** have just as much responsibility to keep in contact with their partner's parents as with their own .............................................. | 1 | 2 | 3 | 4 | 5 | 6 | 7 | 8 | 9 |
| c. | [Partners in a heterosexual marriage]*# [People who are married]** should *not* be expected to visit their partner's relatives if they do not want to ............. | 1 | 2 | 3 | 4 | 5 | 6 | 7 | 8 | 9 |
| d. | Except for emergencies, adult children should not take financial assistance or loans from their parents ... | 1 | 2 | 3 | 4 | 5 | 6 | 7 | 8 | 9 |
| e. | It is the responsibility of adult children to be with their parents in times of serious illness even if the children have moved some distance from the parents ........ | 1 | 2 | 3 | 4 | 5 | 6 | 7 | 8 | 9 |
| f. | If a person's parent has a medical bill and cannot pay, the person is morally obligated to pay the debt ....... | 1 | 2 | 3 | 4 | 5 | 6 | 7 | 8 | 9 |
| *#g. | A [man] [woman] in a living-together [gay] [lesbian] couple has just as much responsibility to keep in contact with [his] [her] partner's parents as with [his] [her] own ......................................... | 1 | 2 | 3 | 4 | 5 | 6 | 7 | 8 | 9 |
| *#h. | A [man] [woman] in a living-together [gay] [lesbian] couple should *not* be expected to visit [his] [her] partner's relatives if [he] [she] does not want to ....... | 1 | 2 | 3 | 4 | 5 | 6 | 7 | 8 | 9 |

*SKIP TO QUESTION 21 IF YOU AND YOUR PARTNER ARE MARRIED.*

| | | | | | | | | | | |
|---|---|---|---|---|---|---|---|---|---|---|
| $i. | People in an unmarried living-together couple have just as much responsibility to keep in contact with their partner's parents as with their own............ | 1 | 2 | 3 | 4 | 5 | 6 | 7 | 8 | 9 |
| $j. | People in an unmarried living-together couple should *not* be expected to visit their partner's relatives if they do not want to........................... | 1 | 2 | 3 | 4 | 5 | 6 | 7 | 8 | 9 |

*IN THE FOLLOWING QUESTIONS ABOUT FINANCIAL MATTERS, PLEASE REMEMBER THAT YOUR ANSWERS ARE COMPLETELY ANONYMOUS.*

21. Do you and your partner both have separate incomes from any source (work, investments, pensions, child-support, etc.)?

   **1** Yes, both have separate incomes

   **2** Only [he] [she] has an income (*SKIP TO QUESTION 23a.*)

   **3** Only [he] [she] has an income (*SKIP TO QUESTION 23a.*)

22. Whose income (from any source) pays for the following expenses, yours or your partner's?

|  | My income pays for all | | | | Both of our incomes contribute equally | | | | [His] [Her] income pays for all | We do not have this expense |
|---|---|---|---|---|---|---|---|---|---|---|
| a. Rent or house payment ..... | 1 | 2 | 3 | 4 | 5 | 6 | 7 | 8 | 9 | X |
| b. Utilities .................. | 1 | 2 | 3 | 4 | 5 | 6 | 7 | 8 | 9 | X |
| c. Groceries ............... | 1 | 2 | 3 | 4 | 5 | 6 | 7 | 8 | 9 | X |
| d. My clothes ............... | 1 | 2 | 3 | 4 | 5 | 6 | 7 | 8 | 9 | X |
| #***e. Expenses for the children living with us ............. | 1 | 2 | 3 | 4 | 5 | 6 | 7 | 8 | 9 | X |

626

|  |  | My income pays for all | | | | Both of our incomes contribute equally | | | | [His] [Her] income pays for all | We do not have this expense |
|---|---|---|---|---|---|---|---|---|---|---|---|
| * **f. | Alimony or child-support payments to a previous spouse.......... | 1 | 2 | 3 | 4 | 5 | 6 | 7 | 8 | 9 | X |
| g. | House cleaning help ....... | 1 | 2 | 3 | 4 | 5 | 6 | 7 | 8 | 9 | X |
| h. | Major household appliances | 1 | 2 | 3 | 4 | 5 | 6 | 7 | 8 | 9 | X |
| i. | Entertainment or food when out for the evening ........ | 1 | 2 | 3 | 4 | 5 | 6 | 7 | 8 | 9 | X |
| j. | My personal spending money (money spent just on myself, not for household expenses) | 1 | 2 | 3 | 4 | 5 | 6 | 7 | 8 | 9 | X |

23a. Do you or your partner currently own your place of residence?

   **1** Yes

   **2** No (IF "NO," SKIP TO QUESTION 24a.)

  b. If "yes," whose name is it in?

   **1** My name

   **2** My partner's name

   **3** Both names

24a. Do you and your partner have a joint checking account?

   **1** Yes

   **2** No (IF "NO," SKIP TO QUESTION 25a.)

  b. If "yes," do you and [he] [she] contribute equally to it?

   **1** Yes, we contribute equally

   **2** No, we both contribute, but I contribute more than [he] [she] does

   **3** No, we both contribute but [he] [she] contributes more than I do

   **4** No, only I contribute to it

   **5** No, only [he] [she] contributes to it

25a. Do you and your partner have a joint savings account?

   **1** Yes

   **2** No (IF "NO," SKIP TO QUESTION 26.)

  b. If "yes," do you and [he] [she] contribute equally to it?

   **1** Yes, we contribute equally

   **2** No, we both contribute, but I contribute more than [he] [she] does

   **3** No, we both contribute, but [he] [she] contributes more than I do

   **4** No, only I contribute to it

   **5** No, only [he] [she] contributes to it

26. Do you have a savings account in your name only?

   **1** Yes

   **2** No

27. Do you have your own personal checking account (one from which only you can write checks)?

   **1** Yes

   **2** No

28. Do you talk with your partner about . . .

    a. . . . how much money *you* should have for personal spending?

        **1** Yes

        **2** No

    b. . . . how much money [he] [she] should have for personal spending?

        **1** Yes

        **2** No

29a. Since you and [he] [she] have been living together, have you invested any of *your own income* in stocks, bonds, real estate, etc.?

        **1** Yes

        **2** No *(IF "NO," SKIP TO QUESTION 30a.)*

    b. Were these investments made with your income only, or did [his] [her] income contribute to their payment?

        **1** I paid for all of them

        **2** I paid for some, and [he] [she] and I paid for some together

        **3** [He] [She] has contributed to all the investments I have made

    c. Of the investments made either entirely or partially with your own income, do you know how much has been invested and where?

        **1** Yes, I know all the details of the investments

        **2** Yes, I know most of the details of the investments

        **3** Yes, I know some of the details of the investments

        **4** No, I do not know any of the details of the investments

    d. How many of these investments were registered jointly (in both names)?

        **1** All

        **2** Most

        **3** About half

        **4** Few

        **5** None

        **6** I do not know

30a. Do you have a life insurance policy?

        **1** Yes

        **2** No *(IF "NO," SKIP TO QUESTION 31a.)*

    b. If "yes," is your partner a beneficiary?

        **1** Yes

        **2** No

31a. Do you have a will?

        **1** Yes

        **2** No *(IF "NO," SKIP TO THE NEXT SECTION - "LIFESTYLE QUESTIONS.")*

    b. If "yes," is your partner a beneficiary?

        **1** Yes

        **2** No

---

## LIFESTYLE QUESTIONS

1. On the average, how many evenings a week do both you and your partner spend at home?

    **0**    **1**    **2**    **3**    **4**    **5**    **6**    **7**

2. During a typical week, how many days do you and your partner have dinner together?

    **0**    **1**    **2**    **3**    **4**    **5**    **6**    **7**

3. Would you prefer to spend more or less time with your partner? . . . . . . . . . . . . . . .

Much more 1    2    3    4    Neither more nor less 5    6    7    8    Much less 9

4. How often do you and your partner spend vacations together (excluding weekend outings)? . . . . . . . . . . . . . . .

Always together 1    2    3    4    Half together and half apart 5    6    7    8    Always apart 9    No vacations X

5. For each of the following leisure activities you do at least twice a year, how often do you and your partner do them together?

Column headers: Always together (1)    Half together and half alone (5)    Always alone (9)    I do this less than twice a year (X)

a. Movies, theatre, concerts, opera, etc. . . . . . . . . . . . . . .
1    2    3    4    5    6    7    8    9    X

b. Ball games and other sports events I go to . . . . . . . . . . . .
1    2    3    4    5    6    7    8    9    X

c. Sports I participate in (like jogging, skiing, volleyball, fishing, etc.) . . . . . . . . . . . . .
1    2    3    4    5    6    7    8    9    X

d. Hobbies (like gardening, crafts, home improvement, car repair, etc.) . . . . . . . . . . .
1    2    3    4    5    6    7    8    9    X

e. Activities of service clubs, political groups, or citizen's associations . . . . . . . . . . . . .
1    2    3    4    5    6    7    8    9    X

f. Church and religious activities . . . . . . . . . . . . . . . .
1    2    3    4    5    6    7    8    9    X

6. How would you describe your political outlook? . . . . . . . . . .

Extremely liberal 1    2    3    4    5    6    7    8    Extremely conservative 9

7. How sympathetic do you feel towards the feminist movement? . . . . . . . . . . . . .

Extremely sympathetic 1    2    3    4    5    6    7    8    Not at all sympathetic 9

*# 8. How active have you been in the gay rights movement?

Extremely active 1    2    3    4    5    6    7    8    Not at all active 9

*# 9a. How often do you go to [a primarily lesbian bar or club] [gay bars or clubs]?

1  Daily or almost every day
2  Three or four times a week
3  Once or twice a week
4  Two or three times a month
5  Once a month
6  Once every few months
7  About once a year
8  Less often than once a year
9  Never

629

**#** b. How often do you go to a primarily male or mixed gay bar or club?

1 Daily or almost every day
2 Three or four times a week
3 Once or twice a week
4 Two or three times a month
5 Once a month
6 Once every few months
7 About once a year
8 Less often than once a year
9 Never

**\*#** 10. If you go to a gay bar or club, how often do you go...? *(CIRCLE ONE ANSWER ON EACH LINE.)*

| | Always | | | | Half the time | | | | Never |
|---|---|---|---|---|---|---|---|---|---|
| a. Alone .................. | 1 | 2 | 3 | 4 | 5 | 6 | 7 | 8 | 9 |
| b. With my partner and possibly other friends ............. | 1 | 2 | 3 | 4 | 5 | 6 | 7 | 8 | 9 |
| c. With friends but *without* my partner .............. | 1 | 2 | 3 | 4 | 5 | 6 | 7 | 8 | 9 |

**\*#** 11. *Excluding bars*, how often do you go to public places where gay men and/or lesbians socialize, such as a coffeehouse, gay or lesbian center, dance, etc.?

1 Daily or almost every day
2 Three or four times a week
3 Once or twice a week
4 Two or three times a month
5 Once a month
6 Once every few months
7 About once a year
8 Less often than once a year
9 Never

12. During the last year, how involved have you been in each of the following activities?

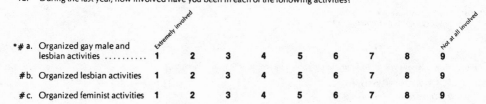

| | Extremely involved | | | | | | | | Not at all involved |
|---|---|---|---|---|---|---|---|---|---|
| **\*#** a. Organized gay male and lesbian activities .......... | 1 | 2 | 3 | 4 | 5 | 6 | 7 | 8 | 9 |
| **#** b. Organized lesbian activities | 1 | 2 | 3 | 4 | 5 | 6 | 7 | 8 | 9 |
| **#** c. Organized feminist activities | 1 | 2 | 3 | 4 | 5 | 6 | 7 | 8 | 9 |

**\*#** 13. How many gay [or lesbian] periodicals do you regularly read or subscribe to?

1 None
2 One
3 Two
4 Three
5 Four or more

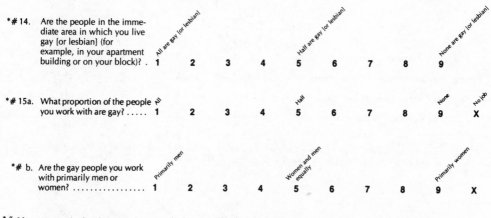

*# 14. Are the people in the immediate area in which you live gay [or lesbian] (for example, in your apartment building or on your block)? . 

All are gay [or lesbian]  1  2  3  4  Half are gay [or lesbian] 5  6  7  8  None are gay [or lesbian] 9

*# 15a. What proportion of the people you work with are gay? . . . . . 

All 1  2  3  4  Half 5  6  7  8  None 9  No job X

*# b. Are the gay people you work with primarily men or women? . . . . . . . . . . . . . . . . 

Primarily men 1  2  3  4  Women and men equally 5  6  7  8  Primarily women 9  X

*# 16a. During the *last five years* have you had any problems on the job because people knew or suspected that you were [a lesbian] [gay]?

  **1** No

  **2** Yes, but only to a very small degree

  **3** Yes, to some degree

  **4** Yes, very much so

  **X** No job

*# b. Have you ever lost or been refused a job because the employer knew or suspected that you were [a lesbian] [gay]?

  **1** Yes, I know for sure that I have

  **2** I think I have

  **3** No

  **X** No job

*#$17. During the *last five years* have you ever been refused a place to live because the landlord/lady or real estate agent knew or suspected that [you were a lesbian] [gay] [you and your partner were not married]?

  **1** Yes, I know for sure that I have

  **2** I think I have

  **3** No

  **X** No chance for this to happen

*# 18. How much do you care whether *heterosexuals* know you are gay?

  **1** I do not care who knows I am gay

  **2** There are a few heterosexuals I do not want to know I am gay

  **3** There are a large number of heterosexuals I do not want to know I am gay

  **4** I do not want any heterosexuals to know I am gay

*#$ 19. Do the following people know that [you are gay] [you and your partner are living together]? *(CIRCLE THE APPROPRIATE NUMBER ON EACH LINE.)*

| | Definitely knows and we have talked about it | Definitely knows but we have never talked about it | Probably knows or suspects | Does not know or suspect | No such person |
|---|---|---|---|---|---|
| a. Your mother . . . . . . . . . . . . . . . . . . . . . . . . . . . . . . . . | 1 | 2 | 3 | 4 | X |
| b. Your father . . . . . . . . . . . . . . . . . . . . . . . . . . . . . . . . | 1 | 2 | 3 | 4 | X |
| c. Your stepmother . . . . . . . . . . . . . . . . . . . . . . . . . . . . | 1 | 2 | 3 | 4 | X |

631

| | Definitely knows and we have talked about it | Definitely knows but we have never talked about it | Probably knows or suspects | Does not know or suspect | No such |
|---|:---:|:---:|:---:|:---:|:---:|
| d. Your stepfather .............................. | 1 | 2 | 3 | 4 | X |
| *# e. Your best heterosexual female friend .............. | 1 | 2 | 3 | 4 | X |
| *# f. Your best heterosexual male friend ................ | 1 | 2 | 3 | 4 | X |
| g. Your supervisor or superior at work ................ | 1 | 2 | 3 | 4 | X |

*#$ 20. How has each of the following persons reacted (or how do you think they *would* react) to the fact that [you and your partner are living together] [ you are gay]? (*CIRCLE THE APPROPRIATE NUMBER ON EACH LINE.*)

| | Accepting (or it would not matter) | Tolerant (but not accepting) | Intolerant (but not rejecting) | Rejecting | No such |
|---|:---:|:---:|:---:|:---:|:---:|
| a. Your mother ................................... | 1 | 2 | 3 | 4 | X |
| b. Your father ................................... | 1 | 2 | 3 | 4 | X |
| c. Your stepmother ............................. | 1 | 2 | 3 | 4 | X |
| d. Your stepfather .............................. | 1 | 2 | 3 | 4 | X |
| *# e. Your best heterosexual female friend .............. | 1 | 2 | 3 | 4 | X |
| *# f. Your best heterosexual male friend ................ | 1 | 2 | 3 | 4 | X |

*# 21. Do your parents think of you and your partner as "a couple"?

    a. Your mother

      1  Yes, I am certain she does

      2  Yes, I feel fairly sure she does

      3  I am not sure whether she does or not

      4  No, I feel fairly sure she does not

      5  No, I am certain she does not

      X  No mother

    b. Your father

      1  Yes, I am certain he does

      2  Yes, I feel fairly sure he does

      3  I am not sure whether he does or not

      4  No, I feel fairly sure he does not

      5  No, I am certain he does not

      X  No father

$ 22. Would your relationship with your parents improve if you were to marry your partner?

    a. Your mother

      1  Yes, considerably

      2  Yes, somewhat

      3  Would stay about the same

      4  Would get worse

      X  Does not apply in my situation

b. Your father

**1** Yes, considerably

**2** Yes, somewhat

**3** Would stay about the same

**4** Would get worse

**X** Does not apply in my situation

$ 23a. How likely is it that you and your partner will get married?............... *Extremely likely* **1**　**2**　**3**　**4**　**5**　**6**　**7**　**8**　**9** *Extremely unlikely*

b. How much would you like to *eventually* marry your partner................. *Would like very much* **1**　**2**　**3**　**4**　**5**　**6**　**7**　**8**　**9** *Would not like at all*

c. How much would you like to be married *now* to your partner?.................. **1**　**2**　**3**　**4**　**5**　**6**　**7**　**8**　**9**

d. How often do you and your partner have *open disagreements or fights* about whether or not you will get married?

**1** Daily or almost every day

**2** Three or four times a week

**3** Once or twice a week

**4** Two or three times a month

**5** Once a month

**6** Once every few months

**7** About once a year

**8** Less than once a year

**9** Never

*# 24. How much do you agree or disagree with each of these statements?

a. Being gay is something that is completely beyond one's control ................. *Strongly agree* **1**　**2**　**3**　**4**　**5**　**6**　**7**　**8**　**9** *Strongly disagree*

b. I would not give up my homosexuality even if I could .... **1**　**2**　**3**　**4**　**5**　**6**　**7**　**8**　**9**

c. I feel my life would be much easier if I were heterosexual **1**　**2**　**3**　**4**　**5**　**6**　**7**　**8**　**9**

d. Being gay is a conscious choice I have made ........ **1**　**2**　**3**　**4**　**5**　**6**　**7**　**8**　**9**

25. Besides your partner and relatives how many *close friends* do you have?

*# a. Lesbians _____

*# b. Gay men _____

c. [Heterosexual] women _____

d. [Heterosexual] men _____

26. What proportion of your close friends are also your partner's friends? ................. *All* **1**　**2**　**3**　**4**　*Half* **5**　**6**　**7**　**8**　*None* **9**

633

27. When you socialize with friends (either away from home or in your home) how often is your partner with you? .................

| Always | | | | Half the time | | | | Never |
|--------|---|---|---|---------------|---|---|---|-------|
| 1 | 2 | 3 | 4 | 5 | 6 | 7 | 8 | 9 |

28. How does your partner feel about your close friends?

   1  [She] [He] likes them all
   2  [She] [He] dislikes one or a few
   3  [She] [He] dislikes most of them
   4  [She] [He] likes all of them
   X  [She] [He] does not know my close friends

29. Of your close friends, with how many did you ever live in a committed sexual relationship or marriage?

   _____

30. How many of your close friends are currently living with a partner or married?

| | All | | | | Half | | | | None | No such close friends |
|---|-----|---|---|---|------|---|---|---|------|----------------------|
| *# a. Lesbian friends ........... | 1 | 2 | 3 | 4 | 5 | 6 | 7 | 8 | 9 | X |
| *# b. Gay male friends .......... | 1 | 2 | 3 | 4 | 5 | 6 | 7 | 8 | 9 | X |
| c. [Heterosexual] female friends ................. | 1 | 2 | 3 | 4 | 5 | 6 | 7 | 8 | 9 | X |
| d. [Heterosexual] male friends ................. | 1 | 2 | 3 | 4 | 5 | 6 | 7 | 8 | 9 | X |

31. How many of your close friends have been living with their current partner for at least five years?

| | All | | | | Half | | | | None | No such close friends |
|---|-----|---|---|---|------|---|---|---|------|----------------------|
| #* a. Lesbian friends ........... | 1 | 2 | 3 | 4 | 5 | 6 | 7 | 8 | 9 | X |
| #* b. Gay male friends .......... | 1 | 2 | 3 | 4 | 5 | 6 | 7 | 8 | 9 | X |
| c. [Heterosexual] female friends ................. | 1 | 2 | 3 | 4 | 5 | 6 | 7 | 8 | 9 | X |
| d. [Heterosexual] male friends ................. | 1 | 2 | 3 | 4 | 5 | 6 | 7 | 8 | 9 | X |

32a. Since you and your partner have been living together, have your close friends sent you Christmas or Channukah cards?

   1  No
   2  Yes, always addressed to me alone
   3  Yes, usually addressed to me alone
   4  Yes, usually addressed to both my partner and to me
   5  Yes, always addressed to both my partner and to me

   b. Since you and your partner have been living together, have you sent Christmas or Channukah cards to your close friends?

   1  No
   2  Yes, always signed from me alone
   3  Yes, usually signed from me alone
   4  Yes, usually signed from me and my partner
   5  Yes, always signed from me and my partner

33. How many of your current close friends . . . *(CIRCLE ONE ANSWER ON EACH LINE)*

a. Were *only* your partner's friends before you and [she] [he] began living together?..

| All | | | | Half | | | | None |
|---|---|---|---|---|---|---|---|---|
| 1 | 2 | 3 | 4 | 5 | 6 | 7 | 8 | 9 |

b. Were *only* your friends before you began living together?...............

| 1 | 2 | 3 | 4 | 5 | 6 | 7 | 8 | 9 |

c. Were friends of you both before you began living together?...............

| 1 | 2 | 3 | 4 | 5 | 6 | 7 | 8 | 9 |

d. Have become your friends, but were not friends of either you or your partner before you began living together ...

| 1 | 2 | 3 | 4 | 5 | 6 | 7 | 8 | 9 |

*#34. How many of your close [gay male] [lesbian] friends believe that many [lesbian] [gay male] couples can stay together more than ten years?...................

| All | | | | Half | | | | None | No close friends of this type |
|---|---|---|---|---|---|---|---|---|---|
| 1 | 2 | 3 | 4 | 5 | 6 | 7 | 8 | 9 | X |

*# 35a. Have you and your partner had a "marriage," "holy union," or other ceremony to symbolize your feelings for each other?

   1  Yes

   2  No *(IF "NO, SKIP TO QUESTION 36)*

*# b. If "yes," was this:

   1  A ceremony in a church involving clergy

   2  A ceremony involving clergy in a location other than a church

   3  A party involving just friends at which an announcement was made

   4  Other (please specify) _____

   _____

*# 36. Have you and your partner ever exchanged rings or other symbols of your relationship?

   1  We have exchanged rings only

   2  We have exchanged other symbols of our relationship only

   3  We have exchanged rings *and* other symbols of our relationship

   4  We have exchanged *neither*

37. Some couples write out a formal agreement concerning various aspects of their relationship or ownership of property (such as homes, cars, or furniture). Do you and your partner have such a document?

   1  No

   2  Yes, concerning property ownership *only*

   3  Yes, concerning other aspects of our relationship *only*

   4  Yes, concerning *both* property ownership and other aspects of our relationship

38a. Have you ever had professional counseling for personal problems *(other than* problems relating to [being gay] or your current relationship?

   1  Yes

   2  No

b. Have you ever had counseling for problems connected with your current relationship?

   1  Yes

   2  No

635

c. Have you and your partner ever attended a workshop or retreat on how to improve or enrich relationships?

   **1**  No

   **2**  Once or twice

   **3**  Three times or more

*#d. Have you ever had counseling regarding your homosexuality?

   **1**  Yes

   **2**  No

*#e. Have you ever received treatment to try to change your homosexuality?

   **1**  Yes

   **2**  No

---

## STATISTICAL INFORMATION

1a.  What is the highest grade you have completed in school?

| *(Elementary)* | | | | | | | | *(High School)* | | | | *(College)* | | | |
|---|---|---|---|---|---|---|---|---|---|---|---|---|---|---|---|
| **1** **2** **3** **4** **5** **6** **7** **8** | **9** | **10** | **11** | **12** | **13** | **14** | **15** | **16** | **17+** |

b.  Are you currently in school?

   **1**  No

   **2**  Yes, attending a four-year college or university full-time

   **3**  Yes, attending a four-year college or university part-time

   **4**  Yes, attending a two-year community college full-time

   **5**  Yes, attending a two-year community college part-time

   **6**  Yes, attending a technical, vocational or trade school

   **7**  Other (specify) _____

c.  Do you have a college degree?

   **1**  No

   **2**  Yes, Bachelor's

   **3**  Yes, Master's

   **4**  Yes, Doctorate

   **5**  Other (specify) _____

d.  Have you ever received any kind of training other than academic training?

   **1**  No

   **2**  Yes, have attended business or technical school

   **3**  Yes, have attended trade school

   **4**  Yes, have attended vocational school in the military

   **5**  Other (specify) _____

e.  If you are thinking about continuing your education, what is the highest level you plan to attain?

   **1**  I am not planning to continue my education

   **2**  High school graduate or equivalent

   **3**  Bachelor's

   **4**  Master's

   **5**  Doctorate

   **6**  Other (specify) _____

2a.  Which of these *best* describes your *current* employment situation?

   **1**  Employed full-time *(SKIP TO QUESTION 2e.)*

   **2**  Employed part-time *(SKIP TO QUESTION 2e.)*

   **3**  Employed but not at work because of temporary illness, strike, etc. *(SKIP TO QUESTION 2e.)*

   **4**  Unemployed *(GO TO QUESTION 2b.)*

   **5**  Retired *(SKIP TO QUESTION 2d.)*

   **6**  Taking care of the household is my full-time job *(GO TO QUESTION 2b.)*

b.  Would you like to be employed? .............   *Yes, very much* **1**   **2**   **3**   **4**   **5**   **6**   **7**   **8**   **9** *No, not at all*

c.  What are the *main* reasons you are not employed? *(CIRCLE ALL ANSWERS THAT APPLY TO YOU.)*

   **1**  Need more education and/or job skill training

   **2**  Do not need additional income

   **3**  Cannot find suitable job

   **4**  Partner does not want me to be employed

   **5**  I do not want to be employed

#** **6**  Cannot find adequate care for my children

#*** **7**  Children are too young

   **0**  Other (please specify) _____

d.  If you are currently *not employed or retired*, what was your last occupation? Give the *specific job description*, rather than just the general type of work. For example, "legal secretary" rather than "clerical," or "machine-shop foreman" rather than "foreman."

_____

*(SKIP TO QUESTION 4)*

e.  If you are *currently employed* what kind of work do you do? Give the *specific job description*, rather than just the general type of work. For example, "legal secretary" rather than "clerical," or "machine-shop foreman" rather than "foreman."

_____

3.  How much satisfaction do you get from your work? .........   *Extremely satisfied* **1**   **2**   **3**   **4**   **5**   **6**   **7**   **8**   **9** *Not at all satisfied*

4.  What is your race?

   **1**  White

   **2**  Black

   **3**  Asian or Asian American

   **4**  [Chicana] [Chicano] or Mexican American

   **5**  Native American or Indian

   **6**  Puerto Rican

   **7**  Other (specify) _____

5.  Are you male or female?

   **1**  Male

   **2**  Female

6.  How tall are you?

   _____ ft.   _____ in.

7.  How much do you weigh?

   _____ lbs.

8a. What is your current religious preference?

1 No religious preference

2 Protestant (specify denomination) _____

3 Catholic

4 Jewish

5 Other (specify) _____

b. About how often do you attend church or synagogue?

1 Daily or almost every day

2 Three or four times a week

3 Once or twice a week

4 Two or three times a month

5 Once a month

6 Once every few months

7 About once a year

8 Less often than once a year

9 Never *(IF "NEVER," SKIP TO QUESTION 8d.)*

*#c. About how often do you attend a gay church or synagogue?

1 Daily or almost every day

2 Three or four times a week

3 Once or twice a week

4 Two or three times a month

5 Once a month

6 Once every few months

7 About once a year

8 Less often than once a year

9 Never

d. Did you receive any kind of religious training or instruction as a child?

1 No

2 Yes, Protestant (specify denomination)_____

3 Yes, Catholic

4 Yes, Jewish

5 Other (specify) _____

e. Overall, how religious would
   you say you are *now?* ......

   Extremely religious 1    2    3    4    5    6    7    8    9 Not at all religious

9. What city or town do you live in?

   _____

10. In what state did you spend most of your adolescence (12 to 18 years)?

   _____

11. Which of the following best describes the community you lived in?

   a. Before your twelfth birthday

      1  Farm

      2  Rural area but not farm

      3  Small town (less than 50,000)

      4  Medium-size town or suburb (50,000 to 99,999)

      5  Small city or large suburb (100,000 to 249,999)

      6  City (250,000 to 500,000)

      7  Large city or metropolis (greater than 500,000)

   b. Between your twelfth and eighteenth birthdays

      1  Farm

      2  Rural area but not farm

      3  Small town (less than 50,000)

      4  Medium-size town or suburb (50,000 to 99,999)

      5  Small city or large suburb (100,000 to 249,999)

      6  City (250,000 to 500,000)

      7  Large city or metropolis (greater than 500,000)


12. When you were about *twelve years old*, what were the occupations of each of your parents? (Again, please give a *specific* job description.)

   a. Father's occupation

      _____

   b. Mother's occupation

      _____


13a. Which of the following best describes your *own* total yearly income *(NOT INCLUDING PARTNER'S INCOME)*? Include all sources, such as wages, salaries, income from investments, interest, etc.

      1  No income

      2  Less than $2,500

      3  $2,500 to $4,999

      4  $5,000 to $7,499

      5  $7,500 to $9,999

      6  $10,000 to $12,499

      7  $12,500 to $14,999

      8  $15,000 to $19,999

      9  $20,000 to $24,999

      10  $25,000 to $29,999

      11  $30,000 to $49,999

      12  $50,000 or more

   b. About how much of your *own* yearly income is *from your own work?*

      1  No income from work

      2  Less than $2,500

      3  $2,500 to $4,999

      4  $5,000 to $7,499

      5  $7,500 to $9,999

**6** $10,000 to $12,499

**7** $12,500 to $14,999

**8** $15,000 to $19,999

**9** $20,000 to $24,999

**10** $25,000 to $29,999

**11** $30,000 to $49,999

**12** $50,000 or more

14a. Are you presently legally married [to a man] [to a woman]?

    **1** I am single and have never been married *(SKIP TO QUESTION 28a.)*

    **2** I am single but have been married (divorced or widowed) *(SKIP TO QUESTION 14d.)*

    **3** I am currently married but not living with my spouse (separated)

  **\*\* 4** I am currently married and living with my spouse

b. If you are married now, how old were you when you and your spouse got married?

    Age _____

c. Did you and your current spouse live together before you got married?

    **1** No

    **2** Yes

    If "yes," for how long?

    _____ years     _____ months

d. How many times altogether have you been married?

    **1** Once

    **2** Twice

    **3** Three times

    **4** Four times

    **5** Five or more times

15. For your previous marriages (*excluding* your current one) how long did each last, how old were you when each began, and how did each end?

| | Length of Marriage | | Age at Marriage | Divorced or Widowed | |
|---|---|---|---|---|---|
| a. First marriage: | _____ years | _____ months | _____ years | **D** | **W** |
| b. Second marriage: | _____ years | _____ months | _____ years | **D** | **W** |
| c. Third marriage: | _____ years | _____ months | _____ years | **D** | **W** |
| d. Fourth marriage: | _____ years | _____ months | _____ years | **D** | **W** |

16. Did you live with your previous spouse(s) before you got married?

| | Yes | No | If "yes" for how long? | |
|---|---|---|---|---|
| a. First marriage: | **Y** | **N** | _____ years | _____ months |
| b. Second marriage: | **Y** | **N** | _____ years | _____ months |
| c. Third marriage: | **Y** | **N** | _____ years | _____ months |
| d. Fourth marriage: | **Y** | **N** | _____ years | _____ months |

640

*IF YOUR FIRST MARRIAGE DID NOT END IN DIVORCE OR PERMANENT SEPARATION, SKIP TO QUESTION 28a.*

**17. When you got married for the *first* time, how likely did you think it was that your marriage would end in divorce or separation?..........................

Extremely likely  1  2  3  4  5  6  7  8  9  Extremely unlikely

**18. Before you met your first spouse, how interested were you in getting married?.......................

Extremely interested  1  2  3  4  5  6  7  8  9  Not at all interested

**19. Do you now consider your first spouse to be your friend?...................................

Very close friend  1  2  3  4  5  6  7  8  9  Not at all

**20  When your first marriage began breaking up, who wanted the marriage to end?

**1** I wanted it to end but [she] [he] did not

**2** We both wanted it to end but I wanted it more

**3** We equally wanted it to end

**4** We both wanted it to end but [she] [he] wanted it more

**5** [She] [He] wanted it to end but I did not

**21. How difficult was the process of ending your first marriage for you emotionally?...................

Extremely difficult  1  2  3  4  5  6  7  8  9  Not at all difficult

**22. How often do you have *any* contact at all with your first spouse (by phone, mail, visits, etc.)?

**1** Daily or almost every day

**2** Three or four times a week

**3** Once or twice a week

**4** Two or three times a month

**5** Once a month

**6** Once every few months

**7** About once a year

**8** Less often than once a year

**9** Never

**23. How much does your partner like your first spouse?.

Very much  1  2  3  4  5  6  7  8  9  Not at all

**24. When your *first* marriage broke up, how interested were you in *ever* getting married again?................

Extremely interested  1  2  3  4  5  6  7  8  9  Not at all interested

641

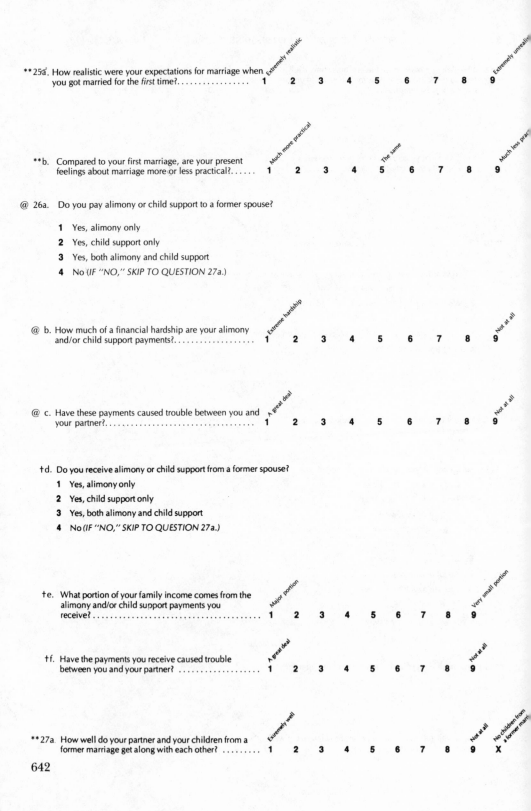

**\*\*25a.** How realistic were your expectations for marriage when you got married for the *first* time?................

Extremely realistic 1　2　3　4　5　6　7　8　9 Extremely unrealistic

**\*\*b.** Compared to your first marriage, are your present feelings about marriage more or less practical?......

Much more practical 1　2　3　4　5　The same 6　7　8　9 Much less practical

**@ 26a.** Do you pay alimony or child support to a former spouse?

**1** Yes, alimony only
**2** Yes, child support only
**3** Yes, both alimony and child support
**4** No *(IF "NO," SKIP TO QUESTION 27a.)*

**@ b.** How much of a financial hardship are your alimony and/or child support payments?.................

Extreme hardship 1　2　3　4　5　6　7　8　9 Not at all

**@ c.** Have these payments caused trouble between you and your partner?................................

A great deal 1　2　3　4　5　6　7　8　9 Not at all

**†d.** Do you receive alimony or child support from a former spouse?
**1** Yes, alimony only
**2** Yes, child support only
**3** Yes, both alimony and child support
**4** No *(IF "NO," SKIP TO QUESTION 27a.)*

**†e.** What portion of your family income comes from the alimony and/or child support payments you receive?....................................

Major portion 1　2　3　4　5　6　7　8　9 Very small portion

**†f.** Have the payments you receive caused trouble between you and your partner? ..................

A great deal 1　2　3　4　5　6　7　8　9 Not at all

**\*\*27a.** How well do your partner and your children from a former marriage get along with each other? .........

Extremely well 1　2　3　4　5　6　7　8　9 Not at all X No children from a former marriage

642

**b. Do you think your partner feels like a parent to your children from a former marriage? . . . . . . . . . . . .
Very much 1 2 3 4 5 6 7 8 9 Not at all X No children from a former marriage

**c. Has there been trouble between you and your partner because you have children from a previous marriage?. . . . . . . . . . . . . . . . . . . . . . . . . . . . . . . . .
A great deal 1 2 3 4 5 6 7 8 9 Not at all X No children from a former marriage

28a. Have you ever lived for over a month with someone with whom you were sexually involved, other than your current partner or a spouse?

1 Yes

2 No *(IF "NO," SKIP TO QUESTION 30.)*

b. If "yes," how many times did this happen?

1 Once

2 Twice

3 Three times

4 Four times

5 Five to ten times

6 Eleven or more times

29. [Did you live with a man or woman]*#, and how long did you live with each?

| | Sex of other person *# | | How long did you live together? | |
|---|---|---|---|---|
| a. First relationship . . . . . . . . . | M | F | _____ years | _____ months |
| b. Second relationship . . . . . . . | M | F | _____ years | _____ months |
| c. Third relationship . . . . . . . . . | M | F | _____ years | _____ months |
| d. Fourth relationship . . . . . . . . | M | F | _____ years | _____ months |

30. How did you and your partner learn about this study *(CIRCLE AS MANY RESPONSES AS APPLY.)*

*# 1 Read about it in a gay or lesbian publication or newspaper

2 Read about it in [some other]*# publication or newspaper

3 Heard the researchers talk about it on TV, radio, or in a public address

4 Heard the study described on the TV or radio news

5 Learned about it in a personal conversation with the researchers

6 Learned about it from someone who had already participated or intended to participate

7 Heard about it from someone who knew about it but who did not intend to participate

*# 8 Saw a notice posted in a gay or lesbian bar, coffee house, community center, etc.

9 Saw a notice posted in a [straight]*# bar, a supermarket, laundromat, etc.

0 Other _____

*# 31. Have you ever taken part in a study of gay people before?

1 Yes

2 No

# INDEX